Stanley Gibbons
Commonwealth Stamp Catalogue

East Africa

with Egypt & Sudan

3rd edition 2014

STANLEY GIBBONS LTD

London and Ringwood

By Appointment to
Her Majesty The Queen
Philatelists
Stanley Gibbons Ltd
London

Published by Stanley Gibbons Ltd
Editorial, Publications Sales Offices
and Distribution Centre:
7 Parkside, Christchurch Road, Ringwood,
Hants BH24 3SH

1st Edition – 2006
2nd Edition – 2010
3rd edition – 2014

British Library Cataloguing in
Publication Data.
A catalogue record for this book is available
from the British Library.

ISBN-10: 0-85259-922-6
ISBN-13: 978-0-85259-922-8

Item No. R2984-14

Printed by
Latimer Trend & Company Ltd, Plymouth

Contents

Stanley Gibbons Holdings Plc

Stanley Gibbons Limited, Stanley Gibbons Auctions
399 Strand, London WC2R 0LX
Tel: +44 (0)207 836 8444
Fax: +44 (0)207 836 7342
E-mail: help@stanleygibbons.com
Website: www.stanleygibbons.com
for all departments, Auction and
Specialist Stamp Departments.

Open Monday–Friday 9.30 a.m. to 5 p.m.
Shop. Open Monday–Friday 9 a.m.
to 5.30 p.m. and Saturday 9.30 a.m.
to 5.30 p.m.

Stanley Gibbons Publications Gibbons Stamp Monthly and Philatelic Exporter
7 Parkside, Christchurch Road,
Ringwood, Hampshire BH24 3SH.
Tel: +44 (0)1425 472363
Fax: +44 (0)1425 470247
E-mail: help@stanleygibbons.com
Publications Mail Order.
FREEPHONE 0800 611622

Monday–Friday 8.30 a.m. to 5 p.m.

Stanley Gibbons (Guernsey) Limited
18–20 Le Bordage, St Peter Port,
Guernsey GY1 1DE.
Tel: +44 (0)1481 708270
Fax: +44 (0)1481 708279
E-mail: investment@stanleygibbons.
com

Stanley Gibbons (Jersey) Limited
18 Hill Street, St Helier, Jersey,
Channel Islands JE2 4UA.
Tel: +44 (0)1534 766711
Fax: +44 (0)1534 766177
E-mail: investment@stanleygibbons.
com

Stanley Gibbons (Asia) Limited
Room 618, 6/F,
100 Queen's Road Central
Central,
Hong Kong
Tel: +852 3180 9370
E-mail: elee@stanleygibbons.com

Benham Collectibles Limited
Unit K, Concept Court,
Shearway Business Park
Folkestone Kent CT19 4RG
E-mail: benham@benham.com

Fraser's
(a division of Stanley Gibbons Ltd)
399 Strand, London WC2R 0LX
Autographs, photographs, letters and
documents
Tel: +44 (0)207 836 8444
Fax: +44 (0)207 836 7342
E-mail: sales@frasersautographs.com
Website: www.frasersautographs.com

Monday–Friday 9 a.m. to 5.30 p.m.
and Saturday 10 a.m. to 4 p.m.

Stanley Gibbons Publications Overseas Representation
Stanley Gibbons Publications are
represented overseas by the following

Australia Renniks Publications PTY LTD
Unit 3 37-39 Green Street,
Banksmeadow, NSW 2019, Australia
Tel: +612 9695 7055
Website: www.renniks.com

Canada Unitrade Associates
99 Floral Parkway, Toronto,
Ontario M6L 2C4, Canada
Tel: +1 416 242 5900
Website: www.unitradeassoc.com

Germany Schaubek Verlag Leipzig
Am Glaeschen 23, D-04420
Markranstaedt, Germany
Tel: +49 34 205 67823
Website: www.schaubek.de

Italy Ernesto Marini S.R.L.
V. Struppa, 300, Genova, 16165, Italy
Tel: +3901 0247-3530
Website: www.ernestomarini.it

Japan Japan Philatelic
PO Box 2, Suginami-Minami,
Tokyo 168-8081, Japan
Tel: +81 3330 41641
Website: www.yushu.co.jp

Netherlands also covers Belgium Denmark, Finland & France Uitgeverij Davo BV
PO Box 411, Ak Deventer, 7400
Netherlands
Tel: +315 7050 2700
Website: www.davo.nl

New Zealand House of Stamps
PO Box 12, Paraparaumu,
New Zealand
Tel: +61 6364 8270
Website: www.houseofstamps.co.nz

New Zealand Philatelic Distributors
PO Box 863
15 Mount Edgecumbe Street
New Plymouth 4615, New Zealand
Tel: +6 46 758 65 68
Website: www.stampcollecta.com

Norway SKANFIL A/S
SPANAV. 52 / BOKS 2030
N-5504 HAUGESUND, Norway
Tel: +47-52703940
E-mail: magne@skanfil.no

Singapore C S Philatelic Agency
Peninsula Shopping Centre #04-29
3 Coleman Street, 179804, Singapore
Tel: +65 6337-1859
Website: www.cs.com.sg

South Africa Peter Bale Philatelics
P O Box 3719, Honeydew,
2040, South Africa
Tel: +27 11 462 2463
Tel: +27 82 330 3925
E-mail: balep@iafrica.com

Sweden Chr Winther Sorensen AB
Box 43, S-310 20 Knaered, Sweden
Tel: +46 43050743
Website: www.collectia.se

USA Regency Superior Ltd
229 North Euclid Avenue
Saint Louis, Missouri 63108, USA

PO Box 8277, St Louis,
MO 63156-8277, USA
Toll Free Tel: (800) 782-0066
Tel: (314) 361-5699
Website: www.RegencySuperior.com
Email: info@regencysuperior.com

Stanley Gibbons
Stamp Catalogues

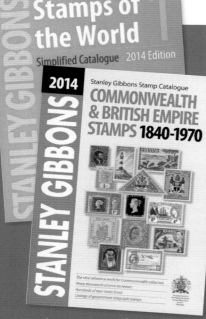

Stamps of the World 1
the World
Simplified Catalogue 2014 Edition

2014
Stanley Gibbons Stamp Catalogue
COMMONWEALTH & BRITISH EMPIRE STAMPS 1840-1970

The vital reference work for Commonwealth collectors
Many thousands of price increases
Hundreds of new items found
Listings of government telegraph stamps

We have catalogues to suit every aspect of stamp collecting

Our catalogues cover stamps issued from across the globe - from the Penny Black to the latest issues. Whether you're a specialist in a certain reign or a thematic collector, we should have something to suit your needs. All catalogues include the famous SG numbering system, making it as easy as possible to find the stamp you're looking for.

1 Commonwealth & British Empire Stamps 1840-1970 (116th edition, 2014)

Commonwealth Country Catalogues

Australia & Dependencies (8th Edition, 2013)
Bangladesh, Pakistan & Sri Lanka (2nd edition, 2010)
Belize, Guyana, Trinidad & Tobago (2nd edition, 2013)
Brunei, Malaysia & Singapore (4th edition, 2013)
Canada (5th edition, 2014)
Central Africa (2nd edition, 2008)
Cyprus, Gibraltar & Malta (3rd edition, 2011)
East Africa with Egypt & Sudan (3rd edition, 2014)
Eastern Pacific (2nd edition, 2011)
Falkland Islands (6th edition, 2013)
Hong Kong (4th edition, 2013)
India (including Convention & Feudatory States) (4th edition, 2013)
Indian Ocean (2nd edition, 2012)
Ireland (4th edition, 2011)
Leeward Islands (2nd edition, 2012)
New Zealand (5th edition, 2014)
Northern Caribbean, Bahamas & Bermuda (3rd edition, 2013)
St. Helena & Dependencies (5th edition, 2014)
Southern Africa (2nd edition, 2008)
Southern & Central Africa (1st edition, 2011)
West Africa (2nd edition, 2012)
Western Pacific (3rd edition, 2014)
Windward Islands & Barbados (2nd edition, 2012)

Stamps of the World 2014

Volume 1 Abu Dhabi – Charkhari
Volume 2 Chile – Georgia
Volume 3 German Commands – Jasdan
Volume 4 Jersey – New Republic
Volume 5 New South Wales – Singapore
Volume 6 Sirmoor – Zululand

We also produce a range of thematic catalogues for use with Stamps of the World.

Great Britain Catalogues

Collect British Stamps (65th edition, 2014)
Collect Channel Islands & Isle of Man (29th edition, 2014)
Great Britain Concise Stamp Catalogue (29th edition, 2014)

Great Britain Specialised

Volume 1 Queen Victoria (16th edition, 2012)
Volume 2 King Edward VII to King George VI (13th edition, 2009)
Volume 3 Queen Elizabeth II Pre-decimal issues (12th edition, 2011)
Volume 4 Queen Elizabeth II Decimal Definitive Issues – Part 1 (10th edition, 2008)
Queen Elizabeth II Decimal Definitive Issues – Part 2 (10th edition, 2010)

Foreign Countries

2   *Austria & Hungary* (7th edition, 2009)
3   *Balkans* (5th edition, 2009)
4   *Benelux* (6th edition, 2010)
5   *Czech Republic, Slovakia & Poland* (7th edition, 2012)
6   *France* (7th edition, 2010)
7   *Germany* (10th edition, 2012)
8   *Italy & Switzerland* (8th edition, 2013)
9   *Portugal & Spain* (6th edition, 2011)
10 *Russia* (7th edition, 2014)
11 *Scandinavia* (7th edition, 2013)
15 *Central America* (3rd edition, 2007)
16 *Central Asia* (4th edition, 2006)
17 *China* (10th edition, 2014)
18 *Japan & Korea* (5th edition, 2008)
19 *Middle East* (7th edition, 2009)
20 *South America* (4th edition, 2008)
21 *South-East Asia* (5th edition, 2012)
22 *United States of America* (7th edition, 2010)

General Philatelic Information and Guidelines to the Scope of Stanley Gibbons Commonwealth Catalogues

These notes reflect current practice in compiling the Stanley Gibbons Commonwealth Catalogues.

The Stanley Gibbons Stamp Catalogue has a very long history and the vast quantity of information it contains has been carefully built up by successive generations through the work of countless individuals. Philately is never static and the Catalogue has evolved and developed over the years. These notes relate to the current criteria upon which a stamp may be listed or priced. These criteria have developed over time and may have differed somewhat in the early years of this catalogue. These notes are not intended to suggest that we plan to make wholesale changes to the listing of classic issues in order to bring them into line with today's listing policy, they are designed to inform catalogue users as to the policies currently in operation.

PRICES

The prices quoted in this Catalogue are the estimated selling prices of Stanley Gibbons Ltd at the time of publication. They are, unless it is specifically stated otherwise, for examples in fine condition for the issue concerned. Superb examples are worth more; those of a lower quality considerably less.

All prices are subject to change without prior notice and Stanley Gibbons Ltd may from time to time offer stamps below catalogue price. Individual low value stamps sold at 399 Strand are liable to an additional handling charge. Purchasers of new issues should note the prices charged for them contain an element for the service rendered and so may exceed the prices shown when the stamps are subsequently catalogued. Postage and handling charges are extra.

No guarantee is given to supply all stamps priced, since it is not possible to keep every catalogued item in stock. Commemorative issues may, at times, only be available in complete sets and not as individual values.

Quotation of prices. The prices in the left-hand column are for unused stamps and those in the right-hand column are for used.

A dagger (†) denotes that the item listed does not exist in that condition and a blank, or dash, that it exists, or may exist, but we are unable to quote a price.

Prices are expressed in pounds and pence sterling. One pound comprises 100 pence (£1 = 100p).

The method of notation is as follows: pence in numerals (e.g. 10 denotes ten pence); pounds and pence, up to £100, in numerals (e.g. 4.25 denotes four pounds and twenty-five pence); prices above £100 are expressed in whole pounds with the '£' sign shown.

Unused stamps. Great Britain and Commonwealth: the prices for unused stamps of Queen Victoria to King George V are for lightly hinged examples. Unused prices for King Edward VIII, King George VI and Queen Elizabeth issues are for unmounted mint.

Some stamps from the King George VI period are often difficult to find in unmounted mint condition. In such instances we would expect that collectors would need to pay a high proportion of the price quoted to obtain mounted mint examples. Generally speaking lightly mounted mint stamps from this reign, issued before 1945, are in considerable demand.

Used stamps. The used prices are normally for fine postally used stamps, but may be for stamps cancelled-to-order where this practice exists.

A pen-cancellation on early issues can sometimes correctly denote postal use. Instances are individually noted in the Catalogue in explanation of the used price given.

Prices quoted for bisects on cover or large piece are for those dated during the period officially authorised.

Stamps not sold unused to the public (e.g. some official stamps) are priced used only.

The use of 'unified' designs, that is stamps inscribed for both postal and fiscal purposes, results in a number of stamps of very high face value. In some instances these may not have been primarily intended for postal purposes, but if they are so inscribed we include them. We only price such items used, however, where there is evidence of normal postal usage.

Cover prices. To assist collectors, cover prices are quoted for issues up to 1945 at the beginning of each country.

The system gives a general guide in the form of a factor by which the corresponding used price of the basic loose stamp should be multiplied when found in fine average condition on cover.

Care is needed in applying the factors and they relate to a cover which bears a single of the denomination listed; if more than one denomination is present the most highly priced attracts the multiplier and the remainder are priced at the simple figure for used singles in arriving at a total.

The cover should be of non-philatelic origin; bearing the correct postal rate for the period and distance involved and cancelled with the markings normal to the offices concerned. Purely philatelic items have a cover value only slightly greater than the catalogue value for the corresponding used stamps. This applies generally to those high-value stamps used philatelically rather than in the normal course of commerce. Low-value stamps, e.g. ¼d. and ½d., are desirable when used as a single rate on cover and merit an increase in 'multiplier' value.

First day covers in the period up to 1945 are not within the scope of the system and the multiplier should not be used. As a special category of philatelic usage, with wide variations in valuation according to scarcity, they require separate treatment.

Oversized covers, difficult to accommodate on an album page, should be reckoned as worth little more than the corresponding value of the used stamps. The condition of a cover also affects its value. Except for 'wreck covers', serious damage or soiling reduce the value where the postal markings and stamps are ordinary ones. Conversely, visual appeal adds to the value and this can include freshness of appearance, important addresses, old-fashioned but legible hand-writing, historic town-names, etc.

The multipliers are a base on which further value would be added to take account of the cover's postal historical importance in demonstrating such things as unusual, scarce or emergency cancels, interesting routes, significant postal markings, combination usage, the development of postal rates, and so on.

Minimum price. The minimum catalogue price quoted is 10p. For individual stamps prices between 10p. and 95p. are provided as a guide for catalogue users. The lowest price charged for individual stamps or sets purchased from Stanley Gibbons Ltd is £1

Set prices. Set prices are generally for one of each value, excluding shades and varieties, but including major colour changes. Where there are alternative shades, etc., the cheapest is usually included. The number of stamps in the set is always stated for clarity. The prices for sets containing se-tenant pieces are based on the prices quoted for such combinations, and not on those for the individual stamps.

Varieties. Where plate or cylinder varieties are priced in used condition the price quoted is for a fine used example with the cancellation well clear of the listed flaw.

Specimen stamps. The pricing of these items is explained under that heading.

Stamp booklets. Prices are for complete assembled booklets in fine condition with those issued before 1945 showing normal wear and tear. Incomplete booklets and those which have been 'exploded' will, in general, be worth less than the figure quoted.

Repricing. Collectors will be aware that the market factors of supply and demand directly influence the prices quoted in this Catalogue. Whatever the scarcity of a particular stamp, if there is no one in the market who wishes to buy it cannot be expected to achieve a high price. Conversely, the same item actively sought by numerous potential buyers may cause the price to rise.

All the prices in this Catalogue are examined during the preparation of each new edition by the expert staff of Stanley Gibbons and repriced as necessary. They take many factors into account, including supply and demand, and are in close touch with the international stamp market and the auction world.

Commonwealth cover prices and advice on postal history material originally provided by Edward B Proud.

GUARANTEE

All stamps are guaranteed originals in the following terms:

If not as described, and returned by the purchaser, we undertake to refund the price paid to us in the original transaction. If any stamp is certified as genuine by the Expert Committee of the Royal Philatelic Society, London, or by BPA Expertising Ltd, the purchaser shall not be entitled to make any claim against us for any error, omission or mistake in such certificate.

Consumers' statutory rights are not affected by the above guarantee.

The recognised Expert Committees in this country are those of the Royal Philatelic Society, 41 Devonshire Place, London W1G, 6JY, and BPA Expertising Ltd, PO Box 1141, Guildford, Surrey GU5 0WR. They do not undertake valuations under any circumstances and fees are payable for their services.

MARGINS ON IMPERFORATE STAMPS

| Superb | Very fine | Fine | Average | Poor |

GUM

Unmounted — Very lightly mounted — Lightly mounted — Mounted/large part original gum (o.g.). — Heavily mounted small part o.g.

CENTRING

Superb — Very fine — Fine — Average — Poor

CANCELLATIONS

Superb — Very fine — Fine — Average — Poor

Superb — Very fine

Fine — Average — Poor

CONDITION GUIDE

To assist collectors in assessing the true value of items they are considering buying or in reviewing stamps already in their collections, we now offer a more detailed guide to the condition of stamps on which this catalogue's prices are based.

For a stamp to be described as 'Fine', it should be sound in all respects, without creases, bends, wrinkles, pin holes, thins or tears. If perforated, all perforation 'teeth' should be intact, it should not suffer from fading, rubbing or toning and it should be of clean, fresh appearance.

Margins on imperforate stamps: These should be even on all sides and should be at least as wide as half the distance between that stamp and the next. To have one or more margins of less than this width, would normally preclude a stamp from being described as 'Fine'. Some early stamps were positioned very close together on the printing plate and in such cases 'Fine' margins would necessarily be narrow. On the other hand, some plates were laid down to give a substantial gap between individual stamps and in such cases margins would be expected to be much wider.

An 'average' four-margin example would have a narrower margin on one or more sides and should be priced accordingly, while a stamp with wider, yet even, margins than 'Fine' would merit the description 'Very Fine' or 'Superb' and, if available, would command a price in excess of that quoted in the catalogue.

Gum: Since the prices for stamps of King Edward VIII, King George VI and Queen Elizabeth are for 'unmounted' or 'never hinged' mint, even stamps from these reigns which have been very lightly mounted should be available at a discount from catalogue price, the more obvious the hinge marks, the greater the discount.

Catalogue prices for stamps issued prior to King Edward VIII's reign are for mounted mint, so unmounted examples would be worth a premium. Hinge marks on 20th century stamps should not be too obtrusive, and should be at least in the lightly mounted category. For 19th century stamps more obvious hinging would be acceptable, but stamps should still carry a large part of their original gum—'Large part o.g.'—in order to be described as 'Fine'.

Centring: Ideally, the stamp's image should appear in the exact centre of the perforated area, giving equal margins on all sides. 'Fine' centring would be close to this ideal with any deviation having an effect on the value of the stamp. As in the case of the margins on imperforate stamps, it should be borne in mind that the space between some early stamps was very narrow, so it was very difficult to achieve accurate perforation, especially when the technology was in its infancy. Thus, poor centring would have a less damaging effect on the value of a 19th century stamp than on a 20th century example, but the premium put on a perfectly centred specimen would be greater.

Cancellations: Early cancellation devices were designed to 'obliterate' the stamp in order to prevent it being reused and this is still an important objective for today's postal administrations. Stamp collectors, on the other hand, prefer postmarks to be lightly applied, clear, and to leave as much as possible of the design visible. Dated, circular cancellations have long been 'the postmark of choice', but the definition of a 'Fine' cancellation will depend upon the types of cancellation in use at the time a stamp was current—it is clearly illogical to seek a circular datestamp on a Penny Black.

'Fine', by definition, will be superior to 'Average', so, in terms of cancellation quality, if one begins by identifying what 'Average' looks like, then one will be half way to identifying 'Fine'. The illustrations will give some guidance on mid-19th century and mid-20th century cancellations of Great Britain, but types of cancellation in general use in each country and in each period will determine the appearance of 'Fine'.

As for the factors discussed above, anything less than 'Fine' will result in a downgrading of the stamp concerned, while a very fine or superb cancellation will be worth a premium.

Combining the factors: To merit the description 'Fine', a stamp should be fine in every respect, but a small deficiency in one area might be made up for in another by a factor meriting an 'Extremely Fine' description.

Some early issues are so seldom found in what would normally be considered to be 'Fine' condition, the catalogue prices are for a slightly lower grade, with 'Fine' examples being worth a premium. In such cases a note to this effect is given in the catalogue, while elsewhere premiums are given for well-centred, lightly cancelled examples.

Stamps graded at less than fine remain collectable and, in the case of more highly priced stamps, will continue to hold a value. Nevertheless, buyers should always bear condition in mind.

The Catalogue in General

Contents. The Catalogue is confined to adhesive postage stamps, including miniature sheets. For particular categories the rules are:
(a) Revenue (fiscal) stamps are listed only where they have been expressly authorised for postal duty.
(b) Stamps issued only precancelled are included, but normally issued stamps available additionally with precancel have no separate precancel listing unless the face value is changed.
(c) Stamps prepared for use but not issued, hitherto accorded full listing, are nowadays foot-noted with a price (where possible).
(d) Bisects (trisects, etc.) are only listed where such usage was officially authorised.
(e) Stamps issued only on first day covers or in presentation packs and not available separately are not listed but may be priced in a footnote.
(f) New printings are only included in this Catalogue where they show a major philatelic variety, such as a change in shade, watermark or paper. Stamps which exist with or without imprint dates are listed separately; changes in imprint dates are mentioned in footnotes.
(g) Official and unofficial reprints are dealt with by footnote.
(h) Stamps from imperforate printings of modern issues which occur perforated are covered by footnotes, but are listed where widely available for postal use.

Exclusions. The following are excluded:
(a) non-postal revenue or fiscal stamps;
(b) postage stamps used fiscally (although prices are now given for some fiscally used high values);
(c) local carriage labels and private local issues;
(d) bogus or phantom stamps;
(e) railway or airline letter fee stamps, bus or road transport company labels or the stamps of private postal companies operating under licence from the national authority;
(f) cut-outs;
(g) all types of non-postal labels and souvenirs;
(h) documentary labels for the postal service, e.g. registration, recorded delivery, air-mail etiquettes, etc.;
(i) privately applied embellishments to official issues and privately commissioned items generally;
(j) stamps for training postal officers.

Full listing. 'Full listing' confers our recognition and implies allotting a catalogue number and (wherever possible) a price quotation.

In judging status for inclusion in the catalogue broad considerations are applied to stamps. They must be issued by a legitimate postal authority, recognised by the government concerned, and must be adhesives valid for proper postal use in the class of service for which they are inscribed. Stamps, with the exception of such categories as postage dues and officials, must be available to the general public, at face value, in reasonable quantities without any artificial restrictions being imposed on their distribution.

For errors and varieties the criterion is legitimate (albeit inadvertent) sale through a postal administration in the normal course of business. Details of provenance are always important; printers' waste and deliberately manufactured material are excluded.

Certificates. In assessing unlisted items due weight is given to Certificates from recognised Expert Committees and, where appropriate, we will usually ask to see them.

Date of issue. Where local issue dates differ from dates of release by agencies, 'date of issue' is the local date. Fortuitous stray usage before the officially intended date is disregarded in listing.

Catalogue numbers. Stamps of each country are catalogued chronologically by date of issue. Subsidiary classes are placed at the end of the country, as separate lists, with a distinguishing letter prefix to the catalogue number, e.g. D for postage due, O for official and E for express delivery stamps.

The catalogue number appears in the extreme left-column. The boldface Type numbers in the next column are merely cross-references to illustrations.

Once published in the Catalogue, numbers are changed as little as possible; really serious renumbering is reserved for the occasions when a complete country or an entire issue is being rewritten. The edition first affected includes cross-reference tables of old and new numbers.

Our catalogue numbers are universally recognised in specifying stamps and as a hallmark of status.

Illustrations. Stamps are illustrated at three-quarters linear size. Stamps not illustrated are the same size and format as the value shown, unless otherwise indicated. Stamps issued only as miniature sheets have the stamp alone illustrated but sheet size is also quoted. Overprints, surcharges, watermarks and postmarks are normally actual size. Illustrations of varieties are often enlarged to show the detail. Stamp booklet covers are illustrated half-size, unless otherwise indicated.

Designers. Designers' names are quoted where known, though space precludes naming every individual concerned in the production of a set. In particular, photographers supplying material are usually named only where they also make an active contribution in the design stage; posed photographs of reigning monarchs are, however, an exception to this rule.

CONTACTING THE CATALOGUE EDITOR
The editor is always interested in hearing from people who have new information which will improve or correct the Catalogue. As a general rule he must see and examine the actual stamps before they can be considered for listing; photographs or photocopies are insufficient evidence.

Submissions should be made in writing to the Catalogue Editor, Stanley Gibbons Publications at the Ringwood office. The cost of return postage for items submitted is appreciated, and this should include the registration fee if required.

Where information is solicited purely for the benefit of the enquirer, the editor cannot undertake to reply if the answer is already contained in these published notes or if return postage is omitted. Written communications are greatly preferred to enquiries by telephone or e-mail and the editor regrets that he or his staff cannot see personal callers without a prior appointment being made. Correspondence may be subject to delay during the production period of each new edition.

The editor welcomes close contact with study circles and is interested, too, in finding reliable local correspondents who will verify and supplement official information in countries where this is deficient.

We regret we do not give opinions as to the genuineness of stamps, nor do we identify stamps or number them by our Catalogue.

TECHNICAL MATTERS

The meanings of the technical terms used in the catalogue will be found in our *Philatelic Terms Illustrated*.

References below to (more specialised) listings are to be taken to indicate, as appropriate, the Stanley Gibbons *Great Britain Specialised Catalogue* in five volumes or the *Great Britain Concise Catalogue*.

1. Printing

Printing errors. Errors in printing are of major interest to the Catalogue. Authenticated items meriting consideration would include: background, centre or frame inverted or omitted; centre or subject transposed; error of colour; error or omission of value; double prints and impressions; printed both sides; and so on. Designs *tête-bêche*, whether intentionally or by accident, are listable. *Se-tenant* arrangements of stamps are recognised in the listings or footnotes. Gutter pairs (a pair of stamps separated by blank margin) are not included in this volume. Colours only partially omitted are not listed. Stamps with embossing omitted are reserved for our more specialised listings.

Printing varieties. Listing is accorded to major changes in the printing base which lead to completely new types. In recess-printing this could be a design re-engraved; in photogravure or photolithography a screen altered in whole or in part. It can also encompass flat-bed and rotary printing if the results are readily distinguishable.

To be considered at all, varieties must be constant.

Early stamps, produced by primitive methods, were prone to numerous imperfections; the lists reflect this, recognising re-entries, retouches, broken frames, misshapen letters, and so on. Printing technology has, however, radically improved over the years, during which time photogravure and lithography have become predominant. Varieties nowadays are more in the nature of flaws and these, being too specialised for this general catalogue, are almost always outside the scope.

In no catalogue, however, do we list such items as: dry prints, kiss prints, doctor-blade flaws, colour shifts or registration flaws (unless they lead to the complete omission of a colour from an individual stamp), lithographic ring flaws, and so on. Neither do we recognise fortuitous happenings like paper creases or confetti flaws.

Overprints (and surcharges). Overprints of different types qualify for separate listing. These include overprints in different colours; overprints from different printing processes such as litho and typo; overprints in totally different typefaces, etc. Major errors in machine-printed overprints are important and listable. They include: overprint inverted or omitted; overprint double (treble, etc.); overprint diagonal; overprint double, one inverted; pairs with one overprint omitted, e.g. from a radical shift to an adjoining stamp; error of colour; error of type fount; letters inverted or omitted, etc. If the overprint is handstamped, few of these would qualify and a distinction is drawn. We continue, however, to list pairs of stamps where one has a handstamped overprint and the other has not.

Albino prints or double prints, one of them being albino (i.e. showing an uninked impression of the printing plate) are listable unless they are particularly common in this form (see the note below Travancore No. 32fa, for example). We do not, however, normally list reversed albino overprints, caused by the accidental or deliberate folding of sheets prior to overprinting (British Levant Nos. 51/8).

Varieties occurring in overprints will often take the form of broken letters, slight differences in spacing, rising spaces, etc. Only the most important would be considered for listing or footnote mention.

Sheet positions. If space permits we quote sheet positions of listed varieties and authenticated data is solicited for this purpose.

De La Rue plates. The Catalogue classifies the general plates used by De La Rue for printing British Colonial stamps as follows:

VICTORIAN KEY TYPE

Die I

1. The ball of decoration on the second point of the crown appears as a dark mass of lines.
2. Dark vertical shading separates the front hair from the bun.
3. The vertical line of colour outlining the front of the throat stops at the sixth line of shading on the neck.
4. The white space in the coil of the hair above the curl is roughly the shape of a pin's head.

Die II

1. There are very few lines of colour in the ball and it appears almost white.

2. A white vertical strand of hair appears in place of the dark shading.

3. The line stops at the eighth line of shading.

4. The white space is oblong, with a line of colour partially dividing it at the left end.

Plates numbered 1 and 2 are both Die I. Plates 3 and 4 are Die II.

GEORGIAN KEY TYPE

Die I

A. The second (thick) line below the name of the country is cut slanting, conforming roughly to the shape of the crown on each side.

B. The labels of solid colour bearing the words "POSTAGE" and "& REVENUE" are square at the inner top corners.

C. There is a projecting "bud" on the outer spiral of the ornament in each of the lower corners.

Die II

A. The second line is cut vertically on each side of the crown.

B. The labels curve inwards at the top.

C. There is no "bud" in this position.

Unless otherwise stated in the lists, all stamps with watermark Multiple Crown CA (w **8**) are Die I while those with watermark Multiple Crown Script CA (w **9**) are Die II. The Georgian Die II was introduced in April 1921 and was used for Plates 10 to 22 and 26 to 28. Plates 23 to 25 were made from Die I by mistake.

2. Paper

All stamps listed are deemed to be on (ordinary) paper of the wove type and white in colour; only departures from this are normally mentioned.

Types. Where classification so requires we distinguish such other types of paper as, for example, vertically and horizontally laid; wove and laid bâtonné; card(board); carton; cartridge; glazed; granite; native; pelure; porous; quadrillé; ribbed; rice; and silk thread.

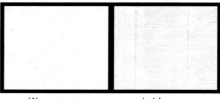

Wove paper   Laid paper

Granite paper   Quadrillé paper

Burelé band

The various makeshifts for normal paper are listed as appropriate. The varieties of double paper and joined paper are recognised. The security device of a printed burelé band on the back of a stamp, as in early Queensland, qualifies for listing.

Descriptive terms. The fact that a paper is handmade (and thus probably of uneven thickness) is mentioned where necessary. Such descriptive terms as "hard" and "soft"; "smooth" and "rough"; "thick", "medium" and "thin" are applied where there is philatelic merit in classifying papers.

Coloured, very white and toned papers. A coloured paper is one that is coloured right through (front and back of the stamp). In the Catalogue the colour of the paper is given in italics, thus:

black/*rose* = black design on rose paper.

Papers have been made specially white in recent years by, for example, a very heavy coating of chalk. We do not classify shades of whiteness of paper as distinct varieties. There does exist, however, a type of paper from early days called toned. This is off-white, often brownish or buffish, but it cannot be assigned any definite colour. A toning effect brought on by climate, incorrect storage or gum staining is disregarded here, as this was not the state of the paper when issued.

"Ordinary" and "Chalk-surfaced" papers. The availability of many postage stamps for revenue purposes made necessary some safeguard against the illegitimate re-use of stamps with removable cancellations. This was at first secured by using fugitive inks and later by printing on paper surfaced by coatings containing either chalk or china clay, both of which made it difficult to remove any form of obliteration without damaging the stamp design.

This catalogue lists these chalk-surfaced paper varieties from their introduction in 1905. Where no indication is given, the paper is "ordinary".

The "traditional" method of indentifying chalk-surfaced papers has been that, when touched with a silver wire, a black mark is left on the paper, and the listings in this catalogue are based on that test. However, the test itself is now largely discredited, for, although the mark can be removed by a soft rubber, some damage to the stamp will result from its use.

The difference between chalk-surfaced and pre-war ordinary papers is fairly clear: chalk-surfaced papers being smoother to the touch and showing a characteristic sheen when light is reflected off their surface. Under good magnification tiny bubbles or pock marks can be seen on the surface of the stamp and at the tips of the perforations the surfacing appears "broken". Traces of paper fibres are evident on the surface of ordinary paper and the ink shows a degree of absorption into it.

Initial chalk-surfaced paper printings by De La Rue had a thinner coating than subsequently became the norm. The characteristics described above are less pronounced in these printings.

During and after the Second World War, substitute papers replaced the chalk-surfaced papers, these do not react to the silver test and are therefore classed as "ordinary", although differentiating them without recourse to it is more difficult, for, although the characteristics of the chalk-surfaced paper remained the same, some of the ordinary papers appear much smoother than earlier papers and many do not show the watermark clearly. Experience is the only solution to identifying these, and comparison with stamps whose paper type is without question will be of great help.

Another type of paper, known as "thin striated" was used only for the Bahamas 1s. and 5s. (Nos. 155a, 156a, 171 and 174) and for several stamps of the Malayan states. Hitherto these have been described as "chalk-surfaced" since they gave some reaction to the silver test, but they are much thinner than usual chalk-surfaced papers, with the watermark showing clearly. Stamps on this paper show a slightly 'ribbed' effect when the stamp is held up to the light. Again, comparison with a known striated paper stamp, such as the 1941 Straits Settlements Die II 2c. orange (No. 294) will prove invaluable in separating these papers.

Glazed paper. In 1969 the Crown Agents introduced a new general-purpose paper for use in conjunction with all current printing processes. It generally has a marked glossy surface but the degree varies according to the process used, being more marked in recess-printing stamps. As it does not respond to the silver test this presents a further test where previous printings were on chalky paper. A change of paper to the glazed variety merits separate listing.

Green and yellow papers. Issues of the First World War and immediate postwar period occur on green and yellow papers and these are given separate Catalogue listing. The original coloured papers (coloured throughout) gave way to surface-coloured papers, the stamps having "white backs"; other stamps show one colour on the front and a different one at the back. Because of the numerous variations a grouping of colours is adopted as follows:

Yellow papers

(1) The original *yellow* paper (throughout), usually bright in colour. The gum is often sparse, of harsh consistency and dull-looking. Used 1912–1920.

(2) The *white-backs*. Used 1913–1914.

(3) A bright lemon paper. The colour must have a pronounced greenish tinge, different from the "yellow" in (1). As a rule, the gum on stamps using this lemon paper is plentiful, smooth and shiny, and the watermark shows distinctly. Care is needed with stamps printed in green on yellow paper (1) as it may appear that the paper is this lemon. Used 1914–1916.

(4) An experimental *orange-buff* paper. The colour must have a distinct brownish tinge. It is not to be confused with a muddy yellow (1) nor the misleading appearance (on the surface) of stamps printed in red on yellow paper where an engraved plate has been insufficiently wiped. Used 1918–1921.

(5) An experimental *buff* paper. This lacks the brownish tinge of (4) and the brightness of the yellow shades. The gum is shiny when compared with the matt type used on (4). Used 1919–1920.

(6) A *pale yellow* paper that has a creamy tone to the yellow. Used from 1920 onwards.

Green papers

(7) The original "green" paper, varying considerably through shades of blue-green and yellow-green, the front and back sometimes differing. Used 1912–1916.

(8) The *white backs*. Used 1913–1914.

(9) A paper blue-green on the surface with *pale olive* back. The back must be markedly paler than the front and this and the pronounced olive tinge to the back distinguish it from (7). Used 1916–1920.

(10) Paper with a vivid green surface, commonly called *emerald-green*; it has the olive back of (9). Used 1920.

(11) Paper with *emerald-green* both back and front. Used from 1920 onwards.

3. Perforation and Rouletting

Perforation gauge. The gauge of a perforation is the number of holes in a length of 2 cm. For correct classification the size of the holes (large or small) may need to be distinguished; in a few cases the actual number of holes on each edge of the stamp needs to be quoted.

Measurement. The Gibbons *Instanta* gauge is the standard for measuring perforations. The stamp is viewed against a dark background with the transparent gauge put on top of it. Though the gauge measures to decimal accuracy, perforations read from it are generally quoted in the Catalogue to the nearest half. For example:

Just over perf 12¾ to just under 13¼ = perf 13
Perf 13¼ exactly, rounded up   = perf 13½
Just over perf 13¼ to just under 13¾ = perf 13½
Perf 13¾ exactly, rounded up   = perf 14

However, where classification depends on it, actual quarter-perforations are quoted.

Notation. Where no perforation is quoted for an issue it is imperforate. Perforations are usually abbreviated (and spoken) as follows, though sometimes they may be spelled out for clarity. This notation for rectangular stamps (the majority) applies to diamond shapes if "top" is read as the edge to the top right.

P 14: perforated alike on all sides (read: "perf 14").

P 14×15: the first figure refers to top and bottom, the second to left and right sides (read: "perf 14 by 15"). This is a compound perforation. For an upright triangular stamp the first figure refers to the two sloping sides and second to the base. In inverted triangulars the base is first and the second figure to the sloping sides.

P 14–15: perforation measuring anything between 14 and 15: the holes are irregularly spaced, thus the gauge may vary along a single line or even along a single edge of the stamp (read: "perf 14 to 15").

P 14 *irregular*: perforated 14 from a worn perforator, giving badly aligned holes irregularly spaced (read: "irregular perf 14").

P *comp(ound)* 14×15: two gauges in use but not necessarily on opposite sides of the stamp. It could be one side in one gauge and three in the other; or two adjacent sides with the same gauge. (Read: "perf compound of 14 and 15".) For three gauges or more, abbreviated as "P 12, 14½, 15 *or compound*" for example.

P 14, 14½: perforated approximately 14¼ (read: "perf 14 or 14½"). It does *not* mean two stamps, one perf 14 and the other perf 14½. This obsolescent notation is gradually being replaced in the Catalogue.

Imperf: imperforate (not perforated)

Imperf×P 14: imperforate at top ad bottom and perf 14 at sides.

P 14×*imperf*: perf 14 at top and bottom and imperforate at sides.

Such headings as "P 13×14 (*vert*) and P 14×13 (*horiz*)" indicate which perforations apply to which stamp format—vertical or horizontal.

Some stamps are additionally perforated so that a label or tab is detachable; others have been perforated for use as two halves. Listings are normally for whole stamps, unless stated otherwise.

Imperf×perf

Other terms. Perforation almost always gives circular holes; where other shapes have been used they are specified, e.g. square holes; lozenge perf. Interrupted perfs are brought about by the omission of pins at regular intervals. Perforations merely simulated by being printed as part of the design are of course ignored. With few exceptions, privately applied perforations are not listed.

In the 19th century perforations are often described as clean cut (clean, sharply incised holes), intermediate or rough (rough holes, imperfectly cut, often the result of blunt pins).

Perforation errors and varieties. Authenticated errors, where a stamp normally perforated is accidentally issued imperforate, are listed provided no traces of perforation (blind holes or indentations) remain. They must be provided as pairs, both stamps wholly imperforate, and are only priced in that form.

Stamps imperforate between stamp and sheet margin are not listed in this catalogue, but such errors on Great Britain stamps will be found in the *Great Britain Specialised Catalogue*.

Pairs described as "imperforate between" have the line of perforations between the two stamps omitted.

Imperf between (horiz pair): a horizontal pair of stamps with perfs all around the edges but none between the stamps.

Imperf between (vert pair): a vertical pair of stamps with perfs all around the edges but none between the stamps.

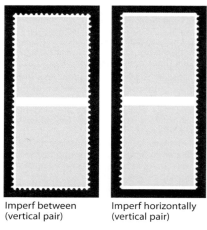

| Imperf between (vertical pair) | Imperf horizontally (vertical pair) |

Where several of the rows have escaped perforation the resulting varieties are listable. Thus:

Imperf vert (horiz pair): a horizontal pair of stamps perforated top and bottom; all three vertical directions are imperf—the two outer edges and between the stamps.

Imperf horiz (vert pair): a vertical pair perforated at left and right edges; all three horizontal directions are imperf—the top, bottom and between the stamps.

Straight edges. Large sheets cut up before issue to post offices can cause stamps with straight edges, i.e. imperf on one side or on two sides at right angles. They are not usually listable in this condition and are worth less than corresponding stamps properly perforated all round. This does not, however, apply to certain stamps, mainly from coils and booklets, where straight edges on various sides are the manufacturing norm affecting every stamp. The listings and notes make clear which sides are correctly imperf.

Malfunction. Varieties of double, misplaced or partial perforation caused by error or machine malfunction are not listable, neither are freaks, such as perforations placed diagonally from paper folds, nor missing holes caused by broken pins.

Types of perforating. Where necessary for classification, perforation types are distinguished.

These include:

Line perforation from one line of pins punching single rows of holes at a time.

Comb perforation from pins disposed across the sheet in comb formation, punching out holes at three sides of the stamp a row at a time.

Harrow perforation applied to a whole pane or sheet at one stroke.

Rotary perforation from toothed wheels operating across a sheet, then crosswise.

Sewing machine perforation. The resultant condition, clean-cut or rough, is distinguished where required.

Pin-perforation is the commonly applied term for pin-roulette in which, instead of being punched out, round holes are pricked by sharp-pointed pins and no paper is removed.

Mixed perforation occurs when stamps with defective perforations are re-perforated in a different gauge.

Punctured stamps. Perforation holes can be punched into the face of the stamp. Patterns of small holes, often in the shape of initial letters, are privately applied devices against pilferage. These (perfins) are outside the scope except for Australia, Canada, Cape of Good Hope, Papua and Sudan where they were used as official stamps by the national administration. Identification devices, when officially inspired, are listed or noted; they can be shapes, or letters or words formed from holes, sometimes converting one class of stamp into another.

Rouletting. In rouletting the paper is cut, for ease of separation, but none is removed. The gauge is measured, when needed, as for perforations. Traditional French terms descriptive of the type of cut are often used and types include:

Arc roulette (percé en arc). Cuts are minute, spaced arcs, each roughly a semicircle.

Cross roulette (percé en croix). Cuts are tiny diagonal crosses.

Line roulette (percé en ligne or en ligne droite). Short straight cuts parallel to the frame of the stamp. The commonest basic roulette. Where not further described, "roulette" means this type.

Rouletted in colour or coloured roulette (percé en lignes colorées or en lignes de coleur). Cuts with coloured edges, arising from notched rule inked simultaneously with the printing plate.

Saw-tooth roulette (percé en scie). Cuts applied zigzag fashion to resemble the teeth of a saw.

Serpentine roulette (percé en serpentin). Cuts as sharply wavy lines.

Zigzag roulette (percé en zigzags). Short straight cuts at angles in alternate directions, producing sharp points on separation. US usage favours "serrate(d) roulette" for this type.

Pin-roulette (originally *percé en points* and now *perforés trous d'epingle*) is commonly called pin-perforation in English.

4. Gum

All stamps listed are assumed to have gum of some kind; if they were issued without gum this is stated. Original gum (o.g.) means that which was present on the stamp as issued to the public. Deleterious climates and the presence of certain chemicals can cause gum to crack and, with early stamps, even make the paper deteriorate. Unscrupulous fakers are adept in removing it and regumming the stamp to meet the unreasoning demand often made for "full o.g." in cases where such a thing is virtually impossible.

The gum normally used on stamps has been gum arabic until the late 1960s when synthetic adhesives were introduced. Harrison and Sons Ltd for instance use *polyvinyl alcohol,* known to philatelists as PVA. This is almost invisible except for a slight yellowish tinge which was incorporated to make it possible to see that the stamps have been gummed. It has advantages in hot countries, as stamps do not curl and sheets are less likely to stick together. Gum arabic and PVA are not

distinguished in the lists except that where a stamp exists with both forms this is indicated in footnotes. Our more specialised catalogues provide separate listing of gums for Great Britain.

Self-adhesive stamps are issued on backing paper, from which they are peeled before affixing to mail. Unused examples are priced as for backing paper intact, in which condition they are recommended to be kept. Used examples are best collected on cover or on piece.

5. Watermarks

Stamps are on unwatermarked paper except where the heading to the set says otherwise.

Detection. Watermarks are detected for Catalogue description by one of four methods: (1) holding stamps to the light; (2) laying stamps face down on a dark background; (3) adding a few drops of petroleum ether 40/60 to the stamp laid face down in a watermark tray; (4) by use of the Stanley Gibbons Detectamark, or other equipment, which work by revealing the thinning of the paper at the watermark. (Note that petroleum ether is highly inflammable in use and can damage photogravure stamps.)

Listable types. Stamps occurring on both watermarked and unwatermarked papers are different types and both receive full listing.

Single watermarks (devices occurring once on every stamp) can be modified in size and shape as between different issues; the types are noted but not usually separately listed. Fortuitous absence of watermark from a single stamp or its gross displacement would not be listable.

To overcome registration difficulties the device may be repeated at close intervals *(a multiple watermark),* single stamps thus showing parts of several devices. Similarly, a *large sheet watermark* (or *all-over watermark)* covering numerous stamps can be used. We give informative notes and illustrations for them. The designs may be such that numbers of stamps in the sheet automatically lack watermark: this is not a listable variety. Multiple and all-over watermarks sometimes undergo modifications, but if the various types are difficult to distinguish from single stamps notes are given but not separate listings.

Papermakers' watermarks are noted where known but not listed separately, since most stamps in the sheet will lack them. Sheet watermarks which are nothing more than officially adopted papermakers' watermarks are, however, given normal listing.

Marginal watermarks, falling outside the pane of stamps, are ignored except where misplacement caused the adjoining row to be affected, in which case they may be footnoted.

Watermark errors and varieties. Watermark errors are recognised as of major importance. They comprise stamps intended to be on unwatermarked paper but issued watermarked by mistake, or stamps printed on paper with the wrong watermark. Varieties showing letters omitted from the watermark are also included, but broken or deformed bits on the dandy roll are not listed unless they represent repairs.

Watermark positions. The diagram shows how watermark position is described in the Catalogue. Paper has a side intended for printing and watermarks are usually impressed so that they read normally when looked through from that printed side. However, since philatelists customarily detect watermarks by looking at the back of the stamp the watermark diagram also makes clear what is actually seen.

Illustrations in the Catalogue are of watermarks in normal positions (from the front of the stamps) and are actual size where possible.

Differences in watermark position are collectable varieties. This Catalogue now lists inverted, sideways inverted and reversed watermark varieties on Commonwealth stamps from the 1860s onwards except where the watermark position is completely haphazard.

Great Britain inverted and sideways inverted watermarks can be found in the *Great Britain Specialised Catalogue* and the *Great Britain Concise Catalogue*.

Where a watermark comes indiscriminately in various positions our policy is to cover this by a general note: we do not give separate listings because the watermark position in these circumstances has no particular philatelic importance.

AS DESCRIBED (Read through front of stamp)		AS SEEN DURING WATERMARK DETECTION (Stamp face down and back examined)
GvR	Normal	ЯvƆ
ЯvƆ	Inverted	ӨΛЯ
ЯvƆ	Reversed	GvR
ӨΛЯ	Reversed and Inverted	ЯvƆ
GvR	Sideways	ЯvƆ
GvR	Sideways Inverted	ЯvƆ

Standard types of watermark. Some watermarks have been used generally for various British possessions rather than exclusively for a single colony. To avoid repetition the Catalogue classifies 11 general types, as under, with references in the headings throughout the listings being given either in words or in the form ("W w **9**") (meaning "watermark type w **9**"). In those cases where watermark illustrations appear in the listings themselves, the respective reference reads, for example, W **153**, thus indicating that the watermark will be found in the normal sequence of illustrations as (type) **153**.

The general types are as follows, with an example of each quoted.

W	Description	Example
w **1**	Large Star	St. Helena No. 1
w **2**	Small Star	Turks Is. No. 4
w **3**	Broad (pointed) Star	Grenada No. 24
w **4**	Crown (over) CC, small stamp	Antigua No. 13
w **5**	Crown (over) CC, large stamp	Antigua No. 31
w **6**	Crown (over) CA, small stamp	Antigua No. 21
w **7**	Crown CA (CA over Crown), large stamp	Sierra Leone No. 54
w **8**	Multiple Crown CA	Antigua No. 41
w **9**	Multiple Script CA	Seychelles No. 158
w **9***a*	do. Error	Seychelles No. 158a
w **9***b*	do. Error	Seychelles No. 158b
w **10**	V over Crown	N.S.W. No. 327
w **11**	Crown over A	N.S.W. No. 347

CC in these watermarks is an abbreviation for "Crown Colonies" and CA for "Crown Agents". Watermarks w **1**, w **2** and w **3** are on stamps printed by Perkins, Bacon; w **4** onwards on stamps from De La Rue and other printers.

w **1**
Large Star

w **2**
Small Star

w **3**
Broad-pointed Star

Watermark w **1**, *Large Star*, measures 15 to 16 mm across the star from point to point and about 27 mm from centre to centre vertically between stars in the sheet. It was made for long stamps like Ceylon 1857 and St. Helena 1856.

Watermark w **2**, *Small Star* is of similar design but measures 12 to 13½mm from point to point and 24 mm from centre to centre vertically. It was for use with ordinary-size stamps such as Grenada 1863–71.

When the Large Star watermark was used with the smaller stamps it only occasionally comes in the centre of the paper. It is frequently so misplaced as to show portions of two stars above and below and this eccentricity will very often help in determining the watermark.

Watermark w **3**, *Broad-pointed Star*, resembles w **1** but the points are broader.

| w **4** | w **5** |
| Crown (over) CC | Crown (over) CC |

Two *Crown (over) CC* watermarks were used: w **4** was for stamps of ordinary size and w **5** for those of larger size.

| w **6** | w **7** |
| Crown (over) CA | CA over Crown |

Two watermarks of *Crown CA* type were used, w **6** being for stamps of ordinary size. The other, w **7**, is properly described as *CA over Crown*. It was specially made for paper on which it was intended to print long fiscal stamps: that some were used postally accounts for the appearance of w **7** in the Catalogue. The watermark occupies twice the space of the ordinary Crown CA watermark, w **6**. Stamps of normal size printed on paper with w **7** watermark show it *sideways*; it takes a horizontal pair of stamps to show the entire watermark.

| w **8** | w **9** |
| Multiple Crown CA | Multiple Script CA |

Multiple watermarks began in 1904 with w **8**, *Multiple Crown CA*, changed from 1921 to w **9**, *Multiple Script CA*. On stamps of ordinary size portions of two or three watermarks appear and on the large-sized stamps a greater number can be observed. The change to letters in script character with w **9** was accompanied by a Crown of distinctly different shape.

It seems likely that there were at least two dandy rolls for each Crown Agents watermark in use at any one time with a reserve roll being employed when the normal one was withdrawn for maintenance or repair.

Both the Mult Crown CA and the Mult Script CA types exist with one or other of the letters omitted from individual impressions. It is possible that most of these occur from the reserve rolls as they have only been found on certain issues. The MCA watermark experienced such problems during the early 1920s and the Script over a longer period from the early 1940s until 1951.

During the 1920s damage must also have occurred on one of the Crowns as a substituted Crown has been found on certain issues. This is smaller than the normal and consists of an oval base joined to two upright ovals with a circle positioned between their upper ends. The upper line of the Crown's base is omitted, as are the left and right-hand circles at the top and also the cross over the centre circle.

Substituted Crown

The *Multiple Script CA* watermark, w **9**, is known with two errors, recurring among the 1950–52 printings of several territories. In the first a crown has fallen away from the dandy-roll that impresses the watermark into the paper pulp. It gives w **9a**, *Crown missing*, but this omission has been found in both "Crown only" (*illustrated*) and "Crown CA" rows. The resulting faulty paper was used for Bahamas, Johore, Seychelles and the postage due stamps of nine colonies

w **9a**: Error, Crown missing

w **9b**: Error, St. Edward's Crown

When the omission was noticed a second mishap occurred, which was to insert a wrong crown in the space, giving w **9b**, St. Edward's Crown. This produced varieties in Bahamas, Perlis, St. Kitts-Nevis and Singapore and the incorrect crown likewise occurs in (Crown only) and (Crown CA) rows.

w **10**
V over Crown

w **11**
Crown over A

Resuming the general types, two watermarks found in issues of several Australian States are: w **10**, *V over Crown*, and w **11**, *Crown over A*.

w **12**
Multiple St. Edward's
Crown Block CA

w **13**
Multiple PTM

The *Multiple St. Edward's Crown Block CA* watermark, w **12**, was introduced in 1957 and besides the change in the Crown (from that used in Multiple Crown Script CA, w **9**) the letters reverted to block capitals. The new watermark began to appear sideways in 1966 and these stamps are generally listed as separate sets.

The watermark w **13**, *Multiple PTM*, was introduced for new Malaysian issues in November 1961.

w **14**
Multiple Crown CA Diagonal

By 1974 the two dandy-rolls the "upright" and the "sideways" for w **12** were wearing out; the Crown Agents therefore discontinued using the sideways watermark one and retained the other only as a stand-by. A new dandy-roll with the pattern of w **14**, *Multiple Crown CA Diagonal,* was introduced and first saw use with some Churchill Centenary issues.

The new watermark had the design arranged in gradually spiralling rows. It is improved in design to allow smooth passage over the paper (the gaps between letters and rows had caused jolts in previous dandy-rolls) and the sharp corners and angles, where fibres used to accumulate, have been eliminated by rounding.

This watermark had no "normal" sideways position amongst the different printers using it. To avoid confusion our more specialised listings do not rely on such terms as

"sideways inverted" but describe the direction in which the watermark points.

w **15**
Multiple POST OFFICE

During 1981 w **15**, *Multiple POST OFFICE* was introduced for certain issues prepared by Philatelists Ltd, acting for various countries in the Indian Ocean, Pacific and West Indies.

w **16**
Multiple Crown Script CA Diagonal

A new Crown Agents watermark was introduced during 1985, w **16**, *Multiple Crown Script CA Diagonal*. This was very similar to the previous w **14**, but showed "CA" in script rather than block letters. It was first used on the omnibus series of stamps commemorating the Life and Times of Queen Elizabeth the Queen Mother.

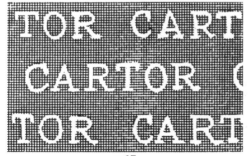

w **17**
Multiple CARTOR

Watermark w **17**, *Multiple CARTOR*, was used from 1985 for issues printed by this French firm for countries which did not normally use the Crown Agents watermark.

w **18**

In 2008, following the closure of the Crown Agents Stamp Bureau, a new Multiple Crowns watermark, w **18** was introduced

In recent years the use of watermarks has, to a small extent, been superseded by fluorescent security markings. These are often more visible from the reverse of the stamp (Cook Islands from 1970 onwards), but have occurred printed over the design (Hong Kong Nos. 415/30). In 1982 the Crown Agents introduced a new stock paper, without watermark, known as "C-Kurity" on which a fluorescent pattern of blue rosettes is visible on the reverse, beneath the gum. This paper was used for issues from Gambia and Norfolk Island.

6. Colours

Stamps in two or three colours have these named in order of appearance, from the centre moving outwards. Four colours or more are usually listed as multicoloured.

In compound colour names the second is the predominant one, thus:

orange-red = a red tending towards orange;
red-orange = an orange containing more red than usual.

Standard colours used. The 200 colours most used for stamp identification are given in the Stanley Gibbons Stamp Colour Key. The Catalogue has used the Stamp Colour Key as standard for describing new issues for some years. The names are also introduced as lists are rewritten, though exceptions are made for those early issues where traditional names have become universally established.

Determining colours. When comparing actual stamps with colour samples in the Stamp Colour Key, view in a good north daylight (or its best substitute; fluorescent "colour matching" light). Sunshine is not recommended. Choose a solid portion of the stamp design; if available, marginal markings such as solid bars of colour or colour check dots are helpful. Shading lines in the design can be misleading as they appear lighter than solid colour. Postmarked portions of a stamp appear darker than normal. If more than one colour is present, mask off the extraneous ones as the eye tends to mix them.

Errors of colour. Major colour errors in stamps or overprints which qualify for listing are: wrong colours; one colour inverted in relation to the rest; albinos (colourless impressions), where these have Expert Committee certificates; colours completely omitted, but only on unused stamps (if found on used stamps the information is footnoted) and with good credentials, missing colours being frequently faked.

Colours only partially omitted are not recognised, Colour shifts, however spectacular, are not listed.

Shades. Shades in philately refer to variations in the intensity of a colour or the presence of differing amounts of other colours. They are particularly significant when they can be linked to specific printings. In general, shades need to

be quite marked to fall within the scope of this Catalogue; it does not favour nowadays listing the often numerous shades of a stamp, but chooses a single applicable colour name which will indicate particular groups of outstanding shades. Furthermore, the listings refer to colours as issued; they may deteriorate into something different through the passage of time.

Modern colour printing by lithography is prone to marked differences of shade, even within a single run, and variations can occur within the same sheet. Such shades are not listed.

Aniline colours. An aniline colour meant originally one derived from coal-tar; it now refers more widely to colour of a particular brightness suffused on the surface of a stamp and showing through clearly on the back.

Colours of overprints and surcharges. All overprints and surcharges are in black unless stated otherwise in the heading or after the description of the stamp.

7. Specimen Stamps

Originally, stamps overprinted SPECIMEN were circulated to postmasters or kept in official records, but after the establishment of the Universal Postal Union supplies were sent to Berne for distribution to the postal administrations of member countries.

During the period 1884 to 1928 most of the stamps of British Crown Colonies required for this purpose were overprinted SPECIMEN in various shapes and sizes by their printers from typeset formes. Some locally produced provisionals were handstamped locally, as were sets prepared for presentation. From 1928 stamps were punched with holes forming the word SPECIMEN, each firm of printers using a different machine or machines. From 1948 the stamps supplied for UPU distribution were no longer punctured.

Stamps of some other Commonwealth territories were overprinted or handstamped locally, while stamps of Great Britain and those in overseas postal agencies (mostly of the higher denominations) bore SPECIMEN overprints and handstamps applied by the Inland Revenue or the Post Office.

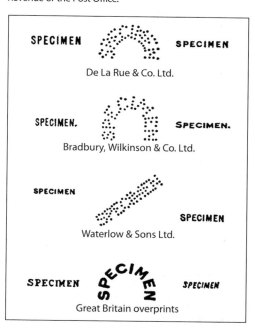

Some of the commoner types of overprints or punctures are illustrated here. Collectors are warned that dangerous forgeries of the punctured type exist.

The *Stanley Gibbons Commonwealth Catalogues* record those Specimen overprints or perforations intended for distribution by the UPU to member countries. In addition the Specimen overprints of Australia and its dependent territories, which were sold to collectors by the Post Office, are also included.

Various Perkins Bacon issues exist obliterated with a "CANCELLED" within an oval of bars handstamp.

Perkins Bacon "CANCELLED"
Handstamp

This was applied to six examples of those issues available in 1861 which were then given to members of Sir Rowland Hill's family. 75 different stamps (including four from Chile) are recorded with this handstamp although others may possibly exist. The unauthorised gift of these "CANCELLED" stamps to the Hill family was a major factor in the loss of the Agent General for the Crown Colonies (the forerunner of the Crown Agents) contracts by Perkins Bacon in the following year. Where examples of these scarce items are known to be in private hands the catalogue provides a price.

For full details of these stamps see *CANCELLED by Perkins Bacon* by Peter Jaffé (published by Spink in 1998).

All other Specimens are outside the scope of this volume.

Specimens are not quoted in Great Britain as they are fully listed in the Stanley Gibbons *Great Britain Specialised Catalogue*.

In specifying type of specimen for individual high-value stamps, "H/S" means handstamped, "Optd" is overprinted and "Perf" is punctured. Some sets occur mixed, e.g. "Optd/Perf". If unspecified, the type is apparent from the date or it is the same as for the lower values quoted as a set.

Prices. Prices for stamps up to £1 are quoted in sets; higher values are priced singly. Where specimens exist in more than one type the price quoted is for the cheapest. Specimen stamps have rarely survived even as pairs; these and strips of three, four or five are worth considerably more than singles.

8. Luminescence

Machines which sort mail electronically have been introduced in recent years. In consequence some countries have issued stamps on fluorescent or phosphorescent papers, while others have marked their stamps with phosphor bands.

The various papers can only be distinguished by ultraviolet lamps emitting particular wavelengths. They are separately listed only when the stamps have some other means of distinguishing them, visible without the use of these lamps. Where this is not so, the papers are recorded in footnotes or headings.

For this catalogue we do not consider it appropriate that collectors be compelled to have the use of an ultraviolet lamp before being able to identify stamps by our listings. Some experience will also be found necessary in interpreting the results given by ultraviolet. Collectors using the lamps, nevertheless, should exercise great care in their use as exposure to their light is potentially dangerous to the eyes.

Phosphor bands are listable, since they are visible to the naked eye (by holding stamps at an angle to the light and looking along them, the bands appear dark). Stamps existing with or without phosphor bands or with differing numbers of bands are given separate listings. Varieties such as double bands, bands omitted, misplaced or printed on the back are not listed.

Detailed descriptions appear at appropriate places in the listings in explanation of luminescent papers; see, for example, Australia above No. 363, Canada above Nos. 472 and 611, Cook Is. above 249, etc.

For Great Britain, where since 1959 phosphors have played a prominent and intricate part in stamp issues, the main notes above Nos. 599 and 723 should be studied, as well as the footnotes to individual listings where appropriate. In general the classification is as follows.

Stamps with phosphor bands are those where a separate cylinder applies the phosphor after the stamps are printed. Issues with "all-over" phosphor have the "band" covering the entire stamp. Parts of the stamp covered by phosphor bands, or the entire surface for "all-over" phosphor versions, appear matt. Stamps on phosphorised paper have the phosphor added to the paper coating before the stamps are printed. Issues on this paper have a completely shiny surface.

Further particularisation of phosphor – their methods of printing and the colours they exhibit under ultraviolet – is outside the scope. The more specialised listings should be consulted for this information.

9. Coil Stamps

Stamps issued only in coil form are given full listing. If stamps are issued in both sheets and coils the coil stamps are listed separately only where there is some feature (e.g. perforation or watermark sideways) by which singles can be distinguished. Coil stamps containing different stamps *se-tenant* are also listed.

Coil join pairs are too random and too easily faked to permit of listing; similarly ignored are coil stamps which have accidentally suffered an extra row of perforations from the claw mechanism in a malfunctioning vending machine.

10. Stamp Booklets

Stamp booklets are now listed in this catalogue.

Single stamps from booklets are listed if they are distinguishable in some way (such as watermark or perforation) from similar sheet stamps.

Booklet panes are listed where they contain stamps of different denominations *se-tenant*, where stamp-size labels are included, or where such panes are otherwise identifiable. Booklet panes are placed in the listing under the lowest denomination present.

Particular perforations (straight edges) are covered by appropriate notes.

11. Miniature Sheets and Sheetlets

We distinguish between "miniature sheets" and "sheetlets" and this affects the catalogue numbering. An item in sheet form that is postally valid, containing a single stamp, pair, block or set of stamps, with wide, inscribed and/or decorative margins, is a miniature sheet if it is sold at post offices as an indivisable entity. As such the Catalogue allots a single MS number and describes what stamps make it up. The sheetlet or small sheet differs in that the individual stamps are intended to be purchased separately for postal purposes. For sheetlets, all the component postage stamps are numbered individually and the composition explained in a footnote. Note that the definitions refer to post office sale—not how items may be subsequently offered by stamp dealers.

12. Forgeries and Fakes

Forgeries. Where space permits, notes are considered if they can give a concise description that will permit unequivocal detection of a forgery. Generalised warnings, lacking detail, are not nowadays inserted, since their value to the collector is problematic.

Forged cancellations have also been applied to genuine stamps. This catalogue includes notes regarding those manufactured by "Madame Joseph", together with the cancellation dates known to exist. It should be remembered that these dates also exist as genuine cancellations.

For full details of these see *Madame Joseph Forged Postmarks* by Derek Worboys (published by the Royal Philatelic Society London and the British Philatelic Trust in 1994) or *Madame Joseph Revisited* by Brian Cartwright (published by the Royal Philatelic Society London in 2005).

Fakes. Unwitting fakes are numerous, particularly "new shades" which are colour changelings brought about by exposure to sunlight, soaking in water contaminated with dyes from adherent paper, contact with oil and dirt from a pocketbook, and so on. Fraudulent operators, in addition, can offer to arrange: removal of hinge marks; repairs of thins on white or coloured papers; replacement of missing margins or perforations; reperforating in true or false gauges; removal of fiscal cancellations; rejoining of severed pairs, strips and blocks; and (a major hazard) regumming. Collectors can only be urged to purchase from reputable sources and to insist upon Expert Committee certification where there is any kind of doubt.

The Catalogue can consider footnotes about fakes where these are specific enough to assist in detection.

ACKNOWLEDGEMENTS

We are grateful to individual collectors, members of the philatelic trade and specialist societies and study circles for their assistance in improving and extending the Stanley Gibbons range of catalogues. The addresses of societies and study circles relevant to this volume are:

Aden & Somaliland Study Group
UK Representative – Mr M. Lacey
P.O. Box 9, Winchester, Hampshire
SO22 5RF

GB Overprints Society
Secretary - Mr A. Stanford
P.O. Box 2675, Maidenhead
SL6 9ZN

East Africa Study Circle
Honorary secretary – Mr. M. Vesey-FitzGerald
Vernalls Orchard, Gosport Lane
Lyndhurst, Hampshire SO43 7BP

Egypt Study Circle
Secretary – Mr M. Murphy,
109 Chadwick Road, Peckham, London
SE15 4PY

Sudan Study Group
Secretary – Mr B.A. Gardner, Chimneys,
Mapledurwell, Basingstoke, Hants
RG25 2LH

Abbreviations

Printers

A.B.N. Co.	American Bank Note Co, New York.
B.A.B.N.	British American Bank Note Co. Ottawa
B.D.T.	B.D.T. International Security Printing Ltd, Dublin, Ireland
B.W.	Bradbury Wilkinson & Co, Ltd.
Cartor	Cartor S.A., La Loupe, France
C.B.N.	Canadian Bank Note Co, Ottawa.
Continental	Continental Bank Note Co. B.N. Co.
Courvoisier	Imprimerie Courvoisier S.A., La-Chaux-de-Fonds, Switzerland.
D.L.R.	De La Rue & Co, Ltd, London.
Enschedé	Joh. Enschedé en Zonen, Haarlem, Netherlands.
Format	Format International Security Printers Ltd., London
Harrison	Harrison & Sons, Ltd. London
J.W.	John Waddington Security Print Ltd., Leeds
P.B.	Perkins Bacon Ltd, London.
Questa	Questa Colour Security Printers Ltd, London
Walsall	Walsall Security Printers Ltd
Waterlow	Waterlow & Sons, Ltd, London.

General Abbreviations

Alph	Alphabet
Anniv	Anniversary
Comp	Compound (perforation)
Des	Designer; designed
Diag	Diagonal; diagonally
Eng	Engraver; engraved
F.C.	Fiscal Cancellation
H/S	Handstamped
Horiz	Horizontal; horizontally
Imp, Imperf	Imperforate
Inscr	Inscribed
L	Left
Litho	Lithographed
mm	Millimetres
MS	Miniature sheet
N.Y.	New York
Opt(d)	Overprint(ed)
P or P-c	Pen-cancelled
P, Pf or Perf	Perforated
Photo	Photogravure
Pl	Plate
Pr	Pair
Ptd	Printed
Ptg	Printing
R	Right
R.	Row

Recess	Recess-printed
Roto	Rotogravure
Roul	Rouletted
S	Specimen (overprint)
Surch	Surcharge(d)
T.C.	Telegraph Cancellation
T	Type
Typo	Typographed
Un	Unused
Us	Used
Vert	Vertical; vertically
W or wmk	Watermark
Wmk s	Watermark sideways

(†) = Does not exist
(–) (or blank price column) = Exists, or may exist, but no market price is known.
/ between colours means "on" and the colour following is that of the paper on which the stamp is printed.

Colours of Stamps
Bl (blue); blk (black); brn (brown); car, carm (carmine); choc (chocolate); clar (claret); emer (emerald); grn (green); ind (indigo); mag (magenta); mar (maroon); mult (multicoloured); mve (mauve); ol (olive); orge (orange); pk (pink); pur (purple); scar (scarlet); sep (sepia); turq (turquoise); ultram (ultramarine); verm (vermilion); vio (violet); yell (yellow).

Colour of Overprints and Surcharges
(B.) = blue, (Blk.) = black, (Br.) = brown, (C.) = carmine, (G.) = green, (Mag.) = magenta, (Mve.) = mauve, (Ol.) = olive, (O.) = orange, (P.) = purple, (Pk.) = pink, (R.) = red, (Sil.) = silver, (V.) = violet, (Vm.) or (Verm.) = vermilion, (W.) = white, (Y.) = yellow.

Arabic Numerals
As in the case of European figures, the details of the Arabic numerals vary in different stamp designs, but they should be readily recognised with the aid of this illustration.

٠	١	٢	٣	٤	٥	٦	٧	٨	٩
0	1	2	3	4	5	6	7	8	9

Features Listing

An at-a-glance guide to what's in the Stanley Gibbons catalogues

Area	Feature	Collect British Stamps	Stamps of the World	Thematic Catalogues	Comprehensive Catalogue, Parts 1-22 (including Commonwealth and British Empire Stamps and country catalogues)	Great Britain Concise	Specialised catalogues
General	SG number	√	√	√	√	√	√
General	Specialised Catalogue number						√
General	Year of issue of first stamp in design	√	√	√	√	√	√
General	Exact date of issue of each design				√	√	√
General	Face value information	√	√	√	√	√	√
General	Historical and geographical information	√	√	√	√	√	√
General	General currency information, including dates used	√	√	√	√	√	√
General	Country name	√	√	√			
General	Booklet panes				√	√	√
General	Coil stamps				√		√
General	First Day Covers	√				√	√
General	Brief footnotes on key areas of note	√	√	√		√	√
General	Detailed footnotes on key areas of note				√	√	√
General	Extra background information				√	√	√
General	Miniature sheet information (including size in mm)	√	√	√	√	√	√
General	Sheetlets				√		
General	Stamp booklets				√	√	√
General	Perkins Bacon "Cancelled"				√		
General	PHQ Cards	√				√	√
General	Post Office Label Sheets					√	
General	Post Office Yearbooks	√				√	√
General	Presentation and Souvenir Packs	√				√	√
General	Se-tenant pairs	√				√	√
General	Watermark details - errors, varieties, positions				√	√	√
General	Watermark illustrations	√			√	√	√
General	Watermark types	√			√	√	√
General	Forgeries noted				√		√
General	Surcharges and overprint information	√	√	√	√	√	√
Design and Description	Colour description, simplified		√	√			
Design and Description	Colour description, extended	√			√	√	√
Design and Description	Set design summary information	√	√	√	√	√	√
Design and Description	Designer name				√	√	√
Design and Description	Short design description	√	√	√	√	√	√

Area	Feature	Collect British Stamps	Stamps of the World	Thematic Catalogues	Comprehensive Catalogue, Parts 1-22 (including Commonwealth and British Empire Stamps and country catalogues)	Great Britain Concise	Specialised catalogues
Design and Description	Shade varieties				√	√	√
Design and Description	Type number	√	√		√	√	√
Illustrations	Multiple stamps from set illustrated	√			√	√	√
Illustrations	A Stamp from each set illustrated in full colour (where possible, otherwise mono)	√	√	√	√	√	√
Price	Catalogue used price	√	√	√	√	√	√
Price	Catalogue unused price	√	√	√	√	√	√
Price	Price - booklet panes				√	√	√
Price	Price - shade varieties				√	√	√
Price	On cover and on piece price				√	√	√
Price	Detailed GB pricing breakdown	√			√	√	√
Print and Paper	Basic printing process information	√	√	√	√	√	√
Print and Paper	Detailed printing process information, e.g. Mill sheets				√		√
Print and Paper	Paper information				√		√
Print and Paper	Detailed perforation information	√			√	√	√
Print and Paper	Details of research findings relating to printing processes and history						√
Print and Paper	Paper colour	√	√		√	√	√
Print and Paper	Paper description to aid identification				√	√	√
Print and Paper	Paper type				√	√	√
Print and Paper	Ordinary or chalk-surfaced paper				√	√	√
Print and Paper	Embossing omitted note						√
Print and Paper	Essays, Die Proofs, Plate Descriptions and Proofs, Colour Trials information						√
Print and Paper	Glazed paper				√	√	√
Print and Paper	Gum details				√		√
Print and Paper	Luminescence/Phosphor bands - general coverage	√			√	√	√
Print and Paper	Luminescence/Phosphor bands - specialised coverage						√
Print and Paper	Overprints and surcharges - including colour information	√	√	√	√	√	√
Print and Paper	Perforation/Imperforate information	√	√		√	√	√
Print and Paper	Perforation errors and varieties				√	√	√
Print and Paper	Print quantities				√		√
Print and Paper	Printing errors				√	√	√
Print and Paper	Printing flaws						√
Print and Paper	Printing varieties				√	√	√
Print and Paper	Punctured stamps - where official				√		
Print and Paper	Sheet positions				√	√	√
Print and Paper	Specialised plate number information						√
Print and Paper	Specimen overprints (only for Commonwealth & GB)				√	√	√
Print and Paper	Underprints					√	√
Print and Paper	Visible Plate numbers	√			√	√	√
Print and Paper	Yellow and Green paper listings				√		√
Index	Design index	√			√	√	

International Philatelic Glossary

English	French	German	Spanish	Italian
Agate	Agate	Achat	Agata	Agata
Air stamp	Timbre de la poste aérienne	Flugpostmarke	Sello de correo aéreo	Francobollo per posta aerea
Apple Green	Vert-pomme	Apfelgrün	Verde manzana	Verde mela
Barred	Annulé par barres	Balkenentwertung	Anulado con barras	Sbarrato
Bisected	Timbre coupé	Halbiert	Partido en dos	Frazionato
Bistre	Bistre	Bister	Bistre	Bistro
Bistre-brown	Brun-bistre	Bisterbraun	Castaño bistre	Bruno-bistro
Black	Noir	Schwarz	Negro	Nero
Blackish Brown	Brun-noir	Schwärzlichbraun	Castaño negruzco	Bruno nerastro
Blackish Green	Vert foncé	Schwärzlichgrün	Verde negruzco	Verde nerastro
Blackish Olive	Olive foncé	Schwärzlicholiv	Oliva negruzco	Oliva nerastro
Block of four	Bloc de quatre	Viererblock	Bloque de cuatro	Bloco di quattro
Blue	Bleu	Blau	Azul	Azzurro
Blue-green	Vert-bleu	Blaugrün	Verde azul	Verde azzuro
Bluish Violet	Violet bleuâtre	Bläulichviolett	Violeta azulado	Violtto azzurrastro
Booklet	Carnet	Heft	Cuadernillo	Libretto
Bright Blue	Bleu vif	Lebhaftblau	Azul vivo	Azzurro vivo
Bright Green	Vert vif	Lebhaftgrün	Verde vivo	Verde vivo
Bright Purple	Mauve vif	Lebhaftpurpur	Púrpura vivo	Porpora vivo
Bronze Green	Vert-bronze	Bronzegrün	Verde bronce	Verde bronzo
Brown	Brun	Braun	Castaño	Bruno
Brown-lake	Carmin-brun	Braunlack	Laca castaño	Lacca bruno
Brown-purple	Pourpre-brun	Braunpurpur	Púrpura castaño	Porpora bruno
Brown-red	Rouge-brun	Braunrot	Rojo castaño	Rosso bruno
Buff	Chamois	Sämisch	Anteado	Camoscio
Cancellation	Oblitération	Entwertung	Cancelación	Annullamento
Cancelled	Annulé	Gestempelt	Cancelado	Annullato
Carmine	Carmin	Karmin	Carmín	Carminio
Carmine-red	Rouge-carmin	Karminrot	Rojo carmín	Rosso carminio
Centred	Centré	Zentriert	Centrado	Centrato
Cerise	Rouge-cerise	Kirschrot	Color de ceresa	Color Ciliegia
Chalk-surfaced paper	Papier couché	Kreidepapier	Papel estucado	Carta gessata
Chalky Blue	Bleu terne	Kreideblau	Azul turbio	Azzurro smorto
Charity stamp	Timbre de bienfaisance	Wohltätigkeitsmarke	Sello de beneficenza	Francobollo di beneficenza
Chestnut	Marron	Kastanienbraun	Castaño rojo	Marrone
Chocolate	Chocolat	Schokolade	Chocolate	Cioccolato
Cinnamon	Cannelle	Zimtbraun	Canela	Cannella
Claret	Grenat	Weinrot	Rojo vinoso	Vinaccia
Cobalt	Cobalt	Kobalt	Cobalto	Cobalto
Colour	Couleur	Farbe	Color	Colore
Comb-perforation	Dentelure en peigne	Kammzähnung, Reihenzähnung	Dentado de peine	Dentellatura e pettine
Commemorative stamp	Timbre commémoratif	Gedenkmarke	Sello conmemorativo	Francobollo commemorativo
Crimson	Cramoisi	Karmesin	Carmesí	Cremisi
Deep Blue	Blue foncé	Dunkelblau	Azul oscuro	Azzurro scuro
Deep bluish Green	Vert-bleu foncé	Dunkelbläulichgrün	Verde azulado oscuro	Verde azzurro scuro
Design	Dessin	Markenbild	Diseño	Disegno

English	French	German	Spanish	Italian
Die	Matrice	Urstempel. Type, Platte	Cuño	Conio, Matrice
Double	Double	Doppelt	Doble	Doppio
Drab	Olive terne	Trüboliv	Oliva turbio	Oliva smorto
Dull Green	Vert terne	Trübgrün	Verde turbio	Verde smorto
Dull purple	Mauve terne	Trübpurpur	Púrpura turbio	Porpora smorto
Embossing	Impression en relief	Prägedruck	Impresión en relieve	Impressione a relievo
Emerald	Vert-eméraude	Smaragdgrün	Esmeralda	Smeraldo
Engraved	Gravé	Graviert	Grabado	Inciso
Error	Erreur	Fehler, Fehldruck	Error	Errore
Essay	Essai	Probedruck	Ensayo	Saggio
Express letter stamp	Timbre pour lettres par exprès	Eilmarke	Sello de urgencia	Francobollo per espresso
Fiscal stamp	Timbre fiscal	Stempelmarke	Sello fiscal	Francobollo fiscale
Flesh	Chair	Fleischfarben	Carne	Carnicino
Forgery	Faux, Falsification	Fälschung	Falsificación	Falso, Falsificazione
Frame	Cadre	Rahmen	Marco	Cornice
Granite paper	Papier avec fragments de fils de soie	Faserpapier	Papel con filamentos	Carto con fili di seta
Green	Vert	Grün	Verde	Verde
Greenish Blue	Bleu verdâtre	Grünlichblau	Azul verdoso	Azzurro verdastro
Greenish Yellow	Jaune-vert	Grünlichgelb	Amarillo verdoso	Giallo verdastro
Grey	Gris	Grau	Gris	Grigio
Grey-blue	Bleu-gris	Graublau	Azul gris	Azzurro grigio
Grey-green	Vert gris	Graugrün	Verde gris	Verde grigio
Gum	Gomme	Gummi	Goma	Gomma
Gutter	Interpanneau	Zwischensteg	Espacio blanco entre dos grupos	Ponte
Imperforate	Non-dentelé	Geschnitten	Sin dentar	Non dentellato
Indigo	Indigo	Indigo	Azul indigo	Indaco
Inscription	Inscription	Inschrift	Inscripción	Dicitura
Inverted	Renversé	Kopfstehend	Invertido	Capovolto
Issue	Émission	Ausgabe	Emisión	Emissione
Laid	Vergé	Gestreift	Listado	Vergato
Lake	Lie de vin	Lackfarbe	Laca	Lacca
Lake-brown	Brun-carmin	Lackbraun	Castaño laca	Bruno lacca
Lavender	Bleu-lavande	Lavendel	Color de alhucema	Lavanda
Lemon	Jaune-citron	Zitrongelb	Limón	Limone
Light Blue	Bleu clair	Hellblau	Azul claro	Azzurro chiaro
Lilac	Lilas	Lila	Lila	Lilla
Line perforation	Denteleure en lignes	Linienzähnung	Dentado en linea	Dentellatura lineare
Lithography	Lithographie	Steindruck	Litografía	Litografia
Local	Timbre de poste locale	Lokalpostmarke	Emisión local	Emissione locale
Lozenge roulette	Percé en losanges	Rautenförmiger Durchstich	Picadura en rombos	Perforazione a losanghe
Magenta	Magenta	Magentarot	Magenta	Magenta
Margin	Marge	Rand	Borde	Margine
Maroon	Marron pourpré	Dunkelrotpurpur	Púrpura rojo oscuro	Marrone rossastro
Mauve	Mauve	Malvenfarbe	Malva	Malva
Multicoloured	Polychrome	Mehrfarbig	Multicolores	Policromo
Myrtle Green	Vert myrte	Myrtengrün	Verde mirto	Verde mirto
New Blue	Bleu ciel vif	Neublau	Azul nuevo	Azzurro nuovo
Newspaper stamp	Timbre pour journaux	Zeitungsmarke	Sello para periódicos	Francobollo per giornali
Obliteration	Oblitération	Abstempelung	Matasello	Annullamento
Obsolete	Hors (de) cours	Ausser Kurs	Fuera de curso	Fuori corso
Ochre	Ocre	Ocker	Ocre	Ocra

English	French	German	Spanish	Italian
Official stamp	Timbre de service	Dienstmarke	Sello de servicio	Francobollo di
Olive-brown	Brun-olive	Olivbraun	Castaño oliva	Bruno oliva
Olive-green	Vert-olive	Olivgrün	Verde oliva	Verde oliva
Olive-grey	Gris-olive	Olivgrau	Gris oliva	Grigio oliva
Olive-yellow	Jaune-olive	Olivgelb	Amarillo oliva	Giallo oliva
Orange	Orange	Orange	Naranja	Arancio
Orange-brown	Brun-orange	Orangebraun	Castaño naranja	Bruno arancio
Orange-red	Rouge-orange	Orangerot	Rojo naranja	Rosso arancio
Orange-yellow	Jaune-orange	Orangegelb	Amarillo naranja	Giallo arancio
Overprint	Surcharge	Aufdruck	Sobrecarga	Soprastampa
Pair	Paire	Paar	Pareja	Coppia
Pale	Pâle	Blass	Pálido	Pallido
Pane	Panneau	Gruppe	Grupo	Gruppo
Paper	Papier	Papier	Papel	Carta
Parcel post stamp	Timbre pour colis postaux	Paketmarke	Sello para paquete postal	Francobollo per pacchi postali
Pen-cancelled	Oblitéré à plume	Federzugentwertung	Cancelado a pluma	Annullato a penna
Percé en arc	Percé en arc	Bogenförmiger Durchstich	Picadura en forma de arco	Perforazione ad arco
Percé en scie	Percé en scie	Bogenförmiger Durchstich	Picado en sierra	Foratura a sega
Perforated	Dentelé	Gezähnt	Dentado	Dentellato
Perforation	Dentelure	Zähnung	Dentar	Dentellatura
Photogravure	Photogravure, Heliogravure	Rastertiefdruck	Fotograbado	Rotocalco
Pin perforation	Percé en points	In Punkten durchstochen	Horadado con alfileres	Perforato a punti
Plate	Planche	Platte	Plancha	Lastra, Tavola
Plum	Prune	Pflaumenfarbe	Color de ciruela	Prugna
Postage Due stamp	Timbre-taxe	Portomarke	Sello de tasa	Segnatasse
Postage stamp	Timbre-poste	Briefmarke, Freimarke, Postmarke	Sello de correos	Francobollo postale
Postal fiscal stamp	Timbre fiscal-postal	Stempelmarke als Postmarke verwendet	Sello fiscal-postal	Fiscale postale
Postmark	Oblitération postale	Poststempel	Matasello	Bollo
Printing	Impression, Tirage	Druck	Impresión	Stampa, Tiratura
Proof	Épreuve	Druckprobe	Prueba de impresión	Prova
Provisionals	Timbres provisoires	Provisorische Marken. Provisorien	Provisionales	Provvisori
Prussian Blue	Bleu de Prusse	Preussischblau	Azul de Prusia	Azzurro di Prussia
Purple	Pourpre	Purpur	Púrpura	Porpora
Purple-brown	Brun-pourpre	Purpurbraun	Castaño púrpura	Bruno porpora
Recess-printing	Impression en taille douce	Tiefdruck	Grabado	Incisione
Red	Rouge	Rot	Rojo	Rosso
Red-brown	Brun-rouge	Rotbraun	Castaño rojizo	Bruno rosso
Reddish Lilac	Lilas rougeâtre	Rötlichlila	Lila rojizo	Lilla rossastro
Reddish Purple	Poupre-rouge	Rötlichpurpur	Púrpura rojizo	Porpora rossastro
Reddish Violet	Violet rougeâtre	Rötlichviolett	Violeta rojizo	Violetto rossastro
Red-orange	Orange rougeâtre	Rotorange	Naranja rojizo	Arancio rosso
Registration stamp	Timbre pour lettre chargée (recommandée)	Einschreibemarke	Sello de certificado lettere	Francobollo per raccomandate
Reprint	Réimpression	Neudruck	Reimpresión	Ristampa
Reversed	Retourné	Umgekehrt	Invertido	Rovesciato
Rose	Rose	Rosa	Rosa	Rosa
Rose-red	Rouge rosé	Rosarot	Rojo rosado	Rosso rosa
Rosine	Rose vif	Lebhaftrosa	Rosa vivo	Rosa vivo
Roulette	Percage	Durchstich	Picadura	Foratura
Rouletted	Percé	Durchstochen	Picado	Forato
Royal Blue	Bleu-roi	Königblau	Azul real	Azzurro reale
Sage green	Vert-sauge	Salbeigrün	Verde salvia	Verde salvia

English	French	German	Spanish	Italian
Salmon	Saumon	Lachs	Salmón	Salmone
Scarlet	Écarlate	Scharlach	Escarlata	Scarlatto
Sepia	Sépia	Sepia	Sepia	Seppia
Serpentine roulette	Percé en serpentin	Schlangenliniger Durchstich	Picado a serpentina	Perforazione a serpentina
Shade	Nuance	Tönung	Tono	Gradazione de colore
Sheet	Feuille	Bogen	Hoja	Foglio
Slate	Ardoise	Schiefer	Pizarra	Ardesia
Slate-blue	Bleu-ardoise	Schieferblau	Azul pizarra	Azzurro ardesia
Slate-green	Vert-ardoise	Schiefergrün	Verde pizarra	Verde ardesia
Slate-lilac	Lilas-gris	Schierferlila	Lila pizarra	Lilla ardesia
Slate-purple	Mauve-gris	Schieferpurpur	Púrpura pizarra	Porpora ardesia
Slate-violet	Violet-gris	Schieferviolett	Violeta pizarra	Violetto ardesia
Special delivery stamp	Timbre pour exprès	Eilmarke	Sello de urgencia	Francobollo per espressi
Specimen	Spécimen	Muster	Muestra	Saggio
Steel Blue	Bleu acier	Stahlblau	Azul acero	Azzurro acciaio
Strip	Bande	Streifen	Tira	Striscia
Surcharge	Surcharge	Aufdruck	Sobrecarga	Soprastampa
Tête-bêche	Tête-bêche	Kehrdruck	Tête-bêche	Tête-bêche
Tinted paper	Papier teinté	Getöntes Papier	Papel coloreado	Carta tinta
Too-late stamp	Timbre pour lettres en retard	Verspätungsmarke	Sello para cartas retardadas	Francobollo per le lettere in ritardo
Turquoise-blue	Bleu-turquoise	Türkisblau	Azul turquesa	Azzurro turchese
Turquoise-green	Vert-turquoise	Türkisgrün	Verde turquesa	Verde turchese
Typography	Typographie	Buchdruck	Tipografía	Tipografia
Ultramarine	Outremer	Ultramarin	Ultramar	Oltremare
Unused	Neuf	Ungebraucht	Nuevo	Nuovo
Used	Oblitéré, Usé	Gebraucht	Usado	Usato
Venetian Red	Rouge-brun terne	Venezianischrot	Rojo veneciano	Rosso veneziano
Vermilion	Vermillon	Zinnober	Cinabrio	Vermiglione
Violet	Violet	Violett	Violeta	Violetto
Violet-blue	Bleu-violet	Violettblau	Azul violeta	Azzurro violetto
Watermark	Filigrane	Wasserzeichen	Filigrana	Filigrana
Watermark sideways	Filigrane couché	Wasserzeichen liegend	Filigrana acostado	Filigrana coricata
Wove paper	Papier ordinaire, Papier uni	Einfaches Papier	Papel avitelado	Carta unita
Yellow	Jaune	Gelb	Amarillo	Giallo
Yellow-brown	Brun-jaune	Gelbbraun	Castaño amarillo	Bruno giallo
Yellow-green	Vert-jaune	Gelbgrün	Verde amarillo	Verde giallo
Yellow-olive	Olive-jaunâtre	Gelboliv	Oliva amarillo	Oliva giallastro
Yellow-orange	Orange jaunâtre	Gelborange	Naranja amarillo	Arancio giallastro
Zig-zag roulette	Percé en zigzag	Sägezahnartiger Durchstich	Picado en zigzag	Perforazione a zigzag

Guide to Entries

(A) **Country of Issue** – When a country changes its name, the catalogue listing changes to reflect the name change, for example Namibia was formerly known as South West Africa, the stamps in Southern Africa are all listed under Namibia, but split into South West Africa and then Namibia.

(B) **Country Information** – Brief geographical and historical details for the issuing country.

(C) **Currency** – Details of the currency, and dates of earliest use where applicable, on the face value of the stamps.

(D) **Illustration** – Generally, the first stamp in the set. Stamp illustrations are reduced to 75%, with overprints and surcharges shown actual size.

(E) **Illustration or Type Number** – These numbers are used to help identify stamps, either in the listing, type column, design line or footnote, usually the first value in a set. These type numbers are in a bold type face – **123**; when bracketed (**123**) an overprint or a surcharge is indicated. Some type numbers include a lower-case letter – **123a**, this indicates they have been added to an existing set.

(F) **Date of issue** – This is the date that the stamp/set of stamps was issued by the post office and was available for purchase. When a set of definitive stamps has been issued over several years the Year Date given is for the earliest issue. Commemorative sets are listed in chronological order. Stamps of the same design, or issue are usually grouped together, for example some of the New Zealand landscapes definitive series were first issued in 2003 but the set includes stamps issued to May 2007.

(G) **Number Prefix** – Stamps other than definitives and commemoratives have a prefix letter before the catalogue number.
Their use is explained in the text: some examples are A for airmail, D for postage due and O for official stamps.

(H) **Footnote** – Further information on background or key facts on issues.

(I) **Stanley Gibbons Catalogue number** – This is a unique number for each stamp to help the collector identify stamps in the listing. The Stanley Gibbons numbering system is universally recognized as definitive.
    Where insufficient numbers have been left to provide for additional stamps to a listing, some stamps will have a suffix letter after the catalogue number (for example 214a). If numbers have been left for additions to a set and not used they will be left vacant.
    The separate type numbers (in bold) refer to illustrations (see **E**).

(J) **Colour** – If a stamp is printed in three or fewer colours then the colours are listed, working from the centre of the stamp outwards (see **R**).

(K) **Design line** – Further details on design variations

(L) **Key Type** – Indicates a design type on which the stamp is based. These are the bold figures found below each illustration, for example listed in Cameroon, in the West Africa catalogue, is the Key type A and B showing the ex-Kaiser's yacht *Hohenzollern*. The type numbers are also given in bold in the second column of figures alongside the stamp description to indicate the design of each stamp. Where an issue comprises stamps of similar design, the corresponding type number should be taken as indicating the general design. Where there are blanks in the type number column it means that the type of the corresponding stamp

is that shown by the number in the type column of the same issue. A dash (–) in the type column means that the stamp is not illustrated. Where type numbers refer to stamps of another country, e.g. where stamps of one country are overprinted for use in another, this is always made clear in the text.

(M) **Coloured Papers** – Stamps printed on coloured paper are shown – e.g. "brown/*yellow*" indicates brown printed on yellow paper.

(N) **Surcharges and Overprints** – Usually described in the headings. Any actual wordings are shown in bold type. Descriptions clarify words and figures used in the overprint. Stamps with the same overprints in different colours are not listed separately. Numbers in brackets after the descriptions are the catalogue numbers of the non-overprinted stamps. The words "inscribed" or "inscription" refer to the wording incorporated in the design of a stamp and not surcharges or overprints.

(O) **Face value** – This refers to the value of each stamp and is the price it was sold for at the Post Office when issued. Some modern stamps do not have their values in figures but instead it is shown as a letter, for example Great Britain use 1st or 2nd on their stamps as opposed to the actual value.

(P) **Catalogue Value** – Mint/Unused. Prices quoted for Queen Victoria to King George V stamps are for lightly hinged examples.

(Q) **Catalogue Value** – Used. Prices generally refer to fine postally used examples. For certain issues they are for cancelled-to-order.

Prices
Prices are given in pence and pounds. Stamps worth £100 and over are shown in whole pounds:

Shown in Catalogue as	Explanation
10	10 pence
1.75	£1.75
15.00	£15
£150	£150
£2300	£2300

Prices assume stamps are in 'fine condition'; we may ask more for superb and less for those of lower quality. The minimum catalogue price quoted is 10p and is intended as a guide for catalogue users. The lowest price for individual stamps purchased from Stanley Gibbons is £1.
    Prices quoted are for the cheapest variety of that particular stamp. Differences of watermark, perforation, or other details, often increase the value. Prices quoted for mint issues are for single examples, unless otherwise stated. Those in *se-tenant* pairs, strips, blocks or sheets may be worth more. Where no prices are listed it is either because the stamps are not known to exist (usually shown by a †) in that particular condition, or, more usually, because there is no reliable information on which to base their value.
All prices are subject to change without prior notice and we cannot guarantee to supply all stamps as priced. Prices quoted in advertisements are also subject to change without prior notice.

(R) **Multicoloured** – Nearly all modern stamps are multicoloured (more than three colours); this is indicated in the heading, with a description of the stamp given in the listing.

(S) **Perforations** – Please see page xiii for a detailed explanation of perforations.

A Country of issue

Bangladesh

B Country Information

In elections during December 1970 the Awami League party won all but two of the seats in the East Pakistan province and, in consequence, held a majority in the National Assembly. On 1 March 1971 the Federal Government postponed the sitting of the Assembly with the result that unrest spread throughout the eastern province. Pakistan army operations against the dissidents forced the leaders of the League to flee to India from where East Pakistan was proclaimed independent as Bangladesh. In early December the Indian army moved against Pakistan troops in Bangladesh and civilian government was re-established on 22 December 1971.

From 20 December 1971 various Pakistan issues were overprinted by local postmasters, mainly using handstamps. Their use was permitted until 30 April 1973. These are of philatelic interest, but are outside the scope of the catalogue.

C Currency

(Currency. 100 paisa = 1 rupee)

D Illustration

5c
N.Z.GOVERNMENT LIFE INSURANCE OFFICE

L 17

E Illustration or Type number

F Date of issue

1978 (8 Mar). No. *L* 57 surch with Type *L* **16**. Chalky paper.

L63	L **14**	25c. on 2½c. ultramarine, green and buff	75	1·75

(Des A. G. Mitchell. Litho Harrison)

1981 (3 June). P 14½.

G Number prefix

L64	L **17**	5c. multicoloured	10	10
L65		10c. multicoloured	10	10
L66		20c. multicoloured	15	15
L67		30c. multicoloured	25	25
L68		40c. multicoloured	30	30
L69		50c. multicoloured	30	45
L64/9	*Set of 6*		1·00	1·25

H Footnote

Issues for the Government Life Insurance Department were withdrawn on 1 December 1989 when it became the privatised Tower Corporation.

(Des G. R. Bull and G. R. Smith. Photo Harrison)

I Stanley Gibbons catalogue number

1959 (2 Mar). Centenary of Marlborough Province. T **198** and similar horiz designs. W **98** (sideways). P 14½×14.

772		2d. green	30	10
773		3d. deep blue	30	10
774		8d. light brown	1·25	2·25
772/4	*Set of 3*		1·60	2·25

J Colour

K Design line

Designs:—3d. Shipping wool, Wairau Bar, 1857; 8d. Salt industry, Grassmere.

1915 (12 July). Stamps of German Kamerun. Types *A* and *B*, surch as T **1** (Nos. B1/9) or **2**. (Nos. B10/13) in black or blue.

L Key type column

B1	A	1½d. on 3pf. (No. k7) (B.)	13·00	42·00
		a. Different fount "d"	£150	£350

340	**41**	2d. purple (1903)	£350	£325
341	**28**	3d. bistre-brown (1906)	£700	£600
342	**37**	4d. blue and chestnut/*bluish* (1904)	£300	£350
		a. Blue and yellow-brown/*bluish*	£300	£350

M Coloured papers

N Surcharges and overprints

1913 (1 Dec). Auckland Industrial Exhibition. Nos. 387aa, 389, 392 and 405 optd with T **59** by Govt Printer, Wellington.

O Face value

412	**51**	½d. deep green	20·00	55·00
413	**53**	1d. carmine	25·00	48·00
		a. "Feather" flaw	£225	
414	**52**	3d. chestnut	£130	£250
415		6d. carmine	£160	£300
412/15	*Set of 4*		£300	£600

P Catalogue value – Mint

Q Catalogue value – Used

These overprinted stamps were only available for letters in New Zealand and to Australia.

(Des Martin Bailey. Litho Southern Colour Print)

R Multicoloured stamp

2008 (2 July). Olympic Games, Beijing. T **685** and similar diamond-shaped designs. Multicoloured. Phosphorised paper. P 14½.

3056	50c. Type **685**	1·00	85

S Perforations

British Occupation of Italian Colonies

PRICES FOR STAMPS ON COVER TO 1945	
Nos. M1/21	from × 4
Nos. MD1/5	from × 10
Nos. S1/9	from × 4

The above prices refer to covers from the territories concerned, not examples used in Great Britain.

MIDDLE EAST FORCES

For use in territory occupied by British Forces in Eritrea (1942), Italian Somaliland (from 13 April 1942), Cyrenaica (1943), Tripolitania (1943), and some of the Dodecanese Islands (1945).

PRICES. Our prices for used stamps with "M.E.F." overprints are for examples with identifiable postmarks of the territories in which they were issued. These stamps were also used in the United Kingdom with official sanction, from the summer of 1950 onwards, and with U.K. postmarks are worth considerably less.

PRINTERS. Considerable research has been undertaken to discover the origins of Nos. M1/10. It is now suggested that Nos. M1/5, previously assigned to Harrison and Sons, were produced by the Army Printing Services, Cairo, and that the smaller printing, Nos. M6/10, previously identified as the work of the Army Printing Services, Cairo, was from GHQ, Middle East Land Forces, Nairobi.

M.E.F. M.E.F.

(M **1**) Opt. 14 mm long. Regular lettering and upright oblong stops.

(M **2**) Opt. 13½ mm long. Regular lettering and square stops.

M.E.F. M.E.F.

(M **2a**) Opt. 13½ mm long. Rough lettering and round stops.

Sliced "M" (R. 6/10)

(Illustrations twice actual size)

1942 (2 Mar). Stamps of Great Britain optd. W **127**. P 15×14.

(a) With Type M 1

M1	**128**	1d. scarlet (No. 463)	3·50	4·75
		a. Sliced "M"	£150	£180
M2		2d. orange (No. 465)	3·00	6·00
		a. Sliced "M"	£110	
M3		2½d. ultramarine (No. 466)	3·00	2·00
		a. Sliced "M"	£150	£170
M4		3d. violet (No. 467)	2·75	30
		a. Sliced "M"		
M5	**129**	5d. brown	2·75	1·00
		a. Sliced "M"	£150	£150

(b) With Type M 2

M6	**128**	1d. scarlet (No. 463)	55·00	26·00
		a. Optd with Type M 2a	45·00	18·00
		b. Nos. M6/a se-tenant vert.	£200	£150
M7		2d. orange (No. 465)	90·00	£160
		a. Optd with Type M 2a	80·00	£140
		b. Nos. M7/a se-tenant vert.	£425	£650
M8		2½d. ultramarine (No. 466)	70·00	10·00
		a. Optd with Type M 2a	65·00	8·00
		b. Nos. M8/a se-tenant vert.	£325	80·00
M9		3d. violet (No. 467)	£140	60·00
		a. Optd with Type M 2a	£130	55·00
		ab. Opt double	†	£6500
		b. Nos. M9/a se-tenant vert.	£600	£325
M10	**129**	5d. brown	£500	£130
		a. Optd with Type M 2a	£450	£110
		b. Nos. M10/a se-tenant vert	£1700	£900

See note after No. M21.

Nos. M6/10 were issued in panes of 60 (6×10), rows 2, 3, and 7 being overprinted with Type M **2** and the other seven rows with Type M **2a**.

M.E.F.

(M **3**) Optd 13½ mm long. Regular lettering and upright oblong stops.

(Illustration twice actual size)

1943 (1 Jan)–**47**. Stamps of Great Britain optd with Type M **3** by Harrison & Sons. W **127**, P 15×14 (1d. to 1s.); W **133**, P 14 (others).

M11	**128**	1d. pale scarlet (No. 486)	1·50	10
M12		2d. pale orange (No. 488)	2·25	1·25
M13		2½d. light ultramarine (No. 489)	2·25	10
M14		3d. pale violet (No. 490)	1·50	10
M15	**129**	5d. brown	4·00	10
M16		6d. purple	65	10
M17	**130**	9d. deep olive-green	85	10
M18		1s. bistre-brown	50	10
M19	**131**	2s.6d. yellow-green	7·00	1·00
M20		5s. red (27.1.47)	29·00	17·00
M21	**132**	10s. ultramarine (27.1.47)	42·00	10·00
M11/21 *Set of 11*			85·00	27·00
M18s/21s Optd "SPECIMEN" *Set of 4*			£650	

The overprint on No. M15 should not be confused with the other overprints on the 5d. value. It can be distinguished from No. M5 by the ½ mm difference in length; and from No. M10 by the more intense colour, thicker lettering and larger stops.

POSTAGE DUE STAMPS

M.E.F.

(MD **1**)

1942 (2 Mar). Postage Due stamps of Great Britain Nos. D27/30 and D33 optd with Type MD **1**, in blue-black.

MD1	D **1**	½d. emerald	40	13·00
MD2		1d. carmine	40	1·75
		w. Wmk sideways inverted*	—	90·00
MD3		2d. agate	2·00	1·25
MD4		3d. violet	50	4·25
MD5		1s. deep blue	4·00	13·00
		s. Optd "SPECIMEN"	£190	
MD1/5 *Set of 5*			6·50	30·00

*No. MD2w shows the Crown pointing to the left, *as seen from the back of the stamp.*

CYRENAICA

In June 1949 the British authorities recognised the leader of the Senussi, Amir Mohammed Idris Al-Senussi, as Amir of Cyrenaica with autonomy in internal affairs.

(Currency. 10 millièmes = 1 piastre, 100 piastres = 1 Egyptian pound)

24 Mounted Warrior

25 Mounted Warrior

(Recess Waterlow)

1950 (16 Jan). P 12½.

136	**24**	1m. brown	4·50	8·50
137		2m. carmine	4·50	8·50
138		3m. orange-yellow	4·50	7·00
139		4m. blue-green	4·50	8·50
140		5m. grey-black	4·50	8·00
141		8m. orange	4·50	4·50
142		10m. violet	4·50	2·50
143		12m. scarlet	4·50	4·00
144		20m. blue	4·50	2·50
145	**25**	50m. ultramarine and purple-brown	19·00	10·00
146		100m. carmine and black	28·00	12·00
147		200m. violet and deep blue	38·00	40·00
148		500m. orange-yellow and green	65·00	90·00
136/148 *Set of 13*			£170	£180

POSTAGE DUE STAMPS

D 26

(Recess Waterlow)

1950 (16 Jan). P 12½.

D149	D **26**	2m. brown	60·00	£110
D150		4m. blue-green	60·00	£110
D151		8m. scarlet	60·00	£120
D152		10m. orange	60·00	£120
D153		20m. orange-yellow	60·00	£140
D154		40m. blue	60·00	£180
D155		100m. grey-brown	60·00	£200
D149/155 *Set of 7*			£375	£900

On 24 December 1951 Cyrenaica united with Tripolitania, Fezzan and Ghadames to form the independent Kingdom of Libya, whose issues are listed in our Part 13 (*Africa since Independence F—M*) catalogue.

ERITREA

From early 1950 examples of Nos. E1/32 exist precancelled in manuscript by a black or blue horizontal line for use by British troops on concession rate mail.

BRITISH MILITARY ADMINISTRATION
(Currency. 100 cents = 1 shilling)

B. M. A.
ERITREA

B. M. A.
ERITREA

10
CENTS
(E **1**)

5 SHILLINGS
(E **2**)

SH. 50
Normal

SH .50
Misplaced Stop

1948 (27 May)–**49**. Stamps of Great Britain surch as Types E **1** or E **2**.

E1	**128**	5c. on ½d. pale green	2·75	65
E2		10c. on 1d. pale scarlet	2·00	2·50
E3		20c. on 2d. pale orange	3·00	2·25
E4		25c. on 2½d. light ultramarine	2·00	60
E5		30c. pale violet	2·50	4·50
E6	**129**	40c. on 5d. brown	2·75	4·25
E7		50c. on 6d. purple	2·25	1·00
E7a	**130**	65c. on 8d. bright carmine (1.2.49)	7·00	2·00
E8		75c. on 9d. deep olive-green	3·75	75
E9		1s. on 1s. bistre-brown	2·50	50
E10	**131**	2s.50c. on 2s.6d. yellow-green	13·00	12·00
		a. Misplaced stop (R. 4/7)	£170	£190
E11		5s. on 5s. red	14·00	24·00
E12	**132**	10s. on 10s. ultramarine	28·00	24·00
E1/12 *Set of 13*			75·00	70·00

BRITISH ADMINISTRATION

1950 (6 Feb). As Nos. E1/12, but surch "B.A. ERITREA" and new values instead of "B.M.A." etc.

E13	**128**	5c. on ½d. pale green	1·50	8·00
E14		10c. on 1d. pale scarlet	40	3·00
E15		20c. on 2d. pale orange	1·50	80
E16		25c. on 2½d. light ultramarine	1·00	60
E17		30c. on 3d. pale violet	40	2·25
E18	**129**	40c. on 5d. brown	3·00	1·75
E19		50c. on 6d. purple	40	20
E20	**130**	65c. on 8d. bright carmine	6·50	1·50
E21		75c. on 9d. deep olive-green	2·00	25
E22		1s. on 1s. bistre-brown	40	15
E23	**131**	2s.50c. on 2s.6d. yellow-green	10·00	5·50
E24		5s. on 5s. red	10·00	12·00
E25	**132**	10s. on 10s. ultramarine	75·00	70·00
E13/25 *Set of 13*			£100	95·00

1951 (28 May*). Nos. 503/4, 506/7 and 509/11 of Great Britain surch "B.A. ERITREA" and new values.

E26	**128**	5c. on ½d. pale orange	3·00	4·00

E27		10c. on 1d. light ultramarine	2·75	75
E28		20c. on 2d. pale red-brown	3·00	30
E29		25c. on 2½d. pale scarlet	3·00	30
E30	**147**	2s.50c. on 2s.6d. yellow-green	21·00	30·00
E31	**148**	5s. on 5s. red	23·00	32·00
E32		10s. on 10s. ultramarine	29·00	32·00
E26/32 *Set of 7*			75·00	90·00

*This is the local release date. The stamps were placed on sale in London on 3 May.

POSTAGE DUE STAMPS

B. M. A.
ERITREA

10 CENTS
(ED **1**)

1948 (27 May). Postage Due stamps of Great Britain Nos. D27/30 and D33 surch as Type ED **1**.

ED1	D **1**	5c. on ½d. emerald	10·00	22·00
		a. No stop after "A"	—	£450
ED2		10c. on 1d. carmine	10·00	24·00
		a. No stop after "B" (R. 1/9)	£190	£350
ED3		20c. on 2d. agate	17·00	16·00
		a. No stop after "A"	70·00	
		b. No stop after "B" (R. 1/9)	£200	£275
ED4		30c. on 3d. violet	13·00	17·00
ED5		1s. on 1s. deep blue	21·00	32·00
ED1/5 *Set of 5*			65·00	£100

1950 (6 Feb). As Nos. ED1/5, but surch "B.A. ERITREA" and new values instead of "B.M.A." etc.

ED6	D **1**	5c. on ½d. emerald	16·00	60·00
ED7		10c. on 1d. carmine	16·00	21·00
		a. "C" of "CENTS" omitted	£4750	
		ab. "C" omitted and vertical oblong for "E" of "CENTS"	£8000	
ED8		20c. on 2d. agate	16·00	25·00
		a. No stop after "A"	£450	
ED9		30c. on 3d. violet	20·00	45·00
		w. Wmk sideways-inverted*	—	70·00
ED10		1s. on 1s. deep blue	21·00	45·00
		a. No stop after "A" (R. 2/13)	£650	
ED6/10 *Set of 5*			80·00	£170

No. ED7a, and probably No. ED7ab, occurred on R. 7/17, but the error was quickly corrected.

*No. ED9w shows the Crowns pointing to the left, *as seen from the back of the stamp.*

Stamps of Ethiopia were used in Eritrea after 15 September 1952 following federation with Ethiopia.

SOMALIA

BRITISH OCCUPATION

E.A.F.

(S **1** "East Africa Forces")

1943 (15 Jan)–**46**. Stamps of Great Britain optd with Type S **1**, in blue.

S1	**128**	1d. pale scarlet	1·50	2·00
S2		2d. pale orange	1·75	2·00
S3		2½d. light ultramarine	2·00	3·50
S4		3d. pale violet	1·75	15
S5	**129**	5d. brown	2·50	40
S6		6d. purple	2·25	1·50
S7	**130**	9d. deep olive-green	2·75	4·25
S8		1s. bistre-brown	3·75	15
S9	**131**	2s.6d. yellow-green (14.1.46)	38·00	14·00
S1/9 *Set of 9*			50·00	25·00
S8s/9s Optd "SPECIMEN" *Set of 2*			£350	

The note *re* used prices above Type M **1** of Middle East Forces also applies to the above issue.

BRITISH MILITARY ADMINISTRATION
(Currency. 100 cents = 1 shilling)

1948 (27 May). Stamps of Great Britain surch "B.M.A./SOMALIA" and new values, as Types E **1** and E **2** of Eritrea.

S10	**128**	5c. on ½d. pale green	1·25	2·00
S11		15c. on 1½d. pale red-brown	1·75	15·00
S12		20c. on 2d. pale orange	3·00	6·00
S13		25c. on 2½d. light ultramarine	2·25	4·50
S14		30c. on 3d. pale violet	2·25	9·00
S15	**129**	40c. on 5d. brown	1·25	20
S16		50c. on 6d. purple	50	20
S17	**130**	75c. on 9d. deep olive-green	2·00	28·00
S18		1s. on 1s. bistre-brown	1·25	20
S19	**131**	2s.50c. on 2s.6d. yellow-green	9·00	25·00
		a. Misplaced stop (R. 4/7)	£130	£275

S20		5s. on 5s. red	20·00	65·00
S10/20		Set of 11	40·00	£140

For illustration of No. S19a, see previous column above No. E1 of Eritrea.

BRITISH ADMINISTRATION

1950 (2 Jan). As Nos. S10/20, but surch "B.A./SOMALIA" and new values, instead of "B.M.A." etc.

S21	**128**	5c. on ½d. pale green	20	3·00
S22		15c. on 1½d. pale red-brown	75	17·00
S23		20c. on 2d. pale orange	75	7·50
S24		25c. on 2½d. light ultramarine	50	14·00
S25		30c. on 3d. pale violet	1·25	9·00
S26	**129**	40c. on 5d. brown	55	2·00
S27		50c. on 6d. purple	50	1·00
S28	**130**	75c. on 9d. deep olive-green	2·00	12·00
S29		1s. on 1s. bistre-brown	60	1·50
S30	**131**	2s.50c. on 2s.6d. yellow-green	8·50	35·00
S31		5s. on 5s. red	20·00	55·00
S21/31		Set of 11	32·00	£140

Somalia reverted to Italian Administration on 1 April 1950 later becoming independent. Later issues will be found listed in our Part 8 (*Italy and Switzerland*) catalogue.

TRIPOLITANIA

BRITISH MILITARY ADMINISTRATION

(Currency. 100 centesimi = 1 Military Administration lira)

Normal	Misaligned surcharge (R. 8/8, 18/8)

1948 (1 July). Stamps of Great Britain surch "B.M.A./TRIPOLITANIA" and new values, as Types E **1** and E **2** of Eritrea, but expressed in M(ilitary) A(dministration) L(ire).

T1	**128**	1l. on ½d. pale green	1·00	4·00
T2		2l. on 1d. pale scarlet	50	15
T3		3l. on 1½d. pale red-brown	50	50
		a. Misaligned surch	60·00	70·00
T4		4l. on 2d. pale orange	50	70
		a. Misaligned surch	60·00	80·00
T5		5l. on 2½d. light ultramarine	50	20
T6		6l. on 3d. pale violet	50	40
T7	**129**	10l. on 5d. brown	50	15
T8		12l. on 6d. purple	50	20
T9	**130**	18l. on 9d. deep olive-green	1·50	1·75
T10		24l. on 1s. bistre-brown	2·50	3·00
T11	**131**	60l. on 2s.6d. yellow-green	9·50	17·00
T12		120l. on 5s. red	29·00	29·00
T13	**132**	240l. on 10s. ultramarine	32·00	£150
T1/13		Set of 13	70·00	£180

BRITISH ADMINISTRATION

1950 (6 Feb). As Nos. T1/13, but surch "B.A. TRIPOLITANIA" and new values, instead of "B.M.A." etc.

T14	**128**	1l. on ½d. pale green	6·00	13·00
T15		2l. on 1d. pale scarlet	5·00	40
T16		3l. on 1½d. pale red-brown	3·75	13·00
		a. Misaligned surch	£130	£250
T17		4l. on 2d. pale orange	4·25	4·50
		a. Misaligned surch	£140	£170
T18		5l. on 2½d. light ultramarine	2·25	70
T19		6l. on 3d. pale violet	3·75	3·25
T20	**129**	10l. on 5d. brown	3·75	4·00
T21		12l. on 6d. purple	5·00	50
T22	**130**	18l. on 9d. deep olive-green	8·00	2·75
T23		24l. on 1s. bistre-brown	7·50	3·75
T24	**131**	60l. on 2s.6d. yellow-green	18·00	12·00
T25		120l. on 5s. red	38·00	40·00
T26	**132**	240l. on 10s. ultramarine	55·00	90·00
T14/26		Set of 13	£140	£170

1951 (3 May). Nos. 503/7 and 509/11 of Great Britain surch "B.A. TRIPOLITANIA" and new values.

T27	**128**	1l. on ½d. pale orange	55	9·50
T28		2l. on 1d. light ultramarine	55	1·00
T29		3l. on 1½d. pale green	55	8·00
T30		4l. on 2d. pale red-brown	55	1·25
T31		5l. on 2½d. pale scarlet	60	7·50
T32	**147**	60l. on 2s.6d. yellow-green	19·00	40·00
T33	**148**	120l. on 5s. red	19·00	40·00
T34	**149**	240l. on 10s. ultramarine	50·00	85·00
T27/34		Set of 8	80·00	£170

POSTAGE DUE STAMPS

1948 (1 July). Postage Due stamps of Great Britain Nos. D27/30 and D33 surch "B.M.A./TRIPOLITANIA" and new values, as Type ED **1** of Eritrea, but expressed in M(ilitary) A(dministration) L(ire).

TD1	D **1**	1l. on ½d. emerald	6·00	65·00
		a. No stop after "A"	90·00	
TD2		2l. on 1d. carmine	2·50	55·00
		a. No stop after "A"	50·00	
		b. No stop after "M" (R. 1/17)	£160	
TD3		4l. on 2d. agate	13·00	50·00
		a. No stop after "A" (R. 2/12, R. 3/8)	£170	
		b. No stop after "M" (R. 1/17)	£325	
TD4		6l. on 3d. violet	7·50	26·00
TD5		24l. on 1s. deep blue	29·00	£110
TD1/5		Set of 5	50·00	£275

1950 (6 Feb). As Nos. TD1/5, but surch "B.A. TRIPOLITANIA" and new values, instead of "B.M.A." etc.

TD6	D **1**	1l. on ½d. emerald	15·00	£110
		a. No stop after "B" (R. 11/10)	£250	
TD7		2l. on 1d. carmine	9·50	32·00
		a. No stop after "B" (R. 11/10)	£130	
TD8		4l. on 2d. agate	11·00	50·00
		a. No stop after "B" (R. 11/10)	£140	
TD9		6l. on 3d. violet	19·00	80·00
		a. No stop after "B" (R. 11/10)	£275	
		w. Wmk sideways-inverted*	35·00	£140
TD10		24l. on 1s. deep blue	55·00	£180
		a. No stop after "A" (R. 11/2)	£700	
		b. No stop after "B" (R. 11/10)	£700	
TD6/10		Set of 5	95·00	£400

*No. TD9w shows the Crowns pointing to the left, *as seen from the back of the stamp.*

Tripolitania became part of the independent kingdom of Libya on 24 December 1951.

Egypt

TURKISH SUZERAINTY

In 1517 Sultan Selim I added Egypt to the Ottoman Empire, and it stayed more or less under Turkish rule until 1805, when Mohammed Ali became governor. He established a dynasty of governors owing nominal allegiance to the Sultan of Turkey until 1914.

Khedive Ismail
18 January 1863–26 June 1879

He obtained the honorific title of Khedive (viceroy) from the Sultan in 1867.

The operations of British Consular Post Offices in Egypt date from August 1839 when the first packet agency, at Alexandria, was opened. Further agencies at Suez (1 January 1847) and Cairo (1856) followed. Alexandria became a post office on 17 March 1858 with Cairo following on 23 February 1859 and Suez on 1 January 1861.

Great Britain stamps were issued to Alexandria in March 1858 and to the other two offices in August/September 1859. "B O1" cancellations as Type **2** were issued to both Alexandria and Cairo. Cancellations with this number as Types **8**, **12** and **15** were only used at Alexandria.

Before 1 July 1873 combination covers showing Great Britain stamps and the first issue of Egypt exist with the latter paying the internal postage to the British Post Office at Alexandria.

The Cairo office closed on 30 June 1873 and the other two on 30 March 1878. Suez continued to function as a transit office for a number of years.

Stamps issued after 1877 can be found with the Egyptian cancellation "Port Said", but these are on letters posted from British ships.

For cancellations used during the 1882 and 1885 campaigns, see BRITISH FORCES IN EGYPT at the end of the listing.

For illustrations of the handstamp and postmark types see BRITISH POST OFFICES ABROAD notes following GREAT BRITAIN.

ALEXANDRIA
CROWNED-CIRCLE HANDSTAMPS

CC1   CC **1b**   ALEXANDRIA (R.) (13.5.1843)...... *Price on cover*   £3250

Stamps of GREAT BRITAIN cancelled "B 01" as in Types **2** (also used at Cairo), **8**, **12** or **15**.

1858 (Mar)–**78**.

Z1	½d. rose-red (1870–79) .... *From*	22·00
	Plate Nos. 5, 6, 8, 10, 13, 14, 15, 19, 20.	
Z2	1d. rose-red (1857)..	7·50
Z3	1d. rose-red (1861) (Alph IV)..........................	
Z4	1d. rose-red (1864–79) .... *From*	11·00
	Plate Nos. 71, 72, 73, 74, 76, 78, 79, 80, 81, 82,	
	83, 84, 85, 86, 87, 88, 89, 90, 91, 92, 93, 94,	
	95, 96, 97, 98, 99, 101, 102, 103, 104, 106, 107,	
	108, 109, 110, 111, 112, 113, 114, 115, 117,	
	118, 119, 120, 121, 122, 123, 124, 125, 127,	
	129, 130, 131, 133, 134, 136, 137, 138, 139,	
	140, 142, 143, 144, 145, 146, 147, 148, 149,	
	150, 152, 154, 156, 157, 158, 159, 160, 162,	
	163, 165, 168, 169, 170, 171, 172, 174, 175,	
	177, 179, 180, 181, 182, 183, 185, 188, 190,	
	198, 200, 203, 206, 210, 220.	
Z5	2d. blue (1858–69) .... *From*	11·00
	Plate Nos. 7, 8, 9, 13, 14, 15.	
Z6	2½d. rosy mauve (1875) (blued *paper*)................ *From*	65·00
	Plate Nos. 1, 2.	
Z7	2½d. rosy mauve (1875–6) (Plate Nos. 1, 2, 3)	35·00
Z8	2½d. rosy mauve *(Error of Lettering)*....................................	£1800
Z9	2½d. rosy mauve (1876–79) .... *From*	25·00
	Plate Nos. 3, 4, 5, 6, 7, 8, 9.	
Z10	3d. carmine-rose (1862)	£120
Z11	3d. rose (1865) (Plate No. 4)	60·00
Z12	3d. rose (1867–73)	25·00
	Plate Nos. 4, 5, 6, 7, 8, 9.	
Z13	3d. rose (1873–76) .... *From*	27·00
	Plate Nos. 11, 12, 14, 15, 16, 18, 19.	
Z15	4d. rose (1857)	42·00
Z16	4d. red (1862) (Plate Nos. 3, 4) .... *From*	42·00
Z17	4d. vermilion (1865–73) .... *From*	29·00
	Plate Nos. 7, 8, 9, 10, 11, 12, 13, 14.	
Z18	4d. vermilion (1876) (Plate No. 15)..............	£160
Z19	4d. sage-green (1877) (Plate No. 15)..............	£110
Z20	6d. lilac (1856)	50·00
Z21	6d. lilac (1862) (Plate Nos. 3, 4) .... *From*	45·00
Z22	6d. lilac (1865–67) (Plate Nos. 5, 6)............ *From*	32·00
Z23	6d. lilac (1867) (Plate No. 6)......................	42·00
Z24	6d. violet (1867–70) (Plate Nos. 6, 8, 9) .... *From*	38·00
	a. Imperf (Plate No. 8)............................	£4500

Z25	6d. buff (1872–73) (Plate Nos. 11, 12) .... *From*	55·00
Z26	6d. chestnut (1872) (Plate No. 11)................	27·00
Z27	6d. grey (1873) (Plate No. 12)......................	80·00
Z28	6d. grey (1874–76) Plate Nos. 13, 14, 15.......... *From*	24·00
Z29	9d. straw (1862)	£160
Z30	9d. bistre (1862)	
Z31	9d. straw (1865)	
Z32	9d. straw (1867)	
Z33	10d. red-brown (1867)	£140
Z34	1s. green (1856)..	£130
Z35	1s. green (1862)	75·00
Z36	1s. green (1862) ("K" *variety*)	
Z37	1s. green (1865) (Plate No. 4)	35·00
Z38	1s. green (1867–73) Plate Nos. 4, 5, 6, 7 .... *From*	18·00
Z39	1s. green (1873–77) .... *From*	30·00
	Plate Nos. 8, 9, 10, 11, 12, 13.	
Z40	2s. blue (1867)	£110
Z41	5s. rose (1867–74) (Plate Nos. 1, 2).................... *From*	£250

CAIRO
CROWNED-CIRCLE HANDSTAMPS

CC2   CC **6**   CAIRO (R. or Blk.) (23.3.1859)..... *Price on cover*   £5000

Cancellation "B 01" as Type **2** (also issued at Alexandria) was used to cancel mail franked with Great Britain stamps between April 1859 and June 1873.

SUEZ
CROWNED-CIRCLE HANDSTAMPS

CC3   CC **1**   SUEZ (B. or Black) (16.7.1847)   *Price on cover*   £6000

Stamps of GREAT BRITAIN cancelled "B 02" as in Types **2** and **8**, or with circular date stamp as Type **5**.

1859 (Aug)–**78**.

Z42	½d. rose-red (1870–79)	38·00
	Plate Nos. 6, 10, 11, 12, 13, 14.	
Z43	1d. rose-red (1857)...................................... *From*	12·00
Z44	1d. rose-red (1864–79) .... *From*	15·00
	Plate Nos. 73, 74, 78, 79, 80, 81, 83, 84, 86, 87,	
	90, 91, 93, 94, 96, 97, 100, 101, 106, 107, 108,	
	110, 113, 118, 119, 120, 121, 122, 123, 124,	
	125, 129, 130, 131, 134, 136, 137, 138, 140,	
	142, 143, 144, 145, 147, 148, 149, 150, 151,	
	152, 153, 154, 156, 158, 159, 160, 161, 162,	
	163, 164, 165, 166, 167, 169, 170, 174, 176,	
	177, 178, 179, 180, 181, 182, 184, 185, 186,	
	187, 189, 190, 205.	
Z45	2d. blue (1858–69) .... *From*	18·00
	Plate Nos. 8, 9, 13, 14, 15.	
Z46	2½d. rosy mauve (1875) (blued *paper*) .... *From*	75·00
	Plate Nos. 1, 2, 3.	
Z47	2½d. rosy mauve (1875–76) .... *From*	40·00
	Plate Nos. 1, 2, 3.	
Z48	2½d. rosy mauve *(Error of Lettering)*	£2250
Z49	2½d. rosy mauve (1876–79) .... *From*	30·00
	Plate Nos. 3, 4, 5, 6, 7, 8, 9, 10.	
Z50	3d. carmine-rose (1862)	£150
Z51	3d. rose (1865) (Plate No. 4)	80·00
Z52	3d. rose (1867–73) (Plate Nos. 5, 6, 7, 8, 10)	
Z53	3d. rose (1873–76) (Plate Nos. 12, 16) .... *From*	32·00
Z54	4d. rose (1857)	65·00
Z55	4d. red (1862) (Plate Nos. 3, 4) .... *From*	55·00
Z56	4d. vermilion (1865–73) .... *From*	32·00
	Plate Nos. 7, 8, 9, 10, 11, 12, 13, 14.	
Z57	4d. vermilion (1876) (Plate No. 15)................	£150
Z58	4d. sage-green (1877) (Plate No. 15)................	65·00
Z59	6d. lilac (1856)	65·00
Z60	6d. lilac (1862) (Plate Nos. 3, 4) .... *From*	50·00
Z61	6d. lilac (1865–67) (Plate Nos. 5, 6)............ *From*	42·00
Z62	6d. lilac (1867) (Plate No. 6)......................	55·00
Z63	6d. violet (1867–70) (Plate Nos. 6, 8, 9) .... *From*	42·00
Z64	6d. buff (1872–73) (Plate Nos. 11, 12) .... *From*	70·00
Z65	6d. pale chestnut (Plate No. 12) (1872)............	£3000
Z66	6d. chestnut (1872) (Plate No. 11)..................	38·00
Z67	6d. grey (1873) (Plate No. 12)	£100
Z68	6d. grey (1874–76) .... *From*	32·00
	Plate Nos. 13, 14, 15, 16.	
Z69	8d. orange (1876)	
Z70	9d. straw (1862)	£250
	a. Thick paper.	
Z71	9d. bistre (1862)	
Z72	9d. straw (1867)	
Z73	10d. red-brown (1867)	£225
Z74	1s. green (1856)..	£170
Z75	1s. green (1862)	95·00
Z76	1s. green (1862) ("K" *variety*)	
Z77	1s. green (1865) (Plate No. 4)	55·00
Z78	1s. green (1867–73) Plate Nos. 4, 5, 6, 7 .... *From*	26·00
Z79	1s. green (1873–77) .... *From*	38·00
	Plate Nos. 8, 9, 10, 11, 12.	
Z80	2s. blue (1867)	£190
Z81	5s. rose (1867–74) (Plate Nos. 1, 2).................... *From*	£375

PRICES FOR STAMPS ON COVER	
Nos. 1/41	from × 8
Nos. 42/3	from × 30
Nos. 44/83	from × 5
Nos. 84/97	from × 2
Nos. D57/70	from × 12
Nos. D71/86	from × 5
Nos. D84/103	from × 2
Nos. O64/87	from × 5
Nos. O88/101	from × 2

(Currency: 40 paras = 1 piastre)

1  2  (3)

(Typo (1pi) or litho (others) Pellas Brothers, Genoa. Inscr (T **3**) applied typo (1, 2pi.) or litho (others))

1866 (1 Jan). Various designs as T **1** with black inscriptions as T **3**. The lowest group of characters indicates the value. 1pi. no wmk, others W **2** (inverted). P 12½.

1	5pa. grey		55·00	35·00
	a. Greenish grey		55·00	35·00
	b. Imperf (pair)		£200	
	c. Imperf between (pair)		£375	
	d. Perf 12½×13 and compound		75·00	55·00
	e. Perf 13		£325	£375
	w. Wmk upright		£400	£250
2	10pa. brown		65·00	35·00
	a. Imperf (pair)		£180	
	b. Imperf between (pair)		£400	
	c. Perf 12½×13 and compound		95·00	55·00
	d. Perf 12½×15		£300	£325
	e. Perf 13		£250	£275
	w. Wmk upright		85·00	38·00
3	20pa. pale blue		80·00	38·00
	a. Greenish blue		80·00	38·00
	b. Imperf (pair)		£275	
	c. Imperf between (pair)		£450	
	d. Perf 12½×13 and compound		£120	80·00
	e. Perf 13		£500	£325
	w. Wmk upright		80·00	38·00
4	1pi. claret		70·00	5·00
	a. Imperf (pair)		£120	
	b. Imperf between (pair)		£450	
	c. Perf 12½×13 and compound		£100	20·00
	d. Perf 13		£400	£250
	e. Perf 12½×15		£350	
5	2pi. yellow		£100	50·00
	a. Orange-yellow		£100	50·00
	b. Imperf (pair)			
	c. Imperf between (pair)		£475	£400
	d. Bisected diag (1pi.) (on cover)		†	£2750
	e. Perf 12½×13 and compound		£160	65·00
	f. Perf 12½×15		£180	
	w. Wmk upright		£100	50·00
6	5pi. rose		£300	£190
	a. Imperf (pair)			
	b. Imperf between (pair)		£1200	
	c. Perf 12½×13 and compound		£350	
	d. Error. Inscr 10pi., perf 12½×15		£1000	£900
	da. Imperf		£550	
	e. Perf 13		£750	
	w. Wmk upright		£300	£190
7	10pi. slate		£350	£300
	a. Imperf (pair)		£700	
	b. Imperf between (pair)		£2250	
	c. Perf 12½×13 and compound		£500	£475
	d. Perf 13		£1900	
	w. Wmk upright		£325	£300

The 2pi. bisected was authorised for use between 16 and 31 July 1867 at Alexandria or Cairo.

Stamps perforated 12½, 12½×13 and compound, and 13 occur in the same sheets with the 13 gauge usually used on the top, left-hand, right-hand or bottom rows. Each sheet of 200 contained one stamp perforated 13 all round, two 13 on three sides, one 13 on two adjacent sides, eighteen 13×12½, eight 12½×13, eight 13 on one side and eighteen 13 at top or bottom. So many sheets were received imperforate or part-perforated that some stock was passed to V. Penasson of Alexandria who applied the 12½×15 gauge.

The two halves of each background differ in minor details of the ornamentation. All values can be found with either half at the top.

Proofs of all values exist on smooth paper, without watermark. Beware of forgeries.

All values also exist with the watermark reversed (same price as upright) or inverted and reversed (same price as inverted).

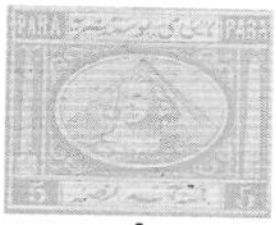

4  5

6

(Des F. Hoff. Litho V. Penasson, Alexandria)

1867 (1 Aug)–**71**. W **6** (impressed on reverse). P 15×12½.

11	**4**	5pa. orange-yellow	48·00	8·00
		a. Imperf (pair)		
		b. Imperf between (horiz pair)	£190	
		x. Wmk impressed on face		
12		10pa. dull lilac	90·00	13·00
		b. Bright mauve (7.69)	65·00	9·00
		ba. Bisected diag (5pa.) (on piece) (17.11.71)	†	£750
		w. Wmk inverted	£300	£200
		x. Wmk impressed on face		
13		20pa. deep blue-green	£130	13·00
		a. Pale blue-green	£130	13·00
		b. Yellowish green (7.69)	£130	12·00
		x. Wmk impressed on face		
14	**5**	1pi. dull rose-red to rose	28·00	1·00
		a. Lake	£170	
		b. Imperf (pair)	£110	
		c. Imperf between (horiz pair)	£190	
		d. Bisected diag (20pa.) (on piece)	†	£750
		e. Rouletted	60·00	
		w. Wmk inverted	55·00	30·00
		x. Wmk impressed on face		
15		2pi. bright blue	£140	17·00
		a. Pale blue	£140	17·00
		b. Imperf (pair)	£650	
		c. Imperf between (pair)	£475	
		d. Bisected diag (1pi.) (on cover)	†	—
		e. Perf 12½	£250	
16		5pi. brown	£300	£180
		x. Wmk impressed on face		

Each value was engraved four times, the resulting blocks being used to form sheets of 200. There are therefore four types showing minor variations for each value.

No. 12ba was used on newspapers from Alexandria between 17 November 1871 and 20 January 1872.

Stamps printed both sides, both imperf and perf, come from printer's waste. The 1pi. rose without watermark is a proof.

7    8 (Side panels transposed and inverted)

8a (I)   8a (II)

WATERMARK 8a. There are two types of this watermark which, as they are not always easy to distinguish, we do not list separately. Type II is slightly wider and less deep and the crescent is flatter than in Type I. The width measurement for Type I is generally about 14 mm and for Type II about 15 mm, but there is some variation within the sheets for both types.

Nos. 26/43, 45/7a, 49/a, 50/1 and 57 come with Type I only. Nos. 44a, 48/a, 52, 54b, 73/7 and 78 exist with both types of watermark (but No. 83 and official overprints on these stamps still require research); our prices are generally for Type II. Other watermarked issues between 1888 and 1907 have Type II watermarks only.

1872 (1 Jan)–**75**. T **7** (the so-called "Penasson" printing*). Thick opaque paper. W **8**a. P 12½×13½.

A. LITHOGRAPHED

26	**7**	20pa. blue (shades)	£150	60·00
		a. Imperf (pair)		£2000
		b. Imperf between (pair)	—	£2000
		c. Perf 13½	£250	65·00
		w. Wmk inverted	£275	80·00
27		1pi. red (shades)	£275	17·00
		a. Perf 13½	£550	35·00
		w. Wmk inverted	£650	35·00

B. TYPOGRAPHED

28	**7**	5pa. brown (shades)	9·50	6·50
		a. Perf 13½	25·00	9·50
		w. Wmk inverted	£100	50·00
29		10pa. mauve	6·00	3·00
		a. Perf 13½	6·00	3·25
		w. Wmk inverted	40·00	25·00
30		20pa. blue (shades)	65·00	4·75
		a. Perf 13½	90·00	20·00
		w. Wmk inverted	60·00	30·00
31		1pi. rose-red	70·00	1·00
		a. Bisected (20pa.) (on piece with No. 31) (7.75)	†	£700
		b. Perf 13½	90·00	3·50
		w. Wmk inverted	65·00	25·00
32		2pi. chrome-yellow	90·00	4·00
		a. Bisected (1pi.) (on piece) (7.74)	†	£750
		b. Perf 13½	21·00	4·75
		w. Wmk inverted		
33		2½pi. violet	90·00	26·00
		a. Perf 13½	£750	£200
		w. Wmk inverted	£100	32·00
34		5pi. yellow-green	£200	48·00
		a. Tête-bêche (pair)	£8000	
		b. Perf 13½	£300	55·00
		w. Wmk inverted	£225	90·00

*It is now accepted that stamps in both processes were printed by the Government Printing Works at Bûlâq, Cairo, although Penasson may have been involved in the production of the dies.

The lithographed and typographed stamps each show the characteristic differences between these two processes:—

The typographed stamps show the coloured lines of the design impressed into the paper and an accumulation of ink along the margins of the lines.

The lithographed stamps are essentially flat in appearance, without the heaping of the ink. Many of the 20pa. show evidence of retouching, particularly of the outer frame lines.

The 1p. bisected was used at Gedda, on 5 July 1875, or Scio, and the 2pi. vertically bisected at Gallipoli or Scio.

See also footnote below No. 41.

1874 (Nov)–**75**. Typo from new stereos at Bûlâq, on thinner paper. W **8**a. P 12½.

35	**8**	5pa. brown (3.75)	29·00	3·75
		a. Tête-bêche (vert pair)	55·00	55·00
		b. Tête-bêche (horiz pair)	£275	£300
		c. Imperf (pair)		
		d. Imperf between (pair)	£100	£120
		ew. Wmk inverted	29·00	3·75
		f. Perf 13½×12½	30·00	3·75
		fa. Tête-bêche (vert pair)	65·00	65·00
		fb. Tête-bêche (horiz pair)	£325	£350
		fw. Wmk inverted	30·00	3·75
36	**7**	10pa. grey-lilac (shades) (8.75)	17·00	4·25
		a. Tête-bêche (vert pair)	£140	£160
		b. Tête-bêche (horiz pair)		
		c. Imperf (pair)		
		dw. Wmk inverted	17·00	4·25
		e. Perf 13½×12½	42·00	3·50
		ea. Tête-bêche (vert pair)	£150	£170
		eb. Tête-bêche (horiz pair)		
		ew. Wmk inverted	42·00	3·75
37		20pa. grey-blue (shades) (2.75)	£100	3·00
		b. Bisected diag (10pa.) (on cover)	†	—
		cw. Wmk inverted	£100	3·00
		d. Perf 13½×12½	13·00	3·00
		da. Imperf between (pair)	£300	
		dw. Wmk inverted	13·00	3·00
38		1pi. red (shades) (4.75)	11·00	65
		a. Tête-bêche (vert pair)	90·00	90·00
		b. Tête-bêche (horiz pair)	£300	£300
		c. Imperf (pair)		
		d. Imperf between (pair)	£400	£400
		ew. Wmk inverted	13·00	1·50
		f. Perf 13½×12½	85·00	1·25
		fa. Tête-bêche (vert pair)	£375	£375
		fb. Tête-bêche (horiz pair)		
		fw. Wmk inverted	90·00	7·50
39		2pi. yellow (12.74)	85·00	4·50
		a. Tête-bêche (pair)	£400	£400
		bw. Wmk inverted	£100	7·50
		c. Perf 13½×12½	5·50	6·50
		ca. Tête-bêche (pair)	£450	£400

		cb. Bisected diag (1pi.) (on cover) (13.4.75)	†	£3500
		cw. Wmk inverted	7·50	7·00
		d. Perf 12½×13½	75·00	16·00
		da. Tête-bêche (pair)	£950	
		dw. Wmk inverted	95·00	19·00
40		2½pi. violet	8·50	6·50
		a. Tête-bêche (pair)	£350	
		bw. Wmk inverted	12·00	8·00
		c. Perf 12½×13½	75·00	19·00
		ca. Tête-bêche (pair)	£1000	£100
		cw. Wmk inverted	65·00	25·00
41		5pi. green	60·00	20·00
		a. Imperf (pair)	†	—
		b. Wmk inverted	£100	50·00
		c. Perf 12½×13½	£350	£275

The 2pi. bisected was used at Gedda and are all postmarked 13 April.

The 1872 printings have a thick line of colour in the top margin of the sheet and the other margins are all plain, an exception being the 5pa., which on the majority of the sheets has the line at the right-hand side of the sheet. The 1874–75 printings have a wide fancy border all round every sheet.

The 1872 printings are on thick opaque paper, with the impressions sharp and clear. The 1874–75 printings are on thinner paper, often semi-transparent and oily in appearance, and having the impressions very blurred and badly printed. These are only general distinctions and there are a number of exceptions.

The majority of the 1874–75 stamps have blind or defective perforations, while the 1872 stamps have clean-cut perfs.

The two printings of the 5pa. to 1pi. values can be identified by their perforation gauges, which are always different; the 5pa. also differs in the side panels (Types **7** and **8**). Only the perf 12½×13½ varieties of the three higher values may need to be distinguished. As well as the general points noted above the following features are also helpful:

2pi. In the 1872 issue the left-hand Arabic character in the top inscription is one complete shape, resembling an inverted "V" with a horizontal line on top. In the 1874 issue the character has three separate components, a line with two dots below.

2½pi. There is a distinct thinning of the frame line in the top right-hand corner of the 1872 issue. This sometimes takes the form of a short white line within the frame.

5pi. In the 1872 issue the top frame line is split for its entire length; in the 1874 issue the line is solid for all or most of its length. The 1872 printing always has a white dot above the "P" of "PIASTRE"; this dot appears on only a few positions of the 1874 printing.

There seem to be many different compositions of the sheets containing the tête-bêche varieties, settings being known with 1, 3, 9 and 10 inverted stamps in various sheets. Sheets of the 5pa. are known with 9 of the 20 horizontal rows inverted, giving vertical tête-bêche pairs; four stamps were inverted within their row giving four horizontal tête-bêche pairs.

Examples of some values exist without watermark due to the paper being misplaced on the press.

(9)

1878 (Dec). No. 40 surch as T **9** at Bûlâq. P 12½.

42	**7**	5pa. on 2½pi. violet	6·50	6·00
		a. Surch inverted	70·00	70·00
		b. Tête-bêche (pair)	£3750	
		c. Imperf (pair)	£900	
		dw. Wmk inverted	7·50	7·50
		e. Perf 12½×13½	6·50	8·00
		ea. Surch inverted	£140	£140
		eb. Tête-bêche (pair)		
		ew. Wmk inverted	8·00	10·00
43		10pa. on 2½ pi. violet	11·00	10·00
		a. Surch inverted	75·00	75·00
		b. Tête-bêche (pair)	£2000	
		dw. Wmk inverted	15·00	15·00
		e. Perf 12½×13½	16·00	15·00
		ea. Surch inverted	£110	£110
		eb. Tête-bêche (pair)	£2000	
		ew. Wmk inverted	25·00	25·00

10	11	12

13   14   15

(Typo De La Rue)

1879 (1 Apr). Ordinary paper. W **8**a (inverted on 10pa.). P 14.

44	10	5pa. deep brown	4·75	1·75
		a. Pale brown	4·75	1·75
		w. Wmk inverted	£120	£100
45	11	10pa. reddish lilac	70·00	3·00
		w. Wmk upright	†	£100
46	12	20pa. pale blue	80·00	2·50
		w. Wmk inverted	95·00	15·00
47	13	1pi. rose	45·00	20
		a. Pale rose	45·00	20
		w. Wmk inverted	65·00	10·00
48	14	2pi. orange	45·00	50
		a. Orange-yellow	42·00	1·25
		w. Wmk inverted	45·00	2·00
49	15	5pi. green	70·00	15·00
		a. Blue-green	70·00	14·00
		w. Wmk inverted	65·00	15·00

See also Nos. 50/6.

Khedive Tewfik
26 June 1879–7 January 1892

British troops were landed in Egypt in 1882 to secure the Suez Canal against a nationalist movement led by Arabi Pasha. Arabi was defeated at Tel-el-Kebir and British troops remained in Egypt until 1954. A British resident and consul-general advised the Khedive. Holders of this post were Sir Evelyn Baring (Lord Cromer), 1883–1907; Sir Eldon Gorst, 1907–11; and Lord Kitchener, 1911–14.

1881–1902. Colours changed. Ordinary paper. W **8**a (inverted on No. 50). P 14.

50	11	10pa. claret (1.81)	65·00	11·00
51		10pa. bluish grey (25.1.82)	24·00	1·75
		w. Wmk inverted	45·00	3·00
52		10pa. green (15.12.84)	3·00	2·75
		w. Wmk inverted	30·00	10·00
53	12	20pa. rose-carmine (15.12.84)	25·00	55
		a. Bright rose	25·00	50
		w. Wmk inverted	40·00	7·00
54	13	1pi. blue (15.12.84)	11·00	70
		a. Deep ultramarine	11·00	70
		b. Pale ultramarine	6·50	50
		cw. Wmk inverted	27·00	10·00
		d. Chalk-surfaced paper. Ultramarine (1902)	3·00	10
		da. Blue	3·00	10
		dw. Wmk inverted	75·00	40·00
55	14	2pi. orange-brown (1.8.93)	12·00	30
		aw. Wmk inverted	80·00	40·00
		b. Chalk-surfaced paper (1902)	12·00	1·00
		ba. Orange	23·00	1·00
		bw. Wmk inverted	—	30·00
56	15	5pi. pale grey (15.12.84)	20·00	50
		a. Slate	20·00	50
		bw. Wmk inverted		
		c. Chalk-surfaced paper. Slate-grey (1902)	16·00	15
		cw. Wmk inverted	—	£100

(17)

1884 (1 Feb). Surch with T **17** at Bûlâq.

57	15	20pa. on 5pi. green	7·00	1·75
		a. Surch inverted	65·00	60·00
		w. Wmk inverted	50·00	30·00

(New Currency: 1000 milliemes = 100 piastres = £1 Egyptian)

18   19   20

21   22

1888 (1 Jan)–**1909**. Ordinary paper. W **8**a. P 14.

58	18	1m. pale brown	3·25	10
		a. Deep brown	3·25	10
		bw. Wmk inverted	25·00	4·00
		c. Chalk-surfaced paper. Pale brown (1902)	3·75	10
		ca. Deep brown	3·75	10
		cw. Wmk inverted	40·00	5·00
59	19	2m. blue-green	3·50	30
		a. Green	1·50	10
		bw. Wmk inverted	40·00	5·00
		c. Chalk-surfaced paper. Green (1902)	1·50	10
		cw. Wmk inverted	40·00	5·00
60	20	3m. maroon (1.1.92)	8·50	2·50
61		3m. yellow (1.8.93)	9·00	75
		a. Orange-yellow	5·00	15
		bw. Wmk inverted	45·00	15·00
		c. Chalk-surfaced paper. Orange-yellow (1902)	3·25	10
		cw. Wmk inverted	75·00	30·00
62	21	4m. verm (chalk-surfaced paper) (1906)	5·50	10
		a. Bisected (2m.) (on cover) (11.09)	†	
		w. Wmk inverted	—	60·00
63		5m. rose-carmine	9·00	55
		a. Bright rose	4·75	10
		b. Aniline rose	5·50	10
		cw. Wmk inverted	—	75·00
		d. Chalk-surfaced paper. Rose (1902).	3·00	10
		da. Deep aniline rose	6·00	35
64	22	10p. mauve (1.1.89)	15·00	1·00
		a. Aniline mauve	18·00	1·00
		bw. Wmk inverted	—	50·00
		c. Chalk-surfaced paper. Mauve (1902)	22·00	50

No. 62a was used at Gizira in conjunction with the 1m. value and the Official, No. O64.

No. 63d exists in coils constructed from normal sheets.

Kedive Abbas Hilmi
7 January 1892–19 December 1914

A set of three values, in a common design showing Cleopatra and a Nile boat, was prepared in 1895 for the Nile Winter Fête, but not issued. Examples survive from the De La Rue archives.

29 Nile Feluccas   **30** Cleopatra from Temple of Dendera   **31** Ras-el-Tin Palace, Alexandria

32 Pyramids of Giza   **33** Sphinx   **34** Colossi of Amenophis III at Thebes

35 Archway of Ptolemy III, Karnak   **36** Citadel, Cairo

37 Rock Temple of Abu Simbel

38 Aswân Dam

(Typo D.L.R.)

1914 (8 Jan). W **8***a*. P 13½×14 (1m. to 10m.) or 14 (20m. to 200m.).

73	**29**	1m. sepia	1·25	40
		w. Wmk inverted	—	75·00
74	**30**	2m. green	3·75	20
		w. Wmk inverted	—	40·00
75	**31**	3m. yellow-orange	3·50	35
		a. Double impression		
		w. Wmk inverted	—	40·00
76	**32**	4m. vermilion	5·00	65
		w. Wmk inverted	—	40·00
77	**33**	5m. lake	4·25	10
		a. Wmk sideways star to right* (booklets)	10·00	25·00
		aw. Wmk sideways star to left	10·00	25·00
		w. Wmk inverted	15·00	10·00
78	**34**	10m. dull blue	8·00	10
		w. Wmk inverted	25·00	25·00
79	**35**	20m. olive	8·00	30
		w. Wmk inverted	60·00	40·00
80	**36**	50m. purple	25·00	1·75
		w. Wmk inverted	—	50·00
81	**37**	100m. slate	25·00	1·50
82	**38**	200m. maroon	35·00	4·25
73/82 *Set of* 10			£100	8·50

*The normal sideways watermark shows the star to the right of the crescent, *as seen from the back of the stamp*.

All the above exist imperforate, but imperforate stamps without watermark are proofs.

See also Nos. 84/95.

BRITISH PROTECTORATE

On 18 December 1914, after war with Turkey had begun, Egypt was declared to be a British protectorate. Abbas Hilmi was deposed, and his uncle, Hussein Kamil, was proclaimed Sultan of Egypt.

Sultan Hussain Kamil

19 December 1914–9 October 1917

(**39**)

1915 (15 Oct). No. 75 surch with T **39**, at Bûlâq.

83	**31**	2m. on 3m. yellow-orange	1·00	2·25
		a. Surch inverted	£225	£200
		b. Surch double, one albino	£140	
		w. Wmk inverted	4·00	

Sultan Ahmed Fuad

9 October 1917–15 March 1922

40   (A)   (B)

41 Statue of Rameses II, Luxor   **42**

(Typo Harrison)

1921–22. As Nos. 73/82 and new designs (15m.). W **40**. P 14 (20, 50, 100m.) or 13½×14 (others).

84	**29**	1m. sepia (A)	1·50	4·25
		a. Two dots omitted (B) (R. 10/10)	35·00	55·00
		w. Wmk inverted	10·00	8·50
85	**30**	2m. green	9·50	5·00
		a. Imperf between (pair)		
		w. Wmk inverted	16·00	10·00
86		2m. vermilion (1922)	7·00	3·00
		w. Wmk inverted	16·00	10·00
87	**31**	3m. yellow-orange	10·00	6·50
		w. Wmk inverted	17·00	10·00
88	**32**	4m. green (1922)	9·00	6·50
		w. Wmk inverted	—	10·00
89	**33**	5m. lake (1.21)	8·00	2·00
		a. Imperf between (pair)		
		w. Wmk inverted	15·00	10·00
90		5m. pink (11.21)	16·00	20
		w. Wmk inverted	20·00	10·00
91	**34**	10m. dull blue	13·00	1·00
		w. Wmk inverted	—	10·00
92		10m. lake (9.22)	4·00	1·00
		w. Wmk inverted	—	10·00
93	**41**	15m. indigo (3.22)	12·00	20
		w. Wmk inverted	—	8·00
94	**42**	15m. indigo	45·00	5·50
		w. Wmk inverted	48·00	10·00
95	**35**	20m. olive	12·00	30
		w. Wmk inverted	21·00	10·00
96	**36**	50m. purple	11·00	1·50
		w. Wmk inverted	20·00	12·00
97	**37**	100m. slate (1922)	90·00	7·50
84/97 *Set of* 14			£225	40·00

The 15m. Type **42** was printed first; but because the Arabic inscription at right was felt to be unsuitable the stamps were withheld and the corrected Type **41** printed and issued. Type **42** was released later.

STAMP BOOKLETS

1903 (1 Jan). Black on pink cover inscr "Egyptian Post Office" in English and French. Stapled.

SB1	121m. booklet containing twenty-four 5m. (No. 63*c*) in blocks of 6	£4000

1903 (1 July). Black on blue cover inscr "Egyptian Post Office" in English and French. Stapled.

SB2	73m. booklet containing twenty-four 3m. (No. 61ab) in blocks of 6	

1911 (1 July). Black on pink cover inscr "Egyptian Post Office" in English and Arabic. Stapled.

SB3	120m. Contents as No. SB1	£3000

1914 (8 Jan). Black on pink cover inscr "Egyptian Post Office" in English and Arabic. Stapled.

SB4	125m. booklet containing twenty-four 5m. (No. 77a) in blocks of 6	

1919 (1 Jan). Black on pink cover inscr "Egyptian Post Office" in English and Arabic. Stapled.

SB5	120m. Contents as No. SB4	£2000

1921 (12 June). Deep blue on pink cover inscr "POST OFFICE" in English and Arabic. Stapled.

SB6	120m. booklet containing twenty-four 5m. (No. 89) in blocks of 6	
	a. Stitched	£1600

1921 (Nov). Deep blue or pink cover inscr "POST OFFICE" in English and Arabic. Stapled.

SB7	120m. booklet containing twenty-four 5m. (No. 90) in blocks of 6	£1200

POSTAGE DUE STAMPS

D 16   D 23   D 24

(Des L. Barkhausen. Litho V. Penasson, Alexandria)

1884 (1 Jan). W **6** (impressed on reverse). P 10½.

D57	D **16**	10pa. red	60·00	9·00
		a. Imperf (pair)	£110	
		b. Imperf between (pair)	£120	
		x. Wmk impressed on face	£120	
D58		20pa. red	£120	42·00
		x. Wmk impressed on face		
D59		1pi. red	£140	50·00
		x. Wmk impressed on face		

D60		2pi. red	£225	12·00
		w. Wmk inverted	£325	22·00
		x. Wmk impressed on face		
D61		5pi. red	15·00	48·00
		x. Wmk impressed on face		

1886 (1 Aug)–**87**. No wmk. P 10½.

D62	D **16**	10pa. rose-red (1887)	75·00	20·00
		a. Imperf between (pair)	95·00	
D63		20pa. rose-red	£250	50·00
		a. Imperf between (pair)		
D64		1pi. rose-red	40·00	10·00
		a. Imperf between (pair)	£130	£130
D65		2pi. rose-red	42·00	4·00
		a. Imperf between (pair)	£130	

Specialists distinguish four types of each value in both these issues.

(Litho V. Penasson, Alexandria)

1888 (1 Jan). No wmk. P 11½.

D66	D **23**	2m. green	26·00	30·00
		a. Imperf between (pair)	£200	£190
		b. Imperf (pair)		
D67		5m. rose-carmine	50·00	30·00
		a. Imperf between (pair)		
D68		1p. blue	£140	35·00
		a. Imperf between (pair)	£180	
D69		2p. orange	£150	19·00
D70		5p. grey	£225	£200
		a. With stop after left-hand "PIASTRES"	£300	£225

Specialists distinguish four types of each value. No. D70a occurs on all examples of one of these types in the sheet except that on R. 2/1. Beware of forgeries of the 5p.

(Typo De La Rue)

1889 (Apr)–**1907**. Ordinary paper. W **8**a. P 14.

D71	D **24**	2m. green	10·00	50
		a. Bisected (1m.) (on cover with unbisected 2m.) (2.98)	†	£300
		bw. Wmk inverted	11·00	3·00
		c. Chalk-surfaced paper (1906)	17·00	50
D72		4m. maroon	4·50	50
		aw. Wmk inverted	5·00	1·00
		b. Chalk-surfaced paper (1906)	4·50	50
D73		1p. ultramarine	5·50	50
		aw. Wmk inverted	8·50	3·00
		b. Chalk-surfaced paper (1906)	6·50	50
D74		2p. orange	5·50	70
		bw. Wmk inverted	5·00	70
		c. Chalk-surfaced paper (1907)	5·00	70

No. D71a was authorised for use on Egyptian Army letters from the Sudan campaign which were only charged 3m. postage due.
See also Nos. 84/6 for stamps with watermark sideways.

(D **26**)

(D **27**)

Slanting 'I' (R. 5/2)

Type D 26

The Arabic figure at right is less than 2 mm from the next character, which consists of a straight stroke only.

Type D 27

The distance is 3 mm and the straight character has a comma-like character above it. There are other minor differences.

1898 (7 May)–**1907**. No. D74 surch at Bûlâq. Ordinary paper.

(a) With Type D 26

D75	D **24**	3m. on 2p. orange	2·75	7·50
		a. Surch inverted	60·00	75·00
		b. Pair, one without surch	£200	
		c. Arabic "2" for "3"	60·00	
		d. Arabic "3" over "2"	£100	

No. D75c occurred in the first printing on positions 10, 20, 30, 40, 50 and 60 of the pane of 60 (the Arabic figure is the right-hand character of the second line—see illustration on page xvii). In the second printing the correct figure was printed on top to form No. D75d. The error was corrected in subsequent printings.

(b) With Type D 27 (11.04)

D76	D **24**	3m. on 2p. orange	6·50	20·00
		a. Surch inverted	50·00	60·00

		b. Chalk-surfaced paper (1907)	6·50	20·00
		ba. Surch inverted	60·00	70·00
		bb. Surch double	£250	
		bc. Slanting 'I'	50·00	

1914–15. As Nos. D71/3 but wmk sideways*.

D84	D **24**	2m. bright green (1915)	27·00	5·50
		w. Wmk star to left of crescent	35·00	16·00
D85		4m. maroon	27·00	23·00
		w. Wmk star to left of crescent	38·00	
D86		1p. dull ultramarine	40·00	14·00
		w. Wmk star to left of crescent	35·00	15·00

*The normal sideways watermark shows star to right of crescent, *as seen from the back of the stamp.*

D **43**

D **44**

(Typo Harrison)

1921 (Apr)–**22**. Chalk-surfaced paper. W **40** (sideways*). P 14×13½.

D98	D **43**		3·50	7·50
		w. Wmk stars below crescents	12·00	7·50
D99		2m. scarlet (1922)	2·25	3·75
		w. Wmk stars below crescents	9·50	6·00
D100		4m. scarlet	8·50	23·00
D101		4m. green (1922)	9·00	3·25
		w. Wmk stars below crescents	15·00	7·50
D102	D **44**	10m. deep slate-blue (11.21)	14·00	28·00
D103		10m. lake (1922)	8·50	2·75
		w. Wmk stars below crescents	13·00	5·00
D98/103 Set of 6			40·00	60·00

*The normal sideways watermark shows the stars above the crescents.

OFFICIAL STAMPS

O **25**

O.H.H.S.
اميري

(O **28**)

"O.H.H.S."

(O **29**)

(Typo De La Rue)

1893 (1 Jan)–**1914**. Ordinary paper. W **8**a. P 14.

O64	O **25**	(–) chestnut	4·25	10
		a. Chalk-surfaced paper (1903)	6·50	50
		bw. Wmk inverted	9·50	
		c. Wmk sideways star to right. Chalk-surfaced paper (1914)	12·00	12·00
		cw. Wmk sideways star to left		

From January 1907 No. O64 was used on most official mail to addresses within Egypt. In 1907 it was replaced by Nos. O73/8, but the use of No. O64 for unregistered official mail to Egyptian addresses was resumed on 1 January 1909.
After No. O64c was withdrawn in 1915 the remaining stock was surcharged 1p., 2p., 3p. or 5p. for fiscal use.

1907 (1 Feb–Aug). Nos. 54da, 56c, 58c, 59c, 61c and 63d optd with Type O **28** by De La Rue.

O73	**18**	1m. pale brown	1·75	30
O74	**19**	2m. green	4·25	10
		a. Opt double		
O75	**20**	5m. orange-yellow	6·00	1·25
O76	**21**	5m. rose	10·00	10
O77	**13**	1p. blue	4·50	20
O78	**15**	5p. slate-grey (Aug)	16·00	9·00
O73/8 Set of 6			38·00	9·00

Nos. O73/8 were used on all official mail from February 1907 until 1 January 1909 after which their use was restricted to registered items and those sent to addresses overseas.

1913 (Nov). No. 63d optd at Bûlâq.

*(a) With Type O **29***

O79	**21**	5m. rose	—	£325
		a. Opt inverted	—	£6000

*(b) As Type O **29** but without inverted commas*

O80	**21**	5m. rose	11·00	70
		a. No stop after "S" (R. 11/10)	60·00	16·00
		b. Opt inverted	—	75·00

O.H.H.S.
اميري

(O **38**)

O.H.H.S.
أميرى

(O **39**)

O.H.H.S.
أميرى

(O **43**)

1914 (Dec)–**15**. Stamps of 1902–6 and 1914 optd with Type O **38** at Bûlâq.

O83	29	1m. sepia (1.15)	2·75	5·50
		a. No stop after "S" (R. 10/10)	15·00	28·00
		w. Wmk inverted	†	—
O84	19	2m. green (3.15)	6·50	12·00
		a. No stop after "S"	18·00	28·00
		b. Opt inverted	35·00	35·00
		c. Opt double	£325	
O85	31	3m. yellow-orange (3.15)	4·50	7·00
		a. No stop after "S" (R. 10/10)	16·00	28·00
O86	21	4m. vermilion (12.14)	8·50	6·50
		a. Opt inverted	£190	£140
		b. Pair, one without opt		
O87	33	5m. lake (1.15)	4·25	3·25
		a. No stop after "S" (R. 10/10)	16·00	23·00
O83/7	*Set of 5*		24·00	30·00

No. O84a occurs on three positions from the first printing and on two different positions from the second. Nos. O83a, O85a and O87a usually show a faint trace of the stop.

1915 (Oct). Nos. 59ab, 62 and 77 optd lithographically with Type O **39** at Bûlâq.

O88	19	2m. green	6·50	5·50
		a. Opt inverted	20·00	20·00
		b. Opt double	25·00	
O89	21	4m. vermilion	13·00	13·00
O90	33	5m. lake	17·00	2·00
		a. Pair, one without opt	£275	

1922. Nos. 84, etc optd lithographically with Type O **43** at Bûlâq.

O98	29	1m. sepia (A) (28.6)	3·50	18·00
		a. Two dots omitted (B)	£200	
		w. Wmk inverted		
O99	30	2m. vermilion (16.6)	12·00	27·00
O100	31	3m. yellow-orange (28.6)	65·00	£130
O101	33	5m. pink (13.3)	24·00	7·00

Egypt was declared to be an independent kingdom on 15 March 1922, and Sultan Ahmed Fuad became king.

Later stamp issues will be found listed in Part 19 (*Middle East*) of this catalogue.

EGYPTIAN POST OFFICES ABROAD

From 1865 Egypt operated various post offices in foreign countries. No special stamps were issued for these offices and use in them of unoverprinted Egyptian stamps can only be identified by the cancellation. Stamps with such cancellations are worth more than the used prices quoted in the Egypt listings.

Such offices operated in the following countries. An * indicates that details will be found under that heading elsewhere in the catalogue.

ETHIOPIA

MASSAWA. *Open Nov 1867 to 5 Dec 1885. Postmark types A (also without REGIE), B, C, D. An Arabic seal type is also known on stampless covers.*
SENHIT (near Keren). *Open 1878 to April 1885. Only one cover, cancelled "Mouderie Senhit" in 1879, is known, together with one showing possible hand-drawn cancellation.*

A post office is also recorded at Harar in 1878, but no postal marking has so far been reported.

SOMALILAND*
Unoverprinted stamps of Egypt used from 1876 until 1884.

SUDAN*
Unoverprinted stamps of Egypt used from 1867 until 1897.

TURKISH EMPIRE

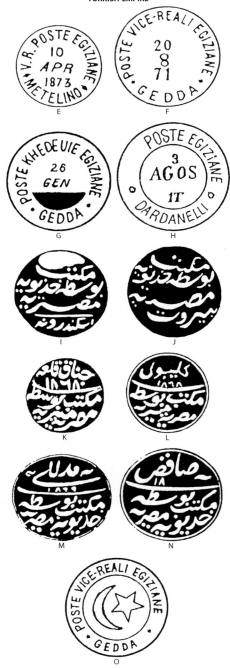

The offices are listed according to the spelling on the cancellation. The present-day name (if different) and country are given in brackets.
ALESSANDRETTA (Iskenderun, Turkey). *Open 14 July 1870 to Feb 1872. Postmark types E, I.*

BAIROUT (Beirut, Lebanon). *Open 14 July 1870 to Feb 1872. Postmark types E, J.*

CAVALA (Kavala, Greece). *Open 14 July 1870 to Feb 1872. Postmark type E.*

COSTANTINOPOLI (Istanbul, Turkey). *Open 13 June 1865 to 30 June 1881. Postmark types E, F, O.*

DARDANELLI (Canakkle, Turkey). *Open 10 June 1868 to 30 June 1881. Postmark types H, K.*

DJEDDAH, see GEDDA.

GALIPOLI (Gelibolu, Turkey). *Open 10 June 1868 to 30 June 1881. Postmark types E, L.*

GEDDA, DJEDDAH (Jeddah, Saudi Arabia). *Open 8 June 1865 to 30 June 1881. Postmark types F, G (also with year replacing solid half-circle), O (all spelt GEDDA), D (spelt DJEDDAH).*

JAFFA (Jaffa, Israel). *Open 14 July 1870 to Feb 1872. Postmark type E.*

LAGOS (Port Logo, Greece). *Open 14 July 1870 to Feb 1872. Postmark type E.*

LATAKIA (Syria). *Open 14 July 1870 to Feb 1872. Postmark type E.*

LEROS (Aegean Is.) *Open July 1873 to January 1874 and May to October 1874. Postmark type E.*

MERSINA (Mersin, Turkey). *Open 14 July 1870 to Feb 1872. Postmark type E.*

METELINO (Lesbos, Greece). *Open 14 July 1870 to 30 June 1881. Postmark types E, M.*

RODI (Rhodes, Greece). *Open 13 Aug 1872 to 30 June 1881. Postmark type E.*

SALONNICCHI (Thessaloniki, Greece). *Open 14 July 1870 to Feb 1872. Postmark type E.*

SCIO (Chios, Aegean Is.). *Open 14 July 1870 to 30 June 1881. Postmark types E, N.*

SMIRNE (Izmir, Turkey). *Open 14 Nov 1865 to 30 June 1881. Postmark types E (also without "V. R."), F.*

TENEDOS (Bozcaada, Turkey). *Open 14 July 1870 to March 1871. Postmark type E.*

TRIPOLI (Lebanon). *Open 14 July 1870 to Feb 1872. Postmark type E.*

VOLO (Volos, Greece). *Open 14 July 1870 to Feb 1872. Postmark type E.*

BRITISH FORCES IN EGYPT

Following the rise of a nationalist movement led by Arabi Pasha, and serious disturbances in Alexandria, British troops landed at Ismalia in August 1882 and defeated the nationalists at Tel-el-Kebir on 13 September. A British Army Post Office detachment landed at Alexandria on 21 August and provided a postal service for the troops, using Great Britain stamps, from various locations until it was withdrawn on 7 October.

During the Gordon Relief Expedition of 1884–85 a postal detachment was sent to Suakin on the Red Sea. This operated between 25 March and 30 May 1885 using Great Britain stamps.

ZA 1

Stamps of GREAT BRITAIN cancelled with Type ZA **1**.

1882 (Aug–Oct).

ZA1	½d. rose-red (Plate No. 20)	
ZA2	½d. green (1880)	£300
ZA3	1d. Venetian red (1880)	£600
ZA4	1d. lilac (1881)	£175
ZA5	2½d. blue (1881) (Plate Nos. 21, 22, 23)	£100

1885. Used at Suakin.

ZA6	½d. slate-blue (1884)	£500
ZA7	1d. lilac (1881)	£300
ZA8	2½d. lilac (1884)	£225
ZA9	5d. dull green (1884)	£500

From 1 November 1932 to 29 February 1936 members of the British Forces in Egypt and their families were allowed to send letters to the British Isles at reduced rates. Special seals, which were on sale in booklets at N.A.A.F.I. Institutes and Canteens, were used instead of Egyptian stamps. These seals were stuck on the back of the envelopes, letters bearing the seals being franked on the front with a hand-stamp inscribed "EGYPT POSTAGE PREPAID" in a double circle surmounted by a crown.

PRICES FOR STAMPS ON COVER		
Nos.	A1/9	*from* × 5
No.	A10	*from* × 1·5
No.	A11	*from* × 5
No.	A12	*from* × 75
No.	A13	*from* × 20
No.	A14	*from* × 100
No.	A15	*from* × 20

A **1**

A **2**

(Des Lt-Col. C. Fraser. Typo Hanbury, Tomsett & Co. Ltd, London)

1932 (1 Nov)–**33**. P 11.

(a) Inscr "POSTAL SEAL"

A1	A **1**	1p. deep blue and red	95·00	5·00

(b) Inscr "LETTER SEAL"

A2	A **1**	1p. deep blue and red (8.33)	50·00	85

(Des Sgt. W. F. Lait. Litho Walker & Co, Amalgamated Press, Cairo)

1932 (26 Nov)–**35**. Christmas Seals. P 11½.

A3	A **2**	3m. black/*azure*	50·00	70·00
A4		3m. brown-lake (13.11.33)	7·50	50·00
A5		3m. deep blue (17.11.34)	7·00	32·00
A6		3m. vermilion (23.11.35)	1·25	50·00
		a. Pale vermilion (19.12.35)	13·00	32·00

A **3**

(Des Miss Waugh. Photo Harrison)

1934 (1 June)–**35**.

(a) P 14½×14

A7	A **3**	1p. carmine	55·00	85
A8		1p. green (5.12.34)	6·50	6·00

(b) P 13½×14

A9	A **3**	1p. carmine (24.4.35)	5·50	4·50

(A **4**)

1935 (6 May). Silver Jubilee. As No. A9, but colour changed and optd with Type A **4**, in red.

A10	A **3**	1p. ultramarine	£300	£180

Xmas 1935
3 Milliemes

(A **5**)

1935 (16 Dec). Provisional Christmas Seal. No. A9 surch with Type A **5**.

A11	A **3**	3m. on 1p. carmine	16·00	70·00

The seals and letter stamps were replaced by the following Army Post stamps issued by the Egyptian Postal Administration. No. A9 was accepted for postage until 15 March 1936.

A **6** King Fuad I

A **7** King Farouk

W **48** of Egypt

(Types A **6**/A **7**. Photo Survey Dept, Cairo)

1936. W **48** of Egypt. P 13½ × 14.

A12	A **6**	3m. green (1.12.36)	1·00	2·75
A13		10m. carmine (1.3.36)	8·00	10
		w. Wmk inverted		

1939 (16 Dec). W **48** of Egypt. P 13×13½.

A14	A **7**	3m. green	7·50	10·00
A15		10m. carmine	9·50	10
		w. Wmk inverted		

These stamps were withdrawn in April 1941 but the concession, without the use of special stamps, continued until October 1951 when the postal agreement was abrogated.

MILITARY TELEGRAPH STAMPS

Military Telegraph stamps were provided for the pre-payment of non-official messages sent by the army telegraph system. They were used by army personnel for private communications, newspaper reporters and the local population (when the army was in control of the telegraph system).

The 'unadopted die' stamps, (T T **1**/3 of Bechuanaland inscribed "MILITARY TELEGRAPHS") were supplied for use in Bechuanaland, Egypt and Sudan.

Operations in Egypt commenced in 1884 and on 1 May 1885 the telegraph system in upper Egypt was transferred to military control.

1885. Nos. MT1/8 of Bechuanaland.

(a) Wmk Orb. P 14

MT1	1d. lilac and black	£250
MT2	3d. lilac and brown	
MT3	6d. lilac and green	

(b) Wmk script "VR" (sideways). P 13½

MT4	1s. green and black	
MT5	2s. green and blue	
MT6	5s. green and mauve	
MT7	10s. green and red	£750

(c) Wmk Two Orbs (sideways). P 14×13½

MT8	£1 lilac and black	

The survival rate of unsurcharged military telegraph stamps used in Egypt is very low.

Used prices for Nos. MT1/8 are for stamps with identifiable Egypt cancellations. For mint prices see Bechuanaland Nos. T1/8.

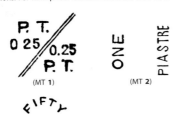

(MT **1**)   (MT **2**)

(MT **3**)   (MT **4**)

1886 (July). Nos. MT1/8 handstamped locally as T MT **1**/4.

MT9	MT **1**	"0.1 P.T." on 1d. lilac and black	£100
		a. bisected (0.05pt) (on piece)	† —
MT10		"0.25 P.T." on 3d. lilac and brown	£100
		a. bisected (0.125pt) (on piece)	† —
MT11	MT **2**	"ONE PIASTRE" on 6d. lilac and green	£100
MT12	MT **3**	"FIVE PIASTRES" on 1s. green and black	£100
MT13		"TEN PIASTRES" on 2s. green and blue	£275
MT14		"TWENTY FIVE PIASTRES" on 5s. green and mauve	£375
MT15		"FIFTY PIASTRES" on 10s. green and red	£750
MT16	MT **4**	"HUNDRED PIASTRES" on £1 lilac and black	£1600

(MT **5**)

TWENTY-FIVE   ONE HUNDRED

PIASTRES   PIASTRES
(MT **6**)   (MT **7**)

1887 (Feb). Nos. MT1/8 and additional values surch in London as T MT **5**/7.

MT17	MT **5**	"ONE DIME" on 1d. lilac and black	50·00
MT18		"TWO DIMES" on 2d. lilac and blue	50·00
MT19		"FIVE DIMES" on 3d. lilac and brown	50·00
MT20		"ONE PIASTRE" on 6d. lilac and green	75·00
MT21		"TWO PIASTRES" on 8d. lilac and carmine	75·00
MT22	MT **6**	"FIVE PIASTRES" on 1s. green and black	75·00
MT23		"TEN PIASTRES" on 2s. green and blue	£110
MT24		"TWENTY-FIVE PIASTRES" on 5s. green and mauve	£225
MT25		"FIFTY PIASTRES" on 10s. green and red	£375
MT26	MT **7**	"ONE HUNDRED PIASTRES" on £1 lilac and black	£550

The London surcharges were withdrawn in Spring 1890. The usage was limited as nearly all the stamps were returned to England and destroyed.

SUEZ CANAL COMPANY

PRICES FOR STAMPS ON COVER	
Nos. 1/4	from × 20

100 Centimes = 1 Franc

On 30 November 1855 a concession to construct the Suez Canal was granted to Ferdinand de Lesseps and the Compagnie Universelle du Canal Maritime de Suez was formed. Work began in April 1859 and the canal was opened on 17 November 1869. In November 1875 the Khedive sold his shares in the company to the British Government, which then became the largest shareholder.

The company transported mail free of charge between Port Said and Suez from 1859 to 1867, when it was decided that payment should be made for the service and postage stamps were introduced in July 1868. Letters for destinations beyond Port Said or Suez required additional franking with Egyptian or French stamps.

The imposition of charges for the service was not welcomed by the public and in August the Egyptian Government agreed to take it over.

1

(Litho Chezaud, Aine & Tavernier, Paris)

1868 (8 July). Imperf.

1	1	1c. black	£250	£1000
2		5c. green	85·00	£500
3		20c. blue	75·00	£500
4		40c. pink	£130	£750

Shades of all values exist.

Stamps can be found showing parts of the papermaker's watermark "LA+-F" (La Croix Frères).

These stamps were withdrawn from sale on 16 August 1868 and demonetised on 31 August.

Many forgeries exist, unused and cancelled. The vast majority of these forgeries show vertical lines, instead of cross-hatching, between "POSTES" and the central oval. It is believed that other forgeries, which do show cross-hatching, originate from the plate of the 40c. value which is missing from the company's archives. These are, however, on thin, brittle paper with smooth shiny gum.

Kenya

INDEPENDENT

(Currency. 100 cents = 1 East Africa, later Kenya Shilling)

1 Cattle Ranching

2 Wood-carving

3 National Assembly

(Des V. Whiteley. Photo Harrison)

1963 (12 Dec). Independence. T **1/3** and similar designs. P 14×15 (small designs) or 14½ (others).

1	5c. brown, deep blue, green and bistre.......	10	55
2	10c. brown..	10	10
3	15c. magenta...	1·00	10
4	20c. black and yellow-green.........................	15	10
5	30c. black and yellow....................................	15	10
6	40c. brown and light blue.............................	15	30
	a. Printed on the gummed side...................	£100	
7	50c. crimson, black and green......................	60	10
8	65c. deep turquoise-green and yellow	55	65
9	1s. multicoloured...	20	10
10	1s.30 brown, black and yellow-green	5·00	30
11	2s. multicoloured...	1·25	40
12	5s. brown, ultramarine and yellow-green ...	1·25	1·25
13	10s. brown and deep blue..............................	9·00	3·00
14	20s. black and rose.......................................	4·00	10·00
1/14 Set of 14		21·00	15·00

Designs: As T **1/2**—15c. Heavy industry; 20c. Timber industry; 30c. Jomo Kenyatta and Mt Kenya; 40c. Fishing industry; 50c. Kenya flag 65c. Pyrethrum industry. As T **3**—1s.30, Tourism (Treetops Hotel); 2s. Coffee industry; 5s. Tea industry; 10s. Mombasa Port; 20s. Royal College, Nairobi.

The 10c. was produced in coils of 1000 in addition to normal sheets.

4 Cockerel

(Des M. Goaman. Photo J. Enschedé)

1964 (12 Dec). Inauguration of Republic. T **4** and similar vert designs. Multicoloured. P 13×12½.

15	15c. Type **4**...	15	15
16	30c. President Kenyatta	15	10
17	50c. Lion...	15	10
18	1s.30 Hartlaub's Turaco..................................	2·00	50
19	2s.50 Nandi flame...	20	4·00
15/19 Set of 5		2·40	4·25

5 Thomson's Gazelle

6 Sable Antelope

For a full range of Stanley Gibbons catalogues, please visit **www.stanleygibbons.com**

7 Greater Kudu

15c. Grey flaw under snout of Aardvark resembles antheap (Pl. 1A, R. 10/5)

(Des Rena Fennessy. Photo Harrison)

1966 (12 Dec)–**71**. Various designs as T **5/7**. Chalk-surfaced paper. P 14×14½ (5c. to 70c.) or 14½ (others).

20	5c. orange, black and sepia...............................	20	20
21	10c. black and apple-green.................................	10	10
	a. Glazed, ordinary paper (13.7.71)	1·00	5·00
22	15c. black and orange...	10	10
	a. "Antheap"..	9·00	
	b. Glazed, ordinary paper (13.7.71)	1·00	1·00
23	20c. ochre, black and blue	10	15
	a. Glazed, ordinary paper (22.1.71)	1·00	1·50
24	30c. Prussian blue, blue and black	20	10
25	40c. black and yellow-brown	60	30
	a. Glazed, ordinary paper (19.2.71)	1·25	3·00
26	50c. black and red-orange.................................	60	10
	a. Glazed, ordinary paper (19.2.71)	14·00	5·00
27	65c. black and light green..................................	1·25	2·00
28	70c. black and claret (15.9.69)	5·00	1·75
	a. Glazed, ordinary paper (19.2.71)	29·00	15·00
29	1s. olive-brown, black and slate-blue	30	10
	a. Glazed, ordinary paper (22.1.71)	1·25	85
30	1s.30 indigo, light olive-green and black...........	4·00	20
31	1s.50 black, orange-brown and dull sage green (15.9.69)	3·00	3·00
	a. Glazed, ordinary paper (22.1.71)	3·50	6·00
32	2s.50 yellow, black and olive-brown	4·25	1·25
	a. Glazed, ordinary paper (22.1.71)	2·00	6·50
33	5s. yellow, black and emerald.........................	75	70
	a. Glazed, ordinary paper (22.1.71)	2·00	12·00
34	10s. yellow-ochre, black and red-brown	2·00	3·00
35	20s. yellow-ochre, yellow-orange, black and gold..	7·50	13·00
20/35 Set of 16		26·00	23·00
21a/33a Set of 10		50·00	50·00

Designs: As T **5/6**—15c. Aardvark ("Ant Bear"); 20c. Lesser Bushbaby; 30c. Warthog; 40c. Common Zebra; 50c. African Buffalo; 65c. Black Rhinoceros; 70c. Ostrich. As T **7**—1s.30, African Elephant; 1s.50, Bat-eared Fox; 2s.50, Cheetah; 5s. Savanna Monkey ("Vervet Monkey"); 10s. Giant Ground Pangolin; 20s. Lion.

On chalk-surfaced paper, all values except 30c., 50c. and 2s.50 exist with PVA gum as well as gum arabic but the 70c. and 1s.50 exist with PVA gum only. The stamps on glazed, ordinary paper exist with PVA gum only.

Nos. 21 and 26 exist in coils constructed from normal sheets.

8 Perna Tellin (*Tellina perna*)

9 Ramose Murex (*Murex ramosus*)

(10)

50c.	A. Inscr "*Janthina globosa*".	
	B. Inscr "*Janthina janthina*".	
70c.	C. Inscr "*Nautilus pompileus*".	
	D. Inscr "*Nautilus pompilius*".	

(Des Rena Fennessy. Photo Harrison)

1971 (15 Dec)–**74**. T **8/9** and similar perf designs showing sea shells. Multicoloured.

*(a) Size as T***8**. P 14½×14*

36	5c. Type **8**..	10	30
37	10c. Episcopal Mitre (*Mitra mitra*) (yellow-green background)......................................	15	10
	a. Olive-green background (21.1.74).............	1·00	10
38	15c. Purplish Clanculus (*Clanculus puniceus*)	15	20
39	20c. Humpback Cowrie (*Cypraea mauritania*)	15	20
40	30c. Variable Abalone (*Haliotis varia*)..............	20	10

41	40c. Flame Top Shell (*Trochus flammulatus*)..	20	10
42	50c. Common Purple Janthina (*Janthina globosa*) (A)............................	30	20
43	50c. Common Purple Janthina (*Janthina janthina*) (B) (21.1.74)................	13·00	3·00
44	60c. Bull-mouth Helmet (*Cypraecassis rufa*)..	30	1·75
45	70c. Chambered, Pearly Nautilus (*Nautilus pompileius*) (C).....................	45	1·50
46	70c. Chambered, Pearly Nautilus (*Nautilus pompilius*) (D) (21.1.74)...........	12·00	6·50

(b) Size as T9. P 14

47	1s. Type **9** (yellow-buff background)............	30	10
	a. Buff background (21.1.74)	40	10
48	1s.50 Trumpet Triton (*Charonia tritonis*)...........	1·00	10
49	2s50. Trapezium Horse Conch (*Fasciolaria trapezium*)............................	1·00	10
50	5s. Great Green Turban (*Turbo marmoratus*) (pale olive-yellow background)...............	1·00	10
	a. Pale olive-bistre background (13.6.73)	1·00	10
51	10s. Textile or Cloth of Gold Cone (*Conus textile*)	1·50	15
52	20s. Scorpion Conch (*Lambis Scorpius*) (grey background)...........................	4·00	1·00
	a. Bluish slate background (12.9.73).............	1·50	25
36/52a Set of 17		30·00	13·00

1975 (17 Nov). Nos. 48/9 and 52 surch as T **10**.

53	2s. on 1s.50 Trumpet Triton (*Charonia tritonis*)..................................	6·00	6·00
54	3s. on 2s.50 Trapezium Horse Conch (*Fasciolaria trapezium*).................	9·50	23·00
55	40s. on 20s. Scorpion Conch (*Lambis Scorpius*)	6·00	15·00
53/5 Set of 3		19·00	40·00

The surcharge on No. 55 does not have a dot beneath the stroke following the face value.

For commemorative stamps, issued between 1964 and 1976, inscribed "UGANDA KENYA TANGANYIKA AND ZANZIBAR" (or "TANZANIA UGANDA KENYA") see under KENYA, UGANDA AND TANGANYIKA.

11 Microwave Tower   **12** Akii Bua, Ugandan Hurdler

(Des H. Nickelsen. Litho Format)

1976 (15 Apr). Telecommunications Development. T **11** and similar multicoloured designs. P 14.

56	50c. Type **11**	10	10
57	1s. Cordless switchboard (*horiz*)................	10	10
58	2s. Telephones	20	30
59	3s. Message Switching Centre (*horiz*)............	25	45
56/9 Set of 4		55	75
MS60 120×120 mm. Nos. 56/9. Imperf.............		1·10	2·50

Nos. 56/7 and 59 exist imperforate from stock dispersed by the liquidator of Format International Security Printers Ltd.

(Des Beryl Moore. Litho Format)

1976 (7 July*). Olympic Games, Montreal. T **12** and similar horiz designs. Multicoloured. P 14½.

61	50c. Type **12**	10	10
62	1s. Filbert Bayi, Tanzanian runner................	15	10
63	2s. Steve Muchoki, Kenyan boxer................	30	35
64	3s. Olympic flame and East African flags....	70	50
61/4 Set of 4		1·10	85
MS65 129×154 mm. Nos. 61/4. P 13.................		5·00	7·50

*This is the local date of issue; the Crown Agents released the stamps two days earlier.

Nos. 61 and 63 exist imperforate from stock dispersed by the liquidator of Format International Security Printers Ltd.

13 Diesel-hydraulic Train, Tanzania–Zambia Railway

(Des H. Moghul. Litho Format)

1976 (4 Oct). Railway Transport. T **13** and similar horiz designs. Multicoloured. P 14½.

66	50c. Type **13**	35	10
67	1s. Nile Bridge, Uganda................	60	15
68	2s. Nakuru Station, Kenya................	1·25	1·00
69	3s. Uganda Railway Class A steam locomotive, 1896....................	1·25	1·50
66/9 Set of 4		3·00	2·50
MS70 154×103 mm. Nos. 66/9. P 13...............		7·00	8·00

Nos. 66/70 exist imperforate from stock dispersed by the liquidator of Format International Security Printers Ltd.

14 Nile Perch   **15** Maasai Manyatta (village), Kenya

(Des Adrienne Kennaway. Litho Format)

1977 (10 Jan). Game Fish of East Africa. T **14** and similar vert designs. Multicoloured. P 14*.

71	50c. Type **14**	25	10
72	1s. Nile Mouthbrooder ("Tilapia ")..................	30	10
73	3s. Sailfish	60	60
74	5s. Black Marlin	80	80
71/4 Set of 4		1·75	1·40
MS75 153×129 mm. Nos. 71/4....................		7·50	4·00

*On No. **MS75** the right-hand side of the 5s. value is perforated 13½.

(Des Rena Fennessy. Litho Questa)

1977 (15 Jan). Second World Black and African Festival of Arts and Culture, Nigeria. T **15** and similar horiz designs. Multicoloured. P 13½.

76	50c. Type **15**	15	10
77	1s. "Heartbeat of Africa" (Ugandan dancers)	15	10
78	2s. Makonde sculpture, Tanzania	60	1·25
79	3s. "Early Man and Technology" (skinning hippopotamus)	75	2·00
76/9 Set of 4		1·50	3·00
MS80 132×109 mm. Nos. 76/9...................		3·50	5·50

16 Rally-car and Villagers

(Des BG. Studios. Litho Questa)

1977 (5 Apr). 25th Anniv of Safari Rally. T **16** and similar horiz designs. Multicoloured. P 14.

81	50c. Type **16**	15	10
82	1s. President Kenyatta starting rally	15	10
83	2s. Car fording river	40	60
84	5s. Car and elephants	1·25	1·50
81/4 Set of 4		1·75	2·00
MS85 126×93 mm. Nos. 81/4....................		3·00	6·50

17 Canon Kivebulaya

(Des Beryl Moore. Litho Questa)

1977 (30 June). Centenary of Ugandan Church. T **17** and similar horiz designs. Multicoloured. P 14×13½.

86	50c. Type **17**	10	10
87	1s. Modern Namirembe Cathedral	10	10
88	2s. The first Cathedral	30	55

89	5s. Early congregation, Kigezi....................	50	1·25
86/9	*Set of 4*	85	1·50
MS90	126×94 mm. Nos. 86/9...............................	1·00	2·50

18 Sagana Royal Lodge, Nyeri, 1952

(Des G. Vasarhelyi (50s.), J. Cooter (others). Litho Questa)

1977 (20 July). Silver Jubilee. T **18** and similar multicoloured designs. P 13½.

91	2s. Type **18**..	15	15
92	5s. Treetops Hotel (*vert*)..........................	20	35
93	10s. Queen Elizabeth and President Kenyatta..	30	60
94	15s. Royal visit, 1972.................................	45	1·00
91/4	*Set of 4*...	1·00	1·90
MS95	Two sheets: (a) 140×60 mm, No. 94; (b) 152×127 mm, 50s. Queen and Prince Philip in Treetops Hotel *Set of 2 sheets*...........................	2·00	1·40

19 Pancake Tortoise

(Des Rena Fennessy. Litho Questa)

1977 (26 Sept). Endangered Species. T **19** and similar horiz designs. Multicoloured. P 14.

96	50c. Type **19**..	30	10
97	1s. Nile Crocodile......................................	40	10
98	2s. Hunter's Hartebeest...........................	1·00	40
99	3s. Red Colobus..	1·25	50
100	5s. Dugong...	1·50	2·25
96/100	*Set of 5*	4·00	1·60
MS101	127×101 mm. Nos. 97/100.......................	4·50	3·00

20 Kenya–Ethiopia Border Point

(Des R. Granger Barrett. Litho Questa)

1977 (10 Nov). Nairobi–Addis Ababa Highway. T **20** and similar horiz designs. Multicoloured. P 14.

102	50c. Type **20**..	15	10
103	1s. Archer's Post	15	10
104	2s. Thika Flyover.......................................	30	25
105	5s. Marsabit Game Lodge.........................	50	75
102/5	*Set of 4*...	1·00	1·00
MS106	144×91 mm. Nos. 102/5.............................	1·75	3·50

21 Gypsum   **22** Amethyst

(Des Rena Fennesey. Photo Harrison)

1977 (10 Dec*). Minerals. Multicoloured designs.

(a) Vert as T **21**. *P 14½×14*

107	10c. Type **21**..	1·25	20
108	20c. Trona..	2·00	20
109	30c. Kyanite...	2·00	20

110	40c. Amazonite..	1·40	10
111	50c. Galena..	1·40	10
112	70c. Silicified wood..................................	7·50	1·00
113	80c. Fluorite..	7·50	60

(b) Horiz as T **22**. *P 14*

114	1s. Type **22**..	1·40	10
	a. Gold (face value and inscr) omitted.......		
115	1s.50 Agate..	1·50	30
	a. Gold (face value and inscr) omitted.......	£325	
116	2s. Tourmaline..	1·50	20
	a. Gold (face value and inscr) omitted.......	£275	
117	3s. Aquamarine...	1·75	55
	a. Gold (face value and inscr) omitted.......	£250	
118	5s. Rhodolite Garnet................................	1·75	1·10
119	10s. Sapphire..	1·75	1·50
120	20s. Ruby..	4·50	2·50
121	40s. Green Grossular Garnet......................	18·00	20·00
107/21	*Set of 15*	48·00	25·00

*This is the local issue date. The stamps were released in London on 9 December.

23 Joe Kadenge (Kenya) and Forwards

(Des H. Moghul. Litho Questa)

1978 (10 Apr). World Cup Football Championship, Argentina. T **23** and similar horiz designs showing footballers. Multicoloured. P 14×13½.

122	50c. Type **23**..	10	10
123	1s. Mohamed Chuma (Tanzania) and Cup presentation...	10	10
124	2s. Omari Kidevu (Zanzibar) and goalmouth scene....................................	30	70
125	3s. Polly Ouma (Uganda) and three forwards..	40	95
122/5	*Set of 4*	70	1·60
MS126	136×81 mm. Nos. 122/5.............................	2·75	3·50

24 Boxing

(Des H. Moghul. Photo Heraclio Fournier)

1978 (17 July). Commonwealth Games, Edmonton. T **24** and similar horiz designs. Multicoloured. P 13×14.

127	50c. Type **24**..	15	10
128	1s. Welcoming Olympic Games Team, 1968...	15	10
129	3s. Javelin throwing..................................	50	1·00
130	5s. President Kenyatta admiring boxer's trophy...	60	1·60
127/30	*Set of 4*	1·10	2·50

25 "Overloading is Dangerous"

(Des H Moghul. Litho Walsall)

1978 (18 Sept). Road Safety. T **25** and similar horiz designs. Multicoloured. P 13½.

131	50c. Type **25**..	40	10
132	1s. "Speed does not pay"........................	60	10
133	1s.50 "Ignoring Traffic Signs may cause death"..	75	55
134	2s. "Slow down at School Crossing"......	1·00	80
135	3s. "Never cross a continuous line".......	1·10	2·00

| 136 | 5s. "Approach Railway Level Crossing with extreme caution" | 1·75 | 3·25 |
| 131/6 | Set of 6 | 5·00 | 6·00 |

26 President Kenyatta at Mass Rally, 1963

27 Freedom Fighters, Namibia

(Des Beryl Moore. Litho J.W.)

1978 (16 Oct). Kenyatta Day. T **26** and similar horiz designs. Multicoloured. P 14.

137	50c. "Harambee Water Project"	15	10
138	1s. Handing over of Independence Instruments, 1963	15	10
139	2s. Type **26**	30	35
140	3s. "Harambee, 15 Great Years"	60	1·00
141	5s. "Struggle for Independence, 1952"	80	2·00
137/41	Set of 5	1·75	3·00

(Des L. Curtis. Litho Questa)

1978 (11 Dec*). International Anti-Apartheid Year. T **27** and similar horiz designs. P 14×14½.

142	50c. multicoloured	15	10
143	1s. black and cobalt	15	10
144	2s. multicoloured	30	30
145	3s. multicoloured	50	65
146	5s. multicoloured	55	1·00
142/6	Set of 5	1·50	1·90

Designs:—1s. International seminar on apartheid, racial discrimination and colonialism in South Africa; 2s. Steve Biko's tombstone; 3s. Nelson Mandela; 5s. Bishop Lamont.

*This is the local date of issue; the Crown Agents released the stamps the previous day.

28 Children Playing

(Des Beryl Moore. Litho Walsall)

1979 (5 Feb). International Year of the Child. T **28** and similar horiz designs. Multicoloured. P 13½×14.

147	50c. Type **28**	15	10
148	2s. Child fishing	30	50
149	3s. Children singing and dancing	45	90
100	**150** 5s. Children working with camels	1·00	2·25
147/50	Set of 4	1·50	3·00

29 "The Lion and the Jewel"

30 Blind Telephone Operator

(Des Beryl Moore. Litho Enschedé)

1979 (6 Apr). Kenya National Theatre. T **29** and similar horiz designs. Multicoloured. P 13×13½.

151	50c. Type **29**	15	10
152	1s. Scene from "Utisi"	15	10
153	2s. "Entertainment past and present" (programmes from past productions)	25	30
154	3s. Kenya National Theatre	35	45
155	5s. Nairobi City Players production of "Genesis"	50	75
151/5	Set of 5	1·25	1·50

(Des H. Moghul. Litho Harrison)

1979 (29 June*). 50th Anniv of Salvation Army Social Services. T **30** and similar multicoloured designs. P 13½×13 (50c., 1s.) or 13×13½ (others).

156	50c. Type **30**	30	10
157	1s. Care for the Aged	30	10
158	3s. Village polytechnic (horiz)	50	1·25
159	5s. Vocational training (horiz)	85	2·25
156/9	Set of 4	1·75	3·25

*This is the local date of issue; the Crown Agents released the stamps on 4 June.

31 "Father of the Nation" (Kenyatta's funeral procession)

32 British East Africa Company 1890 1a. Stamp

(Des H. Moghul. Litho Questa)

1979 (21 Aug*). 1st Death Anniv of President Kenyatta. T **31** and similar vert designs. Multicoloured. P 13½×14.

160	50c. Type **31**	10	10
161	1s. "First President of Kenya" (Kenyatta receiving independence)	10	10
162	3s. "Kenyatta the politician" (speaking at rally)	30	50
163	5s. "A true son of Kenya" (Kenyatta as a boy carpenter)	40	95
160/3	Set of 4	75	1·50

*This is the local date of issue; the Crown Agents did not release the stamps until 29 August.

(Des J.W. Litho Harrison)

1979 (27 Nov). Death Centenary of Sir Rowland Hill. T **32** and similar vert designs showing stamps. P 14×14½.

164	50c. multicoloured	15	10
165	1s. multicoloured	15	10
166	2s. black, magenta and yellow-ochre	20	40
167	5s. multicoloured	35	1·00
164/7	Set of 4	75	1·40

Designs:—1s. Kenya, Uganda and Tanganyika 1935 1s.; 2s. Penny Black; 5s. 1964 Inauguration of Republic 2s.50, commemorative.

33 Roads, Globe and Conference Emblem

(Des H. Moghul. Litho Questa)

1980 (10 Jan). I.R.F. (International Road Federation) African Highway Conference, Nairobi. T **33** and similar horiz designs. Multicoloured. P 14×13½.

168	50c. Type **33**	15	10
169	1s. New weighbridge, Athi River	15	10
170	3s. New Nyali Bridge, Mombasa	40	85
171	5s. Highway to Jomo Kenyatta International Airport	50	2·00
168/71	Set of 4	1·10	2·75

34 Mobile Unit in action, Masailand

(Des Beryl Moore. Litho Questa)

1980 (20 Mar). Flying Doctor Service. T **34** and similar multicoloured designs. P 14½.

| 172 | 50c. Type **34** | 15 | 10 |

173	1s. Donkey transport to Turkana airstrip (vert)		20	10
174	3s. Surgical team in action at outstation (vert)		65	1·00
175	5s. Emergency airlift from North Eastern Province		90	1·60
172/5 Set of 4			1·60	2·50
MS176 146×133 mm. Nos. 172/5			1·60	2·75

35 Statue of Sir Rowland Hill

36 Pope John Paul II

(Des J.W. Litho Questa)

1980 (6 May). London 1980 International Stamp Exhibition. P 14.

177	**35** 25s. multicoloured		1·00	2·50
MS178 114×101 mm. No. 177			1·00	2·75

(Des Sister Frances Randal. Litho Italian Govt Ptg Works, Rome)

1980 (8 May). Papal Visit. T **36** and similar multicoloured designs. P 13.

179	50c. Type **36**		35	10
180	1s. Pope John Paul II, cathedral and coat of arms (vert)		35	10
181	5s. Pope John Paul II, Papal and Kenyan flags on dove symbol (vert)		55	65
182	10s. President Moi, Pope John Paul hand map of Africa		1·00	1·50
179/82 Set of 4			2·00	2·00

37 Blue-spotted Stingray

38 National Archives

(Des Adrienne Kennaway. Litho Harrison)

1980 (27 June). Marine Life. T **37** and similar vert designs. Multicoloured. P 14.

183	50c. Type **37**		30	10
184	2s. Allard's Anemonefish		80	65
185	3s. Four-coloured Nudibranch (Chromodoris quadricolor)		80	1·40
186	5s. Eretmochelys imbricata		1·50	2·25
183/6 Set of 4			3·00	4·00

(Des A. Odhuno; adapted L. Curtis. Litho Questa)

1980 (9 Oct). Historic Buildings. T **38** and similar horiz designs. Multicoloured. P 14.

187	50c. Type **38**		10	10
188	1s. Provincial Commissioner's Office, Nairobi		15	10
189	1s.50 Nairobi House		20	20
190	2s. Norfolk Hotel		25	50
191	3s. McMillan Library		35	95
192	5s. Kipande House		55	1·60
187/92 Set of 6			1·40	3·00

39 "Disabled Enjoys Affection"

(Des H. Moghul. Litho Enschedé)

1981 (10 Feb). International Year for Disabled Persons. T **39** and similar horiz designs. Multicoloured. P 14×13.

193	50c. Type **39**		15	10
194	1s. President Moi presenting Kenyan flag to Disabled Olympic Games team captain		15	10
195	3s. (Blind people climbing Mount Kenya, 1975)		55	65
196	5s. Disabled artist at work		70	1·00
193/6 Set of 4			1·40	1·60

40 Longonot Complex

(Des H. Moghul. Litho Harrison)

1981 (15 Apr). Satellite Communications. T **40** and similar horiz designs. Multicoloured. P 14×14½.

197	50c. Type **40**		15	10
198	2s. "Intelsat V"		40	35
199	3s. "Longonot I"		45	55
200	5s. "Longonot II"		60	85
197/200 Set of 4			1·40	1·60

41 Kenyatta Conference Centre

(Des L. Curtis. Litho Questa (MS206) or J.W. (others))

1981 (17 June*). O.A.U. (Organisation of African Unity) Summit Conference, Nairobi. T **41** and similar horiz designs in black, bistre-yellow and new blue (1s.) or multicoloured (others). P 13½.

201	50c. Type **41**		15	10
202	1s. "Panaftel" earth stations		15	10
203	3s. Parliament Building		25	40
204	5s. Jomo Kenyatta International Airport		50	65
205	10s. O.A.U. flag		60	60
201/5 Set of 5			1·50	2·00
MS206 110×110 mm. No. 205. P 14½×14			1·10	1·50

*This is the local date of issue; the Crown Agents did not release the stamps until 24 June.

42 St. Paul's Cathedral

43 Giraffe

(Des A. Theobald. Litho Questa)

1981 (29 July). Royal Wedding. T **42** and similar vert designs. Multicoloured. P 14.

207	50c. Prince Charles and President Daniel Arap Moi		10	10
208	3s. Type **42**		15	20
209	5s. Royal Yacht Britannia		25	30
210	10s. Prince Charles on safari in Kenya		40	55
207/10 Set of 4			70	1·00

MS211 85×102 mm. 25s. Prince Charles and Lady
Diana Spencer 75   80
Nos. 207/10 also exist perforated 12 (*price for set of* 4 70p *mint*,
£1.40 *used*) from additional sheetlets of five stamps and one label.
Insufficient supplies of No. MS211 were received by 29 July for
a full distribution, but subsequently the miniature sheet was freely
available.

(Des Rena Fennessy. Litho Questa)

1981 (31 Aug). Rare Animals. T **43** and similar vert designs.
Multicoloured. P 14½.

212	50c. Type **43**	15	10
213	2s. Bongo	25	25
214	5s. Roan Antelope	40	1·00
215	10s. Agile Mangabey	60	2·25
212/15 *Set of 4*		1·25	3·25

44 "Technical
Development"

45 Kamba

(Des H. Moghul, adapted L. Curtis. Litho Questa)

1981 (16 Oct). World Food Day. T **44** and similar vert designs.
Multicoloured. P 14.

216	50c. Type **44**	10	10
217	1s. "Mwea rice projects"	15	10
218	2s. "Irrigation schemes"	30	55
219	5s. "Breeding livestock"	60	1·75
216/19 *Set of 4*		1·00	2·25

(Des Adrienne Kennaway. Litho Harrison)

1981 (18 Dec). Ceremonial Costumes (1st series). T **45** and similar vert
designs. Multicoloured. P 14½×13½.

220	50c. Type **45**	40	10
221	1s. Turkana	45	10
222	2s. Giriama	1·25	85
223	3s. Masai	1·60	2·50
224	5s. Luo	1·75	4·25
220/4 *Set of 5*		5·00	7·00

See also Nos. 329/33, 413/17 and 515/19.

46 *Australopithecus boisei*

(Des Adrienne Kennaway. Litho Format)

1982 (19 Jan). "Origins of Mankind". Skulls. T **46** and similar horiz
designs. Multicoloured. P 13½×14.

225	50c. Type **46**	1·75	30
226	2s. *Homo erectus*	3·25	1·50
227	3s. *Homo habilis*	3·25	3·75
228	5s. *Proconsul africanus*	3·75	5·00
225/8 *Set of 4*		11·00	9·50

47 Tree-planting

1982 (9 June). 75th Anniv of Boy Scout Movement (Nos. 229, 231, 233
and 235) and 60th Anniv of Girl Guide Movement (Nos. 230, 232,
234 and 236). T **47** and similar horiz designs. Multicoloured. P 14½.

229	70c. Type **47**	40	80
	a. Horiz pair. Nos. 229/30	80	1·60
230	70c. Paying homage	40	80
231	3s.50 "Be Prepared"	1·00	2·00
	a. Horiz pair. Nos. 231/2	2·00	4·00
232	3s.50 "International Friendship"	1·00	2·00
233	5s. Helping disabled	1·25	2·50
	a. Horiz pair. Nos. 233/4	2·50	5·00
234	5s. Community service	1·25	2·50
235	6s.50 Paxtu Cottage (Lord Baden-Powell's home)	1·25	2·75
	a. Horiz pair. Nos. 235/6	2·50	5·50
236	6s.50 Lady Baden-Powell	1·25	2·75
229/36 *Set of 8*		7·00	14·00
MS237 112×112 mm. Nos. 229, 231, 233 and 235		3·75	3·00

The two designs of each value were printed together, *se-tenant*, in
horizontal pairs throughout the sheet.

48 Footballer displaying Shooting Skill

(Des Adnenne Kennaway. Litho Harrison)

1982 (5 July). World Cup Football Championships, Spain. T **48** and
similar triangular designs showing footballers silhouetted against
world map. Multicoloured. P 12½.

238	70c. Type **48**	1·00	65
239	3s.50 Heading	2·00	2·75
240	5s. Goalkeeping	2·50	4·25
241	10s. Dribbling	3·50	8·00
238/41 *Set of 4*		8·00	14·00
MS242 101×76 mm. 20s. Tackling. P 13×14		5·50	4·00

49 Cattle Judging   **50** Micro-wave
Radio System

(Des H. Moghul. Litho Harrison)

1982 (28 Sept). 80th Anniv of Agricultural Society of Kenya. T **49** and
similar vert designs. Multicoloured. P 14½.

243	70c. Type **49**	40	10
244	2s.50 Farm machinery	1·00	1·00
245	3s.50 Musical ride	1·25	2·00
246	6s.50 Agricultural Society emblem	1·50	4·25
243/6 *Set of 4*		3·75	6·50

(Des H. Moghul. Photo Courvoisier)

1982 (21 Oct). I.T.U. Plenipotentiary Conference, Nairobi. T **50** and
similar vert designs. Multicoloured. P 11½.

247	70c. Type **50**	50	10
248	3s.50 Sea-to-shore service link	1·75	1·75
249	5s. Rural telecommunications system	2·25	3·75
250	6s.50 I.T.U. emblem	2·50	4·50
247/50 *Set of 4*		6·25	9·00

(51)   **52** Container Cranes

1982 (22 Nov). No. 113 surch with T **51**, in white on a black panel.

251	70c. on 80c. Fluorite	1·00	1·25

(Des R. Vigurs. Litho Questa)

1983 (20 Jan). 5th Anniv of Kenya Ports Authority. T **52** and similar
horiz designs. P 14.

252	70c. Type **52**	85	10

253	2s. Port by night	1·75	1·90
254	3s.50 Container cranes (different)..........	2·50	3·50
255	5s. Map of Mombasa Port..................	3·25	4·50
252/5 Set of 4		7·50	9·00
MS256 125×85 mm. Nos. 252/5......		7·50	9·50

53 Shade
Zambarau

54 Waridi Kikuba

(Des Rena Fennessy. Photo Harrison)

1983 (15 Feb). Flowers. Multicoloured.

(a) Vert designs as T53. P 14½×14

257	10c. Type **53**	40	40
258	20c. Kilua Kingulima........................	55	40
259	30c. Mwalika Mwiya.........................	55	40
260	40c. Ziyungi Buluu..........................	55	40
261	50c. Kilua Habashia.........................	55	30
262	70c. Chanuo Kato............................	60	20
262a	80c. As 40c. (7.8.85)	4·50	5·50
262b	1s. Waridi Kikuba (5.8.85*)	4·50	80

*(b) Vert designs as T **54**. P 14*

263	1s. Type **54**	65	20
264	1s.50 Mshomoro Mtambazi................	1·75	60
265	2s. Papatuo Boti............................	1·75	60
266	2s.50 Tumba Mboni..........................	1·75	60
266a	3s. Mkuku Mrembo (12.8.85)............	14·00	12·00
267	3s.50 Mtongo Mbeja.........................	1·50	1·50
	a. Gold (inscr and face value) omitted.......		
267b	4s. Mnukia Muuma (7.8.85)..............	4·75	8·00
268	5s. Nyungu Chepuo........................	1·25	1·50
268a	7s. Mlua Miba (7.8.85)....................	6·50	11·00
269	10s. Muafunili...............................	1·25	1·50
270	20s. Mbake Nyanza.........................	1·25	2·50
271	40s. Njuga Pagwa...........................	2·00	8·00
257/71 Set of 20		45·00	50·00

*Earliest known postmark date.

55 Coffee Plucking

56 Examining Parcels

(Des C. Fernandes. Litho Harrison)

1983 (14 Mar). Commonwealth Day. T **55** and similar multicoloured designs. P 14×14½ (70c., 2s.) or 14½×14 (others).

272	70c. Type **55**	10	10
273	2s. President Daniel Arap Moi............	15	20
274	5s. Satellite view of Earth (horiz).......	35	45
275	10s. Masai dance (horiz)..................	65	1·00
272/5 Set of 4		1·10	1·50

(Des H. Moghul. Litho Harrison)

1983 (11 May). 30th Anniv of Customs Co-operation Council. T **56** and similar vert designs. Multicoloured. P 14.

276	70c. Type **56**	25	10
277	2s.50 Customs Headquarters, Mombasa..........	65	30
278	3s.50 Customs Council Headquarters, Brussels........	75	40
279	10s. Customs patrol boat.................	2·40	2·50
276/9 Set of 4		3·50	3·00

For a full range of Stanley Gibbons catalogues,
please visit **www.stanleygibbons.com**

57 Communications
via Satellite

58 Craftsman (freighter) in Kilindini
Harbour

(Des C. Fernandes Harrison)

1983 (4 July). World Communications Year. T **57** and similar multicoloured designs. P 14×14½ (70c., 2s.50) or 14½×14 (others).

280	70c. Type **57**.................................	60	10
281	2s.50 "Telephone and Postal Services".........	1·50	1·75
282	3s.50 Communications by sea and air (horiz).	2·00	3·00
283	5s. Road and rail communications (horiz)..	2·50	4·00
280/3 Set of 4		6·00	8·00

(Des C. Fernandes. Litho Harrison)

1983 (22 Sept). 25th Anniv of Intergovernmental Maritime Organization. T **58** and similar horiz designs. Multicoloured. P 14.

284	70c. Type **58**.................................	1·10	10
285	2s.50 Life-saving devices..................	2·00	1·40
286	3s.50 Mombasa container terminal.......	2·50	2·50
287	10s. Marine park...........................	3·25	8·50
284/7 Set of 4		8·00	11·00

59 President Moi signing Visitors' Book

(Des H. Moghul. Litho Harrison)

1983 (31 Oct). 29th Commonwealth Parliamentary Conference. T **59** and similar multicoloured designs. P 14.

288	70c. Type **59**.................................	25	10
289	2s.50 Parliament building, Nairobi (vert)........	90	1·25
290	5s. State opening of Parliament (vert)..	1·60	3·00
288/90 Set of 3		2·50	3·75
MS291 122×141 mm. Nos. 288/90......		2·75	6·50

60 Kenyan and British Flags

(Des A. Theobald. Litho Harrison)

1983 (10 Nov). Royal Visit. T **60** and similar horiz designs. Multicoloured. P 14.

292	70c. Type **60**.................................	50	10
293	3s.50 Sagana State Lodge..................	2·00	1·50
294	5s. Treetops Hotel........................	2·25	2·75
295	10s. Queen Elizabeth II and President Moi ...	3·50	7·00
292/5 Set of 4		7·50	10·00
MS296 126×100 mm. 25s. Designs as Nos. 292/5, but without face values. Imperf..................		4·50	7·50

61 President Moi

(Des H. Moghul. Litho Harrison)

1983 (9 Dec). 20th Anniv of Independence. T **61** and similar horiz designs. Multicoloured. P 14½.

297	70c. Type **61**.................................	10	10
298	2s. President Moi planting tree	15	20

299	3s.50 Kenyan flag and emblem	25	35
300	5s. School milk scheme	40	50
301	10s. People of Kenya	75	1·10
297/301 Set of 5		1·60	2·00
MS302 126×93 mm. 25s. Designs as Nos. 297 and 299/301, but without face values. Imperf		1·50	2·75

62 White-backed Night Heron

(Des Agnes Odero. Litho Harrison)

1984 (6 Feb). Rare Birds of Kenya. T **62** and similar vert designs. Multicoloured. P 14½×13½.

303	70c. Type **62**	1·50	30
304	2s.50 Quail Plover	2·50	2·50
305	3s.50 Taita Olive Thrush	3·25	3·75
306	5s. Mufumbiri Shrike ("Yellow Gonolek")	3·75	4·25
307	10s. White-winged Apalis	4·50	7·00
303/7 Set of 5		14·00	16·00

63 Radar Tower

64 Running

(Des C. Fernandes. Litho Harrison)

1984 (2 Apr). 40th Anniv of International Civil Aviation Organization. T **63** and similar multicoloured designs. P 14.

308	70c. Type **63**	30	10
309	2s.50 Kenya School of Aviation (horiz)	75	70
310	3s.50 Boeing 707 taking off from Moi airport (horiz)	1·10	1·50
311	5s. Air traffic control centre	1·50	2·50
308/11 Set of 4		3·25	4·25

(Des Jennifer Toombs. Litho Harrison)

1984 (21 May). Olympic Games, Los Angeles. T **64** and similar horiz designs. P 14½.

312	70c. black, bright yellow-green and bronze green	25	10
313	2s.50 black, bright magenta and reddish violet	50	55
314	5s. black, pale turquoise-blue and steel blue	1·00	2·25
315	10s. black, bistre-yellow and brown	3·75	6·00
312/15 Set of 4		5·00	8·00
MS316 130×121 mm. 25s. Designs as Nos 312/15 but without face values. Imperf		3·25	3·25

Designs:—2s.50, Hurdling; 5s. Boxing; 10s. Hockey.

65 Conference and Kenya Library Association Logos

66 Doves and Cress

(Des C. Fernandes. Harrison)

1984 (28 June). 50th Conference of the International Federation of Library Associations. T **65** and similar horiz designs. Multicoloured. P 14½.

317	70c. Type **65**	10	10
318	3s.50 Mobile library	50	60
319	5s. Adult library	65	1·25
320	10s. Children's library	1·00	3·25
317/20 Set of 4		2·00	4·50

(Des K. Bisley. Litho Harrison)

1984 (23 Aug). 4th World Conference on Religion and Peace. T **66** and similar vert designs, each showing a different central symbol. Multicoloured. P 14½.

321	70c. Type **66**	20	20
322	2s.50 Arabic inscription	80	1·10
323	3s.50 Peace emblem	1·25	1·75
324	6s.50 Star and Crescent	1·75	4·00
321/4 Set of 4		3·50	6·25

67 Export Year Logo

68 Knight and Nyayo National Stadium

(Litho Harrison)

1984 (1 Oct). Kenya Export Year. T **67** and similar multicoloured designs. P 14½.

325	70c. Type **67**	30	10
326	3s.50 Forklift truck with air cargo (horiz)	1·75	2·00
327	5s. Loading ship's cargo	2·50	3·00
328	10s. Kenyan products (horiz)	3·75	6·50
325/8 Set of 4		7·50	10·50

(Des Adnenne Kennaway. Litho Harrison)

1984 (5 Nov). Ceremonial Costumes (2nd series). Vert designs as T **45**. Multicoloured. P 14½×13½.

329	70c. Luhya	80	15
330	2s. Kikuyu	2·00	1·75
331	3s.50 Pokomo	2·50	2·25
332	5s. Nandi	3·00	3·00
333	10s. Rendile	4·00	6·50
329/33 Set of 5		11·00	12·00

(Des Bisley Advertising. Litho Harrison)

1984 (21 Dec). 60th Anniv of International Chess Federation. T **68** and similar horiz designs showing Staunton chess pieces. Multicoloured. P 14½.

334	70c. Type **68**	2·25	40
335	2s.50 Rook and Fort Jesus	3·25	1·75
336	3s.50 Bishop and National Monument	3·75	2·00
337	5s. Queen and Parliament Building	4·00	3·75
338	10s. King and Nyayo Fountain	6·00	8·00
334/8 Set of 5		17·00	14·00

69 Cooking with Wood-burning Stove and Charcoal Fire

(Des H. Moghul. Litho J. W.)

1985 (22 Jan). Energy Conservation. T **69** and similar horiz designs. Multicoloured. P 13½.

339	70c. Type **69**	20	10
340	2s. Solar energy panel on roof	65	75
341	3s.50 Production of gas from cow dung	75	1·25
342	10s. Ploughing with oxen	2·25	6·00
339/42 Set of 4		3·50	7·25
MS343 110×85 mm. 20s. Designs as Nos. 339/42, but without face values		2·50	2·50

70 Crippled Girl Guide making Table-mat

(Des Kenya Advertising Corporation. Litho J.W.)

1985 (27 Mar). 75th Anniv of Girl Guide Movement. T **70** and similar horiz designs. Multicoloured. P 13½.

344	1s. Type **70**	50	15
345	3s. Girl Guides doing community service ...	1·25	1·00
346	5s. Lady Olave Baden-Powell (founder)........	1·75	2·25
347	7s. Girl Guides gardening..............................	2·75	6·00
344/7 *Set of 4*		5·50	8·50

71 Stylised Figures and Globe   **72** Man with Malaria

(Des and litho Harrison)

1985 (8 May). World Red Cross Day. T **71** and similar horiz designs. P 14½.

348	1s. black and rosine..	80	15
349	4s. multicoloured....................................	3·00	3·00
350	5s. multicoloured....................................	3·25	3·50
351	7s. multicoloured....................................	4·50	6·00
348/51 *Set of 4*		10·50	11·50

Designs:—4s. First aid team; 5s. Hearts containing crosses ("Blood Donation"); 7s. Cornucopia ("Famine Relief').

(Des H. Moghul. Litho Harrison)

1985 (25 June). 7th International Congress of Protozoology, Nairobi. T **72** and similar vert designs. Multicoloured. P 14½.

352	1s. Type **72**....................................	2·00	25
	a. Red (country name and value) omitted		
353	3s. Child with Leishmaniasis....................	4·00	2·75
354	5s. Cow with Trypanosomiasis..................	4·50	4·25
355	7s. Dog with Babesiosis...........................	7·50	8·50
352/5 *Set of 4*		15·00	14·00

73 Repairing Water   **74** The Last Supper
Pipes

(Des J. Tobula and Harrison. Litho Harrison)

1985 (15 July). United Nations Women's Decade Conference. T **73** and similar perf designs. Multicoloured. P 14½.

356	1s. Type **73**....................................	20	10
357	3s. Traditional food preparation....................	60	70
358	5s. Basket-weaving....................................	75	1·25
359	7s. Dressmaking....................................	1·00	3·00
356/9 *Set of 4*		2·25	4·50

(Des Eucharistic Congress Secretariat. Litho J.W.)

1985 (17 Aug*). 43rd International Eucharistic Congress, Nairobi. T **74** and similar horiz designs. Multicoloured. P 13½.

360	1s. Type **74**....................................	50	10
361	3s. Village family ("The Eucharist and the		
	Christian Family")....................................	2·00	1·50
362	5s. Congress altar, Uhuru Park....................	2·25	2·75
363	7s. St. Peter Clover's Church, Nairobi	2·50	5·50
360/3 *Set of 4*		6·50	8·75
MS364	117×80 mm. 25s. Pope John Paul II.................	8·50	7·00

*This is the local date of issue. The Crown Agents released the stamps on 15 August and this date also appears on first day covers serviced by Kenya Posts and Telecommunications Corporation.

75 Black Rhinoceros

(Des Rena Fennessy. Litho Harrison)

1985 (10 Dec). Endangered Animals. T **75** and similar horiz designs. Multicoloured. P 14½.

365	1s. Type **75**....................................	2·75	40
366	3s. Cheetah....................................	3·50	2·75
367	5s. De Brazza's Monkey	3·75	4·00
368	10s. Grevy's Zebra....................................	7·50	9·00
365/8 *Set of 4*		16·00	14·50
MS369	129×122 mm. 25s. Endangered species		
(122×114 *mm*). Imperf........		10·00	7·00

76 *Borassus aethiopum*   **77** Dove and U.N.
Logo (from poster)

(Des Rena Fennessy. Litho Questa)

1986 (24 Jan). Indigenous Trees. T **76** and similar horiz designs. Multicoloured. P 14½.

370	1s. Type **76**....................................	1·25	15
371	3s. *Acacia xanthophloea*	3·50	2·50
372	5s. *Ficus natalensis*....................................	4·50	4·50
373	7s. *Spathodea nilotica*...............................	6·00	9·50
370/3 *Set of 4*		13·50	15·00
MS374	117×96 mm. 25s. Landscape with trees		
(109×90 *mm*). Imperf........		3·25	4·00

(Des Advertising Link. Litho Questa)

1986 (30 Apr*). International Peace Year. T **77** and similar multicoloured designs. P 14.

375	1s. Type **77**....................................	30	10
376	3s. U.N. General Assembly (*horiz*)..................	1·00	75
377	7s. Nuclear explosion....................................	2·50	3·25
378	10s. Quotation from Wall of Isaiah, U.N.		
	Building, New York (*horiz*)....................	3·50	3·75
375/8 *Set of 4*		6·50	7·00

*This is the local date of issue. The Crown Agents released the stamps on 17 April and this date also appears on first day covers serviced by Kenya Posts and Telecommunications Corporation.

78 Dribbling the Ball   **79** Rural Post Office and Telephone

(Des C. Fernandes. Litho Harrison)

1986 (8 May). World Cup Football Championship, Mexico. T **78** and similar multicoloured designs. P 14½.

379	1s. Type **78**....................................	65	15
380	3s. Scoring from a penalty	2·00	1·25
381	5s. Tackling....................................	2·50	2·00
382	7s. Cup winners....................................	3·00	3·50
383	10s. Heading the ball....................................	4·00	4·25
379/83 *Set of 5*		11·00	10·00
MS384	110×86 mm. 30s. Harambee Stars football		
team (102×78 *mm*). Imperf		3·75	3·75

(Des H. Moghul. Litho Cartor)

1986 (11 June). "Expo '86" World Fair, Vancouver. T **79** and similar horiz designs. Multicoloured. P 13½×13.

385	1s. Type **79**	50	15
386	3s. Container depot, Embakasi	2·50	1·75
387	5s. Piper PA-30B Twin Commanche airplane landing at game park airstrip..	4·00	2·75
388	7s. Container ship	4·25	4·50
389	10s. Transporting produce to market	4·50	5·25
385/9	Set of 5	14·00	13·00

On 15 July 1986 Kenya was scheduled to release a set of five stamps, 1, 3, 4, 7 and 10s., for the Commonwealth Games at Edinburgh. A political decision was taken at the last moment not to issue the stamps, but this instruction did not reach some of the sub-post offices until the morning of 15 July. About two hundred stamps, mainly the 1s. value, were sold by these sub-post offices before the instruction arrived. Examples of the 1s. exist used on commercial mail from Kenyatta College sub-post office from 17 July 1986 onwards.

80 Telephone, Computer and Dish Aerial

(Des H. Moghul. Litho Harrison)

1986 (16 Sept). African Telecommunications. T **80** and similar horiz designs. Multicoloured. P 14½.

390	1s. Type **80**	35	10
391	3s. Telephones of 1876, 1936 and 1986	1·00	85
392	5s. Dish aerial, satellite, telephones and map of Africa	1·25	1·25
393	7s. Kenyan manufacture of telecommunications equipment	1·75	2·25
390/3	Set of 4	4·00	4·00

81 Mashua   **82** The Nativity

(Des Mukund Arts. Litho Mardon Printers Ltd, Zimbabwe)

1986 (30 Oct). Dhows of Kenya. T **81** and similar horiz designs. Multicoloured. P 14½.

394	1s. Type **81**	1·25	20
395	3s. Mtepe	2·75	1·50
396	5s. Dan La Mwao	3·25	3·00
397	10s. Jahazi	6·00	7·00
394/7	Set of 4	12·00	10·50
MS398	118×80 mm. 25s. Lamu dhow and map of Indian Ocean	5·00	5·50

(Des Mukund Arts. Litho Courvoisier)

1986 (5 Dec). Christmas. T **82** and similar multicoloured designs. Granite paper. P 11½.

399	1s. Type **82**	60	10
400	3s. Shepherd and sheep	1·50	55
401	5s. Angel and slogan "LOVE PEACE UNITY" (horiz)	2·25	1·60
402	7s. The Magi riding camels (horiz)	3·00	3·00
399/402	Set of 4	6·50	4·75

83 Immunization   **84** Akamba Woodcarvers

(Des Judith D'Inca. Litho Harrison)

1987 (6 Jan). 40th Anniv of United Nations Children's Fund. T **83** and similar vert designs. Multicoloured. P 14.

403	1s. Type **83**	45	10
404	3s. Food and nutrition	1·00	70
405	4s. Oral rehydration therapy	1·50	1·50
406	5s. Family planning	1·50	1·50
407	10s. Female literacy	2·25	4·00
403/7	Set of 5	6·00	7·00

(Des C. Fernandes. Litho Questa)

1987 (25 Mar). Tourism. T **84** and similar horiz designs. Multicoloured. P 14½.

408	1s. Type **84**	55	10
409	3s. Tourists on beach	3·25	1·75
410	5s. Tourist and guide at view point	4·00	4·00
411	7s. Pride of lions	6·00	7·00
408/11	Set of 4	12·50	11·50
MS412	118×81 mm. 30s. Geysers	11·00	12·00

(Des Mukund Arts. Litho Harrison)

1987 (20 May). Ceremonial Costumes (3rd series). Vert designs as T **45**. Multicoloured. P 14½×13½.

413	1s. Embu	1·00	10
414	3s. Kisii	2·75	70
415	5s. Samburu	3·25	1·75
416	7s. Taita	4·00	4·25
417	10s. Boron	4·25	4·75
413/17	Set of 5	14·00	10·50

85 Telecommunications by Satellite

(Des Mukund Arts. Litho Harrison)

1987 (1 July). 10th Anniv of Kenya Posts and Telecommunications Corporation. T **85** and similar triangular designs. Multicoloured. P 13½.

418	1s. Type **85**	85	30
419	3s. Rural post office, Kajiado	1·90	2·00
420	4s. Awarding trophy, Welfare Sports	2·00	3·00
421	5s. Village and telephone box	2·50	3·00
422	7s. Speedpost labels and outline map of Kenya	3·50	6·00
418/22	Set of 5	9·75	13·00
MS423	110×80 mm. 25s. Corporation flag	2·50	2·75

Nos. 418/22 were each printed as horizontal tête-bêche pairs within the sheet.

86 Volleyball   **87** Aloe volkensii

(Des C. Fernandes. Litho D.L.R.)

1987 (5 Aug). 4th All-Africa Games, Nairobi. T **86** and similar multicoloured designs. P 14½×14.

424	1s. Type **86**	20	10
425	3s. Cycling	85	65
426	4s. Boxing	35	1·25
427	5s. Swimming	40	1·25
428	7s. Steeplechasing	60	2·25
424/8	Set of 5	2·25	5·00
MS429	117×80 mm. 30s. Kasarani Sports Complex (horiz). P 14×14½	2·50	2·75

(Des Advertising Link. Litho Cartor)

1987 (10 Nov). Medicinal Herbs. T **87** and similar vert designs. Multicoloured. P 13½×14.

430	1s. Type **87**	85	10
431	3s. Cassia didymobotrya	2·25	1·25

432	5s. *Erythrina abyssinica*	3·00	2·75
433	7s. *Adenium obesum*	3·75	5·00
434	10s. Herbalist's clinic	4·00	6·00
430/4	*Set of 5*	12·50	13·50

88 *Epamera sidus*   **89** *Papilio rex*

(Des Rena Fennessy. Photo Harrison)

1988 (15 Feb)–**90**. Butterflies. Multicoloured.

(a) Vert designs as T88. P 15×14

434*a*	10c. *Cyrestis camillus* (1.3.89)	1·50	2·25
435	20c. Type **88**	30	70
436	40c. *Cynthia cardui*	50	70
437	50c. *Colotis evippe*	50	70
438	70c. *Precis westermanni*	50	70
439	80c. *Colias electo*	50	70
440	1s. *Eronia leda*	50	30
440*a*	1s.50 *Papilio dardanus* (18.5.90)	5·50	30

(b) Vert designs as T89. P 14½

441	2s. Type **89**	70	40
442	2s.50 *Colotis phisadia*	75	90
443	3s. *Papilio desmondi*	80	90
444	3s.50 *Papilio demodocus*	80	60
445	4s. *Papilio phorcas*	85	1·00
446	5s. *Charaxes druceanus*	90	70
447	7s. *Cymothoe teita*	1·00	2·50
448	10s. *Charaxes zoolina*	1·00	1·75
449	20s. *Papilio dardanus*	1·25	4·00
450	40s. *Charaxes cithaeron*	2·00	8·50
434*a*/50	*Set of 18*	18·00	25·00

Examples of the 1s. value were used in error at Kisumu from 2 February 1988.

Nos. 434*a*, 437 and 440 also exist in coil form.

90 Samburu Lodge and Crocodiles

(Des Advertising Link. Litho Questa)

1988 (31 May). Kenyan Game Lodges. T **90** and similar horiz designs. Multicoloured. P 14½.

451	1s. Type **90**	70	10
452	3s. Naro Moru River Lodge and rock climbing	1·00	60
453	4s. Mara Serena Lodge and zebra with foal	1·25	1·40
454	5s. Voi Safari Lodge and buffalo	1·25	1·40
455	7s. Kilimanjaro Buffalo Lodge and giraffes	2·50	2·75
456	10s. Meru Mulika Lodge and rhinoceroses	2·75	3·25
451/6	*Set of 6*	8·50	8·50

91 Athletes and Stadium, Commonwealth Games, Brisbane, 1982

(Des D. Ashby. Litho Harrison)

1988 (10 June). Expo '88 World Fair, Brisbane, and Bicentenary of Australian Settlement. T **91** and similar horiz designs. Multicoloured. P 14½.

457	1s. Type **91**	40	10

458	3s. Flying Doctor Service de Haviland DHA–3 Drover 3 and Piper PA-30B Twin Commance aircraft	2·75	1·25
459	4s. H.M.S. *Sirius* (frigate), 1788	3·00	2·25
460	5s. Ostrich and emu	3·25	2·50
461	7s. Queen Elizabeth II, President Arap Moi of Kenya and Prime Minister Hawke of Australia	3·00	4·25
457/61	*Set of 5*	11·00	9·25
MS462	117×80 mm. 30s. Entrance to Kenya Pavilion	1·90	2·00

92 W.H.O. Logo and Slogan   **93** Handball

(Des Mukund Arts. Litho National Printing & Packaging, Zimbabwe)

1988 (1 July). 40th Anniv of World Health Organization. T **92** and similar horiz designs. P 14½.

463	1s. greenish blue, gold and ultramarine	25	10
464	3s. multicoloured	85	70
465	5s. multicoloured	1·25	1·50
466	7s. multicoloured	1·75	2·50
463/6	*Set of 4*	3·75	4·25

Designs:—3s. Mother with young son and nutritious food; 5s. Giving oral vaccine to baby; 7s. Village women drawing clean water from pump.

(Des H. Moghul. Litho D.L.R.)

1988 (1 Aug). Olympic Games, Seoul. T **93** and similar vert designs. Multicoloured. P 14½×14.

467	1s. Type **93**	45	10
468	3s. Judo	75	55
469	5s. Weightlifting	1·00	1·00
470	7s. Javelin	1·00	2·00
471	10s. Relay racing	1·50	3·00
467/71	*Set of 5*	4·25	6·00
MS472	110×78 mm. 30s. Tennis	2·25	2·75

94 Calabashes   **95** Pres. Arap Moi taking Oath, 1978

(Des Mukund Arts. Litho D.L.R.)

1988 (20 Sept). Kenyan Material Culture (1st issue). T **94** and similar multicoloured designs. P 14½×14 (vert) or 14×14½ (horiz).

473	1s. Type **94**	30	10
474	3s. Milk gourds	75	55
475	5s. Cooking pots (*horiz*)	85	85
476	7s. Winnowing trays (*horiz*)	1·25	1·75
477	10s. Reed baskets (*horiz*)	1·60	2·50
473/7	*Set of 5*	4·25	5·00
MS478	118×80 mm. 25s. Gourds, calabash and horn (*horiz*)	1·50	1·60

See also Nos. 646/50.

(Des Mukund Arts. Litho Harrison)

1988 (13 Oct). 10th Anniv of "Nyayo" Era. T **95** and similar horiz designs. Multicoloured. P 13½×14½.

479	1a. Type **95**	30	10
480	3s. Building soil conservation barrier	1·00	70
481	3s.50 Passengers boarding bus	3·00	1·40
482	4s. Metalwork shop	1·25	1·50
483	5s. Moi University, Eldoret	1·25	1·50
484	7s. Aerial view of hospital	3·00	3·50
485	10s. Pres. Arap Moi and Mrs. Thatcher at Kapsabet Telephone Exchange	8·00	7·00
479/85	*Set of 7*	16·00	14·00

96 Kenya Flag

(Des Mukund Arts. Photo Courvoisier)

1988 (9 Dec). 25th Anniv of Independence. T **96** and similar horiz designs. Multicoloured. Granite paper. P 11½.

486	1s. Type **96**	75	10
487	3s. Coffee picking	80	50
488	5s. Proposed Kenya Posts and Telecommunications Headquarters building	1·00	1·10
489	7s. Kenya Airways Airbus Industrie A310-300 *Harambee Star*	5·50	4·00
490	10s. New diesel locomotive No. 9401	7·50	6·00
486/90 *Set of 5*		14·00	10·50

97 Gedi Ruins, Malindi

98 125th Anniversary and Kenya Red Cross Logos

(Des Mukund Arts. Litho National Printing & Packaging, Zimbabwe)

1989 (15 Mar). Historic Monuments. T **97** and similar multicoloured designs. P 14½.

491	1s.20 Type **97**	60	10
492	3s.40 Vasco Da Gama Pillar, Malindi (vert)	1·40	1·75
493	4s.40 Ishiakani Monument, Kiunga	1·50	2·50
494	5s.50 Fort Jesus, Mombasa	1·75	2·50
495	7s.70 She Burnan Omwe, Lamu (vert)	2·50	4·50
491/5 *Set of 5*		7·00	10·00

99 Female Giraffe and Calf

100 *Lentinus sajor-caju*

(Des H. Moghul. Litho Cartor)

1989 (8 May). 125th Anniv of International Red Cross. T **98** and similar horiz designs. Mulicoloured. P 14×13½.

496	1s.20 Type **98**	50	10
497	3s.40 Red Cross workers with car crash victim	1·25	90
498	4s.40 Disaster relief team distributing blankets	1·40	1·60
499	5s.50 Henri Dunant (founder)	1·50	2·25
500	7s.70 Blood donor	1·75	3·50
496/500 *Set of 5*		5·75	7·50

(Des Doreen McGuinness. Litho Walsall)

1989 (12 July). Reticulated Giraffe. T **99** and similar vert designs. Multicoloured. P 14½.

501	1s.20 Type **99**	1·75	30
502	3s.40 Giraffe drinking	3·25	3·00
503	4s.40 Two giraffes	3·75	4·00
504	5s.50 Giraffe feeding	4·50	5·50
501/4 *Set of 4*		12·00	11·50
MS505 80×110 mm. 30s. Designs as Nos. 501/4, but without face values		5·50	7·00

Designs from No. **MS**505 are without the Worldwide Fund for Nature logo.

For a full range of Stanley Gibbons catalogues, please visit **www.stanleygibbons.com**

(Des Dvora Bochman. Litho Questa)

1989 (6 Sept). Mushrooms. T **100** and similar vert designs. Multicoloured. P 14½.

506	1s.20 Type **100**	1·50	30
507	3s.40 *Agaricus bisporus*	2·50	2·00
508	4s.40 *Agaricus bisporus* (different)	2·75	2·50
509	5s.50 *Termitomyces schimperi*	3·50	3·50
510	7s.70 *Lentinus edodes*	4·25	5·50
506/10 *Set of 5*		13·00	12·50

101 Independence Monuments

102 EMS Speedpost Letters and Parcel

(Des Conference and Exhibitions Secretariat, Nairobi. Litho Cartor)

1989 (9 Nov). Birth Centenary of Jawaharlal Nehru (Indian statesman). T **101** and similar vert designs. Multicoloured. P 13½×14.

511	1s.20 Type **101**	1·50	30
512	3s.40 Nehru with graduates and open book	3·50	1·75
513	5s.50 Jawaharlal Nehru	4·50	4·00
514	7s.70 Industrial complex and cogwheels	4·75	6·50
511/14 *Set of 4*		13·00	11·00

(Des Mukund Arts. Litho Harrison)

1989 (20 Dec). Ceremonial Costumes (4th series). Vert designs as T **45**. Multicoloured. P 14½×13½.

515	1s.20 Kipsigis	1·50	20
516	3s.40 Rabai	2·50	1·60
517	5s.50 Duruma	3·00	2·75
518	7s.70 Kuria	4·00	4·25
519	10s. Bajuni	4·25	6·00
515/19 *Set of 5*		13·50	13·50

(Des Conference and Exhibitions Secretariat, Nairobi. Litho Cartor)

1990 (23 Mar). 10th Anniv of Pan African Postal Union. T **102** and similar multicoloured designs. P 14×13½ (horiz) or 13½×14 (vert).

520	1s.20 Type **102**	15	10
521	3s.40 Mail runner	35	35
522	5s.50 Mandera Post Office	55	70
523	7s.70 EMS Speedpost Letters and globe (vert)	80	1·60
524	10s. P.A.P.U. logo (vert)	90	1·60
520/4 *Set of 5*		2·50	3·75

103 "Stamp King" with Tweezers and Magnifying Glass

104 Moi Golden Cup

(Des D. Miller. Photo Courvoisier)

1990 (3 May). Stamp World London 90 International Stamp Exhibition. T **103** and similar horiz designs. Granite paper. P 11½.

525	1s.50 multicoloured	45	10
526	4s.50 multicoloured	1·50	1·25
527	6s.50 black, bright carmine and azure	1·60	2·00
528	9s. multicoloured	2·00	4·00
525/8 *Set of 4*		5·00	6·50
MS529 113×77 mm. Nos. 525/8		5·00	7·00

Designs:—4s.50, Penny Black and Kenya Stamp Bureau postmark; 6s.50, Early British cancellations; 9s. Ronald Ngala Street Post Office, Nairobi.

(Secretariat Des Conference & Exhibitions Litho Harrison)

1990 (21 Mar). World Cup Football Championship Italy. Trophies. T **104** and similar vert designs. Multicoloured. P 14½.

530	1s.50 Type **104**	75	10

531	4s.50 East and Central Africa Challenge Cup	2·25	1·75
532	6s.50 East and Central Africa Club Championship Cup	3·25	3·75
533	9s. World Cup	3·50	7·00
530/3 Set of 4		8·75	11·00

105 K.A.N.U. Flag

(Des Mukund Arts. Litho Harrison)

1990 (11 June). 30th Anniv of Kenya African National Union. T **105** and similar horiz designs. Multicoloured. P 14½.

534	1s.50 Type **105**	15	10
535	2s.50 Nyayo Monument	15	15
536	4s.50 Party Headquarters	35	35
537	5s. Jomo Kenyatta (founder)	40	40
538	6s.50 President Arap Moi	50	85
539	9s. President Mai addressing rally	70	1·90
540	10s. Queue of voters	80	1·90
534/40 Set of 7		2·75	5·00

106 Desktop Computer

(Secretariat Des Conference & Exhibitions Litho Questa)

1990 (12 July). 125th Anniv of International Telecommunications Union. T **106** and similar horiz designs. Multicoloured. P 14½.

541	1s.50 Type **106**	15	10
542	4s.50 Telephone switchboard assembly, Gilgil	35	50
543	6s.50 "125 YEARS"	45	1·00
544	9s. Urban and rural telecommunications	70	2·25
541/4 Set of 4		1·50	3·50

107 Queen Mother at British Museum, 1988

108 Queen Elizabeth at Hospital Garden Party, 1947

(Des D. Miller. Litho Questa)

1990 (4 Aug). 90th Birthday of Queen Elizabeth the Queen Mother. P 14×15 (10s.) or 14½ (40s.).

545	**107**	10s. multicoloured	1·25	1·50
546	**108**	40s. black and brown-olive	2·75	4·50

109 Kenya 1988 2s. Definitive

110 Adult Literacy Class

(Des D. Miller. Litho D.L.R.)

1990 (5 Sept). Centenary of Postage Stamps in Kenya. T **109** and similar vert designs. Multicoloured. P 14×14½.

547	1s.50 Type **109**	1·40	10

548	4s.50 East Africa and Uganda 1903 1a.	2·75	90
549	6s.50 British East Africa Co 1890 ½a. optd on G.B. 1d.	3·25	2·00
550	9s. Kenya and Uganda 1922 20c	3·75	3·50
551	20s. Kenya, Uganda, Tanzania 1971 2s.50, Railway commemorative	6·75	9·50
547/51 Set of 5		16·00	14·50

(Des H. Moghul. Litho Cartor)

1990 (30 Nov). International Literacy Year. T **110** and similar vert designs. Multicoloured. P 13½×14.

552	1s.50 Type **110**	30	10
553	4s.50 Teaching by radio	1·00	1·10
554	6s.50 Technical training	1·25	2·00
555	9s. International Literacy Year logo	2·00	3·50
552/5 Set of 4		4·00	6·00

111 National Flag

112 Symbolic Man and Pointing Finger

(Des H. Moghul. Litho Cartor)

1991 (29 Nov). Olympic Games, Barcelona (1992) (1st issue). T **111** and similar horiz designs. Multicoloured. P 14×13½.

556	2s. Type **111**	1·10	10
557	6s. Basketball	2·75	1·40
558	7s. Hockey	2·75	2·25
559	8s.50 Table tennis	2·50	3·75
560	11s. Boxing	2·50	4·25
556/60 Set of 5		10·50	10·50

See also Nos. 580/4.

(Des H. Mogul. Litho Cartor)

1992 (31 Jan). AIDS Day. T **112** and similar vert designs. Multicoloured. P 13½×14.

561	2s. Type **112**	1·00	15
562	6s. Victim and drugs	2·50	1·25
563	8s.50 Male and female symbols	3·00	4·00
564	11s. Symbolic figure and hypodermic syringe	4·50	6·00
561/4 Set of 4		10·00	10·50

 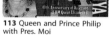 

113 Queen and Prince Philip with Pres. Moi

114 Leopard

(Des D. Miller. Litho Cartor)

1992 (6 Feb). 40th Anniv of Queen Elizabeth II's Accession. T **113** and similar horiz designs. Multicoloured. P 14×13½.

565	3s. Type **113**	50	10
566	8s. Marabou Storks in tree	2·00	75
567	11s. Treetops Hotel	1·00	85
568	14s. Three portraits of Queen Elizabeth	1·00	1·00
569	40s. Queen Elizabeth II	2·00	4·50
565/9 Set of 5		6·00	6·50

(Des Dvora Bachman. Litho National Printing & Packaging, Zimbabwe)

1992 (8 May). Kenya Wildlife. T **114** and similar vert designs. Multicoloured. P 14×14½.

570	3s. Type **114**	2·25	45
571	8s. Lion	3·00	2·00
572	10s. Elephant	8·00	3·75
573	11s. Buffalo	3·00	4·00
574	14s. Black Rhinoceros	10·00	7·00
570/4 Set of 5		24·00	15·00

115 International Harvester Safari Truck, 1926

116 Kenyan Athlete winning Race

(Des Dvora Bochman. Litho National Printing & Packaging, Zimbabwe)

1992 (24 June). Vintage Cars. T **115** and similar horiz designs. Multicoloured. P 14½×14.

575	3s. Type **115**	2·25	30
576	8s. Fiat "509", 1924	3·50	2·00
577	10s. Hupmobile, 1923	3·75	3·50
578	11s. Chevrolet "Box Body", 1928	3·75	3·75
579	14s. Bentley/Parkward, 1934	4·25	7·00
575/9	Set of 5	16·00	15·00

(Des Dvora Bochman. Litho National Printing & Packaging, Zimbabwe)

1992 (24 July). Olympic Games, Barcelona. (2nd series). T **116** and similar vert designs. Multicoloured. P 14×14½.

580	3s. Type **116**	1·00	10
581	8s. Men's judo	2·00	1·25
582	10s. Kenyan women's volleyball players	2·50	2·50
583	11s. Kenyan men's 4×100 metres relay runners	2·50	2·75
584	14s. Men's 10,000 metres	2·75	5·50
580/4	Set of 5	9·75	11·00

117 Holy Child, Joseph and Animals

118 Asembo Bay Lighthouse, Lake Victoria

(Secretariat Des Conference & Exhibitions Litho Cartor)

1992 (14 Dec). Christmas. T **117** and similar vert designs. Multicoloured. P 13½×14.

585	3s. Type **117**	30	10
586	8s. Mary with Holy Child	75	80
587	11s. Christmas tree	1·00	80
588	14s. Adoration of the Magi	1·25	2·25
585/8	Set of 4	3·00	3·25

(Des H. Moghul. Litho Questa)

1993 (25 Jan). Lighthouses. T **118** and similar vert designs. Multicoloured. P 14½.

589	3s. Type **118**	2·75	55
590	8s. Old Ras Serani lighthouse, Mombasa	4·00	2·50
591	11s. New Ras Serani lighthouse, Mombasa	4·25	4·25
592	14s. Gingira, Lake Victoria	5·00	7·00
589/92	Set of 4	14·50	13·00

119 Superb Starling

120 Yellow-billed Hornbill

(Des Dvora Bochman. Photo Courvoisier)

1993 (22 Feb)–**96**. Birds. Multicoloured. Granite paper.

(a) Vert designs as T119. P 15×14

593	50c. Type **119**	15	1·25
594	1s. Red and Yellow Barbet	25	80
594a	1s.50 Lady Ross's Turaco (14.2.94)	65	1·25
595	3s. Black-throated Honeyguide ("Greater Honeyguide")	50	20
595a	5s. African Fish Eagle (14.2.94)	80	1·00
595b	6s. Vulturine Guineafowl (30.8.96)	7·00	1·75
596	7s. Malachite Kingfisher	70	30
597	8s. Speckled Pigeon	70	20
598	10s. Cinnamon-chested Bee Eater	70	20
599	11s. Scarlet-chested Sunbird	70	25
600	14s. Bagalafecht Weaver ("Reichenow's Weaver")	75	30

(b) Vert designs as T120. P 14½

601	50s. Type **120**	1·25	2·00
602	80s. Lesser Flamingo	1·60	3·00
603	100s. Hadada Ibis	1·90	3·50
593/603	Set of 14	16·00	14·50

No. 595a was initially issued in coils, but was subsequently supplied in sheets.

Nos. 593 and 594 also issued in coils.

121 Nurse bandaging boy's legs

122 Maendeleo House, Nairobi

(Des Conference and Exhibitions Secretariat, Nairobi. Litho National Printing & Packaging, Zimbabwe)

1993 (1 July). 17th World Congress of Rehabilitation International. T **121** and similar designs. P 14½.

611	3s. multicoloured	70	10
612	8s. multicoloured	1·10	70
613	10s. multicoloured	1·25	1·40
614	11s. multicoloured	1·25	1·60
615	14s. black, new blue and yellow-orange	1·50	2·50
611/15	Set of 5	5·25	5·50

Designs: Horiz—8s. Singing group on crutches; 10s. Vocational training; 11s. Wheelchair race. Vert—14s. Congress emblem.

(Des Conference and Exhibitions Secretariat, Nairobi. Litho Cartor)

1994 (17 Mar). 40th Anniv of Maendeleo Ya Vianawake Organization. T **122** and similar multicoloured designs. P 14×13½ (horiz) or 13½×14 (vert).

616	3s.50 Type **122**	1·00	20
617	9s. Planting saplings	1·40	70
618	11s. Rural family planning clinic (*vert*)	1·00	1·60
619	12s.50 Women carrying water	1·90	2·75
620	15s.50 Improved wood-burning cooking stove (*vert*)	2·25	3·50
616/20	Set of 5	7·50	8·00

123 Ansellia africana

124 Emblem and K.I.C.C. Building, Nairobi

(Des Dvora Bochman. Litho Cartor)

1994 (27 June). Orchids. T **123** and similar vert designs. Multicoloured. P 13½×14.

621	3s.50 Type **123**	2·25	30
622	9s. *Aerangis luteoalba var rhodosticta*	3·00	85
623	12s.50 *Polystachya bella*	3·25	2·00
624	15s.50 *Brachycorythis kalbreyeri*	3·75	3·75
625	20s. *Eulophia guineensis*	4·50	5·50
621/5	Set of 5	15·00	11·50

(Des and litho Questa)

1994 (21 Nov). 30th Anniv of African Development Bank. T **124** and similar horiz design. Multicoloured. P 14½.

626	6s. Type **124**	1·00	25
627	25s. Isinya-Kajiado project	3·50	5·00

125 Kenyan Family

126 Paul Harris (founder of Rotary)

(Des Micro General Service Ltd. Litho Questa)

1994 (22 Dec). International Year of the Family. T **125** and similar multicoloured designs. P 14½.

628	6s. Type **125**	85	10
629	14s.50 Nurse with mother and baby	3·00	1·40
630	20s. School children and teacher (horiz)	3·25	3·75
631	25s. Emblem (horiz)	3·25	4·25
628/31	Set of 4	9·25	8·50

(Des Omak Design. Litho Cartor)

1994 (29 Dec). 50th Anniv of Rotary Club of Mombasa. T **126** and similar vert designs. Multicoloured. P 13½×14.

632	6s. Type **126**	40	10
633	14s.50 Anniversary logo	1·00	70
634	17s.50 Administering polio vaccine	1·40	2·25
635	20s. Women at stand pipe	1·50	2·50
636	25s. Rotary emblem	1·60	2·75
632/6	Set of 5	5·50	7·50

127 Donkey

128 Male Golfer in Bunker

(Des H. Moghul. Litho Walsall)

1995 (13 Jan). Kenya Society for Prevention of Cruelty to Animals. T **127** and similar vert designs. Multicoloured. P 14½.

637	6s. Type **127**	50	10
638	14s.50 Cow	60	45
639	17s.50 Sheep	65	1·00
640	20s. Dog	2·25	2·50
641	25s. Cat	2·25	2·50
637/41	Set of 5	5·50	6·00

(Des Conference and Exhibitions Secretariat. Litho Questa)

1995 (28 Feb). Golf. T **128** and similar vert designs. Multicoloured. P 14½.

642	6s. Type **128**	1·25	20
643	17s.50 Female golfer on fairway	2·50	1·75
644	20s. Male golfer teeing-off	2·50	3·00
645	25a. Head of golf club	2·75	3·25
642/5	Set of 4	8·00	7·50

129 Perfume Containers

(Des Lari & Loiruk Graphic Studio. Litho Cartor)

1995 (24 Mar). Kenyan Material Culture (2nd issue). T **129** and similar horiz designs. Multicoloured. P 14×13½.

646	6s. Type **129**	30	10
647	14s.50 Basketry	75	75
648	17s.50 Preserving pots	85	1·25
649	20s. Gourds	1·10	1·75
650	25s. Wooden containers	1·25	2·00
646/50	Set of 5	3·75	5·25

130 Tsetse Fly

131 Maize

(Des Design Box Associates. Litho Enschedé)

1995 (29 Sept). 25th Anniv of I.C.I.P.E. Insect Pests. T **130** and similar vert designs. Multicoloured. P 13½.

651	14s. Type **130**	60	30
652	26s. Tick	90	80
653	32s. Wild Silkmoth	1·10	1·10
654	33s. Maize Borer	1·25	1·75
655	40s. Locust	1·75	2·50
651/5	Set of 5	5·00	5·75

(Des Dvora Bochman. Litho Cartor)

1995 (16 Oct). 50th Anniv of Food and Agriculture Organization. T **131** and similar vert designs. Multicoloured. P 13½×14.

656	14s. Type **131**	75	30
657	28s. Cattle	1·25	80
658	32s. Chickens	1·75	1·60
659	33s. Fisherman with catch	2·00	2·50
660	40s. Fruit	2·50	3·50
656/60	Set of 5	7·50	8·00

132 Kenyan and United Nations Flags over Headquarters, Nairobi

(Des O. Karenga. Litho Enschedé)

1995 (24 Oct). 50th Anniv of United Nations. T **132** and similar horiz designs. P 13½.

661	23s. multicoloured	85	70
662	26s. multicoloured	95	95
663	32s. multicoloured	1·25	1·40
664	40s. brt greenish blue, dp carmine & black	1·75	2·50
661/4	Set of 4	4·25	5·00

Designs:—26s. Multi-racial group with emblem; 32s. United Nations helmet; 40s.50th anniversary emblem.

133 Swimming

(Des I.G.P.C. Studios)

1996 (5 Jan). Olympic Games, Atlanta (1st issue). Events and Gold Medal Winners. T **133** and similar multicoloured designs. Litho. P 14.

665	14s. Type **133**	1·00	1·10
	a. Sheetlet. Nos. 665/7 and 686/8	6·00	7·00
666	20s. Archery	1·00	1·10
667	20s. Weightlifting	1·00	1·10
668	20s. Pole vault (vert)	1·00	1·10
	a. Sheetlet. Nos. 668/76	8·00	9·00
669	20s. Equestrian (vert)	1·00	1·10
670	20s. Diving (vert)	1·00	1·10
671	20s. Sprinting (vert)	1·00	1·10
672	20s. Athlete carrying Olympic Torch (vert)	1·00	1·10
673	20s. Hurdling (vert)	1·00	1·10
674	20s. Kayak (vert)	1·00	1·10

675	20s. Boxing (*vert*)	1·00	1·10
676	20s. Gymnastics (*vert*)	1·00	1·10
677	25s. Greg Louganis (U.S.A.) (diving, 1984 and 1988) (*vert*)	1·25	1·40
	a. Sheetlet. Nos. 677/85	10·00	11·00
678	25s. Cassius Clay (U.S.A.) (boxing, 1960) (*vert*)	1·25	1·40
679	25s. Nadia Comaneci (Rumania) (gymnastics, 1980) (*vert*)	1·25	1·40
680	25s. Daley Thompson (Great Britain) (decathlon, 1980 and 1984) (*vert*)	1·25	1·40
681	25a. Kipchoge Keino (Kenya) (running, 1968) (*vert*)	1·25	1·40
682	25s. Kornelia Enders (Germany) (swimming, 1976) (*vert*)	1·25	1·40
683	25s. Jackie Joyner-Kersee (U.S.A.) (long jump, 1988) (*vert*)	1·25	1·40
684	25s. Michael Jordan (U.S.A.) (basketball, 1984) (*vert*)	1·25	1·40
685	25s. Shun Fujimoto (Japan) (gymnastics, 1972) (*vert*)	1·25	1·40
686	32s. Javelin	1·25	1·40
687	40s. Fencing	1·25	1·40
688	50s. Discus	1·50	1·75
665/88 *Set of 24*		24·00	27·00

MS689 Two sheets, each 79×109 mm. (a) 100s. Athlete with medal (vert). (b) 100s. Athlete carrying Olympic Torch (different) (vert) *Set of 2 sheets* .... 7·50 10·00

Nos. 665/7 with 686/8, 668/76 and 677/85 were printed together, *se-tenant*, in sheetlets of 6 (Nos. 665/7, 686/8) or 9 (Nos. 668/76 and 677/85) with the backgrounds forming composite designs.

See also Nos. 702/6.

134 Lions

135 Water Buck

(Des O. Karenga. Litho Cartor)

1996 (31 Jan). Tourism. Multicoloured.

(a) Designs as T134. P 14×13½

690	6s. Type **134**	30	10
691	14s. Mt Kenya	35	30
692	20s. Sailboards	55	70
693	25s. Hippopotami	1·25	1·50
694	40s. Couple in traditional dress	1·25	2·50
690/4 *Set of 5*		3·25	4·50

MS695 100×80 mm. 50s. Female Giraffe and calf (vert). P 13×13½ .... 3·25 3·75

(b) Horiz designs as T135. P 13×13½

696	20s. Type **135**	1·75	2·25
	a. Booklet pane. Nos. 696/701	9·50	
697	20s. Pair of Rhinoceroses	1·75	2·25
698	20s. Cheetah	1·75	2·25
699	20s. Group of Oryx	1·75	2·25
700	20s. Pair of Giraffes	1·75	2·25
701	20s. Monkey and Bongo	1·75	2·25
696/701 *Set of 6*		9·50	12·00

Nos. 696/701 were only available from 480s. stamp booklets. Booklet pane No. 696a exists in two versions which differ in the order of the stamps.

136 Women's 10,000 Metres

137 Red Cross Emblem

(Des Design Box Associates. Litho Cartor)

1996 (18 July). Olympic Games, Atlanta (2nd issue). T **136** and similar vert designs. Multicoloured. P 13½×14.

702	6s. Type **136**	35	10
703	14s. Steeple-chasing	55	30
704	20s. Victorious athletes with flag	80	80
705	25s. Boxing	80	1·00
706	40s. Men's 1500 metres	1·40	2·50
702/6 *Set of 5*		3·50	4·25

(Des Dvora Bochman. Litho National Printing & Packaging, Zimbabwe)

1996 (30 Aug). Kenya Red Cross Society. T **137** and similar vert designs. P 14½.

707	6s. scarlet-vermilion and black	25	10
708	14s. multicoloured	45	35
709	20s. multicoloured	70	80
710	25s. multicoloured	80	95
711	40s. multicoloured	1·40	2·00
707/11 *Set of 5*		3·25	3·75

Designs:—14s. Giving blood; 20s. Immunization; 25s; Refugee child with food; 40s. Cleaning the environment.

138 Impala

139 Kenya Lions Club Logo

(Des H. Moghul. Litho Harrisons)

1996 (10 Sept). East African Wildlife Society. T **138** and similar vert designs. Multicoloured. P 14½.

712	6s. Type **138**	20	10
713	20s. Colobus Monkey	60	70
714	25a. African Elephant	1·75	1·50
715	40s. Black Rhinoceros	2·50	3·50
712/15 *Set of 4*		4·50	5·25

(Des Dvora Bochman. Litho Enschedé)

1996 (31 Oct). Work of Lions Club International in Kenya. T **139** and similar vert designs. Multicoloured. P 13½.

716	6s. Type **139**	15	10
717	14s. Eye operation	55	45
718	20s. Two disabled children in wheelchair	70	1·25
719	25s. Modern ambulance	1·00	1·50
716/19 *Set of 4*		2·10	3·00

140 C.O.M.E.S.A. Logo

141 *Haplochromis cinctus*

(Des O. Karenga. Litho Cartor)

1997 (15 Jan). Inauguration of Common Market for Eastern and Southern Africa. T **140** and similar vert design. Multicoloured. P 13½×14.

720	6s. Type **140**	15	15
721	20s. Kenyan flag and logo	85	1·10

(Des C. Newman. Litho Cartor)

1997 (31 Jan). Endangered Species. Lake Victoria Cichlid Fishes. T **141** and similar horiz designs. Multicoloured. P 14×13½.

722	25s. Type **141**	75	1·00
723	25s. *Haplochromis* "Orange Rock Hunter"	75	1·00
724	25s. *Haplochromis chilotes*	75	1·00
725	25s. *Haplockromis nigricans*	75	1·00
722/5 *Set of 4*		2·75	3·50

142 Class 94 Diesel-electric Locomotive No. 9401, 1981

(Des Design Box. Litho Cartor)

1997 (20 Feb). Kenya Railway Locomotives. T **142** and similar horiz designs. Multicoloured. P 14×13½.

726	6s. Type **142**	70	15
727	14s. Class 87 diesel-electric No. 8721, 1964.	1·10	40
728	20s. Class 59 Garratt steam No. 5905, 1955.	1·50	65
729	25s. Class 57 Garratt steam No. 5701, 1939.	1·50	1·10
730	30s. Class, 23 steam No. 2305, 1923	1·75	2·50
731	40s. Class 10 steam No 1001, 1914)	1·90	3·00
726/31 *Set of 6*		7·50	7·00

143 Orange

144 Crocodile

(Des H. Moghul. Litho Walsall)

1997 (28 Feb). Fruits of East Africa. T **143** and similar vert designs. Multicoloured. P 14½.

732	6s. Type **143**	65	60
733	14s. Pineapple	1·25	1·00
734	20s. Mango	2·00	2·25
735	25s. Pawpaw	2·25	2·50
732/5 *Set of 4*		5·50	5·75

(Des Design Box Associates. Litho Enschedé)

1997 (9 Oct). Local Tourist Attractions. T **144** and similar horiz designs. Multicoloured. P 13½.

736	10s. Type **144**	1·25	25
737	27s. Lake Bogoria hot springs	2·00	1·50
738	30s. Warthogs	2·00	1·75
739	33s. Windsurfing	2·00	2·25
740	42s. Traditional huts	3·25	3·25
736/40 *Set of 5*		8·50	8·00

145 Girl Guides Anniversary Logo

146 Portuguese Ships arriving at Malindi

(Des O. Karenga. Litho Questa)

1997 (21 Nov). 75th Anniv of Kenyan Girl Guides. T **145** and similar vert designs. Multicoloured. P 14½.

741	10s. Type **145**	55	70
	a. Horiz pair. Nos. 741/2	1·10	1·40
742	10s. Lord Baden Powell	55	70
743	27s. Girl Guides hiking	90	1·10
	a. Horiz pair. Nos. 743/4	1·75	2·10
744	27s. Rangers in camp	90	1·10
745	33s. Girl Guides planting seedlings	1·00	1·25
	a. Horiz pair. Nos. 745/6	2·00	2·50
746	33s. Boy Scouts giving first aid	1·00	1·25
747	42s. Boy Scouts in camp	1·25	1·25
	a. Horiz pair. Nos. 747/8	2·50	2·50
748	42s. Brownies entertaining the elderly	1·25	1·25
741/8 *Set of 8*		6·50	7·50

Nos. 741/2, 743/4, 745/6 and 747/8 were each printed together, se-tenant, in horizontal pairs throughout the sheets.

(Des G. Decker. Litho Cartor)

1998 (15 Apr). 500th Anniv of Vasco da Gama's Arrival at Malindi. T **146** and similar horiz designs. Multicoloured. P 13½×13.

749	10s. Type **146**	65	25
750	24s. Portuguese ships	1·40	80
751	33s. Map of Africa	1·75	2·00
752	42s. Vasco da Gama Pillar and harbour	2·00	2·50
749/52 *Set of 4*		5·25	5·00

147 Lion

(Des Mukund Arts Ltd. Litho Questa)

1998 (10 June). 18th Anniv of Pan African Postal Union. Wildlife. T **147** and similar horiz designs. Multicoloured. P 14½.

753	10s. Type **147**	1·50	25
754	24s. Buffalo	2·00	80
755	33s. Grant's Gazelle	2·25	2·50
756	42s. Cheetah	3·25	4·50
753/6 *Set of 4*		8·00	7·25
MS757 94×76 mm. 50s. Hirola Gazelle		3·00	3·25

148 Pres. Arap Moi taking Oath, 1998

(Des Mukund Arts Ltd. Litho Cartor)

1998 (8 Dec). Daniel Arap Moi's 5th Presidential Term. P 13½.

758	**148**	14s. multicoloured	1·50	80

149 Leatherback Turtle

(Des T. Visser. Litho Enschedé)

2000 (13 Apr). Turtles. T **149** and similar horiz designs. Multicoloured. P 13½.

759	17s. Type **149**	1·10	35
760	20s. Green Sea Turtle	1·40	40
761	30s. Hawksbill Turtle	1·75	1·25
762	47s. Olive Ridley Turtle	2·50	3·50
763	59s. Loggerhead Turtle	3·00	4·50
759/63 *Set of 5*		8·75	9·00

150 Kenya Postal Corporation Logo

(Des O. Karenga. Litho Cartor)

2000 (31 May). East Africa Postal Administrations' Co-operation. T **150** and similar horiz designs. Multicoloured (except 17s.). P 14×13½.

764	17s. Type **150** (bright red, new blue & black)	1·00	35
765	35s. Uganda Post Ltd logo	1·75	1·75
766	50s. Tanzania Posts Corporation logo	2·00	3·00
764/6 *Set of 3*		4·25	4·50
MS767 100×80 mm. 70s. As 50s. P 13½×13		4·00	4·75

151 Cotton

152 Tea

(Des Mukund Arts Ltd. Photo Courvoisier)

2001 (28 Feb). Crops. Multicoloured.

(a) Vert designs as T151. P 15×14

768	2s. Type **151**	10	30
769	4s. Bananas	15	30
770	5s. Avocado	15	30
771	6s. Cassava	15	30
772	8s. Arrow Root	25	30
773	10s. Paw paw	25	30
774	19s. Orange	50	35
775	20s. Pyrethrum	50	35
776	30s. Groundnuts	80	55
777	35s. Coconut	1·00	60
778	40s. Sisal	1·25	70
779	50s. Cashew Nuts	1·40	85

(b) Vert designs as T152. P 14½

780	60s. Type **152**	1·50	1·00
781	80s. Maize	2·00	1·40
782	100s. Coffee	2·25	1·75
783	200s. Finger Millet	4·25	3·75
784	400s. Sorghum	7·50	8·00
785	500s. Sugar Cane	9·00	9·50
768/85	*Set of 18*	30·00	27·00

(c) Coil stamps. Perf 14½×imperf

785a	5s. Avocado	50	1·50
785b	10s. Paw paw	60	2·00

153 Source of the Nile, Jinja, Uganda

(Des L. osanjo (19s.) G. Dekker (35s.) P. Ndembo (40s.),T. Hinga (50s.). Litho Walsall)

2002 (23 Nov). Historical Sites of East Africa. T **153** and similar multicoloured designs. P 14½ (19s., 40s.) or 13½ (others).

786	19s. Type **153**	1·00	35
787	35s. Lamu Fort, Kenya (35×35 *mm*)	1·50	1·10
788	40s. Olduvai Gorge, Tanzania	2·75	2·75
789	50s. Thimlich Ohinga (ancient settlement), Kenya (35×35 *mm*)	2·75	3·50
786/9	*Set of 4*	7·00	7·00

154 Section of Mombasa Road

(Des design Box.)

2003 (14 Dec). 40th Anniv of Kenya–China Diplomatic Relations. T **154** and similar horiz design. Multicoloured. Litho. P 12.

790	21s. Type **154**	1·50	40
791	66s. Kasarani Stadium	2·75	3·50

155 Lioness and Baby Oryx

156 Risen Christ
(Luciano Finocchiaro)

(Des D. Revankar. Litho Oriental Press)

2004 (19 Nov). Tourism. T **155** and similar horiz designs. Multicoloured. P 14½.

792	21s. Type **155**	1·25	35
793	60s. Leopard and cub	2·25	1·75
794	66s. Zebra and calf	2·25	2·00
795	88s. Bongo and calf	3·50	5·00
792/5	*Set of 4*	8·25	8·25

2005 (1 Apr). Easter. T **156** and similar vert designs showing bronze bas-reliefs, each brownish black, light purple-brown and greenish yellow. P 14×13½.

796	25s. Type **156**	70	45
797	65s. Christ brought before Pilate	1·75	1·60
798	75s. Crucifixion	2·00	2·00
799	95s. Christ praying in Gethsemane	3·00	4·25
796/9	*Set of 4*	6·75	7·50

157 Polio Vaccination

158 Gabbra

(Des G. Obonyo (No. 800) and E. Ongere (Nos. 801/3). Litho Enschedé)

2005 (26 May). Centenary of Rotary International. T **157** and similar horiz designs. Multicoloured. P 13½.

800	25s. Type **157**	60	45
801	65s. Donation of Jaipur feet (prosthetics)	1·60	1·60
802	75s. Don Bosco Centre (Nairobi)	1·75	2·00
803	95s. Donation of sewing machine	2·75	3·75
800/3	*Set of 4*	6·00	7·00

(Des D. Revankar. Litho Oriental Press, Bahrain)

2005 (6 Dec). Traditional Costumes of East Africa (1st series). T **158** and similar vert designs. Litho. P 14½.

804	21s. Type **158**	1·00	35
805	60s. Pokot	2·25	1·75
806	66s. Meru	2·50	2·25
807	88s. Digo	3·50	4·50
804/7	*Set of 4*	8·25	8·00

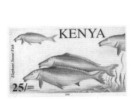

159 Elephant Snout Fish

160 Emblem

(Litho Cartor)

2006 (4 May). Fish of Lake Victoria. T **159** and similar horiz designs. Multicoloured. P 13½×13.

808	25s. Type **159**	1·25	45
809	55s. Sudan catfish	2·25	1·60
810	75s. Nile perch	2·75	2·75
811	95s. Redbreast tilapia	3·75	5·00
808/11	*Set of 4*	9·00	9·00

(Litho Cartor)

2006 (11 Oct). 24th UPU Congress, Nairobi (1st issue). P 14½.

812	**160** 25s. multicoloured	1·00	1·25

No. 812 is perforated in a circle enclosed in an outer perforated square. The UPU Congress was moved to Geneva, Switzerland, due to political unrest in Kenya.

161 Owen and Mzee, 2005

(Litho Cartor)

2006 (15 Dec). Owen and Mzee (baby hippopotamus and giant tortoise), Haller Park, Mombasa. P 13×12½.

813	**161** 25s. multicoloured	1·75	1·75

No. 813 is a triangular stamp laid alternately upright and inverted in the sheet. The two sides are perforated 13 and the bottom 12½.

162 Roan Antelope   **163** Mt. Kenya

2006 (15 Dec). Tourism. 'Kenya The Land of Opportunity'. T **162** and similar square designs. Multicoloured. Litho. P 13.

814	25s. Type **162**	1·25	1·40
	a. Booklet pane. Nos. 814/16	3·25	
815	25s. Weaver bird at nest	1·25	1·40
816	25s. Monkey	1·25	1·40
817	25s. Turkana hut	1·25	1·40
	a. Booklet pane. Nos. 817/19	3·25	
818	25s. Athletes in steeplechase	1·25	1·40
819	25s. Golf course	1·25	1·40
820	25s. Waterfalls, Abadares	1·25	1·40
	a. Booklet pane. Nos. 820/2	3·25	
821	25s. Balloon safari	1·25	1·40
822	25s. Bullfight	1·25	1·40
823	25s. Chimpanzee	1·25	1·40
	a. Booklet pane. Nos. 823/5	3·25	
824	25s. Maasai	1·25	1·40
825	25s. Kit Makaye (rock formation)	1·25	1·40
814/25 *Set of 12*		13·00	15·00

Nos. 814/25 were only issued in 300s. stamp booklets, No. SB13.

(Litho Enschedé)

2007 (28 Feb). Mountains of East Africa. T **163** and similar horiz designs. Multicoloured. P 13½.

826	25s. Type **163**	75	35
827	75s. Mt. Ruwenzori, Uganda	2·50	3·00
828	95s. Mt. Kilimanjaro, Tanzania	2·75	3·75
826/8 *Set of 3*		5·50	6·50

164 African Woman   **165** Oglek

(Litho Cartor)

2007 (30 Oct). Breast Cancer Research. P 13½.

829	**164**	25s. multicoloured	1·25	1·25

(Litho Oriental Press, Bahrain)

2007 (21 Nov). Traditional Costumes of East Africa (2nd series). T **165** and similar vert designs. Multicoloured. P 14½.

830	25s. Type **165**	1·00	35
831	65s. Sabaot	2·25	1·50
832	75s. Ribe	2·50	2·50
833	95s. Elmolo	3·50	4·00
830/3 *Set of 4*		8·50	7·50

166 *Calodendrum capense* (Cape chestnut)

(Litho Oriental Press, Bahrain)

2007 (13 Dec). Centenary of Nairobi Arboretum. T **166** and similar horiz designs. Multicoloured. P 13½×14.

834	25s. Type **166**	75	35
835	65s. Tree Centre and Cupressus torulosa (Bhutan cypress)	2·00	1·50
836	75s. Spathodea campanulata (Nandi flame)	2·25	2·50
837	95s. Monodora myristica (calabash nutmeg)	3·25	4·00
834/7 *Set of 4*		7·50	7·50

167 Sitalunga Gazelle in Saiwa Swamp

(Litho Oriental Press, Bahrain)

2008 (7 Feb). 24th UPU Congress, Nairobi (2nd issue). T **167** and similar horiz designs. Multicoloured. P 14½.

838	25s. Type **167**	75	25
839	65s. Jackson's hartebeest at Ruma Park	2·00	1·50
840	75s. Athlete in steeplechase	2·25	2·50
841	95s. Kenyatta International Conference Centre, Nairobi	3·25	4·00
838/41 Set of 4		7·50	7·50

The UPU Congress was moved to Geneva, Switzerland, due to political unrest in Kenya.

No. 836 has been reported as a sheetlet of six, printed on self-adhesive paper, presented within a commemorative pack.

168 Athletics – Men

2008 (21 Aug). Olympic Games, Beijing. T **168** snd similar designs. Multicoloured. P 14½.

842	25s. Type **168**	1·00	50
843	65s. Ladies Volley Ball	2·50	2·00
844	75s. Athletics – Ladies	3·25	3·75
845	95s. Boxing – Men	4·25	4·75
842/5 *Set of 4*		10·00	10·00

169 Oginga Odinga, Pio Gama Pinto, Tom Mboya and Ronald Ngala (politicians) (Post Independence)

(Litho Oriental Press, Bahrain)

2008 (17 Oct). Heroes of Kenya. T **169** and similar horiz designs. Multicoloured. P 12½×13.

846	25s. Type **169**	70	40
847	65s. Bildad Kaggia, Kung'u Karumba, Jomo Kenyatta, Fred Kubai, Paul Ngei and Achieng' Oneko (The Kapenguria Six)	1·75	1·75
848	75s. Dedan Kimathi (Mau Mau rebellion leader), Elijah Masinde (political and religious leader), Mekatilili Wa Menza (anti colonial leader) and Koitalel Samoei (Nandi rebellion leader) (Pre Independence)	2·25	2·50
849	95s. Kenya Army Peacekeeping Force	2·50	3·25
846/9 Set of 4		6·50	7·25

170 Woman loading Donkey with Water Cans

(Litho Austrian State Ptg Wks, Vienna)

2008 (17 Nov). Centenary of Theosophical Order of Service. Provision of Wells and Boreholes. P 14×13½.

850	**170**	25s. multicoloured	1·25	1·00

171 Madrasa Programme   **172** Blind Man

(Litho Oriental Press, Bahrain)

2008 (13 Dec). Golden Jubilee of the Aga Khan. T **171** and similar
multicoloured designs. P 13 (25, 65s.) or 14½ (75, 95s.).

851	25s. Type **171**	70	40
852	65s. Workers in field (Coastal Rural Support Programme)	1·75	1·75
853	75s. Aga Khan Academy, Mombasa (44×29 mm)	2·25	2·50
854	95s. Aga Khan University Hospital, Nairobi (44×29 mm)	2·50	3·25
851/4 Set of 4..		6·50	7·25

(Litho Oriental Press, Bahrain)

2009 (10 July). Birth Bicentenary of Louis Braille (inventor of Braille
writing for the blind). P 14½.

855	**172**	25s. multicoloured...........................	1·50	1·00

173 Market Stallholder ('Financial Services')

(Litho Austrian State Ptg Wks, Vienna)

2009 (9 Dec). Tenth Anniv of Postal Corporation of Kenya. T **173** and
similar horiz designs. Multicoloured. P 14×13½.

856	25s. Type **173**	90	90
	a. Sheetlet. Nos. 856/64	7·00	7·00
857	25s. Parcels ('We Deliver Peace of Mind!')	90	90
858	25s. Courier and Posta Dispatch vans ('Pick-up Services')	90	90
859	25s. Boy and stamps ('Say it with Stamps!').	90	90
860	25s. Brochures in postbox ('Direct Mail Marketing')	90	90
861	25s. 'Utility Bills Retail Services Salaries' ('Agency Services')	90	90
862	25s. Woman reading letter ('We Deliver Emotions!')	90	90
863	25s. Postman and private letter boxes	90	90
864	25s. 'Financial Services'..............................	90	90
865	65s. Unloading parcels from airplane ('Expedited Mail Service')	90	90
866	75s. Narok Post Office	90	90
867	95s. Water standpipe ('Corporate Social Responsibility')	90	90
856/867 Set of 12		13·50	13·50

Nos. 856/64 were printed together, *se-tenant*, in sheetlets of nine
stamps, and also in separate sheets of 50.

174 Taita African Violet and Amegilla
Bee, Taita Hills

(Litho Cartor)

2010 (25 Mar). Centenary (2009) of the East Africa Natural History
Society. T **174** and similar hexagonal designs. Multicoloured. P 13.

868	25s. Type **174**	90	30
869	65s. Reed frog, Shimba Hills	2·25	1·75
870	75s. Great blue turaco, Kakamega Forest......	3·00	2·25
871	95s. Golden-rumped sengi, Arabuko-Sokoke Forest	2·75	3·25
868/871 Set of 4...		8·00	6·75

175 Elephant

(Litho Austrian State Ptg Wks, Vienna)

2010 (30 Nov). Anniv of PAPU (Pan African Postal Union). P 13½.

872	**175**	25s. multicoloured...........................	50	50

176 Pres. Mwai Kibaki holding
New Constitution

(Litho Oriental Press, Bahrain)

2011 (9 Sept). Promulgation of New Constitution. P 13½.

873	**176**	25s. multicoloured...........................	1·00	1·00

177 *Oplostomus haroldi* (large hive
beetle)

(Litho)

2011 (17 Nov). 40th Anniv of ICIPE (International Centre of Insect
Physiology and Ecology). Insects. T **177** and similar horiz designs.
Multicoloured. P 13.

874	65s. Type **177**	1·50	1·50
	a. Sheetlet. Nos. 874/98	35·00	35·00
875	65s. *Cartoblatta sp.* (cockroach)	1·50	1·50
876	65s. *Mormotomyia hirsuta*	1·50	1·50
877	65s. *Cicindellidae*	1·50	1·50
878	65s. *Nosognatha ruficollis*	1·50	1·50
879	65s. *Hetrodinae sp.*	1·50	1·50
880	65s. *Helopeltis schoutedeni* (and damaged leaves)	1·50	1·50
881	65s. Blister Beetle (*Ceroctis sp.*)	1·50	1·50
882	65s. *Bagrada cruciferarum*	1·50	1·50
883	65s. *Popillia aeneipennis* (chafer)	1·50	1·50
884	65s. Jewel Beetle (*Lampetis sp.*)	1·50	1·50
885	65s. *Oryctes sp.* (Rhinoceros beetle)	1·50	1·50
886	65s. *Homoderus mellyi*	1·50	1·50
887	65s. *Zonocerus variegatus*	1·50	1·50
888	65s. *Leucospidae*	1·50	1·50
889	65s. *Agnoscelis versicolor*	1·50	1·50
890	65s. Tortoise Beetle (*Hispinae*)	1·50	1·50
891	65s. *Curculionidae*	1·50	1·50
892	65s. *Cypholoba perspicillaris*	1·50	1·50
893	65s. *Lycidae*	1·50	1·50
894	65s. Milkweed bugs	1·50	1·50
895	65s. *Mylabris tristigma*	1·50	1·50
896	65s. *Paederus sp.*	1·50	1·50
897	65s. *Pyrops turritus*	1·50	1·50
898	65s. *Tenebrionidae*	1·50	1·50
899	75s. Fig Wasp (perched)	1·50	1·50
	a. Sheetlet. Nos. 899/23	35·00	35·00
900	75s. Rain Tree Bug (*Ptyelus flavescens*)	1·50	1·50
901	75s. Phlebotomus feeding	1·50	1·50
902	75s. Fig Wasp (with ovipositor extended)	1·50	1·50
903	75s. Dragonfly (*Trithemis annulata*)	1·50	1·50
904	75s. Braconid Wasp	1·50	1·50
905	75s. Paper Wasp (*Polistes sp.*)	1·50	1·50
906	75s. *Helopeltis schoutedeni* (in close-up)........	1·50	1·50
907	75s. Dragonfly (*Trithemis sp.*)	1·50	1·50

908	75s. Cicada		1·50	1·50
909	75s. Silverfish		1·50	1·50
910	75s. Stingless Bee		1·50	1·50
911	75s. *Lipotriches sp.*		1·50	1·50
912	75s. *Bombyliidae*		1·50	1·50
913	75s. *Bromophila caffra*		1·50	1·50
914	75s. *Schistocerca gregaria*		1·50	1·50
915	75s. *Plagiotryptus hippiscus*		1·50	1·50
916	75s. *Reduviidae*		1·50	1·50
917	75s. Stalk-eyed Fly (*Diopsidae*)		1·50	1·50
918	75s. Lamyra gulo and wasp prey		1·50	1·50
919	75s. *Dictyopharidae*		1·50	1·50
920	75s. *Rhiniidae cf. Fainia sp.*		1·50	1·50
921	75s. Locust		1·50	1·50
922	75s. *Megastigmus sp.*		1·50	1·50
923	75s. Glossina morsitans feeding		1·50	1·50
874/923	*Set of 50*		70·00	70·00

Nos. 874/98 and 899/923 were each printed together, *se-tenant*, in sheetlets of 25.

178 Flags at UNEP Regional Office, Nairobi

(Litho Austrian State Ptg Wks, Vienna)

2012 (20 Apr). 40th Anniv of UNEP (United Nations Environment Programme) (1st issue). T **178** and similar horiz designs. Multicoloured. P 14.

924	30s. Type **178**		60	60
925	90s. City of Stockholm, Sweden		1·75	1·75
926	110s. Christ the Redeemer statue, Rio de Janeiro		2·25	2·25
924/6	*Set of 3*		4·25	4·25

179 Fauna and Flora (CITES–Convention on International Trade in Endangered Species of Wild Fauna and Flora)

(Litho Austrian State Ptg Wks, Vienna)

2012 (22 June). 40th Anniv of UNEP (United Nations Environment Programme) (2nd issue). T **179** and similar vert designs. Multicoloured. P 14.

927	30s. Type **179**		60	60
928	90s. Globe encircled by human figures (Montreal Protocol on substances that deplete the ozone layer)		1·75	1·75
929	110s. Symbolic globe with green shoots, sun, wind farm and water tap (GREEN economy)		2·25	2·25
927/9	*Set of 3*		4·25	4·25

180 United Nations Energy-neutral Offices, Nairobi

(Litho Austrian State Ptg Wks, Vienna)

2012 (31 Jul). 40th Anniv of UNEP (United Nations Environment Programme) (3rd issue). World Environment Day. T **180** and similar horiz designs. Multicoloured. P 14.

930	30s. Type **180**		60	60
931	90s. Olkaria Geothermal Station		1·75	1·75
932	110s. Turkana Wind Farm		2·25	2·25
930/2	*Set of 3*		4·25	4·25

181 Prof. Wangari Muta Maathai (founder of Green Belt Movement)

182 First Plane to Land in Kenya, 1920

(Litho Austrian State Ptg Wks, Vienna)

2012 (25 Sept). Professor Wangari Muta Maathai's Nobel Peace Prize, 2004. P 14.

933	**181**	30s. multi-coloured	60	60

(Des Kassam Asgarali and Benjamin Mogaka. Litho Cartor)

2013 (11 Dec). 50th Anniv of Independence. T **182** and similar horiz designs. Multicoloured. P 13½.

934	30s. Type **182**	60	60
	a. Sheetlet. Nos. 934/58	15·00	
935	30s. Locomotive, 1904	60	60
936	30s. East Africa Railway and Harbour	60	60
937	30s. Jamhuri High School	60	60
938	30s. Prince of Wales School	60	60
939	30s. Machakos Girls School	60	60
940	30s. Royal Technical College, University of Nairobi	60	60
941	30s. Kenyatta University	60	60
942	30s. Jomo Kenyatta University of Agriculture and Technology	60	60
943	30s. Nairobi City	60	60
944	30s. King George VI Hospital	60	60
945	30s. Kenyatta National Hospital	60	60
946	30s. Jomo Kenyatta International Airport	60	60
947	30s. Mobile Library	60	60
948	30s. Kenya National Library, Nairobi	60	60
949	30s. Horticulture	60	60
950	30s. Poultry farming	60	60
951	30s. Maize farming	60	60
952	30s. Beef farming	60	60
953	30s. Dairy farming	60	60
954	30s. Compulsory Free Primary Education	60	60
955	30s. Kenya National Adult Literacy Survey	60	60
956	30s. Murang'a Road Junction	60	60
957	30s. Globe Cinema Complex	60	60
958	30s. Oil prospecting	60	60
959	75s. Pres. Ururu Kenyatta and Deputy President William Ruto	1·50	1·50
	a. Sheetlet. Nos. 959/83	38·00	
960	75s. Queen Elizabeth II and Prince Philip (Coronation, 1953)	1·50	1·50
961	75s. Lancaster House Conference, 1963	1·50	1·50
962	75s. Dedan Kimathi	1·50	1·50
963	75s. Mau Mau movement	1·50	1·50
964	75s. The Kapenguria Six	1·50	1·50
965	75s. The Kapenguria cells	1·50	1·50
966	75s. The Lowering of the Union Jack	1·50	1·50
967	75s. Munyao Lisoi hoisting of the Kenya Flag on Mt. Kenya, 1963	1·50	1·50
968	75s. Promulgation of the New Constitution	1·50	1·50
969	75s. First Transition	1·50	1·50
970	75s. Second Transition	1·50	1·50
971	75s. Third Transition	1·50	1·50
972	75s. Fourth Transition	1·50	1·50
973	75s. Parliament Building	1·50	1·50
974	75s. First Cabinet, 1963	1·50	1·50
975	75s. Colonial and current Coat of Arms	1·50	1·50
976	75s. Colonial flag and Kenya national flag	1·50	1·50
977	75s. Colonial provincial boundaries and modern county boundaries	1·50	1·50
978	75s. The Judiciary	1·50	1·50
979	75s. Kenyatta Mausoleum	1·50	1·50
980	75s. Old Provincial Commissioner's Office, 2013	1·50	1·50
981	75s. Nyayo House, Nairobi	1·50	1·50
982	75s. First Governor of Nairobi Delamare	1·50	1·50
983	75s. Kenya Defence Force in Somalia	1·50	1·50
984	90s. Fort Jesus, built 1565	1·75	1·75
	a. Sheetlet. Nos. 984/1008	43·00	
985	90s. Kenya–Uganda Railway Line, 1896	1·75	1·75
986	90s. Nyali Bridge, 1900	1·75	1·75
987	90s. 13th-century Gedi ruins	1·75	1·75
988	90s. First Post Office in Mombasa, 1902	1·75	1·75
989	90s. First GPO in Mombasa, 1920	1·75	1·75

990	90s. First GPO in Nairobi, 1944	1·75	1·75
991	90s. Kenya National Archives, 1944	1·75	1·75
992	90s. Macmillian Library, 1925	1·75	1·75
993	90s. Nairobi National Museum, 1890	1·75	1·75
994	90s. Mombasa coins, 1885	1·75	1·75
995	90s. Maasai morans	1·75	1·75
996	90s. Luo traditional homestead	1·75	1·75
997	90s. Karen Blixen Museum	1·75	1·75
998	90s. Kipande House, Nairobi, 2013	1·75	1·75
999	90s. Laikipia Camel Caravan	1·75	1·75
1000	90s. East Africa and Uganda Protectorates 2012–21 5r. blue and dull purple stamp optd Kenya and 1963 65c. pyrethrum industry stamp from Independence set	1·75	1·75
1001	90s. Chuka Drummers	1·75	1·75
1002	90s. Obokono (musical instrument)	1·75	1·75
1003	90s. Vasco Da Gama Pillar, Malindi	1·75	1·75
1004	90s. Naftali Temu winning Olympic gold medal in men's 10000 metres, Mexico City, 1968	1·75	1·75
1005	90s. Athletes Pamela Jelimo and Janeth Jepkosgel with Kenyan flag	1·75	1·75
1006	90s. Ezekial Kemboi winning Olympic gold medal in 3000 metres steeplechase, Athens, 2004	1·75	1·75
1007	90s. David Rudisha winning Olympic gold medal in 800 metres, London, 1912	1·75	1·75
1008	90s. Kenya Rugby Union national team	1·75	1·75
1009	110s. Lion	2·25	2·25
	a. Sheetlet. Nos. 1009/33	55·00	
1010	110s. Elephant	2·25	2·25
1011	110s. Leopard	2·25	2·25
1012	110s. Rhinoceros with calf	2·25	2·25
1013	110s. Buffalo	2·25	2·25
1014	110s. Hippopotamus	2·25	2·25
1015	110s. Cheetah	2·25	2·25
1016	110s. Giraffe	2·25	2·25
1017	110s. Zebra	2·25	2·25
1018	110s. Warthog	2·25	2·25
1019	110s. Wildebeest migration	2·25	2·25
1020	110s. Bongo	2·25	2·25
1021	110s. Impala	2·25	2·25
1022	110s. Hyena	2·25	2·25
1023	110s. Jackal	2·25	2·25
1024	110s. Crocodiles, River Tana	2·25	2·25
1025	110s. Flamingoes, Lake Nakuru	2·25	2·25
1026	110s. Two ostriches	2·25	2·25
1027	110s. Colobus Monkey	2·25	2·25
1028	110s. Falcon	2·25	2·25
1029	110s. Longonot Crater	2·25	2·25
1030	110s. Thompson Falls, Nyahururu	2·25	2·25
1031	110s. Mt. Kenya	2·25	2·25
1032	110s. Lake Turkana	2·25	2·25
1033	110s. Solar Eclipse	2·25	2·25
934/1033	Set of 100	£150	£150

MS1034 110×105 mm. 30s.×4 East African coins, 1910–65; Kenya coins, 1966–2010; East African notes; Kenyan notes .... 2·40 2·40

MS1035 110×105 mm. 30s.×6 Mail runner, 1880; Postman delivering letters at a marketplace, 1902; Street posting box, 1920; Modern delivery van; Letter boxes; Modern posting box .... 3·50 3·50

MS1036 90×125 mm. 150s. Jomo Kenyatta (President 1963–75); Daniel Arap Moi (President 1978–2002); Mwai Kibaki (President 2002–13); Uhuru Kenyatta (President 2013-). Imperf .... 3·00 3·00

Nos. 934/58, 959/83, 984/1008 and 1009/33 were each printed together, *se-tenant*, in sheetlets of 25 (5 ×5).

183 Kenyan and Chinese Flower Vases

(Mr. Maxialing. Litho Henan Post Printing Factory, China)

2013 (20 Dec). 50th Anniv of Diplomatic Relations between Kenya and People's Republic of China. T **183** and similar horiz designs. Multicoloured. P 13½.

1037	30s. Type **183**	60	60
1038	110s. Pres. Uhuru Kenyatta and Xi Jingping of China	2·25	2·25
MS1039 110×80 mm. 150s. As No. 1037		3·00	3·00

STAMP BOOKLETS

1964. Black on blue cover. Stitched.

SB1   5s. booklet containing 10c., 15c., 20c., 30c. and 50c. (Nos. 2/5, 7) in blocks of 4 .... 20·00

1966 (12 Dec). Black on bluish grey (No. SB2) or buff (No. SB3) covers. Stitched.

SB2   3s. booklet containing four 5c., 10c. and eight 30c. (Nos. 20/1, 24), each in blocks of 4 .... 18·00

SB3   5s. booklet containing four 5c., 10c., 50c. and eight 30c. (Nos. 20/1, 24, 26), each in blocks of 4 .... 30·00

1971 (13 Dec). Black on buff (No. SB4) or dull rose (No. SB5) covers. Stitched.

SB4   5s. booklet containing four 10c., 15c., 40c. and eight 30c. (Nos. 37, 38, 40/1), each in blocks of 4 .... 11·00

SB5   10s. booklet containing four 10c., 20c., 30c., 50c. and eight 70c. (Nos. 37, 39/40, 42, 45), each in blocks of 4 .... 18·00

1977 (10 Dec). Black on yellow (No. SB6) or bright rose (No. SB7) covers . Stitched.

SB6   5s. booklet containing ten 50c. (No. 111) in two blocks of 4 and one pair .... 13·00

SB7   10s. booklet containing four 10c., 40c., 80c. and eight 50c. (Nos. 107/8, 110/11, 113), each in blocks of 4 .... 17·00

1983 (14 Feb). Black on pale blue (No. SB8) or pale green (No. SB9) covers . Stitched.

SB8   10s. booklet containing four 10c., 20c., 30c., 50c. and eight 70c. (Nos. 257/9, 261/2), each in blocks of 4 .... 6·50

SB9   20s. booklet containing four 10c., 20c., 30c., 50c. and sixteen 70c. (Nos. 257/9, 261/2), each in blocks of 4 .... 11·00

1988 (15 Feb). Black on greenish yellow (No. SB10) or yellow-orange (No. SB11) covers. Stitched.

SB10   20s. booklet containing eight 20c., 50c., 80c., 1s. (Nos. 435, 437, 439/40), each in blocks of 4 .... 5·00

SB11   40s. booklet containing sixteen 20c., 50c., 80c., 1s. (Nos. 435, 437, 439/40), each in blocks of 4 .... 10·00

B **1**

1993. Brown on pale blue cover. Stitched. As Type B **2**.

SB12   48s. booklet containing eight 50c., 1s, 1s.50, 3s. (Nos. 593, 594, 594a, 595) each in panes of 4 .... 50·00

B **2**

1996 (31 Jan). Tourism "The Land of Contrasts". Multicoloured cover as Type B **2**.

SB13   480s. booklet containing four *se-tenant* panes of six (No. 696a) .... 9·50

B **3**

2006 (15 Dec). Tourism. "The Land of Opportunity". Multicoloured cover, 155×77 mm, as Type B **3**.

SB14   300s. booklet containing four *se-tenant* panes of three (Nos. 814a, 817a, 820a and 823a) .... 13·00

POSTAGE DUE STAMPS

The Postage Due stamps of Kenya, Uganda and Tanganyika were used in Kenya until 2 January 1967.

D **3**

1967 (3 Jan). Chalk-surfaced paper. P 14×13½.

D13	D **3**	5c. scarlet	15	2·75
		a. Perf 14. Ordinary paper. *Dull scarlet* (16.12.69)............................	40	7·50
D14		10c. green...................................	20	2·50
		a. Perf 14. Ordinary paper (16.12.69)	55	4·25
D15		20c. blue	70	2·75
		a. Perf 14. Ordinary paper. *Deep blue* (16.12.69)....................................	55	8·50
D16		30c. brown	80	3·25
		a. Perf 14. Ordinary paper. *Light red-brown* (16.12.69)..............	80	24·00
D17		40c. bright purple	65	5·00
		a. Perf 14. Ordinary paper. *Pale bright purple* (16.12.69)...........	65	24·00
D18		1s. bright orange	1·75	7·00
		a. Perf 14. Ordinary paper. *Dull bright orange* (18.2.70)...............	2·00	24·00
D13/18	*Set of 6*		3·75	21·00
D13a/18a	*Set of 6*		4·50	85·00

1971 (13 July)–**73**. P 14×15.

(a) Chalk-surfaced paper (13.7.71)

D19	D **3**	10c. green....................................	9·00	12·00
D20		20c. deep dull blue.....................	10·00	14·00
D21		30c. red-brown............................	11·00	13·00
D22		1s. dull bright orange...............	17·00	40·00
D19/22	*Set of 4*		42·00	70·00

(b) Glazed, ordinary paper (20.2.73)

D23	D **3**	5c. bright scarlet	1·50	4·75
D24		10c. dull yellow-green	1·50	4·75
D25		20c. deep blue............................	1·50	5·50
D27		40c. bright purple	1·00	8·00
D28		1s. bright orange	1·50	12·00
D23/8	*Set of 5*		6·00	32·00

1973 (12 Dec). Glazed, ordinary paper. P 15.

D29	D **3**	5c. red..	30	4·50
D30		10c. emerald................................	30	4·00
D31		20c. deep blue............................	30	4·25
D32		30c. red-brown............................	30	6·00
D33		40c. bright purple	3·75	10·00
D34		1s. bright orange	95	12·00
D29/34	*Set of 6*		5·50	35·00

1979 (27 Mar). Chalk-surfaced paper. P 14.

D35	D **3**	10c. bright emerald......................	90	5·50
D36		20c. deep dull blue.....................	1·75	7·00
D37		30c. dull red-brown.....................	1·00	6·00
D38		40c. bright reddish purple..........	2·00	10·00
D39		80c. dull red...............................	85	5·50
D40		1s. bright reddish orange.........	85	5·50
D35/40	*Set of 6*		6·50	35·00

1983 (1 Dec). W w **14**. P 14.

D41	D **3**	10c. yellowish green	40	2·25
D42		20c. deep blue............................	40	2·25
D43		40c. bright purple	8·50	13·00
D41/3	*Set of 3*..		8·50	16·00

(Litho Harrison)

1985 (7 Aug)–**87**. Ordinary paper. P 14½×14.

D44	D **3**	30c. red-brown (9.1.87)................	1·00	2·25
D45		40c. bright magenta (9.1.87)	1·00	2·25
D46		80c. dull vermilion (9.1.87).........	1·50	2·50
D47		1s. bright orange (1986)..........	5·00	6·50
D48		2s. violet	2·50	5·00
D44/8	*Set of 5*..		10·00	17·00

No. D47 was issued by the Crown Agents with Nos. D44/6, but was available in Kenya by November 1986.

(Litho Enschedé)

1993 (6 Dec). Ordinary paper. P 14½×14.

D49	D **3**	50c. yellowish green	10	20
D50		1s. yellow-orange.....................	10	20
D51		2s. dull violet...........................	10	25
D52		3s. steel-blue............................	10	25
D53		5s. brown-red...........................	10	25
D54		10s. reddish brown (1998)...........	15	30

D55		20s. deep bright magenta (1998)	30	50
D49/55	*Set of 7*		85	1·75

Nos. D49/55 are from re-drawn plates which differ from Harrison printings of Type D **3** in that "KENYA" is 8½ mm long on the Enschedé instead of 9½ mm and "POSTAGE DUE" 11 mm long instead of 11½ mm. There are other differences in the inner frame at bottom right.

OFFICIAL STAMPS

Intended for use on official correspondence of the Kenya Government only but there is no evidence that they were so used.

OFFICIAL
(O **4**)

(15c. 30c. opt typo; others in photogravure)

1964 (1 Oct). Nos. 1/5 and 7 optd with Type O **4**.

O21	5c. brown, deep blue, green and bistre.......		10
O22	10c. brown..		10
O23	15c. magenta...	1·25	
O24	20c. black and yellow-green......................		20
O25	30c. black and yellow...............................		30
O26	50c. crimson, black and green...................	2·75	
O21/26	*Set of 6*..		4·00

Kenya, Uganda and Tanganyika

BRITISH EAST AFRICA

The area which became British East Africa had been part of the domain of the Zanzibari Sultans since 1794. In 1887 the administration of the province was granted to the British East Africa Association, incorporated as the Imperial British East Africa Company the following year.

Company post offices were established at Lamu and Mombasa in May 1890, British mails having been previously sent via the Indian post office on Zanzibar, opened in 1875.

A German postal agency opened at Lamu on 22 November 1888 and continued to operate until 31 March 1891, using German stamps. These can be identified by the "LAMU/OSTAFRIKA" cancellations and are listed under German East Africa in our Part 7 (*Germany*) catalogue.

PRICES FOR STAMPS ON COVER		
Nos.	1/3	from × 10
Nos.	4/19	from × 30
Nos.	20/1	from × 3
No.	22	—
No.	23	from × 3
No.	24	—
No.	25	from × 1
No.	26	from × 3
Nos.	27/8	from × 8
Nos.	29/30	from × 20
No.	31	from × 10
No.	32	—
Nos.	33/42	from × 10
Nos.	43/7	—
No.	48	from × 15
Nos.	49/64	from × 12
Nos.	65/79	from × 15
Nos.	80/91	from × 8
Nos.	92/6	from × 12
Nos.	97/9	—

(Currency. 16 annas = 1 rupee)

BRITISH EAST AFRICA COMPANY ADMINISTRATION

**BRITISH
EAST AFRICA
COMPANY**

**BRITISH
EAST AFRICA
COMPANY**

HALF ANNA
(1)

1 ANNA
(2)

(Surch D.L.R.)

1890 (23 May). Stamps of Great Britain (Queen Victoria) surch as T **1** or T **2** (1a. and 4a.).

1	½a. on 1d. deep purple (No. 173)	£275	£200
2	1a. on 2d. grey-green and carmine (No. 200)	£500	£275
3	4a. on 5d. dull purple and blue (No. 207a)	£600	£325

The second stamp of each horizontal row on the 4a. on 5d. had the "BRITISH" shifted to the left, placing the "B" directly over the "S" of "EAST". In the normal overprint the "B" is over "ST" as shown in Type (**2**).

A copy of the ½a. with the short crossbar of "F" in "HALF" omitted exists in the Royal Collection but is the only known example.

Following the exhaustion of stocks of Nos. 1/3, stamps of India were used at Mombasa (and occasionally at Lamu) from late July 1890 until the arrival of Nos. 4/19. The following listing is for stamps clearly cancelled with the MOMBASA 21 mm circular date stamp (code "C"). Examples with LAMU circular date stamp are worth much more. Indian stamps used after October 1890, including other values, came from ship mail.

Stamps of INDIA 1882–90 (Nos. 84/101) cancelled at Mombasa between July and October 1890.

Z1	½a. blue-green	£600
Z2	1a. brown-purple	£500
Z3	1a.6p. sepia	£850
Z4	2a. blue	£950
Z5	3a. orange	£950
Z5a	4a. olive-green	£1000
Z6	4a.6p. yellow-green	£350
Z7	8a. dull mauve	£550
Z8	1r. slate	£950

3

4

**5
ANNAS.**
(5)

1a. "ANL" (broken "D") (R. 6/5)

(Litho B.W.)

1890 (13 Oct)–**95**. P 14.

4	**3**	½a. dull brown	9·00	12·00
		a. Imperf (pair)	£1500	£700
		b. *Deep brown* (21.10.93)	70	10·00
		ba. Imperf (pair)	£900	£375
		bb. Imperf between (horiz pair)	£1700	£650
		bc. Imperf between (vert pair)	£1300	£500
		c. *Pale brown* (16.1.95)	1·00	16·00
5		1a. blue-green	9·50	14·00
		aa. "ANL" (broken "D")	£1000	£1000
		a. Imperf (pair)	£4750	£1200
		ab. Ditto. "ANL" (broken "D")	£20000	
		b. *Deep blue-green* (16.1.95)	1·00	
6		2a. vermilion	5·00	6·00
		a. Imperf (pair)	£4500	£1300
7	**3**	2½a. black/*yellow-buff* (9.91)	£100	32·00
		aa. Imperf (pair)	£5500	
		a. Imperf between (horiz pair)	£8000	
		b. *Black/pale buff* (9.92)	£100	11·00
		c. *Black/bright yellow* (21.10.93)	4·75	7·50
		cb. Imperf (pair)	£1200	£500
		cc. Imperf between (horiz pair)	£1400	£450
		cd. Imperf between (vert pair)	£1400	£600
8		3a. black/*dull red* (30.3.91)	22·00	23·00
		a. *Black/bright red* (21.10.93)	3·00	15·00
		ab. Imperf (pair)	£1200	£450
		ac. Imperf between (horiz pair)	£900	£425
		ad. Imperf between (vert pair)	£700	£400
9		4a. yellow-brown	2·50	13·00
		a. Imperf (pair)	£4750	£1600
10		4a. grey (*imperf*)	£1200	£1400
11		4½a. dull violet (30.3.91)	35·00	18·00
		a. *Brown-purple* (21.10.93)	2·50	20·00
		ab. Imperf (pair)	£2000	£450
		ac. Imperf between (horiz pair)	£1500	£950
		ad. Imperf between (vert pair)	£1100	£500
12		8a. blue	5·50	9·50
		a. Imperf (pair)	£9000	£1400
13		8a. grey	£275	£225
14		1r. carmine	6·00	9·00
		a. Imperf (pair)	£15000	£1600
15		1r. grey	£225	£225
16	**4**	2r. brick-red	14·00	50·00
17		3r. slate-purple	11·00	55·00
18		4r. ultramarine	12·00	55·00
19		5r. grey-green	30·00	75·00
4/9, 11/19 *Set of* 15			£550	£650

For the 5a. and 7½a. see Nos. 29/30.

The paper of Nos. 7, 7b, 7c, 8 and 8a is coloured on the surface only.

Printings of 1890/92 are on thin paper having the outer margins of the sheets imperf and bearing sheet watermark "PURE LINEN WOVE BANK" and "W. C. S. & Co." in a monogram, the trademark of the makers, Messrs. William Collins, Sons & Co.

1893/94 printings are on thicker coarser paper with outer margins perforated through the selvedge and without watermark. Single specimens cannot always be distinguished by lack of watermark alone. Exceptions are the 1893 printings of the 2½a. and 3a. which were on Wiggins Teape paper showing a sheet watermark of "1011" in figures 1 centimetre high.

Nos. 7 (coloured through) and 16/19 on thick unwatermarked paper are from a special printing made for presentation purposes.

The printings of the 4a., 8a. and 1r. values in grey were intended for fiscal purposes, but in the event, were made available for postal use.

Forgeries of the 4a., 8a., 1r. grey and 2 to 5r. exist. The latter are common and can be distinguished by the scroll above "LIGHT" where there are five vertical lines of shading in the forgeries and seven in the genuine stamps. Forged cancellations exist on the commoner stamps. Beware of "imperf" stamps made by trimming margins of stamps from marginal rows.

1891. Mombasa Provisionals.

(a) New value handstamped in dull violet, with original face value obliterated and initials added in black manuscript

20	**3**	"½ on 2a. vermilion ("A.D.") Anna" (January)............................	£11000	£1100
		a. "½ Anna" double............................	†	£13000
		b. Original face value not obliterated............................	†	£3750
21		"1 Anna" on 4a. brown ("A.B.") (February).	£18000	£2250

(b) Manuscript value and initials in black

22	**3**	"½ on 2a. vermilion ("A.D.") Anna" (original face value not obliterated) (January).............	†	£4750
23		"½ on 2a. vermilion ("A.B.") Anna" (February)............................	£11000	£1100
		a. Error. "½ Annas" ("A.B.")	†	£1200
24		"½ on 3a. black/*dull red* ("A.B.") Anna" (May)............................	£18000	£2250
25		"1 Anna" on 3a. black/*dull red* ("V.H.M.") (June)............................	£16000	£1300
26		"1 Anna" on 4a. brown ("A.B.") (March)......	£10000	£2000

A.D. = Andrew Dick, Chief Accountant.
A.B. = Archibald Brown, Cashier of the Company.
V.H.M. = Victor H. Mackenzie, Bank Manager.
Nos. 23 and 26 exist with manuscript surcharges in different hands. Examples with a heavy surcharge applied with a thick nib were mainly used at Lamu. Most of the surviving unused examples show this style, but used examples are worth a premium over the prices quoted.

(Surch B.W.)

1894 (1 Nov). Surch as T **5**.

27	**3**	5a. on 8a. blue	75·00	95·00
28		7½a. on 1r. carmine	75·00	95·00
27s/8s		Handstamped "SPECIMEN" Set of 2...............	95·00	

Forgeries exist.

1895 (16 Jan). No wmk. P 14.

29	**3**	5a. black/*grey-blue*	1·25	12·00
30		7½a. black	1·25	18·00
29s/30s		Handstamped "SPECIMEN" Set of 2	75·00	

The date quoted is that of earliest known use of stamps from this consignment.
These two stamps have "LD" after "COMPANY" in the inscription.
The paper of No. 29 is coloured on the surface only.

1895 (Feb). No. 8 surch with manuscript value and initials ("T.E.C.R.").
Original face value obliterated in manuscript.

31	**3**	"½ anna" on 3a. black/*dull red* (19.2).........	£600	55·00
32		"1 anna" on 3a. black/*dull red* (22.2).........	£10000	£7000

T.E.C.R. = T.E.C. Remington, Postmaster at Mombasa.
Similar manuscript surcharges on the black/*bright red* shade (No. 8a) are believed to be forgeries.
The Company experienced considerable financial problems during 1894 with the result that the British Government agreed to assume the administration of the territory, as a protectorate, on 1 July 1895.

IMPERIAL ADMINISTRATION

BRITISH
EAST
AFRICA
(6)

$2\frac{1}{2}$
(7)

(Handstamped at Mombasa)

1895 (9 July). Handstamped with T **6**.

33	**3**	½a. deep brown..	80·00	35·00
		a. *Pale brown*	£120	50·00
		b. *Dull brown*	†	£3500
		c. Double	£475	£450
		d. Inverted...	£7500	
34		1a. blue-green..	£200	£120
		a. Double	£750	£500
		b. "ANL" (broken "D") (R. 6/5)...................	£3500	£500
		c. *Deep blue-green*	†	£4250
35		2a. vermilion...	£200	£100
		a. Double	£850	£550
36		2½a. black/*bright yellow*	£200	65·00
		a. Double	£850	£600
		b. *Black/pale buff*	†	£3000
37		3a. black/*dull red*	£100	55·00
38		4a. yellow-brown...	65·00	42·00
		a. Double	£600	£500
39		4½a. dull violet	£225	£100
		a. Double	£900	£650
		b. *Brown-purple*	£1200	£1000
		ba. Double	£3250	£2250
40		5a. black/*grey-blue*	£300	£150
		a. Double	£1100	£850
		b. Inverted...	†	£5000
41		7½a. black	£140	90·00

		a. Double...	£850	£650
42		8a. blue...	£100	80·00
		a. Double...	£750	£650
		b. Inverted..	£8000	
43		1r. carmine...	65·00	55·00
		a. Double...	£700	£550
44	**4**	2r. brick-red..	£500	£325
45		3r. slate-purple..	£275	£160
		a. Double...	£1200	£1000
		b. Inverted..		
46		4r. ultramarine...	£200	£180
		a. Double...	£1000	£900
47		5r. grey-green...	£450	£300
		a. Double...	£1500	£1400
33/47		*Set of 15*..	£2750	£1600

Forgeries exist.
The ½a. stamps used for this issue were mainly from the 1893–94 printings on thicker paper, but two used examples are known on the 1890 thin paper printing with sheet watermark (No. 4). The 1a stamps were mostly from the 1890 thin paper printing (No. 5), but one example is known from the 1895 printing on thick paper (No. 5b). The 2½a. stamps were mainly from the 1893 printing (No. 7c), but three used examples have been reported from the 1892 printing on thin pale buff paper (No. 7b).

1895 (29 Sept). No. 39 surch with T **7** by The Zanzibar Gazette.

48	**3**	2½a. on 4½a. dull violet (R.)	£225	85·00
		a. Opt (T **6**) double	£1200	£950

British
East
Africa
(8)

British
East
Africa
(9)

SETTING OF TYPE 8. This consisted of 120 impressions in 10 horizontal rows of 12 stamps. This matched the size of the pane for all the Indian issues to 1r. with the exception of the 6a. The sheets of this value contained four panes, each 8×10, which meant that the outer vertical margins also received the overprint.
The setting of Type 9 is not known.
Although only the one setting was used for the low values it is known that some of the overprint errors occurred, or were corrected, during the course of the various printings.

(Overprinted at the offices of The Zanzibar Gazette)

1895 (27 Oct)–**96**. Stamps of India (Queen Victoria) optd with T **8** or **9** (2r. to 5r.). W **13** (Elephant Head) (6a.) or W **34** (Large Star) (others) of India.

49		½a. blue-green (No. 85) (8.11.95)	7·00	5·50
		a. "Brltsh" for "British"...............................	£10000	£8000
		b. "Br1tish" for "British" (R. 10/12)	£550	
		c. "Afr1ca" for "Africa" (R. 1/11)	£750	
		d. Opt double, one albino...........................	£225	
		e. "Briti" for "British" (R. 1/6)...................	£4000	
50		1a. plum (No. 89) (8.11.95)	6·50	6·00
		a. "Brltsh" for "British"...............................	£18000	£5500
		b. "Br1tish" for "British" (R. 10/12)	£600	£650
		c. "Afr1ca" for "Africa" (R. 1/11)	£800	
		d. "Briti" for "British" (R. 1/6)...................	£4250	
51		1a.6p. sepia (No. 90) (23.11.95)	4·25	4·00
		a. "Br1tish" for "British" (R. 10/12)	£650	£550
		b. "Afr1ca" for "Africa" (R. 1/11)	£850	
52		2a. blue (No. 92) (28.10.95)	9·00	3·00
		a. "Brltsh" for "British"...............................	£10000	£8500
		b. "Br1tish" for "British" (R. 10/12)	£550	£275
		c. "Afr1ca" for "Africa" (R. 1/11)	£850	£375
		d. "h" of "British" inserted by hand	£2500	
53		2a.6p. yellow-green (No. 103)	14·00	2·50
		c. "Brltsh" for "British"...............................	†	£5500
		d. "Eas" for "East" (R. 2/12)......................	£1200	£1500
		e. "Br1tish" for "British" (R. 10/12)	£750	£300
		f. "Afr1ca" for "Africa" (R. 1/11)	£950	£400
		g. "Briti" for "British" (R. 1/6)...................	£4500	
		h. Opt double...	£1200	
54		3a. brown-orange (No. 94) (18.12.95)	23·00	11·00
		a. "Br1tish" for "British" (R. 10/12)	£750	£550
		b. "Afr1ca" for "Africa" (R. 1/11)	£1100	
		c. Opt double, one albino...........................	£750	
55		4a. olive-green (No. 95) (18.12.95)	50·00	42·00
		a. *Slate-green*	28·00	28·00
		ab. "Br1tish" for "British" (R. 10/12)	£950	£650
		ac. "Afr1ca" for "Africa" (R. 1/11)	£1300	£850
56		6a. pale brown (No. 81) (18.12.95)	50·00	50·00
		a. "Br1tish" for "British" (R. 10/8)	£2000	
		b. "Afr1ca" for "Africa" (R. 1/7)	£2500	
		c. "E st" for "East"	†	—
		d. Opt double, one albino...........................	£300	
57		8a. dull mauve (No. 98) (18.12.95)	£100	70·00
		a. "Br1tish" for "British" (R. 10/12)		
		b. "Afr1ca" for "Africa" (R. 1/11)		
		c. *Magenta* (1896)	30·00	55·00
		ca. "Br1tish" for "British" (R. 10/12)	£950	£900

	cb. "Afr1ca" for "Africa" (R. 1/11)	£1100	£950
	cc. Inverted "a" for "t" of "East" (R. 2/12)	†	£25000
58	12a. purple/*red* (No. 100) (18.12.95)	22·00	38·00
	a. "Br1tish" for "British" (R. 10/12)	£850	£900
	b. "Afr1ca" for "Africa" (R. 1/11)	£1300	£1400
59	1r. slate (No. 101) (18.12.95)	£100	70·00
	a. "Br1tish" for "British" (R. 10/12)		
	b. "Afr1ca" for "Africa" (R. 1/11)		
60	1r. green and aniline carmine (No. 106) (1896)	50·00	£130
	a. Inverted "a" for "t" of "East" (R. 2/12)	£18000	
	b. "Br1tish" for "British" (R. 10/12)	£2250	
	c. "Afr1ca" for "Africa" (R. 1/11)	£2250	
	d. Opt double, one sideways	£425	£900
	e. Opt double, one albino	£750	
61	2r. carm and yellow-brown (No. 107) (18.12.95)	£120	£180
	a. "B" handstamped	£8500	£8500
62	3r. brown and green (No. 108) (18.12.95)	£140	£190
	a. "B" handstamped	£8500	£8500
	b. Opt double, one albino	£2000	
63	5r. ultramarine and violet (No. 109) (18.12.95)	£150	£200
	a. Opt double	£3500	
	b. "B" handstamped	£7500	£6500
	c. Opt double, one albino	£2000	
49/63 *Set of* 15		£650	£900

The relative horizontal positions of the three lines of the overprint vary considerably but the distance vertically between the lines of the overprint is constant.

In both the "Br1tish" and "Afr1ca" errors the figure one is in a smaller type size.

There are other varieties, such as inverted "s" in "British", wide and narrow "B", and inverted "V" for "A" in "Africa" (R. 1/1 and R. 6/7).

During the overprinting of Nos. 61/3 the "B" of "British" sometimes failed to print so that only traces of the letter appeared. It was replaced by a handstamped "B" which is often out of alignment with the rest of the overprint. The handstamp is known double.

The 2, 3 and 5r., normally overprinted in larger type than the lower values, are also known with a smaller overprint, for use as specimen stamps for the U.P.U. These were not issued for postal purposes (*Price* £475 *un per set*). The lower values were reprinted at the same time using similar type to the original overprint.

Forgeries exist.

2½

(**10**)

11

1895 (19 Dec). No. 51 surch locally with T **10** in bright red.

64	2½ on 1½a. sepia	£120	50·00
	a. Inverted "1" in fraction (R. 5/7, 10/7)	£1200	£650
	b. "Br1tish" for "British" (R. 10/12)	£1800	
	c. "Afr1ca" for "Africa" (R. 1/11)	£1800	

The setting of Type **10** was in 5 horizontal rows of 12 stamps, repeated twice for each pane.

No. 51 also exists surcharged with T **12**, **13** and **14** in brown-red. These stamps were sent to the Postal Union authorities at Berne, but were never issued to the public (*Price unused*: T **12** £110, T **13** £225, T **14** £150).

(Recess D.L.R.)

1896 (26 May)–**1901**. Wmk Crown CA. P 14.

65	**11**	½a. yellow-green	6·00	80
		x. Wmk reversed	£450	£300
66		1a. carmine-rose	15·00	40
		a. Bright rose-red	14·00	40
		b. Rosine (1901)	30·00	4·50
		w. Wmk inverted	£225	£160
		x. Wmk reversed	£350	£190
		y. Wmk inverted and reversed	†	£400
67		2a. chocolate	12·00	8·00
		x. Wmk reversed	†	£200
68		2½a. deep blue	18·00	2·50
		a. Violet-blue	25·00	3·25
		b. Inverted "S" in "ANNAS" (R. 1/1)	£250	80·00
		w. Wmk inverted	†	£325
		x. Wmk reversed	£325	£190
69		3a. grey	9·50	14·00
		x. Wmk reversed	£180	£250
70		4a. deep green	8·50	4·50
71		4½a. orange-yellow	17·00	18·00
72		5a. yellow-bistre	8·50	8·00
73		7½a. mauve	11·00	25·00
		x. Wmk reversed	†	£450
74		8a. grey-olive	11·00	7·00
75		1r. pale dull blue	80·00	27·00
		a. Ultramarine	£140	70·00
76		2r. orange	70·00	32·00
77		3r. deep violet	70·00	38·00
78		4r. carmine-lake	70·00	80·00
79		5r. sepia	70·00	42·00
		a. Thin "U" in "RUPEES" (R. 3/2)	£1800	£1400
		x. Wmk reversed	†	£800
65/79 *Set of* 15			£400	£275
65s/79s Optd "SPECIMEN" *Set of* 15			£325	

Examples of some values exist apparently without watermark or with double-lined lettering from the marginal watermark due to the paper being misplaced on the press.

(Overprinted at the offices of *The Zanzibar Gazette*)

1897 (2 Jan). Nos. 156/7, 159 and 165/7 of Zanzibar optd with T **8**. Wmk Single Rosette.

80	½a. yellow-green and red	60·00	50·00
81	1a. indigo and red	£100	95·00
82	2a. red-brown and red	50·00	23·00
83	4½a. orange and red	60·00	30·00
	a. No right serif to left-hand "4" (R. 1/1)	£1400	
	b. No fraction bar at right (R. 2/1)	£1400	£850
84	5a. bistre and red	65·00	48·00
	a. "Bri" for "British"	£2000	£2000
85	7½a. mauve and red	70·00	50·00
	a. "Bri" for "British"	£2500	
	b. Optd on front and back		
80/5 *Set of* 6		£375	£250

Nos. 84a and 85a appear to have occurred when the type was obscured during part of the overprinting.

The above six stamps exist with an overprint similar to T **8** but normally showing a stop after "Africa". These overprints (in red on the 1a.) were made officially to supply the U.P.U. (*Price* £300 *un per set*). However, the stop does not always show. Pieces are known showing overprints with and without stop *se-tenant* (including the red overprint on the 1a.).

Stamps of Zanzibar, wmk "Multiple Rosettes" and overprinted with T **8** are forgeries.

2½ (**12**) 2½ (**13**) 2½ (**14**)

SETTING OF TYPES 12/14. The setting of 60 (6×10) contained 26 examples of Type **12**, 10 of Type **13** and 24 of Type **14**.

1897 (2 Jan). Nos. 157 and 162 of Zanzibar optd with T **8** and further surch locally, in red.

86	**12**	2½ on 1a. indigo and red	£130	70·00
		b. Opt Type **8** double	£7500	
87	**13**	2½ on 1a. indigo and red	£325	£120
88	**14**	2½ on 1a. indigo and red	£150	75·00
		a. Opt Type **8** double	£7500	
89	**12**	2½ on 3a. grey and red	£130	65·00
90	**13**	2½ on 3a. grey and red	£325	£120
91	**14**	2½ on 3a. grey and red	£150	70·00
86/91 *Set of* 6			£1100	£475

Both the notes after No. 85 also apply here.

A special printing for U.P.U. requirements was made with the 2½ surcharge on the 1a. and 3a. stamps overprinted as T **8** but *with stop* after "Africa". It also included a "2" over "1" error in T **14**. (*Price*, £2500, either value).

15

(Recess D.L.R.)

1897 (Nov)–**1903**. Wmk Crown CC. P 14.

92	**15**	1r. grey-blue	£120	48·00
		a. Dull blue (1901)	£100	60·00
		b. Bright ultramarine (1903)	£550	£400
93		2r. orange	£140	£150
94		3r. deep violet	£180	£190
95		4r. carmine	£500	£550
		x. Wmk reversed	£850	£950
		y. Wmk inverted and reversed	£1600	
96		5r. deep sepia	£450	£550
97		10r. yellow-bistre	£450	£600
		s. Optd "SPECIMEN"	85·00	
		x. Wmk reversed	£1400	
98		20r. pale green (f.c. £110)	£1200	£2500
		s. Optd "SPECIMEN"	£150	
99		50r. mauve (f.c. £300)	£2500	£9000
		s. Optd "SPECIMEN"	£375	
		x. Wmk reversed	£2750	£9000
		xs. Optd "SPECIMEN"	£400	
92s/6s Optd "SPECIMEN" *Set of* 5			£250	

On 1 April 1901 the postal administrations of British East Africa and Uganda were merged. Subsequent issues were inscribed "EAST AFRICA AND UGANDA PROTECTORATES".

EAST AFRICA AND UGANDA PROTECTORATES

For earlier issues see BRITISH EAST AFRICA and UGANDA.
For the issues of the Mandated Territory of Tanganyika and the war-time issues that preceded them, see TANGANYIKA.

PRICES FOR STAMPS ON COVER TO 1945	
Nos. 1/43	from × 3
Nos. 44/75	from × 2
Nos. 76/95	from × 3
Nos. 96/105	—
Nos. 110/23	from × 2
Nos. 124/7	from × 3
Nos. 128/30	from × 5
Nos. 131/54	from × 3
Nos. D1/12	from × 8

PRINTERS. All the stamps issued between 1903 and 1927 were typographed by De La Rue & Co. Ltd, London.

USED HIGH VALUES. Beware of cleaned fiscally cancelled examples with faked postmarks.

1

2

1903 (24 July)–**04**. P 14.

(a) Wmk Crown CA

1	**1**	½a. green (16.2.04)	5·00	20·00
2		1a. grey and red	1·75	1·25
3		2a. dull and bright purple (24.7.03)	8·50	2·50
		w. Wmk inverted	£200	£180
4		2½a. blue	12·00	50·00
5		3a. brown-purple and green	26·00	65·00
6		4a. grey-green and black	11·00	22·00
7		5a. grey and orange-brown	19·00	50·00
8		8a. grey and pale blue	25·00	48·00

(b) Wmk Crown CC. Ordinary paper

9	**2**	1r. green	24·00	60·00
		a. Chalk-surfaced paper	80·00	£120
10		2r. dull and bright purple	80·00	90·00
11		3r. grey-green and black	£150	£250
12		4r. grey and emerald-green	£150	£275
13		5r. grey and red	£150	£275
14		10r. grey and ultramarine	£400	£550
		a. Chalk-surfaced paper	£500	£600
		w. Wmk inverted	£1000	
15		20r. grey and stone	£700	£1700
		s. Optd "SPECIMEN"	£160	
16		50r. grey and red-brown (f.c. £200)	£2000	£4000
		s. Optd "SPECIMEN"	£400	
		w. Wmk inverted (f.c. £500)	£4750	£500
1/13	*Set of 13*		£600	£1100
1s/14s	Optd "SPECIMEN" *Set of 14*		£450	

1904–07. Wmk Mult Crown CA. Ordinary paper (½a. to 8a.) or chalk-surfaced paper (1r. to 50r.).

17	**1**	½a. grey-green	8·50	3·00
		a. Chalk-surfaced paper	13·00	3·25
18		1a. grey and red	8·00	80
		a. Chalk-surfaced paper	14·00	1·75
19		2a. dull and bright purple	3·25	2·75
		a. Chalk-surfaced paper	3·50	2·75
20		2½a. blue	8·00	30·00
21		2½a. ultramarine and blue	7·50	17·00
22		3a. brown-purple and green	3·75	42·00
		a. Chalk-surfaced paper	4·25	45·00
23		4a. grey-green and black	7·50	18·00
		a. Chalk-surfaced paper	8·00	18·00
24		5a. grey and orange-brown	8·00	15·00
		a. Chalk-surfaced paper	6·50	30·00
25		8a. grey and pale blue	7·00	8·50
		a. Chalk-surfaced paper	7·00	21·00
26	**2**	1r. green (1907)	29·00	70·00
		w. Wmk inverted	£1100	£800
27		2r. dull and bright purple (1906)	42·00	65·00
28		3r. grey-green and black (1907)	85·00	£130
29		4r. grey and emerald-green (1907)	£110	£180
		w. Wmk inverted	£900	

30		5r. grey and red (1907)	£150	£170
31		10r. grey and ultramarine (1907)	£325	£375
		w. Wmk inverted	£950	£1000
32		20r. grey and stone (1907)	£750	£1300
33		50r. grey and red-brown (1907)		
		(f.c. £400)	£2500	£4000
17/30	*Set of 13*		£425	£650

(New Currency. 100 cents = 1 rupee)

1907–08. Wmk Mult Crown CA. Chalk-surfaced paper (10, 12, 25, 50, 75c.). P 14.

34	**1**	1c. brown	2·50	15
35		3c. grey-green	19·00	70
		a. Blue-green	24·00	4·00
36		6c. red	3·00	10
37		10c. lilac and pale olive	10·00	8·50
38		12c. dull and bright purple	10·00	2·75
39		15c. bright blue	28·00	8·50
40		25c. grey-green and black	20·00	7·00
41		50c. grey-green and orange-brown	15·00	14·00
42		75c. grey and pale blue (1908)	4·50	42·00
34/42	*Set of 9*		£100	75·00
34s/42s	Optd "SPECIMEN" *Set of 9*		£250	

Original

Redrawn

1910. T **1** redrawn. Printed from a single plate. Wmk Mult Crown CA. P 14.

43		6c. red	23·00	30

In the redrawn type a fine white line has been cut around the value tablets and above the name tablet separating the latter from the leaves above, EAST AFRICA AND UGANDA is in shorter and thicker letters and PROTECTORATES in taller letters than in No. 36

3

4

**4
cents**
(5)

1912–21. Wmk Mult Crown CA. Chalk-surfaced paper (25c. to 500r.). P 14.

44	**3**	1c. black	30	1·75
45		3c. green	2·00	60
		a. Deep blue-green (1917)	4·50	1·75
		w. Wmk inverted	†	—
46		6c. red	1·25	40
		a. Scarlet (1917)	24·00	3·00
		w. Wmk inverted	—	£600
		y. Wmk inverted and reversed	—	£600
47		10c. yellow-orange	2·00	50
		a. Orange (1921)	13·00	6·00
		w. Wmk inverted	£650	
48		12c. slate-grey	2·75	50
		a. Wmk sideways		
49		15c. bright blue	2·75	80
		w. Wmk inverted	†	£600
50		25c. black and red/yellow	50	1·25
		a. White back (5.14)	50	4·50
		as. Optd "SPECIMEN"	38·00	
		b. On lemon (1916)	11·00	11·00
		bs. Optd "SPECIMEN"	42·00	
		c. On orange-buff (1921)	48·00	18·00
		d. On pale yellow (1921)	14·00	7·00
51		50c. black and lilac	1·50	1·25
52		75c. black/green	1·50	17·00
		a. White back (5.14)	1·00	16·00
		as. Optd "SPECIMEN"	40·00	
		b. On blue-green, olive back	8·00	7·50
		bs. Optd "SPECIMEN"	48·00	
		c. On emerald, olive back (1919)	45·00	£150
		d. On emerald back (1921)	12·00	60·00
53	**4**	1r. black/green	1·75	4·25
		aw. Wmk inverted	£700	
		b. On emerald back (1919)	5·00	50·00
54		2r. red and black/blue	22·00	38·00
		w. Wmk inverted	£425	
55		3r. violet and green	27·00	£110
56		4r. red and green/yellow	55·00	£100
		a. On pale yellow	£130	£190
57		5r. blue and dull purple	60·00	£150
58		10r. red and green/green	£225	£350
59		20r. black and purple/red	£450	£450
60		20r. purple and blue/blue (1918)	£500	£750

61		50r. dull rose-red and dull greyish green (f.c. £75)		£850	£900
		a. Carmine and green		£1200	£1200
		s. Optd "SPECIMEN"		£250	
62		100r. purple and black/red (f.c. £250)		£8500	£3250
		s. Optd "SPECIMEN"		£550	
63		500r. green and red/green (f.c. £750)		£35000	
		s. Optd "SPECIMEN"		£1100	
44/58 Set of 15				£350	£700
44s/60s Optd "SPECIMEN" Set of 17				£800	

For values in this series overprinted "G.E.A." (German East Africa) see Tanganyika Nos. 45/62.

1919 (7 Apr). No. 46a surch with T **5** by the Swift Press, Nairobi.

64	**3**	4c. on 6c. scarlet (shades)	1·25	15
		a. Bars omitted	50·00	70·00
		b. Surch double	£140	£250
		c. Surch inverted	£325	£425
		d. Pair, one without surch	£2000	£2250
		e. Surch on back	£450	
		s. Handstamped "SPECIMEN"	60·00	

1921–22. Wmk Mult Script CA. Chalk-surfaced paper (50c. to 50r.). P 14.

65	**3**	1c. black	80	1·75
		w. Wmk inverted	£425	£425
66		3c. green	6·00	13·00
		a. Blue-green	23·00	18·00
67		6c. carmine-red	9·00	18·00
68		10c. orange (12.21)	8·50	1·25
		w. Wmk inverted	†	£600
69		12c. slate-grey	9·00	£140
70		15c. bright blue	11·00	20·00
71		50c. black and dull purple	14·00	£120
72	**4**	2r. red and black/blue	75·00	£180
73		3r. violet and green	£150	£375
74		5r. blue and dull purple	£180	£300
75		50r. carmine and green (f.c. £400)	£3000	£8000
		s. Optd "SPECIMEN"	£475	
65/74 Set of 10			£425	£1000
65s/74s Optd "SPECIMEN" Set of 10			£375	

For values in this series overprinted "G.E.A." see Tanganyika Nos. 63/73.

KENYA AND UGANDA
(New Currency. 100 cents = 1 East Africa shilling)

On 23 July 1920, Kenya became a Crown Colony with the exception of the coastal strip, previously part of the Sultan of Zanzibar's territories, which remained a protectorate.

The northern province of Jubaland was ceded to Italy on 29 June 1925 and later incorporated into Italian Somaliland.

6	**7**

1922 (1 Nov)–**27**. Wmk Mult Script CA. P 14.

(a) Wmk upright. Ordinary paper

76	**6**	1c. pale brown	1·00	4·25
		a. Deep brown (1923)	1·50	3·50
		ax. Wmk reversed	£325	
77		5c. dull violet	5·50	75
		a. Bright violet	11·00	1·50
78		5c. green (1927)	2·00	30
79		10c. green	1·50	30
		w. Wmk inverted		
80		10c. black (5.27)	4·00	20
81		12c. jet-black	12·00	38·00
		a. Grey-black	12·00	26·00
82		15c. rose-carmine	1·25	10
83		20c. dull orange-yellow	3·25	10
		a. Bright orange	6·00	10
84		30c. ultramarine	4·25	50
85		50c. grey	2·50	10
86		75c. olive	9·00	9·00

(b) Wmk sideways. Chalk-surfaced paper*

87	**7**	1s. green	5·50	2·50
88		2s. dull purple	8·00	18·00
		w. Wmk Crown to right of CA	£180	£250
89		2s.50 brown (1.10.25)	19·00	£110
90		3s. brownish grey	18·00	6·50
		a. Jet-black	55·00	50·00
91		4s. grey (1.10.25)	35·00	£120
		w. Wmk Crown to right of CA	75·00	£225
92		5s. carmine-red	24·00	22·00
		w. Wmk Crown to right of CA	—	£500
93		7s.50 orange-yellow (1.10.25)	£120	£275

94		10s. bright blue		70·00	70·00
		w. Wmk Crown to right of CA (f.c. £275)			
95		£1 black and orange (f.c. £20)		£200	£300
96		£2 green and purple (1.10.25) (f.c. £150)		£1000	£1800
		s. Optd "SPECIMEN"		£275	
97		£3 purple and yellow (1.10.25) (f.c. £250)		£1600	
		s. Optd "SPECIMEN"		£325	
98		£4 black and magenta (1.10.25) (f.c. £275)		£2750	
		s. Optd "SPECIMEN"		£425	
99		£5 black and blue (f.c. £120)		£3000	
		s. Optd "SPECIMEN"		£475	
		w. Wmk Crown to right of CA		£3250	
100		£10 black and green (f.c. £325)		£13000	
		s. Optd "SPECIMEN"		£700	
		w. Wmk Crown to right of CA (f.c. £375)		£22000	
101		£20 red and green (1.10.25) (f.c. £800)		£27000	
		s. Optd "SPECIMEN"		£1100	
102		£25 black and red (f.c. £475)		£35000	
		s. Optd "SPECIMEN"		£1200	
		w. Wmk Crown to right of CA		£45000	
103		£50 black and brown (f.c. £650)		£45000	
		s. Optd "SPECIMEN"		£1500	
104		£75 purple and grey (1.10.25) (f.c. £3000)		£130000	
		s. Optd "SPECIMEN"		£3000	
105		£100 black and red (1.10.25) (f.c. £2000)		£140000	
		s. Optd "SPECIMEN"		£3250	
76/95 Set of 20				£475	£850
76s/95s Optd "SPECIMEN" Set of 20				£750	

Nos. 87/94 were printed in two operations sometimes causing shade differences between the head and the frame.

*The normal sideways watermark shows Crown to left of CA, as seen from the back of the stamp.

KENYA, UGANDA AND TANGANYIKA

The postal administrations of Kenya, Tanganyika and Uganda were amalgamated on 1 January 1933. On the independence of the three territories the combined administration became the East African Posts and Telecommunications Corporation.

8 South African Crowned Cranes   **9** Dhow on Lake Victoria

10 Lion   **11** Kilimanjaro

12 Nile Railway Bridge, Ripon Falls   **13** Mt. Kenya

14 Lake Naivasha   I   II

(Des 1c., 20c., 10s., R. C. Luck, 10c., £1, A. Ross, 15c., 2s., G. Gill Holmes, 30c., 5s., R. N. Ambasana, 65c., L. R. Cutts. T **10** typo, remainder recess D.L.R.).

1935 (1 May)–37. Wmk Mult Script CA. Chalk-surfaced paper (10c., £1). P 12×13 (**10**), 14 (**9** and **14**) and 13 (remainder).

110	**8**	1c. black and red-brown	1·00	1·50
111	**9**	5c. black and green (I)	3·25	20
		a. Rope joined to sail (II) (1937)	35·00	7·50
		b. Perf 13×12 (I)	£9000	£950
		ba. Rope joined to sail (II) (1937)	£800	£225
112	**10**	10c. black and yellow	6·50	60
113	**11**	15c. black and scarlet	3·50	10
		a. Frame double, one albino	†	—
114	**8**	20c. black and orange	3·50	20
115	**12**	30c. black and blue	4·75	1·00
116	**9**	50c. bright purple and black (I)	5·00	10
117	**13**	65c. black and brown	7·00	2·00
118	**14**	1s. black and green	5·00	1·00
		a. Perf 13×12 (1936)	£1400	£130
119	**11**	2s. lake and purple	12·00	4·50
120	**14**	3s. blue and black	17·00	15·00
		a. Perf 13×12 (1936)	£2250	
121	**12**	5s. black and carmine	25·00	27·00
122	**8**	10s. purple and blue	95·00	£120
123	**10**	£1 black and red	£275	£375
110/23		Set of 14	£400	£500
110s/23s		Perf "SPECIMEN" Set of 14	£475	

14a Windsor Castle

Diagonal line by turret (Plate 2A R. 10/1 and 10/2)

Dot to left of chapel (Plate 2B R. 8/3)

Dot by flagstaff (Plate 4 R. 8/4)

Dash by turret (Plate 4 R. 3/6)

Line through "0" of 1910 (R. 4/2)

(Des H. Fleury. Recess D.L.R.)

1935 (6 May). Silver Jubilee. Wmk Mult Script CA. P 13½×14.

124		20c. light blue and olive-green	2·00	10
		f. Diagonal line by turret	£120	50·00
		g. Dot to left of chapel	£250	90·00
		h. Dot by flagstaff	£250	90·00
		i. Dash by turret	£325	£120
125		30c. brown and deep blue	3·00	3·00
		f. Diagonal line by turret	£200	£225
		g. Dot to left of chapel	£475	
		h. Dot by flagstaff	£475	
		i. Dash by turret	£500	
126		65c. green and indigo	2·00	2·75
		f. Diagonal line by turret	£250	

127		g. Dot to left of chapel	£425	£450
		1s. slate and purple	2·25	5·50
		f. Diagonal line by turret	£225	£300
		g. Dot to left of chapel	£475	
		h. Dot by flagstaff	£475	
		l. Line through "0" of 1910	£140	£180
124/7		Set of 4	8·25	10·00
124s/7s		Perf "SPECIMEN" Set of 4	£160	

For illustrations of the other plate varieties see Omnibus section following Zanzibar.

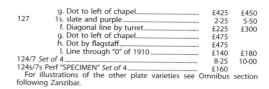
14b King George VI and Queen Elizabeth

Broken leaf (R. 6/1)

(Des and recess D.L.R)

1937 (12 May). Coronation. Wmk Mult Script CA. P 11×11½.

128	**14b**	5c. green	20	10
129		20c. orange	40	30
		a. Broken leaf	65·00	
130		30c. bright blue	60	1·75
128/30		Set of 3	1·10	1·90
128s/30s		Perf "Specimen" Set of 3	£140	

15 Dhow on Lake Victoria

Damaged left-hand value tablet (Frame Pl 2–2, with Centre Pl 4A or 4B, R. 9/6)

Retouched value tablet (Frame Pl 2–2, with Centre Pls 4A, 4B, 5, 6 or 7, R. 9/6)

1c. 'Tadpole' flaw (Frame Pl 2–2, with centre Pl 4B R. 10/8)

1c. Break in bird's breast (Frame Pl 2–2, with Centre Pls 4A or 4B, R. 2/5)

Sky retouch (Pl 7A, R. 10/6)

Damage on mountain (Pl 7B, R. 6/7. August 1948 ptg. Retouched in June 1949 for 10c. and 1s.)

10c., 1s. Mountain retouch (Covering the peak and the slopes to the left) (Pl 7B, R. 6/7)

10c., 1s. Mountain retouch (Covering the peak and the hills to its right) (Pl 7B, R. 5/10)

50c. With dot    Dot removed

In the 50c. printing of 14 June 1950 using Frame-plate 3, the dot was removed by retouching on all but five stamps (R. 5/2, 6/1, 7/2, 7/4 and 9/1). In addition, other stamps show traces of the dot where the retouching was not completely effective.

PERFORATIONS. In this issue, to aid identification, the perforations are indicated to the nearest quarter.

(T **10** typo, others recess D.L.R.)

1938 (11 Apr)–54. As T **8** to **14** (but with portrait of King George VI in place of King George V, as in T **15**). Wmk Mult Script CA. Chalk-surfaced paper (£1).

131	**8**	1c. black & red-brown (P 13¼) (2.5.38).	4·75	85
		a. Perf 13¼×13¾. *Black and chocolate-brown* (1942)	30	50
		ab. "A" of "CA" missing from wmk	£300	
		ac. Damaged value tablet	£100	
		ad. Retouched value tablet	45·00	70·00

		ae. Break in bird's breast	90·00	
		af. 'Tadpole' flaw	£100	£200
		ag. *Black and deep chocolate-brown* (10.6.46)	2·25	3·50
		ah. Ditto. Retouched value tablet	50·00	80·00
		ai. *Black and red-brown* (26.9.51)	7·00	6·50
132	**15**	5c. black and green (II) (P 13×11¾)	5·00	50
133		5c. reddish brown and orange (P 13×11¾) (1.6.49)	2·00	6·00
		a. Perf 13×12½ (14.6.50)	3·50	4·00
134	**14**	10c. red-brown and orange (P 13×11¾) (2.5.38)	2·25	10
		aw. Wmk inverted	†	£2750
		b. Perf 14 (22.4.41)	£130	8·50
135		10c. black and green (P 13×11¾) (1.6.49)	30	2·00
		a. Mountain retouch (R. 6/7)	95·00	£130
		ab. Mountain retouch (R. 5/10)	£450	£550
		b. Sky retouch	£200	
		c. Perf 13×12½ (14.6.50)	4·25	10
136		10c. brown and grey (P 13×12½) (1.4.52)	1·75	55
137	**11**	15c. black and rose-red (P 13¼) (2.5.38)	32·00	55
		a. Perf 13¾×13¼ (2.43)	6·50	3·75
		ab. "A" of "CA" missing from wmk	£1700	
138		15c. black and green (P 13¾ × 13¼) (1.4.52)	3·00	6·00
139	**8**	20c. black and orange (P 13¼) (2.5.38).	42·00	30
		a. Perf 14 (19.5.41)	55·00	1·75
		b. Perf 13¼×13¾ (25.2.42)	9·50	10
		ba. *Deep black and deep orange* (21.6.51)	28·00	2·25
		bw. Wmk inverted	†	
140	**15**	25c. black and carmine-red (P 13×12½) (1.4.52)	1·75	2·25
141	**12**	30c. black and dull violet-blue (P 13¼) (2.5.38)	55·00	40
		a. Perf 14 (3.7.41)	£160	11·00
		b. Perf 13¼×13¾ (10.5.42)	3·25	10
142		30c. dull purple and brown (P 13¼ × 13¾) (1.4.52)	1·75	40
143	**8**	40c. black and blue (P 13¼×13¾) (1.4.52)	1·75	3·50
144	**15**	50c. purple and black (II) (P 13×11¾) (2.5.38)	21·00	1·00
		a. Rope not joined to sail (I) (R. 2/5).	£300	£250
		b. *Dull claret and black* (29.7.47)	£110	11·00
		c. *Brown-purple and black* (4.48)	£120	10·00
		d. *Reddish purple and black* (28.4.49).	50·00	6·50
		e. Ditto. Perf 13×12½ (10.49)	11·00	55
		ea. Dot removed (14.6.50)	28·00	55
		eb. Ditto. In pair with normal	£500	£140
		ew. Wmk inverted	†	£4750
145	**14**	1s. black and yellowish brown (P 13×11¾) (2.5.38)	32·00	30
		a. *Black and brown* (9.42)	18·00	30
		ab. Damage on mountain	—	£1100
		ac. Mountain retouch (R. 6/7)	£1400	£475
		ad. Mountain retouch (R. 5/10)	£2750	£650
		aw. Wmk inverted	†	£3750
		b. Perf 13×12½ (10.49)	19·00	60
		ba. *Deep black and brown* (clearer impression) (14.6.50)	40·00	2·25
146	**11**	2s. lake-brown & brown-purple (P 13¼) (*shades*) (2.5.38)	£130	2·75
		a. Perf 14 (1941)	80·00	17·00
		b. Perf 13¾×13¼ (24.2.44)	48·00	30
147	**14**	3s. dull ultramarine and black (P 13×11¾) (2.5.38)	50·00	8·00
		a. *Deep violet-blue and black* (29.4.47)	85·00	16·00
		ab. Damage on mountain	£5000	£2250
		ac. Perf 13×12½ (14.6.50)	50·00	8·00
148	**12**	5s. black and carmine (P 13¼) (2.5.38)	£150	19·00
		a. Perf 14 (1941)	50·00	2·75
		b. Perf 13¼×13¾ (24.2.44)	50·00	1·75
149	**8**	10s. purple and blue (P 13¼) (2.5.38)	£140	30·00
		a. Perf 14. *Reddish purple and blue* (1941)	50·00	22·00
		b. Perf 13¼×13¾ (24.2.44)	55·00	7·50
150	**10**	£1 black and red (P 11¾ × 13) (12.10.38)	£500	£160
		a. Perf 14 (1941)	40·00	24·00
		ab. Ordinary paper (24.2.44)	40·00	24·00
		b. Perf 12½ (21.1.54)	18·00	40·00
		131/50a (*cheapest*) Set of 20	£250	50·00
		131s/50s Perf "SPECIMEN" Set of 13	£950	

No. 131ab occurs once in some sheets, always in the sixth vertical row.

The two varieties described as 'Mountain retouch', Nos. 135a/ab and 145ac/ad, are found on printings from June 1949 onwards.

The first printing of the 50c. utilised the King George V centre plate on which each impression had been individually corrected to show the rope joined to sail. R. 2/5 was missed, however, and this continued to show Type I until replaced by a further printing from a new plate in September 1938.

Stamps perf 14, together with Nos. 131a, 137a, 139b, 141b, 146b, 148b and 149b, are the result of air raid damage to the De La Rue works which destroyed the normal perforators. Dates quoted for these stamps represent earliest known postmarks.

10c
KENYA
TANGANYIKA
UGANDA
(16)

70c. on 1s. A screw head in the surcharging forme appears as a crescent moon (R. 20/4)

1941 (1 July)–**42**. Pictorial Stamps of South Africa variously surch as T **16** by Government Printer, Pretoria. Inscr alternately in English and Afrikaans.

		Unused pair	Used pair	Used single
151	5c. on 1d. grey and carmine (No. 56)	1·75	1·75	15
152	10c. on 3d. ultramarine (No. 59)	6·00	9·00	30
153	20c. on 6d. green and vermilion (No. 61c)	4·00	3·50	20
154	70c. on 1s. brown and chalky blue (No. 62) (20.4.42)	22·00	5·00	45
	a. Crescent moon flaw	70·00	75·00	
151/4 Set of 4		30·00	17·00	1·00
151s/4s Handstamped "SPECIMEN" Set of 4 pairs		£650		

16a Houses of Parliament, London

1946 (11 Nov). Victory. As Nos. 110/11 of Antigua.

155	**16a**	20c. red-orange	50	10
156		30c. blue	50	75
155s/6s Perf "SPECIMEN" Set of 2			£120	

Examples of Nos. 155/6 were pre-released at Lindi on 15 October 1946.

16b King George VI and Queen Elizabeth

16c

1948 (1 Dec). Royal Silver Wedding. As Nos. 112/13 of Antigua.

157	**16b**	20c. orange	40	30
158	**16c**	£1 scarlet	50·00	70·00

16d Hermes, Globe and Forms of Transport

16e Hemispheres, Jet-powered Vickers Viking Airliner and Steamer

16f Hermes and Globe

16g U.P.U. Monument

1949 (10 Oct). 75th Anniv of Universal Postal Union. Wmk Mult Script CA.

159	**16d**	20c. red-orange	15	10
160	**16e**	30c. deep blue	1·75	2·25
16f		a. "A" of "CA" missing from wmk	£1100	
161	**16g**	50c. grey	45	60
162		1s. red-brown	50	40
159/62 Set of 4			2·50	3·00

17 Lake Naivasha

17a Queen Elizabeth II

(Recess D.L.R.)

1952 (1 Feb). Visit of Princess Elizabeth and Duke of Edinburgh. Wmk Mult Script CA. P 13×12½.

163	**17**	10c. black and green	30	1·50
164		1s. black and brown	1·60	2·00

1953 (2 June). Coronation. As No 120 of Antigua.

165		20c. black and red-orange	30	10

1954 (28 Apr). Royal Visit. As No. 171 but inscr "ROYAL VISIT 1954" below portrait.

166		30c. black and deep ultramarine	75	30

18 Owen Falls Dam

19 Giraffe

20 African Elephants

21 Lion

22 Mount Kilimanjaro

23 Royal Lodge, Sagana

24 Queen Elizabeth II

(Des G. Gill Holmes (10, 50c.), H. Grieme (15c, 1s.30, 5s.),
R. McLellan Sim (10s.), De La Rue (65c, 2s., £1), O.C. Meronti (others).
Recess D.L.R.)

1954 (1 June)–**59**. Designs as T **18/24**. Wmk Mult Script CA. P 13 (£1);
others, 12½×13 (vert) or 13×12½ (horiz).

167	18	5c. black and deep brown	1·75	50
		a. Vignette inverted	†	£60000
168	19	10c. carmine-red	2·25	10
169	20	15c. black and light blue (28.3.58)	1·50	1·50
		a. Redrawn. Stop below "c" of "15 c" (29.4.59)	1·00	1·25
170	21	20c. black and orange	2·00	10
		a. Imperf (pair)	£1500	£1700
171	18	30c. black and deep ultramarine	1·50	10
		a. Vignette inverted	†	£30000
172	20	40c. bistre-brown (28.3.58)	1·25	75
		w. Wmk inverted		
173	19	50c. reddish purple	3·50	10
		a. Claret (23.1.57)	8·50	40
174	22	65c. bluish green & brown-purple (1.12.55)	2·75	1·50
175	21	1s. black and claret	3·75	10
176	20	1s.30 deep lilac and orange (1.12.55)	18·00	10
177	22	2s. black and green	16·00	1·25
		a. Black and bronze-green (19.4.56)	25·00	2·75
178	20	5s. black and orange	35·00	3·50
179	23	10s. black and deep ultramarine	42·00	5·50
180	24	£1 brown-red and black	19·00	22·00
		a. Venetian red and black (19.4.56)	65·00	27·00
167/80		Set of 14	£130	32·00

Only one example of No. 167a and three of No. 171a have been
found, all being used.

The 5, 10 and 50c. exist from coils made up from normal sheets.

25 Map of E. Africa
showing Lakes

(Recess Waterlow)

1958 (30 July). Centenary of Discovery of Lakes Tanganyika and
Victoria by Burton and Speke. W w **12**. P 12½.

181	25	40c. blue and deep green	1·00	40
182		1s.30 green and violet	1·00	1·60

26 Sisal   **27** Cotton

28 Mt Kenya and Giant Plants   **29** Queen Elizabeth II

5c. "Snake" variety (Pl 2, R. 6/2)

15c. Serif at left of base of "Y" in
"TANGANYIKA" (Pl 1, R. 2/7). This was later
retouched but traces still remain

1s. Re-entry. Whole of "TANGANYIKA" is doubled (Pl 1-1 and 1-2,
R. 9/4).

(Des M. Goaman. Photo (5c. to 65c.), recess (others) D.L.R.)

1960 (1 Oct)–**62**. Designs as T **26/9**. W w **12**. P 15×14 (5c. to 65c.), 13
(20s.) or 14 (others).

183		5c. Prussian blue	10	15
		a. "Snake" variety (Pl 2, R. 6/2)	£140	
184		10c. yellow-green	10	10
185		15c. dull purple	30	10
		a. "Serif" variety	14·00	
		b. "Serif" retouched	14·00	
186		20c. magenta	20	10
187		25c. bronze-green	3·25	1·25
188		30c. vermilion	15	10
189		40c. greenish blue	15	20
190		50c. slate-violet	15	10
191		65c. yellow-olive	30	2·00
192		1s. deep reddish violet and reddish purple	1·50	10
		a. Blackish lilac and reddish purple (23.1.62)	14·00	1·50
		b. Re-entry	38·00	
193		1s.30 chocolate and brown-red	6·50	15
194		2s. deep grey-blue and greenish blue	9·00	40
195		2s.50 olive-green and deep bluish green	11·00	2·75
196		5s. rose-red and purple	4·75	60
197		10s. blackish green and olive-green	16·00	7·00
		a. Imperf (pair)	£1700	
198		20s. violet-blue and lake	28·00	30·00
183/98		Set of 16	70·00	40·00

Designs: Vert as T **26/7**—15c. Coffee; 20c. Blue Wildebeest; 25c.
Ostrich; 30c. Thomson's Gazelle; 40c. Manta; 50c. Common Zebra; 65c.
Cheetah. Horiz as T **28**—1s.30, Murchison Falls and Hippopotamus;
2s. Mt Kilimanjaro and Giraffe; 2s.50, Candelabra Tree and Black
Rhinoceros; 5s. Crater Lake and Mountains of the Moon; 10s.
Ngorongoro Crater and African Buffalo.

The 10c. and 50c. exist in coils with the designs slightly shorter
in height, a wider horizontal gutter every eleven stamps and, in the
case of the 10c. only, printed with a coarser 200 screen instead of the
normal 250. (Price for 10c., 10p. unused.) Plate 2 of 30c. shows coarser
200 screen. (Price 25p. unused.).

PRINTERS. All the following stamps were printed in photogravure by
Harrison, unless otherwise stated.

30 Land Tillage

(Des V. Whiteley)

1963 (21 Mar). Freedom from Hunger. T **30** and similar horiz design.
P 14½.

199	30	15c. blue and yellow-olive	30	10
200	–	30c. red-brown and yellow	45	10
201	30	50c. blue and orange-brown	60	10
202	–	1s.30 red-brown and light blue	1·10	1·75
199/202		Set of 4	2·25	1·75

Design:—30c., 1s.30, African with Corncob.

31 Scholars and Open Book

1963 (28 June). Founding of East African University. P 14½.

203	**31**	30c. lake, violet, black and greenish blue..	10	10
204		1s.30 lake, blue, red and light yellow-brown	20	30

32 Red Cross Emblem

(Des V. Whiteley)

1963 (2 Sept). Centenary of Red Cross. P 14½.

205	**32**	30c. red and blue..	1·50	30
206		50c. red and yellow-brown	1·75	1·25

33 Chrysanthemum Emblems   **34**

... (East African "Flags")

35 East African "Flags"

(Des V. Whiteley)

1964 (21 Oct). Olympic Games: Tokyo. P 14½.

207	**33**	30c. yellow and reddish violet..................	15	10
208	**34**	50c. deep reddish violet and yellow......	20	10
209	**35**	1s.30 orange-yellow, deep green and light blue	50	10
210		2s.50 magenta, deep violet-blue and light blue	60	2·50
207/10 *Set of 4*..			1·25	2·50

KENYA, UGANDA AND TANZANIA

The following stamps were issued by the East African Postal Administration for use in Uganda, Kenya and Tanzania, excluding Zanzibar.

36 Rally Badge   **37** Cars *en route*

1965 (15 Apr*). 13th East African Safari Rally. P 14.

211	**36**	30c. black, yellow and turquoise............	10	10
212		50c. black, yellow and brown	10	10
		a. Imperf (pair)......................................	£850	
213	**37**	1s.30 deep bluish green, yellow-ochre and blue	35	10
214		2s.50 deep bluish green, brown-red and light blue..	60	2·00
211/14 *Set of 4*			1·00	2·00

*This is the local release date. The Crown Agents in London issued the stamps the previous day.

38 I.T.U. Emblem and Symbols

1965 (17 May). I.T.U. Centenary. P 14½.

215	**38**	30c. gold, chocolate and magenta	20	10
216		50c. gold, chocolate and grey	30	10
217		1s.30 gold, chocolate and blue	60	10
218		2s.50 gold, chocolate and turquoise-green	1·10	2·25
215/18 *Set of 4*..			2·00	2·25

39 I.C.Y. Emblem

1965 (4 Aug). International Co-operation Year. P 14½×14.

219	**39**	30c. deep bluish green and gold...........	20	10
220		50c. black and gold..................................	25	10
221		1s.30 ultramarine and gold.......................	50	10
222		2s.50 carmine-red and gold.....................	1·00	3·50
219/22 *Set of 4*..			1·75	3·50

40 Game Park Lodge, Tanzania

(Des Rena Fennessy)

1966 (4 Apr). Tourism. T **40** and similar horiz designs. Multicoloured. P 14½.

223		30c. Type **40**...	50	10
224		50c. Murchison Falls, Uganda..................	65	10
		a. Blue omitted......................................	£425	
225		1s.30 Lesser Flamingoes, Lake Nakuru, Kenya	3·00	30
226		2s.50 Deep Sea Fishing, Tanzania	2·00	2·25
223/6 *Set of 4*..			5·50	3·00

41 Games Emblem

(Des Harrison)

1966 (2 Aug). Eighth British Empire and Commonwealth Games: Jamaica. P 14½.

227	**41**	30c. black, gold, turq-green & grey........	10	10
228		50c. black, gold, cobalt and cerise........	15	10
229		1s.30 black, gold, rosine and deep bluish green	20	10
230		2s.50 black, gold, lake and ultramarine ..	35	1·50
227/30 *Set of 4*..			70	1·50

42 U.N.E.S.C.O. Emblem

(Des Harrison)

1966 (3 Oct). 20th Anniv of U.N.E.S.C.O. P 14½×14.
231	**42**	30c. black, emerald and red	65	10
232		50c. black, emerald and light brown.......	75	10
233		1s.30 black, emerald and grey..................	1·75	20
234		2s.50 black, emerald and yellow................	2·50	6·00
231/4	*Set of 4*		5·00	6·00

43 de Havilland DH.89 Dragon Rapide

(Des R. Granger Barrett)

1967 (23 Jan). 21st Anniv of East African Airways. T **43** and similar horiz designs. P 14½.
235	30c. slate-violet, greenish blue and myrtle-green	30	10
236	50c. multicoloured	40	10
	a. Red omitted..	£700	
237	1s.30 multicoloured	85	30
238	2s.50 multicoloured	1·25	3·00
235/8	*Set of 4*	2·50	3·00

Designs:—50c. Vickers Super VC-10; 1s.30, Hawker Siddeley Comet 4B; 2s.50, Fokker F.27 Friendship.

44 Pillar Tomb   **45** Rock Painting

(Des Rena Fennessy)

1967 (2 May). Archaeological Relics. T **44/5** and similar designs. P 14½.
239	30c. ochre, black and deep reddish purple ..	15	10
240	50c. orange-red, black and greyish brown....	65	10
241	1s.30 black, greenish yellow and deep yellow-green	85	15
242	2s.50 black, ochre and brown-red......................	1·40	2·50
239/42	*Set of 4*	2·75	3·00

Designs:—1s.30, Clay head; 2s.50, Proconsul skull.

48 Unified Symbols of Kenya, Tanzania, and Uganda

(Des Rena Fennessy)

1967 (1 Dec). Foundation of East African Community. P 14½×14.
243	**48**	5s. gold, black and grey...........................	40	1·50

49 Mountaineering

(Des Rena Fennessy)

1968 (4 Mar). Mountains of East Africa. T **49** and similar horiz designs. Multicoloured. P 14.
244	30c. Type **49**...	15	10
245	50c. Mount Kenya	30	10
246	1s.30 Mount Kilimanjaro...............................	60	10
247	2s.50 Ruwenzori Mountains	90	2·25
244/7	*Set of 4*	1·75	2·25

50 Family and Rural Hospital

(Des Rena Fennessy. Litho D.L.R.)

1968 (13 May). 20th Anniv of World Health Organization. T **50** and similar horiz designs. P 13½.
248	30c. deep yellow-green, lilac and chocolate	10	10
249	50c. slate-lilac, lilac and black............................	15	10
250	1s.30 yellow-brown, lilac and chocolate..........	20	15
251	2s.50 grey, black and reddish lilac	30	1·90
248/51	*Set of 4*	60	2·00

Designs:—50c. Family and nurse; 1s.30, Family and microscope; 2s.50, Family and hypodermic syringe.

51 Olympic Stadium, Mexico City

(Des V. Whiteley)

1968 (14 Oct). Olympic Games, Mexico. T **51** and similar designs. P 14.
252	30c. light green and black...................................	10	10
253	50c. black and blue-green...................................	15	10
254	1s.30 carmine-red, black and grey.....................	25	15
255	2s.50 blackish brown and yellow-brown..........	35	1·50
252/5	*Set of 4*	70	1·60

Designs: *Horiz*—50c. High-diving boards; 1s.30, Running tracks. *Vert*—2s.50, Boxing ring.

52 *Umoja* (railway ferry)

(Des A. Grosart)

1969 (20 Jan). Water Transport. T **52** and similar horiz designs. P 14.
256	30c. deep blue, light blue and slate-grey......	40	10
	a. Slate-grey omitted..	60·00	
257	50c. multicoloured...	50	10
258	1s.30 bronze-grn, greenish blue & blue	90	20
259	2s.50 red-orange, dp blue & pale blue	1·50	3·25
256/9	*Set of 4*	3·00	3·25

Designs:—50c. S.S. *Harambee*; 1s.30, M.V. *Victoria*; 2s.50, *St. Michael*.

53 I.L.O. Emblem and Agriculture

54 Pope Paul VI and Ruwenzori Mountains

(Des Rena Fennessy)

1969 (14 Apr). 50th Anniv of International Labour Organization. T **53** and similar horiz designs. P 14.
260	30c. black, green and greenish yellow............	10	10
261	50c. black, plum, cerise and rose	10	10

262		1s.30 black, orange-brown and yellow-orange.	10	10
263		2s.50 black, ultramarine and turquoise-blue..	20	90
260/3	*Set of 4*		35	1·00

Designs:—50c. I.L.O. emblem and building work; 1s.30, I.L.O. emblem and factory workers; 2s.50, I.L.O. emblem and shipping.

(Des Harrison)

1969 (31 July). Visit of Pope Paul VI to Uganda. P 14.

264	**54**	30c. black, gold and royal blue	15	10
265		70c. black, gold and claret	20	10
266		1s.50 black, gold and deep blue	25	20
267		2s.50 black, gold and violet	30	1·40
264/7	*Set of 4*		80	1·50

55 Euphorbia Tree shaped as Africa and Emblem

56 Marimba

(Des Rena Fennessy. Litho B.W.)

1969 (8 Dec). Fifth Anniv of African Development Bank. P 13½.

268	**55**	30c. deep bluish green, gold and blue-green	10	10
269		70c. deep bluish green, gold and reddish purple	15	10
270		1s.50 deep bluish green, gold and light turquoise-blue	30	10
271		2s.50 deep bluish green, gold and orange-brown	35	1·40
268/71	*Set of 4*		75	1·50

(Des Rena Fennessy. Litho B.W.)

1970 (16 Feb). Musical Instruments. T **56** and similar horiz designs. P 11×12.

272		30c. buff, yellow-brown and bistre-brown	15	10
273		70c. olive-green, yellow-brown and yellow	25	10
274		1s.50 chocolate and yellow	50	10
275		2s.50 salmon, yellow and chocolate	75	2·50
272/5	*Set of 4*		1·50	2·50

Designs:— 70c. Amadinda; 1s.50, Nzomari; 2s.50, Adeudeu.

57 Satellite Earth Station

(Des V. Whiteley. Litho J.W.)

1970 (18 May). Inauguration of East African Satellite Earth Station. T **57** and similar horiz designs. P 14½×14.

276		30c. multicoloured	10	10
277		70c. multicoloured	15	10
278		1s.50 black, slate-violet and pale orange	30	10
279		2s.50 multicoloured	60	2·25
276/9	*Set of 4*		1·00	2·25

Designs:— 70c. Transmitter in daytime; 1s.50, Transmitter at night; 2s.50, Earth and satellite.

58 Athlete

59 "25" and U.N. Emblem

(Des Rena Fennessy. Litho Walsall)

1970 (13 July). Ninth Commonwealth Games. P 14×14½.

280	**58**	30c. orange-brown and black	10	10
281		70c. olive-green and black	10	10
282		1s.50 slate-lilac and black	15	10
283		2s.50 turquoise-blue and black	20	1·25
280/3	*Set of 4*		40	1·40

(Des Rena Fennessy)

1970 (19 Oct). 25th Anniv of United Nations. P 14½.

284	**59**	30c. multicoloured	10	10
285		70c. multicoloured	10	10
286		1s.50 multicoloured	20	10
287		2s.50 multicoloured	45	2·00
284/7	*Set of 4*		70	2·00

60 Balance and Weight Equivalents

(Des and litho J.W.)

1971 (4 Jan). Conversion to Metric System. T **60** and similar horiz designs. Multicoloured. P 14½×14.

288		30c. Type **60**	10	10
289		70c. Fahrenheit and Centigrade Thermometers	10	10
290		1s.50 Petrol Pump and Liquid Capacities	15	10
291		2s.50 Surveyors and Land Measures	35	2·00
288/91	*Set of 4*		60	2·00

61 Class 11 Tank Locomotive

(Des Rena Fennessy)

1971 (5 Apr). Railway Transport. T **61** and similar horiz designs. Multicoloured. P 14.

292		30c. Type **61**	15	10
293		70c. Class 90 diesel-electric locomotive	25	10
294		1s.50 Class 59 steam locomotive	50	20
295		2s.50 Class 30 steam locomotive	90	2·25
292/5	*Set of 4*		1·60	2·25
MS296	120×88 mm. Nos. 292/5		5·50	10·00

62 Syringe and Cow

(Des Rena Fennessy. Litho)

1971 (5 July). O.A.U. Rinderpest Campaign. T **62** and similar horiz design. P 14.

297	**62**	30c. black, pale yell-brn & pale yell-grn	10	10
298		70c. black, pale slate-blue & pale yell-brn	10	10
299	**62**	1s.50 black, plum & pale yellow-brn	15	10
300		2s.50 black, brown-red pale yell-brn	25	70
297/300	*Set of 4*		45	85

Design:—70c., 2s.50, As T **62**, but with bull facing right.

63 Livingstone meets Stanley

(Des and litho J.W.)

1971 (28 Oct). Centenary of Livingstone and Stanley meeting at Ujiji. P 13½×14.

301	**63**	5s. multicoloured	30	75

64 President Nyerere and Supporters

65 Flags and Trade Fair Emblem

(Des G. Drummond. Litho J.W.)

1971 (9 Dec). Tenth Anniv of Tanzanian Independence. T **64** and similar horiz designs. Multicoloured. P 13½.

302	30c. Type **64**	10	10
303	70c. Ujamaa village	15	10
304	1s.50 Dar es Salaam University	30	25
305	2s.50 Kilimanjaro International Airport	1·25	3·25
302/5	Set of 4	1·60	3·25

(Des Trade Fair Publicity Agents. Litho Questa)

1972 (23 Feb). All-Africa Trade Fair. P 13½×14.

306	**65** 30c. multicoloured	10	10
307	70c. multicoloured	10	10
308	1s.50 multicoloured	20	10
309	2s.50 multicoloured	30	80
306/9	Set of 4	60	90

66 Child with Cup

(Des Rena Fennessy. Litho Questa)

1972 (24 Apr). 25th Anniv of UNICEF. T **66** and similar horiz designs. Multicoloured. P 14×14½.

310	30c. Type **66**	10	10
311	70c. Children with ball	10	10
312	1s.50 Child at blackboard	10	10
313	2s.50 Child and tractor	25	80
310/13	Set of 4	35	90

67 Hurdling

(Des G. Vasarhelyi. Litho J.W.)

1972 (28 Aug). Olympic Games, Munich. T **67** and similar horiz designs. Multicoloured. P 14.

314	40c. Type **67**	10	10
315	70c. Running	10	10
316	1s.50 Boxing	20	15
317	2s.50 Hockey	45	1·75
314/17	Set of 4	70	1·75
MS318	131×98 mm. Nos. 314/17	3·75	7·00

68 Kobs

(Des G. Drummond. Litho D.L.R.)

1972 (9 Oct). Tenth Anniv of Ugandan Independence. T **68** and similar horiz designs. Multicoloured. P 14.

319	40c. Type **68**	30	10
320	70c. Conference Centre	30	10
321	1s.50 Makerere University	65	30
322	2s.50 Coat of Arms	1·00	3·50
319/22	Set of 4	2·00	3·50
MS323	132×120 mm. Nos. 319/22. P 13×14	3·50	3·50

69 Community Flag

(Des Rena Fennessy. Litho)

1972 (1 Dec). Fifth Anniv of East African Community. P 14½×14.

324	**69**	5s. multicoloured	55	1·90

70 Run-of-the-wind Anemometer

71 "Learning by Serving"

(Des P. Powell. Litho)

1973 (1 Mar*). I.M.O./W.M.O. Centenary. T **70** and similar multicoloured designs. P 14½.

325	40c. Type **70**	10	10
326	70c. Weather balloon (vert)	20	10
327	1s.50 Meteorological rocket	30	15
328	2s.50 Satellite receiving aerial	55	2·25
325/8	Set of 4	1·00	2·25

No. 325 exists with country name at foot instead of at top, and also with country name omitted (or with imprint or plate numbers in lieu). These are because of faulty registration of the perforation comb.

*This is the local release date. The Crown Agents in London did not place the stamps on sale until 5 March.

(Des Rena Fennessy. Litho)

1973 (16 July). 24th World Scout Conference, Nairobi. T **71** and similar vert designs. P 14.

329	40c. multicoloured	10	10
330	70c. Venetian red, reddish violet and black..	15	10
331	1s.50 cobalt, reddish violet and black	35	15
332	2s.50 multicoloured	80	2·00
329/32	Set of 4	1·25	2·00

Designs:—70c. Baden-Powell's grave, Nyeri; 1s.50, World Scout emblem; 2s.50, Lord Baden-Powell.

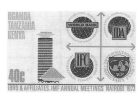

72 Kenyatta Conference Centre

(Des Marketing Communications Ltd, Nairobi; adapted J. Cooter. Litho D.L.R.)

1973 (29 Sept*). I.M.F./World Bank Conference. T **72** and similar designs. P 13½×14 (1s.50) or 14×13½ (others).

333	40c. sage-green, light greenish grey & black	10	10
334	70c. orange-brown, greenish grey and black	10	10
335	1s.50 multicoloured	25	35
336	2s.50 orange, greenish grey and black	35	1·75
333/6	Set of 4	65	2·00
MS337	166×141 mm. Nos. 333/6. Imperf	1·40	4·75

Designs:—Nos. 334/6 show different arrangements of Bank emblems and the Conference Centre, the 1s.50 being vertical.

*This is the local release date. The Crown Agents in London issued the stamps on 24 September.

73 Police Dog-handler

74 Tea Factory

(Des C. Abbott. Litho Questa)

1973 (24 Oct)–**74.** 50th Anniv of Interpol. T **73** and similar vert designs. P 14.

338	40c. yellow, blue and black	55	15
339	70c. turquoise-green, orange-yellow & black	90	15
340	1s.50 light violet, yellow and black	1·50	90
341	2s.50 light yellow-green, red-orange and black (I)	3·75	7·00
342	2s.50 light yellow-green, red-orange, and black (II) (25.2.74)	3·75	7·00
338/42 Set of 5		9·50	13·50

Designs:—70c. East African Policeman; 1s.50, Interpol emblem; 2s.50, Interpol H.Q.

Nos. 341/2. Type I inscribed "St. Clans"; Type II corrected to "St. Cloud".

(Des G. Drummond. Litho Enschedé)

1973 (12 Dec). 10th Anniv of Kenya's Independence. T **74** and similar horiz designs. Multicoloured. P 13×13½.

343	40c. Type **74**	10	10
344	70c. Kenyatta Hospital	15	10
345	1s.50 Nairobi Airport	50	50
346	2s.50 Kindaruma hydro-electric scheme	65	2·25
343/6 Set of 4		1·25	2·25

75 Party H.Q.

(Des PAD Studio. Litho D.L.R.)

1974 (12 Jan). Tenth Anniv of Zanzibar's Revolution. T **75** and similar horiz designs. Multicoloured. P 13½.

347	40c. Type **75**	10	10
348	70c. Housing scheme	15	10
349	1s.50 Colour TV	35	35
350	2s.50 Amaan Stadium	70	3·25
347/50 Set of 4		1·10	3·50

76 "Symbol of Union"

(Des Jennifer Toombs. Litho Questa)

1974 (26 Apr). Tenth Anniv of Tanganyika Zanzibar Union. T **76** and similar horiz designs. Multicoloured. P 14½.

351	40c. Type **76**	10	10
352	70c. Handclasp and map	15	10
353	1s.50 "Communications"	35	30
354	2s.50 Flags of Tanu, Tanzania and Afro-Shirazi Party	70	3·00
351/4 Set of 4		1·10	3·00

77 East African Family ("Stability of the Home")

(Des locally; adapted PAD Studio. Litho)

1974 (15 July). 17th Social Welfare Conference, Nairobi. T **77** and similar horiz designs. P 14½.

355	40c. greenish yellow, lake-brown and black	10	10
356	70c. multicoloured	10	10
357	1s.50 olive-green, yellow-green and black	20	30
358	2s.50 light rose, reddish violet and black	1·00	2·00
355/8 Set of 4		1·25	2·25

Designs:—70c. Dawn and drummer (U.N. Second Development Plan); 1s.50, Agricultural scene (Rural Development Plan); 2s.50, Transport and telephone ("Communications").

78 New Postal H.Q., Kampala

(Des Rena Fennessy. Litho)

1974 (9 Oct). Centenary of Universal Postal Union. T **78** and similar horiz designs. Multicoloured. P 14½.

359	40c. Type **78**	10	10
360	70c. Mail-train and post-van	20	10
361	1s.50 U.P.U. Building, Berne	15	20
362	2s.50 Loading mail into Vickers Super VC-10	55	1·50
359/62 Set of 4		85	1·60

79 Family-planning Clinic

(Des C. Abbott. Litho)

1974 (16 Dec). World Population Year. T **79** and similar horiz designs. P 14.

363	40c. multicoloured	10	10
364	70c. deep reddish violet and scarlet	10	10
365	1s.50 multicoloured	15	20
366	2s.50 apple-green, blue-green & bluish blk	30	1·90
363/6 Set of 4		55	2·00

Designs:—70c. "Tug of war"; 1s.50, Population "scales"; 2s.50, W.P.Y. emblem.

80 Serenera Wild-Life Lodge, Tanzania

(Des R. Granger Barrett. Litho)

1975 (26 Feb*). East Africa Game Lodges. T **80** and similar horiz designs. Multicoloured. P 14.

367	40c. Type **80**	15	10
368	70c. Mweya Safari Lodge, Uganda	20	10
369	1s.50 "Ark"—Aberdare Forest Lodge, Kenya	35	35
370	2s.50 Paraa Safari Lodge, Uganda	60	2·50
367/70 Set of 4		1·10	2·75

*This is the local release date. The Crown Agents in London issued the stamps on 24 February.

81 Kitana (wooden comb), Bajun of Kenya

82 International Airport, Entebbe

(Des Mrs. Gombe of the E.A.P.T.; adapted C. Abbott. Litho Questa)

1975 (5 May). African Arts. T **81** and similar vert designs. Multicoloured. P 13½.

371	50c. Type **81**	10	10
372	1s. Earring, Chaga of Tanzania	15	10
373	2s. Okoco (armlet), Acholi of Uganda	35	75
374	3s. Kitete (Kamba gourd), Kenya	85	1·75
371/4	*Set of 4*	1·10	2·40

(Des PAD Studio. Litho State Ptg Wks, Warsaw)

1975 (28 July). O.A.U. Summit Conference, Kampala. T **82** and similar multicoloured designs. P 11.

375	50c. Type **82**	30	10
376	1s. Map of Africa and flag (*vert*)	30	10
377	2s. Nile Hotel, Kampala	30	90
378	3s. Martyrs' Shrine, Namugongo (*vert*)	40	1·90
375/8	*Set of 4*	1·10	2·75

83 Ahmed ("Presidential" Elephant)

84 Maasai Manyatta (village), Kenya

(Des locally. Litho State Ptg Wks, Warsaw)

1975 (11 Sept). Rare Animals. T **83** and similar vert designs. Multicoloured. P 11.

379	50c. Type **83**	40	10
380	1s. Albino buffalo	40	10
381	2s. Ahmed in grounds of National Museum	1·25	1·50
382	3s. Abbott's Duiker	1·25	3·00
379/82	*Set of 4*	3·00	4·25

(Des Rena Fennessy. Litho Questa)

1975 (3 Nov). Second World Black and African Festival of Arts and Culture, Nigeria (1977). T **84** and similar horiz designs. Multicoloured. P 13½×14.

383	50c. Type **84**	15	10
384	1s. "Heartbeat of Africa" (Ugandan dancers)	15	10
385	2s. Makonde sculpture, Tanzania	50	85
386	3s. "Early Man and Technology" (skinning hippopotamus)	75	1·40
383/6	*Set of 4*	1·40	2·25

For similar stamps see Nos. 76/80 of Kenya and the corresponding issues of Tanzania and Uganda.

85 Fokker F.27 Friendship at Nairobi Airport

(Des local artist. Litho State Security Ptg Wks, Warsaw)

1976 (2 Jan). 30th Anniv of East African Airways. T **85** and similar triangular designs. Multicoloured. P 11½.

387	50c. Type **85**	1·00	30
	a. Black (aircraft) and blue omitted	†	£2250
388	1s. Douglas DC-9 at Kilimanjaro Airport	1·10	30
389	2s. Vickers Super VC-10 at Entebbe Airport	3·50	3·50
390	3s. East African Airways crest	3·75	4·25
387/90	*Set of 4*	8·50	7·50

Two black plates were used for each of Nos. 387/9: one for the frame and the other for the centre. No. 387a, three used copies of which are known, has the printing from the blue and centre black plates omitted.

Further commemorative issues were released during 1976–78, using common designs, but inscribed for one republic only. These are listed under KENYA, TANZANIA, or UGANDA.

Co-operation between the postal services of the three member countries virtually ceased after 30 June 1977, the postal services of Kenya, Tanzania and Uganda then operating independently.

STAMP BOOKLETS

1912–17. Black on pink cover. Letter rate given as 6 cents per oz. Stapled.

SB1	1r.80, booklet containing twelve 3c. and twenty four 6c. (Nos. 45/6), each in blocks of 6	£2000
	a. Letter rate 6 cents per ½oz. Contains Nos. 45a/6a	
SB2	2r. booklet containing six 3c. and thirty 6c. (Nos. 45/6), each in blocks of 6	£2000

1938. Black on pink cover. Stapled.

SB3	3s.40, booklet containing twelve 15c. and eight 20c. (Nos. 137, 139), each in blocks of 4	£275

1950–52. Blue on yellow cover. Stapled.

SB4	1s. booklet containing four 5c. and eight 10c. (Nos. 133a, 135c), each in blocks of 4	£650
	a. Contents as SB4, but 10c. changed to No. 136. Stitched (1952)	50·00

1954 (3 Sept). Blue on yellow cover. Stitched.

SB6	1s. booklet containing four 5c. and eight 10c. (Nos. 167/8), each in blocks of 4	3·00

1958 (16 Jan). Black on yellow cover. Stitched.

SB7	5s. booklet containing four 5c., 20c., 30c., 50c. and eight 10c. (Nos. 167/8, 170/1, 173), each in blocks of 4	21·00

1958 (16 Dec)–**59**. Black on rose-red cover. Stitched.

SB8	5s. booklet containing 10c., 15c., 20c., 30c. and 50c. (Nos. 168/9, 170/1, 173), in blocks of 4	80·00
	a. Contents as No. SB8, but 15c. changed to No. 169a (20.4.59)	50·00

1961 (1 Feb). Black on rose-red cover. Stitched.

SB9	5s. booklet containing 10c., 15c., 20c., 30c. and 50c. (Nos. 184/6, 188, 190) in blocks of 4	18·00

OFFICIAL STAMPS

For use on official correspondence of the Tanganyika Government.

OFFICIAL
(O **1**)

OFFICIAL
£1 Broken "O" in "OFFICIAL" (R. 1/6).

1959 (1 July). Nos. 167/71, 173 and 175/80 optd as Type O **1**.

O1	**18**	5c. black and deep brown	10	1·25
O2	**19**	10c. carmine-red	30	1·25
O3	**20**	15c. black and light blue (No. 169a)	75	1·25
O4	**21**	20c. black and orange	20	20
		a. Opt double	—	£1500
O5	**18**	30c. black and deep ultramarine	15	80
O6	**19**	50c. reddish purple	1·75	20
O7	**21**	1s. black and claret	20	75
O8	**20**	1s.30 orange and deep lilac	9·50	2·50
O9	**22**	2s. black and bronze-green	1·25	1·00
O10	**20**	5s. black and orange	11·00	4·00
O11	**23**	10s. black and deep ultramarine	3·25	7·50
		a. Opt at top	4·25	2·75
O12	**24**	£1 brown-red and black	6·50	25·00
		a. Broken "O"	70·00	£180
O1/12		*Set of 12*	30·00	35·00

The 30c., 50c., 1s. and 1s.30 exist with overprint double, but with the two impressions almost coincident.

OFFICIAL
(O **2**)

OFFICIAL
(O **3**)

1960 (18 Oct). Nos. 183/6, 188, 190, 192 and 196 optd with Type O **2** (cents values) or O **3**.

O13		5c. Prussian blue	10	3·00
O14		10c. yellow-green	10	3·00
O15		15c. dull purple	10	3·00
		a. "Serif" variety	13·00	
		b. "Serif" retouched	13·00	
O16		20c. magenta	10	75
O17		30c. vermilion	10	10
O18		50c. slate-violet	30	1·00
O19		1s. deep reddish violet and reddish purple	30	10
		a. Re-entry	25·00	
O20		5s. rose-red and purple	22·00	65
O13/20		*Set of 8*	22·00	10·50

The use of these overprints ceased on 8 December 1961.

POSTAGE DUE STAMPS

D **1**   D **2**

(Typo Waterlow)

1928 (Sept)–**33**. Wmk Mult Script CA. P 15×14.

D1	D **1**	5c. violet	2·50	75
D2		10c. vermilion	2·50	15
D3		20c. yellow-green	4·00	3·75
D4		30c. brown (1931)	24·00	18·00
D5		40c. dull blue	6·50	14·00
D6		1s. grey-green (1933)	70·00	£140
D1/6 Set of 6			95·00	£160
D1s/6s Optd or Perf (30c., 1s.) "SPECIMEN" Set of 6			£325	

(Typo D.L.R.)

1935 (1 May)–**60**. Wmk Mult Script CA. P 14.

D7	D **2**	5c. violet	2·75	1·75
D8		10c. scarlet	30	50
D9		20c. green	40	50
D10		30c. brown	1·50	50
		a. Bistre-brown (19.7.60)	3·00	9·50
D11		40c. ultramarine	1·50	3·00
D12		1s. grey	19·00	19·00
D7/12 Set of 6			23·00	23·00
D7s/12s Perf "SPECIMEN" Set of 6			£275	

Somaliland Protectorate

Egyptian post offices were opened in Somaliland during 1876 and the stamps of Egypt were used there until the garrisons were withdrawn in 1884.

Cancellations for these offices have been identified as follows (for illustrations of postmark types see SUDAN).

BARBARA (Berbera). Open 1876 to 1 November 1884. Circular datestamp as Sudan Type I.

ZEILA. Open 1876 to 1 November 1884. Circular datestamp as Sudan Types G and I, sometimes inscr ZEJLA. One example with seal type cancellation as Sudan Type B is also known.

Stamps of India were used at the two post offices from 1 January 1887 until 1903 usually cancelled with circular datestamps or the "B" obliterator used by all offices controlled from Bombay.

The Protectorate Post Office was established on 1 June 1903, when control of British Somaliland was transferred from the Indian Government to the British Foreign Office.

PRICES FOR STAMPS ON COVER TO 1945	
Nos. 1/11	from × 25
Nos. 12/13	—
Nos. 18/22	from × 12
Nos. 23/4	—
Nos. 25/30	from × 30
Nos. 32/59	from × 12
Nos. 60/92	from × 6
Nos. 93/104	from × 3
Nos. 105/16	from × 4
Nos. O1/13	from × 20
Nos. O4/9f	—
Nos. O10/13	from × 20
Nos. O14/15	

(Currency. 12 pies = 1 anna; 16 annas = 1 rupee)

BRITISH SOMALILAND
(1)

2   3

SETTINGS OF TYPE 1

In all printings the ½, 1, 2, 2½, 3, 4, 8, 12a. and 1r. values were overprinted from a setting of 240 (2 panes 12×10, one above the other), covering the entire sheet at one operation.

The 6a., which was in sheets of 320 (4 panes, each 8×10), had a modified setting of 160, applied twice to each sheet.

The high values were overprinted in sheets of 96 (8 panes, each 4×3).

The settings for the low value stamps contained two slightly different styles of overprint, identified by the position of "B" of "BRITISH". Type A shows this letter over the "M" of "SOMALILAND" and Type B over the "OM".

For the first printing with the overprint at the top of the design the 240 position setting showed all the stamps in the upper pane and 63 in the lower as Type A, with the remaining 57 as Type B. When the setting was used for the printing with overprint at foot it was amended slightly so that one of the Type A examples in the upper pane became a Type B.

The 6a. value with overprint at top shows 250 examples of Type A and 70 as Type B in each sheet. This proportion altered in the printing with overprint at foot to 256 as Type A and 64 as Type B.

OVERPRINT VARIETIES

Missing second "I" in "BRITISH"—Occurs on the stamps with overprint at top from R. 2/6 of the upper pane and R. 5/1 of the lower, although it is believed that the example on the 2½a. (No. 4a) only occurs from the second position. On the later printing with overprint at foot a similar error can be found on R. 7/12 of the upper pane. Some examples of both these errors show traces of the letter remaining, but the prices quoted are for stamps with it completely omitted.

Figure "1" for first "I" in "BRITISH"—Occurs on R. 6/4 of the upper pane for all printings of the 240 impression setting. In addition it has been reported from R. 7/12 of the Queen Victoria 2½, 12a. and 1r. with overprint at foot. Both versions of the 6a. show the variety on R. 6/4 of the upper left and upper right panes.

Curved overprint—Occurs on R. 3/4 of the top right-hand pane of the high values.

"SUMALILAND"—Occurs on R. 2/9 of the upper pane for all low values with the overprint at foot, except the 6a. A similar variety occurs on the high values from the same series on R. 1/3 of the top left pane.

"SOMAL.LAND"—Occurs on R. 7/5 of the lower pane from the 240 impression setting with the overprint at foot. In addition the Edwardian values of this series also have an example on R. 6/7. The 6a. has examples of the flaw on R. 6/9 and R. 7/5 of both the lower right and left panes. A similar variety occurs on the high values from the same series at R. 3/4 of the third pane in the right-hand column.

1903 (1 June). Nos. 80, 94, 96, 98, 100, 106/9, 114/16 and 118 of India (Queen Victoria) optd with T **1**, at top of stamp, in Calcutta. Wmk Elephant Head (6a.) or Star (others).

1	½a. yellow-green	2·75	4·25
	a. "BRIT SH"	£170	£275
	b. "BR1TISH"	£200	£275
2	1a. carmine	2·75	3·75
	a. "BRIT SH"	£200	£275
	b. "BR1TISH"	£200	
3	2a. pale violet	2·25	1·50
	a. "BRIT SH"	£400	£500
	b. "BR1TISH"	£325	
	c. Opt double	£800	
4	2½a. ultramarine	2·00	1·75
	a. "BRIT SH"	£650	
	b. "BR1TISH"	£400	
5	3a. brown-orange	3·25	3·00
	a. "BRIT SH"	£800	
	b. "BR1TISH"	£400	£450
6	4a. slate-green	3·50	2·75
	a. "BR1TISH"	£425	£475
7	6a. olive-bistre	6·50	4·50
	a. "BR1TISH"	£300	£350
8	8a. dull mauve	3·75	5·00
	a. "BR1TISH"	£425	£550
9	12a. purple/red	5·00	7·00
	a. "BR1TISH"	£500	£600
10	1r. green and aniline carmine	7·50	10·00
	a. "BR1TISH"	£475	
11	2r. carmine and yellow-brown	32·00	42·00
	a. Curved opt	£700	
12	3r. brown and green	27·00	55·00
	a. Curved opt	£650	
13	5r. ultramarine and violet	48·00	65·00
	a. Curved opt	£700	
1/13 Set of 13		£130	£190

1903 (1 Sept–2 Nov). Stamps of India optd with T **1**, at bottom of stamp, in Calcutta.

(a) On Nos. 80, 100, 106/9 and 118 (Queen Victoria)

18	2½a. ultramarine (2.11)	6·50	8·50
	a. "BR1TISH"	£200	
	b. "SUMALILAND"	£250	
	c. "SOMAL.LAND"	£275	
	d. "BRIT SH"	£1500	
19	6a. olive-bistre (2.11)	8·00	7·00
	a. "BR1TISH"	£300	
	b. "SOMAL.LAND"	£180	
20	12a. purple/red (2.11)	10·00	14·00
	a. "BR1TISH"	£425	
	b. "SUMALILAND"	£325	£500
	c. "SOMAL.LAND"	£375	
21	1r. green and aniline carmine (2.11)	9·00	11·00
	a. "BR1TISH"	£475	
	b. "SUMALILAND"	£475	
	c. "SOMAL.LAND"	£500	
22	2r. carmine and yellow-brown (2.11)	£130	£200
	a. Curved opt	£850	£1300
	b. "SUMALILAND"	£850	
	c. "SOMAL.LAND"	£850	
23	3r. brown and green (2.11)	£140	£200
	a. Opt double, both inverted with one albino	£900	
	b. Curved opt	£900	
	c. "SUMALILAND"	£900	
	d. "SOMAL.LAND"	£900	
	e. Opt. double, one albino	£1100	
24	5r. ultramarine and violet (2.11)	£130	£200
	a. Curved opt	£900	
	b. "SUMALILAND"	£900	
	c. "SOMAL.LAND"	£900	

(b) On Nos. 122/4, 127/8 and 133 (King Edward VII)

25	½a. green	2·25	55
	a. "BRIT SH"	£550	
	b. "BR1TISH"	£130	
	c. "SUMALILAND"	£130	£140
	d. "SOMAL.LAND"	80·00	95·00
26	1a. carmine (8.10)	1·25	30
	a. "BRIT SH"	£350	
	b. "BR1TISH"	£130	£140
	c. "SUMALILAND"	£130	£140
	d. "SOMAL.LAND"	60·00	70·00
27	2a. violet (2.11)	2·00	2·00
	a. "BRIT SH"	£1300	
	b. "BR1TISH"	£250	

	c. "SUMALILAND"		£225	
	d. "SOMAL.LAND"		£120	
28	3a. orange-brown (2.11)		2·50	2·00
	a. "BR1TISH"		£275	£350
	b. "SUMALILAND"		£225	
	c. "SOMAL.LAND"		£140	£170
29	4a. olive (2.11)		1·50	2·75
	a. "BR1TISH"		£200	
	b. "SUMALILAND"		£190	
	c. "SOMAL.LAND"		£140	
30	8a. purple (2.11)		2·75	2·00
	a. "BR1TISH"		£375	
	b. "SUMALILAND"		£375	
	c. "SOMAL.LAND"		£225	
18/30 *Set of 13*			£400	£600

(Typo D.L.R.)

1904 (15 Feb–3 Sept).

(a) Wmk Crown CA. P 14

32	2	½a. dull green and green	2·25	4·25
33		1a. grey-black and red (3.9)	19·00	3·25
34		2a. dull and bright purple (3.9)	2·25	2·50
35		2½a. bright blue (3.9)	9·50	3·75
36		3a. chocolate and grey-green (3.9)	2·50	5·00
37		4a. green and black (3.9)	4·00	7·50
38		6a. green and violet (3.9)	9·50	17·00
39		8a. grey-black and pale blue (3.9)	8·50	9·00
40		12a. grey-black and orange-buff (3.9)	14·00	11·00

(b) Wmk Crown CC. P 14

41	3	1r. green (3.9)	18·00	40·00
42		2r. dull and bright purple (3.9)	60·00	90·00
43		3r. green and black (3.9)	70·00	£130
44		5r. grey-black and red (3.9)	70·00	£140
32/44 *Set of 13*			£250	£425
32s/44s Optd "SPECIMEN" *Set of 13*			£225	

1905 (July)–**11**. Ordinary paper. Wmk Mult Crown CA. P 14.

45	2	½a. dull green and green	1·25	7·50
46		1a. grey-black and red (10.7.05)	26·00	10·00
		a. Chalk-surfaced paper (1906)	21·00	1·60
47		2a. dull and bright purple	9·00	19·00
		a. Chalk-surfaced paper (1909)	20·00	15·00
48		2½a. bright blue	3·00	10·00
49		3a. chocolate and grey-green	2·00	16·00
		a. Chalk-surfaced paper (1911)	16·00	50·00
50		4a. green and black	4·25	23·00
		a. Chalk-surfaced paper (1911)	22·00	55·00
51		6a. green and violet	3·00	25·00
		a. Chalk-surfaced paper (1911)	40·00	80·00
52		8a. grey-black and pale blue	8·00	11·00
		a. Chalk-surfaced paper. *Black and blue* (27.1.11)	27·00	70·00
53		12a. grey-black and orange-buff	6·50	10·00
		a. Chalk-surfaced paper. *Black and orange-brown* (9.11.11)	17·00	70·00

1909 (30 Apr–May). Wmk Mult Crown CA. P 14.

58	2	½a. bluish green (May)	45·00	40·00
59		1a. red	2·50	2·00
		s. Optd "SPECIMEN"	40·00	
45/59 *Set of 11*			95·00	£140

4   5

(Typo D.L.R.)

1912 (Sept)–**19**. Chalk-surfaced paper (2a. and 3a. to 5r.). Wmk Mult Crown CA. P 14.

60	4	½a. green (11.13)	65	12·00
		w. Wmk inverted	15·00	65·00
61		1a. red	2·50	50
		a. *Scarlet* (1917)	3·00	1·25
62		2a. dull and bright purple (12.13)	3·50	16·00
		a. *Dull purple and violet-purple* (4.19)	27·00	50·00
63		2½a. bright blue (10.13)	1·00	8·50
64		3a. chocolate and grey-green (10.13)	2·25	10·00
		w. Wmk inverted	£120	
65		4a. green and black (12.12)	2·50	10·00
66		6a. green and violet (4.13)	2·50	10·00
67		8a. grey-black and pale blue (10.13)	3·50	
68		12a. grey-black and orange-buff (10.13)	3·50	21·00
69	5	1r. green (11.12)	19·00	24·00
70		2r. dull purple and purple (4.19)	28·00	80·00
71		3r. green and black (4.19)	85·00	£170

72		5r. black and scarlet (4.19)	90·00	£250
60/72 *Set of 13*			£225	£550
60s/72s Optd "SPECIMEN" *Set of 13*			£300	

1921. Chalk-surfaced paper (2a. and 3a. to 5r.). Wmk Mult Script CA. P 14.

73	4	½a. blue-green	2·75	16·00
74		1a. carmine-red	3·50	70
75		2a. dull and bright purple	4·25	1·00
76		2½a. bright blue	1·00	9·50
77		3a. chocolate and green	2·50	7·50
78		4a. green and black	2·50	13·00
79		6a. green and violet	1·50	13·00
80		8a. grey-black and pale blue	2·00	10·00
81		12a. grey-black and orange-buff	8·50	15·00
82	5	1r. dull green	8·50	48·00
83		2r. dull purple and purple	26·00	55·00
84		3r. dull green and black	42·00	£120
85		5r. black and scarlet	95·00	£200
73/85 *Set of 13*			£180	£450
73s/85s Optd "SPECIMEN" *Set of 13*			£300	

Examples of most values are known showing a forged Berbera postmark dated "21 OC 1932".

Kite and vertical log (Plate "2A" R. 10/6)

Kite and horizontal log (Plate "2B" R. 10/6)

Bird by turret (Plate "7" R. 1/5)

1935 (6 May). Silver Jubilee. As Nos. 91/4 of Antigua, but ptd by Waterlow. P 11×12.

86		1a. deep blue and scarlet	2·50	4·25
		m. "Bird" by turret	£160	£200
87		2a. ultramarine and grey	2·75	4·25
		k. Kite and vertical log	£140	£190
88		3a. brown and deep blue	2·50	22·00
		k. Kite and vertical log	£180	£325
		l. Kite and horizontal log	£170	£325
89		1r. slate and purple	10·00	25·00
		k. Kite and vertical log	£225	
		l. Kite and horizontal log	£190	£350
86/9 *Set of 4*			16·00	50·00
86s/9s Perf "SPECIMEN" *Set of 4*			£110	

For illustrations of plate varieties see Omnibus section following Zanzibar.

1937 (13 May). Coronation. As Nos. 95/7 of Antigua, but ptd by D.L.R. P 14.

90		1a. scarlet	15	50
91		2a. grey-black	55	2·00
92		3a. bright blue	1·10	1·25
90/2 *Set of 3*			1·60	3·25
90s/2s Perf "SPECIMEN" *Set of 3*			95·00	

6 Berbera Blackhead Sheep

7 Greater Kudu

8 Somaliland Protectorate

(Des H. W. Claxton. Recess Waterlow)

1938 (10 May). Portrait to left. Wmk Mult Script CA. P 12½.

93	**6**	½a. green	2·50	8·00
94		1a. scarlet	1·50	3·00
95		2a. maroon	4·00	4·75
96		3a. bright blue	18·00	19·00
97	**7**	4a. sepia	6·00	14·00
98		6a. violet	16·00	12·00
99		8a. grey	8·00	14·00
100		12a. red-orange	19·00	42·00
101	**8**	1r. green	15·00	90·00
102		2r. purple	26·00	90·00
103		3r. bright blue	25·00	55·00
104		5r. black	32·00	55·00
		a. Imperf between (horiz pair)	£28000	
93/104 *Set of 12*			£150	£350
93s/104s Perf "SPECIMEN" *Set of 12*			£325	

Examples of most values are known showing a forged Berbera postmark dated "15 AU 38".

> Following the Italian Occupation, from 19 August 1940 until 16 March 1941, the stamps of ADEN were used at Berbera from 1 July 1941 until 26 April 1942.

9 Berbera
Blackhead Sheep

5 Cents
(10)

1 Shilling
(11)

(Recess Waterlow)

1942 (27 Apr). As T **6/8** but with full-face portrait of King George VI, as in T **9**. Wmk Mult Script CA. P 12½.

105	**9**	½a. green	25	55
106		1a. scarlet	25	10
107		2a. maroon	70	20
108		3a. bright blue	2·25	20
109	**7**	4a. sepia	3·00	30
110		6a. violet	3·00	20
111		8a. grey	4·00	20
112		12a. red-orange	3·25	2·00
113	**8**	1r. green	3·25	3·00
114		2r. purple	5·50	10·00
115		3r. bright blue	10·00	18·00
116		5r. black	16·00	11·00
105/16 *Set of 12*			45·00	42·00
105s/16s Perf "SPECIMEN" *Set of 12*			£300	

1946 (15 Oct). Victory. As Nos. 110/11, of Antigua.

117		1a. carmine	10	10
		a. Perf 13½	14·00	50·00
118		3a. blue	10	10
117s/18s Perf "SPECIMEN" *Set of 2*			85·00	

1949 (28 Jan). Royal Silver Wedding. As Nos. 112/13 of Antigua.

119		1a. scarlet	10	10
120		5r. black	4·50	6·50

1949 (24 Oct*). 75th Anniv of U.P.U. As Nos. 114/17 of Antigua. Surch with face values in annas.

121		1a. on 10c. carmine	20	50
122		3a. on 30c. deep blue (R.)	1·25	5·00
123		6a. on 50c. purple	35	3·75
124		12a. on 1s. red-orange	90	1·75
121/4 *Set of 4*			2·40	10·00

*This is the local date of issue. The Crown Agents released these stamps in London on 10 October.

(New Currency. 100 cents = 1 shilling)

1951 (1 Apr). 1942 issue surch as T **10/11**.

125		5c. on ½a. green	40	3·25
126		10c. on 2a. maroon	40	2·00
127		15c. on 3a. bright blue	1·75	3·25
128		20c. on 4a. sepia	2·00	30

129		30c. on 6a. violet	2·00	2·00
130		50c. on 8a. grey	2·50	30
131		70c. on 12a. red-orange	4·25	9·50
132		1s. on 1r. green	2·50	2·25
133		2s. on 2r. purple (21.4.51)*	5·50	24·00
134		2s. on 3r. bright blue	14·00	11·00
135		5s. on 5r. black (R.)	24·00	16·00
125/35 *Set of 11*			55·00	65·00

*Earliest reported date.

1953 (2 June). Coronation. As No. 120 of Antigua.

136		15c. black and green	30	20

12 Camel and Gurgi

13 Sentry,
Somaliland Scouts

14 Somali Stock Dove

15 Martial Eagle

16 Berbera Blackhead
Sheep

17 Sheikh Isaaq's Tomb,
Mait

18 Taleh Fort

(Recess B.W.)

1953 (15 Sept)–**58**. T **12/18**. Wmk Mult Script CA. P 12½.

137	**12**	5c. slate-black	15	60
138	**13**	10c. red-orange	2·25	1·25
		a. Salmon (20.3.58)	17·00	3·50
139	**12**	15c. blue-green	60	70
140		20c. scarlet	60	40
141	**13**	30c. reddish brown	2·25	40
142	**14**	35c. blue	5·50	1·75
143	**15**	50c. brown and rose-carmine	6·50	55
144	**16**	1s. light blue	1·25	30
145	**17**	1s.30 ultramarine and black (1.9.58)	23·00	4·00
146	**14**	2s. brown and bluish violet	28·00	7·50
147	**15**	5s. red-brown and emerald	35·00	11·00
148	–	10s. brown and reddish violet	32·00	38·00
137/48 *Set of 12*			£120	60·00

OPENING OF THE LEGISLATIVE COUNCIL 1957 **(19)**	LEGISLATIVE COUNCIL UNOFFICIAL MAJORITY, 1960 **(20)**

1957 (21 May). Opening of Legislative Council. Nos. 140 and 144 optd with T **19**.

149		20c. scarlet	10	15
150		1s. light blue	30	15

1960 (5 Apr). Legislative Council's Unofficial Majority. Nos. 140 and 145 optd as T **20**.

151		20c. scarlet	50	15
152		1s.30 ultramarine and black	1·50	15

OFFICIAL STAMPS

SERVICE

BRITISH

BRITISH
SOMALILAND   SOMALILAND
(O 1)   (O 2)

SETTING OF TYPE O 1

The 240 impression setting used for the Official stamps differs considerably from that on the contemporary postage issue with overprint at foot, although the "BR1TISH" error can still be found on R. 6/4 of the upper pane. The Official setting is recorded as consisting of 217 overprints as Type A and 23 as Type B.

OVERPRINT VARIETIES

Figure "1" for first "I" in "BRITISH"—Occurs on R. 6/4 of the upper pane as for the postage issue.

"BRITIS H"—Occurs on R. 8/4 of the lower pane.

1903 (1 June). Nos. O45, O48, O49a and O50/1 of India (Queen Victoria optd "O.H.M.S".) additionally optd with Type O **1** in Calcutta.

O1	½a. yellow-green		7·00	55·00
	a. "BR1TISH"		£475	
	b. "BRITIS H"		£350	£850
O2	1a. carmine		15·00	16·00
	a. "BR1TISH"		£475	£550
	b. "BRITIS H"		£350	£450
O3	2a. pale violet		14·00	55·00
	a. "BR1TISH"		£600	
	b. "BRITIS H"		£475	
O4	8a. dull mauve		12·00	£475
	a. "BR1TISH"		£1600	
	b. "BRITIS H"		£1300	
	c. Stop omitted after "M" of "O.H.M.S." (lower pane R. 10/12)		£4250	
O5	1r. green and carmine		12·00	£750
	a. "BR1TISH"		£1800	
	b. "BRITIS H"		£1500	
O1/5	*Set of 5*		55·00	£1200

No. O4c was caused by an attempt to correct a minor spacing error of the "O.H.M.S." overprint which is known on the equivalent India Official stamp.

SETTING OF TYPE O 2

This 240 impression setting of "BRITISH SOMALILAND" also differs from that used to prepare the postage issue with overprint at foot, although many of the errors from the latter still occur in the same positions for the Official stamps. The setting used for Nos. O6/9f contained 180 overprints as Type A and 60 as Type B.

OVERPRINT VARIETIES

Missing second "I" in "BRITISH"—Occurs R. 7/12 of upper pane as for the postage issue.

Figure "1" for first "I" in "BRITISH"—Occurs R. 6/4 of upper pane as for the postage issue.

"SUMALILAND"—Occurs R. 2/9 of the upper pane as for the postage issue.

"SOMAL.LAND"—Occurs R. 6/7 of the lower pane as for the postage issue.

SERVICE
(O **2a**)

"SERVICE" in wrong fount (Type O **2a**)—Occurs R. 1/7 of lower pane.

1903. Prepared for use but not issued. Nos. 106, 122/4 and 133 of India (1r. Queen Victoria, rest King Edward VII), optd with Type O **2** in Calcutta.

O6	½a. green		40
	a. "BRIT SH"		95·00
	b. "BR1TISH"		85·00
	c. "SUMALILAND"		85·00
	d. "SOMAL.LAND"		85·00
	e. "SERVICE" as Type O **2a**		85·00
O7	1a. carmine		40
	a. "BRIT SH"		95·00
	b. "BR1TISH"		85·00
	c. "SUMALILAND"		85·00
	d. "SOMAL.LAND"		85·00
	e. "SERVICE" as Type O **2a**		85·00
O8	2a. violet		70
	a. "BRIT SH"		£130
	b. "BR1TISH"		£120
	c. "SUMALILAND"		£120
	d. "SERVICE" as Type O **2a**		£120
O9	8a. purple		6·00
	a. "BRIT SH"		£2750
	b. "BR1TISH"		£2250
	c. "SUMALILAND"		£2250
	d. "SERVICE" as Type O **2a**		£2250
O9f	1r. green and aniline carmine		17·00
	fa. "BRIT SH"		£2750
	fb. "BR1TISH"		£2250

	fc. "SUMALILAND"		£2250
	fd. "SOMAL.LAND"		£2250
	fe. "SERVICE" as Type O **2a**		£2250
O6/9f	*Set of 5*		22·00

Used examples of Nos. O6/9f are known, but there is no evidence that such stamps did postal duty.

O.H.M.S.   O.H.M.S.
(O **3**)   (O **4**)

1904 (1 Sept)–**05**. Stamps of Somaliland Protectorate optd with Type O **3** or O **4** (No. O15).

(a) Wmk Crown CA. P 14

O10	**2**	½a. dull green and green	9·50	48·00
		a. No stop after "M"	£300	
O11		1a. grey-black and carmine	4·50	7·00
		a. No stop after "M"	£200	£300
O12		2a. dull and bright purple	£300	70·00
		a. No stop after "M"	£3250	£850
O13		8a. grey-black and pale blue	60·00	£140
		a. No stop after "M"	£600	£950

(b) Wmk Mult Crown CA

O14	**2**	2a. dull and bright purple, (7.05?)	£120	£1100
		a. No stop after "M"	£2500	

(c) Wmk Crown CC

O15	**3**	1r. green	£275	£1100
O10s/13s , O15s Optd "SPECIMEN" *Set of 5*			£150	

SETTING OF TYPE O 3

The anna values were overprinted in sheets of 120 (2 panes 6×10) from a setting matching the pane size. The full stop after the "M" on the fifth vertical column was either very faint or completely omitted. The prices quoted are for stamps with the stop missing; examples with a partial stop are worth much less.

The 1r. value was overprinted from a setting of 60.

All Somaliland Protectorate stamps were withdrawn from sale on 25 June 1960 and until the unification on 1 July, issues of Italian Somalia together with Nos. 353/5 of Republic of Somalia were used. Later issues will be found listed in Part 14 (*Africa since Independence N–Z*) of this catalogue.

Sudan

ANGLO-EGYPTIAN CONDOMINIUM

An Egyptian post office was opened at Suakin in 1867 and the stamps of Egypt, including postage dues and the official (No. O64). were used in the Sudan until replaced by the overprinted "SOUDAN" issue of 1897.

Cancellations have been identified from eleven post offices, using the following postmark types:

BERBER (*spelt* BARBAR). *Open* 1 October 1873 *to* 20 May 1884. *Postmark type* G.

DABROUSSA. *Open* 1891 *onwards. Postmark as type J but with* 11 *bars in arcs.*

DONGOLA. *Open* 1 October 1873 *to* 13 June 1885 *and* 1896 *onwards. Postmark types* F, G, K, L.

GEDAREF. *Open* August 1878 *to* April 1884. *Postmark type* H.

KASSALA. *Open* 15 May 1875 *to* 30 July 1885. *Postmark type* G.

KHARTOUM. *Open* 1 October 1873 *to* 14 December 1885. *Postmark types* E (*spelt* KARTUM), G (*spelt* HARTUM), I (*with or without line of Arabic above date*).

KORTI. *Open* January *to* March 1885 *and* 1897. *Postmark type* K.

SUAKIN. *Open* November 1867 *onwards. Postmark types* A, B, C (*spelt* SUAKIM), D (*spelt* SUAKIM *and also with year replaced by concentric arcs*), I (*spelt* SOUAKIN), J (*spelt* SAWAKIN, *number of bars differs*).

TANI. *Open* 1885. *Postmark type* K.

TOKAR. *Open* 1891 *onwards. Postmark type* J (7 *bars in arcs*).

WADI HALFA. *Open* 1 October 1873 *onwards. Postmark types* F (*spelt* WADI HALFE), G (*spelt* WADI HALFE), I, J (*number of bars differs*).

WADI HALFA CAMP. *Open* 1896 *onwards. Postmark type* I.

Official records also list post offices at the following locations, but no genuine postal markings from them have yet been reported: Chaka, Dara, Debeira, El Abiad, El Fasher, El Kalabat, Faras, Fashoda, Fazogl, Ishkeit, Kalkal, Karkok, Mesellemia, Sara, Sennar and Taoufikia (not to be confused with the town of the same name in Egypt).

The post office at Kassala was operated by Italy from 1894 until 1896, using stamps of Eritrea cancelled with postmark type M.

From the last years of the nineteenth century that part of Sudan lying south of the 5 degree North latitude line was administered by Uganda (the area to the east of the Nile) (until 1912) or by Belgium (the area to the west of the Nile, known as the Lado Enclave) (until 1910).

Stamps of Uganda or East Africa and Uganda were used at Gondokoro and Nimuli between 1901 and 1911, usually cancelled with circular date stamps or, probably in transit at Khartoum, by a lozenge-shaped grid of 18×17 dots.

Stamps of Belgian Congo were used from the Lado Enclave between 1897 and 1910, as were those of Uganda (1901–10) and Sudan (1902–10), although no local postmarks were supplied, examples being initially cancelled in manuscript.

Stamps of Sudan were used at Gambeila (Ethiopia) between 1910 and 10 June 1940 and from 22 March 1941 until 15 October 1956. Sudan stamps were also used at Sabderat (Eritrea) between March 1910 and 1940.

السودان

SOUDAN
(1)

1897 (1 Mar). Nos. 54*b*, 55, 56*a*, 58/*a*, 59*a*, 61*a*, 63 and 64 of Egypt optd as T **1** by Govt Ptg Wks, Búlaq, Cairo.

1		1m. pale brown	4·25	2·00
		a. Opt inverted	£225	
		b. Opt omitted (in vert pair with normal)	£1500	
		c. Deep brown	3·75	2·25
		w. Wmk inverted		
3		2m. green	1·25	1·75
4		3m. orange-yellow	1·40	1·50
5		5m. rose-carmine	1·25	70
		a. Opt inverted	£225	£275
		b. Opt omitted (in vert pair with normal)	£1600	
6		1p. ultramarine	7·00	2·00
7		2p. orange-brown	80·00	16·00
8		5p. slate	80·00	24·00
		a. Opt double	£6000	
		b. Opt omitted (in vert pair with normal).	£6000	
9		10p. mauve	50·00	60·00
1/9 *Set of 8*			£200	£100

Numerous forgeries exist including some which show the characteristics of the varieties mentioned below.

There are six varieties of the overprint on each value. Vertical strips of 6 showing them are worth a premium.

Four settings of the overprint were previously recognised by specialists, but one of these is now regarded as an unauthorised reprint from the original type. Here reprints can only be detected when in multiples. The 2pi. with inverted watermark only exists with this unauthorised overprint so it is not listed.

In some printings the large dot is omitted from the left-hand Arabic character on one stamp in the pane of 60.

Only two examples, one unused and the other used (in the Royal Collection), are known of No. 8a. In both instances one impression is partially albino.

PRINTERS. All stamps of Sudan were printed by De La Rue & Co, Ltd, London, *except where otherwise stated.*

(Currency. 10 milliemes = 1 piastre. 100 piastres = £1 Sudanese)

2 Arab Postman

3

(Des E. A. Stanton. Typo)

1898 (1 Mar). W **3**. P 14.

10	**2**	1m. brown and pink	1·00	3·00
11		2m. green and brown	2·25	2·75
12		3m. mauve and green	2·25	2·25
13		5m. carmine and black	2·00	1·50

14		1p. blue and brown	18·00	2·75
15		2p. black and blue	48·00	3·50
16		5p. brown and green	50·00	17·00
17		10p. black and mauve	42·00	2·25
10/17 *Set of 8*			£150	32·00

4

5 Milliemes

(5)

Damaged stereos (R. 2/5 and 2/6)

1902–21. Ordinary paper. W **4**. P 14.

18	**2**	1m. brown and carmine (5.05)	1·25	65
19		2m. green and brown (11.02)	1·75	10
20		3m. mauve and green (3.03)	2·25	25
21		4m. blue and bistre (20.1.07)	1·50	2·50
22		4m. vermilion and brown (10.07)	1·50	75
23		5m. scarlet and black (12.03)	2·00	10
		w. Wmk inverted	—	£180
24		1p. blue and brown (12.03)	2·25	30
25		2p. black and blue (2.08)	45·00	1·25
26		2p. purple & orange-yellow (*chalk-surfaced paper*) (22.12.21)	11·00	13·00
27		5p. brown and green (2.08)	32·00	30
		a. Chalk-surfaced paper	50·00	4·00
28		10p. black and mauve (2.11)	29·00	4·25
		a. Chalk-surfaced paper	50·00	15·00
18/28 *Set of 11*			£110	21·00

1903 (Sept). No. 16 such at Khartoum with T **5**, in blocks of 30.

29	**2**	5m. on 5 pi. brown and green	6·50	9·50
		a. Surch inverted	£325	£275
		b. Damaged stereos (pair)		£150

The stereos on R. 2/5 and 2/6 were damaged towards the end of production No. 29. They were replaced by new stereos showing a gap between the "m" and second "e" of "Milliemes" (R. 2/5) and a narrower than usual gap between "5" and "M" (R. 2/6).

6

7

1921–23. Chalk-surfaced paper. Typo. W **4**. P 14.

30	**6**	1m. black and orange (4.2.22)	80	4·75
31		2m. yellow-orange and chocolate (1922)	9·00	11·00
		a. Yellow and chocolate (1923)	12·00	16·00
32		3m. mauve and green (25.1.22)	2·50	10
33		4m. green and chocolate (21.3.22)	9·50	12·00
34		5m. olive-brown and black (4.2.22)	2·25	10
35		10m. carmine and black (1922)	7·50	10
36		15m. bright blue and chestnut (14.12.21)	4·50	1·00
30/36 *Set of 7*			32·00	38·00

1927–41. Chalk-surfaced paper. W **7**. P 14.

37	**6**	1m. black and orange	70	10
		a. Ordinary paper (1941)	70	1·25
38		2m. orange and chocolate	75	10
		aw. Wmk inverted	†	£275
		b. Ordinary paper (1941)	1·50	10
39		3m. mauve and green	70	10
		a. Ordinary paper (1941)	2·75	30
40		4m. green and chocolate	60	10

		a. Ordinary paper (1941)	3·75	1·00
		aw. Wmk inverted	75·00	85·00
41		5m. olive-brown and black	60	10
		a. Ordinary paper (1941)	3·00	10
42		10m. carmine and black	1·50	10
		a. Ordinary paper (1941)	7·00	10
43		15m. bright blue and chestnut	4·00	10
		aw. Wmk inverted	†	£275
		b. Ordinary paper (1941)	4·50	10
44	2	2p. purple and orange-yellow	4·50	10
		a. Ordinary paper (1941)	12·00	10
44*b*		3p. red-brown and blue (1.1.40)	10·00	10
		ba. Ordinary paper (1941)	20·00	10
44*c*		4p. ultramarine and black (2.11.36)	4·25	10
45		5p. chestnut and green	1·25	10
		a. Ordinary paper (1941)	13·00	3·50
45*b*		6p. greenish blue and black (2.11.36)	15·00	3·00
		ba. Ordinary paper (1941)	65·00	5·00
45*c*		8p. emerald and black (2.11.36)	15·00	5·00
		ca. Ordinary paper (1941)	75·00	8·50
46		10p. black and reddish purple	9·50	50
		a. Ordinary paper. *Black and bright mauve* (1941)	16·00	70
46*b*		20p. pale blue and blue (17.10.35)	15·00	60
		ba. Ordinary paper (1941)	13·00	20
37/46*b* *Set of* 15			75·00	8·00

The ordinary paper of this issue is thick, smooth and opaque and was a wartime substitute for chalk-surfaced paper.

For similar stamps, but with different Arabic inscriptions, see Nos. 96/111.

AIR MAIL (**8**) **AIR MAIL** (**9**) **AIR** Extended foot to "R" (R. 5/12)

1931 (15 Feb–Mar). Air. Nos. 41/2 and 44 optd with T **8** or **9** (2p.).

47	6	5m. olive-brown and black (Mar)	35	70
48		10m. carmine and black	1·00	17·00
49	2	2p. purple and orange-yellow	85	7·50
		a. Extended foot to "R"	30·00	
47/9 *Set of* 3			2·00	23·00

2½ **2½**

10 Statue of Gen. Gordon

AIR MAIL

(**11**)

1931 (1 Sept)–**37**. Air. Recess. W **7** (sideways*). P 14.

49*b*	10	3m. green and sepia (1.1.33)	2·50	6·50
50		5m. black and green	1·00	10
51		10m. black and carmine	1·00	20
52		15m. red-brown and sepia	40	10
		aw. Wmk sideways inverted (top of G to right)	£200	£180
		b. Perf 11½×12½ (1937)	4·50	10
		bx. Wmk reversed	†	£300
		by. Wmk sideways inverted (top of G to right) and reversed	£400	
53		2p. black and orange	50	10
		ab. Frame printed double, one albino	£800	
		ax. Wmk reversed	£225	
		ay. Wmk sideways inverted (top of G to right) and reversed	£225	
		b. Perf 11½×12½ (1937)	4·50	22·00
53*c*		2½p. magenta and blue (1.1.33)	4·75	10
		cw. Wmk sideways inverted (top of G to right)	—	£300
		cy. Wmk sideways inverted (top of G to right) and reversed	£325	
		d. Perf 11½×12½ (1936)	5·00	10
		da. Aniline magenta and blue	12·00	3·50
		dx. Wmk reversed	£200	
		dy. Wmk sideways inverted (top of G to right) and reversed	£250	£275
54		3p. black and grey	60	15
		a. Perf 11½×12½ (1937)	1·00	35
55		3½p. black and violet	1·50	80
		a. Perf 11½×12½ (1937)	2·50	20·00
		ay. Wmk sideways inverted (top of G to right) and reversed	†	£275
56		4½p. red-brown and grey	13·00	15·00
57		5p. black and ultramarine	1·00	30
		a. Perf 11½×12½ (1937)	3·75	35
57*b*		7½p. green and emerald (17.10.35)	9·50	5·50
		bx. Wmk reversed	£200	
		by. Wmk sideways inverted (top of G to right) and reversed	£200	£200
		c. Perf 11½×12½ (1937)	4·00	10·00
57*d*		10p. brown and greenish blue (17.10.35)	10·00	1·75
		e. Perf 11½×12½ (1937)	8·00	27·00
		ey. Wmk sideways inverted (top of G to right) and reversed	£275	
49*b*/57*d* *Set of* 12 (P 14)			40·00	26·00
52*b*/7*e* *Set of* 8 (P 11½×12½)			30·00	70·00

*The normal sideways watermark shows the top of the G pointing left *as seen from the back of the stamp*.

1932 (18 July). Air. No. 44 surch with T **11**.

58	2	2½p. on 2p. purple and orange-yellow	1·40	3·75

12 Gen. Gordon (after C. Ouless)

13 Gordon Memorial College, Khartoum

14 Gordon Memorial Service, Khartoum (after R. C. Woodville)

1935 (1 Jan). 50th Death Anniv of General Gordon. Recess. W **7**. P 14.

59	12	5m. green	35	10
60		10m. yellow-brown	85	25
61		13m. ultramarine	85	13·00
62		15m. scarlet	1·75	25
63	13	2p. blue	1·75	20
64		5p. orange-vermilion	1·75	40
65		10p. purple	9·00	9·00
66	14	20p. black	32·00	65·00
67		50p. red-brown	£100	£150
59/67 *Set of* 9			£130	£200

7½ PIASTRES
٧ ١/٢ قروش
(**15**)

5 MILLIEMES
٥ مليمات
(**16**)

1935. Air. Nos. 49*b*/51 and 56 surch as T **15** at Khartoum.

68	10	15m. on 10m. black and carmine (Apr)	40	10
		a. Surch double	£1000	£1200
69		2½p. on 3m. green and sepia (Apr)	85	3·25
		a. Second arabic letter from left missing	50·00	£110
		b. Small "½"	2·25	21·00
70		2½p. on 5m. black and green (Apr)	50	1·00
		a. Second Arabic letter from left missing	25·00	60·00
		b. Small "½"	1·25	2·50
		c. Surch inverted	£1000	£1200
		d. Ditto with variety a	£30000	
		e. Ditto with variety b	£4500	£5500
71		3p. on 4½p. red-brown and grey (Apr)	1·75	21·00
72		7½p. on 4½p. red-brown and grey (Mar)	6·50	50·00
73		10p. on 4½p. red-brown and grey (Mar)	6·50	50·00
68/73 *Set of* 6			15·00	£110

Nos. 69a and 70a occur in position 49 of the sheet of 50; the small "½" variety occurs in positions 17, 27, 32, 36, 41, 42 and 46.

The 15m. on 10m. surcharged in red (*Price*, £350) and the 2½p. on 3m. and 2½p. on 5m. in green are from proof sheets; the latter two items being known cancelled (*Price, £225 each, unused*).

There were four proof sheets of the 7½p. on 4½p, two in red and two in black. The setting on these proof sheets showed three errors subsequently corrected before No. 72 was surcharged. Twelve positions showed an Arabic "⅓" instead of "½", one an English "¼" for "½" and another one of the Arabic letters inverted. (*Price for red surcharge*, £350).

1938 (1 July). Air. Nos. 53d, 55, 57*b* and 57*d* surch as T **16** by De La Rue.

74	10	5m. on 2½p. magenta and blue (P 11½×12½)	3·50	10
		w. Wmk sideways inverted (top of G to right)	—	£180

75		3p. on 3½p. black and violet (P 14)	48·00	60·00
		a. Perf 11½×12½	£700	£850
76		3p. on 7½p. green and emerald (P 14)	7·00	6·50
		ax. Wmk reversed		
		ay. Wmk sideways inverted (top of G to right) and reversed.........	90·00	£100
		b. Perf 11½×12½	£700	£850
77		5p. on 10p. brown and greenish blue (P 14)	1·75	4·75
		ax. Wmk reversed	£170	
		b. Perf 11½×12½	£700	£850
74/7 Set of 4			55·00	65·00

A 5p. on 2½p., perf 11½×12½ exists either mint or cancelled from a trial printing (*Price £400 unused*).

5 Mills.

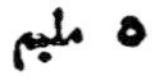

(**17**)    Normal ("Malime")

"Malmime" (Left-hand pane R. 5/1)

"Short "mim" (Right-hand pane R. 3/1)

Broken "lam" (Right-hand pane R. 6/2)

Inserted "5" (Bottom right-hand pane R. 4/5)

1940 (25 Feb). No. 42 surch with T **17** by McCorquodale (Sudan) Ltd, Khartoum.

78	**6**	5m. on 10m. carmine and black	2·00	2·00
		a. "Malmime"	65·00	85·00
		b. Two dots omitted (Right-hand pane R. 8/6)	65·00	85·00
		c. Short "mim"	65·00	85·00
		d. Broken "lam"	65·00	85·00
		e. Inserted "5"	£190	

4½ Piastres

4½ PIASTRES (**18**)

٤١/٢ قرش (**19**)

1940–41. Nos. 41 and 45c surch as T **18** or **19** at Khartoum.

79	**6**	4½p. on 5m. olive-brown & black (9.2.41)	48·00	15·00
80	**2**	4½p. on 8p. emerald and black (12.12.40)	42·00	9·00

20 Tuti Island, R. Nile, near Khartoum

21 Tuti Island, R. Nile near Khartoum

(Des Miss H. M. Hebbert. Litho Security Printing Press, Nasik, India)

1941 (25 Mar–10 Aug). P 14×13½ (T **20**) or P 13½×14 (T **21**).

81	**20**	1m. slate and orange (10.8)	5·00	4·00
82		2m. orange and chocolate (10.8)............	5·00	5·50
83		3m. mauve and green (10.8).................	5·50	20
84		4m. green and chocolate (10.8)..............	1·00	1·50
85		5m. olive-brown and black (10.8)...........	50	10
86		10m. carmine and black (10.8)	29·00	5·50
87		15m. bright blue and chestnut..............	1·50	10
88	**21**	2p. purple and orange-yellow (10.8)........	7·50	60
89		3p. red-brown and blue...................	1·25	10
90		4p. ultramarine and black...............	6·50	10
91		5p. chestnut and green (10.8)............	11·00	13·00
92		6p. greenish blue and black (10.8)........	27·00	2·00

93		8p. emerald and black (10.8)............	30·00	2·00
94		10p. slate and purple (10.8)............	£120	1·25
95		20p. pale blue and blue (10.8)...........	£100	50·00
81/95 Set of 15			£325	75·00

22

23

1m.–15m. "nun" flaw (R. 2/3)

1948 (1 Jan–June). Arabic inscriptions below camel altered. Typo. Ordinary paper (8, 10, 20p.) or chalk-surfaced paper (others). W **7**. P 14.

96	**22**	1m. black and orange............	35	7·00
		a. "nun" flaw	8·00	
97		2m. orange and chocolate..........	80	5·50
		a. "nun" flaw	15·00	
98		3m. mauve and green.............	30	9·00
		a. "nun" flaw	8·00	
99		4m. deep green and chocolate	50	3·25
		a. "nun" flaw	15·00	
100		5m. olive-brown and black.........	12·00	3·00
		a. "nun" flaw	30·00	
		w. Wmk inverted	75·00	
101		10m. rose-red and black............	5·50	10
		a. Centre inverted	†	£40000
		b. "nun" flaw	20·00	
102		15m. ultramarine and chestnut........	5·00	20
		a. "nun" flaw	20·00	
103	**23**	2p. purple and orange-yellow	11·00	5·00
104		3p. red-brown and deep blue...........	7·50	30
105		4p. ultramarine and black..........	4·00	1·75
106		5p. brown-orange and deep green	4·00	7·00
107		6p. greenish blue and black	4·50	3·50
108		8p. bluish green and black	4·50	6·00
109		10p. black and mauve	16·00	10·00
		a. Chalk-surfaced paper (June)	55·00	6·00
110		20p. pale blue and deep blue..........	4·50	50
		a. Perf 13. Chalk-surfaced paper (June)	40·00	£200
111		50p. carmine and ultramarine............	6·50	2·75
96/111 Set of 16			75·00	55·00

A single used example is known of No. 101a.
The 2m. and 4m. are known without the "nun" flaw on R. 2/3.
For similar stamps, but with different Arabic inscriptions, see Nos. 37/46b.

24

25

1948 (1 Oct). Golden Jubilee of "Camel Postman" design. Chalk-surfaced paper. Typo. W **7**. P 13.

112	**24**	2p. black and light blue	50	10

1948 (23 Dec). Opening of Legislative Assembly. Chalk-surfaced paper. Typo. W **7**. P 13.

113	**25**	10m. rose-red and black	1·25	10
114		5p. brown-orange and deep green	1·75	2·75

26 Blue Nile Bridge, Khartoum   **27** Kassala Jebel

28 Sagia (water wheel)

29 Port Sudan

30 Gordon Memorial College

31 *Gordon Pasha* (Nile mail boat)

32 Suakin

33 G.P.O., Khartoum

(Des Col. W. L. Atkinson (2½p., 6p.), G. R. Wilson (3p.), others from photographs. Recess)

1950 (1 July). Air. T **26/33**. W **7**. P 12.

115	**26**	2p. black and blue-green	6·00	1·50
116	**27**	2½p. light blue and red-orange	1·25	1·75
117	**28**	3p. reddish purple and blue	4·50	1·25
118	**29**	3½p. purple-brown and yellow-brown	6·00	6·00
119	**30**	4p. brown and light blue	1·50	3·25
120	**31**	4½p. black and ultramarine	3·00	6·50
		a. Black and steel-blue	20·00	11·00
121	**32**	6p. black and carmine	4·50	3·75
122	**33**	20p. black and purple	2·50	7·50
115/122		*Set of 8*	26·00	28·00

34 Ibex

35 Whale-headed stork

36 Giraffe

37 Baggara girl

38 Shilluk warrior

39 Hadendowa

40 Policeman

41 Cotton Picking

42 Ambatch reed canoe

43 Nuba wrestlers

44 Weaving

45 Saluka farming

46 Gum tapping

47 Darfur chief

48 Stack Laboratory

49 Nile Lechwe

50 Camel postman

(Des Col. W. L. Atkinson (1m., 2m., 4m., 5m., 10m., 3p., 3½p., 20p.), Col. E. A. Stanton (50p.) others from photographs. Typo)

1951 (1 Sept)–**61**. Designs as T **34/50**. Chalk-surfaced paper. W **7**. P 14 (millieme values) or 13 (piastre values).

123	**34**	1m. black and orange	4·00	1·50
124	**35**	2m. black and bright blue	3·50	1·50
125	**36**	3m. black and green	12·00	6·50
126	**37**	4m. black and yellow-green	3·50	6·50
127	**38**	5m. black and purple	2·25	10
		a. Black and reddish purple (8.6.59)	6·50	70
128	**39**	10m. black and pale blue	30	10
129	**40**	15m. black and chestnut	10·00	10
		a. Black and brown-orange (1961)*	6·50	10
130	**41**	2p. deep blue and pale blue	30	10
		a. Deep blue and very pale blue (9.58).*	6·00	1·00
131	**42**	3p. brown and dull ultramarine	22·00	10
		a. Brown and deep blue (11.58)*	11·00	2·75
132	**43**	3½p. bright green and red-brown	2·75	10
		a. Light emerald and red-brown (11.61)*	6·00	10
133	**44**	4p. ultramarine and black	6·50	25
		a. Deep blue and black (7.59)*	8·00	10
134	**45**	5p. orange-brown and yellow-green	3·00	10
135	**46**	6p. blue and black	8·50	2·75
		a. Deep blue and black (8.61)*	16·00	6·50
136	**47**	8p. blue and brown	14·00	5·00
		a. Deep blue and brown (5.60)*	16·00	9·50
137	**48**	10p. black and green	1·50	1·50
138	**49**	20p. blue-green and black	12·00	3·75
139	**50**	50p. carmine and black	20·00	4·75
123/39		*Set of 17*	£100	30·00

*Earliest known postmark date.

SELF-GOVERNMENT

51 Camel Postman

1954 (9 Jan). Self-Government. Chalk-surfaced paper. Typo. W **7**. P 13.

140	**51**	15m. orange-brown and bright green	50	1·25
141		3p. blue and indigo	75	5·00
142		5p. black and reddish purple	50	2·50
140/2		*Set of 3*	1·60	8·00

Stamps as Type **51**, but dated "1953" were released in error at the Sudan Agency in London. They had no postal validity (*Price per set* £18 *un*).

Sudan became an independent republic on 1 January 1956. Later issues will be found in Part 14 (*Africa since Independence N-Z*) of this catalogue.

STAMP BOOKLETS

Nos. SB1/3 have one cover inscribed in English and one in Arabic. Listings are provided for booklets believed to have been issued, with prices quoted for those known to still exist.

1912 (Dec). Black on pink cover, size 74×29 mm. Stapled.
SB1   100m. booklet containing twenty 5m. (No. 23) in pairs   £750

1924. Black on pink cover, size 45×50 mm. Stapled.
SB2   105m. booklet containing twenty 5m. (No. 34) in blocks of 4 ....

1930. Black on pink cover, size 45×50 mm. Stapled.
SB3   100m. booklet containing twenty 5m. (No. 41) in blocks of 4 ....   £1600
Some supplies of No. SB3 included a page of air mail labels.

POSTAGE DUE STAMPS

1897 (1 Mar). Type **D 24** of Egypt, optd with T **1** at Bûlaq.

D1	2m. green	1·75	5·00
	a. Opt omitted (in horiz pair with normal)	£3250	
D2	4m. maroon	1·75	5·00
	a. Bisected (2m.) (on cover)	†	—
D3	1p. ultramarine	10·00	3·50
D4	2p. orange	10·00	7·00
	a. Bisected (1p.) (on cover)	†	£1400
D1/4	Set of 4	21·00	18·00

In some printings the large dot is omitted from the left-hand Arabic character on one stamp in the pane.
No. D1 has been recorded used as a bisect.

D **1** Gunboat *Zafir*

D **2**

1901 (1 Jan)–26. Typo. Ordinary paper. W **4** (sideways). P 14.

D5	D **1**	2m. black and brown	55	60
		a. Wmk upright (1912)	£225	75·00
		b. Chalk-surfaced paper (6.24*)	3·00	12·00
D6		4m. brown and green	2·00	90
		a. Chalk-surfaced paper (9.26*)	12·00	11·00
D7		10m. green and mauve	9·00	3·75
		a. Wmk upright (1912)	£130	60·00
		b. Chalk-surfaced paper (6.24*)	18·00	17·00
D8		20m. ultramarine and carmine	3·25	3·25
D5/8	Set of 4		13·50	7·50

*Dates quoted for the chalk-surfaced paper printings are those of the earliest recorded postal use. These printings were despatched to the Sudan in March 1922 (10m.) or September 1922 (others).
The 4m. is known bisected at Khartoum or Omdurman in November/December 1901 and the 20m. at El Obeid in 1904–05.

1927–30. Chalk-surfaced paper. W **7**. P 14.

D9	D **1**	2m. black and brown (1930)	2·50	2·50
D10		4m. brown and green	1·00	80
D11		10m. green and mauve	1·75	1·60
		a. Ordinary paper...........................	22·00	8·00
D9/11	Set of 3		4·75	4·50

1948 (1 Jan). Arabic inscriptions altered. Chalk-surfaced paper. Typo. W **7**. P 14.

D12	D **2**	2m. black and brown-orange	4·75	50·00
D13		4m. brown and green	11·00	55·00
D14		10m. green and mauve	20·00	21·00
D15		20m. ultramarine and carmine......	20·00	40·00
D12/15	Set of 4		50·00	£150

The 10 and 20m. were reissued in 1979 on Sudan arms watermarked paper.

OFFICIAL STAMPS

1900 (8 Feb). 5 mils of 1897 punctured "S G" by hand. The "S" has 14 and the "G" 12 holes.
O1   5m. rose-carmine ....   60·00   16·00

1901 (Jan). 1m. wmk Quatrefoil, punctured as No. O1.
O2   1m. brown and pink...........................   55·00   30·00
Nos. O1/2 are found with the punctured "SG" inverted, reversed or inverted and reversed.

O.S.G.S.
(O **1**) ("On Sudan Government Service")

O.S.G.S.
(O **2**) ("On Sudan Government Service")

O.S.G.S.
Malformed "O" (lower pane, R. 1/7)

O.S.G.S.
Accent over "G" (upper pane, R. 4/12)

1902. No. 10 optd at Khartoum as Type O **1** in groups of 30 stamps.

O3	**2**	1m. brown and pink..................	3·25	14·00
		a. Oval "O" (No. 19)	40·00	£110
		b. Round stops. (Nos. 25 to 30)	7·50	45·00
		c. Opt inverted	£350	£475
		d. Ditto and oval "O"..............	£4250	£5000
		e. Ditto and round stops.........	£900	£1200
		f. Opt double	£500	
		g. Ditto and round stops.........	£1500	
		h. Ditto and oval "O".............	£5000	

1903–12. T **2** optd as Type O **2**, by D.L.R. in sheets of 120 stamps.

*(i) W **3** (Quatrefoil)*

O4	10p. black and mauve (3.06)	19·00	26·00
	a. Malformed "O"..............................	£150	

*(ii) W **4** (Mult Star and Cresent)*

O5	1m. brown and carmine (9.04)	50	10
	a. Opt double		
	b. Malformed "O"..............................	20·00	10·00
O6	3m. mauve and green (2.04)	2·50	15
	a. Opt double	£850	£850
	b. Malformed "O"..............................	45·00	12·00
	c. Accent over "G".............................		
O7	5m. scarlet and black (1.1.03)	2·50	10
	a. Malformed "O"..............................	45·00	10·00
	b. Accent over "G".............................		
O8	1p. blue and brown (1.1.03)	10·00	10
	a. Malformed "O"..............................	90·00	10·00
	b. Accent over "G".............................		
O9	2p. black and blue (1.1.03)	38·00	20
	a. Malformed "O"..............................	£225	14·00
	b. Accent over "G".............................		
O10	5p. brown and green (1.1.03)	2·75	30
	a. Malformed "O"..............................	55·00	15·00
	b. Accent over "G".............................		
O11	10p. black and mauve (9.12)	4·00	70·00
	a. Malformed "O"..............................	70·00	
O4/11	Set of 8	70·00	85·00

The malformed "O" is slightly flattened on the left-hand side and occurs on position 7 of the lower pane.

1913 (1 Jan)–**22.** Nos. 18/20 and 23/8 punctured "SG" by machine. The "S" has 12 holes and the "G" 13.

O12	**2**	1m. brown and carmine	18·00	25
O13		2m. green and brown (1915)...........	17·00	7·50
O14		3m. mauve and green	27·00	70
O15		5m. scarlet and black	9·50	15
O16		1p. blue and brown	14·00	35
O17		2p. black and blue	35·00	65
O18		2p. purple and orange-yellow (chalk-surfaced paper) (1922)	11·00	9·00
O19		5p. brown and green	50·00	3·00
		a. Chalk-surfaced paper	50·00	8·50
O20		10p. black and mauve (1914)	70·00	50·00
		a. Chalk-surfaced paper	70·00	50·00
O12/20	Set of 9		£225	65·00

1922. Nos. 32/5 punctured "SG" by machine. The "S" has 9 holes and the "G" 10.

O21	**6**	3m. mauve and green	24·00	14·00
O22		4m. green and chocolate	38·00	9·00
O23		5m. olive-brown and black............	9·00	2·50
O24		10m. carmine and black................	9·00	2·50
O21/4	Set of 4		70·00	25·00

1927–30. Nos. 39/42, 44, 45 and 46 punctured "SG" by machine. Nos. O25/8 have 9 holes in the "S" and 10 in the "G"; Nos. O29/31 12 holes in the "S" and 13 in the "G".

O25	**6**	3m. mauve and green (1928)	28·00	5·00
O26		4m. green and chocolate (1930)	90·00	50·00
O27		5m. olive-brown and black............	11·00	10
O28		10m. carmine and black................	30·00	35
O29	**2**	2p. purple and orange-yellow	38·00	1·00
O30		5p. chestnut and green	29·00	3·50
O31		10p. black and reddish purple	60·00	10·00
O25/31	Set of 7		£250	60·00

The use of Nos. O25/31 on internal official mail ceased in 1932, but they continued to be required for official mail to foreign destinations until replaced by Nos. O32/46 in 1936.

S.G.   S.G.   S.G.
(O **3**)   (O **4**)   (O **4a**)

1936 (19 Sept)–**46**. Nos. 37a, 38a, 39/43 optd with Type O **3**, and 44, 44ba, 44c, 45, 45ba, 45ca, 46 and 46ba with Type O **4**. W **7**. P 14.

O32	**6**	1m. black and orange (22.11.46)	2·50	16·00
		a. Opt double	†	£225
O33		2m. orange and chocolate (*ordinary paper*) (4.45)	5·50	9·00
		a. Chalk-surfaced paper	£110	70·00
O34		3m. mauve and green (*chalk-surfaced paper*) (1.37)	5·00	10
O35		4m. green and chocolate (*chalk-surfaced paper*)	9·50	4·75
		a. Ordinary paper		
O36		5m. olive-brown and black (*chalk-surfaced paper*) (3.40)	8·00	10
		a. Ordinary paper	29·00	40
O37		10m. carmine and black (*chalk-surfaced paper*) (6.46)	1·75	10
O38		15m. bright blue and chestnut (*chalk-surfaced paper*) (21.6.37)	14·00	30
		a. Ordinary paper	80·00	4·25
O39	**2**	2p. purple and orange-yellow (*chalk-surfaced paper*) (4.37)	18·00	10
		a. Ordinary paper	50·00	1·00
O39b		3p. red-brown and blue (4.46)	7·50	2·75
O39c		4p. ultramarine and black (*chalk-surfaced paper*) (4.46)	50·00	9·00
		ca. Ordinary paper	80·00	4·50
O40		5p. chestnut and green (*chalk-surfaced paper*)	17·00	10
		a. Ordinary paper	£100	6·50
O40b		6p. greenish blue and black (4.46)	14·00	12·00
O40c		8p. emerald and black (4.46)	7·00	45·00
O41		10p. black and reddish purple (*chalk-surfaced paper*) (10.37)	60·00	23·00
		a. Ordinary paper. *Black and bright mauve* (1941)	60·00	10·00
O42		20p. pale blue and blue (6.46)	38·00	35·00
O32/42		*Set of 15*	£225	£120

1948 (1 Jan). Nos. 96/102 optd with Type O **3**, and 103/111 with Type O **4**.

O43	**22**	1m. black and orange	30	6·50
		a. "nun" flaw	8·00	
O44		2m. orange and chocolate	2·25	1·25
		a. "nun" flaw	15·00	
O45		3m. mauve and green	5·00	12·00
		a. "nun" flaw	20·00	
O46		4m. deep green and chocolate	4·25	7·00
O47		5m. olive-brown and black	3·75	10
		a. "nun" flaw	20·00	
O48		10m. rose-red and black	3·75	3·00
		a. "nun" flaw	20·00	
O49		15m. ultramarine and chestnut	4·50	10
		a. "nun" flaw	20·00	
O50	**23**	2p. purple and orange-yellow	4·50	10
O51		3p. red-brown and deep blue	4·50	10
O52		4p. ultramarine and black	4·00	10
		a. Perf 13 (optd Type O **4a**)	13·00	21·00
O53		5p. brown-orange and deep green	6·50	10
O54		6p. greenish blue and black	3·50	10
O55		8p. bluish green and black	3·50	8·00
O56		10p. black and mauve	8·00	20
O57		20p. pale blue and deep blue	6·00	1·00
O58		50p. carmine and ultramarine	70·00	60·00
O43/58		*Set of 16*	£120	90·00

The "nun" flaw is not known on No. O46.

1950 (1 July). Air. Optd with Type O **4a**.

O59	**26**	2p. black and blue-green (R.)	16·00	4·00
O60	**27**	2½p. light blue and red-orange	1·50	1·75
O61	**28**	3p. reddish purple and blue	1·00	1·00
O62	**29**	3½p. purple-brown and yellow-brown	1·25	12·00
O63	**30**	4p. brown and light blue	1·00	10·00
O64	**31**	4½p. black and ultramarine (R.)	4·75	23·00
		a. *Black and steel-blue*	20·00	27·00
O65	**32**	6p. black and carmine (R.)	1·00	5·00
O66	**33**	20p. black and purple (R.)	4·50	12·00
O59/66		*Set of 8*	28·00	60·00

1951 (1 Sept)–**62?**. Nos. 123/9 optd with Type O **3**, and 130/9 with Type O **4a**.

O67	**34**	1m. black and orange (R.)	50	6·50
O68	**35**	2m. black and bright blue (R.)	50	2·50
O69	**36**	3m. black and green (R.)	14·00	22·00
O70	**37**	4m. black and yellow-green (R.)	10	5·50
O71	**38**	5m. black and purple (R.)	10	10
		a. *Black and reddish purple*		
O72	**39**	10m. black and pale blue (R.)	10	10
O73	**40**	15m. black and chestnut (R.)	1·00	10
		a. *Black and brown-orange*		
O74	**41**	2p. deep blue and pale blue	10	10
		a. Opt inverted	£1200	
		b. *Deep blue and very pale blue* (9.61*)	2·25	10

O75	**42**	3p. brown and dull ultramarine	30·00	10
		a. *Brown and deep blue* (8.60*)	30·00	3·25
O76	**43**	3½p. bright green and red-brown	30	10
		a. *Light emerald and red-brown* (1962?)	8·00	5·50
O77	**44**	4p. ultramarine and black	8·00	10
		a. *Deep blue and black* (1961)	8·50	10
O78	**45**	5p. orange-brown and yellow-green	40	10
O79	**46**	6p. blue and black	70	4·00
		a. *Deep blue and black* (1962?)	15·00	10·00
O80	**47**	8p. blue and brown	1·00	30
		a. *Deep blue and brown* (1962?)	11·00	6·00
O81	**48**	10p. black and green (R.)	70	10
O81a	**49**	10p. black and green (Blk.) (1958)	21·00	4·00
O82	**50**	20p. blue-green and black	1·50	30
		a. Opt inverted	†	£4000
O83		50p. carmine and black	6·00	1·25
O67/83		*Set of 18*	75·00	42·00

The 5, 10 and 15m. values were reissued between 1957 and 1960 with a thinner overprint with smaller stops.
*Earliest known postmark date.

ARMY SERVICE STAMPS

Army

ARMY   OFFICIAL   ARMY   OFFICIAL

Service

(A **1**)   (A **2**)   (A **3**)

1905 (1 Jan). T **2** optd at Khartoum as Types A **1** or A **2**. W **4** (Mult Star and Crescent).

(i) "ARMY" reading up

A1		1m. brown and carmine (A **1**)	9·00	3·75
		a. "!" for "1"	85·00	50·00
		b. Opt Type A **2**	65·00	32·00
		c. Pair. Types A **1** and A **2** se-tenant	£120	£150

(ii) Overprint horizontal

A2		1m. brown and carmine (A **1**)	£550	
		a. "!" for "1"	£6500	
		b. Opt Type A **2**	£4250	

The horizontal overprint exists with either "ARMY" or "OFFICIAL" reading the right way up. It did not fit the stamps, resulting in misplacements where more than one whole overprint appears, or when the two words are transposed.

(iii) "ARMY" reading down

A3		1m. brown and carmine (A **1**)	£180	95·00
		a. "!" for "1"	£1500	£1500
		b. Opt Type A **2**	£1300	£800

1905 (Nov). As No. A1, W **3** (Quatrefoil).

A4		1m. brown and pink (A **1**)	£225	£250
		a. "!" for "1"	£6000	£4000
		b. Opt Type A **2**	£3500	£3500
		c. Pair. Types A **1** and A **2** se-tenant	£5000	

The setting used for overprinting Nos. A1/4 was 30 (6×5). The "!" for "1" variety occurs on R. 5/4 and overprint Type A **2** on R. 1/6 and 2/6 of the setting.

Two varieties of the 1 millieme.

A. 1st Ptg. 14 mm between lines of opt.
B. Later Ptgs. 12 mm between lines.
    All other values are Type B.

1906 (Jan)–**11**. T **2** optd as Type A **3**.

*(i) W **4** (Mult Star and Crescent)*

A5		1m. brown and carmine (Type A)	£700	£450
		a. Opt double, one albino	£750	
A6		1m. brown and carmine (Type B)	3·25	20
		a. Opt double, one diagonal	†	£1600
		b. Opt inverted	£800	£800
		c. Pair, one without opt	†	£7500
		d. "Service" omitted	†	£4750
A7		2m. green and brown	27·00	1·00
		a. Pair, one without opt	£4750	
		b. "Army" omitted	£4500	£4500
A8		3m. mauve and green	25·00	40
		a. Opt inverted	£2000	
A9		5m. scarlet and black	4·75	10
		a. Opt double	£400	£250
		ab. Opt double, one diagonal	£350	
		b. Opt inverted	†	£450
		c. "Army"	†	£2750
		e. Opt double, one inverted	£1800	£700
		f. "Armv" for "Army" (R. 4/9)	£2000	
A10		1p. blue and brown	28·00	15
		a. "Army" omitted	—	£3500
		b. Opt double	†	£3000
A11		2p. black and blue (1.09)	£100	13·00
		a. Opt double	—	£3000
A12		5p. brown and green (5.08)	£180	65·00

| A13 | | 10p. black and mauve (5.11) | £550 | £700 |
| A6s/10s Optd "SPECIMEN" Set of 5 | | | | £130 |

There were a number of printings of these Army Service stamps; the earlier are as Type A **3**; the 1908 printing has a narrower "A" in "Army" and the 1910–11 printings have the tail of the "y" in "Army" much shorter.

The two overprints on No. A11a are almost coincident. The error comes from the 'short "y"' printing.

A variety with no cross-bar to "A" of "Army" is known on some values, but does not appear to be constant.

*(ii) W **3** (Quatrefoil)*

A14		2p. black and mauve	95·00	10·00
A15		5p. brown and green	£130	£250
A16		10p. black and mauve	£160	£425
A14/16 Set of 3			£350	£650
A14s/16s Optd "SPECIMEN" Set of 3				£120

1913 (1 Jan)–**22**. Nos. 18/20 and 23/8 punctured "AS" by machine. The "A" has 12 holes and the "S" 11.

A17	**2**	1m. brown and carmine	50·00	6·00
A18		2m. green and brown	14·00	70
A19		3m. mauve and green	65·00	4·75
A20		5m. scarlet and black	19·00	50
		a. On No. 13		
A21		1p. blue and brown	42·00	1·00
A22		2p. black and blue	80·00	7·00
A23		2p. purple and orange-yellow (*chalk-surfaced paper*) (1922)	£100	55·00
A24		5p. brown and green	95·00	48·00
		a. Chalk-surfaced paper	£110	48·00
A25		10p. black and mauve (1914)	£500	£275
A17/25 Set of 9			£850	£350

1922–24. Nos. 31a and 34/5 punctured "AS" by machine. The "A" has 8 holes and the "S" 9.

A26	**6**	2m. yellow and chocolate (1924)	£100	55·00
A27		5m. olive-brown and black (4.2.22)	24·00	6·50
A28		10m. carmine and black	30·00	9·50
A26/8 Set of 3			£140	65·00

The use of Nos. A17/28 on internal Army mail ceased when the Egyptian units were withdrawn at the end of 1924, but existing stocks continued to be used on Army mail to foreign destinations until supplies were exhausted.

TELEGRAPH STAMPS

From March to May 1885 the Military Telegraph stamps of Great Britain (Bechuanaland Nos. MT1/8) were in use in Sudan. Identifying postmark codes are "SK" (Suakin), "QI" (Quarantine Island), "HQ" (Headquarters), "WR" (Western Redoubt) and "ZA" (No.1 Post and, later, 2nd Brigade HQ).

Telegraph stamps were reintroduced during the Sudan campaign of 1896–8.

(T **1**)

T **2**

1897 (July?). Nos. 5/9 handstamped as Type T **1**.

T1		5m. rose-carmine	7·00	2·00
		a. Opt in blue	21·00	6·00
T2		1p. ultramarine	14·00	4·00
		a. Opt in blue	22·00	10·00
T3		2p. orange-brown	18·00	5·00
T4		5p. slate	24·00	8·00
		a. Opt in blue	40·00	20·00
T5		10p. mauve	18·00	10·00
		a. Opt in blue	70·00	40·00

Handstamp T T **1** is known sideways, diagonal and inverted.

Nos. 1, 3 and 4 are also known handstamped T T **1**, but their authenticity is in doubt.

(Typo D.L.R.)

1898 (1 March). W **3**. P 14.

			Un whole stamp	Used whole stamp	Used half
T6	T **2**	5m. brown-purple and violet	5·00	6·00	75
T7		1p. black and bright carmine	5·00	6·00	75
T8		2p. green and lilac-brown	5·00	6·00	75
T9		5p. violet and black	5·00	6·00	75

PRICES for Nos. T6/17 are for unused whole stamps, used whole stamps or used half stamps. Each stamp has an extra central vertical line of perforations to allow "bisection" in use.

1898 (June). W **8a** of Egypt (sideways). P 14.

| T10 | T **2** | 10p. bright rose and bluish green | 70·00 | 90·00 | 20·00 |

1898–99. W **4**. P 14.

T11	T **2**	5m. brown-purple and violet	1·50	3·00	50
T12		5m. brown and blue (1899)	3·00	5·00	75
T13		1p. black and bright carmine	1·50	3·00	50
T14		2p. green and lilac-brown (1899)	15·00	20·00	2·00
T15		5p. violet and black (1899)	2·00	3·00	50
T16		10p. bright rose and bluish green	2·50	3·50	50
T17		25p. blue and brown (1899)	3·00	5·00	75

The use of telegraph stamps was discontinued in 1902. Postage stamps which had been used for telegraph purposes in parallel with telegraph stamps throughout, were exclusively used thereafter.

Tanzania

GERMAN EAST AFRICA

1893. 64 Pesa = 1 Rupee
1905. 100 Heller = 1 Rupee

In November 1884 Karl Peters, a leader of the German colonial movement, made a treaty with a chief near Usambara, who was declared to be independent of the Sultan of Zanzibar who claimed to rule the mainland of what is now Tanzania. Similar treaties followed, and on 27 February 1885 Germany established a protectorate over the coast of East Africa from the Umba River in the north to the Rovuma River in the south.

LAMU

A postal agency was opened on the island of Lamu, which belonged to the Sultan of Zanzibar, on 22 November 1888 and used unoverprinted stamps of Germany. It closed on 31 March 1891 when the area was transferred to Great Britain.

1888–91. Stamps of Germany cancelled with circular post-mark "LAMU/OSTAFRIKA".

(a) No. 38b (Numeral inscr "DEUTSCHE REICHS-POST")

Z1	7	2m. dull rose (26.10.89)	£7000

(b) Nos. 39/44 (Numeral or Eagle inscr "DEUTSCHE REICHS-POST")

Z2	5	3pf. green (3.2.91)	£5500
Z3		5pf. mauve (13.6.89)	£650
Z4	6	10pf. carmine (8.6.89)	£550
Z5		20pf. bright blue (2.12.88)	£500
Z6		25pf. deep chestnut (9.90)	—
Z7		50pf. dull olive-green (19.1.89)	£1300

(c) Nos. 46/51 (Numeral or Eagle inscr "REICHSPOST")

Z8	8	3pf. brown (6.1.91)	£800
Z9		5pf. green (3.2.91)	£650
		a. Yellow-green (1891)	£650
Z10	9	10pf. rose (6.1.91)	£800
Z11		20pf. ultramarine (3.2.91)	£900
		a. Dull blue (1891)	—
Z12		25pf. orange-yellow (27.2.91)	£1100
Z13		50pf. chocolate (27.2.91)	£1600

Dates are those of earliest known use.
Remainders of Nos. Z3/4 were sold with backdated cancellations; prices quoted are for genuinely used copies, remainders being almost worthless. These remainders, which when on piece are usually on buff-coloured paper, were cancelled as follows: various dates in 1888, 12.3.89, 12.8.89, 21.9.89, 17.12.89, 20.7.90 and 12.8.90.

ZANZIBAR

A postal agency opened in Zanzibar on 27 August 1890 and used unoverprinted stamps of Germany. It closed on 31 July 1891.

1890–91. Stamps of Germany cancelled with circular postmark "ZANZIBAR/KAISERL DEUTSCHE/POSTAGENTUR".

(a) Nos. 38b/d (Numeral inscr "DEUTSCHE REICHS-POST")

Z14	7	2m. mauve (1.9.90)	£5500
		a. Deep claret (9.11.90)	£1900
		b. Dull rose (25.4.91)	£1300

(b) Nos. 46/51 (Numeral or Eagle inscr "REICHSPOST")

Z15	8	3pf. brown (24.3.91)	£450
Z16		5pf. green (4.10.90)	£275
		a. Yellow-green	£225
Z17	9	10pf. rose (31.8.90)	£225
Z18		20pf. ultramarine (31.8.90)	£200
		a. Dull blue	£150
Z19		25pf. orange-yellow (24.3.91)	£900
Z20		50pf. lake-brown (1.9.90)	£800
		a. Chocolate	£450

Dates are those of earliest known use.
Prices quoted are for cancellations in black; most cancellations in blue are worth more.
Examples of Nos. 40/42 of Germany exist with Zanzibar postmarks. These are backdated philatelic cancellations, genuinely used examples being unknown.

OTHER POST OFFICES IN EAST AFRICA

On 4 October 1890 postal agencies were opened at Dar-es-Salaam and Bagamoyo. These were later made post offices. Further agencies were opened on the coast at Tanga (5 May 1891), Lindi (17 May 1891), Kilwa (14 April 1892), Saadani (5 May 1892) and Pangani (15 June 1892). All these used unoverprinted German stamps from these dates.

From 1894 many other offices were opened; unoverprinted German stamps are also known with the following cancellations: Bukoba (opened 14.9.95), Iringa (24.5.98), Kilimatinde (10.1.96), Kilossa (1.4.95), Kisaki (29.4.95 to 15.3.96), Langenburg (5.6.95), Marangu (29.6.95 to 18.5.01), Masinde (15.4.95 to 15.3.96), Mikindani (30.10.94), Mohorro (1.2.94), Moschi (16.4.95), Mpapua (20.4.95), Muanza (1.10.95), Muhesa (12.3.00), Songea (13.5.99), Tabora (15.7.95), Ujiji (8.4.98), Wiedhafen (25.10.99) and Wilhelmsthal (30.4.99).

> **PRICES.** Prices of Nos. Z21/7 are for the most common type of postmark for Dar-es-Salaam found on each stamp; less common types and most cancellations of other offices are worth more. Prices for Nos Z22/5 and Z27 are for cancellations before mid-1893; stamps used after this date are worth about 25% less than those used before.

1890–99. Stamps of Germany cancelled with circular postmarks of German East Africa post offices.

(a) Nos. 38b and 38d/e (Numeral inscr "DEUTSCHEREICHS-POST")

Z21	7	2m. deep claret (29.3.91)	£3750
		a. Dull rose (3.10.91)	55·00
		b. Red-lilac (20.1.99)	70·00

(b) Nos. 46/51 (Numeral or Eagle inscr "REICHSPOST")

Z22	8	3pf. brown (22.1.91)	£130
		a. Grey-brown (1892)	65·00
Z23		5pf. green (4.12.90)	£140
		a. Yellow-green (1890)	80·00
Z24	9	10pf. rose (29.11.90)	80·00
		a. Carmine (1893)	75·00
Z25		20pf. ultramarine (29.10.90)	£130
		a. Dull blue (1891)	£160
Z26		25pf. orange-yellow (2.4.91)	£650
		a. Orange (1894)	£550
Z27		50pf. lake-brown (29.10.90)	£600
		a. Chocolate (1891)	£130

Dates are those of earliest known use. Examples of other shades of the 3pf. (Nos. Z46c/d) are known used from 1898.
Nos. Z21/7 were valid for postage until 30 September 1901.

2 PESA 2	 10 Deutsch-Ostafrika Pesa
(1)	(2)

1893 (1 July). Stamps of Germany surch as T **1**.

1	8	2p. on 3pf. grey-brown	55·00	65·00
		a. Surch 16¾ mm long		
2		3p. on 5pf. green	65·00	70·00
		a. Surch 14¼ mm long	£1200	
		b. Surch 16¼ mm long	£1600	
3	9	5p. on 10pf. rose	£100	£120
4		5p. on 10pf. carmine	55·00	39·00
		a. Surch 14¼ mm long	£2250	
		b. Surch 16¼ mm long	£2250	
5		10p. on 20pf. ultramarine	39·00	20·00
6		25p. on 50pf. pale red-brown	55·00	39·00
		a. Surch 17½ mm long	£130	55·00
1/6	Set of 5 *(cheapest)*		£325	£325

The normal 2p., 3p. and 5p. surcharges are 15¼ mm long and the 25p. 16¾ mm long.

1896 (Apr)**–99.** Stamps of Germany surch as T **2**.

7	8	2p. on 3pf. grey-brown	16·00	16·00
8		2p. on 3pf. bistre-brown (1899)	3·00	50·00
9		2p. on 3pf. reddish brown	£160	£300
10		3p. on 5pf. green	3·25	6·25
11	9	5p. on 10pf. rose	5·50	6·25
13		10p. on 20pf. ultramarine	7·25	7·25
14		25p. on 50pf. chocolate	31·00	38·00
7/14	Set of 5 *(cheapest)*		45·00	65·00

(illustration A: stamp inscribed "DEUTSCH-OSTAFRIKA 15 HELLER 15")

(illustration B: stamp inscribed "DEUTSCH-OSTAFRIKA")

A	B

"YACHT" KEY TYPES. Types A and B, representing the ex-Kaiser's yacht *Hohenzollern*, were in use throughout the German colonies, inscribed with the name of the particular colony for which they were issued.

Type A was printed by typography and Type B was recess-printed, both by Imperial Printing Office, Berlin.

Perforations. Type A (low values) is perforated 14. In Type B (high values) there are three types of perforation, all measuring about 14½. They are distinguishable by the number of holes along the horizontal and down the vertical sides of the stamps thus:—

(a) 26×17 holes
(b) 25×17 holes
(c) 25×16 holes

Wmk Lozenges

Watermark. Some values listed on paper watermarked Lozenges were prepared for use and sold in Berlin, but owing to the war of 1914–18 were not issued in the colonies.

1901 (1 Jan). No wmk.

15	A	2p. brown	4·00	2·20
16		3p. green	4·00	2·75
17		5p. carmine	4·50	3·25
18		10p. ultramarine	7·25	6·75
19		15p. black and orange/*buff*	7·25	9·00
20		20p. black and carmine	10·00	20·00
21		25p. black and purple/*buff*	10·00	20·00
22		40p. black and carmine/*rose*	12·50	31·00
23	B	1r. claret (*a*)	27·00	65·00
24		2r. green (*a*)	13·50	£110
25		3r. blue-black and red (I) (*a*)	£170	£250
15/25		Set of 11	£250	£475

The 2p. imperforate is a proof.

1905 (1 Apr). Change of currency. No wmk.

26	A	2½h. brown	5·50	2·50
27		4h. green (*shades*)	20·00	7·75
28		7½h. carmine	20·00	2·20
29		15h. ultramarine	33·00	8·25
30		20h. black and red/*yellow*	20·00	22·00
31		30h. black and carmine	20·00	8·25
32		45h. black and mauve	39·00	50·00
		a. Black and violet	£100	£120
33		60h. black and carmine/*rose*	50·00	£130
26/33		Set of 8 (*cheapest*)	£190	£200

1905–20. Wmk Lozenges.

34	A	2½h. brown (30.1.06)	1·30	1·30
35		4h. green (12.5.06)	1·30	90
		a. Booklet pane. No. 35×5 plus label (1.10.11)	£850	
		b. Booklet pane. No. 35×4 plus two labels (1913)	85·00	
36		7½h. carmine (13.8.06)	1·60	2·20
		a. Booklet pane. No. 36×5 plus label (1.10.11)	£850	
		b. Booklet pane. No. 36×4 plus two labels (1913)	55·00	
37		15h. ultramarine (*shades*) (27.6.06)	3·00	2·00
38		20h. black and red/*yellow* (1911)	3·25	28·00
39		30h. black and carmine (16.7.09)	3·50	11·00
40		45h. black and mauve (27.6.06)	7·75	80·00
41		60h. black and carmine/*rose* (14.12.05)	42·00	£275
42	B	1r. carmine (*a*) (6.16)	17·00	
		a. 25×17 holes. *Rose* (1919*)	65·00	
43		2r. green (*b*) (1920*)	65·00	
44		3r. blue-black and red (I) (*a*) (10.9.08)	65·00	£325
		a. 25×17 holes (1919*)	45·00	
		b. Frame I, Centre II (*a*) (1919*)	£800	
		c. Frame I, Centre II (*b*) (1919*)	45·00	

*These stamps were only available from Berlin. The 2r. only appeared in the 1920 remainders auction.

The 1913–19 dates relate to the release of the stamps in Berlin.

Supplies of No. 42 reached German East Africa in March 1916. Around 40 examples are known used from June 1916 onwards.

Because of the War, stocks of stamps in the Colony became depleted. At eight post offices between May 1915 and July 1916 postage is known collected in cash; this was indicated by handstamps reading "Fr. lt. Einn/Nachw. in/(town)", sometimes with value shown. In addition, at Morogoro, Dar-es-Salaam and Tanga envelopes were accepted from the public and, on payment, converted into franked envelopes by handstamping with a seal and the words "Frankiert mit 7½ H". These could then be used anywhere.

Unoverprinted "Germania" stamps of Germany salvaged from the German cruiser *Königsberg* and the *Möwe* were distributed to offices at Bagamoyo, Bukoba, Dodoma, Kilwa, Korogwe, Mohorro, Mombo and Pangani. The 3, 5, 10, 20 and 50pf. values are known used on parcel cards, with cancellation dates from 31 December 1915 to

1 June 1916. A small quantity of 1m. stamps were also salvaged but only one used example has been recorded.

An emergency set of stamps was also officially prepared by the Mission printer at Wuga (near Wilhelmsthal) consisting of three values (2½h., 7½h. and 1r.) typographed on ungummed native paper and rouletted. Fresh supplies of German East Africa stamps arrived in March 1916, however, and the set was not issued. The Wuga stamps were hidden by being buried on a plantation near Morogoro in 1916 and were dug up in 1921.

After a prolonged campaign in 1914–18, at the end of which the German forces were invading Rhodesia, General von Lettow-Vorbeck, the German commander, surrendered under the armistice on 14 November 1918. On 17 December 1920 the United Kingdom was given a mandate of the League of Nations to administer the territories of the former German protectorate, except for Ruanda-Urundi (see Part 4 (*Benelux*) of this catalogue) in the west, where the mandate was given to Belgium, and Kionga in the south, which was ceded to Portugal.

STAMP BOOKLETS

Prices are for complete booklets

Booklet No.	Date	Contents and Cover Price	Price
SB1	1.10.11	Yacht 4 panes, No. 35a; 2 panes, No. 36a (1r.55)	£6500
SB2	1913	Yacht 1 pane, No. 35×6; 1 pane, No. 35b; 2 panes, No. 36×6; 1 pane No. 36b (1r.60)	£425

PRICES FOR STAMPS ON COVER TO 1945
The Mafia Island provisionals (Nos. M1/52) are very rare used on cover.

Nos.	N1/5	from × 8
Nos.	45/59	from × 6
Nos.	60/2	—
Nos.	63/73	from × 6
Nos.	74/86	from × 8
Nos.	87/8	—
Nos.	89/92	from × 6
Nos.	93/106	from × 3
No.	107	—

MAFIA ISLAND

BRITISH OCCUPATION

Mafia Island was captured by the British from the Germans in January 1915. Letters were first sent out unstamped, then with stamps handstamped with Type M **1**. Later the military were supplied with handstamps by the post office in Zanzibar. These were used to produce Nos. M11/52.

There is continuing debate about the status of the Mafia provisional issues, but we are satisfied that they were produced with proper authorisation, under wartime conditions.

(Currency. 100 heller = 1 rupee)

G.B.
MAFIA
(M **1**)

(M **3**)

1915 (Jan). German East Africa Yacht types, handstamped with Type M **1**. Wmk Lozenges, or no wmk (1r., 2r.). A. In black (2½h. in blackish lilac). B. In deep purple. C. In reddish violet.

		A	B	C
M1	2½h. brown	£950	†	£225
	a. Pair, one without handstamp	†	†	£4000
M2	4h. green	£900	£1000	£325
	a. Pair, one without handstamp	†	†	£4000
M3	7½h. carmine	£550	£650	£100
	a. Pair, one without handstamp	£8000	†	£2750
M4	15h. ultramarine	£550	£850	£170
	a. Pair, one without handstamp	†	†	£3500
M5	20h. black and red/*yellow*	£850	£850	£350
	a. Pair, one without handstamp	†	£6500	£4000
M6	30h. black and carmine	£900	£1200	£425
	a. Pair, one without handstamp	£8500	†	£3750
M7	45h. black and mauve	£950	£1200	£500
	a. Pair, one without handstamp	£8500	†	£4750
M8	1r. carmine	£13000	†	£8500
M9	2r. green	£14000	†	£9500

M10	3r. blue-black and red	£15000	† £11000

Prices are for unused examples.

A few contemporary Zanzibar stamps (1, 3, 6 and 15c.) and India – I.E.F. ½a and 1a are known with the above handstamp.

(Currency. 100 cents = 1 rupee)

1915 (May). German East Africa Yacht types with handstamped four-line surcharge "G.R.—POST—6 CENTS—MAFIA" in black, green or violet. Wmk Lozenges or no wmk (1r., 2r.).

M11	6c. on 2½h. brown	£1700	£1800
	a. Pair, one without handstamp	†	£7000
M12	6c. on 4h. green	£1800	£1900
	a. Pair, one without handstamp		£7500
M13	6c. on 7½h. carmine	£1700	£1900
	a. Pair, one without handstamp		£7500
M14	6c. on 15h. ultramarine	£1600	£1900
M15	6c. on 20h. black and red/*yellow*	£2500	£2500
M16	6c. on 30h. black and carmine	£3000	£3250
M17	6c. on 45h. black and mauve	£3000	£3000
	a. Pair, one without handstamp		£8500
M18	6c. on 1r. carmine	£40000	
M19	6c. on 2r. carmine	£45000	
M20	6c. on 3r. blue-black and red	£50000	

The 5, 20 and 40 pesa values of the 1901 Yacht issue are also known with the above surcharge as are the contemporary 1c. and 6c. Zanzibar stamps.

1915 (Sept).

*(a) German East African fiscal stamps. "Statistik des Waaren-Verkehrs" (Trade Statistical Charge) handstamped in bluish green or violet, "O.H.B.M.S. Mafia" in a circle, as Type M **3***

M21	24 pesa, vermilion/*buff*	£850	£1300
M22	12½ heller, drab	£950	£1400
	a. Pair, one without handstamp	£12000	
M23	25 heller, dull green	£950	£1400
M24	50 heller, slate	£950	£1400
	a. Pair, one without handstamp	£12000	
M25	1 rupee, lilac	£950	£1400

(b) German East African "Übersetzungs- Gebühren" (Fee) stamp, overprinted as before

M26	25 heller, grey	£950	£1400

G. R
POST
MAFIA
(M **4**)

G. R.
Post
MAFIA.
(M **5**)

*(c) Stamps as above, but with further opt as Type M **4**, in bluish green or violet*

M27	24 pesa, vermilion/*buff*	£1300
M28	12½ heller, drab	£1400
M29	25 heller, dull green	£1400
M30	50 heller, slate	£1400
M31	1 rupee, lilac	£1400
M32	25 heller, grey (No. M26)	£1400
	a. Pair, one without handstamp Type M **4**	£8000

Type M **3** is also known handstamped on the 7½h., 20h. and 30h. values of German East Africa 1905 Yacht issue and also on contemporary 1, 3, 6 and 25c. Zanzibar stamps.

(Currency. 12 pies = 1 anna. 16 annas = 1 rupee)

1915 (Nov)–**16**. Nos. E1/2, E4/9, E11 and E13 of Indian Expeditionary Forces (India King George V optd "I.E.F.") with a further opt Type M **4** handstruck in green, greenish black or dull blue.

M33	3p. grey	40·00	£100
	a. Pair, one stamp without handstamp		£1900
M34	½a. light green	60·00	£100
	a. Pair, one stamp without handstamp	£2500	£1900
M35	1a. aniline carmine	65·00	90·00
M36	2a. purple	£110	£190
M37	2½a. ultramarine	£120	£200
M38	3a. orange	£130	£200
	a. Pair, one stamp without handstamp	†	£3500
M39	4a. olive-green	£190	£275
M40	8a. deep magenta	£350	£450
	a. Pair, one stamp without handstamp	†	£3500
M41	12a. carmine-lake	£450	£600
M42	1r. red-brown and deep blue-green	£475	£700
	a. "I.E.F." opt double, one albino	£1000	
M33/42 *Set of 10*		£1800	£2500

All values exist with the overprint inverted, and several are known with overprint double or sideways.

Type M **4** (a handstamp made up from metal type) was originally applied as a combined overprint and postmark, between November 1915 and July 1916, and can be found tying the 3p., ½a. and 1a. values to piece or cover. A "MAFIA" circular datestamp was supplied from Zanzibar in early July 1916, and from July to September 1916 type M **4** was used as an overprint only, mainly for philatelic purposes.

Until early April 1917 India "I.E.F" stamps were in use on Mafia without additional overprint, but the new overprint type M **5** (a rubber handstamp) was then introduced, producing Nos. M43/52.

1917 (Apr). Nos. E1/2, E4/9, E11 and E13 of Indian Expeditionary Forces (India King George V optd "I.E.F.") with further opt Type M **5** handstruck in green, greenish black, dull blue or violet.

M43	3p. grey	£150	£160
M44	½a. light green	£160	£160
	a. Pair, one without handstamp	†	£3750
M45	1a. aniline carmine	£120	£130
M46	2a. purple	£190	£190
M47	2½a. ultramarine	£200	£200
M48	3a. orange	£225	£225
M49	4a. olive-green	£300	£300
M50	8a. deep magenta	£450	£450
M51	12a. carmine-lake	£450	£550
M52	1r. red-brown and deep blue-green	£600	£700
M43/52 *Set of 10*		£2500	£2750

Stamps with handstamp inverted are known.

Used examples of Nos. M43/52 with black double-ring backdated postmarks of "JA 23 1915" and other dates prior to April 1917 are worth about 50% of the prices quoted.

Nos. M43/52 were in use until August 1918, when they were replaced by the Tanganyika "G.E.A." issue (Nos. 45/61). India "I.E.F." stamps without additional overprint also remained in use during the period.

NYASALAND-RHODESIAN FORCE

This issue was sanctioned for use by the Nyasaland-Rhodesian Force during operations in German East Africa, Mozambique and Nyasaland. Unoverprinted Nyasaland stamps were used by the Force prior to the introduction of Nos. N1/5 and, again, in 1918.

N. F.
(N **1**)

1916 (7 Aug–18 Sept*). Nos. 83, 86, 90/1 and 93 of Nyasaland optd with Type N **1** by Govt Printer, Zomba.

N1	½d. green	1·50	8·00
N2	1d. scarlet	1·50	3·25
N3	3d. purple/*yellow* (15 Sept*)	25·00	17·00
	a. Opt double	†	£22000
N4	4d. black and red/*yellow* (13 Sept*)	50·00	40·00
N5	1s. black/*green* (18 Sept*)	70·00	70·00
N1/5 *Set of 5*		£130	£120
N1s/5s Optd "SPECIMEN" *Set of 5*		£250	

*Earliest known dates of use.

Of No. N3a only six examples were printed, these being the bottom row on one pane issued at M'bamba Bay F.P.O., German East Africa in March 1918.

This overprint was applied in a setting of 60 (10 rows of 6) and the following minor varieties occur on all values: small stop after "N" (R. 1/1); broken "F" (R. 4/3); very small stop after "F" (R. 6/5); no serifs at top left and bottom of "N" (R. 10/1).

TANGANYIKA

BRITISH OCCUPATION OF GERMAN EAST AFRICA

Following the invasion of German East Africa by Allied forces civilian mail was accepted by the Indian Army postal service, using Indian stamps overprinted "I.E.F.". Some offices reverted to civilian control on 1 June 1917 and these used stamps of East Africa and Uganda until the "G.E.A." overprints were ready. The last field post offices, in the southern part of the country, did not come under civilian control until 15 March 1919.

(Currency. 100 cents = 1 rupee)

G.E.A. **G. E. A.** **G.E.A.**
(1) (2) (3)

1917 (Oct)–**21**. Nos. 44/5, 46a/51, 52b, 53/9 and 61 of Kenya, Uganda and Tanganyika optd with T **1** and **2** by De la Rue. Ordinary paper (1c. to 15c.) or chalk-surfaced paper (others). Wmk Mult Crown CA.

45	1c. black (R.)	15	80
	aw. Wmk inverted	£325	
	ay. Wmk inverted and reversed	£190	
	b. Vermilion opt	20·00	16·00
47	3c. green	20	15
48	6c. scarlet	20	10
	a. Wmk sideways	£2250	£2500
	w. Wmk inverted	£350	£250
49	10c. yellow-orange	50	60
	y. Wmk inverted and reversed	£275	
50	12c. slate-grey	50	3·00
	y. Wmk inverted and reversed	£250	
51	15c. bright blue	1·50	4·75
	w. Wmk inverted	£350	

52		25c. black and red/*yellow*		80	5·50
	a.	On pale yellow (1921)		2·00	18·00
	as.	Optd "SPECIMEN"		40·00	
53		50c. black and lilac		2·00	4·75
54		75c. black/*blue-green, olive back* (R.)		1·00	4·75
	a.	On emerald back (1921)		3·50	50·00
	as.	Optd "SPECIMEN"		50·00	
55		1r. black/*green* (R.)		5·50	7·00
	a.	On emerald back (1919)		13·00	65·00
56		2r. red and black/*blue*		13·00	60·00
	x.	Wmk reversed		—	£600
57		3r. violet and green		16·00	80·00
58		4r. red and green/*yellow*		25·00	£120
59		5r. blue and dull green		48·00	£140
60		10r. red and green/*green*		£150	£425
	a.	On emerald back		£180	£600
61		20r. black and purple/*red*		£325	£650
62		50r. carmine and green		£700	£1100
	s.	Optd "SPECIMEN"		£275	
45/61 *Set of* 16				£500	£1400
45s/61s Optd "SPECIMEN" *Set of* 16				£550	

Early printings of the rupee values exist with very large stop after the "E" in "G.E.A." (R. 5/3). There are round stops after "E" varieties, which in one position of later printings became a small stop.
Examples of Nos. 45/55 can also be found handstamped with Type M **5**, but these were not issued.

1921. Nos. 69/74 of Kenya, Uganda and Tanganyika optd with T **1** or **2** by De la Rue. Chalk-surfaced paper (50c. to 5r.). Wmk Mult Script CA.

63		12c. slate-grey		10·00	£110
64		15c. bright blue		8·00	14·00
65		50c. black and dull purple		16·00	£100
66		2r. red and black/*blue*		48·00	£130
67		3r. violet and green		£110	£300
68		5r. blue and dull purple		£160	£400
63/8 *Set of* 6				£300	£950
63s/8s Optd "SPECIMEN" *Set of* 6				£275	

1922. Nos. 65 and 68 of Kenya, Uganda and Tanganyika optd by the Government Printer at Dar-es-Salaam with T **3**. Wmk Mult Script CA.

72		1c. black (R.)		1·75	23·00
73		10c. orange		3·00	14·00
	y.	Wmk inverted and reversed		£200	

No. 73 is known with the overprint inverted, but this is of clandestine origin.

BRITISH MANDATED TERRITORY

(New Currency. 100 cents = 1 shilling)

4 Giraffe   **5** Giraffe

(Recess B.W.)

1922–24. Head in black.

(a) Wmk Mult Script CA. P 15×14

74	**4**	5c. slate-purple		2·25	20
75		10c. green		3·50	85
76		15c. carmine-red		4·00	10
77		20c. orange		5·00	10
78		25c. black		8·00	6·50
79		30c. blue		5·50	5·00
80		40c. yellow-brown		5·50	4·50
81		50c. slate-grey		6·50	1·50
82		75c. yellow-bistre		5·50	22·00

(b) Wmk Mult Script CA (sideways). P 14

83	**5**	1s. green		10·00	26·00
	a.	Wmk upright (1923)		6·00	11·00
84		2s. purple		9·00	26·00
	a.	Wmk upright (1924)		6·50	40·00
85		3s. black		50·00	48·00
86		5s. scarlet		75·00	£120
	a.	Wmk upright (1923)		38·00	95·00
87		10s. deep blue		£200	£425
	a.	Wmk upright (1923)		£100	£180
88		£1 yellow-orange		£400	£600
	a.	Wmk upright (1923)		£350	£550
74/88a *Set of* 15				£550	£850
74s/88s Optd "SPECIMEN" (Nos. 74/82) or "SPECIMEN." *Set of* 15				£700	

On the £1 stamp the words of value are on a curved scroll running across the stamp above the words "POSTAGE AND REVENUE".
Nos. 83/8 are known showing a forged Dodoma postmark, dated "16 JA 22".

1925. As 1922. Frame colours changed.

89	**4**	5c. green		11·00	1·50
90		10c. orange-yellow		11·00	1·50
91		25c. blue		4·50	17·00
92		30c. purple		8·00	26·00
89/92 *Set of* 4				30·00	42·00
89s/92s Optd "SPECIMEN." *Set of* 4				£130	

6   **7**

(Typo D.L.R.)

1927–31. Head in black. Chalk-surfaced paper (5s., 10s., £1). Wmk Mult Script CA. P 14.

93	**6**	5c. green		1·75	10
94		10c. yellow		2·00	10
95		15c. carmine-red		1·75	10
96		20c. orange-buff		2·75	10
97		25c. bright blue		3·75	2·00
98		30c. dull purple		2·75	2·75
98*a*		30c. bright blue (1931)		25·00	30
99		40c. yellow-brown		2·00	8·50
100		50c. grey		2·50	1·00
101		75c. olive-green		2·00	24·00
102	**7**	1s. green		4·25	2·75
103		2s. deep purple		30·00	7·00
104		3s. black		48·00	95·00
105		5s. carmine-red		38·00	26·00
	a.	Ordinary paper		95·00	
106		10s. deep blue		95·00	£150
	a.	Ordinary paper		£475	£650
107		£1 brown-orange		£250	£400
93/107 *Set of* 16				£475	£650
93s/107s Optd or Perf (No. 98as) "SPECIMEN" *Set of* 16				£375	

Examples of Nos. 104/7 are known showing a forged Dar-es-Salaam postmark dated "20 NO 1928".

Tanganyika became part of the joint East African postal administration on 1 January 1933 and subsequently used the stamps of KENYA, UGANDA AND TANGANYIKA.

INDEPENDENT REPUBLIC

8 Teacher and   **9** District Nurse
Pupils   and Child

14 "Maternity"   **15** Freedom Torch
over Mt Kilimanjaro

30c. "UHURU 196" (Pl. 1C, R. 10/10, later corrected)

20s. Mountain flaw (R. 8/8)

(Des V. Whiteley. Photo Harrison)

1961 (9 Dec)–**64**. Independence. T **8/9**, **14/15** and similar designs. P 14×15 (5c., 30c.), 15×14 (10c.,15c., 20c., 50c.) or 14½ (others).

108		5c. sepia and light apple-green	10	10
109		10c. deep bluish green	10	10
110		15c. sepia and blue	10	10
		a. Blue omitted	£1600	
111		20c. orange-brown	10	10
112		30c. black, emerald and yellow	10	10
		a. Inscr "UHURU 196"	£900	£400
		b. "1" inserted after "196"	28·00	
113		50c. black and yellow	10	10
114		1s. brown, blue and olive-yellow	15	10
115		1s.30 red, yellow, black, brown and blue	4·25	10
		a. Red, yellow, black, brown & deep blue (10.3.64)	8·50	1·00
116		2s. blue, yellow, green and brown	1·00	10
117		5s. deep bluish green and orange-red	1·00	50
118		10s. black, reddish purple and light blue	15·00	4·75
		a. Reddish purple (diamond) omitted	£225	£170
119		20s. red, yellow, black, brown and green	4·00	9·00
		a. Mountain flaw	45·00	
108/19 *Set of 12*			23·00	13·50

Designs: *Vert* (as T **9**)—15c. Coffee-picking; 20c. Harvesting maize; 50c. Serengeti lions. *Horiz* (as T **8**)—30c. Tanganyikan flag. (As T **14**)—2s. Dar-es-Salaam waterfront; 5s. Land tillage; 10s. Diamond and mine. *Vert*—20s. Type **15**.

On the corrected version of No. 112a the number "1" is very slightly shorter and the figure is more solid than normal.

19 Pres. Nyerere inaugurating Self-help Project

20 Hoisting Flag on Mt Kilimanjaro

(Photo Harrison)

1962 (9 Dec). Inauguration of Republic. Vert designs as T **19/20**. P 14½.

120		30c. emerald	10	10
121		50c. yellow, black, green, red and blue	10	10
122		1s.30 multicoloured	10	10
123		2s.50 black, red and blue	30	50
120/3 *Set of 4*			55	70

Designs:—1s.30, Presidential emblem; 2s.50, Independence Monument.

Stay up to date with all things philatelic.
Subscribe to **Gibbons Stamp Monthly** –
The UK's number one stamp magazine

23 Map of Republic

24 Torch and Spear Emblem

(Des M. Goaman. Photo Harrison)

1964 (7 July). United Republic of Tanganyika and Zanzibar Commemoration. P 14×14½.

124	**23**	20c. yellow-green and light blue	30	10
125	**24**	30c. blue and sepia	10	10
126		1s.30 orange-brown and ultramarine	10	10
127	**23**	2s.50 purple and ultramarine	2·00	1·75
124/7 *Set of 4*			2·25	1·75

Despite the inscription on the stamps the above issue was only on sale in Tanganyika and had no validity in Zanzibar.

STAMP BOOKLETS

1922–25. Black on red cover.
SB1	3s. booklet containing 5c., 10c., 15c. and 20c. (Nos. 74/7), each in block of 6	£3000
	a. As No. SB1, but contents changed (Nos. 89/90, 76/7) (1925)	

1922–26. Black on red cover. Stapled.
SB2	3s. booklet containing six 10c., and twelve 5c. and 15c. (Nos. 74/6) in blocks of 6	
	a. As No. SB2, but contents changed (Nos. 74, 90, 76) (1925)	
	b. As No. SB2, but contents changed (Nos. 89/90, 76) (1926)	£2500

1927. Black on red covers. Stapled.
SB3	3s. booklet containing six 10c., and twelve 15c. (Nos. 93/5) in blocks of 6	£1400
SB4	3s. booklet containing 5c., 10c. and 15c. (Nos. 93/5), each in block of 10	£1800

1961 (9 Dec). Black on blue-green cover, size 48×46 mm. Stitched.
SB5	5s. booklet containing 10c., 15c., 20c., 30c. and 50c. (Nos. 109/13), each in block of 4	5·00

OFFICIAL STAMPS

OFFICIAL
(O **1**)

OFFICIAL
(O **2**) (3½ mm tall)

1961 (9 Dec). Nos. 108/14 and 117 optd with Type O **1** (10, 15, 20, 50c. or larger (17 mm) 5, 30c.) or with Type O **2** (1s. or larger (22 mm) 5s.).

O1	5c. sepia and light apple-green	10	10
O2	10c. deep bluish green	10	10
O3	15c. sepia and blue	10	10
O4	20c. orange-brown	10	10
O5	30c. black, emerald and yellow	10	10
O6	50c. black and yellow	10	10
O7	1s. brown, blue and olive-yellow	10	10
O8	5s. deep bluish green and orange-red	75	85
O1/8 *Set of 8*		1·00	1·00

ZANZIBAR

An Indian post office opened in Zanzibar in November 1868, but was closed for political reasons on 1 April of the following year. Little has survived from this period. Subsequently mail was forwarded via Seychelles or, later, Aden.

Stamps of INDIA were used in Zanzibar from 1 October 1875 until 10 November 1895, when the administration of the postal service was transferred from India to British East Africa. Separate cancellations for Zanzibar are known from 1 June 1878.

Z **1**

Z **1a**

Stamps of INDIA cancelled with Type Z **1** (1878–79).

1865. (Nos. 54/65).
Z1	1a. deep brown	£500
Z2	2a. orange	£500

1866–78. (Nos. 69/72).
Z2a	4a. green (Die I)	£500
Z3	4a. blue-green (Die II)	£500

1865. (Nos. 54/65).
Z4	½a. blue (Die II)	£500

Surviving covers show that Type Z **1** was normally used as a datestamp, struck clear of the stamps which were obliterated by a rhomboid of bars, but examples of the c.d.s. used as a cancel are known.

Stamps of INDIA cancelled with Type Z **1a**.

1865. (Nos. 54/65).
Z7	2a. orange	£600

In Type Z **1a** the word "ZANZIBAR" is shorter than in Types Z **1** and Z **3**. It was generally used as an arrival mark but cancellations on adhesives are known.

Z **2**

Stamps of INDIA cancelled with Type Z **2** (1879–82).

1865. (Nos. 54/65).
Z10	8p. mauve	£450
Z11	1a. deep brown	19·00
Z12	2a. orange	24·00
	a. Brown-orange	18·00

1866–78. (Nos. 69/72).
Z13	4a. green (Die I)	£120
Z14	4a. blue-green (Die II)	30·00

1868. (Nos. 73/4).
Z15	8a. rose (Die II)	£100

1873. (Nos. 75/6).
Z16	½a. blue (Die II)	19·00

1874. (Nos. 77/9).
Z17	1r. slate	£350

1876. (Nos. 80/2).
Z18	6a. pale brown	£140
Z19	12a. Venetian red	£250

1882. (No. 90).
Z19a	1a.6p. sepia	£225

OFFICIAL STAMPS

1874–82. (Nos. O31/7).
Z19b	1a. brown	£400
Z20	2a. orange	£350
Z21	4a. green (Die I)	£450
Z22	8a. rose (Die II)	£500

Z **3**

Stamps of INDIA cancelled with Type Z **3** (1882–84)

1865. (Nos. 54/65).
Z25	1a. deep brown	60·00
Z26	2a. brown-orange	42·00

1866–78. (Nos. 69/72).
Z26a	4a. green (Die I)	£110
Z27	4a. blue-green (Die II)	50·00

1868. (Nos. 73/4).
Z28	8a. rose (Die II)	80·00

1873. (Nos. 75/6).
Z29	½a. blue (Die II)	38·00

1874. (Nos. 77/9).
Z29a	1r. slate	£225

1876. (Nos. 80/2).
Z30	6a. pale brown	80·00
Z31	12a. Venetian red	£225

1882–83. (Nos. 84/101).
Z32	1a. brown-purple	50·00
Z33	1a.6p. sepia	50·00
Z34	3a. orange	50·00

OFFICIAL STAMPS

1867–73. (Nos. O20/30a).
Z35	2a. orange	£400
Z36	8a. rose	£450

Z **4**   Z **5**

Stamps of INDIA cancelled with Type Z **4** (June 1884–May 1887) (between January and September 1885 the postmark was used without year numerals).

1865. (Nos. 54/65).
Z38	8p. purple	£450
Z39	1a. deep brown	£200
Z40	2a. brown-orange	40·00

1866–78. (Nos. 69/72).
Z41	4a. green (Die I)	£225
Z41a	4a. blue-green (Die II)	38·00

1868. (Nos. 73/4).
Z42	8a. rose (Die II)	42·00

1873. (Nos. 75/6).
Z43	½a. blue (Die II)	30·00

1874. (Nos. 77/9).
Z44	1r. slate	£275

1876. (Nos. 80/2).
Z45	6a. pale brown	95·00
Z45a	12a. Venetian red	£225

1882–86. (Nos. 84/101).
Z46	½a. blue-green	22·00
Z47	1a. brown-purple	27·00
Z48	1a.6p. sepia	21·00
Z49	2a. blue	60·00
Z50	3a. orange	15·00
Z51	4a. olive-green	45·00
Z52	4a.6p. yellow-green	23·00
Z53	8a. dull mauve	60·00
Z54	1r. slate	48·00

OFFICIAL STAMPS

1867–73. (Nos. O20/30a).
Z55	2a. orange	£350

1874–82. (Nos. O31/7).
Z55a	½a. blue	£140
Z56	1a. brown	£140
Z56a	2a. orange	£350

1883–95. (Nos. O37a/48).
Z57	1a. brown-purple	£225

Stamps of INDIA cancelled with Type Z **5** (1887–94).

1865. (Nos. 54/65).
Z58	8p. purple	£400
Z59	2a. brown-orange	£200

1868. (Nos. 73/4).
Z59a	8a. rose (Die II)	£350

1873. (Nos. 75/6).
Z59*b*   ½a. blue (Die II) £160

1876. (Nos. 80/2).
Z60   6a. pale brown ....   21·00
Z61   12a. Venetian red ....   90·00

1882–90. (Nos. 84/101).
Z62   ½a. blue-green ....   7·50
Z63   9p. aniline carmine ....   70·00
Z64   1a. brown-purple ....   6·00
Z65   1a.6p. sepia ....   9·50
Z66   2a. blue ....   7·50
Z67   3a. orange ....   9·00
Z68   3a. brown-orange ....   7·50
Z69   4a. olive-green ....   40·00
Z70   4a.6p. yellow-green ....   12·00
Z71   8a. dull mauve ....   21·00
Z72   12a. purple/*red* ....   70·00
Z73   1r. slate ....   18·00

1891. (No. 102).
Z74   2½a. on 4a.6p. yellow-green ....   8·00

1892–95. (Nos. 103/6).
Z75   2a.6p. yellow-green ....   6·00

OFFICIAL STAMPS

1867–73. (Nos. O20/30*a*).
Z75*a*   4a. green £475

1874–82. (Nos. O31/71).
Z76   ½a. blue £100
Z77   1a. brown £160
Z78   2a. yellow £325

Z 6   Z 7

Stamps of INDIA cancelled with Type Z **6**, inscribed "REG" (registration) or "PAR" (parcel) (1888–95).

1876. (Nos. 80/2).
Z80   6a. pale brown ....   26·00
Z80*a*   12a. Venetian red £200

1882–90. (Nos. 84/101).
Z81   ½a. blue-green ....   45·00
Z82   9p. aniline carmine ....   90·00
Z83   1a. brown-purple ....   9·50
Z84   1a.6p. sepia ....   13·00
Z85   2a. blue ....   14·00
Z86   3a. orange ....   27·00
Z87   3a. brown-orange ....   21·00
Z88   4a. olive-green ....   17·00
Z89   4a.6p. yellow-green ....   27·00
Z90   8a. dull mauve ....   25·00
Z91   12a. purple/*red* ....   80·00
Z92   1r. slate ....   23·00

1891. (No. 102).
Z93   2½a. on 4a.6p. yellow-green ....   35·00

1892–95. (Nos. 103/6).
Z94   2a.6p. yellow-green ....   20·00

Stamps of INDIA cancelled with Type Z **7** (1894–95).

1876. (Nos. 80/2).
Z95   6a. pale brown ....   95·00

1882–90. (Nos. 84/101).
Z100   ½a. blue-green ....   27·00
Z101   9p. aniline carmine £110
Z102   1a. brown-purple ....   35·00
Z103   1a.6p. sepia ....   80·00
Z104   2a. blue ....   26·00
Z105   3a. brown-orange ....   85·00
Z106   4a. olive-green ....   90·00
Z107   8a. dull mauve ....   95·00
Z108   12a. purple/*red* £110
Z109   1r. slate £100

1892–95. (Nos. 103/6).
Z110   2a.6p. yellow-green ....   17·00

1895. (Nos. 107/9).
Z111   2r. carmine and yellow-brown £600

A French post office was opened on the island on 1 February 1889 and this service used the stamps of FRANCE until 1894 when specific stamps for this office were provided. The French postal service on the island closed on 31 July 1904 and it is known that French stamps were again utilised during the final month.

A German postal agency operated in Zanzibar between 27 August 1890 and 31 July 1891, using stamps of GERMANY (see under German East Africa).

PRICES FOR STAMPS ON COVER TO 1945		
Nos. 1/2		
Nos. 3/16	*from ×* 30	
No. 17	*from ×* 8	
No. 18	*from ×* 25	
Nos. 19/21	—	
No. 22	*from ×* 40	
No. 23/5	*from ×* 25	
No. 26	*from ×* 40	
Nos. 27/40	—	
Nos. 41/6	*from ×* 25	
Nos. 156/68	*from ×* 15	
Nos. 169/77	—	
Nos. 178/87	*from ×* 20	
Nos. 188/204	*from ×* 15	
Nos. 205/9	*from ×* 20	
Nos. 210/38	*from ×* 15	
Nos. 239/45	—	
Nos. 246/59	*from ×* 8	
Nos. 260/f	—	
Nos. 261/330	*from ×* 4	
Nos. D1/3	*from ×* 8	
No. D4	*from ×* 1	
No. D5	*from ×* 15	
No. D6	—	
No. D7	*from ×* 1	
Nos. D8/12	*from ×* 15	
No. D13	*from ×* 1	
No. D14	—	
Nos. D15/16	*from ×* 6	
No. D17	*from ×* 4	
Nos. D18/24	*from ×* 15	
Nos. D25/30	*from ×* 30	

PROTECTORATE

(Currency. 12 pies = 1 anna. 16 annas = 1 rupee)

Zanzibar
(1)

1895 (14 Nov)–**96**. Nos. 81, 85, 90/6, 98/101, 103 and 106/9 of India (Queen Victoria) optd with T **1** by Zanzibar Gazette.

(a) In blue

1	½a. blue-green	£25000	£5500
2	1a. plum	£3000	£500
	j. "Zanzidar" (R. 4/6, 8/5)	†	£25000

(b) In black

3	½a. blue-green	4·50	4·75
	j. "Zanzidar" (R. 4/6, 8/5)	£1300	£700
	k. "Zanibar" (R. 7/2)	£1300	£1700
	l. Diaeresis over last "a" (R. 10/5)	£2000	£2000
	m. Opt double, one albino	£225	
4	1a. plum	4·75	3·75
	j. "Zanzidar" (R. 4/6, 8/5)	—	£3500
	k. "Zanibar" (R. 7/2)	£1700	£2000
	l. Diaeresis over last "a" (R. 10/5)	£4750	
5	1a.6p. sepia	5·00	4·75
	j. "Zanzidar" (R. 4/6, 8/5)	£4000	£1200
	k. "Zanibar" (R. 7/2)	£1600	£1700
	l. "Zanzibar" (R. 1/9)		
	m. Diaeresis over last "a" (R. 10/5)	£1600	
6	2a. pale blue	9·00	8·00
7	2a. blue	9·00	8·00
	j. "Zanzidar" (R. 4/6, 8/5)	£7500	£3000
	k. "Zanibar" (R. 7/2)	£6000	£2750
	l. Diaeresis over last "a" (R. 10/5)	£3000	
	m. Opt double	£275	
	n. Opt double, one albino	£250	
8	2½a. yellow-green	9·00	5·00
	j. "Zanzidar" (R. 4/6, 8/5)	£7500	£1800
	k. "Zanibar" (R. 7/2)	£700	£1400
	l. "Zapzibar"		
	n. Diaeresis over last "a" (R.10/5)	£2500	£1900
	o. Second "z" italic (R. 10/1)	£400	£550
	p. Opt double, one albino	£250	
10	3a. brown-orange	12·00	16·00
	j. "Zanzidar" (R. 4/6, 8/5)	£1000	£1900
	k. "Zanibar" (R. 1/9)	£6500	£7000

11		4a. olive-green		20·00	18·00
		j. "Zanzibar" (R. 4/6, 8/5)		£10000	£4250
12		4a. slate-green		21·00	23·00
		l. Diaeresis over last "a" (R. 10/5)		£5000	
		m. Opt double, one albino		£300	
13		6a. pale brown		20·00	11·00
		j. "Zanzibar" (R.4/6, 8/5)		£10000	£4250
		k. "Zanibar" (R. 7/2)		£800	£1400
		l. "Zanzibarr"		£6500	£5000
		m. Opt double		£300	
		n. Opt double, one albino		£170	
		o. Opt triple, two albino		£225	
14		8a. dull mauve		45·00	27·00
		j. "Zanzibar" (R 4/6, 8/5)		£10000	£8000
15		8a. magenta (6.96)		24·00	29·00
		l. Diaeresis over last "a" (R. 10/5)		£8000	
16		12a. purple/red		18·00	10·00
		j. "Zanzibar" (R.4/6, 8/5)		£10000	£4500
17		1r. slate		£120	90·00
		j. "Zanzibar" (R 4/6, 8/5)		£9500	£6000
18		1r. green and aniline carmine (7.96)		21·00	38·00
		j. Opt vert downwards		£425	
19		2r. carmine and yellow-brown		£110	£120
		j. "r" omitted		£28000	
		k. "r" inverted		£4000	£5000
20		3r. brown and green		90·00	£100
		j. "r" omitted		£28000	
		k. "r" inverted		£6000	£6000
		l. Opt double, one albino		£1500	
21		5r. ultramarine and violet		95·00	£130
		j. "r" omitted		£28000	
		k. "r" inverted		£4500	£7500
		l. Opt double one inverted		£850	
		m. Opt double, one albino		£1500	

3/21 Set of 15 ... £500 £500

Forged examples of the blue overprints, Nos. 1/2, can be found on piece with genuine cancellations as type Z 7, dated "13 FE 97".

There were a number of different settings for this overprint. Values to 1r. were initially overprinted from settings of 120 (12×10) including one which showed "Zanzibar" on R. 4/6 and R. 8/5 (soon corrected) and "Zanizbar" on R. 1/9 (also soon corrected). Later supplies of these values were overprinted from settings of 80 (8×10) for the 6a. only or 60 (6×10) for the others. One of these settings included "Zanibar" on R. 7/2. Another late setting, size unknown, showed a diaeresis over last "a" on R. 10/5.

Many forgeries of this overprint exist and also bogus errors.

MINOR VARIETIES. The following minor varieties of type exist on Nos. 1/21:

A. First "Z" antique (sloping serifs) (all values)
B. Broken "p" for "n" (all values to 1r.)
C. Tall second "z" (all values)
D. Small second "z" (all values)
E. Small second "z" and inverted "q" for "b" (all values)
F. Second "z" Gothic (lower limb bent upwards) (½a. to 12a. and 1r.) (No. 18) (black opts only)
G. No dot over "i" (all values to 1r.)
H. Inverted "q" for "b" (all values to 1r.)
I. Arabic "2" for "r" (all values to 1r.) (black opts only)

Varieties D and E are worth the same as normal examples, A (2, 3, 5r.) and C normal plus 50%, G and I from 3 times normal, A (values to 1r.), F and H from 4 times normal and B from 5 times normal.

2½ (2)   2½ (3)   2½ (4)   2¹⁄₂ (5)

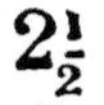

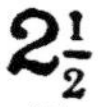

1895–98. Provisionals.

I. Stamps used for postal purposes
(a) No. 5 surch in red (30.11.95)

22	2	2½ on 1½a. sepia		75·00	55·00
		j. "Zanzibar"		£1600	£1300
		k. "Zanizbar"		£4750	£1900
		l. Inverted "1" in "½"		£1100	£900

(b) No. 4 surch in black (11.5.96)

23	3	2½ on 1a. plum		£180	£100
24	4	2½ on 1a. plum		£475	£275
		j. Inverted "1" in "½"		£2750	
25	5	2½ on 1a. plum		£200	£110

2½ (6)   2½ (7)   2½ (8)

(c) No. 6 surch in red (15.8.96)

26	6	2½ on 2a. pale blue		70·00	42·00
		j. Inverted "1" in "½"		£450	£275
		k. Roman "I" in "½"		£250	£160
		l. "Zanzibar" double, one albino		£160	
		m. "Zanzibar" triple, two albino		£300	

27	7	2½ on 2a. pale blue		£190	£100
		j. "2" of "½" omitted		£15000	
		k. "2" for "2½"		£22000	
		l. "1" of "½" omitted		£15000	£6500
		m. Inverted "1" in "½"		£3500	£1700
		n. "Zanzibar" double, one albino		£500	
28	8	2½ on 2a. pale blue		£5000	£2500

No. 28 only exists with small "z" and occurs on R. 2/2 in the setting of 60.

(d) No. 5 surch in red (15.11.96)

29	6	2½ on 1½a. sepia		£180	£170
		j. Inverted "1 in "½"		£1500	£1200
		k. Roman "I" in "½"		£900	£900
		l. Surch double, one albino		£350	
30	7	2½ on 1½a. sepia		£425	£375
		l. Surch double, one albino		£800	
31	8	2½ on 1½a. sepia		£23000	£16000

No. 31 only exists with small "z" and occurs on R. 2/2 in the setting of 60.

II. Stamps prepared for official purposes. Nos. 4, 5 and 7 surch as before in red (1.98)

32	3	2½ on 1a. plum		£250	£650
33	4	2½ on 1a. plum		£450	£950
34	5	2½ on 1a. plum		£275	£650
35	3	2½ on 1½a. sepia		90·00	£225
		j. Diaeresis over last "a"		£8000	
36	4	2½ on 1½a. sepia		£225	£500
37	5	2½ on 1½a. sepia		£130	£300
38	3	2½ on 2a. dull blue		£140	£325
39	4	2½ on 2a. dull blue		£325	£550
40	5	2½ on 2a. dull blue		£160	£375

It is doubtful whether Nos. 32/40 were issued to the public.

1896. Nos. 65/6, 68 and 71/3 of British East Africa (Queen Victoria), optd with T **1**.

41		½a. yellow-green (23 May)		42·00	24·00
42		1a. carmine-rose (1 June)		42·00	17·00
		j. Opt double		£750	£900
		k. Opt double, one albino		£325	
43		2½a. deep blue (R.) (24 May)		90·00	48·00
		j. Inverted "S" in "ANNAS" (R. 1/1)		—	£600
44		4½a. orange-yellow (12 Aug)		50·00	60·00
45		5a. yellow-bistre (12 Aug)		65·00	40·00
		j. "r" omitted		—	£4000
46		7½a. mauve (12 Aug)		55·00	65·00

41/6 Set of 6 ... £300 £225

MINOR VARIETIES. The various minor varieties of type detailed in the note below No. 21 also occur on Nos. 22 to 46 as indicated below:

A. Nos. 23, 25, 27, 30, 35, 38, 41/6
B. Nos. 22/3, 26, 29/30, 32/3, 36, 39, 44/6
C. Nos. 22, 25/6, 32, 36, 38, 40/6
D. Nos. 22/46
E. Nos. 22/46
F. Nos. 22, 25/6, 29, 41/6
G. Nos. 25/6, 29, 35, 37/8, 40/6
H. Nos. 22, 41/6 (on the British East Africa stamps this variety occurs in the same position as variety C)
I. Nos. 26, 29, 35, 38, 41/6

The scarcity of these varieties on the surcharges (Nos. 22/40) is similar to those on the basic stamps, but examples on the British East Africa values (Nos. 41/6) are more common.

PRINTERS. All Zanzibar stamps up to Type **37** were printed by De La Rue & Co.

12    **13**

14 Sultan Seyyid
Hamed-bin-Thwain

No right serif to left-hand "4" (R. 1/1)

No fraction bar at right (R. 2/1)

1896 (Dec). Recess. Flags in red on all values. W **12**. P 14.

156	**13**	½a. yellow-green	4·00	2·00
157		1a. indigo	3·75	1·50
158		1a. violet-blue	7·00	4·50
159		2a. red-brown	3·75	75
160		2½a. bright blue	16·00	1·50
161		2½a. pale blue	18·00	1·50
162		3a. grey	18·00	9·00
163		3a. bluish grey	20·00	11·00
164		4a. myrtle-green	12·00	6·00
165		4½a. orange	8·00	7·00
		a. No right serif to left-hand "4"	£200	£200
		b. No fraction bar at right (R. 2/1)	£200	£200
166		5a. bistre	9·00	4·25
		a. Bisected (2½a.) (on cover)	†	£4500
167		7½a. mauve	6·50	6·50
168		8a. grey-olive	11·00	8·50
169	**14**	1r. blue	25·00	9·00
170		1r. deep blue	32·00	13·00
171		2r. green	30·00	9·50
172		3r. dull purple	32·00	9·50
173		4r. lake	25·00	13·00
174		5r. sepia	32·00	13·00
156/74 *Set of 15*			£200	90·00
156s/74s Optd "SPECIMEN" *Set of 15*			£275	

The ½, 1, 2, 2½, 3 and 8a. are known without wmk, these being from edges of the sheets.

1897 (5 Jan). No. 164 surch as before, in red by the *Zanzibar Gazette*.

175	**3**	2½ on 4a. myrtle-green	90·00	50·00
176	**4**	2½ on 4a. myrtle-green	£300	£275
177	**5**	2½ on 4a. myrtle-green	£110	75·00
175/7 *Set of 3*			£450	£350

There were two settings of the surcharge, the first comprised 26 of Type **3**, 10 of Type **4** and 24 of Type **5**. The composition of the second setting is unknown.

18

1898 (Apr). Recess. W **18**. P 14.

178	**13**	½a. yellow-green	1·50	35
179		1a. indigo	5·50	1·25
		a. Greenish black	6·50	1·50
180		2a. red-brown	9·00	2·00
		a. Deep brown	11·00	2·00
181		2½a. bright blue	5·00	30
182		3a. grey	7·50	75
183		4a. myrtle-green	3·75	1·25
184		4½a. orange	15·00	1·00
		a. No right serif to left-hand "4"	£300	85·00
		b. No fraction bar at right (R. 2/1)	£300	85·00
185		5a. bistre	21·00	2·00
		a. Pale bistre	22·00	2·25
186		7½a. mauve	17·00	2·75
187		8a. grey-olive	21·00	2·50
178/87 *Set of 10*			95·00	12·50

19

20 Sultan Seyyid Hamoud-bin-Mohammed bin Said

1899 (June)–**1901**. Recess. Flags in red. W **18** (Nos. 188/99) or W **12** (others). P 14.

188	**19**	½a. yellow-green	2·75	60

		a. Wmk sideways	21·00	7·00
189		1a. indigo	4·50	20
		a. Wmk sideways	42·00	1·50
190		1a. carmine (1901)	3·75	20
191		2a. red-brown	4·50	1·25
192		2½a. bright blue	4·50	90
193		3a. grey	6·50	3·00
194		4a. myrtle-green	6·50	3·25
195		4½a. orange	18·00	9·00
196		4½a. blue-black (1901)	20·00	14·00
197		5a. bistre	6·50	2·75
198		7½a. mauve	6·50	6·00
199		8a. grey-olive	6·50	5·50
200	**20**	1r. blue	23·00	15·00
201		2r. green	26·00	23·00
202		3r. dull purple	45·00	50·00
203		4r. lake	55·00	70·00
204		5r. sepia	75·00	95·00
188/204 *Set of 17*			£275	£275
188s/204s Optd "SPECIMEN" *Set of 17*			£325	

T W O	T W O	T W O
&	&	&
One Half	Half	Half
(**21**)	(**22**)	(**22a**) Thin open "w" (R. 2/2, 3/4)

(**22b**) Serif to foot of "f" (R. 3/1)

1904 (June). Nos. 194/6 and 198/9 surch as T **21** and **22**, in black or lake (L.) by Zanzibar Gazette in setting of 30 (6×5).

205	**19**	1 on 4½a. orange	4·00	6·00
206		1 on 4½a. blue/black (L.)	6·00	8·00
207		2 on 4a. myrtle-green (L.)	14·00	18·00
208		2½ on 7½a. mauve	17·00	24·00
		a. Opt Type **22a**	90·00	£110
		b. Opt Type **22b**	£150	£190
		c. "Hlaf" for "Half"	£16000	
209		2½ on 8a. grey-olive	30·00	40·00
		a. Opt Type **22a**	£150	£180
		b. Opt Type **22b**	£250	£300
		c. "Hlaf" for "Half"	£15000	£10000
205/9 *Set of 5*			65·00	95·00

23

24

Monogram of Sultan Seyyid Ali bin Hamoud bin Naherud

1904 (8 June). Typo. Background of centre in second colour. W **18**. P 14.

210	**23**	½a. green	2·75	50
211		1a. rose-red	2·75	10
212		2a. brown	4·75	45
213		2½a. blue	4·75	35
214		3a. grey	6·00	2·25
215		4a. deep green	4·25	1·60
216		4½a. black	5·00	2·50
217		5a. yellow-brown	7·00	2·25
218		7½a. purple	8·50	8·00
219		8a. olive-green	6·00	5·50
220	**24**	1r. blue and red	38·00	26·00
		a. Wmk sideways	£100	35·00
221		2r. green and red	42·00	50·00
		a. Wmk sideways	£250	£350
222		3r. violet and red	60·00	90·00
223		4r. claret and red	65·00	£100
224		5r. olive-brown and red	65·00	£100
210/24 *Set of 15*			£275	£350
210s/24s Optd "SPECIMEN" *Set of 15*			£190	

25

26

27 Sultan Ali bin Hamoud

28 View of Port

1908 (May)–**09**. Recess. W **18** (sideways on 10r. to 30r.). P 14.

225	25	1c. pearl-grey (10.09)	2·25	30
226		3c. yellow-green	14·00	10
		a. Wmk sideways	9·00	1·75
227		6c. rose-carmine	11·00	10
		a. Wmk sideways	12·00	2·75
228		10c. brown (10.09)	7·00	2·25
229		12c. violet	19·00	3·50
		a. Wmk sideways	15·00	1·25
230	26	15c. ultramarine	21·00	40
		a. Wmk sideways	19·00	6·00
231		25c. sepia	8·50	1·00
232		50c. blue-green	11·00	7·50
233		75c. grey-black (10.09)	16·00	18·00
234	27	1r. yellow-green	45·00	12·00
		a. Wmk sideways	£100	12·00
235		2r. violet	20·00	16·00
		a. Wmk sideways	£275	75·00
236		3r. orange-bistre	38·00	50·00
237		4r. vermilion	65·00	95·00
238		5r. steel-blue	70·00	70·00
239	28	10r. blue-green and brown	£200	£350
		s. Optd "SPECIMEN"	65·00	
240		20r. black and yellow-green	£600	£800
		s. Optd "SPECIMEN"	90·00	
241		30r. black and sepia	£700	£1000
		a. Wmk upright		
		s. Optd "SPECIMEN"	£110	
242		40r. black and orange-brown	£900	
		s. Optd "SPECIMEN"	£140	
243		50r. black and mauve	£800	
		s. Optd "SPECIMEN"	£140	
244		100r. black and steel-blue	£1200	
		s. Optd "SPECIMEN"	£200	
245		200r. brown and greenish black	£1600	
		s. Optd "SPECIMEN"	£275	
225/38 Set of 14			£300	£250
225s/38s Optd "SPECIMEN" Set of 14			£325	

29 Sultan Kalif bin Harub

30 Sailing Canoe

31 Dhow

1913. Recess. W **18** (sideways on 75c. and 10r. to 200r.). P 14.

246	29	1c. grey	40	75
247		3c. yellow-green	1·50	75
248		6c. rose-carmine	1·75	20
249		10c. brown	1·25	3·50
250		12c. violet	1·50	50
251		15c. blue	3·25	50
252		25c. sepia	1·50	50
253		50c. blue-green	4·00	7·50
254		75c. grey-black	2·75	6·00
		a. Wmk upright	£150	
		as. Optd "SPECIMEN"	95·00	
255	30	1r. yellow-green	21·00	17·00
256		2r. violet	17·00	35·00
257		3r. orange-bistre	23·00	55·00
258		4r. scarlet	38·00	80·00
259		5r. steel-blue	55·00	55·00

260	31	10r. green and brown	£200	£400
260b		20r. black and green	£350	£650
		bs. Optd "SPECIMEN"	80·00	
260c		30r. black and brown	£375	£800
		cs. Optd "SPECIMEN"	85·00	
260d		40r. black and vermilion	£650	£1100
		ds. Optd "SPECIMEN"	£150	
260e		50r. black and purple	£650	£1200
		es. Optd "SPECIMEN"	£140	
260f		100r. black and blue	£850	
		fs. Optd "SPECIMEN"	£170	
260g		200r. brown and black	£1200	
		gs. Optd "SPECIMEN"	£225	
246/60 Set of 15			£325	£600
246s/60as Optd "SPECIMEN" Set of 15			£350	

1914–22. Wmk Mult Crown CA (sideways on 10r.). P 14.

261	29	1c. grey	80	25
262		3c. yellow-green	1·25	10
		a. Dull green	9·00	15
		w. Wmk inverted	†	£225
263		6c. deep carmine	1·00	10
		a. Bright rose-carmine	1·00	10
		aw. Wmk inverted	†	£225
		ay. Wmk inverted and reversed	†	£275
264		8c. purple/pale yellow (1922)	1·00	7·00
265		10c. myrtle/pale yellow (1922)	85	30
266		15c. deep ultramarine	1·50	8·00
268		50c. blue-green	4·75	7·00
269		75c. grey-black	3·00	38·00
270	30	1r. yellow-green	5·50	3·50
271		2r. violet	13·00	14·00
272		3r. orange-bistre	26·00	50·00
273		4r. scarlet	25·00	85·00
		y. Wmk inverted and reversed	£225	
274		5r. steel-blue	17·00	65·00
		w. Wmk inverted	£225	
275	31	10r. green and brown	£225	£750
261/75 Set of 14			£275	£950
261s/75s Optd "SPECIMEN" Set of 14			£350	

1921–29. Wmk Mult Script CA (sideways on 10r. to 30r.). P 14.

276	29	1c. slate-grey	30	11·00
		x. Wmk reversed	£275	
277		3c. yellow-green	3·50	6·00
278		3c. orange-yellow (1922)	40	10
		w. Wmk inverted		
279		4c. green (1922)	60	2·50
280		6c. carmine-red	40	50
281		6c. purple/blue (1922)	45	10
		w. Wmk inverted	†	£375
282		10c. brown	80	16·00
283		12c. violet	50	30
		w. Wmk inverted		
284		12c. carmine-red (1922)	50	40
285		15c. blue	65	15·00
286		20c. indigo (1922)	1·00	30
287		25c. sepia	85	28·00
288		50c. myrtle-green	3·00	7·00
		y. Wmk inverted and reversed	£180	£250
289		75c. slate	2·50	65·00
290	30	1r. yellow-green	7·00	3·50
291		2r. deep violet	3·50	16·00
292		3r. orange-bistre	5·00	7·50
293		4r. scarlet	12·00	48·00
294		5r. Prussian blue	23·00	75·00
		w. Wmk inverted	£325	
295	31	10r. green and brown	£200	£475
296		20r. black and green	£400	£750
		s. Optd "SPECIMEN"	£140	
297		30r. black and brown (1929)	£350	£750
		s. Perf "SPECIMEN"	£150	
276/95 Set of 20			£240	£700
276s/95s Optd "SPECIMEN" Set of 20			£400	

32 Sultan Kalif bin Harub

33

1926–27. T **32** ("CENTS" in serifed capitals). Recess. Wmk Mult Script CA. P 14.

299	32	1c. brown	1·00	10
300		3c. yellow-orange	30	15
301		4c. deep dull green	30	50
302		6c. violet	30	10
303		8c. slate	1·00	4·50
304		10c. olive-green	1·00	40
305		12c. carmine-red	3·00	10
306		20c. bright blue	60	30

307		25c. purple/yellow (1927)	13·00	2·50
308		50c. claret	4·75	35
309		75c. sepia (1927)	32·00	42·00
299/309 Set of 11			50·00	45·00
299s/309s Optd "SPECIMEN" Set of 11			£190	

(New Currency. 100 cents = 1 shilling)

1936 (1 Jan). T **33** ("CENTS" in sans-serif capitals), and T **30/1**, but values in shillings. Recess. Wmk Mult Script CA. P 14×13½–14.

310	**33**	5c. green	10	10
311		10c. black	10	10
312		15c. carmine-red	15	1·25
313		20c. orange	15	10
314		25c. purple/yellow	15	10
315		30c. ultramarine	15	10
316		40c. sepia	15	10
317		50c. claret	30	10
318	**30**	1s. yellow-green	75	10
319		2s. slate-violet	3·25	1·75
320		5s. scarlet	25·00	6·50
321		7s.50 light blue	42·00	38·00
322	**31**	10s. green and brown	42·00	32·00
310/22 Set of 13			£100	70·00
310s/22s Perf "SPECIMEN" Set of 13			£250	

Nos. 310/22 remained current until 1952 and the unused prices are therefore for unmounted examples.

36 Sultan Kalif bin Harub

1936 (9 Dec). Silver Jubilee of Sultan. Recess. Wmk Mult Script CA. P 14.

323	**36**	10c. black and olive-green	3·25	30
324		20c. black and bright purple	4·50	2·75
325		30c. black and deep ultramarine	15·00	35
326		50c. black and orange-vermilion	15·00	6·50
323/6 Set of 4			35·00	9·00
323s/6s Perf "SPECIMEN" Set of 4			£110	

37 Sham Alam (Sultan's dhow)

(38)

1944 (20 Nov). Bicentenary of Al Busaid Dynasty. Recess. Wmk Mult Script CA. P 14.

327	**37**	10c. ultramarine	1·00	5·50
		a. "C" of "CA" missing from wmk	£800	
328		20c. red	1·50	3·75
		a. "C" of "CA" missing from wmk	£800	
329		50c. blue-green	1·50	30
330		1s. dull purple	1·50	1·00
		a. "A" of "CA" missing from wmk	£950	
327/30 Set of 4			5·00	9·50
327s/30s Perf "SPECIMEN" Set of 4			£120	

1946 (11 Nov). Victory. Nos. 311 and 315 optd with T **38**.

331	**33**	10c. black (R.)	20	50
332		30c. ultramarine (R.)	30	50
331s/2s Perf "SPECIMEN" Set of 2			90·00	

1949 (10 Jan). Royal Silver Wedding. As Nos. 112/13 of Antigua.

333		20c. orange	30	1·50
334		10s. brown	25·00	40·00

1949 (10–13 Oct). 75th Anniv of U.P.U. As Nos. 114/17 of Antigua.

335		20c. red-orange (13 Oct)	30	4·00
336		30c. deep blue	1·75	2·00
		a. "C" of "CA" missing from wmk	£900	
337		50c. magenta	1·00	3·25
		a. "A" of "CA" missing from wmk	£900	
338		1s. blue-green (13 Oct)	1·00	4·50
335/8 Set of 4			3·50	12·00

39 Sultan Kalif bin Harub

40 Seyyid Khalifa Schools, Beit-el-Ras

1952 (26 Aug)–**55**. Wmk Mult Script CA. P 12½ (cent values) or 13 (shilling values).

339	**39**	5c. black	10	10
340		10c. red-orange	10	10
341		15c. green	2·25	3·25
		a. Yellow-green (12.11.53)	4·75	3·75
342		20c. carmine-red	75	70
343		25c. reddish purple	1·00	10
344		30c. deep bluish green	1·00	10
		a. Deep green (29.3.55)	16·00	4·75
345		35c. bright blue	1·00	3·50
346		40c. deep brown	1·00	1·25
		a. Sepia (12.11.53)	5·00	2·00
347		50c. violet	3·25	10
		a. Deep violet (29.3.55)	7·50	1·00
348	**40**	1s. deep green and deep brown	60	10
349		2s. bright blue and deep purple	3·00	2·50
350		5s. black and carmine-red	3·50	7·00
351		7s.50 grey-black and emerald	28·00	24·00
352		10s. carmine-red and black	10·00	16·00
339/52 Set of 14			50·00	50·00

41 Sultan Kalif bin Harub

(Photo Harrison)

1954 (26 Aug). Sultan's 75th Birthday. Wmk Mult Script CA. Chalk-surfaced paper. P 13×12.

353	**41**	15c. deep green	10	10
354		20c. rose-red	10	10
355		30c. bright blue	10	10
356		50c. purple	20	10
357		1s.25 orange-red	20	75
353/7 Set of 5			60	1·00

42 Cloves

43 Urnmoja Wema (dhow)

44 Sultan's Barge

45 Map of East African Coast

46 Minaret Mosque

47 Dimbani Mosque

48 Kibweni Palace

(Des W. J. Jennings (T **42**), A. Farhan (T **43**), Mrs. M. Broadbent (T **44**, **46**), R. A. Sweet (T **45**), A. S. B. New (T **47**), B. J. Woolley (T **48**). Recess B.W.)

1957 (26 Aug.). W w **12**. P 11½ (5c., 10c.), 11×11½ (15c., 30c., 1s.25), 14×13½ (20c., 25c., 35c., 50c.), 13½×14 (40c., 1s., 2s.) or 13×13½ (5s., 7s.50, 10s.).

358	**42**	5c. orange and deep green	10	40
359		10c. emerald and carmine-red	10	10
360	**43**	15c. green and sepia	30	2·75
361	**44**	20c. ultramarine	15	10
362	**45**	25c. orange-brown and black	45	1·25
363	**43**	30c. carmine-red and black	20	1·25
364	**45**	35c. slate and emerald	45	20
365	**48**	40c. brown and black	15	10
366	**45**	50c. blue and grey-green	60	30
367	**47**	1s. carmine and black	20	30
368	**43**	1s.25 slate and carmine	3·50	20
369	**47**	2s. orange and deep green	3·75	2·25
370	**48**	5s. deep bright blue	5·00	2·00
371		7s.50 green	16·00	4·00
372		10s. carmine	16·00	6·00
358/72 *Set of 15*			42·00	19·00

49 Sultan Seyyid Sir Abdulla bin Khalifa

(Recess B.W.)

1961 (17 Oct). As T **42/8**, but with portrait of Sultan Sir Abdulla as in T **49**. W w **12**. P 13×13½ (20s.), others as before.

373	**49**	5c. orange and deep green	40	1·25
374		10c. emerald and carmine-red	40	10
375	**43**	15c. green and sepia	75	3·75
376	**44**	20c. ultramarine	40	30
377	**45**	25c. orange-brown and black	2·00	1·75
378	**43**	30c. carmine-red and black	3·00	3·00
379	**45**	35c. slate and emerald	3·50	5·50
380	**48**	40c. brown and black	40	20
381	**45**	50c. blue and grey-green	3·75	10
382	**47**	1s. carmine and black	50	1·50
383	**43**	1s.25 slate and carmine	3·50	7·00
384	**47**	2s. orange and deep green	1·00	3·50
385	**48**	5s. deep bright blue	3·50	11·00
386		7s.50 green	3·50	20·00
387		10s. carmine	4·00	12·00
388		20s. sepia	17·00	28·00
373/88 *Set of 16*			42·00	90·00

50 "Protein Foods"

(Des M. Goaman. Photo Harrison)

1963 (4 June). Freedom from Hunger. W w **12**. P 14×14½.
389	**50**	1s.30 sepia	1·25	75

INDEPENDENT

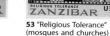

51 Zanzibar Clove

53 "Religious Tolerance" (mosques and churches)

(Photo Harrison)

1963 (10 Dec). Independence. Portrait of Sultan Seyyid Jamshid bin Abdulla. T **51**, **53** and similar vert designs. P 12½.
390		30c. multicoloured	25	1·00
391		50c. multicoloured	25	1·00
392		1s.30, multicoloured	25	4·00
393		2s.50, multicoloured	35	4·75
		a. Green omitted	†	£700
390/3 *Set of 4*			1·00	9·00

Designs:—50c. "To Prosperity" (Zanzibar doorway); 2s.50, "Towards the Light" (Mangapwani Cave).

REPUBLIC

When the Post Office opened on 14 January 1964, after the revolution deposing the Sultan, the stamps on sale had the portrait cancelled by a manuscript cross. Stamps thus cancelled on cover or piece used between January 14 and 17 are therefore of interest.

JAMHURI 1964
(**55**= "Republic")

1964 (17 Jan). Locally handstamped as T **55** in black.

(i) Nos. 373/88

394	**49**	5c. orange and deep green	1·25	65
395		10c. emerald and carmine-red	1·25	10
396	**43**	15c. green and sepia	2·50	2·75
397	**44**	20c. ultramarine	1·75	1·00
398	**45**	25c. orange-brown and black	2·75	20
399	**43**	30c. carmine-red and black	1·50	60
400	**45**	35c. slate and emerald	2·75	1·50
401	**46**	40c. brown and black	1·75	1·25
402	**45**	50c. blue and grey-green	2·75	10
403	**47**	1s. carmine and black	1·50	1·00
404	**43**	1s.25 slate and carmine	1·25	2·00
405	**47**	2s. orange and deep green	2·00	1·75
406	**48**	5s. deep bright blue	1·75	1·75
407		7s.50 green	2·00	1·75
408		10s. carmine	2·00	1·75
409		20s. sepia	2·50	5·50

(ii) Nos. 390/3 (Independence)

410	30c. multicoloured	1·00	2·50
411	50c. multicoloured	60	75
412	1s.30 multicoloured	1·25	1·25
413	2s.50 multicoloured	1·40	2·00
	a. Green omitted	£400	
394/413 *Set of 20*		32·00	27·00

T **55** occurs in various positions—diagonally, horizontally or vertically.

NOTE. Nos. 394 to 413 are the only stamps officially authorised to receive the handstamp but it has also been seen on Nos. 353/7, 389 and the D25/30 Postage Dues. There are numerous errors but it is impossible to distinguish between cases of genuine oversight and those made deliberately at the request of purchasers.

JAMHURI

JAMHURI 1964
(**56**)

1964
(**57**)

1964 (28 Feb). Optd by Bradbury, Wilkinson.

*(i) As T **56** on Nos. 373/88*

414	**49**	5c. orange and deep green	10	10
415		10c. emerald and carmine-red	10	10
416	**43**	15c. green and sepia	20	10
417	**44**	20c. ultramarine	10	10
418	**45**	25c. orange-brown and black	30	10
419	**43**	30c. carmine-red and black	20	10
420	**45**	35c. slate and emerald	30	10
421	**46**	40c. brown and black	10	10
422	**45**	50c. blue and grey-green	30	10
423	**47**	1s. carmine and black	10	10
424	**43**	1s.25 slate and carmine	2·00	1·75
425	**47**	2s. orange and deep green	50	40
426	**48**	5s. deep bright blue	50	35
427		7s.50 green	65	7·00
428		10s. carmine	1·25	8·00
429		20s. sepia	2·25	8·00

The opt T **56** is set in two lines on Types **46/8**.

*(ii) As T **57** on Nos. 390/3 (Independence)*

430	30c. multicoloured	10	10
431	50c. multicoloured	10	10
432	1s.30, multicoloured	10	10
433	2s.50, multicoloured	15	65
	a. Green omitted	£160	
414/33 *Set of 20*		8·00	24·00

The opt T **57** is set in one line on No. 432.

For the set inscribed "UNITED REPUBLIC OF TANGANYIKA AND ZANZIBAR" see Nos. 124/7 of Tanganyika.

58 Axe, Spear and Dagger

59 Zanzibari with Rifle

(Litho German Bank Note Ptg Co, Leipzig)

1964 (21 June). T **58/9** and similar designs inscr. "JAMHURI ZANZIBAR 1964". Multicoloured. P 13×13½ (vert) or 13½×13 (horiz).

434	5c. Type **58**	20	10
435	10c. Bow and arrow breaking chains	30	10
436	15c. Type **58**	30	10
437	20c. As 10c.	50	10
438	25c. Type **59**	50	10
439	30c. Zanzibari breaking manacles	30	10
440	40c. Type **59**	50	10
441	50c. As 30c.	30	10
442	1s. Zanzibari, flag and Sun	30	10
443	1s.30 Hands breaking chains (*horiz*)	30	1·25
444	2s. Hand waving flag (*horiz*)	30	30
445	5s. Map of Zanzibar and Pemba on flag (*horiz*)	1·00	5·00
446	10s. Flag on Map	4·75	7·00
447	20s. National flag (*horiz*)	4·50	25·00
434/47 *Set of 14*		12·50	35·00

68 Soldier and Maps

69 Building Construction

(Litho German Bank Note Ptg Co, Leipzig)

1965 (12 Jan). First Anniv of Revolution. P 13×13½ (vert) or 13½×13 (horiz).

448	**68**	20c. apple-green and deep green	10	10
449	**69**	30c. chocolate and yellow-orange	10	10
450	**68**	1s.30 light blue and ultramarine	10	15
451	**69**	2s.50 reddish violet and rose	10	25
448/51 *Set of 4*			35	55

Type **68** is inscribed "PEMPA" in error for "PEMBA".

70 Planting Rice

(Litho German Bank Note Ptg Co, Leipzig)

1965 (17 Oct). Agricultural Development. T **70** and similar horiz design. P 13×12½.

452	**70**	20c. sepia and blue	10	1·00
453	–	30c. sepia and magenta	10	1·00
454	–	1s.30 sepia and yellow-orange	20	2·00
455	**70**	2s.50 sepia and emerald	30	7·00
452/5 *Set of 4*			60	10·00

Design:—30c., 1s.30, Hands holding rice.

72 Freighter, Tractor, Factory, and Open Book and Torch

73 Soldier

(Litho German Bank Note Ptg Co, Leipzig)

1966 (12 Jan). Second Anniv of Revolution. P 12½×13.

456	**72**	20c. multicoloured	20	20
457	**73**	50c. multicoloured	15	30
458	**72**	1s.30 multicoloured	25	30
459	**73**	2s.50 multicoloured	25	1·75
456/9 *Set of 4*			75	2·25

For stamps with similar inscription or inscribed "TANZANIA" only, and with commemorative date 26th April 1966, see Nos. Z142/5 of TANZANIA.

74 Tree-felling

75 Zanzibar Street

(Litho German Bank Note Ptg Co, Leipzig)

1966 (5 June). Horiz designs as T **74**, and T **75**. P 12½×13 (50c., 10s.) or 13×12½ (others).

460	5c. maroon and yellow-olive	70	80
461	10c. brown-purple and bright emerald	70	80
462	15c. brown-purple and light blue	70	80
463	20c. ultramarine and light orange	40	20
464	25c. maroon and orange-yellow	40	30
465	30c. maroon and ochre-yellow	70	20
466	40c. purple-brown and rose-pink	80	20
467	50c. green and pale greenish yellow	80	20
468	1s. maroon and bright blue	80	20
469	1s. 30 maroon and turquoise	80	3·00
470	2s. brown-purple and light blue-green	80	40
471	5s. rose-red and pale blue	1·25	5·50
472	10s. crimson and pale yellow	2·25	18·00
473	20s. deep purple-brown and magenta	5·00	42·00
460/473 *Set of 14*		14·50	65·00

Designs:—5c., 20s. Type **74**; 10c., 1s. Clove cultivation; 15, 40c. Chair-making; 20c., 5s. Lumumba College; 25c., 4s. 30, Agriculture; 30c., 2s. Agricultural workers; 50c.,10s. Type **75**.

81 "Education"

(Litho D.L.R.)

1966 (25 Sept). Introduction of Free Education. P 13½×13.

474	**81**	50c. black, light blue and orange	10	1·00
475		1s.30 black, light blue and yellow-green	15	1·75
476		2s.50 black, light blue and pink	55	4·50
474/6 *Set of 3*			70	6·50

82 A.S.P. Flag

(Litho D.L.R.)

1967 (5 Feb). Tenth Anniv of Afro-Shirazi Party (A.S.P.). T **82** and similar multicoloured design. P 14.

477	30c. Type **82**	20	1·25
478	50c. Vice-President M. A. Karume of Tanzania, flag and crowd (*vert*)	20	1·00
479	1s.30 As 50c.	20	2·25
480	2s.50 Type **82**	50	3·75
477/80 *Set of 4*		1·00	7·50

84 Voluntary Workers

(Photo Delrieu)

1967 (20 Aug). Voluntary Workers Brigade. P 12½×12.

481	**84**	1s.30 multicoloured	20	2·25
482		2s.50 multicoloured	55	5·50

POSTAGE DUE STAMPS

D 1

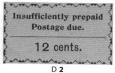

D 2

(Types D **1** and D **2** typo by the Government Printer)

1926–30. Rouletted 10, with imperf sheet edges. No gum.

D1	D **1**	1c. black/*orange*	11·00	£150
D2		2c. black/*orange*	4·50	80·00
D3		3c. black/*orange*	5·00	65·00
		a. "cent.s" for "cents."	£150	£450
D4		6c. black/*orange*	—	£7000
		a. "cent.s" for "cents."		£24000
D5		9c. black/*orange*	2·75	40·00
		a. "cent.s" for "cents."	26·00	£170
D6		12c. black/*orange*	£15000	£12000
		a. "cent.s" for "cents."	†	
		b. "I" of "Insufficiently" omitted	†	£21000
D7		12c. black/*green*	£1500	£600
		a. "cent.s" for "cents."	£4000	£1700
D8		15c. black/*orange*	2·75	42·00
		a. "cent.s" for "cents."	26·00	£180
D9		18c. black/*salmon*	5·50	55·00
		a. "cent.s" for "cents."	50·00	£250
D10		18c. black/*orange*	29·00	90·00
		a. "cent.s" for "cents."	85·00	£375
D11		20c. black/*orange*	4·50	80·00
		a. "cent.s" for "cents."	50·00	£350
D12		21c. black/*orange*	3·50	50·00
		a. "cent.s" for "cents."	42·00	£225
D13		25c. black/*magenta*	£2750	£1300
		a. "cent.s" for "cents."	£7000	£4000
D14		25c. black/*orange*	£19000	£17000
		a. "cent.s" for "cents."	9·50	£110
D15		31c. black/*orange*	70·00	£1200
D16		50c. black/*orange*	21·00	£250
		a. "cent.s" for "cents."	£120	£1700
D17		75c. black/*orange*	80·00	£600
		a. "cent.s" for "cents."	£300	

Initial printings, except the 1c. and 2c., contained the error "cent.s" for "cents" on R. 4/1 in the sheets of 10 (2×5). The error was corrected on subsequent supplies of the 3c., 9c. and 15c.

It is known that examples of these stamps used before early 1929 were left uncancelled on the covers. Uncancelled examples of Nos. D4, D6/7 and D13/14 which are not in very fine condition, must be assumed to have been used.

1930–33. Rouletted 5. No gum.

D18	D **2**	2c. black/*salmon*	27·00	40·00
D19		3c. black/*rose*	3·50	65·00
D21		6c. black/*yellow*	3·25	38·00
D22		12c. black/*blue*	4·50	30·00
D23		25c. black/*rose*	10·00	£140
D24		25c. black/*lilac*	26·00	85·00
D18/24 *Set of 6*			65·00	£350

D **3**

(Typo D.L.R.)

1936 (1 Jan)–**62**. Wmk Mult Script CA. P 14.

D25	D **3**	5c. violet	8·50	14·00
		a. Chalk-surfaced paper (18.7.56)	35	20·00
D26		10c. scarlet	7·00	2·75
		a. Chalk-surfaced paper (6.3.62)	35	12·00
D27		20c. green	2·50	7·00
		a. Chalk-surfaced paper (6.3.62)	35	28·00
D28		30c. brown	18·00	24·00
		a. Chalk-surfaced paper (18.7.56)	35	14·00
D29		40c. ultramarine	10·00	29·00
		a. Chalk-surfaced paper (18.7.56)	75	50·00
D30		1s. grey	16·00	38·00
		a. Chalk-surfaced paper (18.7.56)	1·00	25·00
D25/30 *Set of 6*			55·00	£100
D25a/30a *Set of 6*			2·75	£130
D25s/30s Perf "SPECIMEN" *Set of 6*			£140	

All Zanzibar issues were withdrawn on 1 January 1968 and replaced by Tanzania issues. Zanzibar stamps remained valid for postage in Zanzibar for a limited period.

TANZANIA

The United Republic of Tanganyika and Zanzibar, formed 26 April 1964, was renamed the United Republic of Tanzania on 29 October 1964.

Issues to No. 176, except Nos. Z142/5, were also valid in Kenya and Uganda.

(Currency. 100 cents = 1 shilling)

25 Hale Hydro Electric Scheme

26 Tanzanian Flag

27 National Servicemen

33 Dar-es-Salaam Harbour

38 Arms of Tanzania

(Des V. Whiteley. Photo Harrison)

1965 (9 Dec). T **25/7**, **33**, **38** and similar designs. P 14×14½ (5c., 10c., 20c., 50c., 65c.), 14½×14 (15c., 30c., 40c.), or 14 (others).

128		5c. ultramarine and yellow-orange	10	10
129		10c. black, greenish yellow, green and blue	10	10
130		15c. multicoloured	10	10
131		20c. sepia, grey-green and greenish blue	10	10
132		30c. black and red-brown	10	10
133		40c. multicoloured	1·00	20
134		50c. multicoloured	1·00	10
135		65c. green, red-brown and blue	2·75	2·50
136		1s. multicoloured	1·50	10
137		1s.30 multicoloured	6·50	1·50
138		2s.50 blue and orange-brown	6·50	1·25
139		5s. lake-brown, yellow-green and blue	80	20
140		10s. olive-yellow, olive-green and blue	1·00	3·75
141		20s. multicoloured	7·00	18·00
128/41 *Set of 14*			25·00	25·00

Designs: *Horiz* (as T **25**)—20c. Road-building; 50c. Common Zebras, Manyara National Park; 65c. Mt Kilimanjaro. *Vert* (as T **27**)—30c. Drum, spear, shield and stool; 40 c. Giraffes, Mikumi National Park. Horiz (As T **33**)—1s.30, Skull of *Zinjanthropus* and excavations, Olduvai Gorge, 2s.50, Fishing; 5s. Sisal industry; 10s. State House, Dar-es-Salaam.

Z **39** Pres. Nyerere and First Vice-Pres. Karume within Bowl of Flame

Z **40** Hands supporting Bowl of Flame

(Des J. Ahmed (Type Z **39**), G. Vasarhelyi (Type Z **40**). Photo Enschedé)

1966 (26 April). Second Anniv of United Republic. P 14×13.

Z142	Z **39**	30c. multicoloured	20	45
Z143	Z **40**	50c. multicoloured	20	45
Z144		1s.30, multicoloured	30	45
Z145	Z **39**	2s.50, multicoloured	40	1·25
Z142/5 *Set of 4*			1·00	2·40

Nos. Z142/5 were on sale in Zanzibar only.

39 Black-footed
Cardinalfish

40 Sobrinus
Mudskipper

41 Lionfish

(Des Rena Fennesy. Photo Harrison)

1967 (9 Dec)–**73**. Designs as T **39/41**. Chalk-surfaced paper. P 14×15
(5c. to 70c.) or 14½ (others).

142	5c. magenta, yellow-olive and black	10	2·75
	a. Glazed, ordinary paper (22.1.71)	30	3·50
143	10c. brown and bistre	10	10
	a. Glazed, ordinary paper (27.9.72)	50	2·25
144	15c. grey, turquoise-blue and black	10	2·00
	a. Glazed, ordinary paper (22.1.71)	45	6·00
145	20c. brown and turquoise-green	10	10
	a. Glazed, ordinary paper (16.7.73)	50	9·00
146	30c. sage-green and black	20	10
	a. Glazed, ordinary paper (3.5.71)	15·00	4·50
147	40c. yellow, chocolate and bright green	1·00	10
	a. Glazed, ordinary paper (10.2.71)	1·00	60
148	50c. multicoloured	20	10
	a. Glazed, ordinary paper (10.2.71)	50	3·00
149	65c. orange-yellow, bronze-green and black	2·00	4·50
150	70c. multicoloured (15.9.69)	1·00	3·50
	a. Glazed, ordinary paper (22.1.71)	4·25	10·00
151	1s. orange-brown, slate-blue and maroon .	30	10
	a. Glazed ordinary paper (3.2.71)	1·00	10
152	1s.30 multicoloured	4·00	10
153	1s.50 multicoloured (15.9.69)	2·50	50
	a. Glazed, ordinary paper (27.9.72)	2·25	10
154	2s.50 multicoloured	2·25	3·25
	a. Glazed, ordinary paper (27.9.72)	17·00	10
155	5s. greenish yellow, black and turquoise-green	5·00	2·75
	a. Glazed, ordinary paper (12.12.70*)	3·25	10
156	10s. multicoloured	1·00	3·75
	a. Glazed, ordinary paper (dull blue-green background) (12.12.70*)	1·00	10
	ab. Deep dull green background (12.9.73)	1·75	50
157	20s. multicoloured	1·25	7·00
	a. Glazed, ordinary paper (12.12.70*)	5·50	10
142/57 Set of 16		18·00	27·00
142a/57a Set of 15		45·00	35·00

*Earliest known postmark date.

Designs: Horiz as T **39/40**—15c. White-spotted Puffer; 20c. Thorny
Seahorse; 30c. Dusky Batfish; 40c. Black-spotted Sweetlips 50c. Blue
Birdwrasse; 65c. Bennett's Butterflyfish; 70c. Black-tipped Grouper.
Horiz as T **41**:— 1s.30, Powder-blue Surgeonfish; 1s.50, Yellow-finned
Fusilier; 2s.50, Emperor Snapper; 5s. Moorish Idol; 10s. Painted
Triggerfish; 20s. Horned Squirrelfish.

On chalk-surfaced paper all values except the 30c. exist with PVA
gum as well as gum arabic, but the 70c. and 1s.50 exist with PVA gum
only. Stamps on glazed, ordinary paper come only with PVA gum.

  =

53 Papilio
hornimani

54 Euphaedra neophron

80c
(**55**)

(Des Rena Fennesy. Photo Harrison)

1973 (10 Dec)–**78**. Various vert designs as T **53/4**.

*(a) Size as T **53**. P 14½×14.*

158	5c. light yellow-olive, lt violet-blue and black	60	30
159	10c. multicoloured	60	15

160	15c. light violet-blue and black	60	30
161	20c. reddish cinnamon, orange-yellow and black	70	15
162	30c. yellow, orange and black	70	10
	a. Bistre-yellow, orange and black (20.4.78)	2·75	60
163	40c. multicoloured	70	15
164	50c. multicoloured	1·00	15
165	60c. Lt grey-brown, lemon and reddish brown	1·50	60
166	70c. turquoise-green, pale orange and black	1·50	20
*(b) Size as T **54**. P 14*			
167	1s. multicoloured	1·50	15
168	1s.50 multicoloured	2·00	45
169	2s.50 multicoloured	2·25	80
170	5s. multicoloured (brt green background)	2·00	95
	a. Apple-green background (20.4.78)	6·00	60
171	10s. multicoloured	2·25	6·00
172	20s. multicoloured	2·75	13·00
158/72 Set of 15		18·00	21·00

Butterflies:—10c. *Colotis ione*; 15c. *Amauris hyalites* (s sp
makuyuensis); 20c. *Libythea labdaca* (s sp *laius*); 30c. *Danaus
chrysippus*; 40c. *Asterope rosa*; 50c. *Axiocerses styx*; 60c. *Terias hecabe*;
70c. *Acroea insignis*; 1s.50, *Precis octaoia*; 2s.50, *Charoxes eupale*; 5s.
Charoxes pollux; 10s. *Salamis parhassus*; 20s. *Papilio ophidicephalus*.

Nos. 159 and 164 exist in coils, constructed from normal sheets.

A used example of No. 167 has been seen apparently showing the
yellow colour omitted.

1975 (17 Nov). Nos. 165, 168/9 and 172 surch as T **55**.

173	80c. on 60c. *Terias hecabe*	2·25	2·25
174	2s. on 1s.50 *Precis octavia*	4·00	7·00
175	3s. on 2s.50 *Charoxes eupale*	13·00	32·00
176	40s. on 20s. *Papilio ophidicephalus*	4·75	15·00
173/6 Set of 4		22·00	50·00

1976 (15 Apr). Telecommunications Development. As Nos. 56/60 of
Kenya but inscr "TANZANIA".

177	50c. Microwave Tower	10	10
178	1s. Cordless switchboard	15	10
179	2s. Telephones	25	30
180	3s. Message Switching Centre	30	40
177/80 Set of 4		70	70
MS181 120×120 mm. Nos. 177/80		1·10	1·50

Nos. 177/8 and 180 exist imperforate from stock dispersed by the
liquidator of Format International Security Printers Ltd.

1976 (5 July). Olympic Games, Montreal. As Nos 61/5 of Kenya but
inscr "TANZANIA".

182	50c. Akii Bus, Ugandan hurdler	10	10
183	1s. Filbert Bayi, Tanzanian runner	15	10
184	2s. Steve Muchoki, Kenyan boxer	25	40
185	3s. Olympic flame and East Africa flags	30	40
182/5 Set of 4		70	70
MS186 129×154 mm. Nos. 182/5		2·00	1·75

Nos. 182/4 exist imperforate from stock dispersed by the liquidator
of Format International Security Printers Ltd.

1976 (4 Oct). Railway Transport. As Nos. 66/70 of Kenya but inscr
"TANZANIA".

187	50c. Diesel-hydraulic train, Tanzania Zambia Railway	20	10
188	1s. Nile Bridge, Uganda	25	10
189	2s. Nakuru Station, Kenya	35	30
190	3s. Uganda Railway Class A locomotive, 1896	40	45
187/90 Set of 4		1·10	75
MS191 154×103 mm. Nos. 187/90		2·50	3·50

Nos. 187/91 exist imperforate from stack dispersed by the liquidator
of Format International Security Printers Ltd.

1977 (10 Jan). Game Fish of East Africa. As Nos. 71/5 of Kenya but
inscr "TANZANIA".

192	50c. Nile Perch	15	10
193	1s. Nile Mouthbrooder	15	10
194	3s. Sailfish	50	40
195	5s. Black Marlin	60	60
192/5 Set of 4		1·25	1·00
MS196 153×129 mm. Nos. 192/5		2·75	2·50

1977 (15 Jan). Second World Black and African Festival of Arts and
Culture Nigeria. As Nos 76/80 of Kenya but inscr "TANZANIA".

197	50c. Maasai Manyatta (village), Kenya	15	10
198	1s. "Heartbeat of Africa" (Ugandan dancers)	15	10
199	2s. Makonde sculpture	30	40
200	3s. "Early Man and Technology" (skinning hippopotamus)	75	1·60
197/200 Set of 4		1·25	2·00
MS201 132×190 mm. Nos. 197/200		1·40	2·00

1977 (5 Apr). 25th Anniv of Safari Rally. As Nos. 81/5 of Kenya but
inscr "TANZANIA".

202	50c. Rally-car and villagers	10	10

203	1s. Pres. Kenyatta starting rally.......................	15	10
204	2s. Car fording river	30	40
205	5s. Car and elephants.....................................	1·00	1·10
202/5 *Set of 4*..		1·40	1·50
MS206 126×93 mm. Nos. 202/5.................................		1·40	2·00

1977 (30 June). Centenary of Ugandan Church. As Nos. 86/90 of Kenya but inscr "TANZANIA".

207	50c. Canon Kivebulaya......................................	10	10
208	1s. Modern Namirembe Cathedral..................	15	10
209	2s. The first Cathedral...................................	30	40
210	5s. Early congregation, Kigezi........................	60	1·75
207/10 *Set of 4*..		1·00	2·00
MS211 126×89 mm. Nos. 207/10...............................		1·00	2·00

1977 (26 Sept). Endangered Species. As Nos. 96/101 of Kenya but inscr "TANZANIA".

212	50c. Pancake Tortoise.....................................	40	10
213	1s. Nile Crocodile..	45	10
214	2s. Hunter's Hartebeest.................................	1·25	55
215	3s. Red Colobus monkey................................	1·25	75
216	5s. Dugong...	1·50	1·00
212/16 *Set of 5*..		4·25	2·25
MS217 127×101 mm. Nos. 213/16.............................		3·50	5·00

56 Prince Philip and President Nyerere

(Des G. Vasarhelyi. Litho Questa)

1977 (23 Nov). Silver Jubilee. T **56** and similar horiz designs. Multicoloured. P 14×13½.

218	50c. Type **56**	10	10
219	5s. Pres. Nyerere with Queen and Prince Philip	15	25
220	10s. Jubilee emblem and Commonwealth flags	25	40
221	20s. The Crowning	40	60
218/21 *Set of 4*..		75	1·25
MS222 128×102 mm. Nos. 218/21.............................		75	1·50

57 Improvements in Rural Living Standards

(Des P. Ndembo. Litho J.W.)

1978 (5 Feb). First Anniv of Chama Cha Mapinduzi (New Revolutionary Party). T **57** and similar horiz designs. P 13½×14.

223	50c. multicoloured...	10	10
224	1s. multicoloured..	10	10
225	3s. multicoloured..	25	60
226	5s. black, light green and greenish yellow.	35	1·00
223/6 *Set of 4*..		70	1·40
MS227 142×106 mm. Nos. 223/6...............................		1·00	1·40

Designs:—1s. "Flag raising ceremony, Zanzibar; 3s. Handing over of TANU headquarters, Dodoma; 5s. Chairman Julius Nyerere.

1978 (17 Apr). World Cup Football Championship, Argentina. As Nos. 122/6 of Kenya but inscr "TANZANIA".

228	50c. Joe Kadenge and forwards.......................	10	10
229	1s. Mohamed Chums and cup presentation..	10	10
230	2s. Omari Kidevu and goalmouth scene	30	70
231	3s. Polly Ouma and forwards.........................	40	1·00
228/31 *Set of 4*..		75	1·60
MS232 136×81 mm. Nos. 228/31...............................		2·00	1·75

25th ANNIVERSARY
CORONATION

25th ANNIVERSARY
CORONATION

2nd JUNE 1953
(58)

2nd JUNE 1953
(59)

1978 (2 June). 25th Anniv of Coronation. Nos. 218/22 optd.

A. As T **58**. *P* 14×13½

233A	50c. Type **56**	10	10
234A	5s. Pres. Nyerere with Queen and Prince Philip	20	30
235A	10s. Jubilee emblem and Commonwealth flags	25	50
236A	20s. The Crowning	40	90
233A/6A *Set of 4*		75	1·50
MS237A 128×102 mm. Nos. 233A/6A		75	1·50

B. As T **59**. *P* 12×11½

233B	50c. Type **56**	10	10
234B	5s. Pres Nyerere with Queen and Prince Philip	20	30
235B	10s. Jubilee emblem and Commonwealth flags	25	50
236B	20s. The Crowning	40	90
233B/6B *Set of 4*		75	1·50
MS237B 128×102 mm. Nos. 233B/6B		75	1·50

60 "Do not Drink and Drive"

61 Lake Manyara Hotel

(Des and litho J.W.)

1978 (1 July). Road Safety. T **60** and similar vert designs. P 13½×13.

238	50c. multicoloured...	15	10
239	1s. multicoloured..	20	10
240	3s. orange-red, black and light brown........	45	70
241	5s. multicoloured..	75	1·40
238/41 *Set of 4*..		1·40	2·00
MS242 92×129 mm. Nos. 238/41. P 14......................		1·40	2·00

Designs:—1s. "Show courtesy to young, old and crippled"; 3s. "Observe the Highway Code"; 5s. "Do not drive a faulty vehicle".

(Des M. Raza. Litho B.W.)

1978 (11 Sept). Game Lodges. T **61** and similar horiz designs. Multicoloured. P 13½×13.

243	50c. Type **61**	10	10
244	1s. Lobo Wildlife Lodge................................	10	10
245	3s. Ngorengoro Crater Lodge........................	20	35
246	5s. Ngorongoro Wildlife Lodge......................	30	55
247	10s. Mafia Island Lodge..................................	40	1·10
248	20s. Mikumi Wildlife Lodge............................	75	2·75
243/8 *Set of 6*..		1·50	4·25
MS249 118×112 mm. Nos. 243/8...............................		5·00	7·50

62 "Racial Suppression"

63 Fokker F.27 Friendship

(Des local artist; adapted G. Hutchins. Litho Harrison)

1978 (24 Oct). International Anti-Apartheid Year. T **62** and similar vert designs. P 14½×14.

250	50c. multicoloured...	10	10
251	1s. black, yellowish green and yellow.........	10	10
252	2s.50 multicoloured...	30	1·00
253	5s. multicoloured..	60	1·75
250/3 *Set of 4*..		1·00	2·50
MS254 127×132 mm. Nos. 250/3...............................		1·25	2·75

Designs:—1s. "Racial division"; 2s.50, "Racial harmony"; 5s. "Fall of suppression and rise of freedom".

(Des J. Mzinga; adapted J.W. Litho Walsall)

1978 (28 Dec). 75th Anniv of Powered Flight. T **63** and similar horiz designs. Multicoloured. P 13½.

255	50c. Type **63**	20	10
256	1s. de Havilland DH.84 Dragon Mk I on Zanzibar Island, 1930's	25	10
257	2s. Concorde	1·00	75
258	5s. Wright brothers' *Flyer 1*, 1903	1·25	1·25
255/8 *Set of 4*		2·40	2·00
MS259 133×97 mm. Nos. 255/8		2·75	3·50

64 Corporation Emblem

(Des local artists; adapted BG Studio. Litho Harrison)

1979 (3 Feb). First Anniv of Tanzania Posts and Telecommunications Corporation. T **64** and similar horiz design. Multicoloured. P 14½×14.

260	50c. Type **64**	10	10
261	5s. Headquarters buildings	50	70
MS262 82×97 mm. Nos. 260/1		1·00	1·50

65 Pres. Nyerere (patron of National IYC Committee) with Children

30c
(**66**)

(Des J. Mzinga. Litho B.W.)

1979 (25 June). International Year of the Child. T **65** and similar horiz designs. Multicoloured. P 14½.

263	50c. Type **65**	10	10
264	1s. Day care centre	15	10
265	2s. "Immunisation" (child being vaccinated)	25	45
266	5s. National IYC Committee emblem	40	1·00
263/6 *Set of 4*		80	1·50
MS267 127×91 mm. Nos. 263/6		1·25	1·50

1979 (Aug*–Sept). Nos. 159 and 166 surch as T **66** (No. 269 has horiz bar through original value).

268	10c. + 30c. multicoloured	2·25	2·25
a. Surch inverted		†	—
269	50c. on 70c. turquoise-green, pale orge and blue	3·25	2·25

*The earliest known postmark date for No. 268 is 15 September and for No. 269 30 August.

The face value of No. 268 was 40c.; the 30c. surcharge being added to the original 10c., which was not obliterated. This method was adopted because of difficulties during the actual surcharging. On No. 269 the 70c. face value is obliterated by a bar.

Examples of No. 268a were used at Singida in December 1979.

67 Planting Young Trees

68 Mwenge Satellite Earth Station

(Des J. Mzinga. Litho J.W.)

1979 (24 Sept). Forest Preservation. T **67** and similar vert designs. Multicoloured. P 14×14½.

270	50c. Type **67**	15	10
271	1s. Replacing dead trees with saplings	15	10
272	2s. Rainfall cycle	35	50
273	5s. Forest fire warning	60	1·50
270/3 *Set of 4*		1·10	2·00

(Des and litho J.W.)

1979 (14 Dec). Opening of Mwenge Satellite Earth Station. P 13½.

274	**68**	10c. multicoloured	10	10
275		40c. multicoloured	15	10
276		50c. multicoloured	15	10
277		1s. multicoloured	25	20
274/7 *Set of 4*			55	40

69 Tabata Dispensary, Dar-es-Salaam

(Litho J.W.)

1980 (10 Apr). 75th Anniv of Rotary International. T **69** and similar horiz designs. Multicoloured. P 13.

278	50c. Type **69**	10	10
279	1s. Ngomvu Village water project	10	10
280	5s. Flying Doctor service (plane donation)	35	50
281	20s. Torch and 75th Anniversary emblem	60	2·00
278/81 *Set of 4*		1·00	2·25
MS282 120×101 mm. Nos. 278/81. P 14		1·00	2·25

70 Zanzibar 1896 2r. Stamp and 1964 25c. Definitive

'LONDON 1980'
PHILATELIC EXHIBITION
(**71**)

(Des J.W. Litho Questa)

1980 (21 Apr). Death Centenary of Sir Rowland Hill (1979). T **70** and similar multicoloured designs. P 14.

283	40c. Type **70**	10	10
284	50c. Tanganyika 1962 Independence 50c. commemorative and man attaching stamp to letter (*vert*)	10	10
285	10s. Tanganyika 1922 25c. stamp and 1961 1s.30, definitive	35	75
286	20s. Penny Black and Sir Rowland Hill (*vert*)	60	1·40
283/6 *Set of 4*		1·00	2·00
MS287 158×120 mm. Nos. 283/6		1·00	2·00

1980 (5 May). London 1980 International Stamp Exhibition. Nos. 283/7 optd with T **71**.

288	40c. Type **71**	10	10
289	50c. Tanganyika 1962 Independence 50c. commemorative and man attaching stamp to letter	10	10
290	10s. Tanganyika 1922 25c. stamp and 1961 1s.30, definitive	35	75
291	20s. Penny Black and Sir Rowland Hill	60	1·40
288/91 *Set of 4*		1·00	2·00
MS292 158×120 mm. Nos. 288/91		1·00	2·00

District 920 - 56th Annual Conference, Arusha, Tanzania
(**72**)

1980 (23 June). Annual Conference of District 920, Rotary International, Arusha. Nos. 278/82 optd as T **72**.

293	50c. Type **69**	10	10
294	1s. Ngomvu Village water project	10	10
295	5s. Flying Doctor service (plane donation)	25	50
296	20s. Torch and 75th Anniversary of Rotary International Emblem	65	2·25
293/6 *Set of 4*		1·00	2·25
MS297 120×101 mm. Nos. 293/6		1·25	2·75

73 Conference, Tanzanian Posts and Telecommunications Corporation and UPU Emblems

(Des and litho J.W.)

1980 (1 July). P.A.P.U. (Pan-African Postal Union) Plenipotentiary Conference, Arusha. P 13.

298	**73**	50c. black and bright violet	10	10
299		1s. black and ultramarine	10	10
300		5s. black and orange-red	30	80
301		10s. black and blue-green	65	2·00
298/301 *Set of 4*			1·00	2·75

74 Gidamis Shahanga (marathon)

(Litho J.W.)

1980 (18 Aug). Olympic Games, Moscow. T **74** and similar horiz designs. Multicoloured. P 13.

302	50c. Type **74**	10	15
	a. Horiz strip of 4. Nos. 302/5	1·00	2·75
303	1s. Nzael Kyomo (sprints)	15	15
304	10s. Zakayo Malekwa (javelin)	35	1·00
305	20s. William Lyimo (boxing)	50	1·75
302/5 *Set of 4*		1·00	2·75
MS306 172×117 mm. Nos. 302/305. P 14		1·00	2·25

Nos. 302/305 were printed either in separate sheets or together, *se-tenant*, in horizontal strips of 4 throughout the sheet.

75 Spring Hare   **76** Impala

(Des Rena Fennessy)

1980 (1 Oct)–**85**. Wildlife. Horiz designs as T **75** (10c. to 80c.) or T **76** (1s. to 40s.). Multicoloured.

(a) Litho B.W. P 14 (10c. to 80c.) or 14½ (1s. to 40s.)

307	10c. Type **75**	10	15
308	20c. Large-spotted Genet	10	15
309	40c. Banded Mongoose	10	10
310	50c. Ratel (light blue panel at foot)	10	10
311	75c. Large-toothed Rock Hyrax	10	30
312	80c. Leopard (buff sky)	30	30
313	1s. Type **76**	10	10
314	1s.50 Giraffe	30	20
315	2s. Common Zebra	30	40
316	3s. Buffalo	30	50
317	5s. Lion	40	65
318	10s. Black Rhinoceros	1·00	1·40
319	20s. African Elephant	1·50	1·75
320	40s. Cheetah	1·00	3·25
307/20 *Set of 14*		4·75	8·00

(b) Litho J.W. P 14 (50c., 80c.) or 14×14½ (others) (1984-85)

320a	50c. Ratel (turquoise-blue panel at foot)	1·50	40
320b	80c. Leopard (yellow sky)	16·00	5·00
320c	1s. Type **76**	2·50	60
	ca. Perf 13½	15·00	5·00
	cab. Booklet pane of 4 with margins on three sides	50·00	
320d	1s.50 Giraffe	14·00	5·50
320e	2s. Common Zebra	4·00	3·25
	ea. Perf 13½	15·00	5·00
	eab. Booklet pane of 4 with margins on three sides	50·00	
320f	3s. Buffalo	5·50	6·00
	fa. Perf 13½	15·00	6·00
	fab. Booklet pane of 4 with margins on three sides	50·00	
320g	5s. Lion	7·50	9·00

Both formats of the Waddington printings are slightly smaller than the Bradbury Wilkinson stamps so that Nos. 320a/b measure 19½×16 mm, instead of 20×16½ mm, and the larger designs 40×23½ mm, instead of 40½×24 mm. The Swahili inscriptions on the 1s. and 2s. appear as one word on the Bradbury Wilkinson printings and as two words on those produced by Waddington.

Booklet panes Nos. 320cab, 320eab and 320fab have narrow margins at left, top and bottom.

1980 (22 Nov). Nos. O41 and O43 with "OFFICIAL" opt Type O **1** obliterated by horizontal line.

320h	10c. multicoloured	—	£250

320i	40c. multicoloured	£100	75·00

Nos. 320h/i exist on commercial mail from Morogoro. The date is that of the earliest postmark reported.

77 Ngorongoro Conservation Area Authority Emblem

ROYAL WEDDING H.R.H. PRINCE CHARLES 29th JULY 1981
(78)

(Des D. Kyungu. Litho J.W.)

1981 (2 Feb). 60th Anniv of Ngorongoro and Serengeti National Parks. T **77** and similar horiz designs. P 13.

321	50c. multicoloured	10	10
322	1s. black, gold and deep blue-green	10	10
323	5s. multicoloured	30	60
324	20s. multicoloured	80	2·25
321/4 *Set of 4*		1·10	2·75

Designs:—1s. Tanzania National Parks emblem; 5s. Friends of the Serengeti emblem; 20s. Friends of Ngorongoro emblem.

Nos. 321/4 exist overprinted "75th ANNIVERSARY GIRL GUIDES 1910 1985" or "CONGRATULATIONS TO THE DUKE & DUCHESS OF YORK ON THE OCCASION OF THEIR MARRIAGE", but there is no evidence that these overprints were available from post offices in Tanzania.

1981 (29 July). Royal Wedding. Nos. 220/1 optd with T **78**.

325	10s. Jubilee emblem and Commonwealth flags	30	60
326	20s. Crowning	40	80
MS327 88×97 mm. Nos. 325/6		1·50	2·00

79 Mail Runner

(Des D. Kyungu. Litho State Printing Works, Moscow)

1981 (21 Oct). Commonwealth Postal Administrations Conference, Arusha. T **79** and similar horiz designs. Multicoloured. P 12½×12.

328	50c. Type **79**	10	10
329	1s. Letter sorting	10	10
330	5s. Letter Post symbols	30	1·00
331	10s. Flags of Commonwealth nations	70	2·50
328/31 *Set of 4*		1·00	3·25
MS332 130×100 mm. Nos. 328/31		1·10	3·00

80 Morris Nyunyusa (blind drummer)

(Des and litho Harrison)

1981 (30 Nov). International Year for Disabled Persons. T **80** and similar horiz designs. Multicoloured. P 14.

333	50c. Type **80**	25	10
334	1s. Mgulani Rehabilitation Centre, Dar-es-Salaam	30	10
335	5s. Aids for disabled persons	1·00	2·50
336	10s. Disabled children cleaning school compound	1·50	4·00
333/6 *Set of 4*		2·75	6·00

81 President Mwahmu Julius K. Nyerere

(Litho J.W.)

1982 (13 Jan). 20th Anniv of Independence. T **81** and similar horiz designs. Multicoloured. P 13×13½.

337	50c. Type **81**	10	10
338	1s. Electricity plant, Mtoni	10	10
339	3s. Sisal industry	25	90
340	10s. "Universal primary education"	70	2·50
337/40 *Set of 4*		1·00	3·25
MS341 120×85 mm. Nos. 337/40		1·00	3·00

82 Ostrich   **83** Jella Mtaga

(Des and litho J.W.)

1982 (25 Jan). Birds. T **82** and similar vert designs. Multicoloured. P 13½×13.

342	50c. Type **82**	80	10
343	1s. Secretary Bird	85	10
344	5a. Kori Bustard	3·00	2·75
345	10s. Saddle-bill Stork	3·75	5·50
342/5 *Set of 4*		7·50	7·50

(Des P. Ndembo. Litho J.W.)

1982 (2 June). World Cup Football Championship, Spain. T **83** and similar horiz designs. Multicoloured. P 14.

346	50c. Type **83**	20	10
347	1s. Football stadium	25	10
348	10s. Diego Maradona	2·00	2·25
349	20s. FIFA emblem	3·50	4·50
346/9 *Set of 4*		5·50	6·00
MS350 130×100 mm. Nos. 346/9		7·50	8·00

Nos. 346/9 exist overprinted "CONGRATULATIONS TO THE DUKE & DUCHESS OF YORK ON THE OCCASION OF THEIR MARRIAGE", but there is no evidence that these overprints were available from post offices in Tanzania.

84 "Jade" of Seronera (cheetah) with Cubs

(Des and litho Harrison)

1982 (15 July). Animal Personalities. T **84** and similar horiz designs. Multicoloured. P 14.

351	50c. Type **84**	15	10
352	1s. Female Golden Jackal and cubs (incorrectly inacr "Wild dog")	15	10
353	5s. "Fifi" and two sons of "Gombe" (chimpanzees)	40	1·75
354	10s. "Bahati " of Lake Manyara with twins, "Rashidi" and "Ramadhani" (elephants)	1·00	2·75
351/4 *Set of 4*		1·50	4·25
MS355 120×89 mm. Nos. 351/4. P 14½		1·50	5·00

85 Brick-laying   **86** Ploughing Field

(Des P. Ndembo. Litho J.W.)

1982 (25 Aug). 75th Anniv of Boy Scout Movement. T **85** and similar horiz designs. Multicoloured. P 14.

356	50c. Type **85**	15	10
357	1s. Camping	15	10
358	10s. Tracing signs	50	1·00

359	20s. Lord Baden-Powell	65	1·75
356/9 *Set of 4*		1·25	2·75
MS360 130×100 mm. Nos. 356/9		1·50	3·00

No. **MS**360 exists overprinted "75th ANNIVERSARY GIRL GUIDES 1910-1985", but there is no evidence that this overprint was available from post offices in Tanzania.

(Des P. Ndembo. Litho J.W.)

1982 (16 Oct). World Food Day. T **86** and similar horiz designs. Multicoloured. P 14.

361	50c. Type **86**	10	10
362	1s. Dairy farming	10	10
363	5s. Maize farming	45	60
364	10s. Grain storage	75	1·25
361/4 *Set of 4*		1·10	1·75
MS365 129×99 mm. Nos. 361/4		1·40	2·25

87 Immunization

(Des P. Ndembo. Litho State Printing Works, Moscow)

1982 (1 Dec). Centenary of Robert Koch's Discovery of Tubercle Bacillus. T **87** and similar horiz designs. Multicoloured. P 12½×12.

366	50c. Type **87**	15	10
367	1s. Dr. Robert Koch	15	10
368	5s. International Union Against TB emblem	50	1·25
369	10s. World Health Organization emblem	90	3·00
366/9 *Set of 4*		1·50	4·00

88 Letter Post   **89** Pres. Mwalimu Julius Nyerere

(Litho State Printing Works, Moscow)

1983 (3 Feb). 5th Anniv of Posts and Telecommunications Corporation. T **88** and similar horiz designs. Multicoloured. P 12.

370	50c. Type **88**	10	10
371	1s. Training institute	10	10
372	5s. Satellite communications	35	90
373	10s. U.P.U., I.T.U. and T.P.T.C.C. (Tanzania Poets and Telecommunications Corporation) emblems	60	2·00
370/3 *Set of 4*		1·00	2·75
MS374 126×96 mm. Nos. 370/3		1·50	3·00

(Litho J.W.)

1983 (14 Mar). Commonwealth Day. T **89** and similar horiz designs. Multicoloured. P 14.

375	50c. Type **89**	10	10
376	1s. Athletics and boxing	15	10
377	5s. Flags of Commonwealth countries	40	90
378	10s. Pres. Nyerere and members of British Royal Family	70	1·90
375/8 *Set of 4*		1·10	2·75
MS379 121×100 mm. Nos. 375/8		1·10	2·75

Nos. 375/8 exist overprinted "CONGRATULATIONS TO THE DUKE & DUCHESS OF YORK ON THE OCCASION OF THEIR MARRIAGE", but there is no evidence that these overprints were available from post offices in Tanzania.

90 Eastern and Southern African Management Institute, Arusha, Tanzania

(Des P. Ndembo. Litho State Ptg Wks, Moscow)

1983 (12 Sept). 25th Anniv of the Economic Commission for Africa. T **90** and similar horiz designs. Multicoloured. P 12½×12.

380	50c. Type **90**	15	10

381	1s. 25th Anniversary inscription and UN logo	20	10
382	5s. Mineral collections	2·75	2·75
383	10s. E.C.A. Silver Jubilee logo and O.A.U. flag	2·75	3·50
380/3	Set of 4	5·25	5·75
MS384	132×102 mm. Nos. 380/3	5·75	5·75

91 Telephone Cables

92 Bagamoyo Boma

(Des P. Ndembo. Litho J.W.)

1983 (17 Oct). World Communications Year. T **91** and similar horiz designs. Multicoloured. P 14.

385	50c. Type **91**	10	10
386	1s. W.C.Y. logo	10	10
387	5s. Postal service	50	1·50
388	10s. Microwave tower	75	2·50
385/8	Set of 4	1·25	3·75
MS389	102×92 mm. Nos. 385/88	1·50	3·75

(Des J. de Silva and P. Ndembo. Litho State Ptg Wks, Moscow)

1983 (12 Dec). Historical Buildings. T **92** and similar horiz designs. Multicoloured. P 12½×12.

390	1s. Type **92**	10	10
391	1s.50 Beit el Ajaib, Zanzibar	15	25
392	5s. Anglican Cathedral, Zanzibar	40	1·00
393	10s. Original German Government House and present State House, Dar-es Salaam	75	2·00
390/3	Set of 4	1·25	3·00
MS394	130×100 mm. Nos. 390/3	1·25	3·00

93 Sheikh Abeid Amani Karume (founder of Afro-Shirazi Party)

94 Boxing

(Des P. Ndembo. Litho J.W.)

1984 (18 June). 20th Anniv of Zanzibar Revolution. T **93** and similar horiz designs. Multicoloured. P 14.

395	1s. Type **93**	10	10
396	1s.50 Clove farming	15	25
397	5s. Symbol of Industrial Development	40	1·00
398	10s. New housing schemes	75	2·00
395/8	Set of 4	1·25	3·00
MS399	130×100 mm. 15s. *Mapinduzi* (ferry) and map	1·25	2·50

(Des P. Ndembo. Litho State Ptg Wks, Moscow)

1984 (6 Aug). Olympic Games, Los Angeles. T **94** and similar horiz designs. Multicoloured. P 12½×12.

400	1s. Type **94**	10	10
401	1s.50 Running	15	10
402	5s. Basketball	1·00	60
403	20s. Football	1·60	2·25
400/3	Set of 4	2·50	2·75
MS404	130×100 mm. Nos. 400/3	2·50	2·75

95 Icarus in Flight

(Des P. Ndembo. Litho J.W.)

1984 (15 Nov). 40th Anniv of International Civil Aviation Organization. T **95** and similar horiz designs. Multicoloured. P 13×12½.

405	1s. Type **95**	10	10
406	1s.50 Douglas DC-10, Boeing 737 aircraft and air traffic controller	15	20
407	5s. Boeing 737 undergoing maintenance	55	1·25
408	10s. I.C.A.O. badge	1·10	2·00
405/8	Set of 4	1·75	3·25
MS409	130×100 mm. Nos. 405/8	2·75	3·25

96 Sochi – Conical House

97 Production of Cotton Textiles

(Des P. Ndembo. Litho State Ptg Wks, Moscow)

1984 (20 Dec). Traditional Houses. T **96** and similar horiz designs. Multicoloured. P 12½×12.

410	1s. Type **96**	10	10
411	1s.50 Isyenga–circular type	15	20
412	5s. Tembe–flatroofed type	40	1·25
413	10s. Banda–coastal type	70	2·00
410/13	Set of 4	1·10	3·25
MS414	129×99 mm. Nos. 410/13	1·50	3·25

(Des P. Ndembo. Litho J.W.)

1985 (1 Apr). Fifth Anniv of Southern African Development Co-ordination Conference. T **97** and similar horiz designs. Multicoloured. P 14.

415	1s.50 Type **97**	30	15
416	4s. Diamond mining	2·00	1·50
417	5s. Map of member countries and means of communication	2·00	1·50
418	20s. Flags and signatures of member countries	3·75	4·00
415/18	Set of 4	7·25	6·50
MS419	110×104 mm. Nos. 415/18	8·50	8·00

98 Tortoise

(Des P. Ndembo (15s., 20s.), J. de Silva (others). Litho J.W.)

1985 (8 May). Rare Animals of Zanzibar. T **98** and similar multicoloured designs. P 12½×13 (17s.50) or 13×12½ (others).

420	1s. Type **98**	50	10
421	4s. Leopard	1·00	1·00
422	10s. Civet Cat	1·50	3·25
423	17s.50 Red Colobus Monkey (*vert*)	1·75	5·50
420/3	Set of 4	4·25	9·00
MS424	110×93 mm. 15s. Black Rhinoceros; 20s. Giant Ground Pangolin	1·50	3·50

IMPERFORATE STAMPS. Nos. 425/9, 430/4, 456/68, 474/8, 508/11 and 517/21 exist imperforate from restricted printings reported as being unavailable in Tanzania.

99 The Queen Mother

(Litho Holders Press)

1985 (30 Sept). Life and Times of Queen Elizabeth the Queen Mother. T **99** and similar horiz designs. Multicoloured. P 14.

425	20s. Type **99**	10	25
426	20s. Queen Mother waving to crowd	10	25
427	100s. Oval portrait with flowers	30	1·00
428	100s. Head and shoulders portrait	30	1·00
425/8	Set of 4	70	2·25
MS429	Two sheets, each 125×63 mm. (a) Nos. 425 and 427; (b) Nos. 426 and 428. *Set of 2 sheets*	80	2·75

Designs as Nos. 425/9, but inscr "H.R.H. The Queen Mother" were not issued in Tanzania.

100 Steam Locomotive No. 3022

GOLD MEDAL
HENRY TILLMAN
USA

(101)

(Litho Holders Press)

1985 (7 Oct). Tanzanian Railway Steam Locomotives (1st series). T **100** and similar horiz designs. Multicoloured. P 14.

430	5s. Type **100**	10	20
431	10s. Locomotive No. 3107	15	30
432	20s. Locomotive No. 6004	25	70
433	30s. Locomotive No. 3129	40	1·00
430/3 *Set of 4*		80	2·00
MS434 125×93 mm. Nos. 430/3		80	2·75

See also Nos. 445/50.

1985 (22 Oct). Olympic Games Gold Medal Winners, Los Angeles. Nos. 400/4 optd as T **101**.

435	1s. Type **94** (optd with T **101**)	20	10
436	1s.50 Running (optd "GOLD MEDAL USA")	25	20
437	5s. Basketball (optd "GOLD MEDAL USA")	2·00	1·75
438	20s. Football (optd "GOLD MEDAL FRANCE")	2·00	5·00
435/8 *Set of 4*		4·00	6·25
MS439 130×100 mm. Nos. 435/8		8·00	10·00

102 Cooking and Water Pots

103 Class 64 Diesel Locomotive

(Des J. Mzinga. Litho State Ptg Wks, Moscow)

1985 (4 Nov). Pottery. T **102** and similar horiz designs. Multicoloured. P 12½×12.

440	1s.50 Type **102**	20	10
441	2s. Large pot and frying pot with cover	25	15
442	5s. Trader selling pots	60	35
443	40s. Beer pot	1·75	5·00
440/3 *Set of 4*		2·50	5·00
MS444 129×98 mm. 30s. Water pots		3·50	4·00

(Des P. Ndembo. Litho State Ptg Wks, Moscow)

1985 (25 Nov). Tanzanian Railway Locomotives (2nd series). T **103** and similar horiz designs. P 12½×12.

445	1s.50 multicoloured	40	20
446	2s. multicoloured	40	30
447	5s. multicoloured	60	75
448	10s. multicoloured	75	1·75
449	30s. black, brownish black and red	1·50	3·75
445/9 *Set of 5*		3·25	6·00
MS450 130×100 mm. 15s. black, blackish brown and rose-pink; 20s. black, blackish brown and rose-pink		9·00	8·00

Designs:—2s. Class 36 diesel locomotive; 5s. DFH1013 diesel shunter; 10s. DE1001 diesel-electric locomotive; 15s. Class 30 steam locomotive; 20 a. Class 11 steam locomotive; 30 a. Steam locomotive, Zanzibar, 1906.

Nos. 445/6 and 448/9 exist overprinted "CONGRATULATIONS TO DUKE & DUCHESS OF YORK ON THE OCCASION OF THEIR MARRIAGE", but there is no evidence that these overprints were available from post offices in Tanzania.

104 Young Pioneers

105 Rolls-Royce "20/25" (1936)

(Des P. Ndembo. Litho J.W.)

1986 (20 Jan). International Youth Year. T **104** and similar horiz designs. P 14.

451	1s.50 multicoloured	15	15
452	4s. reddish brown, pale brown and black	20	50
453	10s. multicoloured	50	1·25
454	20s. reddish brown, pale brown and black	1·10	2·50
451/4 *Set of 4*		1·75	4·00

MS455 130×100 mm. 30s. reddish brown, pale brown and black	2·25	3·50

Designs:—1s. Child health care; 10s. Uhuru Torch Race; 20s. Young workers and globe; 30s. Young people farming.

(Litho Holders Press)

1986 (10 Mar). Centenary of Motoring. T **105** and similar horiz designs. Multicoloured. P 14.

456	1s.50 Type **105**	10	10
457	5s. Rolls-Royce "Phantom II" (1933)	15	25
458	10s. Rolls-Royce "Phantom 1" (1926)	25	60
459	30s. Rolls-Royce "Silver Ghost" (1907)	40	2·00
456/9 *Set of 4*		80	2·75
MS460 125×93 mm. Nos. 456/9		80	2·75

106 Rotary Logo and Staunton Queen Chess Piece

(Litho Holders Press)

1986 (17 Mar). World Chess Championships, London and Leningrad. T **106** and similar horiz design. P 14.

461	20s. new blue and magenta	35	50
462	100s. multicoloured	50	2·50
MS463 124×64 mm. Nos. 461/2		1·10	3·25

Design:—100s. Hand moving Rook.

No. 461 also commemorates Rotary International.

Slightly different versions of Nos. 461/2, incorporating the Chess Championship emblem and with "TANZANIA" and face value at top on the 100s., were not issued.

107 Mallard

(Litho Holders Press)

1986 (22 May). Birth Bicentenary of John J. Audubon (ornithologist) (1985). T **107** and similar horiz designs. Multicoloured. P 14.

464	5s. Type **107**	15	35
465	10s. Eider	25	60
466	20s. Scarlet Ibis	30	1·25
467	30s. Roseate Spoonbill	40	1·40
464/7 *Set of 4*		1·00	3·25
MS468 122×91 mm. Nos. 464/7		1·00	3·50

108 Pearls

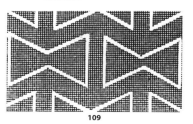

109

(Litho J.W.)

1986 (27 May). Tanzanian Minerals. T **108** and similar horiz designs. Multicoloured. Phosphorised paper (Nos. 469/72). P 14.

469	1s.50 Type **108**	80	15
470	2s. Sapphire	1·10	65
471	5s. Tanzanite	2·00	1·25

472	40s. Diamonds	7·25	10·00
469/72	Set of 4	10·00	11·00
MS473	130×100 mm. 30s. Rubies. W **109**	15·00	15·00

110 Hibiscus calyphyllus   **111** Oryx

(Litho Holders Press)

1986 (25 June). Flowers of Tanzania. T **110** and similar vert designs. Multicoloured. P 14.

474	1s.50 Type **110**	10	10
475	5s. Aloe graminicola	15	25
476	10s. Nersium oleander	20	45
477	30s. Nymphaea caerulea	40	2·00
474/7	Set of 4	75	2·50
MS478	90×119 mm. Nos. 474/7	75	2·50

(Litho Holders Press)

1986 (30 June). Endangered Animals of Tanzania. T **111** and similar vert designs. Multicoloured. P 14.

479	5s. Type **111**	15	15
480	10s. Giraffe	20	35
481	20s. Rhinoceros	25	85
482	30s. Cheetah	25	1·40
479/82	Set of 4	75	2·50
MS483	91×121 mm. Nos. 479/82	75	3·25

Four stamps, 10, 20, 60 and 80s., with accompanying miniature sheets, were prepared in 1986 for the Wedding of the Duke of York. These were not placed on sale in Tanzania at the time, but they are known commercially in the late 1990s. The circumstances surrounding their late release are unclear.

112 Immunization   **113** Angelfish

(Des P. Ndembo. Litho State Ptg Wks, Moscow)

1986 (29 July). U.N.I.C.E.F. Child Survival Campaign. T **112** and similar horiz designs. Multicoloured. P 12½×12.

484	1s.50 Type **112**	35	10
485	2s. Growth monitoring	45	15
486	5s. Oral rehydration therapy	80	40
487	40s. Breast feeding	4·00	5·00
484/7	Set of 4	5·00	5·00
MS488	110×101 mm. 30s. Healthy baby	1·00	1·75

(Des P. Ndembo. Litho State Ptg Wks, Moscow)

1986 (28 Aug). Marine Life. T **113** and similar horiz designs. Multicoloured. P 12½×12.

489	1s.50 Type **113**	70	10
490	4s. Parrotfish	1·50	85
491	10s. Turtle	2·50	2·75
492	20s. Octopus	3·75	5·50
489/92	Set of 4	7·50	8·25
MS493	131×101 mm. 30s. Corals	2·50	2·50

114 Team Captains shaking Hands   **115** Pres. Nyerere receiving Beyond War Award

(Litho Questa)

1986 (30 Oct). World Cup Football Championship Mexico. T **114** and similar horiz designs. Multicoloured. P 14.

494	1s.50 Type **114**	15	10
495	2s. Referee sending player off	15	10
496	10s. Goalkeeper and ball in net	60	1·00
497	20s. Goalkeeper saving ball	1·00	2·25
494/7	Set of 4	1·75	3·00
MS498	95×72 mm. 30s. Winning Argentine team	1·10	1·25

(Des P. Ndembo. Litho Mardon Printers Ltd, Zimbabwe)

1986 (20 Dec). International Peace Year. T **115** and similar horiz designs. Multicoloured. P 14½.

499	1s.50 Type **115**	45	10
500	2s. Children of many races	65	20
501	10s. African cosmonaut and rocket launch...	1·50	2·00
502	20s. United Nations Headquarters, New York	1·75	4·25
499/502	Set of 4	4·00	6·00
MS503	109×86 mm. 30s. International Peace Year symbols	2·75	5·00

116 Mobile Bank Service

(Des P. Ndembo. Litho Questa)

1987 (7 Feb). 20th Anniv of National Bank of Commerce. T **116** and similar horiz designs. Multicoloured. P 14.

504	1s.50 Type **116**	30	10
505	2s. National Bank of Commerce Head Office	50	20
506	5s. Pres. Mwinyi laying foundation stone	80	90
507	20s. Cotton harvesting	2·00	3·25
504/7	Set of 4	3·25	4·00

117 Parade of Young Party Members   **118** Nungu Nungu Hair Style

(Litho Holders Press)

1987 (10 Mar). 10th Anniv of Chama Cha Mapinduzi Party and 20th Anniv of Arusha Declaration. T **117** and similar horiz designs. Multicoloured. P 14.

508	2s. Type **117**	15	10
509	3s. Harvesting coffee	15	10
510	10s. Pres Nyerere addressing Second Peace Initiative Reunion	20	30
511	30s. Presidents Julius Nyerere and Ali Hassan Mwinyi	35	1·50
508/11	Set of 4	75	1·75

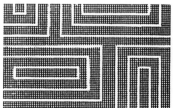

119

(Litho Leigh-Mardon Ltd, Melbourne)

1987 (16 Mar). Traditional Hair Styles. T **118** and similar vert designs. Multicoloured. W **119**. P 14½.

512	1s.50 Type **118**	30	10
513	2s. Upanga wajogoo style	45	20
514	10s. Morani style	80	1·25

515	20s. Twende kilioni style	1·50	2·50
512/15	Set of 4	2·75	3·50
MS516	110×99 mm. 30s. Hair plaiting	3·00	3·75

120 Royal Family on Buckingham Palace Balcony after Trooping the Colour

(Litho Holders Press)

1987 (24 Mar). 60th Birthday of Queen Elizabeth II (1986). T **120** and similar horiz designs. Multicoloured. P 14.

517	5s. Type **120**	15	20
518	10s. Queen and Prince Philip at Royal Ascot	20	25
519	40s. Queen Elizabeth II	50	1·50
520	60s. Queen Elizabeth with crowd	60	2·00
517/20	Set of 4	1·25	3·50
MS521	125×90 mm. Nos. 517/20	1·25	3·50

121 Apis mellifera (bee) **122** Crocodile

(Litho State Ptg Wks, Moscow)

1987 (22 Apr). Insects. T **121** and similar horiz designs. Multicoloured. P 12½×12.

522	1s.50 Type **121**	60	15
523	2s. Prostephanus truncatus (grain borer)	80	25
524	10s. Glossina palpalis (tsetse fly)	1·75	2·00
525	20s. Polistes sp (wasp)	2·50	4·25
522/5	Set of 4	5·00	6·00
MS526	110×101 mm. 30s. Anopheles sp (mosquito)	4·50	7·00

(Des J. Mzinga (3 s., 30s.), P. Ndembo (others). Litho State Ptg Wks, Moscow)

1987 (2 July). Reptiles. T **122** and similar horiz designs. Multicoloured. P 12½×12.

527	2s. Type **122**	1·00	25
528	3s. Black-striped Grass-snake	1·00	30
529	10s. Adder	2·25	2·00
530	20s. Green Mamba	3·00	4·00
527/30	Set of 4	6·50	6·00
MS531	101×101 mm. 30s. Tortoise	1·50	1·25

123 Emblems of Posts/ Telecommunications and Railways **124** Basketry

(Des and litho Questa)

1987 (27 July). 10th Anniu of Tanzania Communications and Transport Corporations. T **123** and similar horiz designs. Multicoloured. P 14.

532	2s. Type **123**	50	30
533	8s. Emblems of Air Tanzania and Harbours Authority	1·25	1·25
MS534	100×66 mm. 20s. Methods of transport and communication	3·75	1·75

(Des P. Ndembo. Litho State Ptg Wks, Moscow)

1987 (15 Dec). Traditional Handicrafts. T **124** and similar horiz designs. Multicoloured. P 12½×12.

535	2s. Type **124**	20	10
536	3s. Decorated gourds	20	15
537	10s. Stools	50	60
538	20s. Makonde carvings	75	85
535/8	Set of 4	1·50	1·50
MS539	89×89 mm. 40s. Makonde carver at work	1·00	1·25

10th Anniversary of TANZANIA ZAMBIA RAILWAY AUTHORITY 1976-1986
(125)

1987 (30 Dec). Tenth Anniv of Tanzania Zambia Railway (1986). Nos. 445/9 optd with T **125**.

540	**103**	1s.50 multicoloured	1·10	45
541	–	2s. multicoloured	1·10	45
542	–	5s. multicoloured	1·75	1·50
543	–	10s. multicoloured	2·50	2·50
544	–	30s. black, brownish black and red	4·00	7·50
540/4		Set of 5	9·50	11·00

126 Mdako (pebble game)

(Des P. Ndembo. Litho State Ptg Wks, Moscow)

1988 (15 Feb). Traditional Pastimes. T **126** and similar horiz designs. Multicoloured. P 12½×12.

545	2s. Type **126**	15	10
546	3s. Wrestling	15	10
547	8s. Bullfighting, Zanzibar	35	30
548	20s. Bao (board game)	70	1·10
545/8	Set of 4	1·25	1·50
MS549	100×90 mm. 30s. Archery	1·25	1·40

127 Plateosaurus

(Des G. Vasarhelyi. Litho Format)

1988 (22 Apr). Prehistoric and Modern Animals. T **127** and similar trapezium-shaped designs. Multicoloured. P 12½.

550	2s. Type **127**	50	65
	a. Tête-bêche (horiz pair)	1·00	1·25
551	3s. Pteranodon	50	65
	a. Tête-bêche (horiz pair)	1·00	1·25
552	5s. Apatosaurus ("Brontosaurus")	60	65
	a. Tête-bêche (horiz pair)	1·10	1·25
553	7s. Lion	60	75
	a. Tête-bêche (horiz pair)	1·10	1·50
554	8s. Tiger	75	80
	a. Tête-bêche (horiz pair)	1·50	1·60
555	12s. Orang-utan	75	1·50
	a. Tête-bêche (horiz pair)	1·50	3·00
556	20s. Elephant	1·10	2·00
	a. Tête-bêche (horiz pair)	2·00	4·00
557	100s. Stegosaurus	1·75	3·00
	a. Tête-bêche (horiz pair)	3·50	6·00
550/7	Set of 8	6·00	9·00

Nos. 550/7 were issued in sheets which had the second and fourth stamps tête-bêche in each horizontal row of five.

128 Marchers with Party Flag **129** Population Symbols on Map

(Des P. Ndembo. Litho Questa)

1988 (1 July). National Solidarity Walk. T **128** and similar horiz designs. Multicoloured. P 14×14½.

558	2s. +1s. Type **128**	25	25
559	3s. +1s. Pres. Mwinyi leading Walk	25	25
MS560	121×121 mm. 50s. +1s. Pres. Ali Hassan Mwinyi (35×25 mm). P 14½	75	85

(Des P. Ndembo. Litho Questa)

1988 (8 Aug). Third National Population Census. T **129** and similar horiz designs. Multicoloured. P 14.

561	2s. Type **129**	10	10
562	3s. Census official at work	10	10
563	10s. Community health care	15	15
564	20s. Population growth 1967-1988	30	30
561/4 *Set of 4*		55	55
MS565 96×91 mm. 40s. Development of modern Tanzania		1·25	1·00

130 Javelin

131 Football

(Litho State Ptg Wks, Moscow)

1988 (5 Sept). Olympic Games, Seoul (1st issue). T **130** and similar horiz designs. Multicoloured. P 12½×12.

566	2s. Type **130**	90	15
567	3s. Hurdling	90	15
568	7s. Long distance running	1·50	40
569	12s. Relay racing	1·75	70
566/9 *Set of 4*		4·50	1·25
MS570 100×70 mm. 40s. Badminton		4·00	1·50

(Des D. Miller. Litho Questa)

1988 (5 Sept). Olympic Games, Seoul (2nd issue). T **131** and similar vert designs. Multicoloured. P 14.

571	10s. Type **131**	30	10
572	20s. Cycling	1·50	25
573	50s. Fencing	70	50
574	70s. Volleyball	80	65
571/4 *Set of 4*		3·00	1·40
MS575 77×92 mm. 100s. Gymnastics		1·50	2·00

(Des D. Miller. Litho Questa)

1988 (5 Sept). Winter Olympic Games, Calgary. Vert designs as T **131**. Multicoloured. P 14.

576	5s. Cross-country skiing	60	20
577	25s. Figure skating	1·25	30
578	50s. Downhill skiing	2·00	80
579	75s. Bobsleighing	2·25	2·50
576/9 *Set of 4*		5·50	3·50
MS580 77×92 mm. 100s. Ice hockey sticks wrapped in Olympic and Canadian colours		2·75	1·25

132 Goat

133 "Love You, Dad" (Pinocchio)

(Litho Questa)

1988 (9 Sept). Domestic Animals. T **132** and similar multicoloured designs. P 14.

581	4s. Typa **132**	30	30
582	5s. Rabbit (*horiz*)	30	30
583	8s. Cows (*horiz*)	40	40
584	10s. Kitten (*horiz*)	1·00	70
585	12s. Pony	2·00	1·00
586	20s. Puppy	2·50	1·75
581/6 *Set of 6*		6·00	4·00
MS587 102×73 mm. 100s. Chicken (*horiz*)		2·50	1·75

(Des Walt Disney Company. Litho Questa)

1988 (9 Sept). Greetings Stamps. T **133** and similar horiz designs showing Walt Disney cartoon characters. Multicoloured. P 14×13½.

588	4s. Type **133**	25	20
589	5s. "Happy Birthday" (Brer Rabbit and Chip n'Dale)	25	20

590	10s. "Trick or Treat" (Daisy and Donald Duck)	40	20
591	12s. "Be kind to Animals" (Ferdie and Mordie with Pluto)	45	20
592	15s. "Love" (Daisy and Donald Duck)	55	35
593	20s. "Let's Celebrate" (Mickey Mouse and Goofy)	70	50
594	30s. "Keep in Touch" (Daisy and Donald Duck)	1·10	1·00
595	50s. "Love you, Mom" (Minnie Mouse with Ferdie and Mordie)	2·00	2·00
588/95 *Set of 8*		5·00	4·25
MS596 Two sheets, each 127×101 mm. (a) 150s. "Let's work together" (Goofy dressed as a fireman). (b) 150s. "Have a super Sunday" (Goofy dressed as American footballer) *Set of 2 sheets*		4·75	4·50

134 *Charaxes varanes*

135 Independence Torch and Mt. Kilimanjaro

(Des Jennifer Toombs. Litho Questa)

1988 (17 Oct). Butterflies. T **134** and similar horiz designs. Multicoloured. P 14½.

597	8s. Type **134**	60	10
598	30s. *Neptis melicerta*	1·10	30
599	40s. *Mylothris chloris*	1·25	40
600	50s. *Charaxes bohemani*	1·40	50
601	60s. *Myrina silenus* (s sp *ficedula*)	1·50	1·00
602	75s. *Papilio phorcas*	2·00	1·50
603	90s. *Cyrestis camillus*	2·50	1·75
604	100s. *Salamis temora*	2·50	1·75
597/604 *Set of 8*		11·50	6·50
MS605 Two sheets, each 80×50 mm. (a) 200s. *Asterope rosa*. (b) 250s. *Kallima rumia* *Set of 2 sheets*		8·00	6·00

(Des R. Vigurs. Litho Questa)

1988 (1 Nov). National Monuments. T **135** and similar vert designs. Multicoloured. P 14.

606	5s. Type **135**	10	10
607	12s. Arusha Declaration Monument	20	15
608	30s. Askari Monument	35	40
609	60s. Independence Monument	55	80
606/9 *Set of 4*		1·10	1·25
MS610 100×89 mm. 100s. Askari Monument statue		1·25	1·40

136 Eye Clinic

137 Loading Patient into Ambulance

(Des P. Ndembo. Litho National Printing & Packaging, Zimbabwe)

1988 (19 Dec). 25th Anniv of Dar-es-Salaam Lions Club. T **136** and similar horiz designs. Multicoloured. P 14½.

611	2s. Type **136**	20	20
612	3s. Family at shallow water well	20	20
613	7s. Rhinoceros and map of Tanzania	3·75	30
614	12s. Club presenting school desks	30	45
611/14 *Set of 4*		4·00	1·00
MS615 100×65 mm. 40s. Lions International logo		1·00	1·00

(Des P. Ndembo. Litho State Ptg Wks, Moscow)

1988 (30 Dec). 125th Anniv of International Red Cross and Red Crescent. T **137** and similar horiz designs. Multicoloured. P 12½×12.

616	2s. Type **137**	50	20
617	3s. Mother and baby health clinic	50	20
618	7s. Red Cross flag	1·00	30
619	12s. Henri Dunant (founder)	1·00	45
616/19 *Set of 4*		2·75	1·00
MS620 90×90 mm. 40s. Members of Red Cross International Committee, 1863		1·00	1·00

138 Paradise Whydah   **139** Bushbaby

(Des S. Barlowe. Litho B.D.T.)

1989 (15 Mar). Birds. T **138** and similar vert designs. Multicoloured. P 13½.

621	20s. Type **138**	1·00	85
	a. Sheetlet. Nos. 621/40	18·00	15·00
622	20s. Black-collared Barbet	1·00	85
623	20s. Bateleur	1·00	85
624	20s. Lilac-breasted Roller and African Open-bill Storks in flight	1·00	85
625	20s. Red-tufted Malachite Sunbird and African Open-bill Stork in flight	1·00	85
626	20s. Dark Chanting Goshawk	1·00	85
627	20s. White-fronted Bee Eater, Carmine Bee Eater and Little Bee Eaters	1·00	85
628	20s. Narina Trogon and Marabou Stork in flight	1·00	85
629	20s. Grey Parrot	1·00	85
630	20s. Hoopoe	1·00	85
631	20s. Masked Lovebird ("Yellow-collared Lovebird")	1·00	85
632	20s. Yellow-billed Hornbill	1·00	85
633	20s. Hammerkop	1·00	85
634	20s. Violet-crested Turaca and flamingos in flight	1·00	85
635	20s. Malachite Kingfisher	1·00	85
636	20s. Greater Flamingos	1·00	85
637	20s. Yellow-billed Storks	1·00	85
638	20s. Whale-headed Stork ("Shoebill Stork")	1·00	85
639	20s. Saddle-bill Stork and Blacksmith Plover	1·00	85
640	20s. South African Crowned Crane	1·00	85
621/40 *Set of 20*		18·00	15·00

MS641 Two sheets, each 105×75 mm. (a) 350s. Helmet Guineafowl (28×42 *mm*). (b) 350s. Ostrich (28×42 mm). P 14 *Set of 2 sheets* ...... 13·00 7·00

Nos. 622/41 were printed together, *se-tenant*, in a sheetlet of 20 forming a composite design of birds at a waterhole.

(Des J. Barbaris (Nos. 642/4, 648, **MS**650a), S. Barlowe (others). Litho Questa)

1989 (20 Mar). Fauna and Flora. T **139** and similar multicoloured designs. P 14.

642	5s. Type **139**	15	25
643	10s. Bushbaby holding insect (*horiz*)	20	25
644	20s. Bushbaby on forked branch	30	30
645	30s. Black Cobra on Umbrella Acacia	60	60
646	45s. Bushbaby at night (*horiz*)	60	60
647	70s. Red-billed Tropic Bird and Tree Ferns	5·00	4·00
648	100s. African Tree Frog on Cocoa Tree	5·00	4·25
649	150s. Black-headed Heron and Egyptian Papyrus	8·00	8·50
642/9 *Set of 8*		18·00	17·00

MS650 Two sheets. (a) 115×85 mm. 350s. African Palm Civet (*horiz*). (b) 65×65 mm. 350s. Pink-backed Pelican and Baobab Tree (*horiz*) *Set of 2 sheets* ...... 13·00 7·00

Nos. 645, 647/9 and **MS**650 are without the World Wildlife Fund logo.

140 Juma Ikangaa (marathon runner)   **141** Drums

(Des W. Storozuk. Litho Questa)

1989 (10 Apr). International Sporting Personalities. T **140** and similar vert designs. Multicoloured. P 14.

651	4s. Type **140**	15	15
652	8s.50 Steffi Graf (tennis player)	1·00	30
653	12s. Yannick Noah (tennis player)	80	40
654	40s. Pele (footballer)	90	65
655	100s. Erhard Keller (speed skater)	1·00	80
656	125s. Sadanoyama (sumo wrestler)	1·25	1·00
657	200s. Taiho (sumo wrestler)	1·75	1·75
658	250s. T. Nakajima (golfer)	5·50	2·75
651/8 *Set of 8*		11·00	7·00

MS659 Two sheets. (a) 100×71 mm. 350s. Joe Louis (boxer). (b) 100×76 mm. 350s. I. Aoki (golfer) *Set of 2 sheets* ...... 14·00 10·00

The captions on Nos. 658 and **MS**659b are transposed.

(Des P. Ndembo. Litho Harrison)

1989 (29 June). Musical Instruments. T **141** and similar horiz designs. Multicoloured. P 14.

660	2s. Type **141**	1·00	25
661	3s. Xylophones	1·00	25
662	10s. Thumbpiano	1·50	1·25
663	20s. Fiddles	1·50	3·75
660/3 *Set of 4*		4·50	5·00

MS664 91×80 mm. 40s. Violins with calabash resonators ...... 1·00 1·00

142 Chains Cha Mapinduzi Party Flag   **143** Class P36 Locomotive, Russia, 1953

(Des P. Ndembo. Litho Questa)

1989 (1 July). National Solidarity Walk. T **142** and similar multicoloured designs. P 14½.

665	5s. +1s. Type **142**	25	25
666	10s. +1s. Marchers with party flag and President Mwinyi	25	25
MS667 122×122 mm. 50s. +1s. President Mwinyi (*vert*)		60	60

(Des W. Wright. Litho B.D.T.)

1989 (22 Aug). Steam Locomotives. T **143** and similar multicoloured designs. P 14.

668	10s. Type **143**	85	35
669	25s. Class 12 streamlined locomotive, Belgium, 1939	95	45
670	60s. Class C62 locomotive, Japan, 1948	1·50	1·00
671	75s. Pennsylvania Railroad Class T1 streamlined locomotive, U.S.A., 1942	1·60	1·25
672	80s. Class WP locomotive, India, 1946	1·75	1·25
673	90s. East African Railways Class 59 Garratt locomotive No. 5919	1·75	1·50
674	150s. Class "People" locomotive No. 1206, China	2·25	2·75
675	200s. Southern Pacific "Daylight" express, USA	2·25	2·75
668/75 *Set of 8*		11·50	10·00

MS676 Two sheets, each 114×85 mm. (a) 350s. Stephenson's *Planet*, Great Britain, 1830 (*vert*). (b) 350s. L.M.S. *Coronation Scot*, Great Britain, 1937 (*vert*) *Set of 2 sheets* ...... 7·00 8·50

143a Union Station

(Des Design Element. Litho Questa)

1989 (17 Nov). "World Stamp Expo '89" International Stamp Exhibition, Washington. Landmarks of Washington. Sheet 78×62 mm. P 14.

MS677 **143a** 500s. multicoloured ...... 4·00 5·50

144 "Luna 3" Satellite orbiting Moon, 1959   Gold–USSR Silver–Brazil Bronze–W.Germany (**145**)

(Des G. Vasarhelyi. Litho Questa)

1989 (22 Nov). History of Space Exploration and 20th Anniv of First Manned Landing on Moon. T **144** and similar horiz designs. Multicoloured. P 14.

678	20s. Type **144**	80	40
679	30s. "Gemini 6" and "7", 1965	90	45
680	40s. Astronaut Edward White in space, 1965	1·00	55
681	60s. Astronaut Aldrin on Moon, 1969	1·60	1·00
682	70s. Aldrin performing experiment, 1969	1·60	1·00
683	100s. "Apollo 15" astronaut and lunar rover, 1971	2·00	1·40
684	150s. "Apollo 18" and "Soyuz 19" docking in space 1975	2·75	2·75
685	200s. Spacelab, 1983	2·75	2·75
678/85	*Set of 8*	12·00	9·25

MS686 Two sheets, each 110×90 mm. (a) 250s. Lunar module *Eagle* and "Apollo 11" emblem. (b) 250s. Projected U.S. space station *Set of 2 sheets* .... 7·50 8·00

1989 (11 Dec). Olympic Medal Winners, Calgary and Seoul. Optd as T **145**.

(a) On Nos. 571/5

687	10s. Type **131** (optd with T **145**)	90	40
688	20s. Cycling (optd "Men's Match Sprint, Lutz Hesslich, DDR")	3·50	1·00
689	50s. Fencing (optd "Epee, Schmitt, W. Germany")	2·25	1·60
690	70s. Volleyball (optd "Men's Team, USA")	3·00	2·75
687/90	*Set of 4*	8·75	5·25

MS691 77×92 mm. 100s. Gymnastics ("Women's Team, Gold-USSR") .... 3·75 4·25

(b) On Nos. 576/80

692	5s. Cross-country skiing (optd "Biathlon, Peter-Roetsch, DDR")	75	40
693	25s. Figure skating (optd "Pairs, Gordeeva & Grinkov, USSR")	1·75	75
694	50s. Downhill skiing (optd "Zurbriggen, Switzerland")	2·50	1·75
695	75s. Bobsleighing (optd "Gold – USSR Silver – DDR Bronze – DDR")	3·00	2·50
692/5	*Set of 4*	7·25	4·75

MS696 77×92 mm. 100s. Ice hockey sticks wrapped in Olympic and Canadian colours (optd "Ice Hockey: Gold–USSR") .... 9·00 9·00

146 Spotted Tilapia

(Des W. Hanson Studio. Litho Questa)

1989 (14 Dec). Reef and Freshwater Fish of Tanzania. T **146** and similar multicoloured design. P 14.

697	9s. Type **146**	75	40
698	13s. Painted Triggerfish	75	40
699	20s. Powder-blue Surgeonfish	1·00	50
700	40s. Red-tailed Butterflyfish	1·60	75
701	70s. Red-tailed Notho	2·00	1·25
702	100s. Ansorge's Neolebias	2·50	1·75
703	150s. Blue Panchax	2·75	3·00
704	200s. Regal Angelfish	2·75	3·00
697/704	*Set of 8*	12·50	10·00

MS705 Two sheets, each 112×83 mm. (a) 350s. Jewel Gichlid (50×38 *mm*). P 14×13½. (b) 350s. Dusky Batfish (38×50 *mm*). P 13½×14 *Set of 2 sheets* ... 12·00 12·00

147 Rural Polling Station

148 Logo

(Des P. Ndembo. Litho State Ptg Wks, Moscow)

1989 (22 Dec). Centenary of Inter-Parliamentary Union. T **147** and similar horiz designs. P 12½×12.

706	9s. multicoloured	10	10
707	13s. multicoloured	10	10
708	80s. multicoloured	40	65
709	100s. black, dull ultramarine and pale blue....	50	85
706/9	*Set of 4*	1·00	1·50

MS710 90×90 mm. 40s. multicoloured .... 70 1·25

Designs:—13s. Parliament Building, Dar-es-Salaam; 40s. Sir William Randal Cremer and Frederic Passy (founders); 80s. Tanzania Parliament in session; 100s. Logo.

(Des P. Ndembo. Litho Cartor)

1990 (10 Jan). Tenth Anniv of Pan-African Postal Union. T **148** and similar horiz designs. P 13½.

711	9s. greenish yellow, dull green and black...	30	20
712	13s. multicoloured	50	20
713	70s. multicoloured	2·00	1·40
714	100s. multicoloured	3·25	2·75
711/14	*Set of 4*	5·50	4·00

MS715 90×90 mm. 40s. multicoloured. P 12½ ... 1·75 2·75

Designs:—13s. Collecting mail from post office box; 40s. Logos of Tanzania Posts and Telecommunications Corporation P.A.P.U. and U.P.U.; 70s. Taking mail to post office; 100s. Mail transport.

149 Admiral's Flag and *Nina*

(Des T. Agana. Litho Questa)

1990 (12 Feb). 500th Anniv of Discovery of America by Columbus (1992) (50, 60, 75, 200s.) and Modern Scientific Discoveries (others). T **149** and similar horiz designs. Multicoloured. P 14.

716	9s. Bell XS-1 aircraft (first supersonic flight, 1947)	75	50
717	13s. *Trieste* (bathyscaphe) (first dive to depth of 35,000 ft, 1960)	75	50
718	50s. Type **149**	1·50	90
719	60s. Fleet flag and *Pinta*	1·50	1·10
720	75s. Standard of Castile and Leon and *Santa Maria*	1·50	1·25
721	150s. Transistor technology	1·25	2·00
722	200s. Arms of Columbus and map of First Voyage	2·75	3·00
723	250s. DNA molecule	2·75	3·00
716/23	*Set of 8*	11·50	11·00

MS724 Two sheets, each 106×78 mm. (a) 350s. Caravels in the Caribbean. (b) 350s. *Voyager II* and Neptune *Set of 2 sheets* .... 7·00 8·50

150 Tecopa Pupfish

(Des J. Genzo. Litho Questa)

1990 (20 Feb). Extinct Species. T **150** and similar multicoloured designs. P 14.

725	25s. Type **150**	1·25	60
726	40s. Thylacine	1·75	1·00
727	50s. Quagga	2·00	1·10
728	60s. Passenger Pigeon	3·00	1·75
729	75s. Rodriguez Saddleback Tortoise	2·25	1·75
730	100s. Toolache Wallaby	2·50	2·00
731	150s. Texas Red Wolf	2·50	2·50
732	200s. Utah Lake Sculpin	2·50	2·50
725/32	*Set of 8*	16·00	12·00

MS733 Two sheets. (a) 102×74 mm. 350s. South Island Whekau. (b) 71×99 mm. 350s. Hawaii O-o (*vert*) *Set of 2 sheets* .... 15·00 12·00

151 Camping

(Des P. Ndembo. Litho State Ptg Wks, Moscow)

1990 (22 Feb). 60th Anniv of Girl Guides Movement in Tanzania. T **151** and similar multicoloured designs. P 12½×12.

734	9s. Type **151**	15	20
735	13s. Guides planting sapling	15	20
736	50s. Guide teaching woman to write	40	65

737	100s. Guide helping at child-care clinic...........	65	1·10
734/7 *Set of 4*		1·25	2·00
MS738 89×89 mm. 40s. Guide teaching child to read (*vert*). P 12×12½		1·00	1·25

152 Fishing

(Des P. Ndembo. Litho State Pig Wks, Moscow)

1990 (25 Apr). 25th Anniv of Union of Tanganyika and Zanzibar. T **152** and similar multicoloured designs. P 12½×12 (horiz) or 12×12½ (vert).

739	9s. Type **152**	55	30
740	13s. Vineyard	55	30
741	50s. Cloves	1·75	1·50
742	100s. Presidents Nyerere and Karume exchanging Union instruments (*vert*).....	2·75	4·50
739/42 *Set of 4*		5·00	6·00
MS743 90×90 mm. 40s. Arms (*vert*)		2·25	3·25

153 Footballer   **154** Miriam Makeba

(Litho B.D.T.)

1990 (1 June). World Cup Football Championship, Italy (1st issue). T **153** and similar vert designs. Multicoloured. P 14.

744	25s. Type **153**	1·50	30
745	60s. Player passing ball..............................	2·00	90
746	75s. Player turning....................................	2·25	1·25
747	200s. Player kicking ball	4·50	5·50
744/7 *Set of 4*		9·25	7·25
MS748 Two sheets, each 105×76 mm. (a) 350s. Two players fighting for possession. (b) 350s. Player kicking ball *Set of 2 sheets*.......................................		12·00	10·00

See also Nos. 789/93 and 794/8.

(Des A. Fagbohun. Litho Questa)

1990 (29 June). Famous Black Entertainers. T **154** and similar vert designs. Multicoloured. P 14.

749	9s. Type **154**	15	10
750	13s. Manu Dibango.....................................	15	10
751	25s. Fela	20	15
752	70s. Smokey Robinson.................................	1·00	40
753	100s. Gladys Knight	1·10	55
754	150s. Eddie Murphy.....................................	2·25	2·25
755	200s. Sammy Davis Jnr.................................	2·50	2·75
756	250f. Stevie Wonder....................................	2·50	3·00
749/56 *Set of 8*		9·00	9·00
MS757 Two sheets, each 69×88 mm. (a) 350s. Bill Cosby (30×39 *mm*). (b) 350s. Michael Jackson (30×39 *mm*). P 14½ *Set of 2 sheets*		4·25	5·00

155 Ring of People round Party Flag

(Litho Cartor)

1990 (6 July). Solidarity Walk, 1990. T **155** and similar multicoloured designs. P 13½.

758	9s. +1s. Type **155**....................................	1·00	1·25
759	13s. +1s. President Mwinyi...........................	1·00	1·25
MS760 90×90 mm. 50s. +1s. Handclasp on map (*vert*). P 12½		1·75	2·25

156 Diesel Train   **157** Pope John Paul II

(Des P. Ndembo. Litho Cartor)

1990 (8 Aug). Tenth Anniv of Southern African Development Co-ordination Conference. T **156** and similar horiz designs. Multicoloured. P 13½.

761	8s. Type **156**...	1·75	50
762	11s.50 Paper-making plant	30	20
763	25s. Tractor factory and ploughing................	35	20
764	100s. Map and national flags	6·00	5·00
761/4 *Set of 4*		7·50	5·50
MS765 89×89 mm. 50s. Map of Southern Africa. P 12½.		3·25	3·75

(Des P. Ndembo. Litho Questa)

1990 (1 Sept). Papal Visit to Tanzania. T **157** and similar multicoloured designs. P 14.

766	10s. Type **157**	20	15
767	15s. Pope in ceremonial robes	25	15
768	20s. Pope giving blessing.............................	30	15
769	100s. Papal coat of arms	80	1·10
766/9 *Set of 4*		1·40	1·40
MS770 172×143 mm. 50s. Pope John Paul II (*horiz*); 50s. St. Joseph's Cathedral, Dar-es-Salaam (*horiz*); 50s. Christ the King Cathedral, Moshi (*horiz*); 50s. Saint Theresa's Cathedral, Tabora (*horiz*); 50s. Cathedral of the Epiphany, Buganda Mwanza (*horiz*); 50s. St. Mathias Mulumba Kalemba Cathedral, Songea (*horiz*)		4·25	4·50
a. Error. Imperf		†	—

158 Mickey and Minnie Mouse in Herby the Love Bug

(Des Walt Disney Co. Litho Questa)

1990 (7 Nov). Motor Cars from Disney Films. T **158** and similar horiz designs. Multicoloured. P 14×13½.

771	20s. Type **158**...	30	30
772	30s. The Absent-minded Professor's car..........	35	35
773	45s. Chitty-Chitty Bang-Bang	45	45
774	60s. Mr. Toad's car	65	65
775	75s. Scrooge's limousine	75	75
776	100s. The Shaggy Dog's car	1·00	1·00
777	150s. Donald Duck's nephews cleaning car......	1·60	1·60
778	200s. Fire engine from *Dumbo*....................	1·75	1·75
771/8 *Set of 8*		6·25	6·25
MS779 Two sheets, each 127×112, (a) 350s. The Mickeymobile. (b) 350s. Croatia De Vil and dog wagon from *101 Dalmations Set of 2 sheets*		8·50	8·50

159 "St. Mary Magdalen in Penitence" (detail)   **160** Klinsmann of West Germany

(Litho Questa)

1990 (7 Nov). Paintings by Titian. T **159** and similar vert designs. Multicoloured. P 13½×14.

780	5s. Type **159**	10	10
781	10s. "Averoldi Polyptych" (detail)	10	10
782	15s. "Saint Margaret" (detail)	15	15
783	50s. "Venus and Adonis" (detail)	40	40
784	75s. "Venus and the Lutenist" (detail)	55	55
785	100s. "Tarquin and Lucretia" (detail)	70	70
786	125s. "Saint Jerome" (detail)	90	90
787	150s. "Madonna and Child in Glory with Saints" (detail)	1·00	1·00
780/7	Set of 8	3·50	3·50

MS788 Three sheets. (a) 95×110 mm. 300s. "Adoration of the Holy Trinity" (detail). (b) 95×110 mm. 300s. "St. Catherine of Alexandria at Prayer" (detail). (c) 110×95 mm. 300s. "The Supper at Emmaus" (detail) *Set of 3 sheets* ... 9·00 10·00

(Des Young Phillips Studio. Litho Questa)

1990 (17 Nov). World Cup Football Championship, Italy (2nd issue). T **160** and similar vert designs. Multicoloured. P 14.

789	10s. Type **160**	50	30
790	60s. Serena of Italy	90	60
791	100s. Nicol of Scotland	1·75	1·75
792	300s. Susie of Yugoslavia	3·25	4·00
789/92	Set of 4	5·75	6·00

MS793 Two sheets, each 85×95 mm. (a) 400s. Montero of Costa Rica. (b) 400s. Seifo of Belgium *Set of 2 sheets* ... 11·00 11·00

161 Throw-in

(Litho Questa)

1990 (17 Nov). World Cup Football Championship, Italy (3rd issue). T **161** and similar horiz designs. Multicoloured. P 14.

794	9s. Type **161**	60	20
795	13s. Penalty kick	60	20
796	25s. Dribbling	85	25
797	100s. Corner kick	3·50	4·00
794/7	Set of 4	5·00	4·25

MS798 82×82 mm. 50s. World Cup and world map ... 3·50 3·75

162 Canoe

(Des M. Raza. Litho State Ptg Works, Moscow)

1990 (24 Nov). Marine Transport. T **162** and similar horiz designs. Multicoloured. P 12½×12.

799	9s. Type **162**	20	20
800	13s. Sailing canoe	25	20
801	25s. Dhow	90	25
802	100s. Freighter	3·75	4·25
799/802	Set of 4	4·50	4·50

MS803 90×90 mm. 40s. Mashua dhow ... 3·25 3·75

163 Lesser Masked Weaver   **164** Lesser Flamingo

(Litho Questa)

1990 (15 Dec)–**91**. Birds. Horiz designs as T **163** (5s. to 30s.) or **164** (40s. to 500s.). Multicoloured. P 14.

804	5s. Type **163**	20	60
	a. Booklet pane. Nos. 804/9 each×2 with margins all round	6·00	
805	9s. African Emerald Cuckoo	30	10
806	13s. Little Bee Eater	60	10

807	15s. Red Bishop	40	10
808	20s. Bateleur	50	10
809	25s. Scarlet-chested Sunbird	50	10
809a	30s. African Wood Pigeon (1.7.91)	50	15
810	40s. Type **164**	50	15
811	70s. Helmet Guineafowl	60	30
812	100s. Eastern White Pelican	75	30
813	170s. Saddle-bill Stork	1·00	85
814	200s. South African Crowned Crane	1·00	90
814a	300s. Pied Crow (1.7.91)	1·00	1·50
814b	400s. White-headed Vulture (1.7.91)	1·00	1·75
815	500s. Ostrich	1·10	1·75
804/15	Set of 15	9·00	7·50

MS816 100×102 mm. 40s. Superb Starling; 60s. Lilac-breasted Roller ... 5·50 6·50

165 Athletics

(Des P. Ndembo. Litho Questa)

1990 (29 Dec). 14th Commonwealth Games, Auckland, New Zealand. T **165** and similar multicoloured designs. P 14.

817	9s. Type **165**	55	20
818	13s. Netball (vert)	80	20
819	25s. Pole vaulting	1·25	25
820	100s. Long jumping (vert)	2·50	3·50
817/20	Set of 4	5·00	3·75

MS821 100×100 mm. 40s. Boxing (vert) ... 1·75 2·50

166 Former German Post Office, Dar-es-Salaam

(Litho Questa)

1991 (10 Jan). 150th Anniv of the Penny Black and "Stamp World London 90" International Stamp Exhibition. T **166** and similar horiz designs. Multicoloured. P 14.

822	50s. Type **166**	90	90
	a. Horiz pair. Nos. 822/3	1·75	1·75
823	50s. *Reichstag* (German mail steamer), 1890	90	90
824	75s. Dhows, Zanzibar	1·25	1·25
	a. Horiz pair. Nos. 824/5	2·50	2·50
825	75s. Cobham's Short S. 5 Singapore I flying boat, Mwanza, Lake Victoria, 1928	1·25	1·25
826	100s. Air Tanzania Fokker F. 27 Friendship over Livingstone's House, Zanzibar	1·75	1·75
	a. Horiz pair. Nos. 826/7	3·50	3·50
827	100s. Mail train at Moshi station	1·75	1·75
828	100s. English mail coach, 1840	1·75	1·75
829	150s. Stephenson's *Rocket* and mail coach, 1838	2·50	2·50
830	200s. Imperial Airways Handley Page H.P.42 at Croydon	2·50	2·50
822/30	Set of 9	13·00	13·00

MS831 Two sheets, each 85×65 mm. (a) 350s. Sir Rowland Hill and Penny Black. (b) 350s. Thurn and Taxis letter of 1860 *Set of 2 sheets* ... 10·00 12·00

Nos. 822/3, 824/5 and 826/7 were each printed together, *se-tenant*, in horizontal pairs throughout the sheets.

Nos. 822/7 and **MS**831a overprinted "40th Anniversary of the Accession H. M. Queen Elizabeth II 1952-1992" are reported as not being issued in Tanzania.

167 Petersberg Railway, Konigswinter, Germany

(Litho Questa)

1991 (10 Jan). Cog Railways. T **167** and similar horiz designs. Multicoloured. P 14.

832	8s. Type **167**	50	30
833	25s. *Waumbek* (locomotive), Mount Washington Railway, USA	70	60
834	50s. Sarajevo-Dubrovnik line, Yugoslavia	85	75
835	100s. Budapest Rack Railway, Hungary	1·25	1·00
836	150s. Steam locomotive No. 97218, Vordenberg-Eisenerz line, Austria	1·75	1·75
837	200s. Last train on Rimutaka Incline, New Zealand, 1955	1·90	1·90
838	250s. "John Stevens" rack and pinion drive locomotive, USA, 1825	1·90	2·00
839	300s. Mt. Pilatus Rack Railway steam railcar, Switzerland	2·00	2·00
832/9 *Set of 8*		9·50	9·25

MS840 Two sheets, each 117×87 mm. (a) 400s. Sylvester Marsh and Presidential excursion train, Mt. Washington Cog Railway, U.S.A. 1869 (51×38 mm). (b) 400s. Steam locomotive, Schneeberg Railway, Austria (51×38 mm). P 13½ *Set of 2 sheets* .... 9·50 10·00

167a Mickey Mouse

167b Archery

(Des Walt Disney Co. Litho Questa)

1991 (10 Jan). International Literacy Year (1st issue). T **167a** and similar multicoloured designs showing Walt Disney cartoon characters illustrating the Alphabet. Multicoloured. P 13½×14.

841/67 1, 2, 3, 5, 10, 15, 18, 20, 25, 30, 35, 40, 45, 50, 55, 60, 75, 80, 90, 100, 120, 125, 145, 150, 160, 175, 200s. *Set of 27* .... 14·00 16·00

MS868 Two sheets, each 128×112 mm. (a) 600s. Tiger Lily and Lost Boys (*horiz*). (b) 600s. Mickey Mouse driving miniature railway locomotive. P 13½×14 *Set of 2 sheets* .... 11·00 12·00

Nos. 841/67 were issued in three sheetlets, each of nine, the first containing Nos. 841/3, 846, 855, 858, 861, 863, 867, the second Nos. 845, 848, 850, 852, 854, 856, 860, 862, 864 and the third Nos. 844, 847, 849, 851, 853, 857, 859, 865/6.

See also Nos. 905/9.

(Litho Questa)

1991 (10 Jan). Olympic Games, Barcelona (1st issue). T **167b** and similar vert designs. Multicoloured. P 14.

869	5s. Type **167b**	50	30
870	10s. Women's gymnastics	50	30
871	25s. Boxing	60	30
872	50s. Canoeing	85	55
873	100s. Volleyball	1·50	1·25
874	150s. Men's gymnastics	1·75	1·75
875	200s. 4 × 100 metres relay	2·25	2·25
876	300s. Judo	2·50	2·50
869/76 *Set of 8*		9·50	8·25

MS877 Two sheets, each 102×71 mm. (a) 400s. Cycling. (b) 400s. 400 metres men's hurdles *Set of 2 sheets* .... 11·00 11·00

See also Nos. 1309/13 and 1404/12.

167c *Phalaenopsis* "Lipperose"

168 Olympic "Soling" Class Yacht Racing

(Litho Questa)

1991 (18 Jan). "EXPO '90" International Garden and Greenery Exhibition, Osaka. Orchids. T **167c** and similar vert designs. Multicoloured. P 14.

878	10s. Type **167c**	25	15
879	25s. *Lycoste* "Aquila"	35	20
880	30s. *Vuylstekearo* "Cambria Plush"	40	20
881	50s. *Vuylstekearo* "Monica Burnham"	55	35
882	90s. *Odontocidium* "Crowborough Plush"	1·00	1·00
883	100s. *Oncidioda* "Crowborough Chelsea"	1·00	1·00
884	250s. *Sophrolaeliocattleya* "Pth Saturn"	1·75	2·00
885	300s. *Laeliocattleya* "Lykas"	1·90	2·50
878/85 *Set of 8*		6·50	6·50

MS886 Two sheets, each 100×69 mm. (a) 400s. *Cymbidium* "Baldoyle Melbury". (b) 400s. *Cymbidium* "Tapestry Long Beach" *Set of 2 sheets* .... 5·50 6·50

(Litho Questa)

1991 (18 Jan). Record-breaking Sports Events. T **168** and similar multicoloured designs. P 14.

887	5s. Type **168**	50	30
888	20s. Olympic downhill skiing	90	35
889	30s. "Tour de France" cycle race	2·50	70
890	40s. Le Mans 24-hour endurance motor race	1·75	75
891	75s. Olympic two-man bobsleighing	2·00	1·10
892	100s. Belgian Grand Prix motor cycle race	3·00	1·75
893	250s. Indianapolis 500 motor race	3·00	3·50
894	300s. Gold Cup power boat championship	3·00	3·75
887/94 *Set of 8*		15·00	11·00

MS895 Two sheets, each 85×64 mm. (a) 600s. Colorado 500 motor cycle race (*vert*). (b) 400s. Schneider Trophy air race (*vert*) *Set of 2 sheets* .... 9·50 11·00

169 Mickey Mouse as Cowboy

(Des Walt Disney Co. Litho Questa)

1991 (20 Feb). Mickey Mouse in Hollywood. T **169** and similar horiz designs showing Walt Disney cartoon characters as actors. Multicoloured. P 14×13½.

896	5s. Type **169**	30	30
897	10s. Mickey as boxer	30	30
898	15s. Mickey as astronaut	30	30
899	20s. Mickey and Minnie as lovers	30	30
900	100s. Mickey as pirate rescuing Minnie	1·50	1·25
901	200s. Mickey and Donald Duck as policemen arresting Big Pete	2·75	2·50
902	350s. Mickey and Donald with Goofy in historical drama	3·00	2·75
903	450s. Mickey, Donald and Goofy as sailors	3·00	2·75
896/903 *Set of 8*		10·50	9·50

MS904 Two sheets, each 127×96 mm. (a) 600s. Mickey, Minnie and Donald in the mummy's tomb. (b) 600s. Mickey as Canadian Mountie rescuing Minnie from Big Pete *Set of 2 sheets* .... 12·00 12·00

170 Women learning to Read

171 Ngorongoro Crater

(Litho Questa)

1991 (15 Mar). International Literacy Year (2nd issue). T **170** and similar horiz designs. Multicoloured. P 14.

905	9s. Type **170**	25	20
906	13s. Teacher with blackboard	30	20
907	25s. Literacy aids	40	25
908	100s. Reading newspaper	2·50	3·00
905/8 *Set of 4*		3·00	3·25

MS909 104×73 mm. 50s. Adult education class .... 2·00 2·50

(Litho National Printing and Packaging, Zimbabwe)

1991 (28 Mar). Historical Craters and Caves. T **171** and similar horiz designs. Multicoloured. P 14×14½.

910	3s. Type **171**	2·75	1·25

911	5s. Prehistoric rock painting, Kondoa Caves	3·25	1·25
912	9s. Inner crater, Mt Kilimanjaro	3·75	1·50
913	12s. Olduvai Gorge	4·75	2·25
910/13	Set of 4	13·00	5·50

MS914 91×92 mm. 10s. Discarded bottles, Amboni Caves; 10s. Rock paintings, Amboni Caves 10s. Entrance to Amboni Caves; 10s. Rock formation, Amboni Caves .... 20·00 11·00

171a "Proclamation of the Vison"

172 Stegosaurus

(Litho Questa)

1991 (28 Apr). 350th Death Anniv of Rubens. Cartoons for Decius Mus Tapestries. T **171a** and similar multicoloured designs. P 14×13½.

915	85s. Type **171a**	1·75	2·00
	a. Sheetlet. Nos. 915/20	9·50	11·00
916	85s. "Divining of the Entrails"	1·75	2·00
917	85s. "Dispatch of the Lictors"	1·75	2·00
918	85s. "Dedication to Death"	1·75	2·00
919	85s. "Victory and Death of Decius Mus"	1·75	2·00
920	85s. "Funeral Rites"	1·75	2·00
915/20	Set of 6	9·50	11·00

MS921 70×100 mm. 500s. "Trophy of War" (detail) (vert). P 13½×14 .... 11·00 13·00

(Litho State Ptg Wks, Moscow)

1991 (3 June). Prehistoric Creatures. T **172** and similar vert designs. Multicoloured. P 12×12½.

922	10s. Type **172**	25	25
923	15s. Triceratops	25	25
924	25s. Edmontosaurus	40	40
925	30s. Plateosaurua	40	40
926	35s. Diplodocus	45	45
927	100s. Iguanodon	1·40	1·50
928	200s. Silviasaurus	2·00	2·50
922/8	Set of 7	4·75	5·00

MS929 90×90 mm. 150s. Rhamphorhynchus .... 2·50 3·00

173 Dairy Farming

174 Pres. Mwinyi leading Walk

(Litho Questa)

1991 (7 June). 20th Anniv of Tanzania Investment Bank. T **173** and similar horiz designs. Multicoloured. P 14.

930	10s. Type **173**	25	20
931	13s. Industrial development	30	20
932	25s. Engineering	35	20
933	100s. Tea picking	2·00	2·50
930/3	Set of 4	2·50	2·75

MS934 93×91 mm. Nos. 930/3 .... 3·00 3·50

(Litho Cartor)

1991 (5 July). National Solidarity Walk. T **174** and similar horiz designs. Multicoloured. P 13½.

935	4s. +1s. Type **174**	75	75
936	30s. +1s. Pres. Mwinyi planting sapling	1·50	1·50

MS937 91×91 mm. 50s. +1s. Pres. Mwinyi sorting cloves. P 12½ .... 2·50 3·00

174a Class 150 Steam Locomotive, 1872 (first locomotive)

(Des K. Gromell. Litho Questa)

1991 (15 Aug). Phila Nippon '91 International Stamp Exhibition, Tokyo. Japanese Railway Locomotives. T **174a** and similar horiz designs. Multicoloured. P 14.

938	10s. Type **174a**	1·25	65
939	25s. Class 4500 steam locomotive, 1902	1·60	90
940	35s. Class C62 steam locomotive, 1948	1·75	1·00
941	50s. Mikado steam locomotive	1·90	1·25
942	75s. Class 6250 steam locomotive, 1915	2·50	1·50
943	100s. Class C11 steam locomotive, 1932	2·75	1·75
944	200s. Class E10 steam locomotive, 1948	3·25	3·25
945	300s. Class 8550 steam locomotive, 1899	3·75	4·00
938/45	Set of 8	17·00	13·00

MS946 Four sheets, each 102×71 mm. (a) 400s. Series 400 electric train. (b) 400s. Class EH10 electric locomotive, 1954. (c) 400s. Class DD51 diesel-hydraulic locomotive, 1962. (d) 400s. Class EF58 electric locomotive Set of 4 sheets ...... 14·00 15·00

175 Zebra and Goldenwinged Sunbird, Ngorongoro Crater

176 Eronia cleodora

(Des Mary Walters. Litho Questa)

1991 (22 Aug). National Game Parks. T **175** and similar horiz designs. Multicoloured. P 14.

947	10s. Type **175**	1·50	70
948	25s. Greater Kudu and Elephant, Ruaha Park	2·00	1·00
949	30s. Sable Antelope and Red and Yellow Barbet, Mikumi Park	2·00	1·00
950	50s. Leopard and Wildebeest, Serengeti Park	1·50	1·25
951	90s. Giraffe and Starred Robin, Ngurdoto Park	3·00	2·25
952	100s. Eland and Abbott's Duiker, Kilimanjaro Park	2·00	1·75
953	250s. Lion and Impala, Lake Manyara Park	3·00	3·75
954	300s. Black Rhinoceros and Ostrich, Tarangire Park	5·00	5·00
947/54	Set of 8	18·00	15·00

MS955 Two sheets, each 99×68 mm. (a) 400s. Blue-breasted Kingfisher and Defassa Waterbuck, Selous Game Reserve. (b) 400s. Paradise Whydah and Oryx, Mkomazi Game Reserve Set of 2 sheets .... 17·00 14·00

(Des I. Maclaury. Litho Questa)

1991 (28 Aug). Butterflies. T **176** and similar vert designs. Multicoloured. P 14.

956	10s. Type **176**	55	45
957	15s. Precis westermanni	70	60
958	35s. Antanartia delius	1·00	90
959	75s. Bematistes aganice	1·75	1·60
960	100s. Kallima jacksoni	1·90	1·75
961	150s. Apaturopsis cleocharis	2·75	2·75
962	200s. Colotis aurigineus	3·00	3·00
963	300s. Iolaus crawshayi	3·25	3·50
956/63	Set of 8	13·00	13·00

MS964 Four sheets, each 117×76 mm. (a) 400s. Charaxes zoolina. (b) 400s. Papilio phoreas. (c) 400s. Charaxes ethalion. (d) 400s. Papilio nohilisSet of 4 sets .... 14·00 15·00

177 Microwave Tower and Dish Aerial

178 Rice Cultivation

(Litho Questa)

1991 (5 Sept). 25th Anniv of Intelsat Satellite System. T **177** and similar horiz designs. Multicoloured. P 14.

965	10s. Type **177**	50	20
966	25s. Satellite picture of Earth	65	30

967	100s. Mwenge "B" Earth station	2·25	1·50
968	500s. Mwenge "A" Earth station	7·75	10·00
965/8	*Set of 4*	10·00	11·00
MS969	90×86 mm. 50s. Satellite links on world map	3·75	3·75

(Litho Cartor)

1991 (16 Sept). 40th Anniv of United Nations Development Programme. T **178** and similar designs. P 13½.

970	10s. multicoloured	15	10
971	15s. multicoloured	20	10
972	100s. multicoloured	1·50	1·60
973	500s. multicoloured	5·50	8·00
970/3	*Set of 4*	6·75	8·75
MS974	90×90 mm. 40s. pale new blue and black. P 12½	1·40	1·75

Designs: Horiz—15s. Vocational and Civil Service training; 100s. Terrace farming. Vert—40s. UNDP anniversary emblem; 500s. Renovated Arab door.

179 Netball

180 TELECOM '91 Logo

(Litho State Ptg Wks, Moscow)

1991 (20 Sept). All-Africa Games, Cairo. T **179** and similar multicoloured designs. P 12½×12 (Nos. 976, 979) or 12×12½ (others).

975	10s. Type **179**	50	30
976	15s. Football (*horiz*)	50	30
977	100s. Tennis	2·50	1·50
978	200s. Athletics	2·75	2·75
979	500s. Baseball (*horiz*)	6·00	8·50
975/9	*Set of 5*	11·00	12·00
MS980	80×60 mm. 500s. Basketball	12·00	10·00

(Litho Cartor)

1991 (1 Oct). TELECOM '91 International Telecommunication Exhibition, Geneva (10, 15s.) and World Telecommunications Day (others). T **180** and similar multicoloured designs. P 13½×14 (vert) or 14×13½ (horiz).

981	10s. Type **180**	20	10
982	15s. "TELECOM '91" logo and address on envelope (*horiz*)	20	10
983	35s. Symbolic telecommunication signals	40	30
984	100s. Symbolic telecommunication signals (*horiz*)	1·10	1·50
981/4	*Set of 4*	1·75	1·75

181 Japanese Bobtail Cat

(Des Mary Walters. Litho Questa)

1991 (28 Oct). Cats. T **181** and similar horiz designs. Multicoloured. P 14.

985	50s. Type **181**	90	80
	a. Sheetlet. Nos. 985/1000	13·00	11·00
986	50s. Cornish Rex	90	80
987	50s. Malayan	90	80
988	50s. Tonkinese	90	80
989	50s. Abyssinian	90	80
990	50s. Russian Blue	90	80
991	50s. Cymric	90	80
992	50s. Somali	90	80
993	50s. Siamese	90	80
994	50s. Himalayan	90	80
995	50s. Singapore	90	80
996	50s. Manx	90	80
997	50s. Oriental Shorthair	90	80
998	50s. Maine Coon	90	80
999	50s. Persian	90	80
1000	50s. Birman	90	80
985/1000	*Set of 16*	13·00	11·00

Nos. 985/1000 were printed together, *se-tenant*, as a sheetlet of 16.

182 Shire Horse

(Des Mary Walters. Litho Questa)

1991 (28 Oct). Horses and Ponies. T **182** and similar horiz designs. Multicoloured. P 14.

1001	50s. Type **182**	90	80
	a. Sheetlet. Nos. 1001/16	13·00	11·00
1002	50s. Thoroughbred	90	80
1003	50s. Kladruber	90	80
1004	50s. Appaloosa	90	80
1005	50s. Hanoverian	90	80
1006	50s. Arab	90	80
1007	50s. Breton	90	80
1008	50s. Exmoor	90	80
1009	50s. Connernara	90	80
1010	50s. Lipizzaner	90	80
1011	50s. Shetland	90	80
1012	50s. Percheron	90	80
1013	50s. Pinto	90	80
1014	50s. Orlov	90	80
1015	50s. Palomino	90	80
1016	50s. Welsh Cob	90	80
1001/16	*Set of 16*	13·00	11·00

Nos. 1001/16 were printed together, *se-tenant*, as a sheetlet of 16, with the backgrounds of each horizontal strip of 4 forming a composite design.

183 Yellow Tetra

184 African Elephant

(Des Mary Walters. Litho Questa)

1991 (28 Oct). Aquarium Fish. T **183** and similar horiz designs. Multicoloured. P 14.

1017	75s. Type **183**	75	75
	a. Sheetlet. Nos. 1017/32	11·00	11·00
1018	75s. Five-banded Barb	75	75
1019	75s. Simpson Platy	75	75
1020	75s. Guppy	75	75
1021	75s. Zebra Danio	75	75
1022	75s. Neon Tetra	75	75
1023	75s. Siamese Fighting Fish	75	75
1024	75s. Tiger Barb	75	75
1025	75s. Two-striped Lyretail	75	75
1026	75s. Fan-tailed Goldfish	75	75
1027	75s. Pearl Gourami	75	75
1028	75s. Freshwater Angelfish	75	75
1029	75s. Clown Loach	75	75
1030	75s. Red Swordtail	75	75
1031	75s. Blue Discus	75	75
1032	75s. Rosy Barb	75	75
1017/32	*Set of 16*	11·00	11·00

Nos. 1017/32 were printed together, *se-tenant*, as a sheetlet of 16, with the backgrounds of each stamp forming a composite design.

(Des Mary Walters. Litho Questa)

1991 (28 Oct). African Elephants. T **184** and similar vert designs. Multicoloured. P 14.

1033	75s. Type **184**	1·25	1·10
	a. Sheetlet. Nos. 1033/48	18·00	16·00
1034	75s. Two elephants fighting	1·25	1·10
1035	75s. Elephant facing forward and tree	1·25	1·10
1036	75s. Elephant facing left and tree	1·25	1·10
1037	75s. Cow elephant and calf facing right standing in water	1·25	1·10
1038	75s. Cow watching over calf in water	1·25	1·10
1039	75s. Two adults and calf in water	1·25	1·10
1040	75s. Cow and calf facing left standing in water	1·25	1·10
1041	75s. Elephant facing right	1·25	1·10
1042	75s. Elephants feeding	1·25	1·10

1043	75s. Elephant feeding	1·25	1·10
1044	75s. Elephant and Zebra	1·25	1·10
1045	75s. Cow and calf drinking	1·25	1·10
1046	75s. Calf suckling	1·25	1·10
1047	75s. Bull elephant	1·25	1·10
1048	75s. Cow with small calf	1·25	1·10
1033/48 Set of 16		18·00	16·00

Nos. 1033/48 were printed together, *se-tenant*, as a sheetlet of 16, with each horizontal strip of 4 forming a composite design.

185 Budgerigar

(Des Mary Walters. Litho Questa)

1991 (28 Oct). Pet Birds. T **185** and similar horiz designs. Multicoloured. P 14.

1049	75s. Type **185**	90	80
	a. Sheetlet. Nos. 1049/64	13·00	11·00
1050	75s. Orange-breasted Bunting ("Rainbow Bunting")	90	80
1051	75s. Golden-fronted Leafbird	90	80
1052	75s. Black-headed Caique	90	80
1053	75s. Java Sparrow	90	80
1054	75s. Diamond Firetail Finch	90	80
1055	75s. Peach-faced Lovebird	90	80
1056	75s. Golden Conure	90	80
1057	75s. Military Macaw	90	80
1058	75s. Yellow-faced Parrotlet	90	80
1059	75s. Sulphur-crested Cockatoo	90	80
1060	75s. White-fronted Amazon ("Spectacled Amazon Parrot")	90	80
1061	75s. Paradise Tanager	90	80
1062	75s. Gouldian Finch	90	80
1063	75s. Masked Lovebird	90	80
1064	75s. Hill Mynah	90	80
1049/64 Set of 16		13·00	11·00

1000 Nos. 1049/64 were printed together, *se-tenant*, as a sheetlet of 16, forming a composite design.

185a "Peasant Woman Sewing"

186 Indian Elephant

(Litho Questa)

1991 (20 Nov). Death Centenary of Vincent van Gogh (artist) (1990). T **185a** and similar multicoloured designs. P 13½×14.

1065	10s. Type **185a**	70	30
1066	15s. "Head of Peasant Woman with Greenish Lace Cap"	75	35
1067	35s. "Flowering Orchard"	1·25	60
1068	75s. "Portrait of a Girl"	2·00	1·00
1069	100s. "Portrait of a Woman with Red Ribbon"	2·25	2·00
1070	150s. "Vase with Flowers"	3·00	3·00
1071	200s. "Houses in Antwerp"	3·25	3·50
1072	400a. "Seated Peasant Woman with White Cap"	6·00	7·50
1065/72 Set of 8		18·00	15·00
MS1073 Two sheets, each 127×112 mm. (a) 400s. "Bulb Fields" (*horiz*). (b) 400s. "The Parsonage Garden at Nuenen in the Snow" (*horiz*). Imperf Set of 2 sheets		15·00	16·00

(Des J. Puvilland. Litho State Ptg Wks, Moscow)

1991 (28 Nov). Elephants. T **186** and similar multicoloured designs. P 12×12½ (vert) or 12½×12 (horiz).

1074	10s. Type **186**	1·00	50
1075	15s. Indian Elephant uprooting tree	1·25	65
1076	25s. Indian Elephant with calf	1·60	80
1077	30s. African Elephant	1·60	80
1078	35s. Head of African Elephant (*horiz*)	1·60	85

1079	100s. African Elephant and calf bathing (*horiz*)	3·50	2·50
1080	200s. Two African Elephants (*horiz*)	5·00	5·50
1074/80 Set of 7		14·00	10·50
MS1081 90×90 mm. 400s. Mammoth (*horiz*)		4·00	4·50

187 Class Em Steam Locomotive, Russia, 1930,

(Litho State Ptg Wks, Moscow)

1991 (10 Dec). Locomotives of the World. T **187** and similar multicoloured designs. P 12½×12 (horiz) or 12×12½ (vert).

1082	10s. Type **187**	20	25
1083	15s. "Hikari" express train, Japan, 1964	30	35
1084	25s. Russian steam locomotive, 1834 (*vert*)	35	45
1085	35s. TGV express train, France, 1979	45	55
1086	60s. Diesel railcar No. R16-01, France, 1972	70	80
1087	100s. High Speed Train 125, Great Britain, 1972	1·10	1·40
1088	300s. Russian steam locomotive, 1833 (*vert*)	2·50	3·00
1082/8 Set of 7		5·00	6·00
MS1089 91×91 mm. 100s. French electric locomotive, 1952 (*vert*)		1·60	2·00

No. 1088 is inscribed "1837" in error.

187a Disney Characters in "Joy", 1968

(Des Walt Disney Co. Litho Questa)

1991 (24 Dec). Christmas. Walt Disney Christmas Cards. T **187a** and similar multicoloured designs. P 14×13½ (horiz) or 13½×14 (vert).

1090	10s. Type **187a**	40	20
1091	25s. Mickey, Donald, Pluto and Goofy hanging up stockings, 1981	65	40
1092	35s. Characters from Disney film *Robin Hood*, 1973	80	45
1093	75s. Mickey looking at Christmas tree, 1967	1·40	90
1094	100s. Goofy, Mickey, Donald and Chip n' Dale on film set, 1969 (*vert*)	1·75	1·25
1095	150s. Mickey on giant bauble, 1976 (*vert*)	2·25	2·00
1096	200s. Clarabelle Cow with electric cow bell, 1935 (*vert*)	2·50	2·50
1097	300s. Mickey's nephews with book, 1935 (*vert*)	3·50	3·50
1090/7 Set of 8		12·00	10·00
MS1098 Two sheets, each 127×102 mm. (a) 500s. Mickey handing out presents, 1935 (*vert*). (b) 500s. Disney cartoon characters, 1968 (*vert*) Set of 2 sheets		15·00	15·00

188 Bruce Lee

189 Sand Tilefish

(Des J. Iskowitz. Litho Questa)

1992 (14 Feb). Entertainers. T **188** and similar vert designs. P 13½.

1099/134	75s. ×36 multicoloured Set of 36	25·00	27·00

TANZANIA

MS1135 Four sheets, each 78×108 mm. 500s. × 4 multicoloured (Bruce Lee, Marilyn Monroe, Elvis Presley, Kouyate & Kouyate each 28×42 mm). P 14 Set of 4 sheets .... 23·00 26·00
Nos. 1099/134 were issued as four sheetlets, each in nine different designs, depicting Bruce Lee, Marilyn Monroe, Elvis Presley and black entertainers (Scott Joplin, Sammy Davis Jnr Joan Armatrading, Louis Armstrong, Miriam Makeba, Lionel Ritchie, Whitney Houston, Bob Marley, Tina Turner).

(Des P. Ndembo. Litho State Ptg Wks, Moscow)

1992 (9 Mar). Fish. T **189** and similar horiz designs. Multicoloured. P 12½×12.

1136	10s. Type **189**	35	40
1137	15s. Five-banded Cichlid	40	45
1138	25s. Pearly Lamprologus	50	60
1139	35s. Jewel Cichlid	60	70
1140	60s. Two-striped Lyretail	80	1·00
1141	100s. Reef Stonefish	1·25	1·50
1142	300s. Ahl's Lyretail	2·50	4·00
1136/42 Set of 7		5·75	7·50
MS1143 90×90 mm. 100s. Oarfish		1·60	2·00

190 Chimpanzee in Tree

191 Pope John Paul II in Dominican Republic, 1979

(Des Mary Walters. Litho Questa)

1992 (30 Mar). Common Chimpanzee. T **190** and similar vert designs. Multicoloured. P 14.

1144	10s. Type **190**	75	50
1145	15s. Feeding	80	55
1146	35s. Two chimpanzees	1·40	85
1147	75s. Adult male with arms folded	2·00	1·25
1148	100s. Breaking branch	2·25	1·50
1149	150s. Young chimpanzee in tree	3·00	3·00
1150	200s. Female holding young	3·50	3·75
1151	300s. Chimpanzee sitting in tree	4·75	5·00
1144/51 Set of 8		17·00	15·00
MS1152 Two sheets, each 99×68 mm. (a) 400a. Eating termites. (b) 400s. Swinging through trees Set of 2 sheets		7·00	7·00

(Litho Questa)

1992 (13 Apr). Papal Visits. T **191** and similar vert designs. P 14.
1153/272 100s.×120 multicoloured Set of 120 .... £110 75·00
Nos. 1153/272 were issued in ten sheetlets, each of 12 different designs arranged round a common block of four stamp sized labels.

192 Balcony

193 Gogo Costume

(Des J. da Silva. Litho State Ptg Wks, Moscow)

1992 (15 Apr). Zanzibar Stone Town. T **192** and similar multicoloured designs. P 12½×12 (200s.) or 12×12½ (others).

1273	10s. Type **192**	65	25
1274	20s. Bahlnara Mosque	90	35
1275	30s. High Court Building	1·25	40
1276	200s. National Museum (horiz)	7·00	8·50
1273/6 Set of 4		9·00	8·50
MS1277 91×91 mm. 150s. Old Fort (horiz); 300s. Maruhubi ruins (horiz). P 12½×12		7·00	6·00

(Des P. Ndembo. Litho National Printing and Packaging, Zimbabwe)

1992 (30 Apr). Traditional Costumes. T **193** and similar vert designs. Multicoloured. P 14½.

1278	3s. Type **193**	1·25	1·00
1279	5s. Swahili	1·25	1·00

1280	9s. Hehe and Makonde	1·75	1·10
1281	12s. Maasai	2·00	1·50
1278/81 Set of 4		5·50	4·25
MS1282 91×91 mm. 40s. Mwarusha		4·50	4·75

194 Melisa and Mike (chimpanzees)

(Des P. Ndembo. Litho B.D.T.)

1992 (29 May). Chimpanzees of the Gombe. Multicoloured. P 14.

*(a) Horiz designs as T **194***

1283	10s. Type **194**	1·00	55
1284	15s. Leakey and David Greybeard	1·25	65
1285	30s. Fifi termiting	1·60	1·10
1286	35s. Galahad	1·60	1·25
1283/6 Set of 4		5·00	3·25
MS1287 90×90 mm. 100s. Fifi, Flo and Faben		2·50	2·75

(b) Vert designs showing individual chimpanzees

1288	10s. Leakey	1·00	1·00
	a. Sheetlet. Nos. 1288/95	8·00	8·00
1289	15s. Fifi	1·00	1·00
1290	20s. Faben	1·00	1·00
1291	30s. David Greybeard	1·00	1·00
1292	35s. Mike	1·00	1·00
1293	50s. Galahad	1·00	1·00
1294	100s. Melisa	1·25	1·25
1295	200s. Flo	1·75	1·75
1288/95 Set of 8		8·00	8·00

Nos. 1288/95 were printed together, se-tenant, in sheetlets of 8.

195 Sorghum Farming, Serena

196 Giant Spider Conch (Lambis truncata)

(Des P. Ndembo. Litho Questa)

1992 (22 June). 25th Anniv of National Bank of Commerce. T **195** and similar multicoloured designs. P 14.

1296	10s. Type **195**	75	15
1297	15s. Samora Avenue Branch and computer operator (vert)	85	25
1298	35s. Training centre	1·25	90
1299	40s. Women dyeing textiles	1·25	1·50
1296/9 Set of 4		3·50	2·50
MS1300 111×117 mm. 30s. Bank Head Office		1·25	1·75

(Litho State Ptg Wks, Moscow)

1992 (30 June). Shells. T **196** and similar vert designs. Multicoloured. P 12×12½.

1301	10s. Type **196**	25	30
1302	15s. Bull-mouth Helmet (Cypraecassis rufa)	30	35
1303	25s. Rugose Mitre (Vexillum ragosum)	40	50
1304	30s. Lettered Cone (Conus litteratus)	40	50
1305	35s. True Heart Cockle (Corculum cardissa)	40	50
1306	50s. Ramose Murex (Murex rammus)	50	70
1307	250s. Indian Volute (Melo melo)	1·50	3·25
1301/7 Set of 7		3·25	5·50
MS1308 91×91 mm. 300s. Giant Clam (Tridacna gigas)		2·75	4·00

197 Basketball

198 British-designed Radar, Pearl Harbor

96

(Des A. Nabola. Litho State Ptg Wks, Moscow)

1992 (23 July). Olympic Games, Barcelona (2nd issue). T **197** and similar vert designs. Multicoloured. P 12×12½.

1309	40a. Type **197**	45	30
1310	100s. Billiards	75	60
1311	200s. Table Tennis	1·25	1·40
1312	400s. Darts	2·75	4·00
1309/12	Set of 4	4·75	5·50
MS1313	91×8 mm. 500s. Weightlifting	3·00	4·25

(Des J. Batchelor. Litho Questa)

1992 (1 Aug). 50th Anniv of Japanese Attack on Pearl Harbor. T **198** and similar horiz designs. Multicoloured. P 14½.

1314	75s. Type **198**	2·25	1·40
	a. Sheetlet. Nos. 1314/23	20·00	12·00
1315	75s. Winston Churchill	2·25	1·40
1316	75s. Sinking of H.M.S. *Repulse* (battle cruiser)	2·25	1·40
1317	75s. Sinking of H.M.S. *Prince of Wales* (battleship)	2·25	1·40
1318	75s. Surrender of Singapore	2·25	1·40
1319	75s. Sinking of H.M.S. *Hermes* (aircraft carrier)	2·25	1·40
1320	75s. Japanese attack on Malayan airfield	2·25	1·40
1321	75a. Japanese gun crew, Hong Kong	2·25	1·40
1322	75s. Japanese landing craft	2·25	1·40
1323	75s. *Haguro* (Japanese cruiser)	2·25	1·40
1314/23	Set of 10	20·00	12·00

Nos. 1314/23 were printed together, *se-tenant*, in sheetlets of 10 with the stamps arranged in two horizontal strips of 5 separated by a gutter showing H.M.S. *Exeter* at Battle of Java Sea.

199 French Resistance Monument and Medal

(Litho Questa)

1992 (1 Aug). Birth Centenary of Charles de Gaulle (French statesman) (1990). T **199** and similar multicoloured designs. P 14.

1324	25s. Type **199**	50	40
1325	30s. Free French tank on Omaha Beach, D-Day	50	40
1326	150s. Concorde at Charles de Gaulle Airport.	10·00	7·50
1324/6	Set of 3	10·00	7·50
MS1327	115×92 mm. 500s. Free French local Cross of Lorraine opt on Petain 1f.50 and De Gaulle label postmarked 25 August 1944 (39×51 *mm*)	10·00	12·00

200 Scout Badge, Giraffe and Elephant

(Litho Questa)

1992 (1 Aug). 50th Death Anniv of Lord Baden-Powell (founder of Boy Scout movement) (1991). T **200** and similar multicoloured designs. P 14.

1328	10s. Type **200**	80	50
1329	15s. Scouts in boat	80	50
1330	400s. John Glenn's space capsule	6·00	8·50
1328/30	Set of 3	7·00	8·50
MS1331	90×117 mm. 500s. Tanzanian Scout (39×51 *mm*). P 13½	4·25	6·50

201 Marcella Sembrich as Zerlina in *Don Giovanni*

202 Lucky Omens

201a "A Picador, mounted on a Chula's Shoulders, spears a Bull" (Goya)

(Litho Questa)

1992 (1 Aug). Death Bicentenary of Mozart. T **201** and similar designs. P 14.

1332	10s. black and deep mauve	1·75	40
1333	50s. multicoloured	3·50	1·10
1334	300s. black and deep mauve	11·00	10·00
1332/4	Set of 3	14·50	10·50
MS1335	115×87 mm. 500s. grey-brown, stone and black	12·00	12·00

Designs: Horiz—50s. Planet Jupiter (Symphony No. 41); 300s. Luciano Pavarotti as Idamente in *Idomeneo*. Vert (35×47 *mm*)—500s. Wolfgang Amadeus Mozart.

(Litho B.D.T.)

1992 (1 Aug). Granada '92 International Stamp Exhibition, Spain. Paintings. T **201a** and similar designs. P 13.

1336	25s. Indian red and black	60	40
1337	35s. multicoloured	70	50
1338	50s. multicoloured	85	60
1339	75s. multicoloured	1·25	1·00
1340	100s. black, brown and flesh	1·75	1·50
1341	150s. Indian red and black	2·25	2·25
1342	200s. Indian red and black	2·50	2·50
1343	300s. multicoloured	3·00	3·50
1336/43	Set of 8	11·50	11·00
MS1344	Two sheets, each 121×95 mm. (a) 400s. multicoloured. (b) 400s. multicoloured. Imperf Set of 2 sheets	9·50	11·00

Designs: Vert—35s. "Philip IV at Fraga " (Velasquez); 50s. "Head of a Stag" (Velasquez); 75s. "The Cardinal-Infante Ferdinand as a Hunter" (Velasquez); 100s. "The Dream of Reason brings forth Monsters" (Goya); 300s. "Pablo de Valladolid" (Velasquez). Horiz—150s. "Another Madness (of Martincho) in the Plaza de Zaragoza" (Goya); 200s. "Recklessness of Martincho in the Plaza de Zaragoza" (Goya). (111×86 *mm*)—400s. (No. MS1344a) "Two Men at Table" (Velasquez); 400s. (No. MS1344b) "Seascape" (Mariana Salvador Maella).

(Des P. Ndembo. Litho State Ptg Wks, Moscow)

1992 (30 Sept). 500th Anniv of Discovery of America by Columbus. T **202** and similar multicoloured designs. P 12×12½ (vert) or 12½×12 (horiz).

1345	10s. Type **202**	20	20
1346	15s. Map and compass	25	25
1347	25s. Look-out in crow's nest	35	35
1348	30s. Amerindians sighting ships (*horiz*)	40	40
1349	35s. *Pinta* and *Nina* (*horiz*)	55	45
1350	75s. *Santa Maria* (*horiz*)	90	80
1351	250s. Wreck of *Santa Maria*	1·75	2·50
1345/51	Set of 7	4·00	4·50
MS1352	93×93 mm. 200s. Columbus	1·75	2·50

203 Superb Starling

15th Anniversary
(204)

(Des P. Ndembo. Litho State Ptg Wks, Moscow)

1992 (15 Oct). Birds. T **203** and similar multicoloured designs. P 12×12½.

1353	5s. Type **203**	60	50
1354	10s. Golden Bishop ("Canary")	70	50
1355	15a. Four-coloured Bush Shrike	80	55
1356	25a. Grey-headed Kingfisher	90	55
1357	30s. Common Kingfisher	90	55
1358	35s. Yellow-billed Oxpecker	90	55

1359	150a. Black-throated Honeyguide	2·50	3·00
1353/9	*Set of 7*	6·50	5·50
MS1360	93×92 mm. 300s. European Cuckoo (*horiz*). P 12½×12	2·75	3·50

1992 (15 Oct). 15th Death Anniv of Elvis Presley. Nos. 1117/25 optd with T **204**.

1361	75s. Looking pensive	95	85
	a. Sheetlet. Nos. 1361/9	7·50	7·00
1362	75s. Wearing black and yellow striped shirt	95	85
1363	75s. Singing into microphone	95	85
1364	75s. Wearing wide-brimmed hat	95	85
1365	75s. With microphone in right hand	95	85
1366	75s. In Army uniform	95	85
1367	75s. Wearing pink shirt	95	85
1368	75s. In yellow shirt	95	85
1369	75s. In jacket and bow tie	95	85
1361/9	*Set of 9*	7·50	7·00

205 Iguanodon

(Des S. Barlowe. Litho Questa)

1992 (5 Nov). African Dinosaurs. T **205** and similar horiz designs. Multicoloured. P 14.

1370	100s. Type **205**	1·10	90
	a. Sheetlet. Nos. 1370/85	16·00	13·00
1371	100s. Saltasaurus	1·10	90
1372	100s. Cetiosaurus	1·10	90
1373	100s. Camarasaurus	1·10	90
1374	100s. Spinosaurus	1·10	90
1375	100s. Stegosaurus	1·10	90
1376	100s. Allosaurus	1·10	90
1377	100s. Ceratosaurus	1·10	90
1378	100s. Lesothosaurus	1·10	90
1379	100s. Anchisaurus	1·10	90
1380	100s. Ornithomimus	1·10	90
1381	100s. Baronyx	1·10	90
1382	100s. Pachycephalosaurus	1·10	90
1383	100s. Heterodontosaurus	1·10	90
1384	100s. Dryosaurus	1·10	90
1385	100s. Coelophysis	1·10	90
1370/85	*Set of 16*	16·00	13·00

Nos. 1370/85 were printed together, *se-tenant*, in aheetlets of 16, forming a composite design.

206 Spotted Tilapia

(Litho B.D.T.)

1992 (5 Nov). Fish. T **206** and similar horiz designs. Multicoloured. P 13½.

1386	100s. Type **206**	1·00	1·00
	a. Sheetlet. Nos. 1386/97	11·00	11·00
1387	100s. Butterfly Barb	1·00	1·00
1388	100s. Blunthead Moliro Cichlid	1·00	1·00
1389	100s. Angel Squeaker	1·00	1·00
1390	100s. Dickfeld's Julie	1·00	1·00
1391	100a. Nile Mouthbrooder	1·00	1·00
1392	100a. Blue-finned Notho	1·00	1·00
1393	100s. Crabro Mbuna	1·00	1·00
1394	100s. Pearl-scaled Lamprologus	1·00	1·00
1395	100s. Zebra Mbuna	1·00	1·00
1396	100s. Marlier's Julie	1·00	1·00
1397	100s. Brichard's Chalinochromis	1·00	1·00
1386/97	*Set of 12*	11·00	11·00

MS1398 Three sheets, each 71×55 mm. (a) 500a. Palmqvist's Notho. (b) 500s. Electric Blue Haplochromis. (c) 500s. Short Lamprologus *Set of 3 sheets* | 11·00 | 12·00

Nos. 1386/97 were printed together, *se-tenant*, in sheetlets of 12, forming a composite design.

207 Hunting Birds with Catapults

207a Men's 4000 Metre Pursuit Cycling

(Litho Cartor)

1992 (25 Nov). Traditional Hunting. T **207** and similar horiz designs. Multicoloured. P 13½.

1399	20s. Type **207**	1·75	50
1400	70s. Hunting antelope with bow and arrow	1·75	80
1401	100s. Hunting antelopes with dogs	3·00	1·50
1402	150s. Hunting lion with spears and shields	3·25	4·25
1399/1402	*Set of 4*	8·75	6·25

MS1403 100×100 mm. 40s. Traditional hunting weapons. P 12½×12 | 3·75 | 4·50

(Litho Questa)

1992 (30 Nov). Olympic Games, Albertville and Barcelona (3rd issue). T **207a** and similar multicoloured designs. P 14.

1404	20s. Type **207a**	2·00	85
1405	40s. Men's double sculls rowing (*horiz*)	70	20
1406	50s. Waterpolo (*horiz*)	80	20
1407	70s. Women's single luge (*horiz*)	90	30
1408	100s. Marathon (*horiz*)	95	50
1409	150s. Women's asymmetrical bars gymnastics (*horiz*)	2·00	2·25
1410	200s. Ice hockey	4·50	3·00
1411	400s. Men's rings gymnastics	4·50	6·00
1404/11	*Set of 8*	14·50	12·00

MS1412 Two sheets, each 100×71 mm. (a) 500s. Tennis. (b) 500s. Football *Set of 2 sheets* | 13·00 | 13·00

207b Donald Duck in *Sea Scouts*, 1939

208 Couroupita guianensis

(Des Walt Disney & Co. Litho Questa)

1992 (30 Nov). Mickey's Portrait Gallery. T **207b** and similar multicoloured designs showing Walt Disney cartoon characters. P 13½×14.

1413	25s. Type **207b**	40	30
1414	25s. Minnie Mouse in *Hawaiian Holiday*, 1937	40	30
1415	25s. Pluto in *Society Dog Show*, 1939	40	30
1416	35s. Donald in *Fire Chief*, 1940	55	40
1417	50s. Donald in *Truant Officer Donald*, 1941	65	50
1418	75s. Goofy in *Clock Cleaners*, 1937	85	60
1419	100s. Goofy in *Goofy and Wilbur*, 1939	1·00	85
1420	100s. Mickey Mouse in *Magician Mickey*, 1937	1·00	85
1421	200s. Minnie in *The Nifty Nineties*, 1941	1·75	1·25
1422	300s. Mickey and Pluto in *Society Dog Show*, 1939	2·00	1·75
1423	400s. Pluto and pups in *Pluto's Quin-Puplets*, 1937	2·25	2·00
1424	500s. Daisy and Donald in *Mr. Duck Steps Out*, 1940	2·25	2·00
1413/24	*Set of 12*	12·00	10·00

MS1425 Three sheets. (a) 127×102 mm. 600s. Goofy in *Forever Goofy*. P 13½×14. (b) 127×102 mm. 600s. Daisy in *Don Donald*, 1937. P 13½×14. (c) 112×104 mm. 600s. Mickey and Minnie in *Brave Little Tailor*, 1938 (*horiz*). P 14×13½ *Set of 3 sheets* | 9·50 | 11·00

(Des Jennifer Toombs. Litho Questa)

1992 (1 Dec). Botanical Gardens of the World. Rio de Janeiro. T **208** and similar vert designs showing African Plants. Multicoloured. P 14½×14.

1426/45	70s.×20 *Set of 20*	16·00	18·00
MS1446	110×74 mm. 500s. Avenue of Royal Palms	4·75	5·50

Nos. 1426/45 were issued as a *se-tenant* sheetlet of 20 (5×4).

209 Abyssinian Cat

209a Baltimore and Ohio Tunnel Locomotive No. 5, 1904

(Litho State Ptg Wks, Moscow)

1992 (3 Dec). Cats. T **209** and similar vert designs. Multicoloured. P 12×12½.

1447	20s. Type **209**	55	45
1448	30s. Havana cat	55	45
1449	50s. Persian black cat	65	55
1450	70s. Persian blue cat	75	65
1451	100s. European silver tabby cat	1·00	85
1452	150s. Persian silver tabby cat	1·25	1·25
1453	200s. Maine Coon cat	1·50	1·50
1447/53	*Set of 7*	5·50	5·00
MS1454	90×90 mm. 300s. European cat	2·75	3·00

(Des W. Hanson. Litho B.D.T.)

1992 (10 Dec). Genova '92 International Stamp Exhibition. Toy Trains manufactured by Lionel. T **209a** and similar horiz designs. Multicoloured. P 14.

1455	10s. Type **209a**	70	35
1456	20s. "Liberty Bell" locomotive No. 385E, 1930	80	45
1457	30s. Armoured rail car No. 203, 1917	85	40
1458	50s. Open trolley No. 202, 1910-14	1·25	60
1459	70s. "Macy Special" electric locomotive No. 405	1·50	85
1460	100s. "Milwaukee Road" bi-polar electric locomotive, 1929	1·60	95
1461	200s. New York Central Type S locomotive, 1912	2·00	2·25
1462	300s. Locomotive No. 7, 1914	2·25	3·25
1455/62	*Set of 8*	10·00	8·00
MS1463	Two sheets. (a) 91×75 mm. 500s. Display model locomotive in clear plastic, 1947. (b) 71×89 mm. 500s. Mickey and Minnie Mouse on clockwork handcar, 1936 *Set of 2 sheets*	6·50	7·50

210 Count Ferdinand von Zeppelin

210a "Young Draughtsman sharpening Pencil

(Des W. Wright and W. Hanson (Nos. 1464, 1471, **MS**1475a), W. Wright and L. Fried (Nos. 1466, 1473, **MS**1475c), J. Genzo (Nos. 1474, **MS**1475e), W. Wright (others). Litho B.D.T.)

1992 (15 Dec). Anniversaries and Events. T **210** and similar multicoloured designs. P 14.

1464	30s. Type **210**	60	30
1465	70s. *Santa Maria*	1·50	1·00
1466	70s. "Apollo-Soyuz" link-up, 1975	1·00	1·00
1467	150s. African Elephant	3·00	1·00
1468	150s. Child being offered apple	1·00	1·50
1469	200s. Zebra	1·50	1·50
1470	200s. Trying on lasses	1·10	1·50
1471	300s. Airship L2-127 *Graf Zeppelin*, 1929	1·75	2·00
1472	300s. Christopher Columbus	2·00	2·00

1473	400s. Space shuttle	2·75	2·75
1474	400s. Wolfgang Amadeus Mozart (*vert*)	4·25	3·50
1464/74	*Set of 11*	19·00	17·00
MS1475	Five sheets. (a) 110×82 mm. 500s. LZ-5 Zeppelin airship (b) 114×81 mm. 500a. Head of Columbus. (c) 110×82 mm. 500 s. "Voyager 2" apace probe. (d) 114×81 mm. 500s. African Elephant (*different*). (e) 110×68 mm. 500s. Queen of the Night from *The Magic Flute* (*vert*) *Set of 5 sheets*	17·00	19·00

Anniversaries and Events:—Nos. 1464, 1471, **MS**1475a, 75th death anniv of Count Ferdinand von Zeppelin; Nos. 1465, 1472, **MS**1475b 500th anniv of Discovery of America by Columbus; Nos. 1466, 1473, **MS**1475c, International Space Year; Nos. 1467, 1469, **MS**1475d, Earth Summit '92, Rio; No. 1468, International Conference on Nutrition, Rome; No. 1470, 75th anniv of International Association of Lions Clubs; Nos. 1474, **MS**1475e, Death bicent of Mozart.

(Litho Walsall)

1992 (15 Dec). Bicentenary of the Louvre, Paris. Paintings by Jean Chardin. T **210a** and similar multicoloured designs. P 12.

1476	100s. Type **210a**	85	85
	a. Sheetlet. Nos. 1476/83	6·00	6·00
1477	100s. "The Buffet"	85	85
1478	100s. "Return from the Market"	85	85
1479	100s. "The Hard-working Mother"	85	85
1480	100s. "Grace"	85	85
1481	100s. "The Copper Water Urn"	85	85
1482	100s. "The House of Cards"	85	85
1483	100s. "Boy with a Top"	85	85
1476/83	*Set of 8*	6·00	6·00
MS1484	100×70 mm. 500s. "The Ray" (85×52 *mm*). P 14½	3·50	4·00

Nos. 1476/83 were printed together, *se-tenant*, in sheetlets of 8 stamps and one centre label.

211 Carved Head

212 Russian Cycle, 1813

(Litho State Ptg Wks, Moscow)

1992 (24 Dec). Makonde Art. T **211** and similar vert designs showing various carvings. P 12×12½.

1485	20a. multicoloured	15	15
1486	30a. multicoloured	15	15
1487	50s. multicoloured	20	20
1488	70s. multicoloured	30	30
1489	100s. multicoloured	40	40
1490	150s. multicoloured	70	70
1491	200s. multicoloured	80	80
1485/91	*Set of 7*	2·40	2·40
MS1492	91×91 mm. 350s. multicoloured	1·75	2·25

(Litho State Ptg Wks, Moscow)

1992 (30 Dec). Bicycles of the World. T **212** and similar horiz designs. Multicoloured. P 12½×12.

1493	20s. Type **212**	20	20
1494	30s. German, 1840	20	20
1495	50s. German, 1818	30	30
1496	70s. German, 1850	30	40
1497	100s. Italian, 1988	35	50
1498	150s. Swedish, 1982	50	80
1499	300s. Italian, 1989	70	1·25
1493/9	*Set of 7*	2·25	3·25
MS1500	90×90 mm. 350a. British penny farthing, 1887	1·00	2·50

213 Seal

(Litho Questa)

1993 (1 Mar). Large Sea Creatures. T **213** and similar horiz designs. Multicoloured. P 14.

1501	20s. Type **213**	75	50
1502	30s. Whale	2·25	80
1503	70s. Shark	1·25	1·00

1504	100s. Walrus..		1·50	1·50
1501/4	Set of 4		5·25	3·50
MS1505	99×91 mm. 500s. Sea Turtle		6·50	6·50

214 Boxing

214a Queen Elizabeth at Coronation (photo by Cecil Beaton)

(Litho State Ptg Wks, Moscow)

1993 (28 May). Sports. T **214** and similar multicoloured designs. P 12×12½.

1506	20s. Type **214**	15	15
1507	50s. Hockey...	1·00	30
1508	70s. Show jumping.................................	40	40
1509	100s. Marathon running	45	45
1510	150s. Football...	60	70
1511	200s. Diving..	70	90
1512	400s. Basketball.......................................	2·00	2·50
1506/12	Set of 7	4·75	5·00
MS1513	91×91 mm. 300s. High jumping (horiz). P 12½×12	1·75	2·25

No 1508 is incorrectly captioned "Horse racing".

(Des Kerri Schiff. Litho Questa)

1993 (10 June). 40th Anniv of Coronation. T **214a** and similar vert designs. P 13½×14.

1514	100s. multicoloured..............................	80	65
	a. Sheetlet. Nos. 1514/17×2	8·00	
1515	100s. multicoloured..............................	1·10	85
1516	200s. blackish lilac and black............	1·40	1·10
1517	300s. multicoloured..............................	1·60	1·25
1514/17	Set of 4	4·50	3·50
MS1518	102×70 mm. 500s. multicoloured. P 14	3·75	3·75

Designs:—150s. Gold salt-cellar; 200s. Prince Philip at Coronation; 300s. Queen Elizabeth II and Prince Andrew. (28½×42½ mm)—500s. "Princess Elizabeth opening the New Broadgate, Coventry" (detail) (Dame Laura Knight).

Nos. 1514/17 were printed together in sheetlets of 8, containing two se-tenant blocks of 4.

215 Macrolepiota rhacodes

216 Geochelone elephantopus (tortoise)

(Des Mary Walters. Litho Questa)

1993 (18 June). Fungi. T **215** and similar vert designs. Multicoloured. P 14.

1519	20s. Type **215**	60	35
1520	40s. Mycena aura	80	50
1521	50s. Chlorophyllum molybdites	80	50
1522	70s. Agaricus campestris.......................	90	60
1523	100s. Volvariella volvacea	1·00	70
1524	150s. Leucoagaricus naucinus	1·40	1·25
1525	200s. Oudemansiella radicata	1·60	1·50
1526	300s. Clitocybe nebularis	1·75	2·00
1519/26	Set of 8	8·00	6·75
MS1527	Two sheets, each 100×70 mm. (a) 500s. Omphalotus olearius. (b) 500s. Lepista nuda Set of 2 sheets	6·50	7·50

(Litho State Ptg Wks, Moscow)

1993 (28 June). Reptiles. T **216** and similar multicoloured designs. P 12×12½ (vert) or 12½×12 (horiz).

1528	20s. Type **216**	20	20

1529	50s. Iguana iguana.................................	30	30
1530	70s. Varanus salvator (lizard) (horiz).....	40	40
1531	100s. Naja oxiana (cobra)......................	45	45
1532	150s. Chamaeleo jacksoni (horiz)	70	70
1533	200s. Eunectes murinus (snake) (horiz)	80	80
1534	250s. Alligator mississippensis (horiz)....	90	90
1528/34	Set of 7	3·25	3·25
MS1535	90×90 mm. 500s. Vipera berus (snake)	2·50	3·50

217 Pancake Tortoise on Rock

218 Elephant

(Des L. Birmingham. Litho Questa)

1993 (30 June). Endangered Species. Pancake Tortoise. T **217** and similar horiz designs. Multicoloured. P 14.

1536	20s. Type **217**	45	35
1537	30s. Drinking	50	40
1538	50s. Under rock	70	80
1539	70s. Tortoise hatching	90	1·00
1536/9	Set of 4	2·25	2·25

(Des L. Birmingham. Litho Questa)

1993 (30 June). Wildlife. T **218** and similar multicoloured designs. P 14.

1540/87	100s.×48 Set of 48	30·00	28·00
MS1588	Two sheets, each 100×71 mm. (a) 500s. Lion cub (horiz). (b) 500s. Elephant calf (horiz) Set of 2 sheets	7·50	8·50

Nos. 1540/87 were issued together, se-tenant, as four sheetlets each of twelve different vertical designs. The species depicted are, in addition to Type **218**, Gazelle, Hartebeest, Duiker, Genet, Civet, Eastern White Pelican, Waterbuck, Blacksmith Plover, Lesser Pied Kingfisher Black-winged Stilt, Bush Pig, Brownhooded Kingfisher, Sable Antelope, Impala, Buffalo, eopard, Aardvark, Hippopotamus, Spotted Hyena, South African Crowned Crane, Crocodile, Greater Flamingo, Baboon, Potto, Lesser Flamingo, Grey-headed Kingfisher, Red Colobus Monkey, Dik-Dik, Aardwolf (incorrectly inscribed "ARDWLF"), Black-backed Jackal, Tree Pangolin, Serval, Yellow-billed Hornbill, Pygmy Mongoose, Bat-eared Fox, Bushbaby, Egyptian Vulture, Ostrich, Greater Kudu, Diana Monkey, Giraffe, Cheetah, Wildebeest, Chimpanzee, Warthog, Zebra and Rhinoceros.

219 Grant's Zebra galloping

220 Valentina Tereshkova (first woman in space)

(Des P. Ndembo. Litho B.D.T.)

1993 (30 June). Wild Animals. T **219** and similar horiz designs. Multicoloured. P 14.

1589	100s. Type **219**	1·00	1·00
	a. Sheetlet. Nos. 1589/94..................	5·50	5·50
1590	100s. Grant's Zebra standing...............	1·00	1·00
1591	100s. Grant's Gazelle doe	1·00	1·00
1592	100s. Grant's Gazelle buck	1·00	1·00
1593	100s. Thomson's Gazelle	1·00	1·00
1594	100s. White-bearded Gnu with calf ...	1·00	1·00
1595	100s. Female Cheetah with cubs	1·00	1·00
	a. Sheetlet. Nos. 1595/1600..............	5·50	5·50
1596	100s. Young Cheetah drinking.............	1·00	1·00
1597	100s. Lioness carrying cub in mouth...	1·00	1·00
1598	100s. Pair of Hunting Dogs	1·00	1·00
1599	100s. Three Hunting Dogs	1·00	1·00
1600	100s. Four Hunting Dogs	1·00	1·00
1589/1600	Set of 12	11·00	11·00

MS1601 Two sheets, each 106×76 mm. (a) 500s. African Elephant. (b) 500s. Rhinoceros *Set of 2 sheets* .... 12·00 10·00

Nos. 1589/94 and 1595/1600 were printed together, *se-tenant*, in sheetlets of 6.

(Des J. Iskowitz. Litho Questa)

1993 (15 July). Famous 20th-century Women. T **220** and similar vert designs. Multicoloured. P 14.

1602	20s. Type **220**	75	65
	a. Sheetlet. Nos. 1602/9	17·00	12·50
1603	40s. Marie Curie (physicist)	2·75	1·50
1604	50s. Indira Gandhi (Prime Minister of India).	4·00	1·50
1605	70s. Wilma Rudolph (Olympic athlete)	1·00	1·50
1606	100s. Margaret Mead (anthropologist)	1·00	1·50
1607	150s. Golda Meir (Prime Minister of Israel).	4·00	2·00
1608	200s. Dr. Elizabeth Blackwell (first female medical doctor)	1·75	2·00
1609	400s. Margaret Thatcher (Prime Minister of Great Britain)	3·75	3·25
1602/9 *Set of 8*		17·00	12·50

MS1610 116×80 mm. 500s. Mother Teresa (humanitarian) .... 4·00 4·00

Nos. 1602/9 were printed together, *se-tenant*, in sheetlets of 8.

221 *Iolaus aphnaeoides*

222 Arthur Ashe (tennis)

(Des Jennifer Toombs. Litho Cartor)

1993 (15 July). Butterflies. T **221** and similar horiz designs. Multicoloured. P 13.

1611/54 100s. × 44 *Set of 44* .... 40·00 30·00

MS1655 Four sheets, each 69×58 mm. (a) 500s. *Cymothoe sangaris.* (b) 500s. *Precis octavia.* (c) 500s. *Charaxes violetta.* (d) 500s. *Papilio nobilis Set of 4 sheets* .... 17·00 17·00

Nos. 1611/54 were printed *se-tenant* in two sheetlets of 12 (Nos. 1611/34) and one of 20 (Nos. 1635/54). The species depicted are *Iolaus aphnaeoides, Charaxes eupale, Danaus formosa, Antanartia hippomene, Mylothris sagala, Charaxes anticlea, Salamis temoro, Nepheronia argia, Acraea pseudolycia, Hypolimnas antevorta, Colotis hildebrandti, Acraea bonasia, Eurema desjardinsi, Myrina silenus, Iolaus ismenias, Charaxes candiope, Precis artaxia, Danaus chrysippus, Axiocerses bambana, Precis orithya, Pinacopteryx eriphia, Iolaus coecolus, Precis hierta, Colotis regina, Euphaedra neophron, Mylothris poppea, Aphaneus flavescens, Eronia leda, Charaxes zoolina, Papilio bromius, Cyrestis camillus, Hypolycaena buxtoni, Charaxes achaemenes, Asterope rosa, Graphium antheus, Charaxes acuminatus, Kallima rumia, Leptosia alcesta, Pseudacraea boisduuali, Iolaus sidus, Salamis parhassus, Charaxes protoclea azota, Charaxes bohemani* and *Papilio ophidicephalus.*

(Des J. Iskowitz. Litho Questa)

1993 (15 July). Black Sporting Personalities. T **222** and similar multicoloured designs. P 14.

1656	20s. Type **222**	50	40
	a. Sheetlet. Nos. 1656/63.	5·00	5·25
1657	40s. Michael Jordan (basketball)	60	60
1658	50s. Daley Thompson (decathlon)	60	40
1659	70s. Jackie Robinson (baseball)	60	40
1660	100s. Kareem Abdul-Jabbar (basketball)	75	60
1661	150s. Florence Joyner (athletics)	75	80
1662	200s. Jesse Owens (athletics)	75	1·00
1663	400s. Jack Johnson (boxing)	1·25	1·75
1656/63 *Set of 8*		5·00	5·25

MS1664 72×101 mm. 500a. Muhammad Ali (boxing) (*horiz*) .... 2·50 3·25

Nos. 1656/63 were printed together, *se-tenant*, in sheetlets of 8.

223 Short-finned Mako

(Litho State Ptg Wks, Moscow)

1993 (27 July). Sharks. T **223** and similar multicoloured designs. P 12½×12.

1665	20s. Type **223**	15	15
1666	30s. Lantern Shark	20	20
1667	50s. Tiger Shark	20	25
1668	70s. African Angelshark	30	35
1669	100s. Longnose Sawshark (*Pristiophorus cirratus*)	35	45
1670	150s. White-tipped Reef Shark	50	65
1671	200s. Scalloped Hammerhead	55	75
1665/71 *Set of 7*		2·00	2·50

MS1672 91×91 mm. 350s. Six-gilled Shark (*vert*) P 12×12½ .... 1·75 2·00

224 Alpha Jet

225 Gordon Setter

(Litho State Ptg Wks, Moscow)

1993 (30 Aug). Military Aircraft. T **224** and similar multicoloured designs. P 12½×12.

1673	20s. Type **224**	20	20
1674	30s. Northrop F-5E	20	25
1675	50s. Dassault Mirage 3NG	25	30
1676	70s. MB 339C	35	45
1677	100s. MiG-31	35	50
1678	150s. C-101 Aviojet	40	70
1679	200s. General Dynamics F-16 Fighting Falcon.	45	80
1673/9 *Set of 7*		2·00	3·00

MS1680 91×91 mm. 500a. EAP fighter (*vert*). P 12×12½ .... 1·40 2·00

(Litho State Ptg Wks, Moscow)

1993 (27 Sept). Dogs. T **225** and similar vert designs. Multicoloured. P 12×12½.

1681	20s. Type **225**	20	20
1682	30s. Zwergschnauzer	25	25
1683	50s. Labrador Retriever	30	30
1684	70s. Wire Fox Terrier	35	45
1685	100s. English Springer Spaniel	40	50
1686	150s. Newfoundlander	60	70
1687	200s. Moscow Toy Terrier	70	80
1681/7 *Set of 7*		2·50	3·00

MS1688 91×91 mm. 350s. Dobermann Pinscher .... 1·75 2·00

226 Rhinoceros, Ngorongoro Crater

227 *Ansellia africana*

(Litho State Ptg Wks, Moscow)

1993 (29 Oct). National Parks. T **226** and similar multicoloured designs. P 12½×12.

1689	20s. Type **226**	20	20
1690	50s. Buffalo, Ngurdoto Crater	20	20
1691	70s. Leopard, Kilimanjaro	25	30
1692	100s. Baboon, Gombe	25	35
1693	150s. Lion, Selous	35	45
1694	200s. Giraffe, Mikumi	65	65
1695	250s. Zebra, Serengeti	65	70
1689/95 *Set of 7*		2·25	2·50

MS1696 91×91 mm. 500s. Elephant, Lake Manyara (*vert*). P 12×12½ .... 1·75 2·00

(Litho Cartor)

1993 (8 Nov). Flowers. T **227** and similar vert designs. Multicoloured. P 13½.

1697	20s. Type **227**	40	20
1698	30s. *Saintpaulia ionantha*	45	25

1699	40s. *Stapelia semota lutes*	50	30
1700	50s. *Impatiens walleriana*	50	30
1701	60s. *Senecio petraeus*	55	35
1702	70s. *Kalanchoe velutina*	65	40
1703	100s. *Kaempferia brachystemon*	85	60
1704	150s. *Nymphaea colorata*	1·25	1·25
1705	200s. *Thunbergia battiscombei*	1·40	1·40
1706	250s. *Crossandra nilotica*	1·40	1·50
1707	300s. *Spathodea campanulata*	1·60	1·75
1708	350s. *Ruttya fruticosa*	1·60	1·75
1697/1708 *Set of 12*		10·00	9·00

MS1709 Two sheets, each 100×70 mm. (a) 500s. *Streptocarpus saxorum.* (b) 500s. *Glorioso verschurii.* P 13 *Set of 2 sheets* .... 5·25 7·00

228 Norman-Arab

229 Berts Warrior

(Litho State Ptg Wks, Moscow)

1993 (30 Nov). Horses. T **228** and similar multicoloured designs. P 12½×12.

1710	20s. Type **228**	40	30
1711	40s. Nonius	50	40
1712	50s. Boulonnais	50	40
1713	70s. Arab	60	60
1714	100a. Anglo-Arab	70	70
1715	150s. Tarpon	90	1·00
1716	200s. Thoroughbred	1·10	1·40
1710/16 *Set of 7*		4·25	4·50

MS1717 91×91 mm. 400s. Anglo-Norman (*vert*). P 12×12½ .... 1·75 2·00

No. 1716 is inscribed "THOROUGBLED" in error.

(Litho State Ptg Wks, Moscow)

1993 (30 Dec). Traditional African Costumes. T **229** and similar vert designs. Multicoloured. P 12×12½.

1718	20s. Type **229**	10	10
1719	40s. Galla	15	15
1720	50s. Guinean	15	15
1721	70s. Goloff	20	25
1722	100s. Peul	30	30
1723	150s. Abyssinian	45	45
1724	200s. Pahuin	55	55
1718/24 *Set of 7*		1·75	1·75

MS1725 91×91 mm. 350s. Zulu.................... 1·10 1·25

229a Boy playing accordian

230 Downhill Skiing

(Litho Questa)

1994 (10 Feb). Hummel Figurines. T **229a** and similar vert designs Multicoloured. P 14.

1726	20s. Type **229a**	30	25
1727	40s. Girl with guitar and boy with lute	35	30
1728	50s. Boy playing euphonium	35	30
1729	70s. Boy playing mouth organ	40	35
1730	100s. Boy with trumpet on fence	50	45
1731	150s. Boy playing recorder	80	80
1732	200s. Boy with trumpet and bird on feet	90	90
1733	300s. Girl playing banjo	1·25	1·40
1734	350s. Boy carrying double bass on back	1·40	1·60
1735	400s. Girls with banjo and song sheet	1·40	1·60
1726/35 *Set of 10*		7·00	7·00

MS1736 Two sheets, each 70×101 mm. (a) 500s. Carol singers. (b) 500s. Angels with trumpets in bell tower *Set of 2 sheets* .... 8·00 8·50

(Litho State Ptg Wks, Moscow)

1994 (12 Feb). Winter Olympic Games, Lillehammer, Norway. T **230** and similar vert designs. Multicoloured. P 12×12½.

1737	40s. Type **230**	20	20
1738	50s. Ice hockey	20	20
1739	70s. Speed skating	30	30
1740	100s. Bobsleighing	35	35
1741	120s. Figure skating	40	40
1742	170s. Free style skiing	55	55
1743	250s. Biathlon	75	75
1737/43 *Set of 7*		2·50	2·50

MS1744 93×91 mm. 500a. Cross-country skiing............ 1·50 2·00

231 Ruud Gullit (Netherlands)

231a Blue-barred Orange Parrotfish and Red Cap White Pearl-scale Goldfish

(Litho Questa)

1994 (14 Feb). World Cup Football Championship, U.S.A. (1st issue). T **231** and similar vert designs. Multicoloured. P 14.

1745	20s. Type **231**	50	30
1746	30s. Kevin Sheedy (Ireland)	50	30
1747	50s. Giuseppe Giannini (Italy)	60	40
1748	70s. Julio Cesar (Brazil)	65	45
1749	250s. John Barnes (England) and Grun (Belgium)	1·50	1·50
1750	300s. Chendo (Spain)	1·50	1·50
1751	350s. Frank Rijkaard (Netherlands)	1·60	2·00
1752	400s. Lothar Matthaeus (Germany)	1·60	2·00
1745/52 *Set of 8*		7·50	7·75

MS1753 Two sheets. (a) 76×106 mm. 500s. Nicola Berti (Italy). (b) 106×76 mm. 500s. Des Walker (England) *Set of 2 sheets* .... 7·50 7·50

See also Nos. 1838/46 and 1892/9.

A further set, inscribed "World Cup - USA 1994", comprising 40s., 120s., 170s., and 250s. with values in the lower right corner is known, dated used examples being cancelled in 1998. The stamps, three of which include spelling mistakes in the captions, were presumably witheld at the time but released later to meet shortages.

(Des W. Hanson. Litho Questa)

1994 (18 Feb). Hong Kong '94 International Stamp Exhibition. T **231a** and similar horiz design. Multicoloured. P 14.

1754	350s. Type **231a**	1·40	1·40
	a. Horiz pair. Nos. 1754/5	2·75	2·75
1755	350s. Regal Angelfish and Red Cap White Pearl-scale Goldfish at left	1·40	1·40

Nos. 1754/5 were printed together, *se-tenant*, in horizontal pairs throughout the sheet with the centre part of each pair forming a composite design.

232 Mickey Mouse, Goofy, Pluto and Donald Duck boarding Airliner

(Des Rosemary DeFiglio. Litho Questa)

1994 (13 Mar). 65th Anniv of Mickey Mouse. T **232** and similar multicoloured designs showing Walt Disney cartoon characters on World Tour. P 14×13½ (horiz) or 13½×14 (vert).

1756	10s. Type **232**	55	25
1757	20s. Daisy Duck and Minnie Mouse dancing, Tonga	65	30
1758	30s. Mickey and Goofy playing bowls, Australia	70	35
1759	40s. Mickey, Donald and Goofy building igloo, Arctic Circle	75	40
1760	50s. Pluto, Goofy, Mickey and Donald on guard at Buckingham Palace, London	75	40

1761	60s. Pluto at Esna Bazaar, Egypt	80	55
1762	70s. Donald being chased by Zsambox herders, Hungary (vert)	80	55
1763	100s. Donald and Daisy on Grand Canal, Venice (vert)	1·25	70
1764	150s. Goofy dancing, Bali (vert)	1·75	1·50
1765	200s. Donald with monks, Thailand (vert)	2·00	1·75
1766	300s. Goofy water skiing at Taj Mahal, India (vert)	2·25	2·50
1767	400s. Mickey, Minnie, Goofy and Donald being carried by Sherpas, Nepal	2·50	2·75
1756/67 Set of 12		13·00	11·00

MS1768 Three sheets. (a) 127×102 mm. 500s. Mickey at Livingstone's memorial, Ujiji (vert). (b) 127×102 mm. 500s. Mickey at Kigoma railway station, Tanzania (vert). (c) 102×127 mm. 500a. Mickey climbing Mt Kilimanjaro (vert) Set of 3 sheets ... 11·00 12·00

233 Bonelli's Eagle ("African Hawk Eagle")　**234** Henry Ford and Model "T"

(Des P. Ndembo. Litho Questa)

1994 (17 Apr). Birds. T **233** and similar multicoloured designs. P 14.

1769	20s. Type 233	1·25	95
	a. Sheetlet. Nos. 1769/74	8·50	6·25
1770	30s. Whale-headed Stork ("Shoe-bill Stork")	1·25	95
1771	50s. Brown Harrier Eagle	1·50	1·10
1772	70s. Black-casqued Hornbill	1·75	1·25
1773	100s. Crowned Cranes	1·75	1·25
1774	150s. Greater Flamingos	2·00	1·25
1775	200s. Pair of Eastern White Pelicans (horiz)	1·75	1·10
	a. Sheetlet. Nos. 1775/80	9·50	6·50
1776	250s. African Jacana and Black Crake (horiz)	1·75	1·10
1777	300s. Pair of Ostriches (horiz)	1·75	1·25
1778	350s. Pair of Helmet Guineafowl (horiz)	1·75	1·25
1779	400s. Malachite Kingfisher (horiz)	1·75	1·25
1780	500s. Pair of Saddle-bill Storks (horiz)	1·75	1·40
1769/80 Set of 12		18·00	12·50

Nos. 1769/74 and 1775/80 were printed together, se-tenant, in sheetlets of 6.

(Litho Questa)

1994 (25 Apr). Centenaries of Henry Ford's First Petrol Engine (Nos. 1781, 1783, **MS**1785a) and Karl Benz's First Four-wheeled Car (others). T **234** and similar horiz designs. Multicoloured. P 14.

1781	200s. Type 234	1·75	1·60
1782	200s. Benz, 1893, and "500 SEL", 1993	1·75	1·60
1783	400s. Ford, 1893, Mustang Cobra and emblem	2·75	2·50
1784	400s. Karl Benz and emblem	2·75	2·50
1781/4 Set of 4		8·00	7·50

MS1785 Two sheets, each 106×71 mm. (a) 500s. Henry Ford outside first factory. (b) 500s. Benz emblem and bonnet of 1937 "540k" Set of 2 sheets . 7·50 8·50

235 Sopwith Pup Biplane　**236** Jahazi (sailing canoe)

(Litho Questa)

1994 (25 Apr). Aviation Anniversaries. T **235** and similar multicoloured designs. P 14.

1786	200s. Type 235	2·50	1·75
1787	200s. Inflating hot-air balloons	2·50	1·75
1788	400s. Hawker Siddeley Harrier and design drawing	3·50	3·00

1789	400s. Jean-Pierre Blanchard and his balloon	3·50	3·00
1786/9 Set of 4		11·00	8·50

MS1790 Two sheets, each 105×71 mm. (a) 500s. Supermarine Spitfire. (b) 500a. Hot-air balloons in flight (vert) Set of 2 sheets ... 10·00 9·00

Anniversaries:—Nos. 1786, 1788, **MS**1790a, 75th anniv of Royal Air Force; Nos. 1787,1789, **MS**1790b, Bicentenary of first balloon flight in the U.S.A.

(Litho State Ptg Wks, Moscow)

1994 (20 May). Sailing Ships. T **236** and similar vert designs. Multicoloured. P 12×12½.

1791	40s. Type 236	15	15
1792	50s. Caravel	15	15
1793	70s. Pirate carrack	25	25
1794	100s. Baltic galeass	25	30
1795	170s. Frigate (inscr "Battle-ship")	35	55
1796	200s. British ship of the line (inscr "Frigate")	40	65
1797	250s. Brig	40	75
1791/7 Set of 7		1·75	2·50

MS1798 91×91 mm. 500s. Clipper ... 1·25 2·00

237 Diatryma　**238** Koala Bear with Cub

(Litho State Ptg Wks, Moscow)

1994 (30 June). Prehistoric Animals. T **237** and similar vert designs. Multicoloured. P 12×12½.

1799	40s. Type 237	60	30
1800	50s. Tyrannosaurus rex	60	30
1801	100s. Uintatherium	80	50
1802	120s. Stiracosaurus	90	80
1803	170s. Diplodocus	1·25	1·50
1804	250s. Archaeopteryx	1·40	1·60
1805	300s. Sordes	1·60	1·90
1799/1805 Set of 7		6·00	6·00

MS1806 91×91 mm. 500s. Dimetrodon ... 1·90 2·25

No. 1799 is inscribed "DIATRUMA" in error.

(Litho State Ptg Wks, Moscow)

1994 (29 July). Endangered Species. T **238** and similar multicolourd designs. P 12½×12.

1807	40s. Type 238	25	25
1808	70s. Giant Panda with cub	35	40
1809	100s. Eagles	45	55
1810	120s. African Elephant with calf	60	70
1811	250s. Caribbean Monk Seals	75	90
1812	400s. Dolphins	80	1·00
1813	500s. Whales	1·25	1·50
1807/13 Set of 7		4·00	4·75

MS1814 90×90 mm. 500s. Tiger (vert). P 12×12½ ... 2·75 2·75

No. 1808 shows the incorrect scientific species name.

239 Pres. Salmin Amour of Zanzibar　**240** Lorry at Customs Post

(Litho State Ptg Wks, Moscow)

1994 (1 Aug). 30th Anniv of Zanzibar Revolution. T **239** and similar multicoloured designs. P 12½×12 (120s.) or 12×12½ (others).

1815	40s. Type 239	40	10
1816	70s. Amani Karume (first President of Zanzibar)	60	20
1817	120s. Harvesting cloves (horiz)	1·00	1·00
1818	250s. Carved door	1·75	2·50
1815/18 Set of 4		3·25	3·75

MS1819 91×91 mm. 500s. Hands clasped over map ... 2·00 2·50

(Litho Cartor)

1994 (23 Aug). 81st/82nd Customs Co-Operation Council Meeting, Arusha. T **240** and similar multicoloured designs. P 14×13½.

1820	20s. Type **240**	1·00	30
1821	50s. Container ship	1·50	40
1822	100s. Passengers and airliner	2·25	1·25
1823	150s. Customs and U.P.U. logos	2·25	2·50
1820/3	*Set of 4*	6·25	4·00
MS1824	99×99 mm. 500s. Customs arms (30×40 mm). P 12½	3·75	3·50

241 Tanzanian Family

242 *Trombidium* sp

(Litho State Ptg Wks, Moscow)

1994 (30 Aug). International Year of the Family. T **241** and similar multicoloured designs. P 12½×12 (170s.) or 12×12½ (others).

1825	40s. Type **241**	35	15
1826	120s. Father playing with children	60	50
1827	170s. Family clinic (*horiz*)	75	1·00
1828	250s. Woman harvesting tobacco	90	1·50
1825/8	*Set of 4*	2·40	2·75
MS1829	91×91 mm. 300s. Emblem	1·60	2·00

(Litho State Ptg Wks, Moscow)

1994 (31 Aug). Arachnids. T **242** and similar multicoloured designs. P 12½×12 (horiz) or 12×12½ (vert).

1830	40s. Type **242**	20	20
1831	50s. *Eurypelma* sp	20	20
1832	100s. *Salticus* sp	30	30
1833	120s. *Micrommata rosea* (*vert*)	35	35
1834	170s. *Araneus* sp (*vert*)	50	50
1835	250s. *Micrathena* sp (*vert*)	70	70
1836	300s. *Araneus diadematus* (*vert*)	80	80
1830/6	*Set of 7*	2·75	2·75
MS1837	92×92 mm. 500a. Claw of *Hadogenes* sp (*vert*)	1·75	2·00

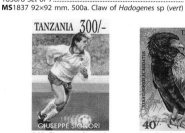
243 Giuseppe Signori (Italy)

244 Bateleur

1994 (26 Sept). World Cup Football Championship, USA (2nd issue). T **243** and similar vert designs. Multicoloured. Litho. P 14.

1838	300s. Type **243**	1·00	1·00
	a. Sheetlet. Nos. 1838/45	7·00	7·00
1839	300s. Ruud Gullit (Netherlands)	1·00	1·00
1840	300s. Roberto Mancini (Italy)	1·00	1·00
1841	300s. Marco van Basten (Netherlands)	1·00	1·00
1842	300s. Dennis Bergkamp (Netherlands)	1·00	1·00
1843	300s. Oscar Ruggeri (Argentina)	1·00	1·00
1844	300s. Frank Rijkaard (Netherlands)	1·00	1·00
1845	300s. Peter Schmeichel (Denmark)	1·00	1·00
1838/45	*Set of 8*	7·00	7·00
MS1846	100×70 mm. 1000s. World Cup trophy	4·00	4·50

Nos. 1838/45 were printed together, *se-tenant*, in sheetlets of 8.

(Litho State Ptg Wks, Moscow)

1994 (30 Sept). Birds of Prey. T **244** and similar multicoloured designs. P 12½×12 (170, 400s.) or 12×12½ (others).

1847	40s. Type **244**	65	40
1848	50s. Ornate Hawk Eagle	65	40
1849	100s. Osprey	85	60
1850	120s. Andean Condor	85	65
1851	170s. African Fish Eagle (*horiz*)	1·00	90
1852	250s. King Vulture	1·10	1·25
1853	400s. Peregrine Falcon (*horiz*)	1·50	1·75
1847/53	*Set of 7*	6·00	5·50
MS1854	90×90 mm. 500s. African White backed Vulture	2·25	2·50

245 Afghan Hound

246 Players and Flags from Group B

(Des G. Bibby. Litho B.D.T.)

1994 (30 Sept). Dogs of the World. T **245** and similar vert designs. Multicoloured. P 14.

1855/63	120s. × 9 (Type **245**; Basenji; Siberian Husky; Irish Setter; Norwegian Elkhound; Bracco Italiano; Australian Cattle Dog; German Short-haired Pointer; Rhodesian Ridgeback)		
	a. Sheetlet. Nos. 1855/63	5·00	5·50
1864/72	120s. × 9 (Alsatian; Japanese Chin; Shetland Sheepdog; Italian Spinone; Great Dane; English Setter; Welsh Corgi; St. Bernard; Irish Wolfhound)		
	a. Sheetlet. Nos. 1864/72	5·00	5·50
1873/81	120s. × 9 (Doberman Pinscher; Chihuahua; Bloodhound; Keeshond; Tibetan Spaniel; Japanese Akita; Tervueren; Chow; Pharaoh Hound)		
	a. Sheetlet. Nos. 1873/81	5·00	5·50
1882/90	120s. × 9 (Alaskan Malamute; Scottish Cairn Terrier; American Fox hound; British Bulldog; Boston Terrier; Borzoi Shar Pei; Saluki; Bernese Mountain Dog)		
	a. Sheetlet. Nos. 1882/90	5·00	5·50
1855/90	*Set of 36*	16·00	17·00
MS1891	Two sheets, each 76×106 mm. 1000s. As No. 1856. (b) 1000s. As No. 1868 *Set of 2 sheets*	11·00	11·00

Nos. 1855/63, 1864/72, 1873/81 and 1882/90 were printed together, *se-tenant*, in sheetlets of 9.

(Litho State Ptg Wks, Moscow)

1994 (30 Sept). World Cup Football Championship, U.S.A. (3rd issue). T **246** and similar horiz designs. Multicoloured. P 12½×12.

1892	40s. Type **246**	45	45
	a. Sheetlet. Nos. 1892/6 and 1898	4·00	4·00
1893	50s. Players and flags from Group C	50	50
1894	70s. Players and flags from Group D	60	60
1895	100s. Players and flags from Group A	65	65
1896	170s. Players and flags from Group A	90	90
1897	200s. Players and World Cup	1·10	1·10
1898	250s. Players and flags from Group F	1·40	1·40
1892/8	*Set of 7*	5·00	5·00
MS1899	92×92 mm. 500s. Player heading ball	3·25	4·00

Nos. 1892/9 have been seen with cancelled-to-order postmarks of 17 June 1994.

In addition to the ordinary sheets Nos. 1892/6 and 1898 were also printed together, *se-tenant*, in sheetlets of 6 with the two vertical rows separated by a gutter containing stamp-sized labels forming a composite design.

247 *Rangaeris amaniensis*

248 *Dicentra spectabilis*

(Des Marilyn Abramowitz. Litho Questa)

1994 (7 Oct). Orchids. T **247** and similar multicoloured designs. P 14.

1900	200s. Type **247**	1·25	90
	a. Sheetlet. Nos. 1900/7	9·00	6·50
1901	200s. *Eulophia macowanii*	1·25	90
1902	200s. *Cytorchis arcuata*	1·25	90
1903	200s. *Centrostigma occultans*	1·25	90
1904	200s. *Cirrhopetalum umbellatum*	1·25	90
1905	200s. *Ansellia gigantea*	1·25	90
1906	200s. *Angraecum ramosum*	1·25	90

1907	200s. *Disa englerana*		1·25	90
1908	200s. *Nervilia stolziana*		1·25	90
	a. Sheetlet. Nos. 1908/15		9·00	6·50
1909	200s. *Satyrium orbiculare*		1·25	90
1910	200s. *Schizochilus sulphureus*		1·25	90
1911	200s. *Disa stolzii*		1·25	90
1912	200s. *Platycoryne mediocris*		1·25	90
1913	200s. *Satyrium breve*		1·25	90
1914	200s. *Eulophia nuttii*		1·25	90
1915	200s. *Disa ornithantha*		1·25	90
1900/15	Set of 16		18·00	13·00

MS1916 Two sheets, each 106×76 mm. (a) 1000s. *Phaius tankervilliae* (*horiz*). (b) 1000s. *Eulophia thomsonii* (*horiz*) Set of 2 sheets ... 8·00 8·50

Nos. 1900/7 and 1908/15 were printed together, *se-tenant*, in sheetlets of 8.

(Litho State Ptg Wks. Moscow)

1994 (31 Oct). Flowers. T **248** and similar vert designs. Multicoloured. P 12×12½.

1917	40s. Type **248**	25	30
1918	100s. *Thunbergia alata*	35	45
1919	120s. *Cyrtanthus minimiflorus*	35	50
1920	170s. *Nepenthes hybrida*	40	70
1921	250s. *Allamanda cathartica*	45	80
1922	300s. *Encyclia pentotis*	45	85
1923	400s. *Protea lacticolor*	50	90
1917/23	Set of 7	2·50	4·00

MS1924 91×92 mm. 500s. *Tradescantia* ... 1·25 1·75

249 *Limenilis sydyi*

(Des Mary Walters. Litho Questa)

1994 (19 Nov). Butterflies. T **249** and similar horiz designs. Multicoloured. P 14.

1925	120s. Type **249**	70	70
	a. Sheetlet. Nos. 1925/33	5·50	5·50
1926	120s. *Agraulis vanillae*	70	70
1927	120s. *Donnas chrysippus*	70	70
1928	120s. *Eurylides marcellus*	70	70
1929	120s. *Artopoetes pryeri*	70	70
1930	120s. *Heliconius charitonius*	70	70
1931	120s. *Limenitis weidemeyerii*	70	70
1932	120s. *Phoebis sennae*	70	70
1933	120s. *Timelaea albescens*	70	70
1934	120s. *Papilio glaucus*	70	70
	a. Sheetlet. Nos. 1934/42	5·50	5·50
1935	120s. *Danaus plexippus*	70	70
1936	120s. *Papilio troilus*	70	70
1937	120s. *Hypolimnas antevorta*	70	70
1938	120s. *Cirrochroa imperatrix*	70	70
1939	120s. *Vanessa atalanta*	70	70
1940	120s. *Limenitis archippus*	70	70
1941	120s. *Hypolimnas pandarus*	70	70
1942	120s. *Anthocharis belia*	70	70
1925/42	Set of 18	11·00	11·00

MS1943 Two sheets, each 101×70 mm. (a) 1000s. *Papilio polyxenes*. (b) 1000s. *Vanessa cardui* Set of 2 sheets ... 8·50 9·00

Nos. 1925/33 and 1934/42 were printed together, *se-tenant*, in sheetlets of 9.

250 Donald Duck and Goofy with Safari Equipment

(Litho Questa)

1994 (26 Nov). Mickey Mouse Safari Club. T **250** and similar multicoloured designs showing Walt Disney cartoon characters on safari. P 14×13½.

1944	70s. Type **250**	55	55
1945	70s. Donald and Mickey Mouse with leopard cubs	55	55

1946	100s. Donald photographing antelope	65	65
1947	100s. Donald between elephant's legs	65	65
1948	120s. Mickey with monkeys	70	70
1949	120s. Donald with hippopotamuses	70	70
1950	150s. Goofy carrying equipment	80	80
1951	150s. Mickey, Donald and Goofy sheltering under elephant's ears	80	80
1952	200s. Goofy with zebras	90	90
1953	200s. Donald, Goofy and Mickey with lion	90	90
1954	250s. Donald filming monkeys	1·00	1·00
1955	250s. Giraffe licking Mickey	1·00	1·00
1944/55	Set of 12	8·25	8·25

MS1956 Three sheets, each 101×121 mm. (a) 1000s. Goofy in tree with camera (*vert*). (b) 1000s. Donald and Goofy with camera (*vert*). (c) 1000s. Donald and Mickey with camera (*vert*). P 13½×14 Set of 3 sheets ... 11·00 12·00

251 Plan indicating Moon Landing Point

(Des G. Vasarhelyi. Litho Questa)

1994 (30 Nov). 25th Anniv of First Moon Landing. T **251** and similar horiz designs. Multicoloured. P 14.

1957	150s. Type **251**	80	80
	a. Sheetlet. Nos. 1957/65	6·50	6·50
1958	150s. Photograph showing Sea of Tranquility	80	80
1959	150s. Lunar surface	80	80
1960	150s. Lift-off	80	80
1961	150s. Jettisoning first stage rocket	80	80
1962	150s. Jettisoning second stage rocket	80	80
1963	150s. Lunar module *Eagle* leaving command module	80	80
1964	150s. *Eagle* descending towards lunar surface	80	80
1965	150s. Armstrong and Aldrin (astronauts) inside *Eagle*	80	80
1966	150s. "Apollo 11" crew in space suits	80	80
	a. Sheetlet. Nos. 1966/74	6·50	6·50
1967	150s. *Eagle* on lunar surface	80	80
1968	150s. Armstrong descending to lunar surface	80	80
1969	150s. Astronaut *Eagle* and experiment	80	80
1970	150s. Astronaut setting-up equipment	80	80
1971	150s. Reflection in astronaut's visor	80	80
1972	150s. Astronaut and USA flag	80	80
1973	150s. Astronaut carrying equipment	80	80
1974	150s. *Eagle* blasting off from Moon	80	80
1975	150s. Command module	80	80
	a. Sheetlet. Nos. 1975/83	6·50	6·50
1976	150s. *Eagle* leaving Moon	80	80
1977	150s. Capsule leaving Moon orbit	80	80
1978	150s. Capsule heading for Earth	80	80
1979	150s. Capsule re-entering Earth's atmosphere	80	80
1980	150s. Capsule in sea	80	80
1981	150s. Recovery crew opening hatch	80	80
1982	150s. Transferring astronauts by helicopter	80	80
1983	150s. Armstrong, Collins and Aldrin (astronaut) after recovery	80	80
1957/83	Set of 27	19·00	19·00

Nos. 1957/65, 1966/74 and 1975/83 were printed together, *se-tenant*, in sheetlets of 9.

252 *Astacus leptodactytus*

(Litho State Ptg Wks, Moscow)

1994 (30 Nov). Crabs. T **252** and similar multicoloured designs. P 12½×12 (horiz) or 12×12½ (vert).

1984	40s. Type **252**	20	30
1985	100s. *Eriocheir sinensis* (*vert*)	35	50
1986	120s. *Caneer opillo* (*vert*)	35	55
1987	170s. *Cardisoma quanhumi*	50	70
1988	250s. *Birgus latro* (*vert*)	65	85
1989	300s. *Menippe mercenaria*	65	90
1990	400s. *Dromia vulgaris* (*vert*)	75	95
1984/90	Set of 7	3·00	4·25

MS1991 92×92 mm. 500s. Coral and crab's claw ... 1·60 2·00

252a Kristin Otto (Germany) (50 metres freestyle swimming), 1988

252b Troops leaving Landing Craft

(Des Kerri Schif. Litho Questa)

1994 (12 Dec). Centenary of International Olympic Committee. Gold Medal Winners. T **252a** and similar vert designs. Multicoloured. P 14.

1992		350s. Type **252a**	1·00	1·00
1993		500s. Carl Lewis (USA) (various track and field events), 1984 and 1988	1·40	1·40
MS1994 74×104 mm. 1000s. Oksana Baiul (Ukraine) (figure skating), 1994			3·50	3·50

(Des J. Batchelor. Litho Questa)

1994 (12 Dec). 50th Anniv of D-Day (1st issue). T **252b** and similar horiz designs. Multicoloured. P 14.

1995		350s. Type **252b**	1·50	1·50
1996		600s. Amphibious tank and troops, Omaha Beach	2·00	2·00
MS1997 104×74 mm. 1000s. Loading landing ship in England			3·50	4·00

253 Supermarine Spitfire over Beaches

254 Deinonychus

(Des R. Vigura. Litho Questa)

1994 (12 Dec). 50th Anniv of D-Day (2nd issue). T **253** and similar horiz designs. Multicoloured. P 14.

1998		200s. Type **253**	85	85
	a.	Sheetlet. Nos. 1998/2003	4·50	4·50
1999		200s. D.U.K.W.s landing on Gold Beach	85	85
2000		200s. Canadian troops landing on Juno Beach	85	85
2001		200s. Canadian cyclists disembarking, Juno Beach	85	85
2002		200s. Amphibious Sherman tank on beach	85	85
2003		200s. German gun implacement	85	85
2004		200s. General Montgomery and British troops on beach	85	85
	a.	Sheetlet. Nos. 2004/9	4·50	4·50
2005		200s. British engineers with AVRE Churchill tank, Gold Beach	85	85
2006		200s. U.S.S. *Thompson* (destroyer) being refuelled	85	85
2007		200s. H.M.S. *Warspite* (battleship)	85	85
2008		200s. Royal Marines on Juno Beach	85	85
2009		200s. Sherman Mark 1 flail tank leaving landing craft	85	85
2010		200s. General Eisenhower and US troops on Omaha Beach	85	85
	a.	Sheetlet. Nos. 2010/15	4·50	4·50
2011		200s. North American P-51 Mustang escorting ships	85	85
2012		200s. U.S. coastguard cutter alongside landing craft	85	85
2013		200s. U.S. troops in landing craft	85	85
2014		200s. U.S. troops landing on Omaha Beach	85	85
2015		200s. U.S. troops on Omaha Beach	85	85
1998/2015 *Set of 18*			13·50	13·50
MS2016 Two sheets, each 99×70 mm. (a) 1000s. U.S. marines amongst beach obstacles. (b) 1000s. U.S. troops landing on Utah Beach *Set of 2 sheets*			8·00	8·50

Nos. 1998/2003, 2004/9 and 2010/15 were each printed together, *se-tenant*, in sheetlets of 6.

No. 2004 is inscribed "COMMANDER-IN-CHEIF" and No. 2010 "OPERATION OVERLOAD", both in error.

(Des G. Bibby. Litho Questa)

1994 (26 Dec). Prehistoric Animals. T **254** and similar designs. P 14.

2017/48 120s.×32 multicoloured		22·00	23·00
MS2049 80×110 mm. 1000s. multicoloured		4·50	5·00

Designs: Vert—No. 2018, Styracosaurus; No. 2019, Anatosaurus; No. 2020, Plateosaurus; No. 2021, Iguanodon; No. 2022, Oviraptor; No. 2023, Dimorphodona; No. 2024, Ornithomimus; No. 2025, Lambeosaurus; No. 2026, Megalosaurus; No. 2027, Cetiosaurus; No. 2028, Hypsilophodon; No. 2029, Rhamphorynchus; No. 2030, Scelidosaurus; No. 2031, Antrodemus; No. 2032, Dimetrodon; No. **MS**2049, Brachiosaurus. Horiz—No. 2033, Brontosaurus; No. 2034, Albertosaurus; No. 2035, Parasaurolophus; No. 2036, Pteranodons; No. 2037, Stegosaurus; No. 2038, Tyrannosaurus rex; No. 2039, Triceratops; No. 2040, Ornitholestea; No. 2041, Camarasaurus; No. 2042, Ankylosaurus; No. 2043, Trachodon; No. 2044, Allosaurus; No. 2045, Corythosaurus; No. 2046, Struthiomimus; No. 2047, Camptosaurus; No. 2048, Heterodontosaurus.

Nos. 2017/32 and 2033/48 were printed together, *se-tenant*, in sheetlets of 16, Nos. 2033/48 forming a composite design.

255 "Hubble" Space Telescope

(Litho State Ptg Wks, Moscow)

1994 (30 Dec). Space Research. T **255** and similar horiz designs. Multicoloured. P 12½×12.

2050		40s. Type **255**	20	30
2051		100s. "Mariner"	35	50
2052		120s. "Voyager 2"	40	55
2053		170s. "Work Package-03"	50	70
2054		250s. Orbiting solar observer	70	85
2055		300s. "Magellan"	70	90
2056		400s. "Galilei"	80	95
2050/6 *Set of 7*			3·25	4·25
MS2057 91×91 mm. 500s. "Fobos"			1·90	2·25

It is understood that the following issues were freely available for postal purposes from Tanzanian post offices. Further issues, for which evidence of normal postal use cannot be found, could be obtained from the Philatelic Bureau in Dar-es-Salaam. Such issues will be found in the Appendix.

70/-

X

(256)

1995 (Feb). No. 906 surch with T **256**.

2058		70s. on 13s. Teacher with blackboard	3·00	1·00
	a.	Surch inverted		

The date quoted for No. 2058 is that of the earliest known postmark.

257 Coconuts

258 Farmer and Maize Crop

(Des P. Ndembo. Litho Questa)

1995 (30 June). Fruit. T **257** and similar horiz designs. Multicoloured. W **119**. P 14.

2059		70s. Type **257**	75	25
2060		100s. Pineapple	95	50
2061		150s. Pawpaw	1·40	1·50
2062		200s. Tomatoes	1·75	2·00
2059/62 *Set of 4*			4·25	3·75
MS2063 91×91 mm. 500s. Type **257**			3·25	3·50

(Des P. Ndembo. Litho Questa)

1995 (24 Oct). 50th Anniv of United Nations and Food and Agriculture Organization. T **258** and similar multicoloured designs (except No. **MS** 2068). W **119**. P 14.

2064	70s. Type **258**	50	25
2065	100s. Ploughing with ox team (horiz)	65	40
2066	150s. Women in spinning mill (horiz)	90	1·25
2067	200s. Child drawing	1·25	1·60
2064/7 Set of 4		3·00	3·25
MS2068 101×97 mm. 500s. U.N. 50th Anniversary logo (horiz) (black and pale blue)		3·00	3·75

100/=

X
(259)

260 Presidents Mwinyi (Tanzania), Moi (Kenya) and Museveni (Uganda)

1995 (Nov?). No. 810 surch with T **259**.

2069	100s. on 40s. Lesser Flamingo	3·00	1·00
	a. Surch inverted		

(Des P. Ndembo. Litho Questa)

1995 (10 Nov). 2nd Anniversary of East African Treaty. T **260** and similar multicoloured designs. P 14.

2070	100s. Type **260**	60	25
2071	150s. Map of East Africa and national flags (vert)	2·75	1·50
2072	180s. Cotton boll (vert)	1·50	1·75
2073	200s. Fishermen on Lake Victoria	1·75	2·00
2070/3 Set of 4		6·00	5·00
MS2074 100×102 mm. 500s. Type **260**		3·50	4·00

261 Plumeria rubra acutifolia

262 Pineapple

1996 (30 July)–**2002**. Flowers. T **261** and similar vert designs. Multicoloured. Litho. P 14½×15.

(a) Without imprint date.

2075	100s. Type **261**	35	15
2076	140s. Lilaceae	50	25
2077	180s. Alamanda	60	25
2078	200s. Lilaceae (different)	70	30
2079	210s. Zinnia	70	40
2080	260s. Malvaviscus penduliflorus	85	45
2081	300s. Canna	1·00	50
2082	380s. Nerium oleander carneum	1·25	1·00
2083	400s. Hibiscus rosa sinensis	1·75	1·75
2084	600s. Catharanthus roseus	1·75	1·75
2085	700s. Bougainvillea formosa	2·00	2·25
2086	750s. Acalypha	2·00	2·25
2075/86 Set of 12		12·00	10·00
MS2087 88×112 mm. 125s.×4 in designs of 210, 300, 380 and 700s. (each 31×36 mm). P 14½		4·00	4·50

(b) With "1997" imprint date.

2088	150s. As 140s.	75	25
2088a	350s. As 210s. (30.12.97)	1·25	90
2088b	400s. Hibiscus rosa-sinensis (30.12.97)	1·25	1·10
2088e	500s. As 600s. (Questa 23.6.02)	1·10	1·25

Nos. 2081 and **MS**2087 are inscribed "Carna", both in error.

(Des P. Ndembo. Litho Cartor)

1996 (16 Sept). East African Fruit. T **262** and similar vert designs. Multicoloured. P 13.

2089	140s. Type **262**	80	40
2090	180s. Orange and limes	1·00	90
2091	200s. Pear and apples	1·40	1·50
2092	300s. Bananas	2·00	2·00
2089/92 Set of 4		4·75	4·50
MS2093 92×92 mm. 300s. No. 2092		2·75	3·00

263 Children's Clinic

264 Couple and setting Sun

(Des A. Nabola. Litho Cartor)

1996 (25 Oct). 25th Anniv of U.N. Volunteers. T **263** and similar horiz designs. Multicoloured. P 13.

2094	140s. Type **263**	1·25	40
2095	200s. Food distribution	1·50	1·00
2096	260s. Clean water supply	1·75	2·00
2097	300s. Public education	2·00	2·50
2094/7 Set of 4		6·00	5·50
MS2098 95×95 mm. 500s. Refugee camp		4·75	5·00

(Des P. Ndembo. Litho Cartor)

1996 (1 Dec). World Aids Day. T **264** and similar multicoloured designs. P 13.

2099	140s. Type **264**	1·50	45
2100	310s. People from various occupations (horiz)	2·25	2·25
2101	370s. Discussion group (horiz)	2·50	2·50
2102	410s. Orphans with foster mother (horiz)	2·75	2·75
2099/102 Set of 4		8·00	7·25
MS2103 95×95 mm. 500s. Type **264**		5·00	5·00

265 Game Reserve

266 Bukoba (ferry) sinking

(Des A. Nabola. Litho Cartor)

1996 (8 Dec). 2nd Anniv of Common Market for Eastern and Southern Africa (COMESA). T **265** and similar horiz designs. Multicoloured. P 13.

2104	140s. Type **265**	2·00	60
2105	180s. Fishermen in canoe	1·50	1·00
2106	200s. Container ship at Dar es Salaam docks	2·25	1·75
2107	300s. Goods train on Tazara railway	4·00	3·50
2104/7 Set of 4		8·75	6·25
MS2108 90×90 mm. 500s. Cotton bolls		4·25	5·00

W **266a**

(Des A. Nbola. Litho Harrison)

1997 (21 May). 1st Anniv of Sinking of Bukoba (ferry). T **266** and similar horiz designs. Multicoloured. W **266a** (sideways). P 14.

2109	140s. Type **266**	75	40
2110	350s. Recovering bodies from wreck	1·60	1·75
2111	370s. Identifying victims	1·75	2·00
2112	410s. Religious service for victims	1·90	2·25
2109/12 Set of 4		5·50	5·75
MS2113 90×90 mm. 500s. Bukoba (ferry). P 14½×14		3·00	3·50

267 Mount Kilimanjaro and Animals

268 Red Hornbill

(Des A. Nbola. Litho B.D.T.)

1997 (9 Oct). Tourist Attractions. T **267** and similar horiz designs. Multicoloured. P 13½.

2114	140s. Type **267**	1·50	40
2115	310s. Members of the Masai tribe	1·75	2·00
2116	370s. Old Stone Town, Zanzibar	1·90	2·25
2117	410s. Buffalo on Ruaha Plains	2·25	2·50
2114/17	*Set of 4*	6·75	6·25
MS2118	87×87 mm. 500s. Mount Kilimanjaro and elephant	3·00	3·50

(Des P. Ndembo. Litho Harrison)

1997 (28 Nov). Coastal Birds. T **268** and similar multicoloured designs. W **266***a* (sideways on horiz designs). P 14.

2119	140s. Type **268**	1·25	50
2120	350s. Sacred Ibis (*horiz*)	2·25	2·00
2121	370s. Gulls (*horiz*)	2·50	2·25
2122	410s. Ring-necked Dove (*horiz*)	2·75	2·50
2119/22	*Set of 4*	8·00	6·50
MS2123	90×90 mm. 500s. Red Hornbill, Sacred Ibis, Gulls and Ring-necked Dove. P 14½×14	2·50	3·00

269 Mount Kilimanjaro and Elephant

270 Tanzania and P.A.P.U. Flags

(Litho B.D.T.)

1997. P 13.

2124	**269** 410s. multicoloured	2·00	1·90

(Litho B.D.T.)

1998 (18 Jan). 18th Anniv of Pan African Postal Union. T **270** and similar horiz designs. Multicoloured. P 13½.

2125	150s. Type **270**	1·50	45
2126	250s. P.A.P.U. logo	1·50	1·25
2127	400s. Postman making E.M.S delivery	2·50	2·50
2128	500s. Two giraffes	3·50	3·00
2125/28	*Set of 4*	8·00	6·50

X

(271)

272 Catapult

1998. (26 Jan). Nos. 805/6 and 808 surch with T **271**.

2129	150s. on 9s. African Emerald Cuckoo	2·50	1·50
2130	150s. on 13s. Little Bee Eater	2·50	1·50
2131	150s. on 20s. Bateleur	2·50	1·50
	a. Surch double, one inverted		
2129/31	*Set of 3*	6·75	4·00

(Des A. Nabola. Litho Questa)

1998 (16 Mar). Traditional Weapons. T **272** and similar horiz designs. Multicoloured. P 14.

2132	150s. Type **272**	1·00	45
2133	250s. Cutlass and club	1·40	1·10
2134	400s. Rifle and ammunition	1·90	2·00
2135	500s. Bow and arrows	2·25	2·50
2132/5	*Set of 4*	6·00	5·50

273 Children carrying Banner

(Des M. Tibasima. Litho Cartor)

1998 (9 Sept). Children's Rights in Tanzania. T **273** and similar multicoloured designs. P 13.

2136	150s. Type **273**	80	40
2137	250s. Teacher with children	1·10	90
2138	400s. Adult with stick and child (*vert*)	1·75	1·90
2139	500s. Child hugging adult (*vert*)	2·00	2·25
2136/9	*Set of 4*	5·00	4·75
MS2140	90×90 mm. 500s. As 250s	2·00	2·25

274 U.P.U. Emblem

275 The Dhow Harbour

(Des A. Nabola. Litho Questa)

1998 (9 Oct). World Stamp Day. T **274** and similar horiz designs. Multicoloured. W **119**. P 14.

2141	150s. Type **274**	80	40
2142	250s. Cancelling mail	1·10	90
2143	400s. Dove carrying air mail letter	1·75	1·90
2144	500s. Woman posting letter	2·00	2·25
2141/4	*Set of 4*	5·00	4·75
MS2145	90×90 mm. 500s. Woman posting letter, dove and U.P.U. emblem	2·00	2·25

(Des P. Ndembo. Litho B.D.T.)

1998 (10 Nov). Tourist Attractions of Zanzibar. T **275** and similar multicoloured designs. P 14.

2146	100s. Type **275**	55	20
2147	150s. Girl on Giant Tortoise in countryside	80	40
2148	250s. Children with Giant Tortoise (*horiz*)	1·10	90
2149	300s. Stone Town street	1·40	1·40
2150	400s. The Old Fort (*horiz*)	1·75	1·90
2151	500s. Red Colobus Monkeys (*horiz*)	2·00	2·25
2146/51	*Set of 6*	7·00	6·25
MS2152	70×100 mm. 600s. Girl on Giant Tortoise in Stone Town street	2·25	2·50

276 Local Post Office

(Litho Questa)

1999 (1 Jan). 5th Anniv of Tanzania Posts Corporation. T **276** and similar multicoloured designs. P 14.

2153	150s. Type **276**	80	40
2154	250s. Post collection van	1·25	90
2155	350s. Counter services	1·60	1·75
2156	400s. Retail facilities	1·75	1·90
2153/6	*Set of 4*	4·75	4·50
MS2157	76×117 mm. 500s. Headquarters (*vert*)	2·00	2·25

277 Blood Pressure Monitoring

(Des P. Ndembo. Litho Questa)

1999 (29 Mar). Millennium. Improvement in Living Standards. T **277** and similar multicoloured designs. P 14.

2158	350s. Type **277**	1·75	1·00
2159	400s. Children playing	1·75	1·10
2160	700s. Maize farming	3·25	3·75
2161	750s. Collecting clean water	3·25	3·75
2158/61	*Set of 4*	9·00	8·75
MS2162	70×101 mm. 1500s. Ostriches (Tourism) (*vert*)	7·00	7·50

278 Rotary Emblem and "50"

(Des A. Nabola. Litho Questa)

1999 (30 June). 50th Anniv of Rotary Club of Dar-es-Salaam. T **278** and similar multicoloured designs. P 14.

2163	150s. Type **278**	70	40
2164	250s. Giving child polio plus vaccine (vert)	90	75
2165	350s. Paul Harris (Rotary founder) (vert)	1·25	1·75
2166	400s. Women collecting clean drinking water from tap (vert)	1·50	2·25
2163/6 *Set of 4*		4·00	4·75
MS2167	70×100 mm. 500s. Rotary emblem and "50" (vert)	2·00	2·75

279 Mail being loaded onto Aeroplane

279a Mask

(Des A. Nabola. Litho Questa)

1999 (10 Aug). 125th Anniv of Universal Postal Union. T **279** and similar horiz designs. Multicoloured. W **119**. P 14.

2168	150s. Type **279**	90	40
2169	300s. Children writing letters	1·25	1·00
2170	350s. U.P.U. members committee meeting	1·40	1·60
2171	400s. Express Mail Service co-ordination	1·60	2·25
2168/71 *Set of 4*		4·75	4·75
MS2172	90×90 mm. 500s. U.P.U. logo	2·00	2·75

1999 (20 Aug). Masks. T **279a** and similar vert designs. Multicoloured. Litho. P 14.

2172a	150s. Type **279a**	70	35
2172b	250s. Mask with blue, red and white face	1·00	75
2172c	300s. Mask with red, black, brown and orange face	1·25	1·25
2172d	350s. Mask with black and white face and rouged cheeks	1·40	1·75
2172a/d *Set of 4*		4·00	3·50
MS2172e	70×100 mm. 1500s. Firebird (two dancers)	4·75	5·50

280 Lilium longiflorum (cool season)

281 Taita Falcon

(Des A. Nabola. Litho Questa)

1999 (6 Oct). Seasonal Flowers. T **280** and similar horiz designs. Multicoloured. W **119**. P 14.

2173	150s. Type **280**	1·00	50
2174	250s. Strelitzia reginae (summer)	1·50	1·10
2175	400s. Zantedeschia (cool season)	2·00	2·00
2176	500s. Iris Apollo (dry season)	2·25	2·50
2173/6 *Set of 4*		6·00	5·50
MS2177	97×90 mm. 600s. As No. 2175	3·00	3·25

No. 2176 is inscribed "Ilis" in error.

(Litho Questa)

1999 (27 Nov). Birds. T **281** and similar horiz designs. Multicoloured. W **119**. P 14.

2178	150s. Type **281**	1·50	55
2179	300s. Banded Green Sunbird	2·25	1·75
2180	400s. Spotted Ground Thrush	2·75	2·50
2181	500s. Fischer's Turaco	3·00	3·00
2178/81 *Set of 4*		8·50	7·00

MS2182	90×90 mm. 600s. Blue Swallow	3·50	3·50

Nos. 2181 and **MS**2182 are inscribed "Taulaco Fisheri" or "atrokaerulea", both in error.

282 Medical Students, Muhimbili University, Tanzania

(**283**)

(Des A. Nabola. Litho Oriental Press, Bahrain)

2000 (5 Mar). Universities of East Africa. T **282** and similar multicoloured designs. P 13.

2183	150s. Type **282**	1·00	40
2184	200s. Students outside Zanzibar University	1·25	55
2185	600s. Makerere University, Uganda (vert)	2·50	2·75
2186	800s. Egerton University, Kenya	3·00	3·50
2183/6 *Set of 4*		7·00	6·50
MS2187	87×87 mm. 500s. Inter University Council for East Africa emblem (84×82 mm). P 14½	2·75	3·25

2000 (6 Apr). No. 813 surch with T **283**.

2188	200s. on 170s. Saddle-billed Stork	1·75	65
	a. Surch double		

A re-print of this surcharge was issued on 23 July 2002 with the typeface shown in a bolder black.

(**284**)

285 Julius Nyerere in Youth and Old Age

2000 (6 Apr). No. 815 surch with T **284**.

2189	800s. on 500s. Ostrich	4·00	3·50

(Des P. Ndembo. Litho Cartor)

2000 (13 Apr). Julius Nyerere (first president of Tanzania, 1962–85) Commemoration. T **285** and similar multicoloured designs. P 13.

2190	200s. Type **285**	90	45
2191	500s. With Edward Sakoine, Prime Minister	2·00	2·25
2192	600s. Nyerere (in close-up) (vert)	2·25	2·50
2193	800s. Wearing Mgolore, local cloth (vert)	2·50	2·75
2190/3 *Set of 4*		7·00	7·00
MS2194	90×90 mm. 1000s. Nyerere's Mausoleum	3·25	4·50

286 Seronera Wildlife Lodge, Serengeti and Lion

287 Children carrying Water Pots on their Heads

(Des P. Ndembo. Litho Oriental Press, Bahrain)

2000 (10 June). Tourist Attractions of Tanzania. T **286** and similar multicoloured designs. P 13.

2195	400s. Type **286**	1·75	1·50
2196	400s. Lake Manyara National Park and elephant	1·75	1·50
2197	400s. Ngorongoro Crater, Wildlife Lodge and rhinoceros	1·75	1·50
2198	400s. Lobo Wildlife Lodge and giraffes	1·75	1·50
2199	400s. Kibo, the central cone of Kilimanjaro, and elephants	1·75	1·50
2200	400s. Fish off Mafia Island	1·75	1·50
2201	400s. Selous Game Reserve and wild dogs	1·75	1·50
2202	400s. Mikumi National Park and elephant	1·75	1·50
2203	500s. Type **286**	1·75	1·60
2204	500s. As No. 2196	1·75	1·60
2205	500s. As No. 2197	1·75	1·60
2206	500s. As No. 2198	1·75	1·60
2207	500s. As No. 2199	1·75	1·60
2208	500s. As No. 2200	1·75	1·60
2209	500s. As No. 2201	1·75	1·60
2210	500s. As No. 2202	1·75	1·60
2211	600s. Type **286**	2·00	1·75
2212	600s. As No. 2196	2·00	1·75

2213	600s. As No. 2197		2·00	1·75
2214	600s. As No. 2198		2·00	1·75
2215	600s. As No. 2199		2·00	1·75
2216	600s. As No. 2200		2·00	1·75
2217	600s. As No. 2201		2·00	1·75
2218	600s. As No. 2202		2·00	1·75
2219	800s. Type **286**		2·25	2·00
2220	800s. As No. 2196		2·25	2·00
2221	800s. As No. 2197		2·25	2·00
2222	800s. As No. 2198		2·25	2·00
2223	800s. As No. 2199		2·25	2·00
2224	800s. As No. 2200		2·25	2·00
2225	800s. As No. 2201		2·25	2·00
2226	800s. As No. 2202		2·25	2·00
2195/226 *Set of 32*			55·00	50·00

MS2227 90×90 mm. 1000s. Lion, giraffes, elephant, rhinoceros and Kilimanjaro (*vert*)............. 3·75 3·50

(Des P. Ndembo. Litho Oriental Press, Bahrain)

2000 (20 July). Work of World Vision (aid organization) in Tanzania (1st series). T **287** and similar horiz designs. Multicoloured. P 13.

2228	200s. Type **287**		80	40
2229	600s. Family making bread		2·00	1·75
2230	800s. Nurse weighing baby at clinic		2·25	2·50
2231	1000s. Children reading		2·50	2·75
2228/31 *Set of 4*			6·75	6·75

MS2232 90×90 mm. 500s. Boy and girl.............. 2·00 2·50

288 Football Match

(Des A. Nabola. Litho Enschedé)

2000 (15 Sept). Olympic Games, Sydney. T **288** and similar multicoloured designs. W **119**. P 13½×14 (horiz) or 14×13½ (vert).

2233	150s. Type **288**		80	40
2234	350s. Basketball game (*vert*)		2·00	1·50
2235	400s. Athletics race (*vert*)		2·00	1·75
2236	800s. Boxing match		3·25	3·50
2233/6 *Set of 4*			7·25	6·25

MS2237 90×90 mm. 500s. Presentation of medals (*vert*) .... 2·00 2·50

289 Gutting Fish

(Des P. Ndembo. Litho Enschedé)

2000 (30 Sept). Zanzibar Millennium. T **289** and similar multicoloured designs. W **119**. P 13½.

2238	150s. Type **289**		1·00	40
2239	200s. Tortoises, baskets of bread and logo		1·40	60
2240	400s. Boy and "Kukuza Hadhi ya Elimu na Uchumi Zanzibar" inscription (*vert*)		2·25	1·75
2241	800s. Girl studying and university graduates (*vert*)		3·75	5·00
2238/41 *Set of 4*			7·75	7·00

MS2242 90×90 mm. 500s. Map and trophy (*vert*)........ 3·25 3·50

230/-

290 Planting Trees (291)

2000 (9 Nov). Environmental Protection. T **290** and similar horiz designs. Multicoloured. Litho. P 13.

2243	200s. Type **290**		80	40
2244	400s. Forest stream		1·75	1·25
2245	600s. Maintenance of sewage works		2·00	2·50
2246	800s. River and forest		2·50	3·25
2243/6 *Set of 4*			6·25	6·75

MS2247 90×90 mm. 1000s. Mt. Kilimanjaro....... 2·75 3·50

2000 (30 Nov)–**2001**. Nos. 808 and 813 surch with T **291**.

2247a	230s. on 20s. Bateleur (20.11.01)		2·50	1·00
2248	230s. on 170s. Saddle-billed Stork		2·50	1·00
	a. Surch double, one inverted			

A re-print of this surcharge was issued on 23 July 2002 with the typeface shown in a bolder black.

292 Old Man in Deckchair (Retirement)

293 Ruins of the Great Mosque, Kilwa Kisiwani

(Des A. Nabola. Litho Enschedé)

2000 (15 Dec). National Social Security Fund. T **292** and similar horiz designs. Multicoloured. W **119**. P 13½.

2249	200s. Type **292**		80	40
2250	350s. Factory worker with eye injury (Employment injury)		1·50	1·00
2251	600s. Man holding prosthetic leg (Invalidity)		2·25	2·75
2252	800s. Mother and baby with nurse (Health insurance)		2·75	3·50
2249/52 *Set of 4*			6·50	7·00

MS2253 90×90 mm. 500s. Pregnant woman (Maternity) .... 2·00 2·50

2000 (29 Dec). Old Buildings and Architecture of Tanzania. T **293** and similar multicoloured designs. Litho. P 13.

2254	150s. Type **293**		60	30
2255	200s. German Boma (fort), Mikindani, Mtwara		75	35
2256	250s. German Boma, Bagamoyo		80	40
2257	300s. Butiama Museum, Mara		90	50
2258	350s. Chief Government Chemist's Offices		95	55
2259	400s. The Old Post Office, Dar es Salaam		1·10	70
2260	500s. Dr. Livingstone's Tembe Lodge, Kwihara, Tabora		1·25	1·00
2261	600s. Original Governor's Palace and State House, Dar es Salaam (*vert*)		1·50	1·40
2262	700s. Traditional houses of the Ngoni-Nyamwezi		1·60	1·60
2263	800s. Palace of Beit Elajaib, Stonetown, Zanzibar		1·75	2·00
2264	900s. Tongoni ruins, Tanga		2·00	2·50
2265	1000s. Karimjee Hall, Dar es Salaam		2·25	2·50
2254/65 *Set of 12*			14·00	12·50

MS2266 100×100 mm. 1500s. The Old Boma, Mikindani, Southern Tanzania .... 3·75 5·00

294 Child Writing

(Des P. Ndembo. Litho Cartor)

2001 (30 Apr). Work of World Vision (aid organization) in Tanzania (2nd series). T **294** and similar multicoloured designs. P 13.

2267	200s. Type **294**		1·00	40
2268	600s. Children laughing		2·25	2·00
2269	800s. Child carrying bananas (*vert*)		2·50	3·00
2270	1000s. Child wearing grey t-shirt (*vert*)		2·75	3·50
2267/70 *Set of 4*			7·75	8·00

MS2270a 90×90 mm. 500s. Children lying on grass..... 2·25 2·75

295 Leopard

(Litho Cartor)

2001 (15 June). Endangered Species. T **295** and similar horiz designs. Multicoloured. P 13.

2271	200s. Type **295**		1·00	50
2272	400s. Rhinoceros		2·75	1·75
2273	600s. Crocodile		2·75	2·75

2274	800s. Wild dogs	3·00	3·75
2271/4	*Set of 4*	8·50	8·00
MS2275	90×90 mm. 600s. Cheetah	3·50	3·75

296 Child receiving Vaccination

297 Dolphins

(Litho Cartor)

2001 (31 July). 50th Anniv of United Nations High Commission for Refugees. T **296** and similar multicoloured designs. P 13.

2276	200s. Type **296**	1·00	40
2277	400s. Refugees in boat on Lake Tanganyika...	1·75	1·00
2278	600s. Female refugee (*vert*)	2·25	2·50
2279	800s. Refugees with possessions on bike	2·50	3·00
2276/9	*Set of 4*	6·75	6·25
MS2280	90×90 mm. 600s. As No. 2278	2·25	3·00

(Litho Cartor)

2001 (30 Aug). Rare Species of Zanzibar. T **297** and similar multicoloured designs. P 13.

2281	250s. Type **297**	1·25	50
2282	300s. Coral plants	1·40	80
2283	450s. Coral reefs	1·90	1·90
2284	800s. Red colobus monkey (*vert*)	3·25	3·50
2281/4	*Set of 4*	7·00	6·00
MS2285	90×90 mm. 700s. Colobus monkeys	3·50	3·75

298 Children in Class

299 Fort Kilwa, Tanzania

(Litho Cartor)

2001 (9 Oct). United Nations Dialogue among Civilisations. T **298** and similar multicoloured designs. P 13.

2286	200s. Type **298**	80	40
2287	400s. People in different dress	1·25	90
2288	600s. Discussion group	2·00	2·50
2289	800s. Couple writing letters	2·25	2·75
2286/9	*Set of 4*	5·50	6·00
MS2290	90×90 mm. 700s. Letter and handshake spanning globe (*vert*)	2·50	3·25

(Litho Cartor)

2001 (19 Oct). Historic Sites of East Africa. T **299** and similar horiz designs. Multicoloured. P 13.

2291	250s. Type **299**	1·00	45
2292	300s. Ruins of Maruhubi Palace, Zanzibar	1·25	65
2293	400s. Old Provincial Office, Nairobi, Kenya (1913)	1·60	1·25
2294	800s. Mparu Tombs, Hoima, Uganda	3·00	3·75
2291/4	*Set of 4*	6·00	5·50
MS2295	90×90 mm. 700s. Map of East Africa with sailing ship	4·25	4·50

300 Hippo in River Rufiji, Selous Game Reserve

(Litho Cartor)

2001 (30 Nov). Scenery of Tanzania. T **300** and similar multicoloured designs. P 13.

2296	200s. Type **300**	1·25	50
2297	400s. Mangapwani Beach, Zanzibar	1·50	1·00
2298	600s. Zebra and mountains, Mikumi National Park	2·50	2·75
2299	800s. Balancing stones, Lake Victoria Mwanza (*vert*)	3·00	3·50
2296/9	*Set of 4*	7·50	7·00
MS2300	90×90 mm. 700s. Giraffes, Ruaha National Park (*vert*)	5·00	5·00

301 Tea Plantation

302 Makonde Masked Dancer

2001 (30 Dec). 40th Anniv of Independence. T **301** and similar multicoloured designs. P 14.

2301	180s. Type **301**	80	30
2302	230s. Tanzania, Uganda and Kenya flags with triple handshake (*vert*)	2·25	1·00
2303	350s. University graduates (*vert*)	1·50	1·00
2304	450s. Lion, leopard, buffalo, rhinoceros, elephant and Mt. Kilimanjaro	3·75	2·25
2305	650s. Operating theatre	3·00	3·50
2306	950s. Minerals	5·50	6·50
2301/6	*Set of 6*	15·00	13·00
MS2307	92×92 mm. 1000s. As 450s	7·50	7·50

(Des. A. Nabola. Litho Enschedé)

2002 (30 Mar). Ceremonial Costumes. T **302** and similar vert designs. Multicoloured. W **119**. P 14.

2308	250s. Type **302**	1·50	50
2309	350s. Mwaka Koga Festival dancers (Zanzibar)	1·75	1·00
2310	400s. Lizombe dancer	1·75	1·75
2311	450s. Zaramo bridal celebration	2·00	2·25
2308/11	*Set of 4*	6·25	5·00
MS2312	90×90 mm. 500s. As No. 2310	2·50	3·00

303 Leopard

304 Mount Kilimanjaro

(Des P. Ndembo. Litho Enschedé)

2002 (30 Apr). Animals of the National Parks. Sheet 105×150 mm containing T **303** and similar vert designs. Multicoloured. W **119**. P 13×14.

MS2313	250s. Type **303**; 250s. Elephant; 250s. Rhinoceros; 250s. Lion; 250s. Buffalo	8·00	8·50

(Des A. Nabola. Litho Enschedé)

2002 (30 June). International Year of Mountains. T **304** and similar horiz designs. Multicoloured. W **119**. P 14.

2314	250s. Type **304**	1·25	50
2315	350s. Usambara Mountains	1·50	1·00
2316	400s. Uluguru Mountains	1·75	1·50
2317	450s. Mwanihara Peak (Udzungwa Mountains)	1·90	2·25
2314/17	*Set of 4*	5·75	4·75
MS2318	90×90 mm. 500s. As Type **303**	2·25	2·75

(**305**)   **306** School Children   (**307**)

2002 (23 July). No. 2077 surch with T **305**.

2319	250s. on 180s. *Alamanda*	1·25	65

2002 (13 Aug). National Population Census. T **306** and similar multicoloured designs. Litho. P 13×13½ (200s.) or 13×13½ (others) (with one elliptical hole on each vert (200s.) or horiz (others) side).

2320	200s. Type **306**	90	40
2321	250s. Group of people (*horiz*)	95	45

2322	350s. Family (horiz)	1·10	70
2323	600s. Boy with emblem and statistics (horiz).	1·90	3·00
2320/3	Set of 4	4·25	4·00

No. **MS**2324 has been left for a miniature sheet, not yet received, to be added to the National Population Census issue.

2002 (30 Aug). No. 810 surch with T **307**.

2325	250s. on 40s. Lesser flamingo	1·25	65
	a. Surch double, one inverted		

308 Raffia Mat Weaving   **309** Ancient City of Kisimkazi, Zanzibar

(Des A. Nabola. Litho Cartor)

2002 (13 Sept). Zanzibar Arts and Crafts. T **308** and similar horiz designs. Multicoloured. P 13½.

2326	200s. Type **308**	80	65
2327	250s. Sewing caps	90	65
2328	350s. Making chair	1·25	1·10
2329	400s. Henna tattoos	1·40	1·75
2326/9	Set of 4	4·00	3·75
MS2330	90×90 mm. 800s. Carved wooden door	3·00	4·00

(Litho Cartor)

2002 (30 Sept). Paintings and Archaeology. T **309** and similar multicoloured designs. P 13½.

2331	250s. Type **309**	1·25	50
2332	400s. Remains of Kaole Town, Bagamoyo (horiz)	1·75	1·25
2333	450s. Kondoa Irangi rock paintings	2·00	2·00
2334	600s. Great Mosque, Kilwa Kisiwani (horiz)	3·25	4·00
2331/4	Set of 4	7·50	7·00
MS2335	90×90 mm. 1000s. As No. 2332. P 13	3·50	4·00

310 Rhinoceros   **311** Lions

(Litho Enschedé)

2003 (22 Apr). The Big Five. T **310** and similar multicoloured designs. W w **119**. P 13½×13 (horiz) or 13×13½ (vert).

2336	400s. Type **310**	2·00	1·25
2337	500s. Elephant	2·25	1·75
2338	600s. Lion	2·25	2·00
2339	800s. Leopard (vert)	2·75	3·25
2340	1000s. Buffalo	3·25	4·00
2336/40	Set of 5	11·00	11·00
MS2341	85×115 mm. 1500m. The Big Five. Imperf	7·00	8·00

(Litho Calcutta Security Printers Ltd, Kanpur)

2003 (30 Apr). Tourism. "The Northern Circuit". T **311** and similar horiz designs. Multicoloured. P 13½×13.

2342	300s. Type **311**	1·50	70
2343	350s. Mt. Kilimanjaro	1·50	80
2344	400s. Zebras	2·00	1·25
2345	500s. Elephants	2·50	1·75
2346	600s. Leopards	2·50	2·75
2347	800s. Rhinoceros	4·50	5·50
2342/7	Set of 6	13·00	11·50
MS2348	97×75 mm. 1000s. Buffalo	4·00	5·00

312 Cotton   **313** Children Eating

(Des P. Ndembo. Litho Calcutta Security Printers Ltd, Kanpur)

2003 (10 June). Cash Crops. T **312** and similar multicoloured designs. P 13×13½ (with one elliptical hole on each vertical (2349/52) or horizontal (**MS**2353) side).

2349	250s. Type **312**	80	40
2350	300s. Cashew nuts	90	50
2351	600s. Sisal	1·75	2·00
2352	800s. Cloves	2·50	3·75
2349/52	Set of 4	5·50	6·00
MS2353	99×81 mm. 1000s. Tea (horiz)	4·00	4·50

(Des P. Ndembo. Litho Cartor)

2003 (3 July). Work of World Vision (aid organization) in Tanzania (3rd series). T **313** and similar multicoloured designs. P 13.

2354	300s. Type **313**	90	50
2355	600s. Children at school	1·75	2·00
2356	800s. Pumping water into bucket (vert)	2·25	2·75
2357	1000s. Distributing mosquito nets	2·50	3·25
2354/7	Set of 4	6·75	7·75
MS2358	90×90 mm. 500s. Three children in ceremonial robes with microphone	2·00	2·50

314 Rufiji Delta View   **315** Nyamwezi Dance, Tabora

(Litho Calcutta Security Printers, Kanpur)

2003 (22 July). Waterfalls and Landscapes. T **314** and similar multicoloured designs. P 13½.

2359	300s. Type **314**	1·25	50
2360	400s. Shore line of Zanzibar coast	1·50	1·00
2361	500s. Riftvalley View (Lake Manyara)	1·75	1·75
2362	800s. Kalambo Falls (vert)	2·50	3·25
2359/62	Set of 4	6·25	6·00
MS2363	105×87 mm. 1000s. Mangroves of coast	3·00	3·50

(Des A. Nabola. Litho Calcutta Security Printers Ltd, Kanpur)

2003 (25 July). Traditional Dances of East Africa. T **315** and similar horiz designs. Multicoloured. P 13 (with one elliptical hole on each horizontal side).

2364	300s. Type **315**	90	45
2365	500s. Luo dance, Kisumu	1·40	1·00
2366	600s. Pemba dance, Zanzibar	1·50	1·75
2367	800s. Baganda dance, Kampala	2·25	3·25
2364/7	Set of 4	5·50	5·75
MS2368	99×81 mm. 1000s. Masai dance, Arusha	2·50	3·25

316 The Old Fort

(Des P. Ndembo. Litho Calcutta Security Printers Ltd, Kanpur)

2003 (30 Sept). Sceneries of Zanzibar. T **316** and similar multicoloured designs. P 13×13½ (vert) or 13½×13 (horiz).

2369	300s. Type **316**	1·00	50
2370	500s. Carved wooden door, Beit al Ajaib (vert)	1·40	1·25
2371	600s. Palm trees, Michamvi beach (vert)	1·50	1·75
2372	800s. Dhow, Beit al Ajaib	2·25	3·25
2369/72	Set of 4	5·50	6·00
MS2373	95×149 mm. Nos. 2369 and 2371/2	4·50	5·50

317 Common Dolphin

(Des A. Nabola. Litho Calcutta Security Printers, Kanpur)

2003 (11 Oct). Marine Mammals. T **317** and similar horiz designs. Multicoloured. P 13½×13.

2374	300s. Type **317**	1·25	50

2375	350s. Sperm Whale	2·00	1·25
2376	400s. Southern Right Whale	2·25	1·75
2377	600s. Dugong	2·75	3·50
2374/7 *Set of 4*		7·50	6·25
MS2378 105×87 mm. 500s. Bottlenose Dolphin		2·25	2·50

318 Prayer on Hija (Tawaf)

319 People working at Computer Terminals

(Litho D.L.R.)

2003 (4 Nov). Religious Festivals. T **318** and similar horiz designs. Multicoloured. W w **119**. P 14.

2379	300s. Type **318**	1·00	50
2380	500s. Choir at Christmas time	1·40	1·00
2381	600s. Birthday memorial of Prophet Muhammad (Maulid)	1·50	1·75
2382	800s. Christmas Day prayers	2·00	3·00
2379/82 *Set of 4*		5·50	5·50
MS2383 90×90 mm. 1000s. Crucifixion		2·50	3·25

(Des P. Ndembo. Litho Cartor)

2004 (19 Jan). 10th Anniv of Posts Corporation. T **319** and similar horiz designs. Multicoloured. P 13.

2384	350s. Type **319**	1·00	45
2385	400s. Overnight mail van	2·00	1·50
2386	600s. Employees participating in meeting	2·00	2·25
2387	800s. EMS postal services mapped on globe	3·00	3·75
2384/7 *Set of 4*		7·25	8·00
MS2388 130×98 mm. Nos. 2384/7		7·25	8·00
MS2389 90×90 mm. 1000s. Post Cargo lorry		4·50	4·75

320 Exchanging Money

321 Guides demonstrating Environmentally Friendly Cooker

(Des P. Ndembo. Litho Calcutta Security Printers, Kanpur)

2004 (3 Feb). Western Union Money Transfer. T **320** and similar horiz designs. Multicoloured. P 13½×13 (horiz) or 13×13½ (vert).

2390	300s. Type **320**	1·00	40
2391	400s. Busalanga primary school	1·50	85
2392	500s. Mother and child with money (*vert*)	1·75	1·60
2393	600s. Globe inside emblem	2·00	2·25
2390/3 *Set of 4*		5·50	4·50
MS2394 89×75 mm. 800s. As Type **320** but without Swahili inscription and Western Union emblem		2·50	3·00

Nos. 2390/**MS**2394 show "2003" inscription date.

(Des A. Nabola. Litho Calcutta Security Printers, Kanpur)

2004 (15 May). 75th Anniv of Girl Guides. T **321** and similar horiz designs. Multicoloured. P 13½×13.

2395	300s. Type **321**	1·00	45
2396	400s. Camp training	1·25	1·00
2397	600s. Bravery training	1·90	2·25
2398	800s. Guides assisting at Mother and Child clinic	2·50	3·50
2395/8 *Set of 4*		6·00	6·50
MS2399 105×85 mm. 1000s. As No. 2397		2·75	3·50

Nos. 2395/**MS**2399 show "2003" inscription date.

322 Overland Vehicle

323 Cheering for Peddle Winners

(Des P. Ndembo. Litho Oriental Press, Bahrain)

2004 (25 May). 40th Anniv of Tanganyika Christian Refugee Service. T **322** and similar horiz designs. Multicoloured. Fluorescent security marking. P 14.

2400	350s. Type **322**	90	45

2401	600s. Drawing fresh water	1·75	1·50
2402	800s. Children in school	2·25	2·50
2403	1000s. Planting saplings	2·50	3·00
2400/3 *Set of 4*		6·75	6·75
MS2404 85×74 mm. 1200s. Combination of designs of Nos. 2400/3 (45×35 *mm*)		3·00	3·50

The logo of Tanzania Posts Corporation is visible as a security marking under U.V. light.

(Des A. Nabola. Litho Cartor)

2004 (25 June). Dhow Events in Zanzibar. T **323** and similar multicoloured designs. P 13.

2405	350s. Type **323**	1·00	50
2406	400s. Punting race	1·10	75
2407	600s. Dhow races	1·75	2·00
2408	800s. Sail boat race	2·25	2·75
2405/8 *Set of 4*		5·50	5·50
MS2409 91×90 mm. 1000s. Dhow (*vert*)		3·00	3·50
MS2409a 130×101 mm. Nos. 2405/8		6·00	6·00

324 Williamson Diamond Mine, Mwadui

325 Removing Water Hyacinth, Mwanza City

(Des A. Nabola. Litho Enschedé)

2004 (30 Jul). Mining. T **324** and similar horiz designs. Multicoloured. P 13½×13.

2410	350s. Type **324**	1·75	65
2411	500s. Semi processed jewels	2·25	1·50
2412	600s. Drillers	2·50	2·50
2413	800s. Small scale gold miners	4·00	4·25
2410/13 *Set of 4*		9·50	8·00
MS2414 130×100 mm. Nos. 2410/13		9·50	9·50
MS2415 90×90 mm. 600s. Unprocessed gemstones		3·25	3·25

(Des A. Nabola. Litho Enschedé)

2004 (17 Aug). 24th Anniv of the Southern African Development Community. T **325** and similar multicoloured designs. P 14×13 (horiz) or 13×14 (vert).

2416	350s. Type **325**	1·00	50
2417	500s. Irrigation of maize, Mbayali District, Mbeya	1·40	1·25
2418	600s. Paddy fields at Igomelo irrigation scheme	1·75	2·00
2419	800s. Installing pipes in new borehole, Mbeya Rural (*vert*)	2·25	3·00
2416/19 *Set of 4*		5·75	6·00
MS2420 130×100 mm. Nos. 2416/19		5·75	6·25
MS2421 90×90 mm. 1000s. Men working in maize fields		3·00	3·50

326 Mwalimu Julius Kambarage Nyerere (facilitator in Burundi Peace negotiations)

350/-

(326a)

350/=

(326b)

2004 (15 Oct). Law and Peace. T **326** and similar horiz designs. Multicoloured. P 14×13.

2422	350s. Type **326**	1·00	45
2423	500s. Burundi returnees at Frontier Reception facility	1·40	1·25
2424	600s. Nelson Mandela and Pres. Benjamin W. Mkapa	1·75	2·00
2425	800s. Presidents Yoweri Museveni of Uganda, Benjamin W. Mkapa, and Domitien Ndayizeye of Burundi	2·25	3·00
2422/5 *Set of 4*		5·75	6·00

MS2426 130×100 mm. Nos. 2422/5 .... 5·75   6·25
MS2427 90×90 mm. 600s. Arusha International
Conference Centre.................................. 1·90   2·25

2004 (20 Oct). Nos. 2075, 2079 and 2252 surch with T **326a/b.**
2427a   350s. on 100s. Type **261** (T **326a**)................... 2·50   1·25
2427b   350s. on 200s. German boma (fort),
      Mikindani, Mtwara (T **326b**) .... 2·50   1·25
2427c   350s. on 210s. Zinnia (T **326a**) .... 2·50   1·25
2427d   400s. on 300s. Canna .... 5·00   2·50
2427a/d Set of 4...................................... 11·50   5·75
    On at least one position in the sheet the "=" on No. 2427b is replaced by a "–".
    On No. 2427d the original value is obliterated by a bold 'x'.

327 Family sitting outside House

(Litho Enschedé)

2004 (4 Nov). Children's Rights (2nd series). T **327** and similar horiz designs. Multicoloured. P 13½×13.
2428   350s. Type **327** .... 1·00   1·00
2429   350s. Teachers and student around table........ 1·00   1·00
2430   400s. Classroom scene............................ 1·10   1·00
2431   500s. Students and child outside house .... 1·25   1·40
2428/31 Set of 4...................................... 4·00   4·00
MS2432 90×90 mm. 1000s. As No. 2431............. 3·00   3·50

2004 (13 Nov). No. 2252 surch with T **327a.**
2432a   350s. on 200s. German boma (fort),
      Mikindani, Mtwara.............................. 1·00   60

328 Mwalimu Julius Kambarage Nyerere   **329** Lionesses

(Des P. Ndembo. Litho Cartor)

2005 (23 Feb). Centenary of Rotary International. T **328** and similar multicoloured designs. P 13.
2433   350s. Type **328** .... 1·00   45
2434   500s. Emblems (vert)............................. 1·25   80
2435   600s. Immunising child........................ 1·75   2·00
2436   600s. Environmental project.................. 1·75   2·00
     a. Sheetlet. Nos. 2436/41................ 9·50   11·00
2437   600s. Self reliance to the handicapped............ 1·75   2·00
2438   600s. Basic Healthcare project (vert)............ 1·75   2·00
2439   600s. Jaipur Foot project....................... 1·75   2·00
2440   600s. Malaria project........................... 1·75   2·00
2441   600s. Eradication of River Blindness project........ 1·75   2·00
2442   800s. Map of East Africa (vert) .... 3·00   3·25
2433/42 Set of 10.................................... 16·00   16·00
MS2443 44×59 mm. 1000s. Rotary emblem (vert)........ 3·25   3·75
    Nos. 2436/41 were printed together, se-tenant, in sheetlets of six stamps. No. 2438 was arranged horizontally in the sheet.

(Des P. Ndembo. Litho Enschedé)

2005 (30 Apr). Safari Circuits. T **329** and similar multicoloured designs. P 13×13½ (vert) or 13½×13 (horiz).
2444   350s. Type **329** .... 1·50   55
2445   500s. Cheetahs (horiz)........................ 1·75   1·00
2446   600s. Red Colobus Monkey................. 2·00   2·00
2447   600s. Elephants (horiz)....................... 2·25   2·25
     a. Sheetlet. Nos. 2447/52................ 12·00   12·00
2448   600s. Rhinoceroses (horiz)................... 2·25   2·25
2449   600s. Giraffes (horiz)......................... 2·25   2·25
2450   600s. Crocodile (horiz)....................... 2·25   2·25
2451   600s. Chimpanzees (horiz)................. 2·25   2·25
2452   600s. Buffaloes (horiz)....................... 2·25   2·25
2453   800s. Zebras (horiz)........................... 2·75   3·00
2444/53 Set of 10.................................... 19·00   18·00
MS2454 90×90 mm. 1000s. Leopard (horiz); 1000s.
Wild Hunting Dogs (horiz).......................... 7·00   8·00
    Nos. 2447/52 were printed together, se-tenant, in sheetlets of six stamps with enlarged illustrated margins.

330 Baron Godefroy de Blonay   **331** Map of Allied Invasion

2005 (2 May). Olympic Games, Athens (2004). T **330** and similar multicoloured designs. Litho. P 13½.
2455   350s. Type **330** .... 1·00   80
2456   350s. Wrestling (horiz) .... 1·00   80
2457   500s. Medal, 1928............................ 1·40   1·25
2458   1000s. Javelin throw (Grecian sculpture) .... 2·75   4·00
2455/8 Set of 4...................................... 5·50   6·25

2005 (2 May). 60th Anniv of D-Day. T **331** and similar multicoloured designs. Litho. P 13½.
MS2459 149×138 mm. 600s.×6, Type **331**; General Dwight D. Eisenhower; US troops landing at Omaha Beach; British Mosquitos; Fleet Admiral Ernest J. King; General George C. Marshall................... 11·00   11·00
MS2460 98×69 mm. 2500s. Battle at Green Beach, Normandy .... 8·00   8·50

332 West Side Lumber Company 3 Truck Shay

2005 (2 May). Bicentenary of Steam Locomotives. T **332** and similar horiz designs. Multicoloured. P 13½.
MS2461 151×104 mm. 1000s.×4, Type **332**; LK & P Saddle tanker; Double headed C&T; Baldwin 4-6-0.. 10·00   11·00
MS2462 100×69 mm. 2500s. Union Pacific locomotive on Heber Valley railroad .... 7·50   8·00

333 Franco Baresi (Italy)

2005 (2 May). Centenary of FIFA (Fédération Internationale de Football Association). T **333** and similar horiz designs. Multicoloured. Litho. P 13½.
MS2463 193×96 mm. 1000s.×4, Type **333**; Daniel Passarella (Argentina); Miroslav Klose (Germany); Michel Platini (France)................................. 9·00   9·50
MS2464 107×86 mm. 2500s. Gianfranco Zola (Italy)..... 6·50   7·00

334 Pope John Paul II as Child and Mother, Emilia Kaczorowska   **335** "Mathias Sandorf"

2005 (2 May). Pope John Paul II Commemoration (1st issue). Sheet, 94×117 mm, containing T **334** and similar horiz designs. Multicoloured. Litho. P 13½.

MS2465 1000s.×4, Type **334**; Visit to Poland; With
Pres. George W. Bush; Visit to Armenia .... 11·00 11·00

2005 (16 May). Death Centenary of Jules Verne (writer). T **335** and similar vert designs. Litho. P 13½.

MS2466 Five sheets, each 98×148 mm. (a) 800s.×4, multicoloured; multicoloured; multicoloured. (b) 800s.×4, multicoloured; multicoloured; multicoloured. (c) 800s.×4, multicoloured; multicoloured; deep blue, deep reddish-lilac and lemon; deep green, deep reddish-lilac and lemon. (d) 800s.×4, deep blue and lemon; deep reddish-lilac and lemon; deep dull purple and lemon; multicoloured. (e) 800s.×4, multicoloured; multicoloured; multicoloured *Set of 5 sheets*................. 27·00 32·00

MS2467 Five sheets. (a) 68×98 mm. 2000l. multicoloured. (b) 68×98 mm. 2000l. multicoloured. (c) 68×98 mm. 2000l. Prussian blue; lemon and violet. (d) 70×101 mm. 2000l. multicoloured. (e) 70×102 mm. 2000s. multicoloured *Set of 5 sheets* ...... 20·00 23·00

Designs—No. MS2466a, Type **335**; "The Steam House, The Demon of Cawnpore"; "Hector Servadac, The Career of a Comet"; "An Antarctic Mystery". No. MS2466b, "The Archipelago on Fire"; "The Vanished Diamond"; "Mistress Branican"; "The Castle of the Carpathians". No. MS2466c, "Around the World in Eighty Days"; "Dr. Ox's Experiment"; "The Purchase of the North Pole"; "Adrift in the Pacific". No. MS2466d, "Invasion of the Sea"; "The Floating Island"; "A Floating City"; "Dick Sands, Boy Captain". No. MS2466e, "Voyages Extraordinaires"; "Twenty Thousand Leagues under the Sea"; "A Floating City"; "Three Englishmen and Three Russians in South Africa". MS2467a, "The Mysterious Island". No. MS2467b, "Around the World in Eighty Days". No. MS2467c, "The Invasion of the Sea". No. MS2467d, "Five Weeks in a Balloon". MS2467e, "The Adventures of a Chinaman".

336 Bull Fighting

(Litho Enschedé)

2005 (30 June). Zanzibar Heritage and Culture. T **336** and similar multicoloured designs. P 13½×13 (horiz) or 13×13½ (vert).

2468	350s. Type **336**	1·00	50
2469	400s. A narrow street, Stone Town (*vert*)	1·25	75
2470	600s. Buibui (outdoor traditional dress) (*vert*)	1·75	2·00
2471	600s. House of Wonders, Beit-al-Ajaib.............	1·75	2·00
	a. Sheetlet. Nos. 2471/6..............................	9·50	11·00
2472	600s. Local Taarabu musicians	1·75	2·00
2473	600s. Fishing...	1·75	2·00
2474	600s. Coconut tree..	1·75	2·00
2475	600s. Khanga (indoor traditional dress)...........	1·75	2·00
2476	600s. Old museum building..............................	1·75	2·00
2477	800s. Clove harvesting, Pemba Island	2·25	2·50
2468/77	*Set of 10*	13·00	14·00

MS2478 90×90 mm. 500s. Modern power boat, Pemba Island .... 1·75 2·00

Nos. 2471/6 were printed together, *se-tenant*, in sheetlets of six stamps.

337 Pope John Paul II with Pres. Bill Clinton

338 Christian Ziege

2005 (22 Aug). Pope John Paul II Commemoration (2nd issue). Litho. P 12½×13.

2479   **337** 1500s. multicoloured .... 5·00 5·00

No. 2479 was printed in sheetlets of four stamps with an enlarged, illustrated left margin.

2005 (22 Aug). 75th Anniv of First World Cup Football Championship, Uruguay. German Players. T **338** and similar vert designs. Multicoloured. Litho. P 13½.

2480	1200s. Type **338**	2·75	3·25
	a. Sheetlet. Nos. 2480/2	7·50	8·75
2481	1200s. Marko Rehmer.....................................	2·75	3·25
2482	1200s. Jens Nowotny	2·75	3·25
2480/2	*Set of 3*	7·50	8·75

MS2483 123×106 mm. 2500s. Rudi Voller .... 6·50 7·50

Nos. 2480/2 were printed together, *se-tenant*, in sheetlets of three stamps with illustrated and inscribed margins.

339 Labeo victorianus

(Des A. Nabola. Litho Cartor)

2005 (30 Aug). Fish of Lake Victoria. T **339** and similar horiz designs. Multicoloured. P 13½.

2484	350s. Type **339**	1·25	55
2485	350s. *Haplochromis* sharpsnout	1·25	1·25
	a. Sheetlet. Nos. 2485/90..........................	6·75	6·75
2486	350s. *Haplochromis chilotes*	1·25	1·25
2487	350s. *Mormyrus kannume*	1·25	1·25
2488	350s. *Clarias gariepinus*................................	1·25	1·25
2489	350s. *Synodontis afrofischeri*	1·25	1·25
2490	350s. *Protopterus aethiopicius*	1·25	1·25
2491	400s. *Lates niloticus*.....................................	1·50	1·00
2492	600s. *Pundamilia nyererei*.............................	2·25	2·00
2493	800s. *Brycinus sadleri*...................................	3·00	3·25
2484/93	*Set of 10*	14·00	13·00

MS2494 90×90 mm. 500s. *Oreochromis niloticus*........... 1·75 2·00

Nos. 2485/90 were printed together, *se-tenant*, in sheetlets of six stamps.

340 Albert Einstein and Commemorative Coins

2005 (22 Sept). 50th Death Anniv of Albert Einstein (physicist). T **340** and similar horiz designs. Multicoloured. Litho. P 13.

2495	1300s. Type **340**	4·00	4·00
	a. Sheetlet. Nos. 2495/7	11·00	11·00
2496	1300s. On the cover of *Time* magazine............	4·00	4·00
2497	1300s. On early Israel stamp...........................	4·00	4·00
2495/7	*Set of 3*	11·00	11·00

MS2498 90×55 mm. 2500s. With hands clasped and inscription .... 8·00 8·50

Nos. 2495/7 were printed together, *se-tenant*, in sheetlets of three stamps with illustrated margins.

341 *Papilio ufipa*   **342** "Diabetes leads to Amputation" (World Diabetes Day)

(Des A. Nabola. Litho Austrian State Ptg Wks, Vienna)

2005 (27 Oct). Butterflies of Tanzania. T **341** and similar horiz designs. Multicoloured. P 14×13½.

2499	350s. Type **341**	1·75	55
2500	500s. *Mylothris sagala mahale*......................	2·00	1·10
2501	600s. Type **341**	2·50	2·50
	a. Sheetlet. Nos. 2501/6..............................	13·50	13·50
2502	600s. *Amauris tartarea tukuyuensis*................	2·50	2·50
2503	600s. *Euphaedra neophron kiellandi*..............	2·50	2·50
2504	600s. *Charaxes lucyae gabrielleae*	2·50	2·50
2505	600s. *Abisara zanzibarica*	2·50	2·50
2506	600s. *Acrae utengulensis*...............................	2·50	2·50
2507	800s. As No. 2504	3·00	3·25

2499/507	*Set of 9*	19·00	18·00
MS2508	90×90 mm. 500s. *Charaxes usambarae maridadi*	2·50	2·75

Nos. 2501/6 were printed together, *se-tenant*, in sheetlets of six stamps. No. 2502 was also printed in ordinary sheets.

(Des P. Ndembo. Litho Enschedé)

2005 (9 Dec). Anniversaries and Events. T **342** and similar horiz designs. Multicoloured. P 13½×13 (horiz) or 13×13½ (vert).

2509	350s. Type **342**	1·25	50
2510	500s. Voters queuing at polling station (General Election)	1·25	1·00
2511	600s. Pope John Paul II on arrival in Tanzania, 1990	2·75	2·25
2512	600s. Presidents J. K. Nyerere (Tanganyika) and Abeid Aman Kurume (Zanzibar) signing Act of Union, 1964	2·75	2·75
	a. Sheetlet. Nos. 2512/17	15·00	15·00
2513	600s. Woman casting vote (General Election)	2·75	2·75
2514	600s. Pope John Paul II greeted by former Pres. and Mrs. Nyerere, 1990	2·75	2·75
2515	600s. Pope John Paul II and Laurean Cardinal Rugambwa, 1990	2·75	2·75
2516	600s. Majimaji Museum, Songea (Cent of Majimaji rebellion)	2·75	2·75
2517	600s. Pres. B. W. Mkapa burning arms after ceasefire, 2001	2·75	2·75
2518	800s. Pope John Paul II, Pres. Mwinyi and Laurean Cardinal Rugambwa, 1990	3·50	3·50
2509/18	*Set of 10*	23·00	22·00
MS2519	90×90 mm. 500s. Majimaji Monument (Cent of Majimaji rebellion) (*vert*)	1·75	2·00

Nos. 2512/17 were printed together, *se-tenant*, in sheetlets of six stamps with enlarged illustrated margins.

343 Rufous-winged Sunbird

(Litho Cartor)

2006 (25 Mar). Endemic Birds of Tanzania. T **343** and similar multicoloured designs. P 13.

2520	350s. Type **343**	1·25	50
2521	500s. Pemba white-eye	1·75	1·00
2522	600s. Kilombero weaver	2·00	1·50
2523	600s. Pemba scops owl	2·25	2·25
	a. Sheetlet. Nos. 2523/8	12·00	12·00
2524	600s. Spike-heeled lark	2·25	2·25
2525	600s. Pemba green pigeon	2·25	2·25
2526	600s. Uluguru bush-shrike	2·25	2·25
2527	600s. Yellow collared love bird	2·25	2·25
2528	600s. Usambara nightjar	2·25	2·25
2529	800s. Usambara eagle owl	3·00	3·00
2520/9	*Set of 10*	19·00	18·00
MS2530	121×82 mm. 500s. Moreau's sunbird (39×51 mm)	2·25	2·50

Nos. 2523/8 were printed together, *se-tenant*, in sheetlets of six stamps with enlarged illustrated margins.

344 New National Stadium, Dar es Salaam

(Litho Stamperija Lithuania)

2006 (9 June). World Cup Football Championship, Germany. T **344** and similar multicoloured designs. P 13½×13 (horiz) or 13×13½ (vert).

2531	350s. Type **344**	80	65
2532	500s. Map of Africa with national flags and World Cup emblem (*vert*)	1·25	90
2533	600s. Pres. Kikwete unveiling World Cup trophy in Dar es Salaam	1·25	1·40
2534	800s. Official mascot (*vert*)	1·75	2·00
2531/4	*Set of 4*	4·50	4·50
MS2535	93×72 mm. Nos. 2531/4. P 13½×13	4·75	5·50
MS2536	85×58 mm. 600s. World Cup trophy	1·60	1·75

The vert designs in **MS**2535 are laid horizontally within the miniature sheet.

345 Cap, Kanzu and Buibui (traditional dress)   346 Mount Kenya

(Litho Stamperija Lithuania)

2006 (30 June). Beauty of Zanzibar. T **345** and similar multicoloured designs. P 13½×13.

2537	350s. Type **345**	80	65
2538	500s. Zanzibar Museum	1·25	90
2539	600s. Maruhubi Palace ruins	1·25	1·10
2540	600s. Green turtle, Mnemba Island	1·25	1·50
	a. Sheetlet. Nos. 2540/5	6·75	8·00
2541	600s. Red colobus monkey	6·75	8·00
2542	600s. Giant tortoise, Changgu Island	1·25	1·50
2543	600s. Zanzibar sunset	1·25	1·50
2544	600s. Dhow sailing near Matemwe	1·25	1·50
2545	600s. Coconut crab, Chumbe Island	1·25	1·50
2546	800s. Climbing a coconut tree	1·75	2·25
2537/46	*Set of 10*	11·00	12·50
MS2547	61×103 mm. 500s. Clove foliage with flowerbuds enlarged (*vert*); 500s. Light Signal Tower (*vert*). P 13×13½	2·50	3·00

Nos. 2540/5 were printed together, *se-tenant*, in sheetlets of six stamps with enlarged illustrated margins.

(Litho Enschedé)

2006 (24 Aug). Famous East African Mountains. T **346** and similar multicoloured designs. P 13½×14 (horiz) or 14×13½ (No. 2550).

2548	350s. Type **346**	80	65
2549	400s. Udzungwa Mountains	90	80
2550	600s. Sanje Falls, Udzungwa Mountains (*vert*)	1·50	1·75
2551	800s. Ruwenzori Range, Uganda	2·00	2·50
2548/51	*Set of 4*	4·75	5·25
MS2552	Two sheets, each 130×100 mm. (a) 1000s. Kibo Summit and Mawenzi, Mount Kilimanjaro; 1000s. Giraffe and Mount Kilimanjaro. (b) Herdsman with cattle and Ol Doinyo Lengai; 1000s. Summit and crater, Ol Doinyo Lengai (*vert*) *Set of 2 sheets*	11·00	12·00

No. **MS**2552(b) has the vert stamp turned sideways within the sheet.

347 Mount Kilimanjaro

(Litho Austrian State Ptg Wks, Vienna)

2006 (24 Aug). Phila Africa 06 Stamp Exhibition, Dar-es-Salaam. P 14×13½.

2553	**347** (EUROPE POSTAGE) multicoloured	1·75	1·75
MS2554	100×100 mm. **347** 600s. multicoloured (49×34 mm). P 13½×14	1·75	2·00

347a Map, Signatories, Victoria Falls and Mount Kilimanjaro

(Litho Beijing Stamp Printing House)

2006 (25 Oct). 30th Anniv of TAZARA Railways. T **347a** and similar horiz designs. Multicoloured. P 12.

2555	350s. Type **347a**	1·50	1·50
	a. Sheetlet. Nos. 2555/60	10·00	10·00
2556	350s. Kenneth Kaunda (Zambian President) and Julius Nyerere (Tanzanian Prime Minister) at inauguration, 1975	1·50	1·50

2557	600s. TAZARA Headquarters, Dar-es-Salaam, Tanzania	2·00	2·00
2558	600s. New Kapiri Mposhi railway station	2·00	2·00
2559	800s. Train on viaduct	2·25	2·25
2560	800s. Train on river bridge	2·25	2·25
2555/60	Set of 6	10·00	10·00

Nos. 2555/60 were printed together, *se-tenant*, in sheetlets of six stamps. Stamps in similar designs were issued by Zambia.

348 Julius Nyerere (first President) holding Torch

349 Wild Dog (Selous Game Reserve)

2006 (9 Dec). 45th Anniv of Independence. T **348** and similar multicoloured designs. Litho. P 13½.

2561	350s. Type **348**	80	65
2562	400s. University of Dar es Salaam (*horiz*)	90	75
2563	600s. Abeid A. Karume (first Vice President) (green border)	1·40	1·10
2564	600s. Rashidi Mfaume Kawawa (second Prime Minister)	1·40	1·60
	a. Sheetlet. Nos. 2564/9	7·50	8·50
2565	600s. Julius Nyerere	1·40	1·60
2566	600s. As No. 2563 but white border	1·40	1·60
2567	600s. Ali Hassan Mwinyi (second President)	1·40	1·60
2568	600s. Benjamin W. Mkapa (third President)	1·40	1·60
2569	600s. Jakaya Mrisho Kikwete (President)	1·40	1·60
2570	800s. Julius Nyerere wearing white hat	1·75	2·00
2561/70	Set of 10	12·00	12·50
MS2571	90×110 mm. 400s. National Uhuru Monument, Arusha	1·40	1·60

Nos. 2564/9 were printed together, *se-tenant*, in sheetlets of six stamps with enlarged illustrated margins.

(Des Paul Ndembo. Litho Austrian State Ptg Wks, Vienna)

2007 (23 Feb). Tanzania Safari. T **349** and similar horiz designs. Multicoloured. P 13½×14 (Nos. 2575/9) or 14 (others).

2572	400s. Type **349**	1·25	75
2573	600s. Warthog with young	1·75	1·50
2574	700s. Two zebras	2·25	2·00
2575	700s. Elephant	2·50	2·50
	a. Sheetlet. Nos. 2575/9	11·00	11·00
2576	700s. Cheetah (wrongly inscr "Leopard *Panthera pardus*")	2·50	2·50
2577	700s. Leopard hiding in foliage (69×49 mm).	2·50	2·50
2578	700s. Two buffaloes	2·50	2·50
2579	700s. Lion and lioness	2·50	2·50
2580	800s. Two monkeys with young	2·50	2·50
2572/80	Set of 9	18·00	17·00
MS2581	90×90 mm. 1000s. Two lionesses (49×34 mm). P 13½×14.	3·00	3·50

Nos. 2575/9 were printed together, *se-tenant*, in sheetlets of five stamps with enlarged illustrated margins.

350 Ruins

351 Crops ("Food Security")

(Des Paul Ndembo. Litho Austrian State Ptg Wks, Vienna)

2007 (26 Apr). Historical Zanzibar. T **350** and similar multicoloured designs. P 14.

2582	400s. Type **350**	1·00	75
2583	600s. Coral reef fish (*horiz*)	1·40	1·10
2584	700s. Bet el Ajaib and cloves	1·50	1·60
2585	700s. Beach (*horiz*)	1·50	1·75
	a. Sheetlet. Nos. 2585/90	8·00	9·50
2586	700s. Kizimbani Persian Bath (*horiz*)	1·50	1·75
2587	700s. Maruhubi ruins (*horiz*)	1·50	1·75

2588	700s. Livingstone House (*horiz*)	1·50	1·75
2589	700s. The Old Dispensary (*horiz*)	1·50	1·75
2590	700s. Cave (*horiz*)	1·50	1·75
2591	800s. Coral formation (*horiz*)	1·60	1·75
2582/91	Set of 10	13·00	14·00
MS2592	90×90 mm. 700s. Colobus monkey	1·75	2·00

Nos. 2585/90 were printed together, *se-tenant*, in sheetlets of six stamps with enlarged illustrated margins.

(Des Paul Ndembo. Litho Austrian State Ptg Wks, Vienna)

2007 (30 May). Work of World Vision (aid organization) in Tanzania (3rd series). T **351** and similar horiz designs. Multicoloured. P 14.

2593	400s. Type **351**	1·00	75
2594	600s. Woman milking goat ("Income Generation and Nutrition")	1·40	1·25
2595	700s. Schoolgirls ("Advocating for Child and Rights")	1·50	1·50
2596	800s. Immunization	1·60	1·75
2597	1000s. Children in class ("Education for Development")	2·25	2·75
2593/7	Set of 5	7·00	7·25
MS2598	90×90 mm. 400s. Type **351**	1·25	1·50
MS2599	100×130 mm. 700s.×3 No. 2595; As Nos. 2596/7	3·75	3·00

352 Minister Prof. Mark Mwandosya Tree planting, Kiroka Secondary School, Morogoro

(Des Amak Nabola. Litho Enschedé)

2007 (5 June). Environmental Care. T **352** and similar horiz designs. Multicoloured. P 14.

2600	400s. Type **352**	1·25	75
2601	400s. Illegal mining causing land degradation and water pollution, Amani Nature Reserve, Tanga	1·50	1·50
	a. Sheetlet. Nos. 2601/6	8·00	8·00
2602	400s. Planting tree seedlings in degraded area, Morogoro	1·50	1·50
2603	400s. Planted trees growing in degraded area	1·50	1·50
2604	400s. Traditional soil and moisture conservation method	1·50	1·50
2605	400s. Tree seedlings	1·50	1·50
2606	400s. Soil erosion caused by agriculture on steep mountains	1·50	1·50
2607	500s. Indigenous fallow lands maintaining soil fertility, Shinyanga	1·50	1·25
2608	700s. Kihansi Waterfalls (habitat of endemic toad *Nectophrynoides asperginis*)	2·25	2·50
2609	800s. Natural regeneration of forest area	2·50	2·75
2600/9	Set of 10	15·00	14·50
MS2610	90×90 mm. 500s. Nguru Mountains catchment area for clean water	1·75	2·00

Nos. 2601/6 were printed together, *se-tenant*, in sheetlets of six stamps.

353 "Let us talk with our children about AIDS"

(Des Amak Nabola. Litho Austrian State Ptg Wks)

2007 (14 July). AIDS Prevention Campaign. T **353** and similar horiz designs. Multicoloured. P 14.

2611	400s. Type **353**	1·50	75
2612	700s. "Be faithful in your marriage"	2·25	1·75
2613	800s. "Fight against AIDS is our duty"	2·50	2·25
2614	1000s. "Examine your health to be free"	3·00	3·50
2611/14	Set of 4	8·25	7·50
MS2615	90×90 mm. 400s. "world aids campaign" and emblem	2·00	2·00
MS2616	100×130 mm. 400s.×4 "Let us get education about AIDS"; "Prevent yourself from new infection"; "Let us sing to stop AIDS"; "Let us not segregate the people with AIDS"	6·00	6·00

354 Children at Zanzibar Madrasa Resource Centre

355 Hehe Tribesman, Iringa

(Litho Oriental Press, Bahrain)

2007 (18 Aug). Golden Jubilee of the Aga Khan. T **354** and similar multicoloured designs. P 14½.

2617	400s. Type **354**	1·25	75
2618	600s. Façade of Aga Khan Hospital, Dar es Salaam (gold border)	1·60	1·25
2619	600s. Façade of Stone Town Cultural Centre, Zanzibar	1·60	1·75
	a. Sheetlet. Nos. 2619/22	5·75	6·25
2620	600s. Balcony and window, Stone Town Cultural Centre, Zanzibar	1·60	1·75
2621	600s. Doctors with patient, Aga Khan Hospital, Dar es Salaam	1·60	1·75
2622	600s. As No. 2609 (white border)	1·60	1·75
2623	700s. Serena Safari Lodge, Lake Manyara	1·75	1·90
2624	800s. Serena Inn, Zanzibar	1·90	2·00
2617/24	*Set of 8*	11·50	11·50
MS2625	90×90 mm. 1000s. Woman at Zanzibar Madrasa Resource Centre (*vert*)	2·50	3·00

(Des Paul Peter Ndembo. Litho Enschedé)

2007 (9 Oct). Ceremonial Costumes. T **355** and similar multicoloured designs. P 14.

2626	400s. Type **355**	1·25	75
2627	600s. Haya girls wearing bark cloth	1·60	1·25
2628	700s. Msewe dancers, Pemba (*horiz*)	1·75	1·75
2629	700s. Maasai girls	1·75	1·75
	a. Sheetlet. Nos. 2629/34	9·50	9·50
2630	700s. Maasai dancing	1·75	1·75
2631	700s. Singida Nyaturu girl	1·75	1·75
2632	700s. Sambaa tribesman	1·75	1·75
2633	700s. Wabena woman grinding maize	1·75	1·75
2634	700s. Wairaq man and woman wearing leather	1·75	1·75
2635	800s. Wabena tribal ceremony	1·90	1·90
2626/35	*Set of 10*	15·00	14·00
MS2636	90×90 mm. 400s. Wanyaturu girls	1·40	1·50

Nos. 2629/34 were printed together, *se-tenant*, in sheetlets of six stamps.

356 People of Tanzania

357 Wildebeest and Zebras grazing

(Des Paul P. Ndembo. Litho Oriental Press, Bahrain)

2007 (9 Oct). Anti-Corruption Campaign. T **356** and similar multicoloured designs.

2637	400s. Type **356**	1·25	75
2638	400s. PCB emblem (yellow background)	1·75	2·00
	a. Sheetlet. Nos. 2638/42	11·00	11·00
2639	500s. Policeman and prisoner	2·00	1·50
2640	600s. Bus driver and policeman	4·00	4·25
2641	700s. Businessman on puppet strings (*vert*)	2·00	2·25
2642	800s. Official refusing bribe	2·25	2·50
2637/42	*Set of 6*	12·00	12·00
MS2643	400s. As No. 2638 (olive-bistre background)	1·25	1·40

No. 2637 was only issued in ordinary sheets.

Nos. 2638/42 were printed together, *se-tenant*, in sheetlets of five with enlarged illustrated margins.

Nos. 2639 and 2641/2 were also issued in ordinary sheets.

2008 (30 Jan). Animals. T **357** and similar multicoloured designs. P 13½.

2644	400s. Type **357**	1·50	75
2645	600s. Lion and lioness (*vert*)	2·00	1·75
2646	700s. Lioness descending from tree, Manyara (*vert*)	2·00	2·00

2647	800s. Giraffes (*vert*)	3·00	3·50
2644/7	*Set of 4*	7·75	7·25
MS2648	110×150 mm. 600s.×6 Leopard descending from tree (*vert*); Young chimpanzee (*vert*); Lioness resting on tree (*vert*); Adult male chimpanzee (*vert*); Cheetah with antelope kill; Baboons	11·00	13·00
MS2649	70×140 mm. 600s.×2 Leopard with cub; Impala	3·75	4·25

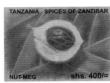

358 Basketball

359 Nutmeg

2008 (8 Apr). Olympic Games, Beijing. T **358** and similar vert designs. Multicoloured. P 12½.

2650	700s. Type **358**	2·75	2·75
	a. Horiz strip of 4. Nos. 2650/3	10·00	10·00
2651	700s. Marathon	2·75	2·75
2652	700s. Swimming	2·75	2·75
2653	700s. Javelin throw	2·75	2·75
2650/3	*Set of 4*	10·00	10·00

Nos. 2650/3 were printed together, *se-tenant*, in sheetlets of four stamps with enlarged illustrated margins.

(Des Paul P. Ndembo. Litho Madras Security Printers, India)

2008 (26 Apr). Spices of Zanzibar. T **359** and similar multicoloured designs. P 13.

2654	400s. Type **359**	1·25	75
2655	600s. Picking cloves	1·75	1·25
2656	700s. Drying cloves (*vert*)	1·90	1·75
2657	1000s. Cardamom seeds	2·75	4·00
2654/7	*Set of 4*	7·00	7·00
MS2658	116×115 mm. 600s.×6 Growing cardamom; Vanilla; Ginger; Mdalasini; Black pepper; Paprika	10·00	12·00
MS2659	101×101 mm. 600s. Binzari	1·90	2·25

360 Turtle

361 Kitulo National Park

(Des Paul P. Ndembo. Litho Austrian State Ptg Wks, Vienna)

2008 (15 Aug). Marine Parks of Tanzania. T **360** and similar multicoloured designs. P 14×13½ (**MS**2664) or 13½ (others).

2660	400s. Type **360**	1·25	75
2661	600s. Dugongs	1·75	1·25
2662	700s. Octopus	1·90	1·75
2663	1000s. Whale shark	2·75	4·00
2660/3	*Set of 4*	7·00	7·00
MS2664	150×140 mm. 600s.×6 Lizard fish; Moray eel; Turtle (facing right); Clear lion fish; Anemone fish; Coelacanth (all 42×32 mm)	12·00	14·00
MS2665	120×80 mm. 600s. Pair of seahorses (35×50 mm)	1·90	2·25

(Des Amak Nabola. Litho Austrian State Ptg Wks, Austria)

2008 (25 Nov). Botanical Gardens of Tanzania. T **361** and similar horiz designs. Multicoloured. P 13½.

2666	400s. Type **361**	1·25	75
2667	600s. Butterfly and chameleon in Amani Forest	2·00	1·50
2668	700s. Monkey and waterfall in Udzungwa Mountains Forest	2·00	2·00
2669	1000s. Forest in Saadani National Park	2·75	4·00
2666/9	*Set of 4*	7·25	7·50
MS2670	127×77 mm. 600s.×6 Wild flowers ('Kitulo, the Garden of God'); Garden House, Vuga-Lushoto; Wild flowers and ferns, Udzungwa Mountains; Shoebill, Lake Rushwa Kagera; Riverside trees, Rufiji river, Selous Game Reserve; Rhinoceros, Ngorongoro crater	14·00	15·00
MS2671	100×150 mm. 600s. Denham's bustard and wild flowers ('Kitulo Botanical Wonderland') (50×35 mm)	2·75	3·00

362 Automated Post Office Counter

363 Pres. George W. Bush

(Litho Austrian State Ptg Wks, Vienna)

2009 (20 Jan). 15th Anniv of Tanzania Posta Corporation. T **362** and similar multicoloured design. P 13½.

2672	400s. Type **362**	1·00	1·00
2673	600s. Posta Headquarters Building (*vert*)	1·50	1·50

2009 (27 Jan). Signing of Millennium Challenge Compact Aid Package by US President George Bush and Pres. Kikwete of Tanzania. Sheet 127×89 mm containing T **363** and similar vert design. Multicoloured. P 13½.

MS2674 Type **363**; Pres. Jakaya Kikwete .... 7·00   8·00

364 Mkuranga Moth

(Litho Cartor)

2009 (30 June). Butterflies (and Moth) of Tanzania. T **364** and similar multicoloured designs. P 13½.

2675	400s. Type **364**	1·50	1·00
2676	600s. Udzungwa Butterfly	1·75	1·25
2677	700s. *Acraea petraea* (butterfly red-brown)	1·90	1·90
2678	800s. *Acraea petraea* (butterfly pale brown)	2·25	2·50
2675/2678 *Set of 4*		6·75	6·00

MS2679 140×173 mm. 600s.×4 *Cymothoe alcimeda*; *Junonuia octavia sesamus*; *Junonia oenone oenone*; *Hypolimnas misippus* .... 6·50   7·00

MS2680 90×60 mm. 600s. Vanessa cardui and sunflowers .... 2·00   2·25

MS2681 120×90 mm. 600s. Axiocerses tjoane (*vert*) ..... 2·00   2·25

The inscription 'Udzungwa Butterfly' on No. 2676 is printed upside down along the foot of the stamp design.

365 Red Colobus Monkey

366 Chimpanzees

(Litho Enschedé)

2009 (31 July). Zanzibar Attractions. T **365** and similar multicoloured designs. P 14.

2682	400s. Type **365**	1·25	60
2683	600s. House of Wonders (*horiz*)	1·50	1·00
2684	700s. Carved door	1·60	1·60
2685	1000s. Coffee seller	2·25	2·75
2682/2685 *Set of 4*		6·00	5·50

MS2686 150×115 mm. 600s.×6 Ngalawa (outrigger canoe); Zanzibar Seafront (*horiz*); Giant tortoise (*horiz*); Face of Red Colobus Monkey; Chake Chake's Courthouse (*horiz*); Zumari player (*horiz*) ...... 9·00   9·00

MS2687 90×90 mm. 600s. Zanzibar Seafront with a Dhow (*horiz*) .... 1·40   1·40

In **MS**2686 the vertical designs are laid sideways within the sheet.

(Litho Enschedé)

2009 (31 Aug). Wild Animals of Tanzania. T **366** and similar multicoloured designs. P 14.

2688	400s. Type **366**	1·00	50

2689	500s. Lion and lioness (*horiz*)	1·25	75
2690	600s. Grant's Red Colobus Monkeys (*horiz*)	1·25	85
2691	700s. Elephants	1·75	1·25
2692	800s. Migrating gnus (*horiz*)	1·75	1·25
2693	1000s. Water buck	2·25	1·75
2694	1800s. Elephant looking for tree foliage	5·00	4·50
2695	2000s. Migrating zebras (*horiz*)	5·50	5·50
2696	2500s. Hunting dogs (*horiz*)	6·00	7·00
2697	3000s. Buffalo (*horiz*)	7·00	8·00
2698	5000s. Zebras, gnu and gazelles grazing (*horiz*)	11·00	12·00
2688/2698 *Set of 11*		40·00	40·00

MS2699 150×115 mm. 600s.×6 Kirk's Red Colobus Monkey; Lioness guarding her cubs; The Udzungwa Monkey; Female Kongoni with her young; Female hippopotamus with baby; Leopard with her cub (all horiz) .... 9·00   9·00

MS2700 90×90 mm. 600s. Male Giraffe (*horiz*) .... 1·75   1·90

367 Mdako Game

(Litho Austrian State Ptg Wks, Vienna)

2009 (30 Dec). Youth and Sports. T **367** and similar horiz designs. Multicoloured. P 14.

2701	400s. Type **367**	1·00	50
2702	600s. Girls playing tennis	1·25	75
2703	700s. Dancing	1·40	1·25
2704	1000s. Boy on swing	2·25	2·50
2701/2704 *Set of 4*		5·50	4·50

MS2705 145×90 mm. 600s.×6 Bao game; Boys playing basketball; Boys playing handball; Boys playing baseball; Athletics (relay race); Girls skipping .... 9·00   9·00

MS2706 130×90 mm. 600s. Football game .... 1·40   1·40

368 Electronic Money Transfer

369 Teacher and Students

(Litho)

2010 (18 Jan). 30th Anniv of PAPU (Pan African Postal Union). T **368** and similar horiz designs. Multicoloured. P 14½.

2707	400s. Type **368**	80	80
2708	500s. Integrating Physical Mail into Digital World	1·00	1·00
2709	700s. Track and Trace of Postal Items	1·40	1·40
2707/9 *Set of 3*		3·00	3·00

MS2710 116×116 mm. 600s. Post Office Internet Café ... 1·25   1·25

(Litho Oriental Press, Bahrain)

2010 (28 Oct). St. Jude's School, Arusha. T **369** and similar horiz designs. Multicoloured. P 13.

2711	400s. Type **369**	80	80
2712	400s. Two students with textbook	80	80
2713	600s. Students in canteen	1·25	1·25
2714	700s. Student	1·40	1·40
2715	800s. School bus	1·60	1·60
2711/15 *Set of 5*		5·25	5·25

MS2716 91×91 mm. Nos. 2712/15 .... 5·00   5·00

370 Ruins of Friday Mosque, Tumbatu

(Litho)

2011 (22 Feb). Wonders of Zanzibar. T **370** and similar multicoloured designs. P 14 (**MS**2722) or 13½ (others).

2717	400s. Giant Tortoise, Prison Island	80	80
2718	600s. Red Colobus Monkey, Jozani Forest (*vert*)	1·25	1·25

2719	700s. Pemba Flying Fox	1·40	1·40
2720	800s. Slave Chambers, Manga Pwani (vert)	1·60	1·60
2717/20 Set of 4		4·50	4·50
MS2721 168×126 mm. 600s.×6 Type **370**; Ruins of Beit el Mtoni palace; Anglican Cathedral; Beit el Jaib palace; Ruins of Maruhubi Palace; Old Fort, Stone Town		7·50	7·50
MS2722 140×79 mm. 600s. Chumbe Island Lighthouse (40×60 mm)		1·25	1·25

371 Truxalis sp.

372 Kibo Peak, Mount Kilimanjaro

(Litho De La Rue)

2011 (15 Apr). Grasshoppers. T **371** and similar horiz designs. Multicoloured. P 14.

2723	500s. Type **371**	1·00	1·00
2724	700s. Common Milkweed Locust (*Phynateus morbillosus*)	1·40	1·40
2725	800s. Common Stick Grasshopper (*Acrida acuminate*)	1·60	1·60
2726	900s. Red Locust (*Nomadacris septemfasciata*)	1·75	1·75
2723/6 Set of 4		5·25	5·25
MS2727 93×90 mm. 600s. Elegent Grasshopper (*Zanocerus elegans*)		1·25	1·25
MS2728 100×100 mm. 700s.×6 The Migratory Locust (*Locusta migroteria*); Foam Locust (*Dictyopharus spumans*); Green Milkweed Locust (*Phymateus yiridipes*); The Edible Grasshopper (*Homorochoryphus nitidulus*); Mole Cricket (*Gryllotalpa africana*); Green Bush Cricket (*Tettigonia viridissima*)		8·25	8·25

(Litho Austrian State Ptg Wks, Vienna)

2011 (16 May). Tourist Attractions. T **372** and similar horiz designs. Multicoloured. Self-adhesive. Die-cut perf 14.

2729	500s. Type **372**	1·00	1·00
	a. Booklet pane. No. 2729×8	8·00	
2730	700s. Pemba Floating Island	1·40	1·40
	a. Booklet pane. No. 2730×8	11·00	
2731	800s. Giraffes, Serengeti National Park	1·60	1·60
	a. Booklet pane. No. 2731×8	12·00	
2732	900s. Lions, Serengeti National Park	1·75	1·75
	a. Booklet pane. No. 2732×8	14·00	
2729/32 Set of 4		5·50	5·50

Nos. 2729/32 were issued in separate booklets, Nos. SB19/22.

373 Grain Storage Baskets

(Litho De La Rue)

2011 (25 Aug). Traditional Grain Storage. T **373** and similar horiz designs. Multicoloured. P 14.

2733	500s. Type **373**	1·00	1·00
2734	700s. Pole hanging	1·40	1·40
2735	800s. Tree hanging	1·60	1·60
2736	900s. Outdoor granary	1·75	1·75
2733/6 Set of 4		5·25	5·25
MS2737 93×90 mm. 600s. Outdoor grain storage		1·25	1·25
MS2738 100×100 mm. 700s.×6 Grain granary; Outdoor granary (cylindrical); Maize granary; Granary container; Outdoor granary (circular); Indoor granary		8·50	8·50

900/

(374)

375 Child drawing Clean Water

2011 (8 Sept). Nos. 809/a surch with T **374**.

2739	900s. on 25s. Scarlet-chested Sunbird	1·75	1·75
2740	900s. on 30s. African Wood Pigeon	1·75	1·75

(Litho Enschedé)

2011 (30 Sept). Work of World Vision (aid organization) in Tanzania (5th series). T **375** and similar horiz designs. Multicoloured. P 14×13.

2741	500s. Type **375**	1·00	1·00
2742	800s. Boy with maize (Food Security)	1·60	1·60
2743	900s. Three boys (Children enjoy Good Health)	1·75	1·75
2744	1000s. Advocating for Child's Right	1·90	1·90
2741/4 Set of 4		5·75	5·75

376 Complete Independence, 9 December 1961

(Litho Oriental Press, Bahrain)

2011 (9 Dec). 50th Anniv of Independence. T **376** and similar multicoloured designs. P 14 (MS2805), 14×13 (MS2806) or 13 (others).

2745	500s. Type **376**	1·00	1·00
	a. Horiz strip of 5. Nos. 2745/9	5·00	5·00
2746	500s. Julius Nyerere and students on adult education program	1·00	1·00
2747	500s. Presidents Nyerere, Kaunda of Zambia and Samora Machel of Mozambique	1·00	1·00
2748	500s. Pres. Nyerere and Hon. Edward Moringe Sakoine, 1982	1·00	1·00
2749	500s. Presidents Nyerere and Samora Machel of Mozambique	1·00	1·00
2750	800s. Pres. Nyerere and Nelson Mandela	1·60	1·60
2751	900s. Pres. Jakaya Kikwete with US Pres. Obama at the White House	1·75	1·75
2745/51 Set of 7		7·50	7·50
MS2752 180×151 mm. 700s.×4 State House; Parliament of Tanzania at Dodoma; University of Dodoma; University of Dar Es Salaam		5·50	5·50
MS2753 181×151 mm. 700s.×8 Julius Kambarage Nyerere ('Father of the Nation'); Alhaj Ali Hassan Mwinyi (2nd President); Benjamin William Mkapa (3rd President); Jakaya Mrisho Kikwete (President of Tanzania); Abeid Aman Karume (1st Vice President of Tanzania, 1st President of Zanzibar); Hon. Rashid Mfaume Kwawa (2nd Prime Minister); Hon. Edward Moringe Sokoine (Prime Minister 1980–4); Julius Kambarage Nyerere (as old man) (all vert)		11·00	11·00
MS2754 181×151 mm. 800s. Pres. Nyerere with Pres. Fidel Castro of Cuba; 800s. Pres. Nyerere with Pres. Kwame Nkrumah of Ghana; As No. 2751; 900s. Pres. Jakaya Kikwete with Pres. Hu Jin Tao of China in Tanzania		6·75	6·75
MS2755 160×150 mm. 900s.×4 Pres. Jakaya Kikwete with Pres. Hu Jin Tao of China in Tanzania; No. 2751; As No. 2750; Pres. Jakaya Kikwete with ex Presidents Ally Hassan Mwinyi and Benjamin William Mkapa		7·00	7·00

Nos. 2745/9 were printed together, *se-tenant*, as horizontal strips of five stamps throughout the sheets.

377 Pot with Three Mouths for serving Beer and Pottery Cow for Water Storage

(Des Paul P. Ndembo. Litho Enschedé)

2012 (15 Mar). Material Culture. T **377** and similar horiz designs. Multicoloured. P 14×13½.

2756	500s. Type **377**	1·00	1·00
2757	700s. Fiddle with calabash resonator	1·40	1·40
2758	800s. Maasai beaded necklaces	1·60	1·60
2759	900s. Container with lid and maize storage container	1·75	1·75

2760	1000s. Milk mugs of bamboo and decorated calabash	1·90	1·90
2756/60	Set of 5	7·00	7·00

MS2761 150×90 mm. 800s.×6 Bao game; Grain storage; Cooking pot and storage pot; Drum and wedding drums; Winnowing trays, storage basket and drinking mug; Fruit storage and dish cover ...... 9·50 9·50

MS2762 90×90 mm. No. 2760 .... 1·90 1·90

378 New House of Representatives Building

(Paul P. Ndembo. Litho Enschedé)

2012 (26 Apr). Zanzibar Attractions (2nd series). T **378** and similar multicoloured designs. P 13×14 (vert) or 14×13 (horiz).

2763	500s. Type **378**	1·00	1·00
2764	700s. Zanzibar doors	1·40	1·40
2765	800s. Ngalawa sailing off the Jambian coast, Zanzibar (vert)	1·60	1·60
2766	900s. Zanzibar indigenous huts	1·75	1·75
2763/6	Set of 4	5·25	5·25

MS2767 151×90 mm. 800s.×6 Dr. Ali Mohammed Shein, President of Zanzibar, harvesting cloves; Dr. Ali Mohammed Shein and 1st Vice President Maalim Seif Sharif Hamad on official tour of Zanzibar; President Ali Mohammed Shein meeting girl students; Dr. Ali Mohammed Shein helping with paddy harvest; Dr. Ali Mohammed Shein, Maalim Seif Sharif Hamad and 2nd Vice President Ambassador Seif Ali Iddi; Dr. Ali Mohammed Shein and 1st Lady Mwanamwema Shein helping with separation of clove buds ...... 9·50 9·50

MS2768 90×90 mm. 1000s. Darajani Market, Stone Town ...... 1·90 1·90

379 Iringa Red Colobus Monkey

380 Mihrab of Kizimkazi Mosque with 12th-century Kufic Inscription

(Litho Enschedé)

2012 (15 Oct). Colobus Monkeys of Tanzania. T **379** and similar multicoloured designs. P 14×13½.

MS2769 90×90 mm. 700s. Zanzibar Red Colobus, Jozani Chwaka Bay National Park ...... 1·40 1·40

MS2770 100×100 mm. 800s.×6 Type **379**; Black & White Colobus (seen from front); Iringa Red Colobus Monkey (looking forward); Black & White Colobus (side view); Iringa Red Colobus Monkey (looking left); Sanje Crested Mangabay Monkey ...... 9·50 9·50

(Des Paul P. Ndembo. Litho Garsu Pasaulis, Lithuania)

2013 (26 Apr). Zanzibar the Mystical Islands. T **380** and similar multicoloured designs. P 13.

2771	600s. Type **380**	1·25	1·25
2772	700s. Bao board (horiz)	1·40	1·40
2773	800s. Traditional wooden charpoys used as beach beds (horiz)	1·60	1·60
2774	900s. Giant Tortoise (horiz)	1·75	1·75
2771/4	Set of 4	5·50	5·50

MS2775 120×100 mm. 700s.×6 Mkumbu – ruins of tombs; Stone pillars at ruins of Maruhubi Palace; Zanzibar Red Colobus Monkey at Jozan Chwaka Bay National Park; Bao board and wooden chests with inlay; Crenellated walls and Palace Museum; Coconut Crab on palm tree, Chumbe Island ...... 8·25 8·25

MS2776 110×90 mm. 1600s. Kibanda Beni – Forodhali Square (horiz) ...... 3·25 3·25

381 Lioness carrying Cub

(Litho)

2013 (31 July). Big Five. T **381** and similar horiz designs. Multicoloured. P 13.

MS2777 110×90 mm. 1600s. Type **381** ...... 3·25 3·25

MS2778 110×90 mm. 1600s. Leopard ...... 3·25 3·25

MS2779 110×90 mm. 1600s. Rhinoceros ...... 3·25 3·25

MS2780 100×120 mm. 1800s.×5 As Type **419**; Elephants; Buffaloes; Leopard; Rhinoceros ...... 16·00 16·00

500/=

500/=

(382) (383)

2013 (1 Aug). Nos. 2644 and 2688 surch as Types 382/3.

2781	500s. on 400s. Type **357** (surch with T **382**)...	4·00	4·00
2782	500s. on 400s. Type **366** (surch h with T **383**).	4·00	4·00

384 Kuria Lady from Mara

(Litho Garsu Pasaulis, Lithuania)

2013 (30 Nov). Ceremonial Costumes of Tanzania. T **384** and similar multicoloured designs. P 13.

2783	600s. Type **384**	1·25	1·25
2784	700s. Nyaturu woman	1·40	1·40
2785	800s. Nyagatwa couple (vert)	1·60	1·60
2786	900s. Zaramo boy in Jando ceremony (vert)..	1·75	1·75
2783/6	Set of 4	5·50	5·50

MS2787 120×100 mm. 700s.×6 Mbunga woman; Makonde woman; Sukuma dancer; Haya Umwinyereko dancer; Kwele widow woman; Ngindo girl in Unyago ceremony (all vert) ...... 8·25 8·25

MS2788 110×90 mm. 1600s. Manyema Kilua dancer... 3·25 3·25

385 Weighing Baby ('Child's road to health')

(Litho Austrian State Ptg Wks, Vienna)

2013 (20 Dec). Work of World Vision (aid organization) in Tanzania (6th series). T **385** and similar multicoloured designs. P 14.

2789	600s. Type **385**	1·25	1·25
2790	800s. 'Child's well being – livelihood' (horiz)...	1·60	1·60

2791	900s. 'Child's Nutrition – Breast feeding'	1·75	1·75
2792	1000s. Drawing water ('Water and Sanitation') (horiz)	1·90	1·90
2789/92	Set of 4	5·75	5·75
MS2793	90×91 mm. No. 2791	1·75	1·75

386 Dr. Ali M. Shein (7th President)

(Litho Enschedé)

2014 (12 Jan). 50th Anniv of Zanzibar Revolution. T 385 and similar multicoloured designs. P 13×14 (vert) or 14×13 (horiz).

2794	500s. Type 386	1·00	1·00
2795	700s. Karume showing Nyerere model of housing development (horiz)	1·40	1·40
2796	800s. Sheikh Abed Karume with revolutionary commanders (horiz)	1·60	1·60
2794/6	Set of 3	3·50	3·50
MS2797	151×115 mm. 600s.×6 Aboud J. Mwinyi (2nd President of Zanzibar); Ali H. Mwinyi (3rd President); Idrisa A. Wakil (4th President); Dr. Salmin A. Juma (5th President); Amani A. Karume (6th President); Dr. Ali M. Shein (7th President)	7·50	7·50
MS2798	151×115 mm. 700s.×2 Seif S. Hamad (1st Vice President of Zanzibar); Ambassador Seif Idd (2nd Vice President)	2·75	2·75
MS2799	91×91 mm. 1000s. Zanzibar House of Representatives building (horiz)	1·90	1·90

STAMP BOOKLETS

1965 (9 Dec). Black on blue (No. SB6) or buff (No. SB7) covers, size 48×46 mm. Stitched.

SB6	3s. booklet containing four 15c. and eight 30c. (Nos. 130, 132) in blocks of 4	5·50
SB7	5s. booklet containing four 15c. and 50c. and eight 30c. (Nos. 130, 132, 134) in blocks of 4	6·00

1965 (9 Dec). Black on blue (No. SB8) or buff (No. SB9) covers, size 48×45 mm. Stitched.

SB8	3s. booklet containing four 15c. and eight 30c. (Nos. 144, 146) in blocks of 4	3·00
SB9	5s. booklet containing 10c., 15c., 20c., 30c. and 50c. and eight 30c. (Nos. 143/6, 148), each in blocks of 4	3·50

1971 (15 Dec). Black printed (No. SB10) or black on claret (No. SB11) covers, size 48×46 mm. Stitched.

SB10	5s. booklet containing four 10c., 15c. and 40c., and eight 30c. (Nos. 143, 144a, 146, 147a) in blocks of 4	26·00
SB11	10s. booklet containing four 10c., 20c., 30c. and 50c., and eight 70c. (Nos. 143, 145/6, 148a, 150a) in blocks of 4	25·00

1973 (13 June). Black printed cover, size 48×46 mm. Stitched.

SB12	5s. booklet containing four 10c., 15c. and 40c., and eight 30c. (Nos. 143a, 144a, 146a, 147a) in blocks of 4	23·00

1973 (10 Dec). Black on yellow (No. SB13) or blue (No. SB14) covers, size 54×41 mm. Stitched.

SB13	5s. booklet containing 5c., 10c., 20c., 40c. and 50c. (Nos. 158/9, 161, 163/4), each in block of 4	12·00
SB14	10s. booklet containing four 10c., 20c., 30c. and 50c., and eight 70c. (Nos. 159, 161/2, 164, 166) in blocks of 4	20·00

1980 (Nov). Black printed (No. SB15) or black on red (No. SB16) covers, size 66×47 mm. Stitched.

SB15	6s. booklet containing eight 10c. and 20c., and four 40c. and 50c. (Nos. 307/10) in blocks of 4.	3·00
SB16	14s. booklet containing four 1s. and two 2s. and 3s. (Nos. 313, 315/16) in pairs	3·50

B 1

1984. Black on green (10s) or red (24s) covers as Type B 1 59×50 mm (10s) or 98×63 mm (24s) stitched.

SB17	10s. booklet containing 20 50c. Waddington printings in panes of 4 (No. 320a)	£200

1984. Black on red cover, 98×63 mm. Stitched.

SB17a	24s. booklet containing four 1s., 2s. and 3s. Waddington printings in panes of 4 (Nos. 320cab, 320eab, 320fab)	£200

1990 (15 Dec). Black on yellow cover as Type B 2, size 99×58 mm. Pane attached by selvedge.

SB18	174s. booklet containing se-tenant pane of twelve (No. 804a)	6·00

B 2 Kibo Peak, Mount Kilimanjaro

2011 (16 May). Tourist Attractions. Multicoloured covers, 98×78 mm, as Type B 2. Self-adhesive.

SB19	4000s. booklet containing pane of eight 500s. (No. 2729a) (Type B 2)	8·00
SB20	5600s. booklet containing pane of eight 700s. (No. 2730a) (Pemba Floating Island)	11·00
SB21	6400s. booklet containing pane of eight 800s. (No. 2731a) (Giraffes)	12·00
SB22	7200s. booklet containing pane of eight 900s. (No. 2732a) (Lions)	14·00

OFFICIAL STAMPS

(Opt photo Harrison)

1965 (9 Dec). Nos. 128/32, 134, 136, 139 optd as Types O 1 (15c., 30c. or larger (17 mm) 5c., 10c., 20c., 50c.), or with O 2 of Tanganyika (1s., 5s.).

O9	5c. ultramarine and yellow-orange	10	2·00
O10	10c. black, greenish yellow, green & blue	10	1·50
O11	15c. multicoloured	10	1·50
O12	20c. sepia, grey-green and greenish blue	10	2·00
O13	30c. black and red-brown	10	1·50
O14	50c. multicoloured	15	1·50
O15	1s. multicoloured	30	1·25
O16	5s. lake-brown, yellow-green and blue	1·75	9·00
O9/16	Set of 8	2·25	18·00

OFFICIAL

(O 3)

(Opt litho Govt Printer, Dar-es-Salaam)

1967 (10 Nov). Nos. 134, 136 and 139 optd as No. O14 (50c.) or with Type O 3 (others).

O17	50c. multicoloured (18.11)	—	14·00
O18	1s. multicoloured (18.11)	20·00	9·00
O19	5s. lake-brown, yellow-green and blue	10·00	16·00

The issue dates given are for the earliest known postmarked examples.

Nos. O9/16 were overprinted by Harrison in photogravure and Nos. O17/19 have litho overprints by the Government Printer, Dar-es-Salaam. On No. O17 the overprint is the same size (17 mm long) as on No. O14.

1967 (9 Dec)–71. Nos. 142/6, 148, 151 and 155 optd as Type O 1, but larger (measuring 17 mm) (5c. to 50c.) or as Type O 2 of Tanganyika (1s. and 5s.). Chalk-surfaced paper.

O20	5c. magenta, yellow-olive and black	10	4·25

O21	a. Glazed, ordinary paper (22.1.71)		3·25	4·75
	10c. brown and bistre		10	1·00
	a. Glazed, ordinary paper (1971)		10·00	4·25
O22	15c. grey turquoise-blue and black		10	6·00
	a. Glazed, ordinary paper (22.1.71)		2·75	5·50
O23	20c. brown and turquoise-green		10	1·00
O24	30c. sage-green and black		10	30
O25	50c. multicoloured		15	1·60
	a. Glazed, ordinary paper (22.1.71)		3·00	5·50
O26	1s. orange-brown, slate-blue and maroon .		30	3·00
	a. Glazed, ordinary paper (3.2.71)		16·00	5·50
O27	5s. greenish yellow, black and turquoise-green		2·50	17·00
	a. Glazed, ordinary paper (3.2.71)		19·00	22·00
O20/7	Set of 8		3·00	30·00
O20a/7a	Set of 6		48·00	42·00

The chalk-surfaced paper exists with both PVA gum and gum arabic, but the glazed, ordinary paper exists PVA gum only.

OFFICIAL
(O 4)

1970 (10 Dec)–**73**. Nos. 142/8, 151 and 155 optd locally by letterpress as Type O **4** (5 to 50c.) or as Type O **2** of Tanganyika, but measuring 28 mm (1s. and 5s.).

(a) Chalk-surfaced paper

O28	5c. magenta, yellow-olive and black		50	9·00
	a. "OFFCIAL" (R.7/6)		—	£130
O29	10c. brown and bistre		85	3·50
	a. "OFFCIAL" (R.7/6)			
O30	20c. brown and turquoise-green		1·25	4·00
O31	30c. sage-green and black		1·50	4·00
O28/31	Set of 4		3·50	18·00

(b) Glazed, ordinary paper (1973)

O32	5c. magenta, yellow-olive and black		20·00	7·00
	a. "OFFCIAL" (R.7/6)		£500	90·00
	b. "OFFICIA" (R.10/9)		—	£110
O33	10c. brown and bistre		—	7·00
	a. "OFFCIAL" (R.7/6)		—	£120
O34	15c. grey, turquoise-blue and black		85·00	7·00
	a. "OFFCIAL" (R.7/6)		—	£110
O35	20c. brown and turquoise-green		—	4·75
O36	40c. yellow, chocolate and bright green		45·00	4·00
	a. Opt double		—	£200
	b. "OFFICIA" (R.10/9)		—	£110
O37	50c. multicoloured		—	4·00
	a. "OFFCIAL" (R.7/6)		—	£100
O38	1s. orange-brown, slate-blue and maroon .		65·00	13·00
	a. Opt double		—	£400
O39	5s. greenish yellow, black and turquoise-green		75·00	55·00

The letterpress overprint can be distinguished from the photogravure by its absence of screening dots and the overprint showing through to the reverse, apart from the difference in length.

"OFFICIAL" handstamps: various "Fish" and "Butterflies" definitives have been reported handstamped "OFFICIAL" in a range of colours. The status of these is unknown, but they are outside the scope of this catalogue.

1973 (10 Dec). Nos. 158/9, 161, 163/4 and 166/70 optd with Type O **1** of Tanganyika (5 to 70c.) or Type O **5** (others).

O40	5c. light yellow-olive, lt violet-blue and black		50	3·25
O41	10c. multicoloured		75	40
O42	20c. reddish cinnamon, orange-yellow & black		1·00	40
O43	40c. multicoloured		1·50	40
O44	50c. multicoloured		1·50	40
O45	70c. turquoise-green, pale orange and black		1·50	1·00
O46	1s. multicoloured		1·50	40
O47	1s.50 multicoloured		2·75	3·75
	a. Pair, one without opt †		†	£650
O48	2s.50 multicoloured		3·25	8·50
O49	5s. multicoloured		3·50	14·00
O40/9	Set of 10		16·00	29·00

No. O47a is due to a paper fold and comes from a sheet used at Kigoma in 1974.

1977 (Feb). Nos. 159, 161 and 163/4 optd locally by letterpress as Type O **4**.

O50	10c. multicoloured		—	4·00
	a. "OFFCIAL" (R. 7/6)		—	80·00
O51	20c. multicoloured		—	4·00
	a. "OFFCIAL" (R. 7/6)		—	£100
	b. Opt double			
	c. Opt inverted			
O52	40c. multicoloured		—	4·00
	a. "OFFCIAL" (R. 7/6)		—	90·00
O53	50c. multicoloured		—	4·00
	a. "OFFCIAL" (R. 7/6)		—	80·00
	b. Opt inverted		†	£400

(O **6**)	(O **6a**)	(O **7**)	(O **7a**)	

1980 (Nov)–**85**.

*(a) Bradbury Wilkinson printings. Nos. 307/12 optd with Type O **6** (10 mm long) and Nos. 313 and 315/17 optd with Type O **7** (13½ mm long)*

O54	10c. Type **75**		20	1·50
O55	20c. Large-spotted Genet		25	1·00
O56	40c. Banded Mongoose		30	1·00
O57	50c. Ratel (light blue panel at foot)		30	40
O58	75c. Large-toothed Rock Hyrax		40	60
O59	80c. Leopard		55	1·50
O60	1s. Type **76**		55	40
O61	2s. Common Zebra		85	2·75
O62	3s. African Buffalo		1·00	3·00
O63	5s. Lion		1·50	4·00
O54/63	Set of 10		5·50	14·00

*(b) John Waddington printings. No. 320a optd with Type O **6a** (8½ mm long) and Nos. 320c/g optd with Type O **7a** (13 mm long) (1984-85)*

O64	50c. Ratel (turquoise-blue panel at foot)		2·75	2·25
O65	1s. Type **76**		3·25	2·50
O66	1s.50 Giraffe		7·50	5·50
O67	2s. Common Zebra		7·00	7·50
O68	3s. African Buffalo		8·00	10·00
O69	5s. Lion		10·00	14·00
O64/9	Set of 6		35·00	38·00

On the Bradbury Wilkinson printings the overprint reads downwards on the 10c., 50c., 2a., 5s. and upwards on the others. All values of the John Waddington printing show the overprint reading upwards.

OFFICIAL
(O 8)

OFFICIAL
(O 9)

1990 (15 Dec)–**91**. Nos. 804/12 optd with Type O **8** (5s. to 30s.) or Type O **9** (40s. to 100s.).

O70	5s. Type **163**		65	2·75
O71	9s. African Emerald Cuckoo		80	1·75
O72	13s. Little Bee Eater		1·00	1·75
O73	15s. Red Bishop		1·00	2·00
O74	20s. Bateleur		1·00	2·00
O75	25s. Scarlet-chested Sunbird		1·00	2·00
O76	30s. African Wood Pigeon (1.7.91)		1·50	2·50
O77	40s. Type **164**		1·25	2·00
O78	70s. Helmet Guineafowl		2·25	3·00
O79	100s. Eastern White Pelican		2·75	4·00
O70/9	Set of 10		12·00	21·00

Official overprints were reported as being used for normal postal purposes during 1992.

OFFICIAL
(O 10)

1996 (30 Dec). Nos. 2075/6, 2078 and 2081 optd with Type O **10**.

O80	100s. *Plumeria rubra acutifolia*		80	1·00
O81	140s. *Liliaceae*		1·00	1·40
O82	200s. *Liliaceae (different)*		1·50	1·75
O83	260s. *Malvaviscus penduliflorus*		1·50	1·75
O84	300s. *Canna*		1·75	2·25
O85	380s. *Nerium oleander carneum*		2·00	2·25
O80/5	Set of 6		7·75	9·50

No. O84 is inscribed "Carna" in error.

POSTAGE DUE STAMPS

Postage Due stamps of Kenya and Uganda were issued for provisional use as such in Tanganyika on 1 July 1933. The postmark is the only means of identification.

The Postage Due stamps of Kenya, Uganda and Tanganyika were used in Tanganyika until 2 January 1967.

D **1**	D **2**

(Litho D.L.R.)

1967 (3 Jan). P 14×13½.

D1	D **1**	5c. scarlet	35	10·00
D2	D **2**	10c. green	45	10·00

D3		20c. deep blue	50	13·00
D4		30c. red-brown	50	15·00
D5		40c. bright purple	50	18·00
D6		1s. orange	80	12·00
D1/6	*Set of 6*		2·75	70·00

1969 (12 Dec)–**71**. Chalk-surfaced paper. P 14×15.

D7	D **1**	5c. scarlet	30	14·00
		a. Glazed, ordinary paper (13.7.71)	4·00	8·00
D8		10c. green	65	6·00
		a. Glazed, ordinary paper (13.7.71)	75	4·25
D9		20c. deep blue	70	13·00
		a. Glazed, ordinary paper (13.7.71)	2·50	9·00
D10		30c. red-brown	65	23·00
		a. Glazed, ordinary paper (13.7.71)	85	6·50
D11		40c. bright purple	2·00	23·00
		a. Glazed, ordinary paper (13.7.71)	6·50	48·00
D12		1s. orange (*glazed, ordinary paper*) (13.7.71)	4·75	38·00
D7/11	*Set of 5*		3·75	70·00
D7a/12	*Set of 6*		17·00	£100

The stamps on chalk-surfaced paper exist only with gum arabic, but the stamps on glazed paper exist only with PVA gum.

1973 (12 Dec). As Nos. D1/6, but glazed ordinary paper. P 15.

D13	D **1**	5c. scarlet	60	10·00
D14		10c. emerald	60	7·00
D15		20c. deep blue	80	11·00
D16		30c. red-brown	95	11·00
D17		40c. bright mauve	1·00	16·00
D18		1s. bright orange	1·50	17·00
D13/18	*Set of 6*		5·00	65·00

(Litho Questa)

1978 (31 July). Chalk-surfaced paper. P 13½×14.

D19	D **1**	5c. brown-red	15	2·75
D20		10c. emerald	20	2·75
D21		20c. steel-blue	30	3·00
D22		30c. red-brown	45	3·75
D23		40c. bright purple	50	5·50
D24		1s. bright orange	70	6·00
D19/24	*Set of 6*		2·10	16·00

1984. Chalk-surfaced paper. P 15×14.

D25	D **1**	10c. emerald	—	15·00
D26		20c. deep dull blue	—	15·00
D27		30c. reddish brown	—	15·00
D28		40c. bright purple	—	15·00
D29		1s. bright orange		

(Litho Questa)

1990 (15 Dec). P 14½×14.

D30	D **2**	50c. myrtle-green	10	75
D31		80c. ultramarine	10	50
D32		1s. orange-brown	15	75
D33		2s. yellow-olive	20	80
D34		3s. purple	20	90
D35		5s. grey-brown	30	1·00
D36		10s. reddish brown	50	1·25
D37		20s. brown-ochre	75	1·50
D38		40s. bright new blue	25	40
D39		60s. bright blue-green	30	60
D40		80s. lemon	30	80
D41		100s. azure	35	95
D30/41	*Set of 12*		3·25	9·50

Appendix

The following stamps have either been issued in excess of postal needs, or have not been made available to the public in reasonable quantities at face value. Miniature sheets, imperforate stamps, etc., are excluded from this section.

Several appendix issues have been seen commercially used, but the circumstances surrounding their release are unclear. For the time being, those sets from which stamps have been seen properly used are indicated in **bold**. We will consider giving them full listing in the next edition of the catalogue and would welcome information on other issues which are known and, in particular, their dates of use.

1985
Life and Times of Queen Elizabeth the Queen Mother. As Nos. 425/8 but embossed on gold foil. 20s. × 2, 100s. × 2.
Tanzanian Railway Locomotives (1st series). As Nos. 430/3, 5, 10, 20, 30s.

1986
Caribbean Royal Visit. Optd in silver and gold on previous issues. (a) Nos. 425/8 20s. × 2, 100s. × 2. (b) On Nos. 430/3, 5, 10, 20, 30s.
Ameripex International Stamp Exhibition, Chicago. Optd on Nos. 425/8. 20s. × 2, 100s. × 2.

1988
Centenary of Statue of Liberty (1986). 1, 2, 3, 4, 5, 6, 7, 8, 9, 10, 12, 15, 18, 20, 25, 30, 35, 40, 45, 50, 60s.
Royal Ruby Wedding. Optd on No. 378. 10s.
125th Anniv of Red Cross. Optd on Nos. 486/7. 5, 40s.
63rd Anniv of Rotary International in Africa. Optd on Nos. 422/3. 10s., 17s.50.

1995
The Beatles. 100s.×18.
Hoofed Animals. 70, 100, 150, 180, 200, 260, 380s.
Fauna of Coral Reefs. 70, 100, 150, 180, 200, 260, 380s.
Singapore '95 International Stamp Exhibition. Trains of the World. 200s.×18.
Centenary of Sierra Club. 150s.×18.
Bats. 70, 100, 150, 180, 200, 260, 380s.
History of Rock and Roll. 250s.×9
90th Anniversary of Rotary International. 600s.
Winter Olympic Games, Lillehammer, Norway. 300, 400s.
Picasso Paintings. 30, 200, 300s.
450th Death Anniversary of Copernicus (astronomer) (1993). 100, 300s.
Polska'93 International Stamp Exhibition, Poznan. 200, 300s.
95th Birthday of Queen Elizabeth the Queen Mother. 250s.×4
Olympic Games, Atlanta 1996. Olympic History. 200s.×18
50th Anniversary of End of Second World War in the Pacific. 250s.×6
50th Anniv of End of Second World War. 250s.×8
Cacti. 70, 100, 150, 180, 200, 260, 380s.
African Reptiles. 200s.×12
Predatory Animals. 70, 100, 150, 200, 250, 280, 300s.
50th Aniversary of United Nations. 250s.×3
50th Aniversary of U.N. Food and Agriculture Organization. 250s.×3
Centenary of Cinema. Biblical Epics. 250s.×9
20th Anniversary of World Tourism Organization. 100, 300, 400s.
Gerry Garcia (rock musician) Commemoration. 200s.
Frogs. 100, 140, 180, 200, 210, 260, 300s.
Fauna of Kilimanjaro. 100s.×16, 250s.×4
Butterflies. 200s.×19, 250, 370, 410s.

1996
Moths and Butterflies. 70, 100, 150, 200, 250, 260, 300s.
Chinese New Year ("Year of the Rat"). 200s.×4
Horses. 250s.×9
Cats. 100, 150, 200, 250s.×9, 300s.×4
Dogs. 70s, 250s.×10, 300s.×4, 600s.
Crocodiles. 100, 150, 200, 250, 260, 300, 380s.
125th Anniversary of the Metropolitan Museum, New York. Paintings. 200s.×18
Elvis Presley Commemoration. 250s.×9
Snakes. 100, 140, 180, 200, 260, 300, 400s.
China 96, International Stamp Exhibition. Deng Xiaoping. 250s.×6
70th Birthday of Queen Elizabeth II. 300s.×3
Famous People. 70, 100, 150, 200s., 250s.×16
Olympic Games Atlanta. 100, 150, 200, 300s.
Birds. 300s.×16
Centenary of Radio. Famous People. 70, 100, 150, 200s.
Flowers. 300s.×16
Fish. 100, 150, 200s.×9, 250, 500s.
Mercedes and Ferrari Cars. 250s.×12
50th Anniversary of U.N.E.S.C.O. 200, 250, 600s.
50th Anniversary of U.N.I.C.E.F. 200, 250, 500s.
90th Anniversary of Rotary. Nos. 985/1000 and 1589/600 overprinted "90th ANNIVERSARY OF ROTARY 1905–1995" and emblem. 50s.×16, 100s.×12.
International Scout Camp, Thailand and 34th World Scout Conf, Norway. Nos. 1001/16 and 1564/75 overprinted either "34th WORLD SCOUT CONFERENCE NORWAY JULY 8–12 1996" or "INTERNATIONAL SCOUT CAMP THAILAND MARCH 25–31 1996", both with Scout emblem. 50s.×16, 100s.×12
Fungi. 300s.×16

1997
Hong Kong 97 International Stamp Exhibition. Portraits of Sun Yat-sen. 300s.×6
Horses. 250s.×12
Chernobyl's Children. 700s.×2
Birds. 140s.×6, 150s., 200s., 370s.×6, 410s., 500s.
Flowers. 200s.×6, 300s.×6
175th Anniv of Brothers Grimm's Third Collection of Fairy Tales. Rumpelstiltskin. 400s.×3
Birth Bicentenary of Hiroshige (Japanese painter). 250s.×6
Golden Wedding of Queen Elizabeth and Prince Philip. 370s.×6
Return of Hong Kong to China. 1000s.×5
Winter Olympic Games, Nagano (1998). 100, 200, 250s.×4, 500, 600s.
World Cup Football Championship, France (1998). 100, 150, 200, 250s.×17, 500, 600s.
African Safari. 250s.×9
Northern Wilderness (Arctic). 250s.×9
Endangered Species. 250s.×24
Seven Wonders of the Ancient World. 370s.×6
Seven Wonders of the Modern World. 140s.×6
Aviation. 100, 150s.×18, 200, 250s.×8, 300, 400, 500s.

1998
Diana, Princess of Wales Commemoration. 150, 250s.
Marine Life. 200s.×12, 250s.×18

Chinese New Year ("Year of the Tiger"). 370s.×4
John Denver Commemoration. 370s. × 4
Classic Cars. 370s.×12
Aircraft. 300s.×18
Exotic Flowers. 250s.×26
Endangered Species. 200s.×12, 370s.×12
Eagles. 370s.×6
Fauna and Flora. 250, 370s.×12, 410, 500, 600s.
International Year of the Ocean (1st issue). 150, 200s.×12, 250, 300s.×9, 400, 500s.
International Year of the Ocean (2nd issue). 1998 Marine Life overprinted with emblem. 200s.×12, 250s.×18
Fungi and Insects. 140, 150, 200, 250s.×19, 370, 410, 500, 600s.
Rudolph the Red-nosed Reindeer (cartoon film). 200s.×12
25th Death Anniv of Pablo Picasso (painter). 400s.×2, 500s.
50th Death Anniv of Mahatma Gandhi. 370s.
1st Death Anniv of Diana, Princess of Wales. 600s.
19th World Scout Jamboree, Chile. 600s.×3
80th Anniv of Royal Air Force. 500s.×4

1999
Chinese New Year ("Year of the Rabbit"). 4×250s.
Marine Life. 200, 250s.×19, 310, 410s.
Balloons. 370s.×6
Tourism booklet. 150s.×24
Space. 70, 100, 150, 200, 250, 370s.
Early Flight. 20, 100, 140s.×2, 150, 200, 250, 370s.×7
Aircraft. 370s.×6
Ships of the 19th Century. 370s.×12
Endangered Species. 100s.×20
Animals. 100, 140, 150, 200, 250, 370s.
Birds of the World. 370s.×12
Birds. 370s.×12
Flora and Fauna. 100, 140, 150, 200, 250, 370s.×13
Orchids. 200, 250, 370s.×13
Dogs of the World. 200s.×9
Cats of the World. 100, 140, 150, 200, 250, 370s.×13
Cats. 200, 250s.×9, 370, 410s.
Cats of the East. 500s.×4
Prehistoric Animals. 400s.×6
50th Anniv of Rotary in Tanzania 150, 250, 350, 400s.
Queen Mother's Century. 600s.×4
APS Stamp Show, Cleveland Birds of Japan 250s.×18
Birds of Japan. 250s.×18
Fashion Designers. 300s.×8
Ballet. 300, 350, 400, 500s.
Hokusai (Japanese artist). 400s.×6
Art of India. 500s.×8
Military Exploits. 150, 250s.×3, 300s.×3, 350s.×3, 400s.×3, 500s.×3
Aircraft. 200, 250s.×9, 300, 400s.
Helicopters. 370s.×6
UFOs. 370s.×12
Locomotives. 400s.×6
History of Trains. 400s.×12
Sailing Vessels of the World. 400s.×12
Fighting Machines of Second World War. 400s.×12
Cars. 400s.×12
China '99. Paintings of Xu Beihong. 150s.×10
China '99. Macau Returns to China. 300s.×4
Underwater Creatures. 150, 250, 300s.×19, 350, 400, 500s.
Flowers. 150, 250, 350s.×18, 400, 500s.
Flowers of Africa. 150, 250, 300, 350, 400s.×13
Flora and Fauna. 150s.×2, 250s.×2, 300s.×2, 350s.×2, 400s.×26, 500s.×2
Fungi. 150, 250, 300, 350, 400s.×13, 500s.
Predators of the Deep. 200, 250, 370s.×7, 410s.
Prehistoric Animals. 200, 250, 370s.×13, 410s.
Sea Birds. 150, 250s.×16, 300, 350, 400, 500s.
Marine Life. 250s.×12, 350, 400, 500s.
African Wildlife. 300s.×8
Central American Rainforest. 350s.×9
Butterflies. 400s.×6
Cats and Dogs. 400s.×12

2000
Orchids. 200, 250, 370s.×13
Flowers. 150, 250, 300s.×19, 350, 400, 500s.
Flora and Faun. 100, 140, 150, 250, 370s.×13

2002
Queen Elizabeth the Queen Mother "In Memoriam". 95th Birthday of Queen Elizabeth the Queen Mother (1995 Appendix). Sheet margin inscribed "IN MEMORIAM 1900–2002". 250s.×4

2004
Mushrooms. 550s.×6
Animals. 550s.×6
Birds. 550s.×6
Butterflies. 550s.×6
Orchids. 550s.×6

2005
Rotary International. 1200s×3

2006
80th Birthday of Queen Elizabeth II. 1200s.×4
250th Birth Anniv of Wolfgang Amadeus Mozart. 1200s.×4

50th Anniv of Jailhouse Rock (film) (Elvis Presley). 1200s.×4
Space: International Space Station. 800s.×6
Space: Mars Reconnaissance Orbiter. 1150s.×4
400th Birth Anniv of Rembrandt van Rijn. 1000s.×4
Endangered Species. Topi antelope (Damaliscus lunatus jimela). 600s.×4
Species of Zanzibar. 1000s.×8

2007
80th Birthday of Pope Benedict XVI. 600s.
Diamond Wedding of Queen Elizabeth II and Duke of Edinburgh. 750s.×2
10th Death Anniv of Diana, Princess of Wales. 750s.×6
50th Death Anniv of Qi Baishi (artist). 1000s.×4
Centenary of First Helicopter Flight. 1200s.×4

2008
Visit of Pope Benedict XVI to United States. 1000s.
Elvis Presley in the Movies. 1200s.×4

2009
Inauguration of US President Barack Obama. 1500s.×4
50 Years of Space Exploration and Satellites. 750s.×6, 1200s.×17, 1500s.
China 2009 International Stamp Exhibition, Luoyang. Peony. 570s.
Michael Jackson Commemoration. 1500s.×8

2010
Centenary of Chinese Aviation. 950s.×4
50th Anniv of Election of Pres. John F. Kennedy. 1400s.×8
Centenary of the Boy Scouts of America. 1900s.×3
Princess Diana Commemoration. 1400s.×8
Star Trek Voyager. 1400s.×4
Star Trek Deep Space Nine. 1400s.×4
50th Anniv of NASA. 1400s.×4
5th Anniv of Pontificate of Pope Benedict XVI. 1400s.×2
Pres. Barack Obama. 1800s.×6
50th Anniv of Jane Goodall's Work with Chimpanzees, Gombe. 2500s.×6

2011
Beijing Expo 2010. Leaders of China. Hu Jin Tao. 900s.×3; 1100s.×4
Whales of the World. 1250s.×6
Beatification of Pope John Paul II. 1800s.×4
10th Anniv of Attack on World Trade Center, New York. 2000s.×3
Animals of the Serengeti. 800s.×4
African Seashells. 1700s.×3
Flowers of Africa. 1500s.×5

2012
Butterflies of Africa. 1700s.×8
Birds of Africa. 1700s.×8
Olympic Games, London. 1300s.×4
Birds of Tanzania. 1000s.×16
70th Birthday of Mohammed Ali. 2000s.×4
Beijing 2012 International Stamp Exhibition. Ceramics of China. 1300s.×16
Lunar New Year. Chinese Zodiac Animals. 450s.×12
Chinese New Year. Year of the Snake. 500s.×2
Chinese New Year. Year of the Snake. Chinese Paintings. 350s.×2
Chinese New Year. Year of the Snake. 2000s.×4
85th Birthday of Pope Benedict XVI. 2000s.×4
Abraham Lincoln Commemoration. 1700s.×4

2013
Election of Pope Francis I. 2000s.×4
Animals of Africa. 2000s.×4
Flora. 1200s×16
Insects of Africa. 2000s.×4
Fruits of Africa. 1500s.×6
China International Collection Expo 2013. 2000s.×4
Cats. 2000s.×8
Birth of Prince George of Cambridge. 2000s.×4
Nelson Mandela Commemoration. 1550s.×12
Sunbirds of Africa. 2000s.×4
Reptiles of Africa. 2000s.×4
Dogs. 2000s.×8

Uganda

PROTECTORATE

Following a period of conflict between Islamic, Protestant and Roman Catholic factions, Uganda was declared to be in the British sphere of influence by the Anglo-German Agreement of July 1890. The British East Africa Company exercised a variable degree of control until 27 August 1894 when the country was declared a British Protectorate.

Before the introduction of Nos. 84/91 the stamps of Uganda were only valid for internal postage. Letters for overseas were franked with British East Africa issues on arrival at Mombasa.

(Currency. 200 cowries = 1 rupee)

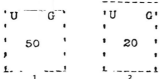

TYPE-WRITTEN STAMPS. Nos. 1/53 were type-written by the Revd. E. Millar at Mengo for the Uganda administration. For all "printings" a thin laid paper was used, and all issues were imperforate and ungummed. The laid lines are invariably horizontal, with the exception of Nos. 19a, 20a and 38b.

The original typewriter used had wide letters, but in late April, 1895 Millar obtained a new machine on which the type face was in a narrower fount.

Each sheet was made up of whatever values were required at the time, so that different values can be found *se-tenant* or *tête-bêche*. These last were caused by the paper being inverted in the machine so that space at the foot could be utilised.

For the first issue the sheets were of 117 (9×13), but with the introduction of the narrower width (Nos. 17 onwards) a larger number of stamps per sheet, 143 (11×13), was adopted.

PRICES. The prices of Nos. 1/53 vary greatly according to condition. The thin paper used is subject to creasing, staining and thinning. Catalogue quality is for fine examples, with borders visible on at least three sides. Used stamps are usually found with manuscript crosses in pencil, crayon or ink; examples with initials, dates or place names may command a premium, but note that stamps cancelled to order with circular datestamps (usually at Kampala in 1898) tend to be worth less.

1895 (20 Mar). Wide letters. Wide stamps, 20 to 26 mm wide.
1	**1**	10 (c.) black	£4250	£2250
2		20 (c.) black	£7500	£1800
		a. "U A" for "U G"	†	£6500
3		30 (c.) black	£2000	£1600
4		40 (c.) black	£6000	£2250
5		50 (c.) black	£1400	£1100
		a. "U A" for "U G"	†	£8500
6		60 (c.) black	£2500	£2250

It is now believed that the 5, 15 and 25 cowries values in this width, formerly listed, do not exist.

1895 (May). Wide stamps with pen-written surcharges, in black.
8	**1**	5 on 10 (c.) black	†	£70000
9		10 on 30 (c.) black	†	£70000
10		10 on 50 (c.) black	†	£70000
11		15 on 10 (c.) black	†	£50000
12		15 on 20 (c.) black	†	£70000
13		15 on 40 (c.) black	†	£60000
14		15 on 50 (c.) black	†	£70000
15		25 on 50 (c.) black	†	£70000
16		50 on 60 (c.) black	†	£70000

The manuscript provisionals, Nos. 9/16 come from the Mission at Ngogwe, most of the manuscript surcharges including the initials of the Revd. G. R. Blackledge stationed there. But No. 8, known only in *se-tenant* form with an unsurcharged pair of No. 1 on cover, was initialled "E.M." by Revd. E. Millar, presumably at Mengo.

1895 (April). Wide letters. Narrow stamps, 16 to 18 mm wide.
17	**1**	5 (c.) black	£3250	£1300
18		10 (c.) black	£3250	£1600
19		15 (c.) black	£2000	£1500
		a. Vertically laid paper	†	£5000
20		20 (c.) black	£3250	£1500
		a. Vertically laid paper	†	£6500
21		25 (c.) black	£1800	£1600
22		30 (c.) black	£8500	£8500
23		40 (c.) black	£8000	£8000
24		50 (c.) black	£3750	£4250
25		60 (c.) black	£8000	£8500

A used pair of No. 19a and two used examples of No. 20a have been seen. With the exception of No. 38b, Nos. 1/53 otherwise show the laid lines horizontal.

To qualify as Nos. 22/5, which are very rare stamps, examples must show borders on both vertical sides and not exceed 18 mm in width. Examples not fulfilling both criteria can only be classified as belonging to the "Wide stamps" group, Nos. 3/6.

1895 (May). Narrow letters. Narrow stamps 16 to 18 mm wide.
26	**2**	5 (c.) black	£1700
27		10 (c.) black	£1800
28		15 (c.) black	£1800
29		20 (c.) black	£1500
30		25 (c.) black	£1700
31		30 (c.) black	£2000
32		40 (c.) black	£1700
33		50 (c.) black	£1800
34		60 (c.) black	£2500

1895 (Nov). Narrow letters. Narrow stamps, 16–18 mm wide. Change of colour.
35	**2**	5 (c.) violet	£700	£650
36		10 (c.) violet	£650	£650
37		15 (c.) violet	£1100	£600
38		20 (c.) violet	£475	£300
		a. "G U" for "U G"		
		b. Vertically laid paper	£3000	
39		25 (c.) violet	£1800	£1600
40		30 (c.) violet	£2250	£1100
41		40 (c.) violet	£2250	£1500
42		50 (c.) violet	£2000	£1500
43		100 (c.) violet	£2500	£3000

Stamps of 35 (c.) and 45 (c.) have been recorded in violet, on vertically laid paper. They were never prepared for postal use, and did not represent a postal rate, but were type-written to oblige a local official. (*Price* £2750 *each, unused*)

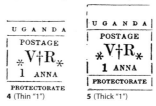

3

1896 (June).
44	**3**	5 (c.) violet	£750	£1000
45		10 (c.) violet	£850	£650
46		15 (c.) violet	£750	£750
47		20 (c.) violet	£400	£225
48		25 (c.) violet	£700	£900
49		30 (c.) violet	£750	£850
50		40 (c.) violet	£900	£900
51		50 (c.) violet	£750	£800
52		60 (c.) violet	£1600	£2000
53		100 (c.) violet	£1500	£2000

(New Currency. 16 annas = 1 rupee)

UGANDA
POSTAGE
V†R
1 ANNA
PROTECTORATE
4 (Thin "1")

UGANDA
POSTAGE
V†R
1 ANNA
PROTECTORATE
5 (Thick "1")

| | **6** | | | **7** | |

In the 2a. and 3a. the dagger points upwards; the stars in the 2a. are level with the top of "VR"; the 8a. is as T **6** but with left star at top and right star at foot. The 1r. has three stars at foot. The 5r. has central star raised and the others at foot.

(Type-set by the Revd. F. Rowling at Lubwa's, in Usoga)

1896 (7 Nov). Thick white wove paper (Nos. 54/8) or thin yellowish paper ruled with vertical lines 9 mm apart (Nos. 59/61).

*(a) Types **4/6***

54	**4**	1a. black	£110	£100
		a. Small "o" in "POSTAGE"	£600	£600
55	**5**	1a. black	23·00	26·00
		a. Small "o" in "POSTAGE"	85·00	£100
56	**6**	2a. black	29·00	35·00
		a. Small "o" in "POSTAGE"	£100	£120
57		3a. black	29·00	45·00
		a. Small "o" in "POSTAGE"	£120	£180
58		4a. black	32·00	38·00
		a. Small "o" in "POSTAGE"	£120	£130
59		8a. black	40·00	48·00
		a. Small "o" in "POSTAGE"	£140	£180
60		1r. black	85·00	£100
		a. Small "o" in "POSTAGE"	£350	£425
61		5r. black	£275	£350
		a. Small "o" in "POSTAGE"	£900	£1100

*(b) Optd "L", in black as in T **7** for local use, by a postal official, R. R. Racey, at Kampala*

70	**4**	1a. black	£190	£170
		a. Small "o" in "POSTAGE"	£1400	£1200
71	**6**	2a. black	£120	£120
		a. Small "o" in "POSTAGE"	£550	£600
72		3a. black	£275	£325
		a. Small "o" in "POSTAGE"	£1700	£2000
73		4a. black	£120	£160
		a. Small "o" in "POSTAGE"	£550	
74		8a. black	£200	£300
		a. Small "o" in "POSTAGE"	£1500	£1900
75		1r. black	£375	£450
		a. Small "o" in "POSTAGE"	£2000	
76		5r. black	£22000	£22000

Tête-bêche pairs of all values may be found owing to the settings of 16 (4×4) being printed side by side or above one another. They are worth a premium. The variety with small "O" occurs on R. 3/1.

8	**9**

UGANDA

(10)

(Recess D.L.R.)

1898 (Nov)–**1902**. P 14.

(a) Wmk Crown CA

84	**8**	1a. scarlet	5·00	4·25
		a. Carmine-rose (1902)	2·25	1·75
86		2a. red-brown	9·00	11·00
87		3a. pale grey	20·00	45·00
		a. Bluish grey	21·00	20·00
		x. Wmk reversed	£325	
88		4a. deep green	13·00	10·00
89		8a. pale olive	15·00	30·00
		a. Grey-green	35·00	50·00

(b) Wmk Crown CC

90	**9**	1r. dull blue	55·00	55·00
		a. Bright blue	65·00	70·00
91		5r. brown	£100	£120
84/91 *Set of 7*			£190	£225
84s/91s Optd "SPECIMEN" *Set of 7*			£180	

Examples of No. 86 are known bisected to pay the 1 anna rate during a shortage of 1a. stamps at the post office in Masindi in late 1899 and early 1900.

Nos. 84/9 exist without watermark or with double-lined lettering from the marginal watermark due to the way in which sheets were cut for printing.

On 1 April 1901 the postal administrations of British East Africa and Uganda were merged. Subsequent issues to 1962 are listed under KENYA, UGANDA and TANGANYIKA.

1902 (Feb). T **11** of British East Africa (Kenya, Uganda, and Tanganyika) optd with T **10**.

92		½a. yellow-green	3·00	2·00
		a. Opt omitted (in pair with normal)	£5000	
		b. Opt inverted (at foot)	£2000	
		c. Opt double	£2500	
		w. Wmk inverted	—	£300
		x. Wmk reversed		
93		2½a. deep blue (R.)	4·50	3·00
		a. Opt double	£600	
		b. Inverted "S" (R. 1/1)	£120	95·00
		x. Wmk reversed	£350	
		y. Wmk inverted and reversed	£350	

The Eastern Province of Uganda was transferred to British East Africa on 1 April 1902.

SELF-GOVERNMENT

(New Currency. 100 cents = 1 East African, later Uganda shilling)

11 Ripon Falls and Speke Memorial

(Des S. Scott. Recess B.W.)

1962 (28 July). Centenary of Speke's Discovery of Source of the Nile. W w **12**. P 14.

95	**11**	30c. black and red	20	25
96		50c. black and slate-violet	20	10
97		1s.30 black and green	1·00	25
98		2s.50 black and blue	2·25	2·25
95/8 *Set of 4*			3·25	2·50

INDEPENDENT

12 Murchison Falls	**13** Tobacco-growing

14 Mulago Hospital

1s.30 Dome flaw - a large white flaw to left of dome of Namirembe Cathedral (Pl. 1A-1A, R. 9/10)

(Des V. Whiteley. Photo Harrison)

1962 (9 Oct)–**64**. Independence. Various designs as T **12/14**. P 15×14 (5c. to 50c.) or 14½ (others).

99		5c. deep bluish green	10	10
100		10c. reddish brown	10	10
		a. Brown (coil)	10	10
		b. Deep yellow-brown (17.10.64)	10	10
101		15c. black, red and green	10	10

102	20c. plum and buff	10	10
103	30c. blue	10	10
104	50c. black and turquoise-green	10	10
105	1s. sepia, red and turquoise-green	1·25	20
106	1s.30 yellow-orange and violet	25	10
	a. Dome flaw	21·00	
107	2s. black, carmine and light blue	50	70
108	5s. vermilion and deep green	8·00	1·50
109	10s. slate and chestnut	4·25	4·00
110	20s. brown and blue	4·50	21·00
99/110	Set of 12	17·00	25·00

Designs: As T **12/13**—10c. Tobacco growing, 15c. Coffee growing; 20c. Ankole cattle; 30c. Cotton; 50c. Mountains of the Moon. As T **14**—1s.30, Cathedrals and Mosque; 2s. Makerere College; 5s. Copper mining; 10s. Cement industry; 20s. Parliament Buildings.

15 South African Crowned Crane

(Photo Harrison)

1965 (20 Feb). International Trade Fair, Kampala. P 14½×14.
111	**15**	30c. multicoloured	15	10
112		1s.30 multicoloured	25	10

16 Black Bee Eater **17** African Jacana

18 Ruwenzori Turaco

(Des Mrs. R. Fennessy. Photo Harrison)

1965 (9 Oct). Birds. Various designs as T **16/18**. P 15×14 (5c., 15c., 20c., 40c., 50c.), 14×15 (10c., 30c., 65c.) or 14½ (others).
113	5c. multicoloured	10	10
114	10c. chestnut, black and light blue	10	10
115	15c. yellow and sepia	20	10
116	20c. multicoloured	20	10
117	30c. black and brown-red	1·50	10
118	40c. multicoloured	1·00	1·75
119	50c. grey-blue and reddish violet	25	10
	a. White bird (grey-blue omitted)	£1500	
120	65c. orange-red, black and light grey	2·50	2·75
121	1s. multicoloured	50	10
122	1s.30 chestnut, black and yellow	5·50	30
123	2s.50 multicoloured	4·25	65
124	5s. multicoloured	7·00	4·00
125	10s. multicoloured	11·00	11·00
126	20s. multicoloured	21·00	38·00
113/26	Set of 14	48·00	48·00

Designs: Vert as T **16**—15c. Orange Weaver; 20c. Narina Trogon; 40c. Blue-breasted Kingfisher; 50c. Whale-headed Stork. Horiz as T **17**—30c. Sacred Ibis; 65c. Red-crowned Bishop. As T **18**. Vert—1s.30, African Fish Eagle; 5s. Lilac-breasted Roller. Horiz—2s.50, Great Blue Turaco; 10s. Black-collared Lovebird; 20s. South African Crowned Crane.
The 15c., 40c., 65c., and 1s. exist with PVA gum as well as gum arabic.

19 Carved Screen

(Des Mrs. R. Fennessy. Photo Harrison)

1967 (26 Oct). 13th Commonwealth Parliamentary Association Conference. T **19** and similar horiz designs. Multicoloured. P 14.
127	30c. Type **19**	10	10
128	50c. Arms of Uganda	10	10
129	1s.30 Parliamentary Building	10	10
130	2s.50 Conference Chamber	15	1·75
127/30	Set of 4	30	1·75

20 Cordia abyssinica **21** Acacia drepanolobium

(Des Mrs. R. Fennessy. Photo Harrison)

1969 (9 Oct)–**74**. Flowers. Various designs as T **20/1**. Chalk-surfaced paper. P 14½×14 (5c. to 70c.) or 14 (others).
131	5c. brown, green and light olive-yellow	10	1·00
	a. Glazed, ordinary paper (11.4.73)	40	10
132	10c. multicoloured	10	10
	a. Glazed, ordinary paper (27.9.72)	40	10
133	15c. multicoloured	40	10
134	20c. bluish violet, yellow-olive and pale sage-green	15	10
	a. Glazed, ordinary paper (27.9.72)	40	10
135	30c. multicoloured	20	10
136	40c. reddish violet, yellow-green and pale olive-grey	20	10
137	50c. multicoloured	20	10
138	60c. multicoloured	45	2·50
	a. Glazed, ordinary paper (9.5.73)	17·00	40
139	70c. multicoloured	25	30
	a. Glazed, ordinary paper (27.9.72)	1·00	45
140	1s. multicoloured	20	10
	a. Glazed, ordinary paper (22.1.71)	1·00	10
141	1s.50 multicoloured (cobalt background)	25	10
	a. Glazed, ordinary paper (3.2.71)	50	10
	b. Azure background (chalk-surfaced paper) (21.1.74)	55	30
142	2s.50 multicoloured	30	1·25
	a. Glazed, ordinary paper (3.2.71)	1·25	10
143	5s. multicoloured	40	1·60
	a. Glazed, ordinary paper (3.2.71)	1·75	10
144	10s. multicoloured	50	4·50
	a. Glazed, ordinary paper (3.2.71)	3·75	10
145	20s. multicoloured	1·00	6·00
	a. Glazed, ordinary paper (22.1.71)	12·00	15
131/45	Set of 15	3·50	15·00
131a/45a	Set of 11	35·00	1·40

Designs: As T **20**—10c. *Grewia similis*; 15c. *Cassia. didymobotrya*; 20c. *Coleus barbatus*; 30c. *Ockna ovata*; 40c. *Ipomoea spathulata*; 50c. *Spathodea nilotica*; 60c. *Oncoba spinosa*; 70c. *Carissa edulis*. As T **21**—1s.50, *Clerodendrum myricoides*; 2s.50, *Acanthus arboreus*; 5s. *Kigelia aethiopium*; 10s. *Erythrina abyssinica*; 20s. *Monodora myristica*.
Some of the glazed ordinary paper printings were available in Uganda some time before the London release dates which are quoted in the listings.

2!

(22)

1975 (29 Sept). Nos. 141/2 and 145a surch as T **22**.
146	2s. on 1s.50 multicoloured	2·00	1·50
147	3s. on 2s.50 multicoloured	18·00	42·00
148	40s. on 20s. multicoloured	4·00	3·50
	a. Surch on No. 145	6·50	3·50
146/8	Set of 3	22·00	42·00

23 Millet   **24** Maize

(Des Mrs. R. Fennessy. Photo Harrison)

1975 (9 Oct). Ugandan Crops. T **23/4** and similar horiz designs. P 14×14½ (10 to 80c.) or 14 (others).

149	10c. black, apple-green and yellow-brown...	10	10
150	20c. multicoloured	10	10
151	30c. multicoloured	10	10
152	40c. multicoloured	10	10
153	50c. multicoloured	10	10
154	70c. black, apple-green and light blue-green	10	15
155	80c. multicoloured	10	15
156	1s. multicoloured	10	10
157	2s. multicoloured	30	30
158	3s. multicoloured	50	45
159	5s. multicoloured	50	75
160	10s. multicoloured	50	1·25
161	20s. apple-green, black and bright purple ...	70	2·50
162	40s. apple-green, black and yellow-orange..	1·10	4·50
149/62 *Set of 14*		3·50	9·00

Designs: As T **23**—20c. Sugar; 30c. Tobacco; 40c. Onions; 50c. Tomatoes; 70c. Tea; 80c. Bananas. As T **24**—2s. Pineapples; 3s. Coffee; 5s. Oranges; 10s. Groundnuts; 20s. Cotton; 40s. Runner Beans.

Face value colours: 5s. green; 10s. brown; 20s. bright purple; 40s. yellow-orange. For 5s. to 40s. with colours changed see Nos. 220/3.

Nos. 149 and 153 exist in coils constructed from normal sheets.

1976 (15 Apr). Telecommunications Development. As Nos. 56/60 of Kenya, but inscr "UGANDA".

163	50c. Microwave tower	10	10
164	1s. Cordless switchboard	10	10
165	2s. Telephone	20	25
166	3s. Message Switching Centre	30	45
163/6 *Set of 4*		60	70
MS167 120×120 mm. Nos. 163/6		90	1·25

Nos. 164 and 166 exist imperforate from stock dispersed by the liquidator of Format International Security Printers Ltd.

1976 (5 July). Olympic Games, Montreal. As Nos. 61/5 of Kenya, but inscr "UGANDA".

168	50c. Akii Bua, hurdler	10	10
169	1s. Filbert Bayi, runner	10	10
170	2s. Steve Muchoki, boxer	30	30
171	3s. East African flags	40	45
168/71 *Set of 4*		75	75
MS172 129×154 mm. Nos. 168/71		4·00	5·00

Nos. 168/70 exist imperforate from stock dispersed by the liquidator of Format International Security Printers Ltd.

1976 (4 Oct). Railway Transport. As Nos. 66/70 of Kenya, but inscr "UGANDA".

173	50c. Diesel-hydraulic train, Tanzania-Zambia railway	15	10
174	1s. Nile Bridge, Uganda	15	10
175	2s. Nakuru Station, Kenya	50	45
176	3s. Uganda Railway Class A locomotive, 1896.	55	55
173/6 *Set of 4*		1·25	1·00
MS177 154×103 mm. Nos. 173/6		2·25	2·50

Nos. 173/7 exist imperforate from stock dispersed by the liquidator of Format International Security Printers Ltd.

1977 (10 Jan). Game Fish of East Africa. As Nos. 71/5 of Kenya, but inscr "UGANDA".

178	50c. Nile Perch	15	10
179	1s. Nile Mouthbrooder	20	10
180	3s. Sailfish	60	40
181	5s. Black Marlin	80	60
178/81 *Set of 4*		1·60	1·00
MS182 153×129 mm. Nos. 178/81		3·25	2·00

On No. **MS**182 the right-hand side of the 5s. value is perforated 13½.

1977 (15 Jan). Second World Black and African Festival of Arts and Culture, Nigeria. As Nos. 76/80 of Kenya, but inscr "UGANDA".

183	50c. Maasai Manyatta (village)	10	10
184	1s. "Heartbeat of Africa" (Ugandan dancers)	10	10
185	2s. Makonde sculpture	25	55
186	3s. "Early Man and Technology" (skinning hippopotamus)	35	85
183/6 *Set of 4*		75	1·40
MS187 132×109 mm. Nos. 183/6		1·25	2·25

1977 (5 Apr). 25th Anniv of Safari Rally. As Nos. 81/5 of Kenya, but inscr "UGANDA".

188	50c. Rally-car and villagers	10	10
189	1s. Starting-line	10	10
190	2s. Car fording river	25	35
191	5s. Car and elephants	80	1·00
188/91 *Set of 4*		1·10	1·40
MS192 126×93 mm. Nos. 188/91		1·50	2·50

1977 (30 June). Centenary of Ugandan Church. As Nos. 86/90 of Kenya, but inscr "UGANDA".

193	50c. Canon Kivebulaya	10	10
194	1s. Modern Namirembe Cathedral	10	10
195	2s. Old Namirembe Cathedral	20	40
196	5a. Early congregation, Kigezi	45	1·10
193/6 *Set of 4*		75	1·50
MS197 126×89 mm. Nos. 193/6		1·00	1·75

80c ═   **(25)**   **26** Shot Putting

1977 (22 Aug). Design as No. 155 surch with T **25** in mauve by Harrison.

198	80c. on 60c. multicoloured	30	20
	a. Surch omitted		£180

A 60c. stamp was to have been added to Nos. 149/62 using the design of the 80c. (bananas), but it was cancelled and those already printed were surcharged to make No. 198.

1977 (26 Sept). Endangered Species. As Nos. 96/101 of Kenya, but inscr "UGANDA".

199	50c. Pancake Tortoise	30	10
200	1s. Nile Crocodile	45	10
201	2s. Hunter's Hartebeest	80	40
202	3s. Red Colobus monkey	1·00	75
203	5s. Dugong	1·00	1·00
199/203 *Set of 5*		3·25	2·00
MS204 127×101 mm. Nos. 200/3		3·75	3·00

1978 (10 Apr). World Cup Football Championship, Argentina (1st issue). As Nos. 122/6 of Kenya but inscr "UGANDA".

205	50c. Joe Kadenge and forwards	15	10
206	1s. Mohamed Chuma and cup presentation	15	10
207	2s. Omari Kidevu and goalmouth scene	30	45
208	5s. Polly Ouma and forwards	50	1·25
205/8 *Set of 4*		1·00	1·60
MS209 136×81 mm. Nos. 205/8		1·50	2·50

(Litho Questa)

1978 (28 Aug). Commonwealth Games, Edmonton. T **26** and similar horiz designs. Multicoloured. P 14.

210	50c. Type **26**	10	10
211	1s. Long jumping	15	10
212	2s. Running	20	40
213	5s. Boxing	40	1·10
210/13 *Set of 4*		75	1·50
MS214 114×85 mm. Nos. 210/13. P 12½×12		1·25	3·00

1978 (11 Sept). World Cup Football Championship, Argentina (2nd issue). Designs as Nos. 205/8 but additionally inscr "WORLD CUP 1978".

215	50c. Polly Ouma and forwards	10	10
216	2s. Omari Kidevu and goalmouth scene	20	50
217	5s. Joe Kadenge and forwards	40	85
218	10s. Mohamed Chuma and cup presentation	70	1·75
215/18 *Set of 4*		1·25	2·75
MS219 140×87 mm. Nos. 215/18. P 12×11½		1·50	2·75

(Litho Questa)

1978. As Nos. 159/62 but printing process and colours changed.

220	5s. multicoloured (face value in blue)	50	70
221	10s. multicoloured (face value in magenta) .	50	85
222	20s. multicoloured (face value in brown)	55	85
223	40s. multicoloured (face value in red)	65	1·10
220/3 *Set of 4*		2·00	3·25

27 Measurements of High Blood Pressure

(Litho Questa)

1978 (25 Sept). "Down with High Blood Pressure". T **27** and similar horiz designs. Multicoloured. P 14×13½.

224	50c. Type **27**	15	10
225	1s. Hypertension and the heart	15	10
226	2s. Fundus of the eye in hypertension	40	45
227	5s. Kidney and high blood pressure	75	1·40
224/7	*Set of 4*	1·25	1·75
MS228	180×115 mm. Nos. 224/7	1·25	2·75

28 Off Loading Cattle

(Litho Questa)

1978 (16 Dec). 75th Anniv of Powered Flight. T **28** and similar horiz designs. Multicoloured. P 14.

229	1s. Type **28**	15	10
230	1s.50 "Domestic services" (passengers boarding Britten Norman Islander light aircraft)	25	15
231	2s.70 Export of Uganda coffee	25	35
232	10s. "Time machines in the air" (Wright *Flyer III* and Concorde)	75	1·50
229/32	*Set of 4*	1·25	1·90
MS233	166×110 mm. Nos. 229/32	1·50	2·75

29 Queen Elizabeth II leaving Owen Falls Dam

(Des BG Studio. Litho Ashton-Potter)

1979 (15 Feb). 25th Anniv of Coronation (1978). T **29** and similar horiz designs. Multicoloured. P 12½×12.

234	1s. Type **29**	15	10
235	1s.50 Regalia	15	10
236	2s.70 Coronation ceremony	30	20
237	10s. Royal family on balcony of Buckingham Palace	50	1·25
234/7	*Set of 4*	1·00	1·50
MS238	150×102 mm. Nos. 234/7	1·40	1·25

30 Dr. Joseph Kiwanuka (first Ugandan bishop)

(Des G. Vasarhelyi. Litho Questa)

1979 (15 Feb). Centenary of Catholic Church in Uganda. T **30** and similar horiz designs. Multicoloured. P 14.

239	1s. Type **30**	10	10
240	1s.50 Lubaga Cathedral	10	10
241	2s.70 Ugandan pilgrimage to Rome, Holy Year, 1975	15	25
242	10s. Friar Lourdel-Mapeera (early missionary)	50	80
239/42	*Set of 4*	75	1·10
MS243	128×91 mm. Nos. 239/42	1·00	2·00

31 Immunisation of Children

(Des J.W. Litho Questa)

1979 (28 June). International Year of the Child. T **31** and similar horiz designs. Multicoloured. P 14.

244	1s. Type **31**	10	10
245	1s.50 Handicapped children at play	15	20
246	2s.70 Ugandan I.Y.C. emblem	15	35
247	10s. Children in class	40	1·10
244/7	*Set of 4*	65	1·60
MS248	136×113 mm. Nos. 244/7	1·10	2·00

UGANDA LIBERATED 1979 (**32**)	**UGANDA LIBERATED 1979** (**33**)	**UGANDA LIBERATED 1979** (**34**)

1979 (12 July). Liberation.

*(a) Nos. 149/55 optd with T **32** and 156/62 with T **33** (12 July)*

249	10c. black, apple-green and yellow-brown	10	10
250	20c. multicoloured	10	10
251	30c. multicoloured	10	10
252	40c. multicoloured	10	10
253	50c. multicoloured	10	10
254	70c. black, apple-green and light blue-green	10	10
255	80c. multicoloured	10	10
	a. Opt double	£110	
256	1s. multicoloured	15	15
257	2s. multicoloured	20	25
258	3s. multicoloured	35	40
259	5s. multicoloured	55	60
260	10s. multicoloured	80	1·25
261	20s. apple-green, black and bright purple	1·00	2·40
262	40s. apple-green, black and yellow-orange	1·50	4·75
	a. Opt double	£130	

*(b) Nos. 210/13 (Commonwealth Games) optd with T **34** (1 Aug)*

263	50c. Type **26**	10	10
264	1s. Long jumping	15	20
265	2s. Running	25	30
266	5s. Boxing	60	65

*(c) Nos. 207, 215 and 217/18 (World Cup Football Championships) optd with T **34** (1 Aug)*

267	50c. Polly Ouma and forwards	10	10
268	2s. Omari Kidevu and goal-mouth scene	20	30
	a. Optd on No. 216	10·00	18·00
269	5s. Joe Kadenge and forwards	55	65
270	10s. Mohamed Chuma and cup presentation	1·00	1·40

*(d) Nos. 220/3 optd with T **33** (1979)*

271	5s. multicoloured	55	60
272	10s. multicoloured	60	1·25
273	20s. multicoloured	60	2·40
274	40s. multicoloured	75	4·75

*(e) Nos. 229/32 (75th Anniv of Powered Flight) until with T **34** (1 Aug)*

275	1s. Type **28**	35	20
276	1s.50 "Domestic services" (passengers boarding Britten Norman Islander light aircraft)	45	25
277	2s.70 Export of Uganda coffee	55	55
278	10s. "Time machines in the air" (Wright *Flyer III* and Concorde)	2·00	2·50

*(f) Nos. 234/7 (25th Anniv of Coronation) optd as T **33** or surch also and No. MS238 additionally inscr "Diplomatic Relations Normalised" with Ugandan and British flags replacing portrait of Amin (12 July)*

279	1s. Type **29**	10	20
280	1s.50 Regalia	15	20
281	2s.70 Coronation ceremony	20	40
282	15s. on 10s. Royal family on balcony of Buckingham Palace	85	1·75
MS283	150×102 mm. Nos. 234/6 and 15s. as No. 237*	1·50	3·25

*The sheet contains unoverprinted stamps; the additional inscriptions and changes in design appear only on the sheet margin.

*(g) Nos. 239/42 (Centenary of Catholic Church in Uganda) optd with T **34** and No. MS243 with additional inscr "FREEDOM OF WORSHIP DECLARED" replacing part of the margin decoration (1 Aug)*

284	1s. Type **30**	10	20
285	1s.50 Lubaga Cathedral	15	25
286	2s.70 Ugandan pilgrimage to Rome, Holy Year, 1975	30	50
287	10s. Friar Lourdel-Mapeera (early missionary)	90	1·75
MS288	128×91 mm. Nos. 239/42*. P 12½×12 (1979)	1·75	2·75

*The sheet contains the original unoverprinted stamps; the additional inscription appears on the sheet margin.

*(h) Nos. 244/8 (International Year of the Child) optd with T **34** (16 Aug)*

289	1s. Type **31**	20	20
290	1s.50 Handicapped children at play	25	25
291	2s.70 Ugandan I.Y.C. emblem	50	60
292	10s. Children in class	1·40	1·75
249/82, 284/7 and 289/92	*Set of 42*	18·00	30·00
MS293	136×113 mm. Nos. 289/92	2·25	3·50

35 Radio Wave Symbol

(Des G. Vasarhelyi. Litho Questa)

1979 (11 Sept). 50th Anniv of International Consultative Radio Committee and International Telecommunications Union. P 14.

294	**35**	1s. multicoloured	10	10
295		1s.50 multicoloured	15	10
296		2s.70 multicoloured	15	35
297		10s. multicoloured	40	1·10
294/7	*Set of 4*		65	1·50

36 20s. Definitive Stamp of 1965 and Sir Rowland Hill

(Des BG Studio. Litho Questa)

1979 (Oct). Death Centenary of Sir Rowland Hill. T **36** and similar horiz designs showing stamps and Sir Rowland Hill. Multicoloured. P 14.

298	1s. Type **36**		10	10
299	1s.50 1967 13th Commonwealth Parliamentary Association Conference 50c. commemorative		15	10
300	2s.70 1962 Independence 20s. commemorative		15	30
301	10s. Uganda Protectorate 1898 1a.		40	1·25
298/301	*Set of 4*		65	1·40
MS302	154×98 mm. Nos. 298/301		65	1·50

37 Impala   **38** Lions with Cub

(Des G. Drummond. Litho Questa)

1979 (3 Dec)–**82**. Wildlife. Horiz designs as T **37** (10 to 80c.) or T **38** (1 to 40s.). Multicoloured. P 14×13½ (10 to 80c.) or 14 (1 to 40s.).

A. Without imprint date

303A	10c. Type **37**		10	20
304A	20c. Large-spotted Genet		10	20
305A	30c. Thomson's Gazelle		10	20
306A	50c. Lesser Bushbaby		10	10
307A	80c. Hunting Dog		10	10
308A	1s. Type **38**		10	10
309A	1s.50 Gorilla		40	10
310A	2s. Common Zebra		35	20
311A	2s.70 Leopard with cub		40	20
312A	3s.50 Black Rhinoceros		50	55
313A	5s. Waterbuck		25	55
314A	10s. African Buffalo		30	1·00
315A	20s. Hippopotamus		65	2·00
316A	40s. African Elephant		1·00	3·50
303A/16A	*Set of 14*		3·50	8·00

B. With imprint date ("1982") at foot of design (1982)

308B	1s. Type **38**		30	10
310B	2s. Common Zebra		40	35
313B	5s. Waterbuck		40	1·10
308B/13B	*Set of 3*		1·00	1·40

For designs as Nos. 308/12 and 315/16, but with face values in revalued currency, see Nos. 433/9.

LONDON 1980
(39)

1980 (6 May). London 1980 International Stamp Exhibition. Nos. 298/302 optd as T **39**.

317	1s. Type **36**		15	10

318	1s.50 1967 13th Commonwealth Parliamentary Association Conference 50c. commemorative		15	10
319	2s.70 1962 Independence 20s. commemorative		25	25
320	10s. Uganda Protectorate 1898 1a.		55	80
317/20	*Set of 4*		1·00	1·10
MS321	154×99 mm. Nos. 317/20		1·00	1·75

40 Rotary Emblem

(Des BG Studio. Litho Questa)

1980 (25 Aug). 75th Anniv of Rotary International. T **40** and similar multicoloured design. P 14.

322	1s. Type **40**		10	10
323	20s. Paul Harris (founder) with wheel-barrow containing "Rotary projects" (*horiz*)		1·25	2·00
MS324	100×76 mm. Nos. 322/3. Imperf		1·25	2·50

41 Football   FOOTBALL GOLD MEDALISTS, C.S.S.R. **(42)**

(Des G. Vasarhelyi. Litho Questa)

1980 (29 Dec). Olympic Games, Moscow. T **41** and similar horiz designs. Multicoloured. P 14.

325	1s. Type **41**		10	10
326	2s. Relay		10	10
327	10s. Hurdles		35	75
328	20s. Boxing		55	2·00
325/8	*Set of 4*		1·25	2·50
MS329	118×90 mm. 2s.70, 3s., 5s., 25s. As Nos. 325/8		1·25	2·25

1980 (29 Dec). Olympic Games, Moscow. Medal Winners. Nos. 325/9 optd as T **42**.

330	1s. Type **41**		10	10
331	2s. Relay		20	25
332	10s. Hurdles		55	90
333	20s. Boxing		85	2·25
330/3	*Set of 4*		1·50	3·00
MS334	118×90 mm. 2s.70, 3s., 5s., 25s. As Nos. 330/3		1·00	2·50

Overprints:—2s. "RELAY GOLD MEDALIST U.S.S.R."; 10s. "HURDLES 110m. GOLD MEDALIST THOMAS MUNKLET, D.D.R."; 20s. "BOXING WELTERWEIGHT SILVER MEDALIST JOHN MUGABI, UGANDA".

43 "Christ in the Storm on the Sea of Galilee" (painting, Rembrandt)

1980 (31 Dec). Christmas. Sheet 79×101 mm. Litho. Imperf.

MS335	**43** 25s. multicoloured		4·25	4·75

44 Heinrich von Stephan and U.P.U. Emblem

45 Tower of London

(Des BG Studio. Litho Questa)

1981 (2 June). 150th Birth Anniv of Heinrich von Stephan (founder of U.P.U.). T **44** and similar horiz designs. Multicoloured. P 14.

336	1s. Type **44**	10	10
337	2s. U.P.U. Headquarters	15	15
338	2s.70 Air mail, 1935	40	20
339	10s. Mail transport by train, 1927	1·10	80
336/9 *Set of 4*		1·60	1·10
MS340 112×95 mm. Nos. 336/9		2·25	1·90

(46) **(47)**

(Des J.W. Litho Questa)

1981 (July). Royal Wedding. T **45** and similar vert designs. Multicoloured. P 14.

*(a) Unissued stamps surch as T **46** (13 July)*

341	10s. on 1s. Prince Charles and Lady Diana Spencer	20	50
	a. Surch on 5s. value	20·00	
	b. Surch on 20s. value	19·00	
	c. Surch omitted	50·00	
	d. Surch inverted		
	e. Surch as Type **47**	15	20
342	50s. on 5s. Type **45**	30	70
	a. Surch omitted	30·00	
	e. Surch as Type **47**	20	30
343	200s. on 20s. Prince Charles at Balmoral	60	2·00
	a. Surch omitted	75·00	
	b. Surch inverted	22·00	
	c. Surch inverted on 1s. value	22·00	
	d. Surch inverted on 5s. value	22·00	
	e. Surch as Type **47**	45	80
341/3 *Set of 3*		1·00	2·75
341e/3e *Set of 3*		70	1·10
MS344 95×80 mm. 250s. on 25s. Royal Mews		3·00	5·50
	a. Surch omitted		
	e. Surch as Type **47**	1·00	1·00

(b) Redrawn with new face values. Background colours changed (29 July)

345	10s. As No. 341	10	15
346	50s. Type **45**	15	20
347	200s. As No. 343	30	40
345/7 *Set of 3*		40	65
MS348 95×80 mm. 250s. As No. MS344		50	65

Nos. 345/7 also exist perforated 12 (*price for set of 3 40p mint or used*) from additional sheetlets of 5 stamps and one label. These stamps have changed background colours.

The issue was originally printed with face values of 1, 5 and 20s. and 25s. for the miniature sheet. Before it could be placed on sale the Uganda currency was devalued and the stamps were surcharged, and later reprinted with corrected face values.

48 "Sleeping Woman before Green Shutters"

(Des J. W. Litho Questa)

1981 (21 Sept). Birth Centenary of Picasso. T **48** and similar multicoloured designs. P 14×13½.

349	10s. Type **48**	10	10
350	20s. "Bullfight"	20	20
351	30s. "Detail of a Nude asleep in a Landscape"	25	30
352	200s. "Interior with a Girl Drawing"	1·10	3·25
349/52 *Set of 4*		1·50	3·50

MS353 120×146 mm. 250s. "Minotaure" (112×139 *mm*). Imperf ... 2·00 4·00

49 Deaf People using Sign Language

(Des Design Images. Litho Format)

1981 (28 Dec). International Year of Disabled Persons. T **49** and similar horiz designs. Multicoloured. P 15.

354	1s. Type **49**	10	10
355	10s. Disabled teacher in classroom	15	10
356	50s. Teacher and disabled children	70	50
357	200s. Blind person with guide dog	1·40	2·00
354/7 *Set of 4*		2·00	2·25
MS358 122×93 mm. Nos. 354/7		3·00	4·00

50 Footballers

(Des G. Vasarhelyi. Litho Questa)

1982 (11 Jan). World Cup Football Championship, Spain. T **50** and similar horiz designs showing World Cup (250s.) or footballers (others). P 14.

359	1s. multicoloured	10	10
360	10s. multicoloured	15	10
361	50s. multicoloured	55	50
362	200s. multicoloured	1·50	2·00
359/62 *Set of 4*		2·00	2·25
MS363 116×77 mm. 250s. multicoloured		2·00	2·50

51 Mpoma Satellite Earth Station

(Des Artists International. Litho Format)

1982 (10 May). "Peaceful Use of Outer Space". T **51** and similar horiz designs. Multicoloured. P 15.

364	5s. Type **51**	25	15
365	10s. *Pioneer II* (satellite)	35	35
366	50s. Space Shuttle	80	2·00
367	100s. *Voyager 2* (satellite)	1·10	2·00
364/7 *Set of 4*		2·25	6·00
MS368 118×89 mm. 150s. Space Shuttle (*different*)		3·75	2·00

No. 364 exists imperforate from stock dispersed by the liquidator of Format International Security Printers Ltd.

52 Dr. Robert Koch

(53)

(Des R. Vigurs. Litho Questa)

1982 (14 June). Centenary of Robert Kochs Discovery of Tubercle Bacillus. T **52** and similar multicoloured designs. P 14.

369	1s. Type **52**	25	10
370	10s. Microscope	70	40
371	50s. Ugandans receiving vaccinations	1·75	2·50

372	100s. Tubercle virus	2·75	4·25
369/72	Set of 4	5·00	6·50
MS373	85×64 mm. 150s. Medical College class room scene (*horiz*)	3·50	2·00

1982 (7 July). 21st Birthday of Princess of Wales. Nos. 345/8 optd with T **53**. P 14.

374	10s. Prince Charles and Lady Diana Spencer.	20	10
375	50s. Type **45**	50	40
376	200s. Prince Charles at Balmoral	1·00	1·00
374/6	Set of 3	1·50	1·25
MS377	95×82 mm. 250s. Royal Mews	2·00	2·00

Nos. 374/6 also exist perforated 12 (*price for set of 3 £1.25 mint or used*) from additional sheetlets of 5 stamps and one label. These stamps have changed background colours.

Nos. 374/7, and the sheetlets, also exist with the top line of the overprint shown as "21st Birthday" instead of "21st BIRTHDAY" as in Type **53** (*Price for set of 3 and miniature sheet £4 mint*).

Examples of an unissued miniature sheet for the 20th Anniversary of Independence, containing a single 150s. stamp showing the State Arms, exist from stock dispersed by the liquidator of Format International Security Printers Ltd.

54 Yellow-billed Hornbill

55 Scout Band

(Des Artists International. Litho Questa)

1982 (12 July). Birds. T **54** and similar vert designs. Multicoloured. P 14.

378	1s. Type **54**	15	10
379	20s. Superb Starling	60	35
380	50s. Bateleur	1·25	1·75
331	100s. Saddle-bill Stork	2·00	2·50
378/81	Set of 4	3·50	4·25
MS382	115×85 mm. 200s. Laughing Dove	7·00	9·00

(Des G. Vasarhelyi. Litho Questa)

1982 (23 Aug). 75th Anniv of Boy Scout Movement. T **55** and similar horiz designs. Multicoloured. P 14.

383	5s. Type **55**	30	10
384	20s. Scout receiving Bata Shoe trophy	70	35
385	50s. Scouts with wheelchair patient	1·00	1·50
386	100s. First aid instruction	1·50	2·75
383/6	Set of 4	3·25	4·25
MS387	112×85 mm. 150s. Lord Baden-Powell	1·75	2·25

56 Swearing-in of Roosevelt

(Des Design Images. Litho Format)

1982 (8 Nov). 250th Birth Anniv of George Washington (Nos. 389/90) and Birth Centenary of Franklin D. Roosevelt (others). T **56** and similar horiz designs. Multicoloured. P 15.

388	50s. Type **56**	30	30
389	200s. Swearing-in of Washington	75	1·25
MS390	100×69 mm. 150s. Washington at Mt. Vernon.	1·00	1·25
MS391	100×70 mm. 150s. Roosevelt at Hyde Park Mansion	1·00	1·25

Nos. 388/91 exist imperforate from stock dispersed by the liquidator of Format International Security Printers Ltd.

57 Italy v West Germany

(Des D. Miller. Litho Format)

1982 (30 Dec). World Cup Football Championship Winners. T **57** and similar horiz designs. Multicoloured. P 14½.

392	10s. Type **57**	25	25
393	200s. Victorious Italian team.	1·00	2·75
MS394	97×117 mm. 250s. Espana '82 emblem with Spanish and Italian flags	1·00	1·50

Nos. 392/4 exist imperforate from stock dispersed by the liquidator of Format International Security Printers Ltd.

58 Dancers

59 "St. George and the Dragon" (Raphael)

(Des and litho Questa)

1983 (14 Mar). Commonwealth Day. Cultural Art. T **58** and similar horiz designs. Multicoloured. P 14.

395	5s. Type **58**	10	10
396	20s. Traditional currency	15	20
397	50s. Homestead	35	55
398	100s. Drums	70	1·10
395/8	Set of 4	1·10	1·75

(Des Design Images. Litho Questa)

1983 (16 Apr). 500th Birth Anniv of Raphael (painter). T **59** and similar vert designs. Multicoloured. P 13½.

399	5s. Type **59**	10	10
400	20s. "St. George and the Dragon" (*different*)	25	20
401	50s. "Crossing the Red Sea" (detail)	50	60
402	200s. "The Expulsion of Heliodorus" (detail)	90	3·00
399/402	Set of 4	1·50	3·50
MS403	126×101 mm. 250s. "The Meeting of Pope Leo the Great and Attila the Hun" (detail)	1·40	1·40

60 Map showing Namibia and U.N. Flag

(Des R. Vigurs. Litho Format)

1983 (15 Aug). Commemorations. T **60** and similar horiz design. Multicoloured. P 15.

404	5s. Type **60**	10	10
405	200s. Seventh Non-aligned Summit Conference logo	60	2·50

Nos. 404/5 exist imperforate from stock dispersed by the liquidator of Format International Security Printers Ltd.

61 Elephants in Grassland

(62)

(Des J. Iskowitz. Litho Format)

1983 (22 Aug). Endangered Species (1st series). T **61** and similar multicoloured designs. P 15.

406	5s. Elephants in "Elephants' Graveyard"	1·50	50
407	10s. Type **61**	1·75	50
408	30s. Elephants at waterhole	3·00	2·50
409	70s. Elephants having dust bath	5·00	5·00
406/9	Set of 4	10·00	9·50
MS410	87×64 mm. 300s. Grevy's Zebra drinking (*vert*)..	4·75	3·25

Nos. 406/9 also exist perforated 14, but have only been seen mint or used on first day covers. There is some evidence that such stamps were produced around 1990.

No. **MS**410 exists imperforate from stock dispersed by the liquidator of Format International Security Printers Ltd.

See also No. 642 for the 10s. redrawn and Nos. 988/92 for these designs with different face values.

1983 (19 Sept). Centenary of Boys' Brigade. Nos. 383/7 optd with T **62** or surch also.
411	5s. Type **55**	10	10
412	20s. Scout receiving Bata Shoe trophy	15	15
413	50s. Scouts with wheelchair patient	20	30
414	400s. on 100s. First aid instruction	1·75	3·50
411/14 *Set of 4*		2·00	3·50
MS415 112×85 mm. 150s. Lord Baden-Powell		1·00	1·25

63 Mpoma Satellite Earth Station   **(64)**

(Des D. Dorfman. Litho Format)

1983 (3 Oct). World Communications Year. T **63** and similar horiz designs. Multicoloured. P 15.
416	20s. Type **63**	35	15
417	50s. Railroad computer and operator	70	85
418	70s. Cameraman filming lions	70	1·50
419	100s. Aircraft cockpit	80	2·25
416/19 *Set of 4*		2·25	4·25
MS420 128×103 mm. 300s. Communications satellite		1·00	1·75

No. 416 has the "o" omitted from "Station".

1983 (7 Oct). Nos. 303, 305/7, 308A, 309 and 313A surch as T **64**.
421	100s. on 10c. Type **37**	1·25	80
422	135s. on 1s. Type **38**	1·50	1·50
423	175s. on 30c. Thomson's Gazelle	1·75	2·00
424	200s. on 50c. Lesser Bushbaby	1·75	2·00
425	400s. on 80c. Hunting Dog	2·75	3·50
426	700s. on 5s. Waterbuck	3·75	8·00
427	1000s. on 1s.50 Gorilla	7·00	13·00
421/7 *Set of 7*		18·00	28·00

65 The Nativity

(Des PAD Studio. Litho Questa)

1983 (12 Dec). Christmas. T **65** and similar horiz designs. Multicoloured. P 14.
428	10s. Type **65**	10	10
429	50s. Shepherds and Angels	20	30
430	175s. Flight into Egypt	60	1·25
431	400s. Angels blowing trumpets	1·00	2·75
428/31 *Set of 4*		1·60	4·00
MS432 85×57 mm. 300s. The Three Kings		1·40	1·75

1983 (19 Dec). Designs as Nos. 308/12 and 315/16 but with face values in revalued currency. Without imprint date.
433	100s. Type **38**	90	35
434	135s. Gorilla	1·25	50
435	175s. Common Zebra	1·40	80
436	200s. Leopard with cub	1·75	1·50
437	400s. Black Rhinoceros	3·00	3·75
438	700s. African Elephant	5·00	8·50
439	1000s. Hippopotamus	9·00	12·00
433/9 *Set of 7*		20·00	25·00

An example of No. 438 is known showing an unissued overprint for the U.P.U. Congress held in Hamburg during 1989.

66 Ploughing with Oxen

(Des J.W. Litho Questa)

1984 (16 Jan). World Food Day. T **66** and similar horiz design. Multicoloured. P 14.
440	10s. Type **66**	15	10
441	300s. Harvesting bananas	1·75	5·50

67 Ruth Kyalisiima, Sportsman of the Year 1983

(Des J. Iskowitz. Litho Format)

1984 (1 Oct). Olympic Games, Los Angeles. T **67** and similar multicoloured designs. P 15.
442	5s. Type **67**	10	10
443	115s. Javelin-throwing	55	1·00
444	155s. Wrestling	60	1·40
445	175s. Rowing	60	1·60
442/5 *Set of 4*		1·60	3·50
MS446 108×79 mm. 500s. Fund-raising walk (*vert*)		1·00	1·25

68 Entebbe Airport

(Des BG Studio. Litho Format)

1984 (29 Oct). 40th Anniv of International Civil Aviation Organization. T **68** and similar horiz designs. Multicoloured. P 15.
447	5s. Type **68**	15	10
448	115s. Loading cargo plane	1·50	1·75
449	155s. Uganda police helicopter	2·50	2·75
450	175s. East African Civil Flying School, Soroti	2·75	3·25
447/50 *Set of 4*		6·25	7·00
MS451 100×70 mm. 250s. Balloon race		2·00	1·75

69 *Charaxes druceanus*

(Des J. Johnson. Litho Questa)

1984 (19 Nov). Butterflies. T **69** and similar horiz designs. Multicoloured. P 14.
452	5s. Type **69**	30	10
453	115s. *Papilio lormieri*	1·75	2·00
454	155s. *Druryia antimachus*	2·10	2·50
455	175s. *Salamis temora*	2·50	3·25
452/5 *Set of 4*		6·00	7·00
MS456 127×90 mm. 250s. *Colotis protomedia*		4·50	2·50

70 Blue-finned Notho

(Des Associated Creative Designers. Litho Format)

1985 (1 Apr–10 June). Lake Fish. T **70** and similar horiz designs. Multicoloured. P 15.
457	5s. Type **70**	30	40
458	10s. Semutundu	40	40
459	50s. Grey Bichir	75	30
460	100s. Walking Catfish	85	30
461	135s. Elephant-snout Fish (10 June)	1·25	1·00
462	175s. Lake Victoria Squeaker	1·25	1·60
463	205s. Brown's Haplochromis	1·25	2·00
464	400s. Nile Perch	1·25	2·25

465	700s. African Lungfish	1·25	3·00
466	1000s. Radcliffe's Barb	1·25	3·50
467	2500s. Electric Catfish (10 June)	1·50	4·50
457/67	Set of 11	10·00	17·00

Nos. 459/67 exist imperforate from stock dispersed by the liquidator of Format International Security Printers Ltd.

Similar horizontal designs with only Latin names for the species were prepared but not issued. Face values were 5, 10, 50, 100, 135 and 175s. in small format and 200, 400, 700 and 1000s. in larger size. The following values were similar to some of the issued stamps; 5s. (400s.), 10s. (2500s.), 135s. (5s.), 175s. (205s.) and 1000s. (1000s.).

The 135s. value has been reported with two different Latin inscriptions *Mormyrus caballas* and *Mormyrus kannume* (No. 461). It is possible that the former was issued on 1 April 1985, with the rest of the set (apart from No. 467), but we have not seen used examples.

71 The Last Supper

(Des Associated Creative Designers. Litho Questa)

1985 (13 May). Easter. T **71** and similar horiz designs. Multicoloured. P 14.

468	5s. Type **71**	10	10
469	115s. Christ showing the nail marks to Thomas	1·40	1·40
470	155s. The raising of the Cross	1·60	2·25
471	175s. Pentecost	1·90	2·75
468/71	Set of 4	4·50	6·00
MS472	99×70 mm. 250s. The last prayer in the Garden	80	1·25

72 Breast Feeding

73 Queen Elizabeth the Queen Mother

(Des Associated Creative Designers. Litho Questa)

1985 (29 July). U.N.I.C.E.F. Child Survival Campaign. T **72** and similar horiz designs. Multicoloured. P 14.

473	5s. Type **72**	10	10
474	115s. Growth monitoring	1·75	1·75
475	155s. Immunisation	2·25	2·50
476	175s. Oral re-hydration therapy	2·50	3·00
473/6	Set of 4	6·00	6·50
MS477	75×55 mm. 500s. Pregnant woman preparing nourishing food	4·25	5·00

(Des J.W. Litho Questa)

1985 (21 Aug). Life and Times of Queen Elizabeth the Queen Mother and Decade for Women. T **73** and similar vert design. Multicoloured. P 14.

478	1000s. Type **73**	1·40	2·10
MS479	57×81 mm. 1500s. The Queen Mother inspecting Kings African Rifles, Kampala	2·25	3·50

74 Sedge Warbler

GOLD MEDALIST BENITA BROWN-FITZGERALD USA

(75)

(Des S. Heinmann. Litho Questa)

1985 (21 Aug). Birth Bicentenary of John J. Audubon (ornithologist) (1st issue). T **74** and similar vert designs. Multicoloured. P 14.

480	115s. Type **74**	1·75	1·50

481	155s. Cattle Egret	2·00	1·75
482	175s. Crested Lark	2·00	2·25
483	500s. Tufted Duck	2·25	4·50
480/3	Set of 4	7·25	9·00
MS484	99×69 mm. 1000s. Tawny Owl	11·00	10·00

See also Nos. 494/8.

1985 (21 Aug). Olympic Gold Medal Winners, Los Angeles. Nos. 442/6 optd or surch as T **75** in gold.

485	5s. Type **67** (optd T **75**)	10	10
486	115s. Javelin-throwing (optd "GOLD MEDALIST-ARTO HAERKOENEN FINLAND")	70	30
487	155s. Wrestling (optd "GOLD MEDALIST ATSUJI MIYAHARA JAPAN")	80	40
488	1000s. on 175s. Rowing (surch "GOLD MEDALIST WEST GERMANY")	3·00	2·00
485/8	Set of 4	4·00	2·50
MS489	108×79 mm. 1200s. on 500s. Fund-raising walk (surch "MEN'S HURDLES EDWIN MOSES USA")	2·25	2·50

On No. **MS**489 only the new value appears on the stamp, the remainder of the surcharge is on the sheet margin.

76 Women carrying National Women's Day Banner

77 Man beneath Tree laden with Produce (F.A.O.)

76a Rock Ptarmigan

(Des and litho Questa)

1985 (1 Nov). Decade for Women. T **76** and similar multicoloured designs. P 14.

490	5s. Type **76**	10	10
491	115s. Girl Guides (*horiz*)	1·75	2·00
492	155s. Mother Teresa (Nobel Peace Prize winner, 1979)	3·00	3·25
490/2	Set of 3	4·25	4·75
MS493	85×59 mm. 1500s. As 115s.	4·00	4·00

Nos. 491 and **MS**493 also commemorate the 75th anniversary of the Girl Guide movement.

(Litho Questa)

1985 (23 Dec). Birth Bicentenary of John J. Audubon (ornithologist) (2nd issue). T **76a** and similar horiz designs showing original paintings. Multicoloured. P 12.

494	5s. Type **76a**	55	10
495	155s. Sage Grouse	1·50	1·75
496	175s. Lesser Yellowlegs	1·50	2·50
497	500s. Brown-headed Cowbird	2·75	4·75
494/7	Set of 4	5·50	8·00
MS498	72×102 mm. 1000s. Whooping Crane. P 14	7·50	9·50

Nos. 494/7 were each printed in sheetlets of 5 stamps and one stamp-size label which appears in the centre of the bottom row.

(Des BG Studio. Litho Format)

1986 (1 Apr). 40th Anniv of United Nations Organization. T **77** and similar designs. P 15.

499	10s. multicoloured	10	10
500	180s. multicoloured	40	30
501	200s. new blue, agate and bright green	40	35
502	250s. new blue, brownish blk & scar-verm.	40	40
503	2000s. multicoloured	1·25	5·00
499/503	Set of 5	2·25	5·50
MS504	69×69 mm. 2500s. multicoloured	1·75	2·75

Designs: Horiz—180s. Soldier of U.N. Peace-Keeping Force; 250s. Hands releasing peace dove. Vert—200s. U.N. emblem; 2000s. Flags of U.N. and Uganda; 2500s. U.N. Building, New York, and flags of member nations.

78 Goalkeeper catching Ball

NRA LIBERATION 1986
(**79**)

(Des Shelley Haas. Litho Questa)

1986 (17 Apr). World Cup Football Championship, Mexico. T **78** and similar multicoloured designs. P 14.

505	10s. Type **78**	10	10
506	180s. Player with ball	60	55
507	250s. Two players competing for ball	70	65
508	2500s. Player running with ball	4·00	6·00
505/8	*Set of 4*	4·75	6·50
MS509	87×66 mm. 3000s. Player kicking ball (*vert*)	4·75	3·50

1986 (30 Apr). Liberation by National Resistance Army. Nos. 462, 464/7 and **MS**493 optd with T **79** or larger (22×8 *mm*) (No. **MS**493).

510	175s. Lake Victoria Squeaker (Sil.)	1·00	70
511	400s. Nile Perch	1·75	1·25
512	700s. African Lungfish (Sil.)	2·50	3·00
513	1000s. Radcliffe's Barb	3·50	4·50
514	2500s. Electric Catfish	4·50	7·50
510/14	*Set of 5*	12·00	15·00
MS514a	85×59 mm. 1500s. Girl Guides	6·50	3·50

Nos. 510/14 also exist with the overprint colours transposed.

79a Tycho Brahe and Arecibo Radio Telescope, Puerto Rico

(Des W. Hanson. Litho Questa)

1986 (30 Apr). Appearance of Halley's Comet (1st issue). T **79a** and similar horiz designs. Multicoloured. P 14.

515	50s. Type **79a**	20	10
516	100s. Recovery of astronaut John Glenn from sea, 1962	35	15
517	140s. "The Star in the East" (painting by (Giotto))	50	30
518	2500s. Death of Davy Crockett at the Alamo, 1835	3·75	6·00
515/18	*Set of 4*	4·25	6·00
MS519	102×70 mm. 3000s. Halley's Comet over Uganda	7·00	6·00

See also Nos. 544/8.

80 Niagara Falls

80a Princess Elizabeth at London Zoo

(Des Mary Walters. Litho Format)

1986 (22 May). Ameripex '86 International Stamp Exhibition, Chicago. American Landmarks. T **80** and similar horiz designs. Multicoloured. P 15.

520	50s. Type **80**	15	10
521	100s. Jefferson Memorial. Washington D.C.	25	15
522	250s. Liberty Bell, Philadelphia	50	35
523	1000s. The Alamo, San Antonio, Texas	1·25	2·50
524	2500s. George Washington Bridge, New York-New Jersey	1·75	5·50
520/4	*Set of 5*	3·50	7·75
MS525	87×64 mm. 3000s. Grand Canyon	2·00	3·25

Nos. 520/4 exist imperforate from stock dispersed by the liquidator of Format International Security Printers Ltd.

(Litho Questa)

1986 (24 May). 60th Birthday of Queen Elizabeth II. T **80a** and similar vert designs. P 14.

526	100s. black and yellow	85	30
527	140s. multicoloured	85	30
528	2500s. multicoloured	3·25	4·50
526/8	*Set of 3*	4·50	4·50
MS529	120×85 mm. 3000s. black and grey-brown	4·00	4·00

Designs:—140s. Queen Elizabeth at race meeting, 1970; 2500s. With Prince Philip at Sandringham, 1982; 3000s. Engagement photograph, 1947.

81 *Gloria* (Colombia)

81a Prince Andrew and Miss Sarah Ferguson

(Des J. Iskowitz. Litho Questa)

1986 (2 July). Centenary of Statue of Liberty. T **81** and similar multicoloured designs showing cadet sailing ships. P 14.

530	50s. Type **81**	70	20
531	100s. *Mircea* (Rumania)	1·10	30
532	140s. *Sagres II* (Portugal) (*horiz*)	1·75	1·00
533	2500s. *Gazela Primiero* (U.S.A.) (*horiz*)	7·00	12·00
530/3	*Set of 4*	9·50	12·00
MS534	113×82 mm. 3000s. Statue of Liberty	3·50	3·50

No. 533 is inscribed "Primero" in error.

(Des and litho Questa)

1986 (23 July). Royal Wedding. T **81a** and similar horiz designs. Multicoloured. P 14.

535	50s. Type **81a**	10	10
536	140s. Prince Andrew with Princess Anne at shooting match	20	20
537	2500s. Prince Andrew and Miss Sarah Ferguson at Ascot	2·75	4·00
535/7	*Set of 3*	2·75	4·00
MS538	88×88 mm. 3000s. Prince Andrew and Miss Sarah Ferguson (*different*)	3·00	3·25

WINNERS

Argentina 3 W. Germany 2
(**82**)

1986 (15 Sept). World Cup Football Championship Winners, Mexico. Nos. 505/9 optd as T **82**, or surch also, in gold.

539	50s. on 10s. Type **78**	10	10
540	180s. Player with ball	25	25
541	250s. Two players competing for ball	35	35
542	2500s. Player running with ball	2·75	4·50
539/42	*Set of 4*	3·00	4·75
MS543	87×66 mm. 3000s. Player kicking ball (*vert*)	4·75	3·25

82a

83 St. Kizito

1986 (15 Oct). Appearance of Halley's Comet (2nd issue). Nos. 515/19 optd with T **82a** (in silver on 3000s.).

544	50s. Type **79a**	20	15
545	100s. Recovery of astronaut John Glenn from sea, 1962	35	20
546	140s. "The Star in the East" (painting by Giotto)	55	40
547	2500s. Death of Davy Crockett at the Alamo, 1835	5·50	7·50
544/7	*Set of 4*	6·00	7·50
MS548	102×70 mm. 3000s. Halley's Comet over Uganda	6·00	5·00

(Des Associated Creative Designers. Litho Questa)

1986 (15 Oct). Christian Martyrs of Uganda. T **83** and similar horiz designs. Multicoloured. P 14.

549	50s. Type **83**	20	10
550	150s. St. Kizito instructing converts	40	35
551	200s. Martyrdom of Bishop James Hannington, 1885	55	45
552	1000s. Burning of Bugandan Christians, 1886	2·25	4·00
549/52 *Set of 4*		3·00	4·50
MS553 89×59 mm. 1500s. King Mwanga of Buganda passing sentence on Christians		1·50	2·25

84 "Madonna of the Cherries" (Titian)

(Litho Questa)

1986 (26 Nov). Christmas. Religious Paintings. T **84** and similar multicoloured designs. P 14.

554	50s. Type **84**	25	15
555	150s. Madonna and Child" (Dürer) (*vert*)	60	30
556	200s. "Assumption of the Virgin" (Titian) (*vert*)	70	40
557	2500s. "Praying Hands" (Dürer) (*vert*)	5·50	8·50
554/7 *Set of 4*		6·25	8·50
MS558 Two sheets, each 102×76 mm. (a) 3000s. "Presentation of the Virgin in the Temple" (Titian). (b) 3000s. "Adoration of the Magi" (Dürer) *Set of 2 sheets*		8·50	10·00

85 Red-billed Fire Finch and Glory Lily

(Litho Format)

1987 (22 July). Flora and Fauna. T **85** and similar horiz designs. Multicoloured. P 15.

559	2s. Type **85**	65	75
560	5s. African Pygmy Kingfisher and Nandi Flame	85	1·00
561	10s. Scarlet-chested Sunbird and Crown of Thorns	95	1·00
562	25s. White Rhinoceros and Yellow-billed Oxpecker	2·25	1·25
563	35s. Lion and Elephant Grass	1·25	1·25
564	45s. Cheetahs and Doum Palm	1·50	1·50
565	50s. Red-cheeked Cordon Bleu and Desert Rose	2·25	2·25
566	100s. Giant Eland and Acacia	2·50	4·00
559/66 *Set of 8*		11·00	11·50
MS567 Two sheets, each 98×67 mm. (a) 150s. Carmine Bee Eaters and Sausage Tree. (b) 150s. Cattle Egret and Zebras *Set of 2 sheets*		11·00	9·50

Nos. 559 and 561/6 exist imperforate from stock dispersed by the liquidator of Format International Security Printers Ltd.

86 Tremml's *Eagle* (longest man-powered flight), 1987

(Des W. Hanson. Litho Format)

1987 (14 Aug). Milestones of Transportation. T **86** and similar horiz designs. Multicoloured. P 15.

568	2s. Type **86**	40	70
569	3s. Junkers W.33 *Bremen* (first east-west transatlantic flight), 1928	40	70
570	5s. Lockheed Vega 5 *Winnie Mae* (Post's first solo round-the-world flight), 1933	50	70
571	10s. *Voyager* (first non-stop round-the-world flight), 1986	60	70
572	15s. Chanute biplane glider, 1896	75	85

573	25s. Airship N.1 *Norge* and Polar Bear (first transpolar flight), 1926	1·50	1·00
574	35s. Curtiss Golden Flyer biplane and U.S.S. *Pennsylvania* (battleship) (first take-off and landing from ship), 1911	1·75	1·25
575	45s. Shepard and "Freedom 7" spacecraft (first American in space), 1961	1·75	1·50
576	100s. Concorde (first supersonic passenger flight)	7·50	7·50
568/76 *Set of 9*		13·50	13·50

Nos. 568/76 exist imperforate from stock dispersed by the liquidator of Format International Security Printers Ltd.

87 Olympic Torch-bearer

(Litho Questa)

1987 (5 Oct). Olympic Games, Seoul (1988) (1st issue). T **87** and similar horiz designs. Multicoloured. P 14.

577	5s. Type **87**	10	10
578	10s. Swimming	20	25
579	50s. Cycling	1·00	1·25
580	100s. Gymnastics	2·00	2·50
577/80 *Set of 4*		3·00	3·75
MS581 100×75 mm. 150s. Boxing		2·00	3·50

See also Nos. 628/32.

88 Child Immunization   **89** Golden-backed Weaver

(Des Associated Creative Designers. Litho Questa)

1987 (8 Oct). 25th Anniv of Independence. T **88** and similar horiz designs. P 14.

582	5s. multicoloured	20	10
583	10s. multicoloured	35	25
584	25s. multicoloured	80	70
585	50s. multicoloured	1·50	1·50
582/5 *Set of 4*		2·50	3·25
MS586 90×70 mm. 100s. black, bright scarlet and greenish yellow		1·75	2·25

Designs:—10s. Mulago Hospital, Kampala; 25s. Independence Monument, Kampala City Park; 50s. High Court, Kampala; 100s. Stylized head of Crested Crane, "25" and Ugandan flag.

(Des Jennifer Toombs. Litho Questa)

1987 (19 Oct). Birds of Uganda. T **89** and similar multicoloured designs. P 14.

587	5s. Type **89**	1·25	80
588	10s. Hoopoe	2·25	1·25
589	15s. Red-throated Bee Eater	2·50	1·25
590	25s. Lilac-breasted Roller	3·00	1·60
591	35s. African Pygmy Goose	3·00	1·75
592	45s. Scarlet-chested Sunbird	3·25	2·75
593	50s. South African Crowned Crane	3·25	2·75
594	100s. Long-tailed Fiscal	5·00	5·50
587/94 *Set of 8*		21·00	16·00
MS595 Two sheets, each 80×60 mm. (a) 150s. African Fish Eagle. (b) 150s. Barn Owl *Set of 2 sheets*		8·00	10·00

90 Hippocrates (physician) and Surgeons performing Operation

(Des L. Nelson. Litho Questa)

1987 (2 Nov). Great Scientific Discoveries. T **90** and similar multicoloured designs. P 14.

596	5s. Type **90**	75	30
597	25s. Einstein and Deep Space (Theory of Relativity)	3·25	1·75
598	35s. Isaac Newton and diagram from *Opticks* (Theory of Colour and Light)	2·75	2·50
599	45s. Karl Benz, early Benz and modern Mercedes cars	3·25	3·00
596/9 *Set of 4*		9·00	6·75
MS600 97×70 mm. 150s. *Challenger* (space shuttle) (*vert*)		4·25	4·00

91 Scout with Album and Uganda Stamps

(Des Mary Walters. Litho Questa)

1987 (20 Nov). World Scout Jamboree, Australia. T **91** and similar horiz designs. Multicoloured. P 14.

601	5s. Type **91**	20	10
602	25s. Scouts planting tree	70	70
603	35s. Canoeing on Lake Victoria	1·00	85
604	45s. Hiking	1·50	1·10
601/4 *Set of 4*		3·00	2·50
MS605 95×65 mm. 150s. Jamboree and Uganda scout emblems		2·50	3·25

92 "The Annunciation"

(Litho Questa)

1987 (18 Dec). Christmas. T **92** and similar multicoloured designs showing scenes from French diptych, c. 1250. P 14.

606	5s. Type **92**	10	10
607	10s. "The Nativity"	20	25
608	50s. "Flight into Egypt"	1·00	1·25
609	100s. "The Adoration of the Magi"	2·00	2·50
606/9 *Set of 4*		3·00	3·50
MS610 76×105 mm. 150s. "Mystic Wine" (tapestry detail) (*vert*)		3·00	4·00

93 Class 12 Light Shunter Locomotive

94 Columbite-Tantalite

(Des BG Studio. Litho Questa)

1988 (18 Jan). Locomotives of East Africa Railways. T **93** and similar horiz designs. Multicoloured. P 14.

611	5s. Type **93**	60	35
612	10s. Class 92 diesel-electric	70	45
613	15s. Steam locomotive No. 2506	90	60
614	25s. Class 11 tank locomotive No. 126	1·25	85
615	35s. Class 24 steam locomotive	1·50	1·10
616	45s. Class 21 steam locomotive	1·75	1·40
617	50s. Class 59 Garratt steam locomotive, 1955	2·00	1·60
618	100s. Class 87 diesel-electric locomotive	3·00	2·40
611/18 *Set of 8*		10·50	8·00
MS619 Two sheets, each 100×74 mm. (a) 150s. Class 31 steam locomotive. (b) 150s. Class 59 Garratt steam locomotive *Set of 2 sheets*		9·50	7·50

(Des Mary Walters. Litho Questa)

1988 (18 Jan). Minerals. T **94** and similar vert designs. Multicoloured. P 14.

620	1s. Type **94**	25	15
621	2s. Galena	30	20
622	5s. Malachite	50	35
623	10s. Cassiterite	70	55
624	35s. Ferberite	2·00	1·50
625	50s. Emerald	2·50	2·00
626	100s. Monazite	3·75	3·00
627	150s. Microcline	4·50	4·00
620/7 *Set of 8*		13·00	10·50

95 Hurdling

(Des BG Studio. Litho Questa)

1988 (16 May). Olympic Games, Seoul (2nd issue). T **95** and similar horiz designs. Multicoloured. P 14.

628	5s. Type **95**	10	10
629	25s. High jumping	40	50
630	35s. Javelin throwing	45	55
631	45s. Long jumping	55	70
628/31 *Set of 4*		1·25	1·60
MS632 85×114 mm. 150s. Olympic medals		1·00	1·50

96 *Spathodea campanulata*

(Des L. Nelson. Litho Format)

1988 (29 July). Flowers. T **96** and similar multicoloured designs. P 15.

633	5s. Type **96**	15	15
634	10s. *Gloriosa simplex*	15	15
635	20s. *Thevetia peruviana* (*vert*)	20	20
636	25s. *Hibiscus schizopetalus*	20	25
637	35s. *Aframomum sceptrum*	20	30
638	45a. *Adenium obesum*	20	35
639	50s. *Kigelia africana* (*vert*)	25	40
640	100s. *Clappertonia ficifolia*	35	75
633/40 *Set of 8*		1·50	2·25
MS641 Two sheets, each 109×79 mm. (a) 150s. *Costus spectabilis*. (b) 150s. *Canarina abyssinica* (*vert*) *Set of 2 sheets*		2·00	2·75

Nos. 633/41 exist imperforate from stock dispersed by the liquidator of Format International Security Printers Ltd.

97 Elephants in Grassland (Type **61** redrawn)

(Litho Questa)

1988 (29 July). Endangered Species (2nd series). P 14.

642	**97** 10s. multicoloured	70·00	4·00

World Wildlife Fund first day covers for No. 642 are cancelled "22 Aug 1983", the issue date of the first series.

98 Red Cross Worker vaccinating Baby

(Des Associated Creative Art Designers. Litho Questa)

1988 (28 Oct). 125th Anniv of International Red Cross. T **98** and similar designs. P 14.

643	10s. bright scarlet, pale yellow and black.....	25	15
644	40s. multicoloured	70	70
645	70s. multicoloured	1·50	2·00
646	90s. multicoloured	2·00	2·25
643/6 *Set of 4*		4·00	4·50
MS647 110×78 mm. 150s. multicoloured		1·00	1·60

Designs: Horiz—10s. "AIDS" with test tube as "I"; 70s. Distributing food to refugees; 90s. Red Cross volunteers with accident victim. Vert—150s. Henri Dunant (founder).

98a "Portrait of a Lady"

99 Giraffes, Kidepo Valley National Park

(Litho Questa)

1988 (31 Oct). 500th Birth Anniv of Titian (artist). T **98a** and similar vert designs. Multicoloured. P 13½×14.

648	10s. Type **98a**....................................	15	15
649	20s. "Portrait of a Man"......................	20	20
650	40s. "Isabella d'Este"..........................	35	35
651	50s. "Vincenzo Mosti"..........................	45	45
652	70s. "Pope Paul III Farnese"................	50	60
653	90s. "Violante"...................................	60	75
654	100s. "Titian's Daughter Lavinia"..........	70	85
655	250s. "Dr. Parma"...............................	1·40	1·90
648/55 *Set of 8*		4·00	4·75
MS656 Two sheets, each 110×95 mm. (a) 350s. "The Speech of Alfonso D'Avalos" (detail). (b) 350s. "Cain and Abel" (detail) *Set of 2 sheets*............		5·50	7·00

(Des Mary Walters. Litho Questa)

1988 (18 Nov). National Parks of Uganda. T **99** and similar vert designs. Multicoloured. P 14.

657	10s. Type **99**	1·75	30
658	25s. Zebras, Lake Mburo National Park	2·00	30
659	100s. African Buffalo, Murchison Falls National Park	2·50	2·50
660	250s. Eastern White Pelicans, Queen Elizabeth National Park	8·00	7·00
657/60 *Set of 4*		13·00	9·00
MS661 97×68 mm. 350s. Roan Antelopes, Lake Mburo National Park..............................		2·50	2·75

100 Doctor examining Child's Eyes

100a Father Christmas with List

(Des L. Watkins. Litho Questa)

1988 (1 Dec). 40th Anniv of World Health Organization. T **100** and similar horiz designs. Multicoloured. P 14.

662	10s. Type **100**..................................	25	15
663	25s. Mental health therapist with patient.....	50	30
664	45s. Surgeon performing operation..........	70	60
665	100s. Dentist treating girl......................	1·40	1·50
666	200s. Doctor examining child	2·00	2·50
662/6 *Set of 5*		4·25	4·50
MS667 107×88 mm. 350s. Delegates approving Declaration of Alma-Ata, 1978		2·50	3·50

(Des Walt Disney Co. Litho Questa)

1988 (2 Dec). Christmas. "Santa's Helpers". T **100a** and similar vert designs showing Walt Disney cartoon characters. Multicoloured. P 13½×14.

668	50s. Type **100a**.................................	1·25	1·00
	a. Sheetlet. Nos. 668/75	9·00	7·00
669	50s. Goofy carrying presents................	1·25	1·00
670	50s. Mickey Mouse on toy train............	1·25	1·00
671	50s. Reindeer at window......................	1·25	1·00
672	50s. Donald Duck's nephew with building blocks..........................	1·25	1·00
673	50s. Donald Duck holding sack............	1·25	1·00
674	50s. Chip n'Dale on conveyor belt........	1·25	1·00
675	50s. Donald Duck's nephew operating conveyor belt............................	1·25	1·00
668/75 *Set of 8*		9·00	7·00
MS676 Two sheets, each 127×102 mm. (a) 350s. Mickey Mouse loading sack of toys on sleigh (*horiz*). P 14×13½. (b) 350s. Mickey Mouse and Chip n'Dale grooming reindeer. P 13½×14 *Set of 2 sheets*..		7·50	8·50

Nos. 668/75 were printed together, *se-tenant* as a composite design, in sheetlets of eight.

**110 M HURDLES
R. KINGDOM
USA**
(101)

1989 (30 Jan). Olympic Gold Medal Winners, Seoul. Nos. 628/32 optd as T **101** or surch also.

677	5s. Type **95** (optd with T **101**)	10	10
678	25s. High jumping (optd "HIGH JUMP G. AVDEENKO USSR")	20	25
679	35s. Javelin throwing (optd "JAVELIN T. KORJUS FINLAND")	25	30
680	300s. on 45s. Long jumping (optd "LONG JUMP C. LEWIS USA")	2·50	3·00
677/80 *Set of 4*		2·75	3·25
MS681 85×114 mm. 350s. on 150s. Olympic medals with medal table optd on sheet margin		3·00	4·00

102 Goalkeeper with Ball

103 1895 5 Cowries Stamp

102a "Fuji and the Great Wave off Kanagawa"

(Des J. Genzo. Litho Questa)

1989 (24 Apr). World Cup Football Championship, Italy (1990) (1st issue). T **102** and similar multicoloured designs. P 14.

682	10s. Type **102**	25	15
683	25s. Player kicking ball (*horiz*)............	55	40
684	75s. Heading ball towards net (*horiz*)............	1·25	1·10
685	200s. Tackling	2·25	2·75
682/5 *Set of 4*		3·75	4·00
MS686 118×87 mm. 300s. Football and World Cup trophy (*horiz*)............................		2·50	3·25

See also Nos. 849/53.

(Litho Questa)

1989 (15 May). Japanese Art. Paintings by Hokusai. T **102a** and similar horiz designs. Multicoloured. P 14×13½.

687	10s. Type **102a**.................................	35	30
688	15s. "Fuji from Lake Sawa"...................	45	35
689	20s. "Fuji from Kajikazawa"..................	50	35
690	60s. "Fuji from Shichirigahama"............	1·50	85

691	90s. "Fuji from Ejiri in Sunshu"	1·75	1·10
692	120s. "Fuji above Lightning"	2·00	1·25
693	200s. "Fuji from Lower Meguro in Edo"	2·75	2·00
694	250s. "Fuji from Edo"	3·00	2·25
687/94	Set of 8	11·00	7·50

MS695 Two sheets, each 102×76 mm. (a) 500s. "The Red Fuji from the Foot". (b) 500s. "Fuji from Umezawa" Set of 2 sheets .... 9·00 9·00

Nos. 687/94 were each printed in sheetlets of 10 containing two horizontal strips of 5 stamps separated by printed labels commemorating Emperor Hirohito.

(Des U. Purins. Litho B.D.T.)

1989 (7 July). Philexfrance 89 International Stamp Exhibition, Paris. T **103** and similar vert designs. P 14.

696	20s. black, brt scarlet and pale grey-brown	60	35
697	70s. black, yellowish green and azure	1·75	1·00
698	100s. black, dull violet and pale brown-rose	2·00	1·75
699	250s. black, orange-yell & pale greenish yellow	3·00	4·25
696/9	Set of 4	6·50	6·50

MS700 176×131 mm. Nos. 696/9 (sold at 500s.) .... 6·50 8·00

Designs:—70s. 1895 10 on 50 cowries stamp; 100s. 1896 25 cowries stamp; 250s. 1896 1 rupee stamp.

104 Scout advising on Immunization

105 Suillus granulatus

(Des Associated Creative Designers. Litho Questa)

1989 (3 Aug). 2nd All African Scout Jamboree Uganda, and 75th Anniv of Ugandan Scout Movement. T **104** and similar multicoloured designs. P 14.

701	10s. Type **104**	40	15
702	70s. Poultry keeping	1·25	1·10
703	90s. Scout on crutches leading family to immunization centre	1·50	2·25
704	100s. Scouts making bricks	1·50	2·25
701/4	Set of 4	4·25	5·25

MS705 99×67 mm. 500s. Ugandan Scout logo (vert) ... 3·25 4·50

(Des Mary Walters. Litho B.D.T.)

1989 (14 Aug). Fungi. T **105** and similar vert designs. Multicoloured. P 14.

706	10s. Type **105**	40	30
707	15s. Omphalotus olearius	55	40
708	45s. Oudemansiella radicata	1·25	1·00
709	50s. Clitocybe nebularis	1·25	1·10
710	60s. Macrolepiota rhacodes	1·40	1·25
711	75s. Lepista nuda	1·60	1·40
712	150s. Suillus luteus	2·75	3·00
713	200s. Agaricus campestris	3·00	3·25
706/13	Set of 8	11·00	10·50

MS714 Two sheets, each 100×68 mm. (a) 350s. Bolbitius vitellinus. (b) 350s. Schizophyllum commune Set of 2 sheets .... 12·00 11·00

106 Saddle-bill Stork

107 Rocket on Launch Pad

(Des S. Barlowe. Litho Questa)

1989 (12 Sept). Wildlife at Waterhole. T **106** and similar vert designs. Multicoloured. P 14½×14.

715	30s. Type **106**	90	75
	a. Sheetlet. Nos. 715/34	16·00	13·00
716	30s. Eastern White Pelican	90	75
717	30s. Marabou Stork	90	75
718	30s. Egyptian Vulture	90	75

719	30s. Bateleur	90	75
720	30s. African Elephant	90	75
721	30s. Giraffe	90	75
722	30s. Goliath Heron	90	75
723	30s. Black Rhinoceros	90	75
724	30s. Common Zebra and Oribi	90	75
725	30s. African Fish Eagle	90	75
726	30s. Hippopotamus	90	75
727	30s. Black-backed Jackal and Eastern White Pelican	90	75
728	30s. African Buffalo	90	75
729	30s. Olive Baboon	90	75
730	30s. Behar Reedbuck	90	75
731	30s. Lesser Flamingo and Serval	90	75
732	30s. Whale-headed Stork ("Shoebill Stork")..	90	75
733	30s. South African Crowned Crane	90	75
734	30s. Impala	90	75
715/34	Set of 20	16·00	13·00

MS735 Two sheets, each 99×68 mm. (a) 500s. Lion. (b) 500s. Long-crested Eagle Set of 2 sheets .... 8·00 9·50

Nos. 715/34 were printed together, se-tenant, in a sheetlet of 20 stamps, forming a composite design showing wildlife at a waterhole.

(Des T. Agana. Litho Questa)

1989 (20 Oct). 20th Anniv of First Manned Landing on Moon. T **107** and similar multicoloured designs. P 14.

736	10s. Type **107**	40	20
737	20s. Lunar module Eagle on Moon	55	30
738	30s. "Apollo 11" command module	65	40
739	50s. Eagle landing on Moon	1·00	60
740	70s. Astronaut Aldrin on Moon	1·25	85
741	250s. Neil Armstrong alighting from Eagle (vert)	4·25	2·75
742	300s. Eagle over Moon	4·25	3·00
743	350s. Astronaut Aldrin on Moon (vert)	4·25	3·25
736/43	Set of 8	15·00	10·00

MS744 Two sheets, each 77×104 mm. (a) 500s. "Saturn" rocket (vert). (b) 500s. "Apollo 11" capsule on parachutes (vert) Set of 2 sheets .... 7·50 8·50

108 Aphniolaus pallene

109 John Hanning Speke and Map of Lake Victoria

(Des S. Heimann. Litho Questa)

1989 (13 Nov). Butterflies. T **108** and similar vert designs showing "UGANDA" in black. Multicoloured. Without imprint date. P 14.

745	5s. Type **108**	45	40
746	10s. Hewitsonia boisduvali	60	25
747	20s. Euxanthe wakefieldi	80	30
748	30s. Papilio echerioides	95	30
749	40s. Acraea semivitrea	1·00	40
750	50s. Colotis antevippe	1·00	40
751	70s. Acraea perenna	1·25	70
752	90s. Charaxes cynthia	1·25	70
753	100s. Euphaedra neophron	1·25	70
754	150s. Cymothoe beckeri	1·50	1·25
755	200s. Vanessula milca	1·50	1·25
756	400s. Mimacraea marshalli	1·75	3·25
757	500s. Axiocerses amanga	1·75	3·50
758	1000s. Precis hierta	2·75	6·50
745/58	Set of 14	16·00	18·00

For these, and similar, designs showing "UGANDA" in blue, see Nos. 864/80.

(Des A. Granberg. Litho Questa)

1989 (15 Nov). Exploration of Africa. T **109** and similar horiz designs. Multicoloured. P 14.

760	10s. Type **109**	1·00	35
761	25s. Sir Richard Burton and map of Lake Tanganyika	1·25	50
762	40s. Richard Lander and Bakota bronze	1·00	65
763	90s. René Caillié and mosque, Timbuktu	1·75	1·00
764	125s. Sir Samuel Baker and Dorcas Gazelle	1·75	1·75
765	150s. Pharaoh Necho and ancient Phoenician merchantship	2·00	2·25
766	250s. Vasco da Gama and 15th-century caravel	4·00	3·75
767	300s. Sir Henry Morton Stanley and Lady Alice (sectional boat)	4·00	4·25
760/7	Set of 8	15·00	13·00

MS768 Two sheets, each 73×103 mm. (a) 500s.
Dr. David Livingstone and steam launch *Ma Robert*;
(b) 500s. Mary Kingsley and map of Ogooué River
Set of 2 sheets .... 8·50 9·50

110 Logo (25th anniv of African Development Bank)

111 *Aerangis kotschyana*

(Des D. Miller. Litho Questa)

1989 (12 Dec). Anniversaries. T **110** and similar horiz designs. Multicoloured. P 14.

769	10s. Type **110**	25	15
770	20s. Arrows and dish aerials (World Telecommunications Day)	25	20
771	75s. Two portraits of Nehru (birth centenary)	4·00	1·75
772	90s. Pan Am Boeing 314A flying boat *Dixie Clipper* (50th anniv of first scheduled trans-Atlantic airmail flight)	2·50	1·75
773	100s. George Stephenson and *Locomotion*,1825 (175th anniv of first practical steam locomotive)	3·50	1·75
774	150s. Concorde cockpit (20th anniv of first test flight)	4·25	3·25
775	250s. *Wapen von Hamburg* and *Leopoldus Primus* (galleons) (800th anniv of Port of Hamburg)	3·50	4·25
776	300s. Concorde and cockpit interior (20th anniv of first test flight)	5·00	4·50
769/76 *Set of 8*		21·00	16·00

MS777 Two sheets (a) 91×87 mm. 500s. Revolutionary with musket and Bastille, Paris (bicentenary of French Revolution). (b) 110×82 mm. 500s. Emperor Frederick I Barbarossa and Hamburg charter (800th anniv of Port of Hamburg) *Set of 2 sheets* .... 10·00 11·00

(Des W. Wright. Litho Questa)

1989 (18 Dec). Orchids. T **111** and similar vert designs. Multicoloured. P 14.

778	10s. Type **111**	30	25
779	15s. *Angraecum infundibulare*	35	30
780	45s. *Cyrtorchis chailluana*	80	70
781	50s. *Aerangis rhodosticta*	85	75
782	100s. *Eulophia speciosa*	1·75	1·50
783	200s. *Calanthe sylvatica*	2·50	2·25
784	250s. *Vanilla imperialis*	2·75	2·40
785	350s. *Polystachya vulcanica*	3·25	2·75
778/85 *Set of 8*		11·00	9·75

MS786 Two sheets, each 110×82 mm. (a) 500s. *Ansellia africana*. (b) 500s. *Ancistrochilus rothschildianus Set of 2 sheets* .... 13·00 11·00

111a "Madonna and Child"

112 *Thevetia peruviana*

(Litho Questa)

1989 (21 Dec). Christmas. Paintings by Fra Angelico T **111a** and similar vert designs. Multicoloured. P 14.

787	10s. Type **111a**	15	10
788	20s. "Adoration of the Magi"	20	15
789	40s. "Virgin and Child enthroned with Saints"	40	30
790	75s. "The Annunciation"	70	60
791	100s. "Virgin and Child" (detail, "St. Peter Martyr" triptych)	85	75

792	150s. "Virgin and Child enthroned with Saints" (*different*)	1·25	1·50
793	250s. "Virgin and Child enthroned"	1·75	2·25
794	350s. "Virgin and Child" (from Annalena altarpiece)	2·00	3·25
787/94 *Set of 8*		6·50	8·00

MS795 Two sheets, each 72×96 mm. (a) 500s. "Virgin and Child" (from Bosco ai Frati altarpiece). (b) 500s. "Madonna and Child with Twelve Angels" *Set of 2 sheets* .... 5·00 6·00

(Des Jennifer Toombs. Litho B.D.T.)

1990 (17 Apr). "EXPO '90" International Garden and Greenery Exhibition, Osaka (1st issue). Flowering Trees. T **112** and similar vert designs. Multicoloured. P 14.

796	10s. Type **112**	15	15
797	20s. *Acanthus eminens*	20	20
798	90s. *Gnidia glauca*	50	50
799	150s. *Oncoba spinosa*	70	70
800	175s. *Hibiscus rosa-sinensis*	75	75
801	400s. *Jacaranda mimosifolia*	1·25	1·75
802	500s. *Erythrina abyssinica*	1·40	1·90
803	700s. *Bauhinia purpurea*	1·60	2·25
796/803 *Set of 8*		6·00	7·50

MS804 Two sheets, each 93×85 mm. (a) 1000s. *Delonix regia*. (b) 1000s. *Cassia didymobotrya Set of 2 sheets* .... 13·00 14·00

See also Nos. 820/8.

112a Allied penetration of German West Wall, 1944

(Des W. Wright. Litho Questa)

1990 (8 June). 50th Anniv of Second World War. T **112a** and similar multicoloured designs. P 14.

805	5s. Type **112a**	50	40
806	10s. Flags of the Allies, VE Day, 1945	70	40
807	20s. Capture of Okinawa, 1945	80	45
808	75s. Appointment of Gen. De Gaulle to command all Free French forces, 1944	1·25	60
809	100s. Invasion of Saipan, 1944	1·60	75
810	150s. Airborne landing, Operation Market Garden, 1944	2·25	1·75
811	200s. MacArthur's return to Philippines, 1944	2·50	1·75
812	300s. *Shoho* (Japanese aircraft carrier) under attack, Coral Sea, 1942	2·75	2·50
813	350s. First Battle of El Alamein, 1942	3·00	2·50
814	500s. Naval Battle of Guadalcanal, 1942	3·25	3·25
805/14 *Set of 10*		17·00	13·00

MS815 112×83 mm. 1000s. Battle of Britain, 1940 (*vert*) .... 4·50 5·50

112b Queen Elizabeth with Corgi

(113)

(Des Young Phillips Studio. Litho Questa)

1990 (5 July). 90th Birthday of Queen Elizabeth the Queen Mother. T **112b** and similar vert designs, showing portraits, 1940–49. P 14.

816	250s. black, deep magenta and new blue	1·60	1·75
	a. Strip of 3. Nos. 816/18	4·25	4·75
817	250s. black deep magenta and new blue	1·60	1·75
818	250s. black, deep magenta and new blue	1·60	1·75
816/18 *Set of 3*		4·25	4·75

MS819 90×75 mm. 1000s. multicoloured .... 3·25 3·50

Designs:— Nos. 817, MS819, Queen Elizabeth wearing feathered hat; No. 818, Queen Elizabeth at wartime inspection.

Nos. 816/18 were printed together, horizontally and vertically se-tenant, in sheetlets of 9 (3×3).

1990 (30 July). EXPO 90 International Garden and Greenery Exhibition, Osaka (2nd issue). Nos. 778/86 optd as T **113** in silver.

820	10s. Type **111**	90	40
821	15s. *Angraecum infundibulare*	90	40
822	45s. *Cyrtorchis chailluana*	1·40	45
823	50s. *Aerangis rhodosticta*	1·40	45
824	100s. *Eulophia speciosa*	2·25	80
825	200s. *Calanthe sylvatica*	3·00	2·75
826	250s. *Vanilla imperialis*	3·25	3·50
827	350s. *Polystachya vulcanica*	3·50	4·50
820/7	Set of 8	15·00	12·00

MS828 Two sheets, each 110×82 mm. (a) 500s. *Ansellia africana*. (b) 500s. *Ancistrochilus rothschildianus* Set of 2 sheets .... 10·00 12·00

The overprint on No. **MS**828 occurs on the sheet margin and includes an additional inscription.

114 P.A.P.U. Emblem

115 Unissued G. B. "V R" Penny Black

(Des L. Fried. Litho B.D.T.)

1990 (3 Aug). Tenth Anniv of Pan-African Postal Union (80s.) and Second United Nations Conference on Least Developed Countries, Paris (750s.). T **114** and similar horiz design. P 14.

829	80s. multicoloured	1·60	1·00

MS830 97×67 mm. 750s. black and new blue .... 4·50 6·50
Design:—750s. Clasped hands.

(Des and litho B.D.T.)

1990 (6 Aug). 150th Anniv of the Penny Black. T **115** and similar vert designs. P 14.

831	25s. multicoloured	60	15
832	50s. brown-lake, blk & pale turquoise-green	80	25
833	100s. multicoloured	1·25	45
834	150s. multicoloured	1·75	1·25
835	200s. multicoloured	2·00	1·50
836	300s. multicoloured	2·25	2·00
837	500s. multicoloured	2·50	3·50
838	600s. multicoloured	2·50	3·50
831/8	Set of 8	12·00	11·00

MS839 Two sheets (a) 107×77 mm. 1000s. multicoloured. (b) 119×85 mm. 1000s. black and rosine Set of 2 sheets .... 10·00 12·00
Designs:—50s. Canada 1858–59 3d. Beaver; 100s. Baden 1851 9k. on green error; 150s. Basel 1845 2½r. Dove; 200s. U.S.A. 1918 24c. Inverted "Jenny" error; 300s. Western Australia 1854 1d. Black Swan; 500s. Uganda 1895 20c. "narrow" typewritten stamp; 600s. Great Britain Twopenny blue; 1000s. (No. **MS**839a), Uganda 1895 20c. "wide" typewritten stamp; 1000s. (No. **MS**839b), Sir Rowland Hill.
No. **MS**839 also commemorates "Stamp World London 90 International Stamp Exhibition."

116 African Jacana

(Des P. Gonzalez. Litho Questa)

1990 (3 Sept). Wild Birds of Uganda. T **116** and similar multicoloured designs. P 14.

840	10s. Type **116**	60	35
841	15s. Southern Ground Hornbill	60	35
842	45s. Kori Bustard (*vert*)	85	50
843	50s. Secretary Bird	85	50
844	100s. Egyptian Geese	1·25	85
845	300s. Goliath Heron (*vert*)	2·25	2·75
846	500s. Ostrich with chicks (*vert*)	2·75	3·50
847	650s. Saddle-bill Stork (*vert*)	3·00	4·00
840/7	Set of 8	11·00	11·50

MS848 Two sheets, each 98×69 mm. (a) 1000s. Lesser Flamingo (*vert*). (b) 1000s. Vulturine Guineafowl (*vert*) Set of 2 sheets .... 9·50 10·00

117 Roger Milla of Cameroun

(Des Young Phillips Studio. Litho Questa)

1990 (21 Sept). World Cup Football Championship, Italy (2nd issue). T **117** and similar horiz designs. Multicoloured. P 14.

849	50s. Type **117**	35	25
850	100s. Ramzy of Egypt	55	45
851	250s. David O'Leary of Ireland	1·25	1·25
852	600s. Littbarsky of West Germany	1·75	2·50
849/52	Set of 4	3·50	4·00

MS853 Two sheets, each 75×90 mm. (a) 1000s. Ali McCoist of Scotland. (b) 1000s. Ekstrom of Sweden Set of 2 sheets .... 9·00 10·00

118 Mickey and Minnie Mouse at Breakfast

(Des Walt Disney Co. Litho B.D.T.)

1990 (19 Oct). Health and Safety Campaign. T **118** and similar multicoloured designs showing Walt Disney cartoon characters. P 13.

854	10s. Type **118**	35	10
855	20s. Donald Duck's nephews doing kerb drill.	45	15
856	50s. Donald and Mickey stopping Big Pete smoking	80	35
857	90s. Mickey stopping Donald choking	1·40	40
858	100s. Mickey and Goofy using seat belts	1·50	45
859	250s. Mickey and Minnie dancing	2·50	2·25
860	500s. Donald Duck's fitness class	3·50	4·50
861	600s. Mickey's nephews showing lights at night	3·75	5·00
854/61	Set of 8	13·00	12·00

MS862 Two sheets, each 135×115 mm. (a) 1000s. Mickey weighing nephew (*vert*). (b) 1000s. Mickey and Pluto walking (*vert*) Set of 2 sheets .... 9·50 10·00

(Litho Questa)

1990 (1 Nov)–**92**. As Nos. 746/55 and new values, showing butterflies, as T **108** with "UGANDA" in blue. Multicoloured. P 14.

A. Without imprint date

864A	10s. *Hewitsonia boisduvali*	30	15
865A	20s. *Euxanthe wakefieldi*	40	20
866A	30s. *Papilio echerioides*	40	20
867A	40s. *Acraea semivitrea*	40	20
869A	70s. *Acraea perenna*	50	30
870A	90s. *Charaxes cynthia*	60	30
871A	100s. *Euphaedra neophron*	60	40
872A	150s. *Cymothoe beckeri*	60	40
873A	200s. *Vanessula milca*	1·00	60
877A	2000s. *Precis hierta*	6·00	7·50
878A	3000s. *Euphaedra eusemoides* (9.10.92)	6·00	9·50
879A	4000s. *Acraea natalica* (9.10.92)	6·50	12·00
880A	5000s. *Euphaedra themis* (9.10.92)	6·50	12·00
864A/80A	Set of 13	27·00	40·00

B. With "1991" imprint date (4.11.91)

865B	20s. *Euxanthe wakefieldi*	60	30
868B	50s. *Colotis antevippe*	60	30
871B	100s. *Euphaedra neophron*	80	40
873B	200s. *Vanessula milca*	1·25	60
874B	400s. *Mimacraea marshalli*	1·75	1·75
875B	500s. *Axiocerses amanga*	1·75	1·75
876B	1000s. *Precis hierta*	5·00	4·50
877B	2000s. *Precis hierta*	5·00	7·50
865B/77B	Set of 8	15·00	15·00

118a "Baptism of Christ" (detail)   120 Damselfly

119 Census Emblem

(Litho Questa)

1990 (17 Dec). Christmas. 350th Death Anniv of Rubens. T **118a** and similar multicoloured designs. P 13½×14.

881	10s. Type **118a**.	10	10
882	20s. "St. Gregory the Great and other Saints" (detail)	15	10
883	100s. "Saints Nereus, Domitilla and Achilleus" (detail)	65	35
884	150s. "St. Gregory the Great and other Saints" (different detail)	90	60
885	300s. "Saint Augustine" (detail)	1·50	1·75
886	400s. "St. Gregory the Great and other Saints" (different detail)	1·60	1·90
887	500s. "Baptism of Christ" (different detail)	1·75	2·00
888	600s. St. Gregory the Great and other Saints (different detail)	1·90	2·75
881/8	*Set of 8*	10·00	12·00

MS889 Two sheets, each 110×71 mm. (a) 1000s. "The Triumph of Faith" (detail) (*horiz*). (b) 1000s. "The Victory of Eucharistic Truth over Heresy" (detail) (*horiz*). P 14×13½ *Set of 2 sheets* .... 12·00 14·00

(Litho Questa)

1990 (28 Dec). National Population and Housing Census. T **119** and similar horiz design. Multicoloured. P 14.

890	20s. Type **119**.	65	50

MS891 105×73 mm. 1000s. Symbolic people and dwellings .... 5·50 6·50

(Des I. Maclaury. Litho B.D.T.)

1991 (8 Jan). Fauna of Uganda's Wetlands. T **120** and similar multicoloured designs. P 14.

892	70s. Type **120**.	1·10	85
	a. Sheetlet of 16. Nos. 892/907	16·00	12·00
893	70s. Purple Swamphen ("Gallinule")	1·10	85
894	70s. Sitatunga	1·10	85
895	70s. Western Reef Heron ("Purple Heron")	1·10	85
896	70s. Bushing	1·10	85
897	70s. Vervet Monkey	1·10	85
898	70s. Long Reed Frog	1·10	85
899	70s. Malachite Kingfisher	1·10	85
900	70s. Marsh Mongoose	1·10	85
901	70s. Painted Reed Frog	1·10	85
902	70s. African Jacana	1·10	85
903	70s. Charaxes butterfly	1·10	85
904	70s. Nile Crocodile	1·10	85
905	70s. Herald Snake	1·10	85
906	70s. Dragonfly	1·10	85
907	70s. Lungfish	1·10	85
892/907	*Set of 16*	16·00	12·00

MS908 118×78 mm. 1000s. Nile Monitor (*horiz*) .... 6·50 7·50

Nos. 892/907 were printed together, *se-tenant*, in sheetlets of 16 forming a composite design.

121 Slug Haplochromis

(Des Susan Fuller. Litho B.D.T.)

1991 (18 Jan). Fish of Uganda. T **121** and similar horiz designs. Multicoloured. P 14.

909	10s. Type **121**	20	10
910	20s. Palmquist's Notho	30	15
911	40s. Silver Distichodus	40	20
912	90s. Sauvage's Haplochromis	70	40
913	100s. Blue Calliurum	75	45
914	350s. Johnston's Haplochromis	2·00	2·00
915	600s. Colour-tailed Haplochromis	3·25	3·75
916	800s. Jewel Cichlid	3·75	4·50
909/16	*Set of 8*	10·00	10·50

MS917 Two sheets, each 100×74 mm. (a) 1000s. Haplochromis. (b) 1000s. Striped Panchax *Set of 2 sheets* .... 16·00 15·00

121a Women's 100 Metres Hurdles   122 South African Railways Class 15f Steam Locomotive, 1938–48

(Des B. Grout. Litho Questa)

1991 (25 Feb). Olympic Games, Barcelona (1992). T **121a** and similar multicoloured designs. P 14.

918	20s. Type **121a**	40	20
919	40s. Long jump	55	20
920	125s. Table tennis	1·40	1·25
921	250s. Football	2·00	2·00
922	500s. Men's 800 metres	2·75	3·75
918/22	*Set of 5*	6·50	6·75

MS923 Two sheets, each 110×71 mm. (a) 1200s. Opening Ceremony at Seoul Games (*horiz*). (b) 1200s. Women's 4×100 metres relay (*horiz*) *Set of 2 sheets* .... 10·00 12·00

(Des O. Fernandez. Litho Walsall)

1991 (2 Apr). African Railway Locomotives. T **122** and similar horiz designs. Multicoloured. P 14.

924	10s. Type **122**	1·00	40
925	20s. Rhodesian Railways 12th Class steam locomotive, 1900s.	1·40	50
926	80s. Class "Tribal" steam locomotive, Tanzam Railway, 1951–56.	2·50	80
927	200s. Steam locomotive, Egypt, 1905	3·50	1·50
928	300s. Mikado steam locomotive, Sudan, 1930.	3·50	2·50
929	400s. East African Railways Class 59 Garratt steam locomotive, 1955.	4·00	3·25
930	500s. East African Railways Mallet steam locomotive, 1900.	4·00	3·25
931	1000s. Type 5 F 1 electric locomotive, South Africa, 1970.	5·00	5·50
924/31	*Set of 8*	22·00	16·00

MS932 Four sheets, each 100×70 mm. (a) 1200s. Atlantic steam locomotive, Egypt, 1900s. (b) 1200s. Rhodesian Railways 12th Class steam locomotive, 1930. (c) 1200s. Benguela Railway Class II steam locomotive, Angola, 1920. (d) 1200s. Natal Govt Mallet steam locomotive, 1905–19 *Set of 4 sheets* .... 19·00 20·00

No. 924 is incorrectly captioned as a Rhodesia Railways 10th Class locomotive.

123 Lord Baden-Powell and Scout Emblem

(Des W. Hanson Studio. Litho Questa)

1991 (27 May). World Scout Jamboree Mount Sorak, Korea. T **123** and similar horiz designs. P 14.

933	20s. multicoloured	70	30
934	80s. multicoloured	1·10	65
935	100s. multicoloured	1·25	75
936	150s. black and pale yellow-olive.	1·75	1·00

937	300s. multicoloured	2·50	2·00
938	400s. multicoloured	2·50	2·75
939	500s. multicoloured	2·75	2·75
940	1000s. multicoloured	3·50	5·00
933/40	Set of 8	14·50	13·50

MS941 Two sheets. (a) 76×115 mm. 1200s. black and stone. (b) 115×76 mm. 1200s. black and dull violet-blue *Set of 2 sheets* .... 14·00 14·00

Designs:—80s. Scouts and Uganda 1982 100s. anniversary stamp; 100s. Scout encampment, New York World's Fair, 1939; 150s. Cover and illustration from *Scouting for Boys*; 300s. Cooking on campfire; 400s. Aldrin and Armstrong on Moon; 500s. Scout salutes; 1000s. Statue to the Unknown Scout, Gillwell Park; 1200s. (**MS**941a) Jamboree emblem; 1200s. (**MS**941b) Lord Baden-Powell, W. Boyce and Revd. L. Hadley.

123a Uncle Scrooge celebrating Ga-No-Iwai

(Des Walt Disney Co. Litho Questa)

1991 (29 May). "Phila Nippon '91" International Stamp Exhibition, Tokyo. T **123a** and similar multicoloured designs showing Walt Disney cartoon characters and Japanese traditions. P 14×13½.

942	10s. Type **123a**	25	20
943	20s. Mickey Mouse removing shoes	35	20
944	70s. Goofy leading cart-horse	80	50
945	80s. Daisy Duck and Minnie Mouse exchanging gifts	90	60
946	300s. Minnie kneeling at doorway	2·25	2·00
947	400s. Donald Duck and Mickey taking a hot volcanic sand bath	2·50	2·25
948	500s. Clarabelle Cow burning incense	2·50	2·25
949	1000s. Mickey and Minnie writing New Year cards	3·25	3·50
942/9	Set of 8	11·50	10·50

MS950 Two sheets, each 127×112 mm. (a) 1200s. Mickey conducting (*vert*). (b) 1200s. Mickey in public bath (*vert*). P 13½×14 *Set of 2 sheets* .... 13·00 13·00

123b "Snowy Landscape with Arles in the Background"

(Litho Walsall)

1991 (26 June). Death Centenary of Vincent van Gogh (artist) (1990). T **123b** and similar multicoloured designs. P 13½.

951	10s. Type **123b**	60	30
952	20s. "Peasant Woman binding Sheaves" (*vert*)	70	30
953	60s. "The Drinkers"	1·00	50
954	80s. "View of Auvers"	1·25	65
955	200s. "Mourning Man" (*vert*)	2·25	1·25
956	400s. "Still Life: Vase with Roses"	2·75	2·50
957	800s. "The Raising of Lazarus"	4·00	4·50
958	1000s. "The Good Samaritan" (*vert*)	4·00	4·50
951/8	Set of 8	15·00	13·00

MS959 Two sheets, each 102×76 mm. (a) 1200s. "First Steps" (95×71 *mm*). (b) 1200s. "Village Street and Steps in Auvers"(95×71 *mm*). Imperf *Set of 2 sheets* . 15·00 16·00

123c Queen Elizabeth II and Prince Charles after Polo Match

(Des D. Miller. Litho Walsall)

1991 (5 July). 65th Birthday of Queen Elizabeth II. T **123c** and similar horiz designs. Multicoloured. P 14.

960	70s. Type **123c**	1·50	45
961	90s. Queen at Balmoral, 1976	1·50	55
962	500s. Queen with Princess Margaret, August 1980	3·00	2·25
963	600s. Queen and Queen Mother leaving St. George's Chapel, Windsor	3·25	2·75
960/3	Set of 4	8·25	5·50

MS964 68×90 mm. 1200s. Separate photographs of Queen and Prince Philip .... 5·50 5·00

(Des D. Miller. Litho Walsall)

1991 (5 July). 10th Wedding Anniv of Prince and Princess of Wales. Horiz designs as T **123c.** Multicoloured. P 14.

965	20s. Prince and Princess of Wales in July 1986	70	15
966	100s. Separate photographs of Prince, Princess and sons	1·75	50
967	200s. Prince Henry and Prince William	1·90	1·00
968	1000s. Separate photographs of Prince and Princess in 1988	7·00	6·50
965/8	Set of 4	10·00	7·25

MS969 68×90 mm. 1200s. Princes William and Henry on Majorca and Prince and Princess of Wales in Cameroon .... 7·50 4·50

124 General Charles de Gaulle   **125** *Volvariella bingensis*

(Litho Questa)

1991 (15 July). Birth Centenary of Charles de Gaulle (French statesman) (1990). T **124** and similar multicoloured designs. P 14.

970	20s. Type **124**	30	20
971	70s. Liberation of Paris, 1944	65	45
972	90s. De Gaulle with King George VI, 1940	75	55
973	100s. Reviewing Free French troops, 1940 (*horiz*)	80	60
974	200s. Broadcasting to France, 1940 (*horiz*)	1·40	1·00
975	500s. De Gaulle in Normandy, 1944 (*horiz*)	2·25	2·00
976	600s. De Gaulle at Albert Hall, 1940 (*horiz*)	2·25	2·25
977	1000s. Inauguration as President, 1959	3·25	3·50
970/7	Set of 8	9·50	9·50

MS978 Two sheets. (a) 104×76 mm. 1200s. De Gaulle entering Paris, 1944. (b) 107×76 mm. 1200s. De Gaulle with Eisenhower, 1942 (*horiz*) *Set of 2 sheets* 12·00 12·00

(Des K. Botis. Litho Questa)

1991 (19 July). Fungi. T **125** and similar multicoloured designs. P 14.

979	20s. Type **125**	40	30
980	70s. *Agrocybe broadwayi*	70	55
981	90s. *Camarophyllus olidus*	80	65
982	140s. *Marasmius arborescens*	1·25	1·10
983	180s. *Marasmiellus subcinereus*	1·40	1·40
984	200s. *Agaricus campestris*	1·40	1·40
985	500s. *Chlorophyllum molybdites*	2·50	2·50
986	1000s. *Agaricus biagensis*	4·00	4·50
979/86	Set of 8	11·00	11·00

MS987 Two sheets, each 96×65 mm. (a) 1200s. *Leucocoprinus cepaestipes* (*horiz*). (b) 1200s. *Laccaria ohiensis* ("*Laccaria lateritia*") (*horiz*) *Set of 2 sheets* .... 9·00 9·50

(Des J. Iskowitz (Nos. 988/91), O. Fernandez (No. **MS**992). Litho Questa (Nos. 988/91) or Cartor (No. **MS**992))

1991 (1 Aug). Endangered Species (3rd series). As Nos. 406/9, but with changed face values, and additional horiz designs as T **61**. Multicoloured. P 14.

988	100s. Elephants in "Elephants' Graveyard"	75	45
989	140s. Type **61**	95	75
990	200s. Elephants at waterhole	1·50	1·25
991	600s. Elephants having dust bath	3·00	4·25
988/91	Set of 4	5·50	6·00

MS992 Two sheets, each 102×74 mm. (a) 1200s. Giraffe. (b) 1200s. Rhinoceros and Red-billed Oxpecker. P 13×12 *Set of 2 sheets* .... 25·00 18·00

126 Anigozanthos manglesii

(127)

20/-

(Des Jennifer Toombs. Litho Questa)

1991 (25 Nov). Botanical Gardens of the World. T **126** and similar vert designs. Multicoloured. P 14½.

993/1032	90s.×20, 100s.×20 Set of 40	25·00	26·00

MS1033 Two sheets, each 110×75 mm. (a) 1400s. The Pagoda, Kew. (b) 1400s. Temple of the Winds, Melbourne Set of 2 sheets ... 16·00 17·00

Nos. 993/1032 were issued together, se-tenant, as two sheetlets of 20. The 90s. values show Anigozanthos manglesii, Banksia grandis, Clianthus formosus, Gossypium sturtianum, Callistemon lanceolatus, Saintpaulia ionantha, Calodendrum capense, Aloe ferox×arborescens, Bolusanthus speciousus, Lithops schwantesii, Protea repens, Plumbago capensis, Clerodendrum thomsoniae, Thunbergia. alata, Schotia latifolia, Epacris impressa, Acacia pycnantha, Telopea speciosissima, Wahlenbergia gloriosa, Eucalyptus globulus from Melbourne, and the 100s. Cypripedium calceolus, Rhododendron thomsonii, Ginkgo biloba, Magnolia campbellii, Wisteria sinensis, Clerodendrum ugandense, Eulophia horsfallii, Aerangis rhodosticta, Abelmoschus moschatus, Gloriosa superba, Carissa edulis, Ockna kirkii, Canarina abyssinica, Nymphaea caerulea, Ceropegia succulenta, Strelitzia reginae, Strongylodon macrobotrys, Victoria amazonica, Orchis militaris and Sophora microphylla from Kew.

1991 (4 Dec). Nos. 569, 573, 597 and 614 surch as T **127**.

1034	20s. on 3s. Junkers W.33 Bremen (first east-west transatlantic flight), 1928	
1034a	20s. on 25s. Airship N.1 Norge and Polar Bear (first transpolar flight), 1926	
1035	20s. on 25s. Einstein and Deep Space (Theory of Relativity)	
1035a	20s. on 25s. Tank locomotive No. 126	

127a "Madonna with Child and Angels"

(Litho Walsall)

1991 (18 Dec). Christmas. Paintings by Piero della Francesca. T **127a** and similar vert designs. Multicoloured. P 12.

1036	20s. Type **127a**	50	20
1037	50s. "The Baptism of Christ"	75	20
1038	80s. "Polyptych of Mercy"	1·00	40
1039	100s. "Polyptych of Mercy" (detail)	1·00	40
1040	200s. "The Annunciation" from "The Legend of the True Cross"	1·75	80
1041	500s. "Pregnant Madonna"	2·75	2·50
1042	1000s. "The Annunciation" from "Polyptych of St. Anthony"	4·00	4·50
1043	1500s. "The Nativity"	5·00	7·50
1036/43	Set of 8	15·00	15·00

MS1044 Two sheets, each 102×127 mm. (a) 1800s. "The Brera Altarpiece". (b) 1800s. "Madonna and Child" from "Polyptych of St. Anthony". P 14 Set of 2 sheets ... 14·00 15·00

128 Boy Scout Monument, New York, and Ernest Thompson (first Chief Scout of U.S.A.)

(Des W. Hanson (Nos. 1045/6, **MS**1050b). W. Wright (Nos. 1047, **MS**1050a). Litho Questa)

1992 (6 Jan). Anniversaries and Events. T **128** and similar multicoloured designs. P 14.

1045	20s. Type **128**	80	30
1046	50s. Treehouse design and Daniel Beard (vert)	85	40
1047	400s. Lilienthal's signature and Flugzeug Nr. 8	1·60	1·75
1048	500s. Demonstrator demolishing Berlin Wall	1·60	2·25
1049	700s. The Magic Flute	9·50	8·50
1045/9	Set of 5	13·00	12·00

MS1050 Two sheets. (a) 114×85 mm. 1200s. Class VL8 electric locomotive leaving tunnel. (b) 117×89 mm. 1500s. Ugandan Boy Scout badge Set of 2 sheets ... 14·00 15·00

Anniversaries and Events:—Nos. 1045/6 **MS**1050b, 50th death anniv of Lord Baden-Powell and World Scout Jamboree, Korea; No. 1047, Centenary of Otto Lilienthal's first gliding experiments; No. 1048, Bicentenary of Brandenburg Gate, Berlin; No. 1049, Death bicentenary of Mozart; No. **MS**1050a, Centenary of Trans-Siberian Railway.

129 U.S.S. Vestal (repair ship) under Attack

(Des W. Hanson Studio. Litho Questa)

1992 (6 Jan). 50th Anniv of Japanese Attack on Pearl Harbor. T **129** and similar horiz designs. Multicoloured. P 14½.

1051	200s. Type **129**	1·75	1·50
	a. Sheetlet. Nos. 1051/60	16·00	13·50
1052	200s. Japanese Mitsubishi A6M Zero-Sen	1·75	1·50
1053	200s. U.S.S. Arizona (battleship) on fire	1·75	1·50
1054	200s. U.S.S. Nevada (battleship) passing burning ships	1·75	1·50
1055	200s. Japanese Aichi D3A "Val" bomber attacking	1·75	1·50
1056	200s. Douglas SBD Dauntless bombers attacking Hiryu (carrier) at Midway	1·75	1·50
1057	200s. Japanese Mitsubishi A6M Zero-Sen aircraft attacking Midway Island	1·75	1·50
1058	200s. U.S. Marine Brewster F2A Buffalo (fighter) defending Midway	1·75	1·50
1059	200s. American Grumman F6F Hellcat aircraft and carrier	1·75	1·50
1060	200s. U.S.S. Yorktown (carrier) torpedoed	1·75	1·50
1051/60	Set of 10	16·00	13·50

Nos. 1051/60 were printed together, se-tenant, in sheetlets of 10 with the stamps arranged in two horizontal strips of 5 forming composite designs separated by a gutter showing photograph of Pearl Harbor model and text.

130 Three Modern Hot Air Balloons

(Litho Questa)

1992 (6 Jan). 120th Anniv of Paris Balloon Post (1990). T **130** and similar horiz designs. Multicoloured. P 14.

1061	200s. Type **130**	1·50	1·50
	a. Sheetlet. Nos. 1061/9	12·00	12·00
1062	200s. Sport balloons and top of Double Eagle II	1·50	1·50
1063	200s. Pro Juventute balloon and top of Branson's Virgin Otsuka Pacific Flyer	1·50	1·50
1064	200s. Blanchard and Jeffries' balloon	1·50	1·50
1065	200s. Nadar's Le Geant and centre of Double Eagle II	1·50	1·50
1066	200s. Branson's Virgin Otsuka Pacific Flyer	1·50	1·50
1067	200s. Montgolfier balloon	1·50	1·50
1068	200s. Double Eagle II basket and Paris balloons of 1870	1·50	1·50
1069	200s. Henri Giffard's balloon Le Grand Ballon Captif	1·50	1·50
1061/9	Set of 9	12·00	12·00

Nos. 1061/9 were printed together, se-tenant, as a sheetlet of 9 forming a composite design.

130a Mickey Mouse and Goofy on African Safari

(Des Walt Disney Co. Litho B.D.T.)

1992 (20 Feb). Mickey's World Tour. T **130a** and similar multicoloured designs showing Walt Disney cartoon characters in different countries. P 13.

1070	20s. Type **130a**	50	20
1071	50s. Mickey charming Pluto's tail, India	70	20
1072	80s. Minnie Mouse, Donald and Daisy Duck as Caribbean calypso band	1·00	25
1073	200s. Goofy pulling Donald and Daisy in rickshaw, China	1·60	60
1074	500s. Mickey and Minnie on camel, Egypt	2·25	1·75
1075	800s. Donald and Pete sumo wrestling, Japan	2·50	2·75
1076	1000s. Goofy bullfighting, Spain	2·50	2·75
1077	1500s. Mickey playing football, Italy	3·00	4·00
1070/7	Set of 8	12·50	11·50

MS1078 Two sheets each 83×104 mm. (a) 2000s. Mickey as Cossack dancer, Russia (*vert*). (b) 2000s. Daisy as Wagnerian diva, Germany (*vert*) *Set of 2 sheets* ... 12·00 13·00

130b Queen Elizabeth II and Lake Victoria   **130c** Kentrosaurus

(Des D. Miller. Litho Questa)

1992 (26 Feb). 40th Anniv of Queen Elizabeth II's Accession. T **130b** and similar horiz designs each showing inset portrait and African scene. Multicoloured. P 14.

1079	100s. Type **130b**	80	25
1080	200s. Lake and mountains	1·25	60
1081	500s. Lakeside fields	2·75	2·25
1082	1000s. River Nile	4·00	4·25
1079/82	Set of 4	8·00	6·50

MS1083 Two sheets, each 74×97 mm. (a) 1800s. Waterfalls. (b) 1800s. Owen Falls Dam *Set of 2 sheets* ... 13·00 11·00

(Des D. Burkhart, Litho Walsall)

1992 (8 Apr). Prehistoric Animals. T **130c** and similar horiz designs. Multicoloured. P 14.

1084	50s. Type **130c**	50	30
1085	200s. Iguanodon	1·00	80
1086	250s. Hypsilophodon	1·10	90
1087	300s. Brachiosaurus	1·25	1·10
1088	400s. Peloneustes	1·40	1·40
1089	500s. Pteranodon	1·50	1·50
1090	800s. Tetralophodon	2·00	2·50
1091	1000s. Megalosaurus	2·00	2·50
1084/91	Set of 8	9·75	10·00

MS1092 Two sheets, each 100×70 mm. (a) 2000s. As 250s. (b) 2000s. As 1000s. *Set of 2 sheets* ... 14·00 13·00

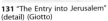

131 "The Entry into Jerusalem" (detail) (Giotto)   **132** Adungu

(Litho Questa)

1992 (7 May). Easter. Religious Paintings. T **131** and similar vert designs. Multicoloured. P 13½×14.

1093	50s. Type **131**	75	20
1094	100s. "Pilate and the Watch" (Psalter of Robert de Lisle)	95	20
1095	200s. "The Kiss of Judas" (detail) (Giotto)	1·60	75
1096	250s. "Christ washing the Feet of the Disciples" (Vita Christi manuscript)	1·60	75
1097	300s. "Christ seized in the Garden" (Melissende Psalter)	1·75	85
1098	500s. "Doubting Thomas" (Vita Christi manuscript)	2·50	1·75
1099	1000s. "The Marys at the Tomb" (detail) (anon)	4·25	4·75
1100	2000s. "The Ascension" (Florentine manuscript)	6·50	8·50
1093/100	Set of 8	18·00	16·00

MS1101 Two sheets, each 72×102 mm. (a) 2500s. "The Piercing of Christ's Side" (detail) (Limoges enamel). (b) 2500s. "Agony at Gethsemane" (detail) (Limoges enamel) *Set of 2 sheets* ... 18·00 19·00

(Des R. Sauber. Litho Questa)

1992 (20 July). Traditional Musical Instruments. T **132** and similar vert designs. Multicoloured. P 14.

1102	50s. Type **132**	60	20
1103	100s. Endingidi	80	35
1104	200s. Akogo	1·25	60
1105	250s. Nanga	1·40	70
1106	300s. Engoma	1·50	1·25
1107	400s. Amakondere	1·75	1·75
1108	500s. Akakyenkye	1·90	2·00
1109	1000s. Ennanga	3·50	5·50
1102/9	Set of 8	11·50	11·00

133 Map of Known World, 1486   **133a** Girl with Washing

(Des A. Granberg. Litho Questa)

1992 (27 July). 500th Anniv of Discovery of America by Columbus and World Colombian Stamp Expo '92 Exhibition, Chicago. T **133** and similar multicoloured designs. P 14.

1110	50s. Type **133**	20	20
1111	100s. Map of Africa, 1508	30	30
1112	150s. Map of West Indies, 1500	50	50
1113	200s. *Nina* and astrolabe	60	60
1114	600s. *Pinta* and quadrant	1·50	1·50
1115	800s. Sand glass	1·60	1·60
1116	900s. 15th-century compass	1·75	1·75
1117	2000s. Map of World, 1492	3·50	3·50
1110/17	Set of 8	9·00	9·00

MS1118 Two sheets, each 95×75 mm. (a) 2500s. Sections of globe, 1492. (b) 2500s. Europe and Africa from map by Henricus Martellus, 1490 (*vert*) *Set of 2 sheets* ... 9·25 10·00

(Litho Questa)

1992 (28 Aug). Hummel Figurines. T **133a** and similar vert designs. Multicoloured. P 14.

1119	50s. Type **133a**	35	20
1120	200s. Girl scrubbing floor	80	50
1121	250s. Girl sweeping floor	90	60
1122	300s. Girl with baby	1·00	70
1123	600s. Boy mountaineer	2·25	2·00
1124	900s. Girl knitting	2·75	2·75
1125	1000s. Boy on stool	2·75	3·00
1126	1500s. Boy with telescope	3·25	3·50
1119/26	Set of 8	12·50	12·00

MS1127 Two sheets, each 97×122 mm. (a) 500s. As No. 1119; 500s. As No. 1120; 500s. As No. 1121; 500s. As No. 1122. (b) 500s. As No. 1123; 500s. As No. 1125; 500s. As No. 1126 *Set of 2 sheets* ... 12·00 13·00

134 Spotted Hyena

(Litho Questa)

1992 (25 Sept). Wildlife. T **134** and similar horiz designs. Multicoloured. P 14.

1128	50s. Type **134**	50	20
1129	100s. Impala	60	25
1130	200s. Giant Forest Hog	85	45
1131	250s. Pangolin	95	65
1132	300s. Golden Monkey	1·10	75
1133	800s. Serval	3·00	3·00
1134	1000s. Small-spotted Genet ("Bush Genet")	3·00	3·25
1135	3000s. Waterbuck	7·50	9·00
1128/35	Set of 8	16·00	16·00
MS1136	Two sheets, each 100×70 mm. (a) 2500s. Gorilla. (b) 2500s. Hippopotamus Set of 2 sheets	10·00	12·00

(Litho Questa)

1992 (2 Oct). Olympic Games, Barcelona. Multicoloured designs as T **207a** of Tanzania. P 14.

1137	50s. Men's javelin	40	20
1138	100s. Men's highjump (horiz)	55	30
1139	200s. Fencing (Pentathlon)	80	45
1140	250s. Men's volleyball	85	60
1141	300s. Women's platform diving	90	60
1142	500s. Men's team cycling	5·00	2·50
1143	1000s. Women's tennis	5·50	6·00
1144	2000s. Boxing (horiz)	6·00	9·50
1137/44	Set of 8	18·00	18·00
MS1145	Two sheets, each 100×70 mm. (a) 2500s. Men's basketball. (b) 2500s. Baseball Set of 2 sheets	18·00	18·00

135 Red-headed Falcon

(Litho Questa)

1992 (9 Oct). Birds. T **135** and similar vert designs. Multicoloured. P 15×14.

1146	20s. Type **135**	55	40
1147	30s. Yellow-billed Hornbill	65	40
1148	50s. Purple Heron	70	30
1149	100s. Regal Sunbird	90	30
1150	150s. White-browed Robin Chat	1·25	40
1151	200s. Shining-blue Kingfisher	1·25	45
1152	250s. Great Blue Turaco	1·25	50
1153	300s. African Emerald Cuckoo	1·40	70
1154	500s. Abyssinian Roller	1·75	1·25
1155	800s. South African Crowned Crane	2·50	2·00
1156	1000s. Doherty's Bush Shrike	3·00	3·00
1157	2000s. Splendid Glossy Starling	3·75	4·25
1158	3000s. Little Bee Eater	5·00	7·50
1159	4000s. Red-faced Lovebird ("Red-headed Lovebird")	6·50	9·00
1146/59	Set of 14	27·00	27·00

135a United Nations Headquarters

136 Goofy in Hawaiian Holiday, 1937

(Des Kerri Schiff. Litho Questa)

1992 (28 Oct). Postage Stamp Mega Event, New York. Sheet 100×70 mm. Multicoloured. P 14.

MS1160	**135a** 2500s. multicoloured	3·75	4·50

CHRISTMAS 1992

THE ANNUNCIATION - ZURBARAN

UGANDA 50/-

137 "The Annunciation" (Zurbaran)

(Des Walt Disney Co. Litho Questa)

1992 (2 Nov). 60th Anniv of Goofy. T **136** and similar multicoloured designs. P 13½.

1162	50s. Type **136**	30	20
1163	100s. Riding pennyfarthing cycle, 1941	40	20
1164	200s. Goofy and Mickey Mouse as firemen, 1935	60	35
1165	250s. Skiing, 1941 (horiz)	70	60
1166	300s. One man band, 1937 (horiz)	70	60
1167	1000s. Asleep against boat, 1938 (horiz)	2·25	2·50
1168	1500s. Ancient Olympic champion, 1942	3·25	3·75
1169	2000s. Pole vaulting, 1942	3·50	3·75
1162/9	Set of 8	10·50	10·50
MS1170	Two sheets. (a) 105×115 mm. 3000s. Goofy and Wilbur the grasshopper, 1939 (horiz). (b) 92×116 mm. 3000s. Wyatt Goofy and Goofy today Set of 2 sheets	12·00	12·00

(Litho Questa)

1992 (16 Nov). Christmas. Religious Paintings by Francisco Zurbaran. T **137** and similar vert designs. Multicoloured. P 13½×14.

1171	50s. Type **137**	65	15
1172	200s. "The Annunciation" (different)	1·25	35
1173	250s. "The Virgin of the Immaculate Conception"	1·40	45
1174	300s. "The Virgin of the Immaculate Conception" (detail)	1·50	50
1175	800s. "Holy Family with Saints Anne, Joachim and John the Baptist"	3·50	3·50
1176	900s. "Holy Family with Saints Anne, Joachim and John the Baptist" (detail)	3·75	4·00
1177	1000s. "Adoration of the Magi"	3·75	4·00
1178	2000s. "Adoration of the Magi" (detail)	5·50	9·00
1171/8	Set of 8	19·00	20·00
MS1179	Two sheets, each 76×102 mm. (a) 2500s. "The Virgin of the Immaculate Conception (different). (b) 2500s. "The Virgin of the Immaculate Conception" (different) Set of 2 sheets	19·00	20·00

Granary - 'Improving household food security'

50/=

UGANDA

138 Man cleaning Granary

(Des W. Wright and L. Fried (Nos. 1184, 1189, **MS**1191a). Litho Questa)

1992 (7 Dec). Anniversaries and Events. T **138** and similar horiz designs. Multicoloured. P 14.

1180	50s. Type **138**	20	15
1181	200s. Mother breast feeding	65	40
1182	250s. Mother feeding baby	70	50
1183	300s. Boy collecting water from pump	75	75
1184	300s. "Voyager 2" passing Jupiter	2·75	1·25
1185	800s. Mother and baby	2·00	2·75
1186	800s. Impala	2·00	2·75
1187	1000s. Mountain Zebra	4·00	4·50
1188	1000s. Count Ferdinand von Zeppelin and airship	4·00	4·50
1189	2000s. "Voyager 2" passing Neptune	8·50	9·00
1190	3000s. Count Ferdinand von Zeppelin and Clement-Bayard airship Fleurus	9·00	11·00
1180/90	Set of 11	30·00	35·00

MS1191 Four sheets, each 115×85 mm. (a) 2500s. "Voyager 2" and Jupiter. (b) 2500s. Warthog. (c) 2500s. Count Ferdinand von Zeppelin with Robert Brothers and Colin Hullin balloon. (d) 2500s. Doctor inoculating boy *Set of 4 sheets* .... 29·00 32·00

Anniversaries and Events—Nos. 1180/3, 1185, United Nations World Health Organization Projects; Nos. 1184, 1189, **MS**1191a, International Space Year; Nos. 1186/7, **MS**1191b Earth Summit '92, Rio; Nos. 1188, 1190, **MS**1191c, 75th death anniv of Count Ferdinand von Zeppelin (airship pioneer); **MS**1191d, 75th anniv of International Association of Lions Clubs.

139 Hands releasing Dove with Lubaga and Kampala Catholic Cathedrals

(Des Susan Rini. Litho Questa)

1993 (1 Feb). Visit of Pope John Paul II. T **139** and similar multicoloured designs. P 14.
1192	50s. Type **139**	75	10
1193	200s. Pope and Kampala Cathedral	1·25	30
1194	250s. Pope and Catholic worshipper	1·40	45
1195	300s. Ugandan bishops and Pope	1·60	60
1196	800s. Pope John Paul II waving	3·00	3·00
1197	900s. Pope and Kampala Cathedral (different)	3·00	3·00
1198	1000s. Pope, national flag and Kampala Cathedral	3·00	3·00
1199	2000s. Pope and national flag	5·50	6·00
1192/9	*Set of 8*	18·00	15·00

MS1200 Two sheets, each 100×70 mm. (a) 3000s. Pope on aircraft steps (*vert*). (b) 3000s. Pope delivering blessing (*vert*) *Set of 2 sheets* ...... 18·00 16·00
A 5000s. value embossed on gold foil exists from a limited printing.

(Litho Walsall)

1993 (5 Apr). Bicentenary of the Louvre, Paris. Paintings by Rembrandt. Multicoloured designs as T **210a** of Tanzania. P 12.
1201	500s. "Self-portrait at Easel"	1·10	1·10
	a. Sheetlet. Nos. 1201/8	8·00	8·00
1202	500s. "Birds of Paradise"	1·10	1·10
1203	500s. "The Carcass of Beef"	1·10	1·10
1204	500s. "The Supper at Emmaus"	1·10	1·10
1205	500s. "Hendrickje Stoffels"	1·10	1·10
1206	500s. "The Artist's Son, Titus"	1·10	1·10
1207	500s. "The Holy Family" (left detail)	1·10	1·10
1208	500s. "The Holy Family" (right detail)	1·10	1·10
1201/8	*Set of 8*	8·00	5·00

MS1209 100×70 mm. 2500s. "The Philosopher in Meditation" (89×57 mm). P 14½ .... 4·50 5·00
Nos. 1201/8 were printed together, *se-tenant*, in sheetlets of 8 stamps and one centre label.

140 Afghan Hound

(Des J. Barbaris. Litho Questa)

1993 (28 May). Dogs of the World. T **140** and similar multicoloured designs. P 14.
1210	50s. Type **140**	1·00	40
1211	100s. Newfoundland	1·40	40
1212	200s. Siberian Huskies	2·00	60
1213	250s. Briard	2·00	75
1214	300s. Saluki	2·00	1·00
1215	800s. Labrador guide-dog (*vert*)	3·50	3·50
1216	1000s. Greyhound	3·75	3·75
1217	1500s. Pointer	4·50	5·00
1210/17	*Set of 8*	18·00	14·00

MS1218 Two sheets, each 103×80 mm. (a) 2500s. Cape Hunting Dog. (b) 2500s. Norwegian Elkhound pup *Set of 2 sheets* .... 21·00 19·00

(Des Kerri Schiff. Litho Questa)

1993 (2 June). 40th Anniv of Coronation. Vert designs as T **214a** of Tanzania. Multicoloured. P 13½.
1219	50s. Queen Elizabeth II at Coronation (photograph by Cecil Beaton)	30	35

	a. Sheetlet. Nos. 1219/22×2	7·00	8·00
1220	200s. Orb and Sceptre	50	60
1221	500s. Queen Elizabeth during Coronation	90	1·10
1222	1500s. Queen Elizabeth II and Princess Margaret	2·25	2·50
1219/22	*Set of 4*	3·50	4·00

MS1223 69×100 mm. 2500s. "The Crown" (detail) (Grace Wheatley) (28½×42½ mm). P 14 ...... 5·00 5·50
Nos. 1219/22 were printed in sheetlets of 8, containing two *se-tenant* blocks of 4.

140a Bupati karma, Prince of Wangga

141 Gutierrez (Uruguay) and Voeller (Germany)

(Des Kerri Schiff. Litho Questa)

1993 (22 Sept). Asian International Stamp Exhibitions. T **140a** and similar vert designs. Multicoloured. P 13½×14.

(a) Indopex '93, Surabaya, Indonesia. Javanese Wayang Puppets
1224	600s. Type **140a**	1·25	1·50
	a. Sheetlet. Nos. 1224/9	6·50	8·00
1225	600s. Rahwana	1·25	1·50
1226	600s. Sondjeng Sandjata	1·25	1·50
1227	600s. Raden Damar Wulan	1·25	1·50
1228	600s. Unidentified puppet	1·25	1·50
1229	600s. Hanaman	1·25	1·50
1224/9	*Set of 6*	6·50	8·00

MS1230 135×105 mm. 2500s. Candi Mendut Temple, Java .... 6·00 7·00

(b) Taipei '93, Taiwan. Funerary Pottery Figures
1231	600s. Tomb guardian god in green armour	1·25	1·50
	a. Sheetlet. Nos. 1231/6	6·50	8·00
1232	600s. Civil official and shrine	1·25	1·50
1233	600s. Tomb guardian god in green and gold armour	1·25	1·50
1234	600s. Civil official in red	1·25	1·50
1235	600s. Chimera (tomb guardian)	1·25	1·50
1236	600s. Civil official in red and green robe	1·25	1·50
1231/6	*Set of 6*	6·50	8·00

MS1237 135×105 mm. 2500s. Statue of the Sacred Mother, Taiyuan .... 6·00 7·00

(c) Bangkok '93, Thailand. Sculptured Figures
1238	600s. Standing Buddha in gilded red sandstone, 13th-15th century	1·25	1·50
	a. Sheetlet. Nos. 1238/43	6·50	8·00
1239	600s. Crowned Buddha in bronze, 13th century	1·25	1·50
1240	600s. Thepanom in stone, 15th century	1·25	1·50
1241	600s. Crowned Buddha in bronze, 12th century	1·25	1·50
1242	600s. Avalokitesvara in bronze, 9th century	1·25	1·50
1243	600s. Lop Buri standing Buddha in bronze, 13th-century	1·25	1·50
1238/43	*Set of 6*	6·50	8·00

MS1244 135×105 mm. 2500s. Buddha, Wat Mahathat 6·00 7·00
Nos. 1224/9, 1231/6 and 1238/43 were each printed together, *se-tenant*, in sheetlets of 6.

(Des Rosemary DeFiglio. Litho Questa)

1993 (1 Oct). World Cup Football Championship, U.S.A. (1994) (1st issue). T **141** and similar multicoloured designs. P 14.
1245	50s. Type **141**	60	20
1246	200s. Tomas Brolin (Sweden)	1·25	50
1247	250s. Gary Lineker (England)	1·50	50
1248	300s. Munoz and Butragueno (Spain)	1·50	65
1249	800s. Carlos Valderrama (Colombia)	2·75	3·00
1250	900s. Diego Maradona (Argentina)	2·75	3·00
1251	1000s. Pedro Troglio (Argentina)	2·75	3·00
1252	2000s. Enzo Scifo (Belgium)	4·00	5·50
1245/52	*Set of 8*	15·00	15·00

MS1253 Two sheets, each 103×72 mm. (a) 2500s. Brazilians celebrating. (b) 2500s. De Napoli (Italy) and Skuhravy (Czechoslovkia) (*horiz*) *Set of 2 sheets* .... 13·00 14·00
See also Nos. 1322/8.

142 York Minster,
England

142a "Virgin with Carthusian
Monks" (detail) (Dürer)

(Des G. Bibby. Litho Questa)

1993 (3 Nov). Cathedrals of the World. T **142** and similar vert designs.
Multicoloured. P 14.

1254	50s. Type **142**	40	15
1255	100s. Notre Dame, Paris	55	20
1256	200s. Little Metropolis, Athens	85	40
1257	250s. St. Patrick's, New York	90	45
1258	300s. Ulm, Germany	95	50
1259	800s. St. Basil's, Moscow	2·50	2·75
1260	1000s. Roskilde, Denmark	2·50	2·75
1261	2000s. Seville, Spain	4·00	5·50
1254/61	Set of 8	11·50	11·50

MS1262 Two sheets, each 70×100 mm. (a) 2500s.
Namirembe, Uganda. (b) 2500s. St. Peter's, Vatican
City Set of 2 sheets ... 13·00 14·00

(Litho Questa)

1993 (19 Nov). Christmas. Religious Paintings. T **142a** and similar vert
designs. Black, pale lemon and red (Nos. 1263, 1265, 1267, 1270
and **MS**1271a) or multicoloured (others).

1263	50s. Type **142a**	50	10
1264	100s. "Sacred Family" (detail) (Raphael)	75	10
1265	200s. "Virgin with Carthusian Monks" (different detail) (Dürer)	1·10	30
1266	250s. "The Virgin of the Rose" (Raphael)	1·25	35
1267	300s. "Virgin with Carthusian Monks" (different detail) (Dürer)	1·25	40
1268	800s. "Sacred Family" (different detail) (Raphael)	2·75	3·00
1269	1000s. "Virgin with Beardless Joseph" (Raphael)	2·75	3·00
1270	2000s. "Virgin with Carthusian Monks" (different detail) (Dürer)	4·25	6·00
1263/70	Set of 8	13·00	11·50

MS1271 Two sheets, each 102×127 mm. (a) 2500s.
"Virgin with Carthusian Monks" (different detail)
(Dürer). (b) 2500s. "Sacred Family" (different detail)
(Raphael) Set of 2 sheets ... 15·00 13·00
Nos. **MS**1271 is inscribed "Canthusian Monks" in error.

143 Mickey Mouse asleep on Stegosaurus

(Des Walt Disney Co. Litho Questa)

1993 (22 Dec). Prehistoric Animals. T **143** and similar horiz designs
showing Walt Disney cartoon characters. Multicoloured.
P 14×13½.

1272	50s. Type **143**	60	20
1273	100s. Minnie Mouse on pteranodon	70	20
1274	200s. Mickey being licked by mamenchisaurus	1·00	40
1275	250s. Mickey doing cave painting	1·10	45
1276	300s. Mickey wind-surfing on dinosaur	1·25	60
1277	500s. Mickey and Donald Duck sliding on diplodocus	1·90	1·40
1278	800s. Mamenchisaurus carrying Mickey	2·75	3·25
1279	1000s. Pluto on triceratops	2·75	3·25
1272/9	Set of 8	11·00	8·75

MS1280 Two sheets, each 128×102 mm. (a) 2500s.
Mickey and Minnie. (b) 2500s. Mickey feeding
tyrannosaurus rex Set of 2 sheets ... 12·00 13·00
No. 1273 is inscribed "PTERANDOM" and No. 1278 "MAMENSHISAURUS",
both in error.

144 "Woman in Yellow"
(Picasso)

145 Passion Fruit

(Litho Questa)

1993 (29 Dec). Anniversaries and Events. T **144** and similar
multicoloured designs. P 14.

1281	100s. Type **144**	40	15
1282	200s. Head of cow and syringe	50	30
1283	250s. "Gertrude Stein" (Picasso)	60	35
1284	500s. Early telescope	3·50	1·50
1285	800s. "Creation" (S. Witkiewicz after J. Glogowski)	2·00	2·50
1286	1000s. Modern telescope	4·50	3·50
1287	1000s. "For the flight to Work" (A. Strumillo)	2·25	3·50
1281/7	Set of 7	12·50	10·50

MS1288 Three sheets. (a) 75×105 mm. 2500s.
"Woman by a Window" (detail) (Picasso).
(b) 105×75 mm. 2500s. Copernicus. (c)
105×75 mm. 2500s. "Temptation of Saint Antony I"
(detail) (S. Witkiewicz) (horiz) Set of 3 sheets ... 18·00 19·00
Anniversaries and Events:—Nos. 1281, 1283, **MS**1288a, 20th death
anniv of Picasso (artist); No. 1282, Pan African Rinderpest Campaign;
Nos. 1284, 1286, **MS**1288b, 450th death anniv of Copernicus
(astronomer); Nos. 1285, 1287, **MS**1288c, Polska '93 International
Stamp Exhibition, Poznan.

(Litho Questa)

1994 (13 Jan). Fruits and Crops. T **145** and similar multicoloured
designs. P 14.

1289	50s. Type **145**	45	10
1290	100s. Sunflower	55	10
1291	150s. Bananas	75	25
1292	200s. Runner beans	85	30
1293	250s. Pineapple	90	55
1294	300s. Jackfruit	1·10	70
1295	500s. Sorghum	2·00	2·00
1296	800s. Maize	3·00	4·00
1289/96	Set of 8	8·75	7·00

MS1297 Two sheets, each 101×71 mm. (a) 2000s.
Sesame. (b) 2000s. Coffee (horiz) Set of 2 sheets ... 12·00 12·00

146 Ford Model "A", 1903

146a Glass Box with
Pavilion Design

(Litho Questa)

1994 (18 Jan). Centenaries of Henry Ford's First Petrol Engine
(Nos. 1298/1301, **MS**1306a) and Karl Benz's First Fourwheeled Car
(others). T **146** and similar multicoloured designs. P 14.

1298	700s. Type **146**	1·25	1·50
	a. Horiz strip of 4. Nos. 1298/1301	4·50	5·50
1299	700s. Ford Model "T" snowmobile, 1932	1·25	1·50
1300	700s. Ford "Mustang"	1·25	1·50
1301	700s. Lotus-Ford racing car; 1965	1·25	1·50
1302	800s. Mercedes-Benz "S600" coupe, 1994	1·25	1·50
	a. Horiz strip of 4. Nos. 1302/5	4·50	5·50
1303	800s. Mercedes-Benz "W196" racing car, 1955	1·25	1·50
1304	800s. Mercedes-Benz "W125" road speed record car, 1938	1·25	1·50
1305	800s. Benz "Viktoria", 1893	1·25	1·50
1298/1305	Set of 8	9·00	11·00

MS1306 Two sheets, each 85×85 mm. (a) 2500s.
Henry Ford (vert). (b) 2500s. Karl Benz (vert) Set of
2 sheets ... 9·00 10·00
Nos. 1298/1301 and 1302/5 were printed together, se-tenant, in
horizontal strips of 4 throughout the sheet.

(Des W. Hanson. Litho Questa)

1994 (18 Feb). Hong Kong '94 International Stamp Exhibition (1st issue). Horiz designs as T **231a** of Tanzania. Multicoloured. P 14.

1307	500s. Hong Kong 1988 60c. Catholic Cathedral stamp and Religious shrines, Repulse Bay	80	1·00
	a. Horiz pair. Nos. 1307/8	1·60	2·00
1308	500s. Uganda 1993 2500s. Namirembe Cathedral stamp and Religious shrines, Repulse Bay (*different*)	80	1·00

Nos. 1307/8 were printed together, *se-tenant*, in horizontal pairs throughout the sheet with the centre part of each pair forming a composite design.

(Des Kerri Schiff. Litho Questa)

1994 (18 Feb). Hong Kong '94 International Stamp Exhibition (2nd issue). Ching Dynasty Snuff Boxes. T **146a** and similar vert designs. Multicoloured. P 14.

1309	200s. Type **146a**	60	70
	a. Sheetlet. Nos. 1309/14	3·25	3·75
1310	200s. Porcelain box with quail design	60	70
1311	200s. Porcelain box with floral design	60	70
1312	200s. Porcelain box with openwork design	60	70
1313	200s. Agate box with carved Lion-dogs	60	70
1314	200s. Agate box with man on donkey design	60	70
1309/14	*Set of 6*	3·25	3·75

Nos. 1309/14 were printed together, *se-tenant*, in sheetlets of 6. Captions for Nos. 1310/11 are transposed.

147 Meteorological Weather Station

(Des Associated Creative Designs. Litho Questa)

1994 (15 Mar). World Meteorological Day. T **147** and similar multicoloured designs. P 14.

1315	50s. Type **147**	70	15
1316	200s. Weather observatory at training school, Entebbe (*vert*)	1·50	55
1317	250s. Satellite link	1·50	70
1318	300s. Recording temperatures	1·75	1·00
1319	400s. Automatic weather station (*vert*)	2·00	2·25
1320	800s. Crops damaged by hailstones	3·00	5·00
1315/20	*Set of 6*	9·50	8·75
MS1321	105×75 mm. 2500s. Barograph	8·00	9·00

147a Georges Grun (Belgium)

(Des J. Iskowitz. Litho Questa)

1994 (27 June). World Cup Football Championship, U.S.A. (2nd issue). T **147a** and similar horiz designs. Multicoloured. P 14.

1322	500s. Type **147a**	1·50	1·75
	a. Sheetlet. Nos. 1322/7	8·00	9·50
1323	500s. Oscar Ruggeri (Argentina)	1·50	1·75
1324	500s. Frank Rijkaard (Netherlands)	1·50	1·75
1325	500s. Magid "Tyson" Musisi (Uganda)	1·50	1·75
1326	500s. Ronald Koeman (Netherlands)	1·50	1·75
1327	500s. Igor Shalimov (Russia)	1·50	1·75
1322/7	*Set of 6*	8·00	9·50
MS1328	Two sheets, each 70×100 mm. (a) 2500s. Ruud Gullit (Netherlands). (b) 2500s. Player and R.F.K. Stadium, Washington D.C. *Set of 2 sheets*	9·00	11·00

Nos. 1322/7 were printed together, *se-tenant*, in sheetlets of 6. No. 1326 is inscribed "DONALD KOEMAN" in error.

148 Milking Cow

(Des Associated Creative Designs. Litho Questa)

1994 (29 June). 50th Anniv of Heifer Project International. P 14.

1329	**148** 100s. multicoloured	1·75	1·00

149 *Lobobunaea goodii* (wings spread)

150 Wooden Stool

(Des D. Burkhart. Litho Questa)

1994 (13 July). Moths. T **149** and similar vert designs. Multicoloured. P 14.

1330	100s. Type **149**	35	20
1331	200s. *Bunaeopsis hersilia*	65	40
1332	300s. *Rufoglanis rosea*	80	60
1333	350s. *Acherontia atropos*	85	75
1334	400s. *Rohaniella pygmaea*	95	95
1335	450s. *Euchloron megaera*	1·00	1·25
1336	500s. *Epiphora rectifascia*	1·10	1·25
1337	1000s. *Polyphychus coryndoni*	1·90	2·50
1330/7	*Set of 8*	7·00	7·00
MS1338	Two sheets, each 117×88 mm. (a) 2500s. As Type **149**. (b) 2500s. *Lobobunaea goodii* (wings folded) *Set of 2 sheets*	9·50	10·00

(Litho Questa)

1994 (18 July). Crafts. T **150** and similar vert designs. Multicoloured. P 14.

1339	100s. Type **150**	25	10
1340	200s. Wood and banana fibre chair	45	30
1341	250s. Raffia and palm leaves basket	50	35
1342	300s. Wool tapestry showing tree planting	55	45
1343	450s. Wool tapestry showing hair grooming	85	90
1344	500s. Wood sculpture of a drummer	95	1·10
1345	800s. Gourds	1·75	2·50
1346	1000s. Bark cloth handbag	2·00	3·25
1339/46	*Set of 8*	6·50	8·00
MS1347	Two sheets, each 100×70 mm. (a) 2500s. Raffia baskets. (b) 2500s. Papyrus hats *Set of 2 sheets*	11·00	13·00

151 Turkish Angora Cat and Blue Mosque

152 Child carrying Building Block

(Des J. Genzo. Litho Questa)

1994 (22 July). Cats. T **151** and similar multicoloured designs. P 14.

1348	50s. Type **151**	60	25
1349	100s. Japanese Bobtail and Mt Fuji	80	25
1350	200s. Norwegian Forest Cat and windmill, Holland	1·00	40
1351	300s. Egyptian Mau and Pyramids (*vert*)	1·40	75
1352	450s. Rex and Stonehenge, England (*vert*)	2·00	1·60
1353	500s. Chartreux and Eiffel Tower, France	2·25	1·75
1354	1000s. Burmese and Shwe Dagon Pagoda (*vert*)	3·25	3·75
1355	1500s. Maine Coon and Pemaquid Point Lighthouse (*vert*)	5·50	6·00
1348/55	*Set of 8*	15·00	13·50
MS1356	Two sheets, each 100×76 mm. (a) 2500s. Russian Blue. (b) 2500s. Manx *Set of 2 sheets*	12·00	12·00

(Des Associated Creative Designs. Litho Questa)

1994 (29 July). 75th Anniv of International Labour Organization. P 14.

1357	**152** 350s. multicoloured	1·75	1·75

152a Alan Shepard Jnr

(Des W Hanson. Litho B.D.T.)

1994 (11 Aug). 25th Anniv of First Moon Landing Astronauts. T **152a** and similar horiz designs. Multicoloured. P 14.

1358	50s. Type **152a**	1·10	1·10
	a. Sheetlet. Nos. 1358/64	9·50	9·50
1359	100s. M. Scott Carpenter	1·25	1·25
1360	200s. Virgil Grissom	1·50	1·50
1361	300s. L. Cordon Cooper Jnr	1·60	1·60
1362	400s. Walter Schirra Jnr	1·75	1·75
1363	500s. Donald Slayton	1·75	1·75
1364	600s. John Glenn Jnr	1·75	1·75
1358/64	Set of 7	9·50	9·50
MS1365	88×91 mm. 3000s. "Apollo 11" anniversary emblem	7·00	7·50

Nos. 1358/64 were printed together, se-tenant, in sheetlets of 7 with 2 stamp-size labels depicting rocket launches.

(Des Kerri Schiff. Litho Questa)

1994 (11 Aug). Centenary of International Olympic Committee. Gold Medal Winners. Multicoloured designs as T **252a** of Tanzania but vert. P 14.

1366	350s. John Akii-Bua (Uganda) (400 metres hurdles), 1972 (horiz)	60	45
1367	900s. Heike Herkel (Germany) (high jump), 1992 (horiz)	1·25	1·75
MS1368	107×76 mm. 2500s. Aleski Urmanov (Russia) (figure skating), 1994	5·50	5·50

(Des J. Batchelor. Litho Questa)

1994 (11 Aug). 50th Anniv of D-Day. Horiz designs as T **252b** of Tanzania. Multicoloured. P 14.

1369	300s. Mulberry Harbour pier	50	40
1370	1000s. Mulberry Harbour floating bridge	1·50	2·00
MS1371	105×76 mm. 2500s. Aerial view of Mulberry Harbour	6·00	6·50

152b Sari Pagoda, Paekyangsa

153 Ugandan Family

(Litho Questa)

1994 (11 Aug). Philakorea '94 International Stamp Exhibition, Seoul. T **152b** and similar horiz designs. Multicoloured. P 14.

1372	100s. Type **152b**	10	10
1373	350s. Ch'omsongdae	50	60
1374	1000s. Pulguksa Temple	1·40	2·75
1372/4	Set of 3	1·75	3·00
MS1375	76×106 mm. 2500s. Bronze mural, Pagoda Park, Seoul	3·00	3·75

(Litho Questa)

1994 (11 Aug). International Year of the Family. P 14.

1376	**153** 100s. multicoloured	40	20

154 Baby Simba

154a Chimpanzee

(Des Alvin White Studios. Litho Questa)

1994 (30 Sept). The Lion King. T **154** and similar multicoloured designs showing characters from Walt Disney's cartoon film. P 14.

1377	100s. Type **154**	40	40

	a. Sheetlet. Nos. 1377/85	3·25	3·25
1378	100s. Mufasa, Simba and Sarabi	40	40
1379	100s. Young Simba and Nala	40	40
1380	100s. Timon	40	40
1381	100s. Rafiki	40	40
1382	100s. Pumbaa	40	40
1383	100s. The Hyenas	40	40
1384	100s. Scar	40	40
1385	100s. Zazu	40	40
1386	200s. Rafiki and Mufasa	40	40
	a. Sheetlet. Nos. 1386/94	3·25	3·25
1387	200s. Rafiki holding Simba with Mufasa and Sarabi	40	40
1388	200s. Rafiki holding Simba aloft	40	40
1389	200s. Scar and Zazu	40	40
1390	200s. Rafiki having vision	40	40
1391	200s. Simba and Scar	40	40
1392	200s. Simba and Nala	40	40
1393	200s. Simba with mane of leaves	40	40
1394	200s. Simba, Nala and Zazu	40	40
1395	250s. Scar and Simba	40	40
	a. Sheetlet. Nos. 1395/1403	3·25	3·25
1396	250s. Mufasa rescues Simba	40	40
1397	250s. Scar killing Mufasa	40	40
1398	250s. Simba falling off cliff	40	40
1399	250s. Timon, Pumbaa and Simba at pool	40	40
1400	250s. Simba, Timon and Pumbaa	40	40
1401	250s. Rafiki with staff	40	40
1402	250s. Simba and Nala	40	40
1403	250s. Simba looking into pool	40	40
1377/1403	Set of 27	9·75	9·75
MS1404	Three sheets. (a) 127×94 mm. 2500s. Jungle animals. P 14×13½. (b) 127×102 mm. 2500s. Simba and Timon on branch. P 14×13½. (c) 127×94 mm. 2500s. Simba with parents and Rafiki (vert). P 13½×14. Set of 3 sheets	13·00	14·00

Nos. 1377/85, 1386/94 and 1395/1403 were each printed together, se-tenant, in sheetlets of 9. 5000s. in a similar design, embossed on gold foil, also exists from a limited printing.

(Des Kerri Schiff. Litho B.D.T.)

1994 (9 Nov). Centenary of Sierra Club (environmental protection society) (1992). Endangered Species. T **154a** and similar multicoloured designs. P 14.

(a) Vert designs

1405	100s. Type **154a**	60	55
	a. Sheetlet. Nos. 1405/12	6·50	7·00
1406	200s. Head of Chimpanzee	80	80
1407	250s. Head of African Wild Dog	80	80
1408	300s. Head of Cheetah	80	90
1409	500s. Geleda Baboon	90	1·00
1410	600s. Geleda Baboon from back	1·00	1·10
1411	800s. Head of Grevy's Zebra	1·10	1·25
1412	1000s. Geleda Baboon sitting on rock	1·25	1·40

(b) Horiz designs

1413	200s. Pair of Cheetahs	80	90
	a. Sheetlet. Nos. 1413/19 plus label	6·50	7·00
1414	250s. Cheetah cubs	80	90
1415	300s. African Wild Dog at rest	90	1·00
1416	500s. Head of African Wild Dog	1·00	1·10
1417	600s. Grevy's Zebra	1·10	1·25
1418	800s. Chimpanzee lying down	1·25	1·40
1419	1000s. Grevy's Zebra feeding	1·40	1·50
1405/19	Set of 15	13·00	14·00

Nos. 1405/12 and 1413/19 were each printed together, se-tenant, in sheetlets of 8 stamps (Nos. 1405/12) or 7 stamps and one label (at top left) (Nos. 1413/19).

155 Terminal Building, Entebbe International Airport

156 Game Poachers

(Des Creative Graphics. Litho B.D.T.)

1994 (14 Nov). 50th Anniv of International Civil Aviation Organization. T **155** and similar horiz design. Multicoloured. P 14.

1420	100s. Type **155**	1·00	20
1421	250s. Control tower, Entebbe International Airport	1·75	1·25

(Des Creative Graphics. Litho B.D.T.)

1994 (15 Nov). Ecology. T **156** and similar vert designs. Multicoloured. P 14.

1422	100s. Type **156**	50	10
1423	250s. Villagers at rubbish dump	90	45
1424	350s. Fishermen	1·25	1·25
1425	500s. Deforestation	1·90	2·25
1422/5 *Set of 4*		4·00	3·50

157 "Adoration of the Christ Child" (Filippino Lippi)

158 "Self-portrait" (Tintoretto)

(Litho Questa)

1994 (5 Dec). Christmas. Religious Paintings. T **157** and similar vert designs. Multicoloured. P 13½×14.

1426	100s. Type **157**	30	10
1427	200s. "The Holy Family rests on the Flight into Egypt" (Annibale Carracci)	50	30
1428	300s. "Madonna with Christ Child and St. John" (Piero di Cosimo)	70	40
1429	350s. "The Conestabile Madonna" (Raphael)	80	65
1430	450s. "Madonna and Child with Angels" (after Antonio Rossellino)	90	1·00
1431	500s. "Madonna and Child with St. John" (Raphael)	1·00	1·00
1432	900s. "Madonna and Child" (Luca Signorelli)	2·00	2·50
1433	1000s. "Madonna with the Child Jesus, St. John and an Angel" (pseudo Pier Francesco Fiorentino)	2·00	2·50
1426/33 *Set of 8*		7·50	7·50

MS1434 Two sheets, each 115×95 mm. (a) 2500s. "The Madonna of the Magnificat" (detail) (Sandro Botticelli). (b) 2500s. "Adoration of the Magi" (detail) (Fra Angelico and Filippo Lippi) *Set of 2 sheets* .... 9·00 10·00

No. 1426 is inscribed "Fillipino" in error.

(Des Pauline Cianciolo. Litho B.D.T.)

1995 (7 Feb). 400th Death Anniv of Jacopo Tintoretto (painter) (1994). T **168** and similar multicoloured designs. P 13.

1435	100s. Type **158**	40	10
1436	300s. "A Philosopher"	80	50
1437	400s. "The Creation of the Animals" (detail) (*horiz*)	1·00	90
1438	460s. "The Feast of Belshazzar" (detail) (*horiz*)	1·10	1·10
1439	500s. "The Raising of the Brazen Serpent"	1·25	1·25
1440	1000s. "Elijah fed by the Angel"	2·50	3·25
1435/40 *Set of 6*		6·25	6·25

MS1441 Two sheets. (a) 114×124 mm. 2000s. "Moses striking Water from a Rock" (detail). (b) 124×114 mm. 200s. "Finding of Moses" (detail) *Set of 2 sheets* .... 8·50 9·50

159 White-faced Whistling Duck ("White-faced Tree-duck")

1995 (24 Apr). Waterfowl and Wetland Birds of Uganda. T **159** and similar horiz designs. Multicoloured. Litho. P 14.

1442	200s. Type **159**	90	85
	a. Sheetlet. Nos. 1442/5	13·00	12·00
1443	200s. Common Shoveler ("European Shoveler")	90	85

1444	200s. Hartlaub's Duck	90	85
1445	200s. Verreaux's Eagle Owl ("Milky Eagle-owl")	90	85
1446	200s. Avocet	90	85
1447	200s. African Fish Eagle	90	85
1448	200s. Spectacled Weaver	90	85
1449	200s. Black-headed Gonolek	90	85
1450	200s. Great Crested Grebe	90	85
1451	200s. Red-knobbed Coot	90	85
1452	200s. Woodland Kingfisher	90	85
1453	200s. Pintail	90	85
1454	200s. Squacco Heron	90	85
1455	200s. Purple Swamphen ("Purple Gallinule")	90	85
1456	200s. African Darter	90	85
1457	200s. African Jacana	90	85
1442/57 *Set of 16*		13·00	12·00

MS1458 Two sheets, each 106×76 mm. (a) 2500s. African Pygmy Goose. (b) 2500s. Fulvous Whistling Duck ("Fulvous Tree-duck") *Set of 2 sheets* .... 9·00 10·00

Nos. 1442/57 were printed together, *se-tenant*, in sheetlets of 16 forming a composite design.

18th World Scout Jamboree Mondial, Holland, August 1995

(**160**)

1995 (1 June). 18th World Scout Jamboree, Netherlands. Nos. 701/4 and **MS**941b optd or surch as T **160**.

1459	100s. Scouts making bricks	25	10
1460	450s. on 70s. Poultry keeping	95	55
1461	800s. on 90s. Scout on crutches leading family to immunization centre	1·75	1·90
1462	1500s. on 10s. Type **104**	3·00	3·50
1459/62 *Set of 4*		5·50	5·50

MS1463 115×76 mm. 2500s. on 1200s. Lord Baden-Powell, W. Boyce and Revd. L. Hadley. .... 4·25 5·00

No. **MS**1463 is overprinted "18th World Scout Jamboree, August 1995, The Netherlands" on the sheet margin with the surcharge appearing on the stamp.

160a Soviet Artillery in Action

161 Dove, Child, Dish Aerial, Food and Emblem

(Den W. Wright. Litho Questa)

1995 (6 July). 50th Anniv of End of Second World War in Europe. T **160a** and similar horiz designs. Multicoloured. P 14.

1464	500s. Type **160a**	1·40	1·25
	a. Sheetlet. Nos. 1464/71	10·00	9·00
1465	500s. Soviet tanks on the Moltke Bridge	1·40	1·25
1466	500s. Kaiser Wilhelm Memorial Church, Berlin	1·40	1·25
1467	500s. Soviet tanks and Brandenburg Gate	1·40	1·25
1468	500s. U.S. Boeing B-17 Flying Fortress	1·40	1·25
1469	500s. Soviet tanks enter Berlin	1·40	1·25
1470	500s. Ruins of the Chancellery	1·40	1·25
1471	500s. The Reichstag on fire	1·40	1·25
1464/71 *Set of 8*		10·00	9·00

MS1472 104×74 mm. 2500s. Hoisting the Soviet flag on the Reichstag (57×42½ *mm*) .... 5·00 6·00

Nos. 1464/71 were printed together, *se-tenant*, in sheetlets of 8 with the stamps arranged in two horizontal strips of 4 separated by a gutter showing map of the Soviet advance.

(Litho Questa)

1995 (6 July). 50th Anniv of United Nations. T **161** and similar multicoloured designs. P 14.

1473	450s. Type **161**	70	50
1474	1000s. Hands releasing bird and insects	1·75	2·50

MS1475 100×70 mm. 2000s. Child's hand holding adult's finger (*horiz*) .... 2·75 3·50

161a Woman peeling Maize

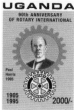

161b Paul Harris (founder) and Logo

(Litho Questa)

1995 (6 July). 50th Anniv of Food and Agriculture Organization. T **161a** and similar vert designs. Multicoloured. P 14.

1476	350s. Type **161a**	55	75
	a. Horiz strip of 3. Nos. 1476/8	1·50	2·40
1477	500s. Woman and child with maize	65	85
1478	1000s. Woman and baby with maize	80	1·10
1476/8 *Set of 3*		1·50	2·40
MS1479	100×70 mm. 2000s. Child and head of cow...	2·50	3·25

Nos. 1476/8 were printed together, *se-tenant*, as horizontal strips of 3 in sheets of 9, each strip forming a composite design.

(Litho Questa)

1995 (6 July). 90th Anniv of Rotary International. T **161b** and similar vert designs. Multicoloured. P 14.

1480	2000s. Type **161b**	2·00	2·75
MS1481	70×100 mm. 2000s. National flag and logo....	2·25	3·00

161c Queen Elizabeth the Queen Mother (pastel drawing)

162 Australian Flag in Form of "VJ"

(Litho Questa)

1995 (6 July)–**2002**. 95th Birthday of Queen Elizabeth the Queen Mother. T **161c** and similar vert designs. P 13½×14.

1482	500s. orange-brown, pale brown and black...	1·90	1·90
	a. Sheetlet. Nos. 1482/5×2	13·00	13·00
	ab. Sheetlet. As No. 1482a, but with top margin additionally inscr "IN MEMORIAM 1900-2002" (15.7.02)	17·00	17·00
1483	500s. multicoloured	1·90	1·90
1484	500s. multicoloured	1·90	1·90
1485	500s. multicoloured	1·90	1·90
1482/5 *Set of 4*		7·00	7·00
MS1486	102×127 mm. 2500s. multicoloured	5·50	5·50
	a. Additionally inscr "IN MEMORIAM 1900-2002" on margin (15.7.02)	8·00	8·00

Designs:— No. 1483, With bouquet of flowers; No. 1484, At desk (oil painting); No. 1845, Wearing turquoise-blue dress; No. **MS**1486, Wearing pale blue dress.

Nos. 1482/5 were printed together in sheetlets of 8, containing two *se-tenant* horizontal strips of 4.

Nos. 1482a and **MS**1486 were re-issued in 2002 with additional memorial inscription and black on the margins.

(Des J. Batchelor. Litho Questa)

1995 (6 July). 50th Anniv of End of Second World War in the Pacific. T **162** and similar horiz designs showing national flags as "VJ". P 14.

1487	600s. scarlet-vermilion, bluish violet and black	1·75	1·50
	a. Sheetlet. Nos. 1487/92	9·50	8·00
1488	600s. scarlet-vermilion, bluish violet and black	1·75	1·50
1489	600s. scarlet vermilion, bluish violet and black	1·75	1·50
1490	600s. multicoloured	1·75	1·50
1491	600s. scarlet-vermilion, pale orange and black	1·75	1·50

1492	600s. scarlet-vermilion and black	1·75	1·50
1487/92 *Set of 6*		9·50	8·00
MS1493	108×76 mm. 2500s. multicoloured	6·00	6·50

Designs:—No. 1487 Type **162** No. 1488 Great Britain; No. 1489, New Zealand; No. 1490, United States of America; No. 1491, People's Republic of China; No. 1492, Canada; No. **MS**1493 American soldier and flag.

Nos. 1487/92 were printed together, *se-tenant*, in sheetlets of 6 with the stamps arranged in two horizontal strips of 3 separated by a gutter showing the raising of the U.S.A. flag on Iwo Jima.

163 Velociraptor

(Des B. Regal. Litho B.D.T.)

1995 (15 July). Prehistoric Animals. T **163** and similar multicoloured designs. P 14.

1494	150s. Type **163**	1·00	65
1495	200s. Head of Psittacosaurus	1·00	65
1496	300s. Archaeopteryx	1·00	1·00
	a. Sheetlet. Nos. 1496/1507	11·00	11·00
1497	300s. Quetzalcoatlus and volcano (*vert*)	1·00	1·00
1498	300s. Pteranodon and volcano (*vert*)	1·00	1·00
1499	300s. Brachiosaurus (*vert*)	1·00	1·00
1500	300s. Tsintaosaur (*vert*)	1·00	1·00
1501	300s. Allosaur (*vert*)	1·00	1·00
1502	300s. Tyrannosaur (*vert*)	1·00	1·00
1503	300s. Apatosaur (*vert*)	1·00	1·00
1504	300s. Giant Dragonfly (*vert*)	1·00	1·00
1505	300s. Dimorphodon (*vert*)	1·00	1·00
1506	300s. Triceratops (*vert*)	1·00	1·00
1507	300s. Compsognathus (*vert*)	1·00	1·00
1508	350s. Head of Dilophosaurus	1·25	1·10
1509	400s. Kentrosaurus	1·40	1·25
1510	500s. Stegosaurus	1·60	1·40
1511	1500s. Pterodaustro	3·00	3·00
1494/1511 *Set of 18*		19·00	18·00
MS1512	Two sheets, each 106×75 mm. (a) 2000s. Head of Parasaurolophus. (b) 2000s. Head of Shunosaurus *Set of 2 sheets*	8·50	8·50

Nos. 1496/1507 were printed together, *se-tenant*, in sheetlets of 12 with the backgrounds forming a composite design. No. 1502 is inscribed "Tyranosaur" and No. 1506 "Tricreatops", both in error.

164 Rough-scaled Bush Viper

165 Bell's Hinged Tortoise

(Des R. Rundo. Litho Questa)

1995 (21 Aug)–**98**. Reptiles. T **164/6** and similar multicoloured designs. P 14×15 (50, 100, 150, 200, 350, 400, 450, 500s.), 13½×13 (300, 600, 700s. (No. 1521a) or 14 (others).

1513	50s. Type **164**	25	10
1514	100s. Pygmy Python	35	10
1515	150s. Three-horned Chameleon	50	20
1516	200s. African Rock Python	60	20
1516a	300s. Armadillo Girdled Lizard (21.4.95)	85	35
1517	350s. Nile Monitor	85	35
1518	400s. Savannah Monitor	1·00	40
1519	450s. Bush Viper	1·00	55
1520	500s. Nile Crocodile	1·00	55
1520a	600s. Spotted Sandveld Lizard (21.4.98)	1·25	70
1521	700s. Type **165**	1·40	1·00
1521a	700s. Bell's Hinged Tortoise (21.4.95)	1·40	1·00
1522	900s. Rhinoceros Viper	1·75	1·25
1523	1000s. Gaboon Viper	1·75	1·40
1524	2000s. Spitting Cobra	3·00	3·25
1525	3000s. Leopard Tortoise (20.11.95)	4·00	4·50
1526	4000s. Puff Adder (20.11.95)	5·00	6·00
1527	5000s. Common House Gecko (20.11.95)	6·50	7·50
1528	6000s. Dwarf Chameleon (20.11.95)	7·00	8·00
1529	10000s. Boomslang (snake) (20.11.95)	11·00	11·00
1513/29 *Set of 20*		45·00	45·00

Sizes:—21×21 mm 50, 100, 150, 200, 350, 400, 450, 500s; 18×20 mm 300, 600, 700s. (No. 1521a); 38½×24½ mm 700s. (No. 1521), 900s. to 10000s.

166 Nsambya Church

(Litho Questa)

1995 (7 Sept). Local Anniversaries. T **166** and similar horiz designs. Multicoloured. P 14.

1530	150s. Type **166**		45	20
1531	450s. Namilyango College		90	70
1532	500s. Figures with symbolic wheel		95	75
1533	1000s. Volunteers with food sacks		1·75	2·50
1530/3	*Set of 4*		3·50	3·75

Anniversaries:—Nos. 1530/1, Centenary of Mill Hill Missionaries in Uganda; No. 1532, Centenary of International Cooperative Alliance; No. 1533, 25th anniversary of U.N. volunteers.

167 Bwindi Forest

(Litho Questa)

1995 (14 Sept). Landscapes. T **167** and similar horiz designs. Multicoloured. P 14.

1534	50s. Type **167**		40	20
1535	100s. Karamoja		50	20
1536	450s. Sunset, Lake Mburo National Park		1·25	80
1537	500s. Sunset, Gulu District		1·25	80
1538	900s. Mist, Kabale District		2·00	2·75
1539	1000s. Ruwenzori Mountains		2·00	2·75
1534/9	*Set of 6*		6·75	6·75

(Litho Questa)

1995 (14 Sept). Waterfalls. Multicoloured designs as T **167**. P 14.

1540	50s. Sipi Falls (*vert*)		40	20
1541	100s. Murchison Falls		50	20
1542	450s. Bujagali Falls		1·25	80
1543	500s. The Two Falls at Murchison		1·25	80
1544	900s. Falls, Ruwenzori Mountains (*vert*)		2·00	2·75
1545	1000s. Falls, Ruwenzori Mountains (*different*) (*vert*)		2·00	2·75
1540/5	*Set of 6*		6·75	6·75

168 Peter Rono (1500 metres), 1988

(Des R. Sauber. Litho Questa)

1995 (21 Sept). Olympic Games Atlanta (1996). T **168** and similar multicoloured designs. P 14.

1546	50s. Type **168**		20	10
1547	350s. Reiner Klimke (dressage), 1984		90	40
1548	450s. German team (cycling time trials), 1988		1·75	70
1549	500s. Grace Birungi (athlete)		90	70
1550	900s. Francis Ogola (athlete)		1·40	1·75
1551	1000s. Nyakana Godfrey (boxer)		1·50	1·75
1546/51	*Set of 6*		6·00	4·75

MS1552 Two sheets, each 106×76 mm. (a) 2500s. Sebastian Coe (1500 metres), 1980 and 1984. (b) 2500s. Rolf Dannenberg (discus), 1984 (*vert*) *Set of 2 sheets* — 7·00 / 8·00

169 Peacock

(Litho Questa)

1995 (2 Oct). Domestic Animals. T **169** and similar horiz designs. Multicoloured. P 14.

1553	200s. Type **169**		80	70
		a. Sheetlet. Nos. 1553/68	11·50	10·00
1554	200s. Pouter Pigeon		80	70
1555	200s. Rock Doves		80	70
1556	200s. Rouen Duck		80	70
1557	200s. Guineafowl		80	70
1558	200s. Donkey		80	70
1559	200s. Shetland ponies		80	70
1560	200s. Palomino horse		80	70
1561	200s. Pigs		80	70
1562	200s. Border Collie		80	70
1563	200s. Merino sheep		80	70
1564	200s. Milch goat		80	70
1565	200s. Black Dutch rabbit		80	70
1566	200s. Lop rabbit		80	70
1567	200s. Somali cat		80	70
1568	200s. Asian cat		80	70
1553/68	*Set of 16*		11·50	10·00

MS1569 Two sheets, each 106×76 mm. (a) 2500s. Saddle-bred horses. (b) 2500s. Oxen *Set of 2 sheets* — 10·00 / 9·00

Nos. 1553/68 were printed together, *se-tenant*, in sheetlets of 16 forming a composite design.

170 Scouts putting Child on Scales

171 Hermann Staudinger (1953 Chemistry)

(Litho Questa)

1995 (18 Oct). Uganda Boy Scouts in the Community. T **170** and similar multicoloured designs. P 14.

1570	150s. Type **170**		50	20
1571	350s. Scouts carrying children		85	45
1572	450s. Checking health cards (*horiz*)		95	70
1573	800s. Holding child for immunization (*horiz*)		1·75	2·00
1574	1000s. Weighing child before immunization		1·90	2·25
1570/4	*Set of 5*		5·00	5·00

(Des R. Cassila. Litho Questa)

1995 (31 Oct). Centenary of Nobel Prize Trust Fund. T **171** and similar vert designs. Multicoloured. P 14.

1575	**300**	300s. Type **171**	90	80
		a. Sheetlet. Nos. 1575/86	9·75	8·75
1576		300s. Fritz Haber (1918 Chemistry)	90	80
1577		300s. Bert Sakmann (1991 Medicine)	90	80
1578		300s. Adolf Windaus (1926 Chemistry)	90	80
1579		300s. Wilhelm Wien (1911 Physics)	90	80
1580		300s. Ernest Hemingway (1954 Literature)	90	80
1581		300s. Richard Willstatter (1915 Chemistry)	90	80
1582		300s. Stanley Cohen (1986 Medicine)	90	80
1583		300s. Hans Jensen (1963 Physics)	90	80
1584		300s. Otto Warburg (1931 Medicine)	90	80
1585		300s. Heinrich Wieland (1927 Chemistry)	90	80
1586		300s. Albrecht Kossel (1910 Medicine)	90	80
1587		300s. Hideki Yukawa (1949 Physics)	90	80
		a. Sheetlet. Nos. 1587/98	9·75	8·75
1588		300s. F. W. de Klerk (1993 Peace)	90	80
1589		300s. Nelson Mandela (1993 Peace)	90	80
1590		300s. Odysseus Elytis (1979 Literature)	90	80
1591		300s. Ferdinand Buisson (1927 Peace)	90	80
1592		300s. Lev Landau (1962 Physics)	90	80
1593		300s. Halldor Laxness (1955 Literature)	90	80
1594		300s. Wole Soyinka (1986 Literature)	90	80
1595		300s. Desmond Tutu (1984 Peace)	90	80
1596		300s. Susumu Tonegawa (1987 Medicine)	90	80
1597		300s. Louis de Brogue (1929 Physics)	90	80
1598		300s. George Seferis (1963 Literature)	90	80
1575/98		*Set of 24*	19·00	17·00

MS1599 Two sheets, each 105×76 mm. (a) 2000s. Nelly Sachs (1966 Literature). (b) 2000s. Werner Forssmann (1956 Medicine) *Set of 2 sheets* — 9·00 / 9·50

Nos. 1575/86 and 1587/98 were each printed together, *se-tenant*, in sheetlets of 12 forming composite designs.

171a "The Virgin and Child"
(Holbein the Younger)

(Litho Questa)

1995 (30 Nov). Christmas. Religious Paintings. T **171a** and similar vert designs. Multicoloured. P 13½×14.

1600	150s. Type **171a**	40	20
1601	350s. "Madonna" (Procaccini)	70	35
1602	500s. "The Virgin and Child" (Pisanello)	95	50
1603	1000s. "Madonna and Child" (Crivelli)	1·75	2·00
1604	1500s. "The Nativity of the Virgin" (Le Nain)	2·25	3·00
1600/4	*Set of 5*	5·50	5·50

MS1605 Two sheets, each 102×127 mm. (a) 2500s. "Madonna and Child" (detail) (Bellini). (b) 2500s. "The Holy Family" (detail) (Andrea del Sarto) *Set of 2 sheets* ... 8·50 8·50

172 *Ansellia africana*

(Litho Questa)

1995 (8 Dec). Orchids. T **172** and similar vert designs. Multicoloured. P 14½×14.

1606	150s. Type **172**	60	40
1607	350s. *Aerangis iuteoalba*	75	75
	a. Sheetlet. Nos. 1607/15	6·00	6·00
1608	350s. *Satyrium sacculatum*	75	75
1609	350s. *Bolusiella maudiae*	75	75
1610	350s. *Habenaria attenuata*	75	75
1611	350s. *Cyrtorchis arcuata*	75	75
1612	350s. *Eulophia angolensis*	75	75
1613	350s. *Tridactyle bicaudata*	75	75
1614	350s. *Eulophia horsfallii*	75	75
1615	350s. *Diaphananthe fragrantissima*	75	75
1616	450s. *Satyricum crassicaule*	85	85
1617	500s. *Polystachya cultriformis*	90	90
1618	800s. *Disa erubescens*	1·40	1·60
1606/18	*Set of 13*	9·50	9·50

MS1619 Two sheets, each 66×76 mm. (a) 2500s. *Rangaeris amaniensis.* (b) 2500s. *Diaphananthe pulchella.* P 13½×14 *Set of 2 sheets* ... 8·50 9·00

Nos. 1607/15 were printed together, *se-tenant*, in sheetlets of 9.

173 Rat and Purple Grapes   **174** Wild Dog and Pup

(Des Y. Lee. Litho B.D.T.)

1996 (29 Jan). Chinese New Year ("Year of the Rat"). T **173** and similar horiz designs. Multicoloured. P 14.

1620	350s. Type **173**	60	65
	a. Block of 4. Nos. 1620/3	2·25	2·40
1621	350s. Rat and radishes	60	65
1622	350s. Rat eating corn	60	65
1623	350s. Rat eating cucumber	60	65
1620/3	*Set of 4*	2·25	2·40

MS1624 100×74 mm. Nos. 1620/3 ... 1·25 1·60

MS1625 106×76 mm. 2000s. Rat and green grapes ... 3·00 3·50

Nos. 1620/3 were printed together, *se-tenant*, as blocks of 4 in sheets of 16.

(Des R. Rundo. Litho Questa)

1996 (27 Mar). Wildlife of Uganda. Multicoloured designs as T **174**. P 14.

(a) Horiz designs

1626	150s. Type **174**	55	55
	a. Sheetlet. Nos. 1626/33	5·00	5·00
1627	200s. African Fish Eagle	60	60
1628	250s. Hippopotamus	65	60
1629	350s. Leopard	60	60
1630	400s. Lion	65	65
1631	450s. Lioness	70	70
1632	500s. Meerkats	75	60
1633	550s. Pair of Black Rhinoceroses	1·00	1·00

(b) Vert designs

1634	150s. Gorilla	50	50
	a. Sheetlet. Nos. 1634/41	5·00	5·00
1635	200s. Cheetah	50	55
1636	250s. African Elephant	70	60
1637	350s. Thomson's Gazelle	60	60
1638	400s. Crowned Crane	80	80
1639	450s. Saddlebill	80	80
1640	500s. Vulture	80	80
1641	550s. Zebra	80	85
1626/41	*Set of 16*	10·00	10·00

MS1642 Two sheets. (a) 72×102 mm. 2000s. Grey Heron (*horiz*). (b) 102×72 mm. 2000s. Giraffe *Set of 2 sheets* ... 7·00 8·00

Nos. 1626/33 and 1634/41 were each printed together, *se-tenant*, in sheetlets of 8 with enlarged left or top margin.

175 Mickey Mouse and Goofy on   **176** "Autumn Pond"
Platform at Calais

(Des Walt Disney Co. Litho Questa)

1996 (15 Apr). Mickey's Orient Express. T **175** and similar horiz designs showing Walt Disney cartoon characters. Multicoloured. P 14×13½.

1643	50s. Type **175**	35	30
1644	100s. Mickey and Goofy at Athens	45	30
1645	150s. Mickey showing Donald Duck his Pullman ticket	60	30
1646	200s. Daisy and Donald Duck in Pullman car	75	30
1647	250s. Mickey and Minnie Mouse in dining car	80	40
1648	300s. Goofy as guard assisting Mickey and Minnie	90	50
1649	600s. Mickey and Donald preparing for bed	1·75	2·00
1650	700s. Mickey and Minnie at Orient Express accident, Frankfurt, 1901	1·90	2·25
1651	800s. Mickey and Goofy building snowman and Orient Express in snowdrift, 1929	2·00	2·25
1652	900s. Disney characters filming Murder on the Orient Express	2·25	2·50
1643/52	*Set of 10*	10·50	10·00

MS1653 Two sheets, each 132×106 mm. (a) 2500s. Donald driving Orient Express. (b) 2500s. Mickey, Minnie and Goofy on observation platform *Set of 2 sheets* ... 9·50 11·00

(Litho Questa)

1996 (8 May). CHINA '96 Ninth Asian International Stamp Exhibition, Peking (1st issue). Paintings by Qi Baishi. T **176** and similar vert designs. Multicoloured. P 15×14.

1654	50s. Type **176**	45	45
	a. Sheetlet. Nos. 1654/63	6·75	6·75
1655	100s. "Partridge and Smartweed"	60	60
1656	150s. "Begonias and Mynah"	70	70
1657	200s. "Chrysanthemums, Cocks and Hens"	70	70
1658	250s. "Crabs"	70	70
1659	300s. "Wisterias and Bee"	75	75
1660	350s. "Smartweed and Ink-drawn Butterflies"	80	80
1661	400s. Lotus and Mandarin Ducks"	85	85
1662	450s. "Lichees and Locust"	90	90
1663	500s. "Millet and Praying Mantis"	95	95
1654/63 Set of 10		6·75	6·75

MS1664 135×114 mm. 800s. "Morning Glories and Locust" (50×38 mm); 800s. "Shrimps" (50×38 mm). P 14×13½ .... 7·50 7·50

The painting titles on 150s. and 200s. are transposed in error with "CHRYSANTHEMUMS" shown as "RYSANTHEMUMS".

Nos. 1654/63 were printed together, se-tenant, in sheetlets of 10.

177 Tomb Mural, Xi'an

1996 (13 May). CHINA '96 Ninth Asian International Stamp Exhibition, Peking (2nd issue). Sheet 140×90 mm. Litho. P 13½×14.

MS1664a **177** 500s. multicoloured .... 2·25 2·25

178 Coprinus disseminatus

179a Queen Elizabeth II

179 Catopsilia philea

1996 (24 June). African Fungi. T **178** and similar vert designs. Multicoloured. Litho. P 14.

1665	150s. Type **178**	50	50
	a. Sheetlet. Nos. 1665/72	5·50	6·00
1666	300s. Coprinus radians	60	60
1667	350s. Hygrophorus coccineus	60	60
1668	400s. Marasmius siccus	70	70
1669	450s. Cortinarius collinitus	80	80
1670	500s. Cortinarius cinnabarinus	80	80
1671	550s. Coltricia cinnamomea	85	90
1672	1000s. Mutinus elegans	1·50	1·75
1665/72 Set of 8		5·50	6·00

MS1673 Two sheets, each 110×80 mm. (a) 2500s. Inocybe sororia. (b) 2500s. Flammulina velutipes Set of 2 sheets .... 6·50 7·00

Nos. 1665/72 were printed together, se-tenant, in sheetlets of 8.

(Des D. Burkhardt. Litho Questa)

1996 (26 June). Butterflies. T **179** and similar horiz designs. Multicoloured. P 14.

1674	50s. Type **179**	50	50
	a. Sheetlet. Nos. 1674/85	7·75	7·75
1675	100s. Dione vanillae	50	50

1676	150s. Metamorpha dido	65	65
1677	200s. Papilio sesostris	70	70
1678	250s. Papilio neophilus	75	75
1679	300s. Papilio thoas	75	75
1680	350s. Diorina periander	75	75
1681	400s. Morpho cipris	75	75
1682	450s. Catonephele numilia	80	80
1683	500s. Heliconius doris	80	80
1684	550s. Prepona antimache	80	80
1685	600s. Eunica alcmena	80	80
1674/85 Set of 12		7·75	7·75

MS1686 Two sheets, each 100×70 mm. (a) 2500s. Caligo mania. (b) 2500s. Heliconius doris (different) Set of 2 sheets .... 6·50 7·00

Nos. 1674/85 were printed together, se-tenant, in sheetlets of 12.

(Litho Questa)

1996 (10 July). 70th Birthday of Queen Elizabeth II. T **179a** and similar vert designs showing different photographs. Multicoloured. P 13½×14.

1687	500s. Type **179a**	1·40	1·40
	a. Strip of 3. Nos. 1687/9	3·75	3·75
1688	500s. In evening dress	1·40	1·40
1689	500s. Wearing red coat and hat	1·40	1·40
1687/9 Set of 3		3·75	3·75

MS1690 125×103 mm. 2000s. Queen Elizabeth II .... 5·00 4·50

Nos. 1687/9 were printed together, se-tenant, in horizontal and vertical strips of 3 throughout sheets of 9.

179b Asian Children

(Litho Questa)

1996 (10 July). 50th Anniv of U.N.I.C.E.F. T **179b** and similar multicoloured designs. P 14.

1691	450s. Type **179b**	1·00	1·10
1692	500s. South American children	1·25	1·40
1693	550s. Boy holding pencil	1·40	1·60
1691/3 Set of 3		3·25	3·50

MS1694 74×104 mm. 2000s. African mother and child (vert) .... 3·50 4·25

179c Darien National Park, Panama

(Des M. Freedman and Dena Rubin. Litho Questa)

1996 (10 July). 50th Anniv of U.N.E.S.C.O. T **179c** and similar horiz designs. Multicoloured. P 14×13½.

1695	450s. Type **179c**	1·40	1·40
1696	500s. Los Glaciares National Park, Argentina	1·50	1·50
1697	550s. Tubbatha Reef Marine Park, Philippines	1·60	1·60
1695/7 Set of 3		4·00	4·00

MS1698 104×74 mm. 2500s. Ruwenzori Mountains National Park Uganda .... 4·25 5·50

No. **MS**1698 is inscribed "RWENZORI" in error.

180 Statue of Menorah, Knesset

180a Ella Fitzgerald

(Des R. Sauber. Litho Questa)

1996 (10 July). 3000th Anniv of Jerusalem. T **180** and similar vert designs. Multicoloured. P 14.
MS1699 114×95 mm. 300s. Type **180**, 500s. Jerusalem Theatre. 1000s. Israel Museum .... 5·00 4·50
MS1700 104×74 mm. 2000s. Grotto of the Nativity...... 5·00 4·50

(Des R. Sauber. Litho Questa)

1996 (10 July). Centenary of Radio. Entertainers. T **180a** and similar vert designs. Multicoloured. P 13½×14.
1701	200s. Type **180a**	35	20
1702	300s. Bob Hope	90	40
1703	500s. Nat "King" Cole	90	70
1704	800s. George Burns and Gracie Allen	1·25	1·75
1701/4 *Set of 4*		3·00	2·75
MS1705 74×104 mm. 2000s. Jimmy Durante		3·00	3·50

181 Electric Locomotive, 1968 (Japan)

(Des J. Puvilland. Litho B.D.T.)

1996 (25 July). Railway Locomotives. T **181** and similar horiz designs. Multicoloured. P 14.
1706	450s. Type **181**	1·00	1·00
	a. Sheetlet. Nos. 1706/11	5·50	5·50
1707	450s. Stephenson's *Rocket*, 1829	1·00	1·00
1708	450s. William Norris's *Austria*, 1843	1·00	1·00
1709	450s. Early American steam locomotive	1·00	1·00
1710	450s. Steam locomotive, 1947 (India)	1·00	1·00
1711	450s. Class 103 electric locomotive (Germany)	1·00	1·00
1712	550s. GWR steam locomotive *Lady of Lynn* (England)	1·00	1·00
	a. Sheetlet. Nos. 1712/17	5·50	5·50
1713	550s. Steam locomotive, 1930 (China)	1·00	1·00
1714	550s. Meyer-Kitson steam locomotive (Chile)	1·00	1·00
1715	550s. Union Pacific "Centennial" diesel locomotive No. 6900 (U.S.A.)	1·00	1·00
1716	550s. Type 581 diesel locomotive (Japan)	1·00	1·00
1717	550s. Class 120 electric locomotive (Germany)	1·00	1·00
1706/17 *Set of 12*		11·00	11·00
MS1718 Two sheets, each 106×76 mm. (a) 2500s. Type 99 steam locomotive (Germany); (b) 2500s. LNER Class A4 steam locomotive *Mallard*, (Great Britain) *Set of 2 sheets*		8·00	8·50

Nos. 1706/11 and 1712/17 were each printed, *se-tenant*, in sheetlets of 6.

182 Postal and Telecommunications Corporation Emblem

(Litho Questa)

1996 (30 Aug). Centenary of Postal Services. T **182** and similar horiz designs. Multicoloured. P 14.
1719	150s. Type **182**	25	20
1720	450s. Loading postbus	2·00	1·75
1721	500s. Modern postal transportation	2·25	2·00
1722	550s. 1896 25c. violet and 1r. black stamps	2·25	2·25
1719/22 *Set of 4*		6·00	5·50

183 Two American River Steamers and 1904 Games, St. Louis

(Litho B.D.T.)

1996 (23 Sept). Olympic Games, Atlanta (1st issue). T **183** and similar multicoloured designs. P 14.
1723	350s. Type **183**	90	45
1724	450s. George Finnegan (U.S.A.) (boxing), 1904	95	75
1725	500s. Chariot racing	1·10	95
1726	800s. John Flanagan (U.S.A.) (hammer), 1904 (*vert*)	1·75	3·00
1723/6 *Set of 4*		4·25	4·75

See also Nos. 1764/81.

184 Mango

184a "Annunciation" (Lorenzo di Credi)

(Litho B.D.T.)

1996 (8 Oct). Fruit. T **184** and similar multicoloured designs. P 14.
1727	150s. Type **184**	55	20
1728	350s. Orange	1·10	50
1729	450s. Pawpaw	1·25	1·10
1730	500s. Avocado	1·40	1·25
1731	650s. Watermelon (*horiz*)	1·75	2·50
1727/31 *Set of 5*		5·50	5·00

(Litho Questa)

1996 (18 Nov). Christmas. Religious Paintings. T **184a** and similar multicoloured designs. P 13½×14.
1732	150s. Type **184a**	60	20
1733	350s. "Madonna of the Loggia" (detail) (Botticelli)	1·10	40
1734	400s. "Virgin in Glory with Child and Angels" (Lorenzetti)	1·25	75
1735	450s. "Adoration of the Child" (Lippi)	1·40	1·25
1736	500s. "Madonna of the Loggia" (Botticelli)	1·50	1·50
1737	550s. "The Strength" (Botticelli)	1·60	2·00
1732/7 *Set of 6*		6·75	5·50
MS1738 Two sheets, each 106×76 mm. (a) 2500s. "Holy Allegory" (Bellini) (*horiz*); (b) 2500s. "The Virgin on the Throne with Child and the Saints" (Ghirlandaio) (*horiz*). P 14×13½ *Set of 2 sheets*		10·00	11·00

184b Sylvester Stallone in *Rocky III*

185 Traditional Costume from Western Uganda

(Des Shannon. Litho Questa)

1996 (21 Nov). 20th Anniv of Rocky (film). Sheet 143×182 mm. Multicoloured. P 14×13½.
MS1739 800s.×3 Type **184b** .... 4·00 5·00

(Litho B.D.T.)

1997 (2 Jan). Traditional Costumes. T **185** and similar multicoloured designs. P 14.
1740	150s. Type **185**	55	30
1741	300s. Acholi headdress	1·00	1·00
	a. Sheetlet. Nos. 1741/6	5·50	5·50
1742	300s. Alur headdress	1·00	1·00
1743	300s. Bwola dance headdress	1·00	1·00
1744	300s. Madi headdress	1·00	1·00
1745	300s. Karimojong headdress with plume	1·00	1·00
1746	300s. Karimojong headdress with two feathers	1·00	1·00

1747	350s. Karimojong women		1·00	1·00
1748	450s. Ganda traditional dress (horiz)		1·10	1·10
1749	500s. Acholi traditional dress (horiz)		1·25	1·50
1740/9	Set of 10		9·00	9·00

Nos. 1741/6 were printed together, se-tenant, in sheetlets of 6.

186 Ox

187 Giraffe running

(Des Y. Lee. Litho Questa)

1997 (24 Jan). Chinese New Year ("Year of the Ox"). T **188** and similar multicoloured designs. P 14.

1750	350s. Type **186**		1·00	1·00
	a. Vert strip of 4. Nos. 1750/3		3·50	3·50
1751	350s. Cow suckling calf		1·00	1·00
1752	350s. Cow and calf lying down		1·00	1·00
1753	350s. Ox lying down		1·00	1·00
1750/3	Set of 4		3·50	3·50
MS1754	111×83 mm. 1750/3		3·50	3·75
MS1755	76×106 mm. 1500s. Young calf (vert)		3·50	3·75

Nos. 1750/3 were printed together, se-tenant, as vertical strips of 4 in sheets of 16.

(Des D. Burkhart. Litho Questa)

1997 (12 Feb). Endangered Species. Rothschild's Giraffe. T **187** and similar multicoloured designs. P 14.

1756	300s. Type **187**		90	90
	a. Horiz strip of 4. Nos. 1756/9		3·25	3·25
1757	300s. Two adult giraffes		90	90
1758	300s. Head of giraffe		90	90
1759	300s. Giraffe with calf		90	90
1756/9	Set of 4		3·25	3·25
MS1760	75×109 mm. 2500s. Head of giraffe (different) (horiz)		5·00	5·00

Nos. 1756/9 were printed together, se-tenant, both horizontally and vertically in sheets of 12 containing three of each design.

188 "The Constitution" on Open Book

189 Kitel Son (Japan) (marathon), 1936

(Litho Questa)

1997 (25 Feb). Promulgation of New Constitution (8 Oct 1995). T **188** and similar multicoloured designs. P 13½×14 (550s.) or 14×13½ (others).

1761	150s. Type **188**		50	20
1762	350s. "The Constitution" on scroll		85	60
1763	550s. "THE CONSTITUTION" on closed book (vert)		1·40	2·00
1761/3	Set of 3		2·50	2·50

(Den J. Puvilland. Litho Questa)

1997 (3 Mar). Olympic Games, Atlanta (2nd issue). Previous Gold Medal Winners. T **189** and similar vert designs. Multicoloured. P 14.

1764	150s. Type **189**		60	70
	a. Sheetlet. Nos. 1764, 1766, 1768, 1770, 1772, 1774, 1776, 1778, 1780		6·25	7·00
1765	150s. Bob Hayes (U.S.A.) (100m), 1964		60	70
	a. Sheetlet. Nos. 1765, 1767, 1769, 1771, 1773, 1775, 1777, 1779, 1781		6·25	7·00
1766	200s. Walter Davis (U.S.A.) (high jump), 1952		65	75
1767	200s. Rod Milburn (110m hurdles), 1972		65	75
1768	250s. Matthes (swimming), 1968		70	80
1769	250s. Filbert Bayi (Tanzania) (athletics), 1976.		70	80
1770	300s. Akii Bua (Uganda) (400m hurdles), 1972		75	85
1771	300s. H. Kipchoge Keino (Kenya) (steeple chase), 1972		75	85
1772	350s. Nordwig (Germany) (pole vault), 1972..		80	90

1773	350s. Ron Ray (U.S.A.) (athletics), 1976		80	90
1774	400s. Wilma Rudolph (U.S.A.) (100m relay), 1960		80	90
1775	400s. Joe Frazer (U.S.A.) (boxing), 1976		80	90
1776	450s. Abebe Bikila (Ethiopia) (marathon), 1964		85	95
1777	450s. Carl Lewis (U.S.A.) (100m), 1984		85	95
1778	500s. Edwin Moses (U.S.A.) (400m hurdles), 1984		90	1·00
1779	500s. Gisela Mauermayer (Germany) (discus), 1936		90	1·00
1780	550s. Rady Williams (U.S.A.) (long jump), 1972		90	1·00
1781	550s. Dietmar Mogenburg (Germany) (high jump), 1984		90	1·00
1764/81	Set of 18		12·50	14·00

Nos. 1764, 1766, 1768, 1770, 1772, 1774, 1776, 1778 and 1780 and 1765, 1767, 1769, 1771, 1773, 1775, 1777, 1779 and 1781 were each printed together, se-tenant, in sheetlets of 9 with the backgrounds forming composite designs. No. 1769 is incorrectly inscribed "Eiilbert" and is dated "1976"; Filbert Bayi did not participate in the 1976 Games.

No. 1779 is incorrectly inscribed "Mauemayer" and wrongly identifies the event as the shotput.

The sheetlets 1764a and 1765a are also known without the inscription "OLYMPIC WINNERS" on each stamp. These are inscribed "OLYMPIC GAMES 1996/ATLANTA" in the top margin. On the sheets as listed this has been trimmed off.

190 "Red Plum Blossom and Daffodil"

(Des Y. Lee. Litho B.D.T.)

1997 (5 Mar). HONG KONG '97 International Stamp Exhibition. Paintings by Wu Changshuo. T **190** and similar multicoloured designs. P 14×15.

1782	50s. Type **190**		45	50
	a. Sheetlet. Nos. 1782/91		5·75	6·25
1783	100s. "Peony"		55	60
1784	150s. "Rosaceae"		60	65
1785	200s. "Pomegranate"		65	70
1786	250s. "Peach, Peony and Plum Blossom"		65	70
1787	300s. "Calyx Canthus"		65	70
1788	350s. "Chrysanthemum"		65	70
1789	400s. "Calabash"		70	75
1790	450s. "Chrysanthemum" (different)		70	75
1791	500s. "Cypress Tree"		70	75
1782/91	Set of 10		5·75	6·25
MS1792	137×105 mm. 550s. "Litchi" (50×37 mm); 1000s. "Water Lily" (50×37 mm). P 14		2·50	3·00

Nos. 1782/91 were printed together, se-tenant, in sheetlets of 10.

191 Woody

192 "Pioneer 10"

(Des Rosemary DeFiglio. Litho Questa)

1997 (2 Apr). Disney's Toy Story (cartoon film). T **191** and similar multicoloured designs. P 13½×14 (vert) or 14×13½ (others).

1793	100s. Type **191**	55	55
	a. Sheetlet. Nos. 1793/8	3·00	3·00
1794	100s. Buzz Lightyear	55	55
1795	100s. Bo Peep	55	55
1796	100s. Hamm	55	55
1797	100s. Slinky	55	55
1798	100s. Rex	55	55
1799	150s. Woody on bed (horiz)	65	65
	a. Sheetlet. Nos. 1799/1807	5·00	5·00
1800	150s. Woody at microphone (horiz)	65	65
1801	150s. Bo Peep (horiz)	65	65
1802	150s. Buzz Lightyear (horiz)	65	65
1803	150s. Slinky and Rex (horiz)	65	65
1804	150s. Woody hiding (horiz)	65	65
1805	150s. "Halt! Who goes there" (horiz)	65	65
1806	150s. Rex, Slinky and Buzz Lightyear (horiz)...	65	65
1807	150s. "You're just an action figure!" (horiz)	65	65
1808	200s. "I'm the only sheriff in these parts" (horiz)	65	65
	a. Sheetlet. Nos. 1808/16	5·00	5·00
1809	200s. Green toy soldiers (horiz)	65	65
1810	200s. Woody and Buzz (horiz)	65	65
1811	200s. Woody pointing (horiz)	65	65
1812	200s. Buzz Lightyear (horiz)	65	65
1813	200s. Green aliens (horiz)	65	65
1814	200s. "This is an intergalactic emergency" (horiz)	65	65
1815	200s. Buzz and Woody argue (horiz)	65	65
1816	200s. Buzz and Woody in buggy (horiz)	65	65
1793/1816	Set of 24	13·00	13·00

MS1817 Three sheets, each 133×108 mm. (a) 133×108 mm. 2000s. Woody; (b) 108×133 mm. 2000s. Buzz Lightyear; (c) 2000s. Buzz Lightyear Set of 3 sheets .... 15·00 15·00

Nos. 1793/8, 1799/1807 and 1808/16 were each printed, *se-tenant*, in sheetlets of 6 (Nos. 1793/8) or 9.

(Des W. Wright. Litho Questa)

1997 (16 Apr). Space Exploration. T **192** and similar multicoloured designs. P 14.

1818	250s. Type **192**	1·25	1·00
	a. Sheetlet. Nos. 1818/25	9·00	7·25
1819	250s. "Voyager 1"	1·25	1·00
1820	250s. "Viking Orbiter"	1·25	1·00
1821	250s. "Pioneer – Venus 1"	1·25	1·00
1822	250s. "Mariner 9"	1·25	1·00
1823	250s. "Galileo" Entry Probe	1·25	1·00
1824	250s. "Mariner 10"	1·25	1·00
1825	250s. "Voyager 2"	1·25	1·00
1826	300s. "Sputnik 1"	1·25	1·00
	a. Sheetlet. Nos. 1826/33	9·00	7·25
1827	300s. "Apollo" space craft	1·25	1·00
1828	300s. "Soyuz" space craft	1·25	1·00
1829	300s. "Intelsat 1"	1·25	1·00
1830	300s. Manned manoeuvring Unit	1·25	1·00
1831	300s. "Skylab"	1·25	1·00
1832	300s. "Telstar 1"	1·25	1·00
1833	300s. Hubble Telescope	1·25	1·00
1818/33	Set of 16	18·00	14·50

MS1834 Two sheets, each 103×73 mm. (a) 2000s. Space Shuttle Challenger (35×61 mm). (b) 2000s. "Viking Lander" on Mars (61×35 mm) Set of 2 sheets .... 9·00 8·50

Nos. 1818/25 and 1826/33 were each printed together, *se-tenant*, in sheetlets of 8 with the backgrounds forming composite designs.

193 Deng Xiaoping and Port

194 Water Hyacinth and Pebbles

(Des Y. Lee. Litho Questa)

1997 (9 May). Deng Xiaoping (Chinese statesman) Commemoration. T **193** and similar horiz design. P 14.

1835	**193** 500s. multicoloured	1·25	1·25
	a. Sheetlet. Nos. 1835/7	4·25	4·50
1836	550s. multicoloured	1·25	1·25

1837	1000s. multicoloured	2·25	2·50
1835/7	Set of 3	4·25	4·50

MS1838 100×70 mm. 2000s. multicoloured (Deng Xiaoping and Shenzhen) .... 3·25 3·75

Nos. 1835/7 were printed together, *se-tenant*, in sheetlets of 3 with an enlarged illustrated margin at right.

(Des R. Martin. Litho Questa)

1997 (14 May). Environmental Protection. T **194** and similar vert designs. Multicoloured. P 14.

1839	500s. Water hyacinth and Lake Victoria (inscr at top left)	1·50	1·25
	a. Sheetlet. Nos. 1839/42	5·50	4·50
1840	500s. Water hyacinth and Lake Victoria (inscr at top right)	1·50	1·25
1841	500s. Type **194**	1·50	1·25
1842	500s. Larger clump of Water hyacinth and pebbles	1·50	1·25
1843	550s. Buffalo	1·50	1·25
	a. Sheetlet. Nos. 1843/6	5·50	4·50
1844	550s. Uganda Kob	1·50	1·25
1845	550s. Guinea Fowl	1·50	1·25
1846	550s. Marabou Stork	1·50	1·25
1839/46	Set of 8	11·00	9·00

MS1847 106×76 mm. 2500s. Gorilla .... 6·00 5·50

Nos. 1839/42 and 1843/6 were each printed together, *se-tenant*, in sheetlets of 4 with the backgrounds forming composite designs, and an enlarged illustrated margin at right.

No. 1845 is inscribed "GUINEA FOWEL" and No. 1846 "MALIBU STORK", both in error.

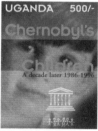

194a Child's Face and UNESCO Emblem

194b Paul Harris and Child drinking

(Litho Questa)

1997 (21 May). 10th Anniv of Chernobyl Nuclear Disaster. P 13½×14.

1848	500s. Type **194a**	1·50	1·25
1849	700s. As Type **194a** but inscribed "CHABAD'S CHILDREN OF CHERNOBYL" at foot	2·25	2·25

(Des J. Iskowitz. Litho Questa)

1997 (2 June). 50th Death Anniv of Paul Harris (founder of Rotary International). T **194b** and similar horiz designs. Multicoloured. P 14.

1850	1000s. Type **194b**	2·50	3·00

MS1851 78×107 mm. 2500s. The first Rotarians .... 3·00 3·75

194c Queen Elizabeth II

(Litho Questa)

1997 (2 June). Golden Wedding of Queen Elizabeth and Prince Philip. T **194c** and similar horiz designs. Multicoloured. P 14.

1852	200s. Type **194c**	1·10	1·25
	a. Sheetlet. Nos. 1852/7	6·00	6·50
1853	200s. Royal coat of arms	1·10	1·25
1854	200s. Queen Elizabeth and Prince Philip at reception	1·10	1·25
1855	200s. Queen Elizabeth and Prince Philip on royal visit	1·10	1·25
1856	200s. Buckingham Palace	1·10	1·25
1857	200s. Prince Philip in military uniform	1·10	1·25
1852/7	Set of 6	6·00	6·50

MS1858 100×70 mm. 2000s. Princess Elizabeth in wedding dress .... 3·25 3·50

Nos. 1852/7 were printed together, *se-tenant*, in sheetlets of 6.

194d Chinese Post Boat

(Des J. Iskowitz. Litho Questa)

1997 (2 June). Pacific '97 International Stamp Exhibition, San Francisco. Death Centenary of Heinrich von Stephan (founder of the U.P.U.). T **194d** and similar horiz designs. P 14.

1859	800s. deep blue	1·10	1·25
	a. Sheetlet. Nos. 1859/61	3·00	3·25
1860	800s. chestnut	1·10	1·25
1861	800s. blue-green	1·10	1·25
1859/61	Set of 3	3·00	3·25

MS1862 82×119 mm. 2500s. dull blue and grey-blue. 3·25 3·75
Designs:—No. 1860 Von Stephan and Mercury; No. 1861, Russian post cart; No. **MS**1862 Von Stephan and French postman on stilts.
Nos. 1859/61 were printed together, *se-tenant*, in sheets of 3 with enlarged right-hand margin.

195 Men's Slalom

196a Fritz Walter (Germany)

196 Main Building, Makerere University

(Litho Questa)

1997 (23 June). Winter Olympic Games, Nagano, Japan (1998). T **195** and similar multicoloured designs. P 14.

1863	350s. Type **195**	50	35
1864	450s. Two-man bobsled	60	45
1865	500s. Ski-jumping (horiz)	70	75
	a. Sheetlet. Nos. 1865/70	3·75	4·00
1866	500s. Giant slalom (horiz)	70	75
1867	500s. Cross-country skiing (horiz)	70	75
1868	500s. Ice hockey (horiz)	70	75
1869	500s. Pairs figure skating (man) (horiz)	70	75
1870	500s. Pairs figure skating (woman) (horiz)	70	75
1871	800s. Women's slalom (horiz)	1·10	1·25
1872	2000s. Men's speed skating (horiz)	2·25	3·00
1863/72	Set of 10	7·75	8·50

MS1873 Two sheets, each 103×72 mm. (a) 2500s. Downhill skiing (horiz). (b) 2500s. Women's figure skating (horiz) Set of 2 sheets 6·50 7·50
Nos. 1865/70 were printed together, *se-tenant*, in sheetlets of 6 with the backgrounds forming a composite design.

(Litho Questa)

1997 (31 July). 75th Anniv of Makerere University. T **196** and similar multicoloured designs. P 14×13½ (horiz) or 13½×14 (vert).

1874	150s. Type **196**	40	20
1875	450s. East African School of Librarianship building (vert)	80	90
1876	500s. Buyana Stock Farm, Makerere University	90	1·00
1877	550s. Ceramic dish from School of Architecture and Fine Arts	1·00	3·25
1874/7	Set of 4	2·75	3·25

1997 (3 Oct). World Cup Football Championship, France (1998). T **196a** and similar multicoloured (except Nos. 1878, 1880, 1883 and 1886) designs. P 13½×14 (vert) or 14×13½ (horiz).

1878	200s. Type **196a** (agate)	50	50
	a. Sheetlet. Nos. 1878 and 1896/1900	3·50	4·00
1879	250s. Paulo Rossi (horiz)	50	50
	a. Sheetlet. Nos. 1879/87	4·00	4·00
1880	250s. Mario Kempes (black) (horiz)	50	50
1881	250s. Gerd Muller (horiz)	50	50
1882	250s. Grzegorz Lato (horiz)	50	50
1883	250s. Joseph Gaetjens (black) (horiz)	50	50
1884	250s. Eusebio Ferreica da Silva (horiz)	50	50
1885	250s. Salvatore Schillaci (horiz)	50	50
1886	250s. Leonidas da Silva (black) (horiz)	50	50
1887	250s. Gary Lineker (horiz)	50	50
1888	250s. Argentine and West German player chasing ball (horiz)	50	50
	a. Sheetlet. Nos. 1888/95 and central label	3·50	3·50
1889	250s. Azteca Stadium (horiz)	50	50
1890	250s. Maradona holding World Cup (horiz)	50	50
1891	250s. Argentine and West German players with goalkeeper (horiz)	50	50
1892	250s. West German player tackling Argentine player (horiz)	50	50
1893	250s. Ball in back of net (horiz)	50	50
1894	250s. Argentine team (horiz)	50	50
1895	250s. Players competing to head ball (horiz)	50	50
1896	300s. Daniel Pasarella, Argentina	55	55
1897	450s. Dino Zoff, Italy	70	70
1898	500s. Bobby Moore, England	80	80
1899	550s. Franz Beckenbauer, West Germany	85	90
1900	600s. Diego Maradona, Argentina	90	1·10
1878/1900	Set of 23	11·00	11·50

MS1901 Two sheets. (a) 102×127 mm. 2000s. Celebrating West German players, 1990 (horiz). (b) 127×102 mm. 2000s. Bobby Moore, 1966 (horiz) Set of 2 sheets 5·50 7·50
Nos. 1878 with 1896/1900, 1879/87 and 1888/95 were each printed together in sheets of 6 (Nos. 1878 with 1896/1900), 9 (Nos. 1879/87) or 8 stamps and 1 central label (Nos. 1888/95) (depicts 1986 World Cup final between Argentina and West Germany).
No. 1883 is inscribed "ADEMIR" in error.

197 Mahatma Gandhi

198 "Cupid and Dolphin" (Andrea del Verrocchio)

(Des J. Iskowitz. Litho Questa)

1997 (5 Oct). 50th Death Anniv of Mahatma Gandhi (1998) (1st issue). T **197** and similar vert designs showing different portraits. P 14.

1902	600s. reddish brown and black	2·50	2·00
1903	700s. reddish brown and black	2·50	2·00

MS1904 73×103 mm. 1000s. multicoloured 5·50 4·50
See also Nos. 2021/2.

(Litho B.D.T.)

1997 (1 Dec). Christmas. Paintings and Sculptures. T **198** and similar multicoloured designs. P 14.

1905	200s. Type **198**	50	20
1906	300s. "The Fall of the Rebel Angels" (Pieter Brueghel the Elder)	70	30
1907	400s. "The Immaculate Conception" (Bartolome Murillo)	85	50
1908	500s. "Music-making Angel" (Rosso Fiorentino)	90	80
1909	600s. "Cupid and Psyche" (Adolphe-William Bouguereau)	1·00	1·25
1910	700s. "Cupid and Psyche" (Antonio Canova)	1·25	1·75
1905/10	Set of 6	4·75	4·25

MS1911 Two sheets, each 105×96 mm. (a) 2500s. Mary and Angels (detail, "The Assumption of the Virgin") (El Greco) (horiz). (b) 2500s. Angel holding baby (detail, "The Assumption of the Virgin") (El Greco) (horiz) Set of 2 sheets 6·00 8·00

199 Diana, Princess of Wales

200 Tiger

(Des Deb Hoeffner. Litho Questa)

1997 (8 Dec). Diana, Princess of Wales Commemoration. P 14.
1912	**199**	600s. multicoloured	1·25	1·40
		a. Sheetlet. No. 1912×6	6·50	

No. 1912 were printed in sheetlets of 6 stamps with an enlarged illustrated right-hand margin.

(Litho Cartor)

1998 (16 Jan). Chinese New Year ("Year of the Tiger"). T **200** and similar horiz designs. Multicoloured. P 13½.
1913	350s. Type **200**	75	75
	a. Sheetlet. Nos. 1913/16	2·75	2·75
1914	350s. Tiger leaping	75	75
1915	350s. Tiger resting	75	75
1916	350s. Tiger yawning	75	75
1913/16	Set of 4	2·75	2·75
MS1917	106×76 mm. 1500s. Tiger	2·25	2·50

Nos. 1913/16 were printed together, se-tenant, in sheetlets of 4.

201 Mountain Gorilla

202 Namugongo Martyrs Shrine, Kampala

(Litho Questa)

1998 (18 Jan). 18th Anniv of Pan African Postal Union. P 14.
1918	**201**	300s. +150s. multicoloured	2·50	3·00

(Des M. Friedman. Litho Questa)

1998 (6 Feb). Tourist Attractions. T **202** and similar multicoloured designs. P 14.
1919	300s. Type **202**	40	30
1920	400s. Kasubi Tombs, Kampala (horiz)	60	40
1921	500s. Tourist launch in Kazinga Channel, Queen Elizabeth Park (horiz)	1·00	80
1922	600s. Elephant, Queen Elizabeth Park (horiz)	1·50	1·50
1923	700s. Bujagali Falls, River Nile at Jinja (horiz)	1·50	2·00
1919/23	Set of 5	4·50	4·50

203 Mother Teresa, 1928

204 Child in Wheelchair

(Des Zina Saunders. Litho B.D.T.)

1998 (9 Feb). Mother Teresa Commemoration. T **203** and similar multicoloured designs. P 14.
1924	300s. Type **203**	95	80
	a. Sheetlet. Nos. 1924/31	7·00	5·75

1925	300s. Holding child (56×42 mm)	95	80
1926	300s. Mother Teresa at United Nations, 1975 (56×42 mm)	95	80
1927	300s. Facing left	95	80
1928	300s. Full face portrait	95	80
1929	300s. With children (56×42 mm)	95	80
1930	300s. Mother Teresa rescuing child (56×42 mm)	95	80
1931	300s. Smiling	95	80
1924/31	Set of 8	7·00	5·75
MS1932	95×81 mm. 2000s. Mother Teresa with Diana, Princess of Wales (50×37 mm)	7·00	6·00

Nos. 1924/31 were printed together, se-tenant, in sheetlets of 8.

(Des R. Sempagala-Mpagi. Litho Questa)

1998 (6 Mar). 30th Anniv of U.N.I.C.E.F. T **204** and similar vert designs. Multicoloured. P 13½×14.
1933	300s. Type **204**	80	30
1934	400s. Child receiving oral vaccination against polio	90	40
1935	600s. Children outside toilet	1·75	1·75
1936	700s. Children in class	1·90	2·25
1933/6	Set of 4	4·75	4·25

205 Pteranodon

206 Rita Dove

(Des G. Bibby. Litho Questa)

1998 (24 Mar). Prehistoric Animals. T **205** and similar multicoloured designs. P 14.
1937	300s. Type **205**	55	30
1938	400s. Diplodocus	65	45
1939	500s. Lambeosaurus	80	60
1940	600s. Centrosaurus	85	95
1941	600s. Cetiosaurus (vert)	1·50	1·50
	a. Sheetlet. Nos. 1941/6	8·00	8·00
1942	600s. Brontosaurus (vert)	1·50	1·50
1943	600s. Brachiosaurus (vert)	1·50	1·50
1944	600s. Deinonychus (vert)	1·50	1·50
1945	600s. Dimetrodon (vert)	1·50	1·50
1946	600s. Megalosaurus (vert)	1·50	1·50
1947	700s. Parasaurolophus	1·50	1·75
1937/47	Set of 11	12·00	11·50
MS1948	Two sheets, each 73×103 mm. (a) 2500s. Tyrannosaurus rex (42×56 mm). (b) 2500s. Iguanodon (42×56 mm) Set of 2 sheets	9·50	11·00

Nos. 1941/6 were printed together, se-tenant, in sheetlets of 6 with the backgrounds forming a composite design.

(Des G. Aagaard. Litho Questa)

1998 (6 Apr). U.N.E.S.C.O. World Literacy Campaign. 20th century Afro-American Writers. T **206** and similar vert designs. Multicoloured. P 14.
1949	300s. Type **206**	1·10	1·10
	a. Sheetlet. Nos. 1949/54	6·00	6·00
1950	300s. Mari Evans	1·10	1·10
1951	300s. Sterling A. Brown	1·10	1·10
1952	300s. June Jordan	1·10	1·10
1953	300s. Stephen Henderson	1·10	1·10
1954	300s. Zora Neale Hurston	1·10	1·10
1949/54	Set of 6	6·00	6·00

Nos. 1949/54 were printed together, se-tenant, in sheetlets of 6.

207 Mickey Mouse and Monster

(208)

(Litho Questa)

1998 (4 May). 70th Birthday of Mickey Mouse. T **207** and similar multicoloured designs showing scenes from cartoon film Runaway Brain. P 14×13½.
1955	400s. Type **207**	90	90

	a. Sheetlet. Nos. 1955/63	7·25	7·25
1956	400s. Mickey and Pluto with newspaper	90	90
1957	400s. Mickey and Pluto in front of television.	90	90
1958	400s. Mickey and Minnie fleeing	90	90
1959	400s. Mickey on television screen	90	90
1960	400s. Monster and hostage Minnie Mouse clinging to skyscraper	90	90
1961	400s. Mickey Mouse throwing lasso	90	90
1962	400s. Mickey circling Monster on lasso	90	90
1963	400s. Mickey and Minnie on rope	90	90
1955/63 *Set of 9*		7·25	7·25

MS1964 Two sheets, each 127×102 mm. (a) 3000s. Mickey and Minnie hugging on roof. P 14×13½. (b) 3000s. Mickey and Minnie on liferaft (*vert*). P 13½×14 *Set of 2 sheets* .... 11·00 11·00

Nos. 1955/63 were printed together, *se-tenant*, in sheetlets of 9.

1998 (13 May). Israel 98 International Stamp Exhibition, Tel-Aviv. Nos. **MS**1699/1700 optd with T **208** and each further optd ISRAEL 98 – WORLD STAMP EXHIBITION TEL AVIV 13–21 MAY 1998 on margin.

MS1965 114×95 mm. 300s. Type **180**; 500s. Jerusalem Theatre; 1000s. Israel Museum .... 3·25 3·25
MS1966 104×74 mm. 2000s. Grotto of the Nativity...... 3·25 3·25

209 *Santa Maria* (Columbus)

(Des L. Schwinger. Litho Cartor)

1998 (2 June). Ships of the World. T **209** and similar multicoloured designs. P 13×13½.

1967	1000s. Type **209**	1·60	1·75
	a. Sheetlet. Nos. 1967/9	4·25	4·75
1968	1000s. *Mayflower* (Pilgrim Fathers)	1·60	1·75
1969	1000s. Barque	1·60	1·75
1970	1000s. Fishing schooner	1·60	1·75
	a. Sheetlet. Nos. 1970/2	4·25	4·75
1971	1000s. Chesapeake oyster boat	1·60	1·75
1972	1000s. Java Sea schooner	1·60	1·75
1967/72 *Set of 6*		8·50	9·50

MS1973 Two sheets, each 100×70 mm. (a) 3000s. Thames barge (27×41 *mm*); (b) 3000s. Felucca (41×27 *mm*). P 13½ *Set of 2 sheets* .... 8·00 8·50

Nos. 1967/9 and 1970/2 were each printed together, *se-tenant*, in sheetlets of 3 with enlarged illustrated left-hand margins.

210 Grumman F4F Wildcat (U.S.A.)   **211** *Onosma* sp.

(Des B. Regal. Litho Questa)

1998 (24 July). Aircraft. T **210** and similar horiz designs. Multicoloured. P 14.

1974	500s. Type **210**	1·50	1·25
	a. Sheetlet. Nos. 1974/9	8·00	6·75
1975	500s. Mitsubishi A6M Zero-Sen (Japan)	1·50	1·25
1976	500s. Supermarine Seafire ("Spitfire") (Great Britain)	1·50	1·25
1977	500s. Hawker Siddeley Harrier (Great Britain)	1·50	1·25
1978	500s. S3A Viking (U.S.A.)	1·50	1·25
1979	500s. Corsair (U.S.A.)	1·50	1·25
1980	600s. Dornier Do-X (flying boat) (1929)	1·50	1·25
	a. Sheetlet. Nos. 1980/5	8·00	6·75
1981	600s. German Zucker mail rocket (1930)	1·50	1·25
1982	600s. North American X-15 rocket plane (1959)	1·50	1·25
1983	600s. Goddard's rocket (1930s)	1·50	1·25
1984	600s. Wright Brothers' *Flyer I* (1903)	1·50	1·25
1985	600s. 160R Sikorsky (first helicopter) (1939)	1·50	1·25
1974/85 *Set of 12*		16·00	13·50

MS1986 Two sheets. (a) 85×110 mm. 2500s. P-40 Tomahawk (U.S.A.) (1940). (b) 110×85 mm. 2500s. SH-346 Seabat recovery helicopter (U.S.A.) *Set of 2 sheets* .... 8·50 8·50

Nos. 1974/9 and 1980/5 were each printed together, *se-tenant*, in sheetlets of 6, forming composite designs.

1998 (23 Sept). Flowers of the Mediterranean. T **211** and similar multicoloured designs. Litho. P 14.

1987	300s. Type **211**	65	65
	a. Sheetlet. Nos. 1987/95	5·25	5·25
1988	300s. *Rhododendron luteum*	65	65
1989	300s. *Paeonia mascula*	65	65
1990	300s. *Geranium macrorrhizum*	65	65
1991	300s. *Cyclamen graecum*	65	65
1992	300s. *Lilium rhodopaedum*	65	65
1993	300s. *Narcissus pseudonarcissus*	65	65
1994	300s. *Paeonia rhodia*	65	65
1995	300s. *Aquilegia amaliae*	65	65
1996	600s. *Paeonia peregrina* (*horiz*)	80	80
	a. Sheetlet. Nos. 1996/2004	6·50	6·50
1997	600s. *Muscari comutatum* (*horiz*)	80	80
1998	600s. *Sternbergia* sp. (*horiz*)	80	80
1999	600s. *Dianthus* sp. (*horiz*)	80	80
2000	600s. *Verbascum* sp. (*horiz*)	80	80
2001	600s. *Aubrieta gracilis* (*horiz*)	80	80
2002	600s. *Galanthus nivalis* (*horiz*)	80	80
2003	600s. *Campanula incurva* (*horiz*)	80	80
2004	600s. *Crocus sieberi* (*horiz*)	80	80
1987/2004 *Set of 18*		11·50	11·50

MS2005 Two sheets. (a) 70×100 mm. 2000s. *Paeonia parnassica*. (b) 100×70 mm. 2000s. *Pancratium maritimum Set of 2 sheets* .... 7·50 8·50

Nos. 1987/95 and 1996/2004 were each printed together, *se-tenant*, in sheetlets of 9.

212 Bohemian Waxwing   **212a** "Woman Reading"

(Litho B.D.T.)

1998 (3 Dec). Christmas. Birds. T **212** and similar multicoloured designs. P 14.

2006	300s. Type **212**	65	30
2007	400s. House Sparrow	75	40
2008	500s. Black-capped Chickadee	85	50
2009	600s. Eurasian Bullfinch	95	90
2010	700s. Painted Bunting	1·10	1·25
2011	1000s. Common Cardinal ("Northern Cardinal")	1·50	2·50
2006/11 *Set of 6*		5·25	5·25

MS2012 Two sheets, each 70×97 mm. (a) 2500s. Winter Wren (*vert*). (b) 2500s. Red-winged Blackbird (*vert*) *Set of 2 sheets* .... 8·50 8·50

No. **MS**2012a is inscribed "Winter Wren" in error.

(Des Diana Catharines. Litho Questa)

1998 (28 Dec). 25th Death Anniv of Pablo Picasso (painter). T **212a** and similar multicoloured designs. P 14½.

2013	500s. Type **212a**	1·00	75
2014	600s. "Portrait of Dora Maar"	1·40	1·25
2015	700s. "Les Demoiselles d'Avignon" (*horiz*)	1·60	1·75
2013/15 *Set of 3*		3·50	3·25

MS2016 127×101 mm. 2500s. "Night Fishing at Antibes" .... 3·50 3·50

No. 2015 is inscribed "Des Moiselles D'Avignon" in error.

212b Cub Scouts greeting President Eisenhower, 1956   **212c** Gandhi as a Young Man

(Des J. Iskowitz. Litho Questa)

1998 (28 Dec). 19th World Scout Jamboree, Chile. T **212b** and similar multicoloured (except No. **MS2020**) designs. P 14.

2017	700s. Type **212b**		85	95
	a. Sheetlet. Nos. 2017/19		2·25	2·50
2018	700s. Scout with "Uncle Dan" Beard, 1940		85	95
2019	700s. Vice-President Hubert Humphrey as Scout leader, 1934		85	95
2017/19 *Set of 3*			2·25	2·50
MS2020 70×100 mm. 2000s. Scout with pet beaver (*vert*) (dull pur, bluish grey and dp reddish brn)			3·00	3·25

Nos. 2017/19 were printed together, *se-tenant*, in sheetlets of 3 with enlarged illustrated margins at top and right.

(Des J. Iskowitz. Litho Questa)

1998 (28 Dec). 50th Death Anniv of Mahatma Gandhi (2nd issue). T **212c** and similar design. P 14.

2021	600s. multicoloured		4·00	3·50
	a. Sheetlet of 4		14·00	12·00
MS2022 98×58 mm. 2500s. orange-brown, dull mauve and black			8·00	7·50

Designs: Horiz—2500s. Gandhi in Bombay law office. No. 2021 was printed in sheetlets of 4 with enlarged illustrated margins at top and left.

213 Diana, Princess of Wales

214 Rabbit

(Litho Questa)

1998 (28 Dec). First Death Anniv of Diana, Princess of Wales. P 14½×14.

2023	**213** 700s. multicoloured		1·40	1·60
	a. Sheetlet of 6		7·50	

No. 2023 was printed in sheetlets of 6 with an enlarged illustrated right-hand margin.

(Des Wong Kang. Litho Questa)

1999 (4 Jan). Chinese New Year ("Year of the Rabbit"). T **214** and similar horiz designs. Multicoloured. P 14.

2024	350s. White rabbit		75	80
	a. Sheetlet. Nos. 2024/7		2·75	3·00
2025	350s. Rabbit with carrot		75	80
2026	350s. Brown and white rabbit		75	80
2027	350s. Type **214**		75	80
2024/7 *Set of 4*			2·75	3·00
MS2028 106×76 mm. 1500s. Rabbit			2·75	3·25

Nos. 2024/7 were printed together, *se-tenant*, in sheetlets of 4.

215 Post Office Emblem and Slogan

216 Iru Hairstyle

(Litho Questa)

1999 (18 Jan). Uganda Post Limited Commemoration. P 14.

2029	**215** 300s. multicoloured		1·50	65

(Litho B.D.T.)

1999 (1 Feb). Hairstyles. T **216** and similar vert designs. Multicoloured. P 14.

2030	300s. Type **216**		80	30
2031	500s. Enshunju hairstyle		1·10	75
2032	550s. Elemungole hairstyle		1·25	1·25
2033	600s. Lango hairstyle		1·25	1·50
2034	700s. Ekikuura hairstyle		1·40	1·75
2030/4 *Set of 5*			5·25	5·00

217 Blue Marlin

1999 (13 Mar). International Year of the Ocean. T **217** and similar horiz designs. Multicoloured. P 14.

2035	500s. Type **217**		95	85
	a. Sheetlet. Nos. 2035/43		7·50	7·00
2036	500s. Arctic Tern		95	85
2037	500s. Common Dolphin		95	85
2038	500s. Blacktip Shark		95	85
2039	500s. Manta Ray		95	85
2040	500s. Blackedge Moray		95	85
2041	500s. Loggerhead Turtle		95	85
2042	500s. Sail-finned Tang		95	85
2043	500s. Two-spotted Octopus		95	85
2044	500s. Atlantic Wolffish		95	85
	a. Sheetlet of 4. Nos. 2044/7		3·50	
2045	500s. Equal Sea Star		95	85
2046	500s. Purple Sea Urchin		95	85
2047	500s. Mountain Crab		95	85
2035/47 *Set of 13*			11·00	10·00
MS2048 Two sheets, each 110×85 mm. (a) 500s. Sea Nettle Jellyfish. (b) 2500s. *Decatopecten striatus* (scallop) *Set of 2 sheets*			7·50	8·00

Nos. 2035/43 and Nos. 2044/7 were each printed together, *se-tenant*, in sheetlets of 9 (with the backgrounds forming a composite design) or 4.

No. 2036 is inscribed "ARTIC TERN" in error.

218 Cows feeding (income generation)

219 L'Hoest's Monkey

(Litho Cartor)

1999 (19 July). International Year of the Elderly. T **218** and similar horiz designs. Multicoloured. P 13×13½.

2049	300s. Type **218**		80	30
2050	500s. Elderly man reading with child		1·25	75
2051	600s. Playing board game		1·40	1·75
2052	700s. Food distribution		1·50	2·25
2049/52 *Set of 4*			4·50	4·50

1999 (19 Nov). Primates. T **219** and similar multicoloured designs. Litho. P 13½×14.

2053	300s. Type **219**		80	30
2054	400s. Diademed Monkey ("Sykes/Blue Monkey")		90	40
2055	500s. Patas Monkey		1·10	70
2056	600s. Red-tailed Monkey		1·25	1·40
2057	700s. Eastern Black and White Colobus		1·40	1·75
2058	1000s. Mountain Gorilla		1·75	3·00
2053/8 *Set of 6*			6·50	6·75
MS2059 73×54 mm. 2500s. Olive Baboon (35×26 *mm*). P 13½			5·00	5·50

219a "Dragon flying over Mount Fuji" (detail)

219b Duchess of York

(Des R. Sauber. Litho Questa)

1999 (24 Nov). 150th Death Anniv of Katsushika Hokusai (Japanese artist). T **219a** and similar vert designs. Multicoloured. P 13½×14.

2060	700s. Type **219a**	1·10	1·10
	a. Sheetlet. Nos. 2060/5	6·00	6·00
2061	700s. "Famous Poses from the Kabuki Theatre" (one woman)	1·10	1·10
2062	700s. "Kitsune No Yomeiri"	1·10	1·10
2063	700s. "Dragon flying over Mount Fuji" (complete picture)	1·10	1·10
2064	700s. "Famous Poses from the Kabuki Theatre" (man and woman)	1·10	1·10
2065	700s. "Girl holding Cloth"	1·10	1·10
2060/5	Set of 6	6·00	6·00
MS2066	100×70 mm. 3000s. "Japanese Spaniel"	4·75	5·00

Nos. 2060/5 were printed together, *se-tenant*, in sheetlets of 6.
No. 2065 is inscribed "GIRL HOLDING CLOTHE" in error.

(Litho Questa)

1999 (24 Nov). "Queen Elizabeth the Queen Mother's Century". T **219b** and similar vert designs. P 14.

2067	1200s. multicoloured	2·50	2·50
	a. Sheetlet. Nos. 2067/70	9·00	9·00
2068	1200s. black and gold	2·50	2·50
2069	1200s. black and gold	2·50	2·50
2070	1200s. multicoloured	2·50	2·50
2067/70	Set of 4	9·00	9·00
MS2071	152×155 mm. 3000s. multicoloured. P 13½×14	6·50	6·50

Designs: (As Type **219b**)— No. 2068, Wedding of Duke and Duchess of York; 1923 No. 2069, Formal portrait of Queen Mother; No. 2070, Queen Mother at evening reception. (37×50 mm)—No. **MS**2071 Queen Mother visiting Cambridge, 1961.

Nos. 2067/70 were printed together, *se-tenant*, as a sheetlet of 4 stamps and a central label with inscribed and embossed margins.
No. **MS**2071 also shows the Royal Arms embossed in gold.

220 Saturn V Rocket Launch

221 Penduline Tit

(Des G. Capasso. Litho Questa)

1999 (24 Nov). 30th Anniv of First Manned Landing on Moon. T **220** and similar vert designs. Multicoloured. P 14×13½.

2072	600s. Type **220**	1·40	1·40
	a. Sheetlet. Nos. 2072/7	7·50	7·50
2073	600s. Command and service module *Columbia*	1·40	1·40
2074	600s. Edwin E. Aldrin descending ladder	1·40	1·40
2075	600s. Saturn V rocket on launch pad	1·40	1·40
2076	600s. Lunar module *Eagle*	1·40	1·40
2077	600s. Edwin E. Aldrin on Moon's surface	1·40	1·40
2078	700s. Mercury mission "Freedom 7", 1961	1·40	1·40
	a. Sheetlet. Nos. 2078/83	7·50	7·50
2079	700s. "Gemini 4", 1965	1·40	1·40
2080	700s. "Apollo 11" command and service module *Columbia*	1·40	1·40
2081	700s. "Vostok 1", 1961	1·40	1·40
2082	700s. Saturn V rocket	1·40	1·40
2083	700s. Apollo 11 lunar module *Eagle*	1·40	1·40
2072/83	Set of 12	15·00	15·00
MS2084	Two sheets, each 76×106 mm. (a) 3000s. Edwin E. Aldrin with scientific experiment. (b) 3000s. "Apollo 11" command module re-entering Earth's atmosphere Set of 2 sheets	15·00	15·00

Nos. 2072/7 and 2078/83 were each printed together, *se-tenant*, in sheetlets of 6 with enlarged illustrated margins with the backgrounds of Nos. 2078/83 forming a composite design.

(Des T. Wood. Litho Questa)

1999 (1 Dec). Birds of Uganda. T **221** and similar vert designs. Multicoloured. P 14.

2085	300s. Type **221**	1·50	60
2086	500s. Grey-headed Kingfisher	1·75	1·40
	a. Sheetlet. Nos. 2086/93	12·00	10·00
2087	500s. Green-headed Sunbird	1·75	1·40
2088	500s. Speckled Pigeon	1·75	1·40
2089	500s. Grey Parrot	1·75	1·40

2090	500s. Barn Owl	1·75	1·40
2091	500s. South African Crowned Crane ("Grey Crowned Crane")	1·75	1·40
2092	500s. Whale-headed Stork ("Shoebill")	1·75	1·40
2093	500s. Black Heron	1·75	1·40
2094	600s. Scarlet-chested Sunbird	1·75	1·40
	a. Sheetlet. Nos. 2094/101	12·00	10·00
2095	600s. Lesser Honeyguide	1·75	1·40
2096	600s. African Palm Swift	1·75	1·40
2097	600s. Swamp Flycatcher	1·75	1·40
2098	600s. Lizard Buzzard	1·75	1·40
2099	600s. Osprey	1·75	1·40
2100	600s. Cardinal Woodpecker	1·75	1·40
2101	600s. Pearl-spotted Owlet	1·75	1·40
2102	700s. Speke's Weaver ("Fox's Weaver")	1·75	1·40
	a. Sheetlet. Nos. 2102/9	12·00	10·00
2103	700s. Chin-spot Flycatcher	1·75	1·40
2104	700s. Blue Swallow	1·75	1·40
2105	700s. Purple-breasted Sunbird	1·75	1·40
2106	700s. Comb Duck ("Knob-billed Duck")	1·75	1·40
2107	700s. Red-collared Whydah ("Widowbird")	1·75	1·40
2108	700s. Ruwenzori Turaco	1·75	1·40
2109	700s. African Cuckoo Hawk	1·75	1·40
2110	1000s. Yellow-fronted Tinkerbird	2·50	2·50
2111	1200s. Zebra Waxbill	2·75	2·75
2112	1800s. Sooty Anteater Chat	3·50	3·50
2085/112	Set of 28	45·00	38·00
MS2113	Two sheets, each 76×106 mm. (a) 3000s. Four-banded Sandgrouse. (b) 3000s. Paradise Whydah Set of 2 sheets	16·00	16·00

Nos. 2086/93, 2094/101 and 2102/9 were each printed together, *se-tenant*, in sheetlets of 8 with the backgrounds forming composite designs.

Nos. 2100/1 are inscribed "Cardinal Woopecker" or "Glaucidium periatum ", both in error.

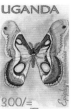

222 *Epiphora bauhiniae* (moth)

223 Postman with Women and Child

(Litho Cartor)

2000 (19 Jan). Moths. T **222** and similar multicoloured designs. P 13½.

2114	300s. Type **222**	80	30
2115	400s. *Phylloxiphia formosa* (horiz)	95	50
2116	500s. *Bunaea alcinoe*	1·25	70
2117	600s. *Euchloron megaera* (horiz)	1·40	1·25
2118	700s. *Argema mimosae*	1·50	1·60
2119	1800s. *Denephila nerii* (horiz)	3·75	6·00
2114/19	Set of 6	8·75	9·25
MS2120	75×52 mm. 3000s. *Lobobunaea angasana* (horiz)	6·50	8·00

2000 (28 Jan). 125th Anniv of Universal Postal Union. T **223** and similar vert designs. Multicoloured. Litho. P 14.

2121	600s. Type **223**	1·25	1·00
2122	700s. American mother and child reading letter by post box	1·40	1·50
2123	1200s. Mail coach	3·50	4·75
2121/3	Set of 3	5·50	6·50

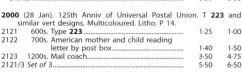

224 *Eulophia paivenna*

225 Short-tailed Admiral

(Des R. Runde. Litho Questa)

2000 (18 Feb). Orchids. T **224** and similar multicoloured designs. P 14.

2124	600s. Type **224**	1·50	1·25
	a. Sheetlet. Nos. 2124/32	12·00	10·00

2125	600s. *Ansellia gigantea*		1·50	1·25
2126	600s. *Anglaecopsis gracillima*		1·50	1·25
2127	600s. *Bonatea steudneri*		1·50	1·25
2128	600s. *Bulbophyllum falcatum*		1·50	1·25
2129	600s. *Aerangis citrata*		1·50	1·25
2130	600s. *Eulophiella Elisabethae*		1·50	1·25
2131	600s. *Aerangis rhodosticta*		1·50	1·25
2132	600s. *Angraecum scottianum*		1·50	1·25
2133	600s. *Angraecum eicheerianum*		1·50	1·25
	a. Sheetlet. Nos. 2133/41		12·00	10·00
2134	600s. *Angraecum leonis*		1·50	1·25
2135	600s. *Arpophyllum giganteum*		1·50	1·25
2136	600s. *Bulbophyllum barbigerum*		1·50	1·25
2137	600s. *Angeraelum giryamae*		1·50	1·25
2138	600s. *Angraecum ellisii*		1·50	1·25
2139	600s. *Disa uniflora*		1·50	1·25
2140	600s. *Eulophia alta*		1·50	1·25
2141	600s. *Ancistrochilius stylosa*		1·50	1·25
2142	700s. *Eulophia orthoplectra*		1·50	1·25
	a. Sheetlet. Nos. 2142/50		12·00	10·00
2143	700s. *Cirrhopetalum umbellatum*		1·50	1·25
2144	700s. *Eulophiella rolfei*		1·50	1·25
2145	700s. *Eulophia porphyroglossa*		1·50	1·25
2146	700s. *Eulophia petersii*		1·50	1·25
2147	700s. *Cyrtorchis arcuata*		1·50	1·25
2148	700s. *Eurychone rothschildiana*		1·50	1·25
2149	700s. *Eulophia quartiniana*		1·50	1·25
2150	700s. *Eulophia stenophylia* (single flower)		1·50	1·25
2151	700s. *Grammangis ellisii*		1·50	1·25
	a. Sheetlet. Nos. 2151/9		12·00	10·00
2152	700s. *Eulophia stenophylia* (several flowers)		1·50	1·25
2153	700s. *Oeoniella polystachys*		1·50	1·25
2154	700s. *Cymbidiella humblotii*		1·50	1·25
2155	700s. *Polystachya bella*		1·50	1·25
2156	700s. *Vanilla polycepis*		1·50	1·25
2157	700s. *Eulophiella roemplerana*		1·50	1·25
2158	700s. *Habenaria englerana*		1·50	1·25
2159	700s. *Ansella frallana*		1·50	1·25
2124/59 *Set of 36*			48·00	40·00

MS2160 Four sheets, each 95×65 mm. (a) 3000s. *Cymbidiella rhodochila* (*horiz*). (b) 3000s. *Calanthe corymbosa* (*horiz*). (c) 3000s. *Ancistrochilus rothschildianus* (*horiz*). (d) 3000s. *Polystachya tayloriana* (*horiz*) *Set of 4 sheets* .... 27·00 27·00

Nos. 2124/32, 2133/41, 2142/50 and 2151/9 were each printed together, *se-tenant* in sheetlets of 9 with the backgrounds forming composite designs.

(Des Jennifer Toombs. Litho Questa)

2000 (24 May). The Stamp Show 2000 International Stamp Exhibition, London. Butterflies. T **225** and similar vert designs. Multicoloured. P 14.

2161	300s. Type **225**		1·50	40
2162	400s. Guineafowl		1·50	60
2163	500s. *Charaxes anticlea*		1·50	1·25
	a. Sheetlet. Nos. 2163/70		11·00	9·00
2164	500s. *Epitola posthumus*		1·50	1·25
2165	500s. Beautiful Monarch		1·50	1·25
2166	500s. Blue-banded Nymph		1·50	1·25
2167	500s. *Euxanthe crossleyi*		1·50	1·25
2168	500s. African Map Butterfly		1·50	1·25
2169	500s. Western Blue Charaxes		1·50	1·25
2170	500s. Noble Butterfly		1·50	1·25
2171	600s. Green-veined Charaxes		1·50	1·25
	a. Sheetlet. Nos. 2171/8		11·00	9·00
2172	600s. Ansorge's Leaf Butterfly		1·50	1·25
2173	600s. Crawshay's Sapphire Blue		1·50	1·25
2174	600s. *Palla ussheri*		1·50	1·25
2175	600s. Friar		1·50	1·25
2176	600s. Blood-red Cymothoe		1·50	1·25
2177	600s. Mocker Swallowtail		1·50	1·25
2178	600s. Green Charaxes ("*Charaxes eupale*")		1·50	1·25
2179	700s. *Acraea pseudolycia*		1·50	1·25
	a. Sheetlet. Nos. 2179/86		11·00	9·00
2180	700s. *Colotis protomedia* ("Veined Yellow")		1·50	1·25
2181	700s. Buxton's Hairstreak		1·50	1·25
2182	700s. *Iolaus isomenias*		1·50	1·25
2183	700s. Veined Swallowtail		1·50	1·25
2184	700s. Fig-tree Blue		1·50	1·25
2185	700s. Scarlet Tip		1·50	1·25
2186	700s. Gaudy Commodore ("*Precis octavia*")		1·50	1·25
2187	1200s. Club-tailed Charaxes		2·50	2·50
2188	1800s. *Cymothoe egesta*		3·50	4·50
2161/88 *Set of 28*			40·00	35·00

MS2189 Two sheets, each 63×69 mm. (a) 3000s. African Monarch. (b) 3000s. Kigezi Swordtail *Set of 2 sheets* .... 14·00 14·00

Nos. 2163/70, 2171/8 and 2179/86 were each printed together, *se-tenant*, in sheetlets of 8 with the backgrounds forming composite designs.

No. 2165 is inscribed "Danasus formosa", No. 2169 "Western Blue Caraxes" and No. 2183 "*Graphium lionidas*", all in error.

225a King Philip II of France   **225b** Pope Agapitus II

(Des R. Sauber. Litho Questa)

2000 (28 June). Monarchs of the Millennium. T **225a** and similar vert designs. P 13½×14.

2190	900s. grey, purple-brown and olive-bistre		2·00	2·00
	a. Sheetlet. Nos. 2190/2		5·50	5·50
2191	900s. grey, purple-brown and olive-bistre		2·00	2·00
2192	900s. grey, purple-brown and olive-bistre		2·00	2·00
2193	900s. dull purple, purple-brown & ol-bistre		2·00	2·00
	a. Sheetlet. Nos. 2193/8		11·00	11·00
2194	900s. multicoloured		2·00	2·00
2195	900s. multicoloured		2·00	2·00
2196	900s. grey, purple-brown and olive-bistre		2·00	2·00
2197	900s. grey, purple-brown and olive-bistre		2·00	2·00
2198	900s. grey, purple-brown and olive-bistre		2·00	2·00
2190/8 *Set of 9*			16·00	16·00

MS2199 Two sheets. (a) 117×137 mm. 3000s. multicoloured. (b) 116×136 mm. 3000s. multicoloured *Set of 2 sheets* .... 8·50 10·00

Designs:—No. 2191 King Richard I of England; No. 2192, King William I of England; No. 2193, Tsar Boris III of Bulgaria; No. 2194, Emperor Charles V of Holy Roman Empire No. 2195, Emperor Pedro II of Brazil; No. 2196, Empress Elizabeth of Austria; No. 2197, Emperor Francis Joseph of Austria; No. 2198 King Frederik of Bohemia No. **MS**2199a, King Mutesa I of Buganda; No. **MS**2199b, King Cwa II of Kabaleega.

Nos. 2190/2 and 2193/8 were each printed together, *se-tenant*, in sheetlets of 3 or 6 with enlarged illustrated bottom margins.

No. 2198 is inscribed "FREDRICH" in error.

(Des R. Sauber. Litho Questa)

2000 (28 June). Popes of the Millennium. T **225b** and simialr vert designs. Multicoloured (except No. **MS**2206). P 13½×14.

2200	900s. Type **225b**		2·50	2·25
	a. Sheetlet. Nos. 2200/5		13·50	12·00
2201	900s. Alexander II		2·50	2·25
2202	900s. Anastasius IV		2·50	2·25
2203	900s. Benedict VIII		2·50	2·25
2204	900s. Benedict VII		2·50	2·25
2205	900s. Callistus		2·50	2·25
2200/5 *Set of 6*			13·50	12·00

MS2206 116×137 mm. 3000s. Celestine III, (grey, purple-brown and buff) .... 8·50 8·50

Nos. 2200/5 were printed together, *se-tenant*, in sheetlets of 6 with an enlarged illustrated top margin.

225c Bow of Merchant Ship (opening of Japan to foreign trade, 1853)

226 Education in the Millennium

(Des Dreamscape Studio. Litho Cartor)

2000 (28 June). New Millennium. People and Events of Nineteenth Century (1850–1900). T **225c** and similar multicoloured designs. P 12½.

2207	300s. Type **225c**		1·50	1·50
	a. Sheetlet. Nos. 2207/23		23·00	23·00
2208	300s. First elevator, 1854		1·50	1·50
2209	300s. Ladle of molten steel (Bessemer Process, 1854)		1·50	1·50
2210	300s. Florence Nightingale (founder of nursing, 1854)		1·50	1·50
2211	300s. Louis Pasteur (French chemist, discovered bacteriology, 1856)		1·50	1·50

2212	300s. Oil gusher (first oil well, 1859)		1·50	1·50
2213	300s. Charles Darwin (*The Origin of Species*, 1859)		1·50	1·50
2214	300s. Gregor Mendel (law of heredity, 1866)		1·50	1·50
2215	300s. Alfred Nobel (invention of dynamite, 1867)		1·50	1·50
2216	300s. Modern freighter in Canal (opening of Suez Canal, 1869)		1·50	1·50
2217	300s. Early telephone (invented 1876)		1·50	1·50
2218	300s. Light bulb (invention of electric light, 1879)		1·50	1·50
2219	300s. Clocks (World's time zones established, 1884)		1·50	1·50
2220	300s. Electric motor (invented 1888)		1·50	1·50
2221	300s. Cinema projector (first motion pictures, 1895)		1·50	1·50
2222	300s. *Monitor and Merrimack* (ironclad warships) (American Civil War, 1861–65) (59×39 *mm*)		1·50	1·50
2223	300s. Olympic Torch and Rings (revival of Games, 1896)		1·50	1·50
2207/23	*Set of 17*		23·00	23·00

Nos. 2207/23 were printed together, *se-tenant*, in sheetlets of 17 including a central label (59×39 *mm*) and inscribed left margin.

2000 (24 July). Anniversaries and Events. T **226** and similar horiz designs. Multicoloured. Litho. P 14½.

2224	300s. Type **226**		80	30
2225	500s. Controlled and open borders (6th anniv of Comesa Treaty)		1·25	60
2226	600s. Flags of member countries (50th anniv of Commonwealth)		3·00	1·75
2227	600s. Aspects of the River Nile in the Millennium		1·75	1·75
2228	700s. Non-traditional exports in the Millennium		1·75	1·75
2229	1200s. World map (50th anniv of Commonwealth)		5·00	3·50
2230	1400s. People and exports crossing border (6th anniv of Comesa Treaty)		3·50	3·75
2231	1800s. Tourism in the Millennium		4·00	5·00
2224/31	*Set of 8*		19·00	16·00

227 Kenya Railways Class A 60 Steam Locomotive

228 "The Nativity" (Drateru Oliver)

(Des R. Sauber. Litho Questa)

2000 (14 Aug). African Railway Locomotives. T **227** and similar horiz designs. Multicoloured. P 14.

2232	300s. Type **227**		85	25
2233	400s. Mozambique Railways Baldwin type		1·00	30
2234	600s. Uganda Railways Class 73 diesel locomotive		1·40	40
2235	700s. South Africa Railways Baby Garrott type		1·40	1·10
2236	700s. Uganda Railways Class 36 diesel locomotive (from back)		1·40	1·40
	a. Sheetlet. Nos. 2236/43		10·00	10·00
2237	700s. Rhodesian Railways 12th Class		1·40	1·40
2238	700s. Rhodesian Railways Garrait type		1·40	1·40
2239	700s. Uganda Railways Class 62 diesel locomotive		1·40	1·40
2240	700s. South African Railways Beyer-Garratt type		1·40	1·40
2241	700s. Sudan Railways oilburning locomotive		1·40	1·40
2242	700s. Nigerian Railways coal train		1·40	1·40
2243	700s. South Africa Railways steam locomotive		1·40	1·40
2244	700s. Uganda Railways Class 36 diesel locomotive (from front)		1·40	1·40
	a. Sheetlet. Nos. 2244/51		10·00	10·00
2245	700s. South African Railways Class 19D		1·40	1·40
2246	700s. Algeria Railways Garrett type		1·40	1·40
2247	700s. Cameroon Railways locomotive No. 194		1·40	1·40
2248	700s. South Africa Railways electric freight locomotive		1·40	1·40
2249	700s. Rhodesian Railways Class 14A		1·40	1·40
2250	700s. Egyptian Railways British-built locomotive		1·40	1·40

2251	700s. Uganda Railways Class 73 diesel locomotive		1·40	1·40
2252	1200s. Uganda Railways Class 82 diesel locomotive		2·25	2·25
2253	1400s. East Africa Railways Beyer-Garratt type		2·50	2·50
2254	1800s. Rhodesian Railways Beyer-Garratt type		3·00	3·25
2255	2000s. East African Railways Garratt type		3·50	4·00
2232/55	*Set of 24*		35·00	32·00

MS2256 Three sheets, each 106×76 mm. (a) 3500s. East Africa Railways steam locomotive (56×42 *mm*). (b) 3500s. Egyptian State Railways locomotive No. 402 (56×42 *mm*). (c) 3500s. Rhodesian Railways Alco type (56×42 *mm*) *Set of 2 sheets* ... 16·00 18·00

Nos. 2236/43 and 2244/51 were each printed together, *se-tenant*, in sheetlets of 8, each containing two horizontal strips of four with an illustration in the centre.

No. 2237 also shows part of the inscription for No. 2236 in error.

2000 (14 Dec). Christmas. Young People's Paintings. T **228** and similar multicoloured designs. Litho. P 14.

2257	300s. Type **228**		75	30
2258	400s. "Baby Jesus and Donkey" (Brenda Tumwebaze) (*horiz*)		80	35
2259	500s. "Angels" (Joseph Mukiibi)		95	45
2260	600s. "Holy Family in Stable" (Paul Serunjogi) (*horiz*)		1·10	50
2261	700s. "Holy Family with Oxon" (Edward Maswere) (*horiz*)		1·25	75
2262	1200s. "Children worshiping baby Jesus" (Ndeba Harriet) (*horiz*)		2·00	3·00
2263	1800s. "Madonna and Child with Shepherd" (Jude Kasagga)		3·00	4·50
2257/63	*Set of 7*		9·00	9·00

MS2264 Two sheets, each 85×110 mm. (a) 3000s. "King with Gift and Christmas Tree" (Nicole Kwiringira). (b) 3000s. "Adoration of the Shepherds" (Michael Tinkamanyire) *Set of 2 sheets* ... 13·00 15·00

229 Snake

(Litho Enschedé)

2001 (5 Jan). Chinese New Year ("Year of the Snake") and "Hong Kong 2001" Stamp Exhibition. T **229** and similar horiz designs showing different snakes. Multicoloured. P 14.

2265	600s. Type **229**		1·75	1·75
	a. Sheetlet. Nos. 2265/8		6·25	6·25
2266	600s. Snake coiled around man		1·75	1·75
2267	600s. Snakes showing fangs		1·75	1·75
2268	600s. Snake on branch		1·75	1·75
2265/8	*Set of 4*		6·25	6·25

MS2269 115×75 mm. 2500s. Cobra ... 10·00 10·00

Nos. 2265/8 were printed together, *se-tenant*, in sheetlets of 4.

230 Bongo

231 Holy Family

(Des P. Lubowa (No. 2270), G. Kawere (No. 2271), F. Ifee (No. 2272), J. Kasagga (No. **MS**2273a), M. Pagril (No. **MS**2273b). Litho Cartor)

2001 (5 Feb). Endangered Wildlife. T **230** and similar multicoloured designs. P 13½×13 (vert) or 13×13½ (horiz).

2270	600s. Type **230**		2·75	2·75
	a. Strip of 3. Nos. 2270/2		7·50	7·50
2271	600s. Black Rhinoceros		2·75	2·75
2272	600s. Leopard (*vert*)		2·75	2·75
2270/2	*Set of 3*		7·50	7·50

MS2273 Two sheets. (a) 110×85 mm. 3000s. Mountain Gorillas. (b) 85×110 mm. 3000s. Parrot (*vert*) *Set of 2 sheets* ... 15·00 15·00

Nos. 2270/2 are printed together, *se-tenant*, as horizontal or vertical strips of 3 in sheets of 9.

2001 (4 Apr). 2000th Birth Anniversary of Jesus Christ. T **231** and similar multicoloured designs. Litho. P 13×13½ (1200s.) or 13½×13 (others).

2274	300s. Type **231**	85	30
2275	700s. Madonna and child	1·75	1·50
2276	1200s. The Nativity (horiz)	3·00	4·00
2274/6	Set of 3	5·00	5·25

232 East African School of Library and Information Science, Makerere

233 Anemometer

2001 (23 Apr). East African Universities. T **232** and similar multicoloured designs. Litho. P 13½×13 (1800s.) or 13×13½ (others).

2277	300s. Type **232**	85	30
2278	400s. Nairobi University	1·00	35
2279	1200s. Nkrumah Hall, University of Dar-es-Salaam	2·75	3·00
2280	1800s. Makerere, Kenyatta and Open Universities (vert)	4·00	5·00
2277/80	Set of 4	7·75	7·75

2001 (28 May). 50th Anniv of World Meteorological Organization (2000). T **233** and similar multicoloured design. Litho. P 13½×13 (300s.) or 13×13½ (2000s.).

2281	300s. Type **233**	1·25	50
2282	2000s. Tropical sun recorder (horiz)	4·50	5·50

234 Working in the Fields

235 "Segawa Kikunojo and Ichikawa Danjuro as Samurai" (Kiyonobu II)

2001 (15 June). 50th Anniv of United Nations High Commissioner for Refugees. Economic Development. T **234** and similar horiz designs. Multicoloured. Litho. P 13×13½.

2283	300s. Type **234**	80	30
2284	600s. Community building project	1·40	70
2285	1200s. Carpentry class	2·50	2·75
2286	1800s. New water supply	3·50	4·75
2283/6	Set of 4	7·50	7·75

(Litho Walsall)

2001 (1 Aug). Philanippon '01 International Stamp Exhibition, Tokyo. Japanese Woodcuts. T **235** and similar vert designs. Multicoloured. P 14.

2287	600s. Type **235**	50	50
2288	700s. "Tchimura Kamezo as Warrior" (Kiyohiro)	1·60	65
2289	1000s. "Ichikawa Danjuro as Shirobei Tadanobu" (Kiyomitsu)	2·00	1·60
2290	1200s. "Actor Arashi Sangoro" (Shunsho)	2·25	2·25
2291	1400s. "Matsumoto Koshiro IV as Juro Sukenari" (Kiyonaga)	2·50	2·75
2292	2000s. "Pheasant on Pine Branch" (Kiyomasu II)	3·50	5·00
2287/92	Set of 6	12·00	11·50
MS2293	68×105 mm. 3500s. "Tale of Ise" (Eishi)	6·00	6·50

236 Blue and Cream Shorthair

(Des T. Wood. Litho Questa)

2001 (23 Aug). Cats and Dogs. T **236** and similar multicoloured designs. P 14.

2294	400s. Tabby British Shorthair (vert)	1·75	50
2295	600s. Type **236**	2·25	2·25
	a. Sheetlet. Nos. 2295/300	12·00	12·00
2296	600s. Manx	2·25	2·25
2297	600s. Angora	2·25	2·25
2298	600s. Red and White British Shorthair	2·25	2·25
2299	600s. Turkish Cat	2·25	2·25
2300	600s. Egyptian Mau	2·25	2·25
2301	700s. Rottweiler	2·25	2·25
	a. Sheetlet. Nos. 2301/6	12·00	12·00
2302	700s. Flat-coated Retriever	2·25	2·25
2303	700s. Samoyed	2·25	2·25
2304	700s. Poodle	2·25	2·25
2305	700s. Maltese	2·25	2·25
2306	700s. Irish Terrier	2·25	2·25
2307	900s. Turkish Cat (vert)	2·25	2·25
2308	1100s. German Shepherd (vert)	2·25	2·25
2309	1200s. Irish Setter (vert)	2·25	2·25
2310	1300s. English Sheepdog	2·25	2·25
	a. Sheetlet. Nos. 2310/15	12·00	12·00
2311	1300s. German Shepherd	2·25	2·25
2312	1300s. Great Dane	2·25	2·25
2313	1300s. Boston Terrier	2·25	2·25
2314	1300s. Bull Terrier	2·25	2·25
2315	1300s. Australian Terrier	2·25	2·25
2316	1400s. Red Tabby Shorthair	2·25	2·25
	a. Sheetlet. Nos. 2316/21	12·00	12·00
2317	1400s. Japanese Bobtail	2·25	2·25
2318	1400s. Siamese	2·25	2·25
2319	1400s. Tabby Persian	2·25	2·25
2320	1400s. Black and White Persian	2·25	2·25
2321	1400s. Russian Blue	2·25	2·25
2294/321	Set of 28	55·00	55·00
MS2322	Four sheets. (a) 106×76 mm. 3500s. American Calico Shorthair (vert). (b) 76×106 mm. 3500s. Blue-eyed British Shorthair (vert). (c) 106×76 mm. 3500s. Bloodhound (vert). (d) 106×76 mm. 3500s. Pointer Set of 4 sheets	32·00	32·00

Nos. 2295/300 (cats), 2301/6 (dogs), 2310/15 (dogs) and 2316/21 (cats) were each printed together, se-tenant, in sheetlets of 6 with inscribed top margins with that on Nos. 2310/15 including the "APS STAMPSHOW, Chicago" logos.

236a Queen Victoria

236b "Storm, Belle-Ile Coast"

(Des H. Friedman. Litho Questa)

2001 (27 Aug). Death Centenary of Queen Victoria. T **236a** and similar vert designs. Multicoloured. P 14.

2323	1000s. Type **236a**	2·25	2·25
	a. Sheetlet. Nos. 2323/8	12·00	12·00
2324	1000s. Queen Victoria in white bonnet	2·25	2·25
2325	1000s. Wearing feathered hat	2·25	2·25
2326	1000s. In evening dress	2·25	2·25
2327	1000s. Queen Victoria wearing choker with pendant	2·25	2·25
2328	1000s. In black dress, looking down	2·25	2·25
2323/8	Set of 6	12·00	12·00
MS2329	107×83 mm. 3500s. Queen Victoria in furred hat	6·50	7·50

Nos. 2323/8 were printed together, se-tenant, in sheetlets of 6, with an enlarged illustrated left margin.

(Litho Questa)

2001 (27 Aug). 75th Death Anniv of Claude-Oscar Monet (French painter). T **236b** and similar multicoloured designs. P 13½.

2330	1200s. Type **236b**	2·50	2·50
	a. Sheetlet. Nos. 2330/3	9·00	9·00
2331	1200s. "Manneporte, Etretat"	2·50	2·50
2332	1200s. "Rocks at Low Tide, Pourville"	2·50	2·50
2333	1200s. "Wild Sea"	2·50	2·50
2330/3	Set of 4	9·00	9·00
MS2334	137×109 mm. 3500s. "Sunflowers" (vert)	6·00	7·00

Nos. 2330/3 were printed together, se-tenant, in sheetlets of 4 with an enlarged top margin showing a photograph of the artist.

236c Princess Elizabeth as a Baby, 1926

237 "Woman combing her Hair" (Toulouse-Lautrec)

(Des H. Friedman. Litho Questa)

2001 (27 Aug). 75th Birthday of Queen Elizabeth II. T **236c** and similar vert designs. Multicoloured. P 14.

2335	1000s. Type **236c**	2·25	2·25
	a. Sheetlet. Nos. 2335/40	12·00	12·00
2336	1000s. Princess Elizabeth aged 5, 1931	2·25	2·25
2337	1000s. Princess Elizabeth in 1939	2·25	2·25
2338	1000s. Queen Elizabeth in 1955	2·25	2·25
2339	1000s. Queen Elizabeth wearing tiara, 1963	2·25	2·25
2340	1000s. Queen Elizabeth in 1999	2·25	2·25
2335/40	Set of 6	12·00	12·00

MS2341 82×106 mm. 3500s. Queen Elizabeth in uniform for Trooping the Colour .... 6·00 7·00

Nos. 2335/40 were printed together, *se-tenant*, in sheetlets of 6, with an enlarged illustrated left margin.

(Litho Questa)

2001 (27 Aug). Death Centenary of Henri de Toulouse-Lautrec (French painter). T **237** and similar vert designs. Multicoloured. P 13½×14.

2342	1500s. Type **237**	4·00	4·00
	a. Sheetlet. Nos. 2342/4	11·00	11·00
2343	1500s. "The Toilette"	4·00	4·00
2344	1500s. "English Girl at the Star Inn, Le Havre"	4·00	4·00
2342/4	Set of 3	11·00	11·00

MS2345 74×109 mm. 3500s. "Aristide Bruant" .... 7·00 8·00

Nos. 2342/4 were printed together, *se-tenant*, in sheetlets of 3, with an illustrated top margin.

237a H.M.S. *Tribune* (submarine)

238 Carrying Ebola Victim on Stretcher

(Des G. Bibby. Litho Questa)

2001 (27 Aug). Centenary of Royal Navy Submarine Service. T **237a** and similar multicoloured designs. P 14.

2346	1000s. Type **237a**	4·00	3·25
2347	1000s. H.M.S. *Royal Oak* (battleship, launched 1914)	4·00	3·25
2348	1000s. H.M.S. *Invincible* (aircraft carrier)	4·00	3·25
2349	1000s. H.M.S. *Dreadnought* (nuclear submarine)	4·00	3·25
2350	1000s. H.M.S. *Ark Royal* (aircraft carrier, launched 1950)	4·00	3·25
2351	1000s. H.M.S. *Cardiff* (destroyer)	4·00	3·25
2346/51	Set of 6	22·00	18·00

MS2352 70×57 mm. 3500s. H.M.S. *Triad* (submarine) (*horiz*) .... 11·00 11·00

Nos. 2346/51 were printed together, *se-tenant*, in sheetlets of 6, with enlarged illustrated margins.

(Litho Cartor)

2001 (16 Nov). U.N. Dialogue among Civilisations (3000s.) and International Year of Volunteers (others). T **238** and similar multicoloured designs. P 13½.

2353	300s. Type **238**	1·00	45
2354	700s. Blood donor session	1·75	80
2355	2000s. Provision of clean water	3·25	3·75
2356	3000s. Children encircling Globe (*vert*)	4·25	6·00
2353/6	Set of 4	9·25	10·00

239 *Amanita excelsa*

240 Long Drums

(Litho Cartor)

2001 (26 Nov). Fungi. T **239** and similar horiz designs. Multicoloured. P 14½.

2357	300s. Type **239**	1·00	30
2358	500s. *Coprinus cinereus*	1·50	50
2359	600s. *Scleroderma aurantium*	1·60	85
2360	700s. *Armillaria mellea*	1·75	1·40
2361	1200s. *Leopiota procera*	3·00	3·00
2362	2000s. *Flammulina velutipes*	5·00	6·00
2357/62	Set of 6	12·50	11·00

MS2363 Two sheets, each 100×70 mm. (a) 3000s. *Amanita phalloides*. (b) 3000s. *Amanita fulva* Set of 2 sheets .... 18·00 17·00

2001 (16 Dec). Christmas. Musical Instruments. T **240** and similar multicoloured designs. Litho. P 14×13½ (vert) or 13½×14 (horiz).

2364	400s. Type **240**	70	25
2365	800s. Animal horn trumpets (*horiz*)	1·25	65
2366	1000s. Bugisu clay drum	1·60	1·00
2367	1200s. Musical bows	1·75	1·75
2368	1400s. Pan pipes	1·90	2·25
2369	2000s. Two-man xylophone (*horiz*)	3·00	4·50
2364/9	Set of 6	9·25	9·25

MS2370 Two sheets. (a) 85×110 mm. 3500s. Eight-stringed giant bow harp. (b) 110×85 mm. 3500s. Nativity (*horiz*) Set of 2 sheets .... 14·00 15·00

241 Namugongo Shrine, Uganda

242 White Horse

(Litho Cartor)

2002 (8 May). Historical Sites of East Africa. T **241** and similar multicoloured designs. P 14½.

2371	400s. Type **241**	65	30
2372	800s. Maruhubi Palace ruins, Zanzibar	1·25	80
2373	1200s. Kings' Burial Grounds, Mparo, Hoima	1·75	2·00
2374	1400s. Old Law Courts, Mombasa (*vert*)	2·00	2·50
2371/4	Set of 4	5·00	5·00

2002 (8 May). Chinese New Year ("Year of the Horse"). T **242** and similar vert designs. Multicoloured. Litho. P 13½×14½.

2375	1200s. Type **242**	2·25	2·25
	a. Sheetlet. Nos. 2375/7	6·00	6·00
2376	1200s. Piebald horse	2·25	2·25
2377	1200s. Dun horse	2·25	2·25
2375/7	Set of 3	6·00	6·00

MS2378 75×105 mm. 3000s. Rearing horse .... 5·50 6·00

Nos. 2375/7 were printed together, *se-tenant*, in sheetlets of three.

242a Young Queen Elizabeth

242b US Flag as Statue of Liberty with Uganda Flag

(Des D. Miller. Litho Questa)

2002 (17 June). Golden Jubilee. T **242a** and similar square designs. Multicoloured. P 14½.

2379	1500s. Type **242a**		3·00	3·00
	a. Sheetlet. Nos. 2379/82		11·00	11·00
2380	1500s. Queen Elizabeth in striped hat		3·00	3·00
2381	1500s. Queen Elizabeth in evening dress		3·00	3·00
2382	1500s. As No. 2379, but Queen Elizabeth looking to her right		3·00	3·00
2379/82	Set of 4		11·00	11·00
MS2383	76×108 mm. 3500s. Queen Elizabeth wearing straw hat . P 14		6·50	7·50

Nos. 2379/82 were printed together, se-tenant, in sheetlets of four, with an illustrated left margin.

2002 (1 July). "United We Stand". Support for Victims of 11 September 2001 Terrorist Attacks. Litho. P 13½×13.

2384	**242b** 1500s. multicoloured		2·00	2·50

No. 2384 was printed in sheetlets of four with an illustrated left margin.

242c Mount Tateyama, Japan

(Litho Cartor)

2002 (1 July). International Year of Mountains. T **242c** and similar horiz designs. Multicoloured. P 13½.

2385	2000s. Type **242c**		3·00	3·00
	a. Sheetlet. Nos. 2385/7		8·00	8·00
2386	2000s. Mount Nikko Semdjoda-Hara, Japan		3·00	3·00
2387	2000s. Mount Hodaka, Japan		3·00	3·00
2385/7	Set of 3		8·00	8·00
MS2388	70×55 mm. 3500s. Mount Fuji, Japan		6·00	7·00

Nos. 2385/7 were printed together, se-tenant, in sheetlets of three with enlarged left margin showing another view of Mount Fuji.

242d Scout from 1930s in Forest

(Litho Cartor)

2002 (1 July). 20th World Scout Jamboree, Thailand. T **242d** and similar multicoloured designs. P 13½.

2389	1400s. Type **242d**		2·25	2·50
	a. Sheetlet. Nos. 2389/92		8·00	9·00
2390	1400s. Scout from 1930s saluting		2·25	2·50
2391	1400s. Two scouts with packs		2·25	2·50
2392	1400s. International Scouts symbol		2·25	2·50
2389/92	Set of 4		8·00	9·00
MS2393	60×78 mm. 3500s. Lord Baden-Powell (vert)		7·50	8·50

Nos. 2389/92 were printed together, se-tenant, in sheetlets of four with enlarged top and left margins.

243 Two Women with Symbol and Makerere University

243a Cross-country Skiing

(Des F. Ifee. Litho Cartor)

2002 (8 July). 8th International Interdisciplinary Congress on Women, Kampala. T **243** and similar multicoloured design. P 13½.

2394	400s. Type **243**		1·00	30
2395	1200s. Arms of Makerere University (vert)		2·50	3·00

(Litho Cartor)

2002 (15 July). Winter Olympic Games, Salt Lake City. T **243a** and similar vert designs. P 13½.

2396	1200s. Type **243a**		2·50	2·75
2397	1200s. Ski-jumping		2·50	2·75
MS2398	82×113 mm. Nos. 2396/7		5·00	5·50

244 Termitomyces microcarpus (fungus)

245 Cetiosaurus

(Des R. Martin. Litho Walsall)

2002 (6 Nov). Flora and Fauna. T **244** and similar multicoloured designs. P 14.

2399	400s. White Rhinoceros (vert)		2·25	1·00
2400	800s. Macrotermes subhyalinus (insect) (vert)		1·50	1·00
2401	1000s. Type **244**		2·25	2·25
	a. Sheetlet. Nos. 2401/6		12·00	12·00
2402	1000s. Agaricus trisulphuratus		2·25	2·25
2403	1000s. Macrolepiota zeyheri		2·25	2·25
2404	1000s. Lentinus stupeus		2·25	2·25
2405	1000s. Lentinus sajor-caju		2·25	2·25
2406	1000s. Lentinus velutinus		2·25	2·25
2407	1000s. Nudaurelia cytherea (caterpillar)		2·25	2·25
	a. Sheetlet. Nos. 2407/12		12·00	12·00
2408	1000s. Locusta migratoria (locust)		2·25	2·25
2409	1000s. Anacridium aegyptium (grasshopper)		2·25	2·25
2410	1000s. Sternotomis bohemanni (longhorn beetle)		2·25	2·25
2411	1000s. Papilio dardanus (butterfly)		2·25	2·25
2412	1000s. Mantis polyspilota (mantid)		2·25	2·25
2413	1200s. Uganda Kob		2·25	2·25
	a. Sheetlet. Nos. 2413/18		12·00	12·00
2414	1200s. Hartebeest		2·25	2·25
2415	1200s. Topi		2·25	2·25
2416	1200s. Olive Baboon		2·25	2·25
2417	1200s. Lion		2·25	2·25
2418	1200s. Common Warthog		2·25	2·25
2419	1200s. Canarina eminii		2·25	2·25
	a. Sheetlet. Nos. 2419/24		12·00	12·00
2420	1200s. Vigna unguiculata		2·25	2·25
2421	1200s. Gardenia ternifolia		2·25	2·25
2422	1200s. Canavalia rosea		2·25	2·25
2423	1200s. Hibiscus calyphyllus		2·25	2·25
2424	1200s. Nymphaea lotus		2·25	2·25
2425	1200s. Gloriosa superba (flower) (vert)		2·25	2·25
2426	1400s. Cyptotrama asprata (fungus) (vert)		2·50	3·00
2399/426	Set of 28		45·00	42·00
MS2427	Four sheets, each 95×70 mm. (a) 4000s. Podoscypha parvula (fungus). (b) 4000s. Glossina austeni (tsetse fly). (c) 4000s. Waterbuck (vert). (d) 4000s. Abutilon grandiflorum (flower) Set of 4 sheets		30·00	32·00

Nos. 2401/6 (fungi), 2407/12 (insects), 2423/28 (mammals) and 2419/24 (flowers) were each printed together, se-tenant, in sheetlets of six with the backgrounds forming composite designs which extend on to the sheetlet margins.

For stamps previously listed as Nos. 2428/33 please see Nos. 1941/6.

246 President John Kennedy

247 Ram (lying down)

(Des R. Rundo. Litho Questa)

2002 (30 Dec). Famous People of the Late 20th Century. Six miniature sheets containing T **246** and similar vert designs. Multicoloured (except Nos. **MS**2434/5). P 14.

*(a) Life and Times of President John F. Kennedy. Two sheets containing portraits as T **246***

MS2434 117×97 mm. 1200s. Type **246**; 1200s. In profile; 1200s. Facing right, speaking; 1200s. Smiling, facing forwards (all brownish grey and black)..........	9·00 10·00
MS2435 125×97 mm. 1400s. Wearing white jacket (blackish brown and black); 1400s. Wearing brown jacket and white tie (light brown and black); 1400s. Wearing brown jacket and dark tie (blackish brown and black); 1400s. Wearing brown jacket and dark tie (light brown and black).........	10·00 11·00

(b) President Ronald Reagan. Two sheets, each containing four different portraits

MS2436 138×115 mm. 1200s. Smiling with mouth open; 1200s. Looking down; 1200s. Smiling with mouth closed; 1200s. Facing forwards..........	9·00 10·00
MS2437 120×95 mm. 1400s. Wearing red necktie (facing right); 1400s. Wearing grey sweater; 1400s. Close up of face; 1400s. Wearing red tie (facing forwards)........	10·00 11·00

(c) Fifth Death Anniv of Diana, Princess of Wales

MS2438 125×150 mm. 1200s. Wearing red dress with white collar; 1200s. Wearing white jacket; 1200s. Wearing red and white jacket and hat; 1200s. Wearing evening dress and necklace..........	9·00 10·00
MS2439 140×115 mm. 2000s. Wearing white blouse; 2000s. Wearing lace blouse; 2000s. Wearing headscarf on visit to Middle East; 2000s. Wearing tiara and white jacket..........	13·00 15·00

(Des Dayna Elefant. Litho Questa)

2003 (24 Feb). Chinese New Year ("Year of the Ram"). Sheet, 107×120 mm, containing T **247** and similar vert designs. Multicoloured. P 14.

MS2440 1000s. Type **247**; 1000s. Ram on hilltop; 1000s. Ram and six rams heads; 1000s. Six rams; 1000s. Ram (looking backwards); 1000s. Ram climbing mountain..........	11·00 12·00

247a "Jacob Blessing the Sons of Joseph" (detail)

247c "Beauty arranging her Hair" (Keisai Eisen)

247b "Group of Personages in the Forest"

(Litho BDT)

2003 (26 May). Paintings by Rembrandt. T **247a** and similar vert designs. Multicoloured. P 14.

2441	400s. Type **247a**..........	80 40
2442	1000s. "A Young Woman in Profile with Fan"....	2·00 1·50
2443	1200s. "The Apostle Peter (Kneeling)"........	2·25 2·00
2444	1400s. "The Painter Hendrick Martensz Sorgh"	2·50 3·00
2441/4 *Set of 4*..........		6·75 6·25

MS2445 185×175 mm. 1400s. "Portrait of Margaretha de Geer"; 1400s. "Portrait of a White Haired Man"; 1400s. "Portrait of Nicolaes Ruts"; 1400s. "Portrait of Catrina Hooghsaet"..........	11·00 12·00
MS2446 138×135 mm. 5000s. "Joseph accused by Potiphar's Wife" (detail)..........	10·00 11·00

(Litho BDT)

2003 (26 May). 20th Death Anniv of Joan Miró (artist). T **247b** and similar multicoloured designs. P 14.

2447	400s. Type **247b**..........	80 40
2448	800s. "Nocturne"..........	1·50 1·25
2449	1200s. "The Smile of a Tear"..........	2·25 2·25
2450	1400s. "Personage before the Sun"..........	2·50 3·00
2447/50 *Set of 4*..........		6·25 6·25

MS2451 132×175 mm. 1400s. "Man's Head III"; 1400s. "Catalan Peasant by Moonlight"; 1400s. "Woman in the Night"; 1400s. "Seated Woman" (all vert)..........	11·00 12·00
MS2452 Two sheets, each 102×82 mm. (a) 3500s. "Self Portrait II". Imperf. (b) 3500s. "Woman with Three Hairs, Birds, and Constellations". Imperf..........	13·00 15·00

(Litho BDT)

2003 (26 May). Japanese Art. T **247c** and similar vert designs. Multicoloured. P 14.

2453	400s. Type **247c**..........	80 40
2454	1000s. "Geishas" (detail) (Kitagawa Tsukimaro)	1·75 1·50
2455	1200s. "True Beauties" (Toyohara Chikanobu) ..	2·00 2·25
2456	1400s. "Geishas" (different detail) (Kitagawa Tsukimaro)..........	2·25 2·75
2453/6 *Set of 4*..........		6·00 6·25

MS2457 150×148 mm. 1200s. "Scene in a Villa" (detail of two women and urn) (Toyohara Kunichika); 1200s. "Scene in a Villa" (detail of two women behind screen) (Toyohara Kunichika); 1200s. "Visiting a Flower Garden" (detail of two women in garden) (Utagawa Kunisada); 1200s. "Visiting a Flower Garden" (detail of woman picking flowers) (Utagawa Kunisada)..........	10·00 11·00
MS2458 90×152 mm. 5000s. "Woman and Children" (detail) (Chikakazu)..........	10·00 11·00

248 Princess Katrina-Sarah Ssangalyambogo and Bulange Building

(Des Multimedia Productions. Litho Oriental Press, Bahrain)

2003 (16 June). Second Birthday of Princess Katrina-Sarah Ssangalyambogo of Buganda. T **248** and similar multicoloured designs. P 13×13½ (horiz) or 13½×13 (vert).

2459	400s. Type **248**..........	80 40
2460	1200s. Princess and Twekobe Palace, Mengo (vert)..........	2·25 2·50
2461	1400s. Princess and royal drum (vert)..........	2·50 2·75
2459/61 *Set of 3*..........		5·00 5·00

249 Princess Elizabeth as Baby

250 Prince William

(Litho BDT)

2003 (15 July). 50th Anniv of Coronation. T **249** and similar vert designs. Multicoloured. P 14.

MS2462 143×77 mm. 2000s. Type **249**; 2000s. Princess Elizabeth; 2000s. Queen Elizabeth II in Garter robes..........	11·00 12·00
MS2463 105×75 mm. 3500s. Queen wearing Imperial State Crown..........	7·50 8·00

(Litho BDT)

2003 (15 July). 21st Birthday of Prince William of Wales. T **250** and similar vert designs. Multicoloured. P 14.

MS2464 124×125 mm. 2000s. Type **250**; 2000s. Prince William as boy holding presents; 2000s. As teenager..........	11·00 12·00
MS2465 105×76 mm. 5000s. Prince William as adult...	9·50 11·00

251 Seville Elegante (1979)

(Des T. Wood and R. Rundo. Litho BDT)

2003 (15 July). Centenary of General Motors Cadillac. T **251** and similar horiz designs. Multicoloured. P 14.
MS2466 118×167 mm. 1200s. Type **251**; 1200s. Eldorado Touring Coupe (1998); 1200s. Escalade (2002); 1200s. Seville Elegante (1983) .... 8·50   9·50
MS2467 89×126 mm. 3500s. Eldorado.............................. 6·00   7·00

252 Corvette (1970)

(Litho BDT)

2003 (15 July). 50th Anniv of General Motors Chevrolet Corvette. T **252** and similar horiz designs. Multicoloured. P 14.
MS2468 145×125 mm. 1400s. Type **252**; 1400s. Corvette (1972); 1400s. Collector Edition Corvette (1982); 1400s. Corvette (1977)........................... 8·00   9·00
MS2469 125×90 mm. 3500s. Collector Edition Corvette (1982) .... 6·00   7·00

253 Endogoro Dance   **254** Women holding Meeting ("Promote Gender Equity and Empower Women")

(Litho Enschedé)

2003 (16 Oct). Cultural Dances and Dresses of East Africa. T **253** and similar vert designs. Multicoloured. P 14.
2470   400s. Type **253** .... 1·00   40
2471   800s. Karimojong dancers..................... 1·75   1·40
2472   1400s. Dance from Teso .... 3·00   3·50
2470/2 Set of 3 .... 5·25   4·75
MS2473 70×105 mm. 1200s. Kiga; 1200s. Acholi; 1200s. Karimojong; 1200s. Ganda.................. 11·00   12·00

(Litho Oriental Press, Bahrain)

2003 (24 Oct). United Nations Millennium Development Goals. T **254** and similar horiz designs. Multicoloured. P 14½.
2474   400s. Type **254** .... 1·00   1·00
2475   400s. Men pushing bicycle for pregnant woman ("Improve Maternal Health")...... 1·00   1·00
2476   600s. Women fetching water ("Ensure Environmental Sustainability") .... 1·25   1·00
2477   1000s. Woman feeding children ("Reduce Child Mortality").. 1·75   1·50
2478   1200s. Couple and storage hut ("Eradicate Extreme Poverty and Hunger")................. 1·90   1·90
2479   1200s. Family outside house ("Combat HIV/ AIDS, Malaria and other diseases")........... 1·90   1·90
2480   1400s. Teacher and schoolchildren ("Achieve Universal Primary Education") .... 2·25   2·25

2481   2000s. Emblem ("Develop a Global Partnership for Development")................. 3·00   4·00
2474/81 Set of 8.. 12·50   13·00

255 Mary and Joseph   **256** Outline of Africa, Boy and Basket of Food

(Des Kasagga Jude. Litho Enschedé)

2003 (10 Nov). Christmas. T **255** and similar vert designs. Multicoloured. P 14.
2482   300s. Type **255** 75   25
2483   400s. Angels and Shepherds 90   30
2484   1200s. Nativity.. 2·25   2·50
2485   1400s. Three Wise Men......................... 2·50   3·00
2482/5 Set of 4 .... 5·75   5·50
MS2486 105×70 mm. 3000s. Nativity (different)........ 7·00   8·00

(Litho Oriental Press, Bahrain)

2004 (31 Aug). International Food Policy Research Institute. Conference on Sustainable Food and Nutrition, Kampala. T **256** and similar horiz design. Multicoloured. Fluorescent security marking. P 14×14½.
2487   400s. Type **256** .... 1·00   50
2488   1400s. As No. 2487 but showing girl.................. 3·00   3·50

257 Adult making Child carry Baby and Bundle of Sticks

(Litho Oriental Press, Bahrain)

2004 (22 Sept). Kids In Need. Prevention of Child Labour. T **257** and similar horiz design. Multicoloured. Fluorescent security marking. P 14×14½.
2489   400s. Type **257** .... 1·00   40
2490   2000s. Speaker and people around blackboard   4·00   4·50

258   Child laughing

(Litho Oriental Press, Bahrain)

2004 (22 Sept). Straight Talk Foundation. Adolescent Health. T **258** and similar multicoloured design. Fluorescent security marking. P 14½.
2491   400s. Type **258** .... 1·00   40
2492   1200s. Boy reading paper........................ 2·50   3·00

259   "Celebrate Rotary 100 Years"

(Litho Oriental Press, Bahrain)

2004 (22 Sept). Centenary of Rotary International. T **259** and similar multicoloured designs. Fluorescent security marking. P 14×14½ (horiz) or 14½×14 (vert).

2493	400s. Type **259**	1·00	40
2494	1200s. Rotary international emblem (vert)........	2·50	3·00

260 Blue and Black Cockerel

2005 (4 Apr). Chinese New Year ("Year of the Rooster"). T **260** and similar horiz designs. Multicoloured. Litho. P 14.

2495	1200s. Type **260**	2·25	2·25
	a. Sheetlet. Nos. 2495/8	8·00	8·00
2496	1200s. Brown and fawn cockerel..........	2·25	2·25
2497	1200s. Grey and white cockerel............	2·25	2·25
2498	1200s. Pink and white cockerel............	2·25	2·25
2495/8	Set of 4	8·00	8·00
MS2499	105×75 mm. 5000s. Yellow cockerel......	10·00	11·00

Nos. 2495/8 were printed together, se-tenant, in sheetlets of four stamps.

261 Sick Man under Blanket ("STOP TB×HIV")

262 Clerodendrum sp.

(Litho Habe Druck, Germany)

2005 (31 May). National Tuberculosis and Leprosy Programme. T **261** and similar vert designs. Multicoloured. P 13.

2500	400s. Type **261**	1·00	1·00
2501	400s. Woman holding baby ("STOP TB")	1·00	1·00
2502	400s. Baby ("STOP TB")	1·00	1·00
2503	400s. Man with artificial leg ("FOR A LEPROSY FREE WORLD")	1·00	1·00
2504	400s. Elderly man wearing blue T shirt ("FOR A LEPROSY FREE WORLD")..........	1·00	1·00
2505	400s. Sick man (wearing white loin cloth) in hospital ("STOP TB×HIV")..........	1·00	1·00
2500/5	Set of 6	5·50	5·50

(Litho Enschedé)

2005 (22 June). Flowering Plants of Uganda. T **262** and similar vert designs. Multicoloured. P 13×13½.

2506	100s. Type **262**	10	15
2507	400s. Calliandra haematocephala..........	50	25
2508	600s. Asteraceae compositae	70	35
2509	850s. Angraecum sp..........	1·10	1·25
2510	900s. Delonix regia	1·10	1·25
2511	1100s. Bidens grantii	1·25	1·40
2512	1200s. Musa sapientum	1·40	1·50
2513	1400s. Begonia coccinea	1·75	1·90
2514	1600s. Impatiens walleriana	2·00	2·25
2515	2000s. Strelitzia reginae	2·25	2·40
2516	5000s. Tecomaria capensis	6·00	6·25
2517	6000s. Ixora hybrida	7·00	7·25
2518	10000s. Datura suaveolens	12·00	12·50
2519	20000s. Cucurbita pepo	24·00	25·00
2506/19	Set of 14	55·00	55·00

263 Synodontis afrofischeri

(Des F. Xavier Ifee. Litho Calcutta Security Printers Ltd, India)

2005 (6 Oct). Fish of Lake Victoria. T **263** and similar horiz designs. Multicoloured. Litho. P 13½.

2520	400s. Type **260**	90	45
2521	600s. Protopterus aethiopicus	1·50	60
2522	1100s. Clarias gariepinus..........	2·25	2·00
2523	1200s. Rastrineobola argentea (inscr "agented")	2·25	2·00
2524	1600s. Bagrus docmac..........	2·75	3·25
2525	2000s. Schilbe (inscr "Schlbe") mystus	3·00	3·75
2520/5	Set of 6..........	11·50	11·00
MS2526	97×77 mm. 1000s.×4, Mormyrus kannume; Barbus jacksonni; Bagrus docmac; Labeo victorianus .	9·00	10·00

264 Map of Africa Emblem

(Litho Oriental Press, Bahrain)

2006 (20 July). Tenth Anniv of Western Union in Africa. T **264** and similar multicoloured designs. P 14½.

2527	400s. Type **264**	85	55
2528	1600s. Globe money transfer emblem..........	2·50	3·00
2529	2000s. Globe and national flags (vert)	2·75	3·50
2527/9	Set of 3..........	5·50	6·25

265 Arms of Bank of Uganda

266 Emblem of Ramsar Convention, Kampala, 2005 and Cattle in Marshland

(Litho Calcutta Security Printers, India)

2006 (3 Oct). 40th Anniv of the Bank of Uganda. T **265** and similar vert designs. Multicoloured. P 13×13½.

2530	400s. Type **265**	85	55
2531	600s. Wildlife and city buildings..........	1·25	75
2532	1600s. Tilapia nilotica (fish)..........	2·50	3·00
2533	2000s. Mountain gorilla..........	3·00	3·75
2530/3	Set of 4..........	7·00	7·25

2007 (2 Feb). Wetlands. T **266** and similar horiz designs. Multicoloured. Litho. P 13×13½.

2534	400s. Type **266**	1·00	55
2535	1600s. River valley with crowned cranes and people observing birds	3·00	3·25
2536	2000s. Banana tree and fishermen in canoe, Lake George..........	3·25	3·75
2534/6	Set of 3	6·50	6·75

267 Emblem

268 Omwenda

(Litho Oriental Press, Bahrain)

2007 (27 Nov). CHOGM (Commonwealth Heads of Government) Meeting, Kampala. T **267** and similar multicoloured designs. P 13½×13 (5000s.) or 13×13½ (others).

2537	400s. Type **267**	75	55
2538	1600s. Boniface Kiprop winning 10,000 metres, Commonwealth Games, 2006...	2·25	2·50

2539	2000s. Dorcas Inzikuru, gold medallist, 3000 metres steeplechase, Commonwealth Games, 2006	2·75	2·75
2540	5000s. Arms of Uganda (vert)	6·50	8·50
2537/40	Set of 4	11·00	13·00

(Litho Oriental Press, Bahrain)

2007 (7 Dec). UPU Congress, Nairobi, Kenya. Costumes of Uganda. T **268** and similar vert designs. Multicoloured. P 13½×13.

2541	1600s. Type **268**	2·50	2·50
	a. Horiz strip of 5. Nos. 2541/5	11·00	11·00
2542	1600s. Ebibaraho	2·50	2·50
2543	1600s. Kikoyi	2·50	2·50
2544	1600s. Kanzu	2·50	2·50
2545	1600s. Gomesi	2·50	2·50
2546	1600s. Karimojong	2·50	2·50
2541/6	Set of 6	12·50	12·50

Nos. 2541/5 were printed together, se-tenant, as horizontal strips of five stamps in sheets of 25.

269 Javelin-thrower

2008 (18 June). Olympic Games, Beijing. T **269** and similar vert designs. Multicoloured. Litho. P 12.

2547	1000s. Type **269**	2·00	2·00
	a. Sheetlet. Nos. 2547/50	7·25	7·25
2548	1000s. Athlete on starting block	2·00	2·00
2549	1000s. Boxer	2·00	2·00
2550	1000s. Swimmer	2·00	2·00
2547/50	Set of 4	7·25	7·25

Nos. 2547/50 were printed together, se-tenant, in sheetlets of four with enlarged illustrated margins.

270 Spotted Hyaena

(Des Owen Bell. Litho)

2008 (18 June). Endangered Species. Spotted Hyaena (*Crocuta crocuta*). T **270** and similar horiz designs. P 13½.

2551	1000s. Type **270**	2·00	2·00
	a. Strip of 4. Nos. 2551/4	7·25	7·25
2552	1000s. Hyaenas around kill	2·00	2·00
2553	1000s. Female with pups	2·00	2·00
2554	1000s. Two young hyaenas	2·00	2·00
2551/4	Set of 4	7·25	7·25
MS2555	113×165 mm. Nos. 2551/4, each ×2	12·00	13·00

Nos. 2551/4 were printed together, se-tenant, as horizontal and vertical strips of four stamps in sheetlets of 16.

The stamps within **MS**2555 are arranged in two blocks of four separated by a horizontal gutter.

271 Jubilee Insurance Company

(Litho Oriental Press, Bahrain)

2008 (30 Sept). Golden Jubilee (2007) of the Aga Khan. T **271** and similar horiz designs. Multicoloured. P 14½.

2556	400s. Type **271**	1·00	1·00
2557	400s. Kampala Serena Hotel	1·00	1·00
2558	400s. Diamond Trust Bank Building	1·00	1·00
2559	1100s. Madrasa Programme	2·00	2·00
	a. Horiz strip of 5. Nos. 2559/63	9·00	9·00
2560	1100s. The Ismaili Jamatkhana, Kampala	2·00	2·00

2561	1100s. Aga Khan High School (Aga Khan Education Services)	2·00	2·00
2562	1100s. Air Uganda plane	2·00	2·00
2563	1100s. Bujagala Hydropower Project	2·00	2·00
2556/63	Set of 8	11·50	11·50

Nos. 2559/63 were printed together, se-tenant, as horizontal strips of five stamps in sheets of 50.

272 Longmen Grottoes, Luoyang   **273** Peony

2009 (10 Apr). China 2009 World Stamp Exhibition, Luoyang (1st issue). Sites and Scenes of China. Sheet 101×147 mm containing T **272** and similar horiz designs. Multicoloured. Litho. P 12.

MS2564	Type **272**; Pearl River, Guangzhou; Twin Temples on Fir Lake, Guilin; Yi Yuan Garden, Shanghai	6·50	7·50

MS2564 contains four stamps and four stamp-size labels.

2009 (10 Apr). China 2009 World Stamp Exhibition, Luoyang (2nd issue). Peony. Litho. P 13.

2565	**273** 1600s. multicoloured	2·25	2·50

No. 2565 was issued in a sheetlet of eight stamps and one central label.

274 Abraham Lincoln in 1857

2009 (10 Apr). Birth Bicentenary of Abraham Lincoln. Sheet 181×142 mm containing T **274** and similar vert designs. Multicoloured. Litho. P 13½.

MS2566	Type **274**; Abraham Lincoln in 1864; In profile, 1863; In 1857 (head and shoulders portrait)	10·00	11·00

275 Barack and Michelle Obama   **276** Michael Jackson

2009 (10 Apr). Inauguration of President Barack Obama. Sheet 151×151 mm containing T **275** and similar horiz designs. Multicoloured. Litho. P 11½.

MS2567	Type **275**; Pres. Obama looking to right (window to his left); Pres. Obama facing camera; Pres. Obama looking to right; Pres. Obama facing camera (window with Christmas tree at top left); As Type **275** but different background (three large windows at top of stamp)	14·00	16·00

No. **MS**2567 contains six stamps: three different photographic portraits, each with two different backgrounds of the White House facade.

2009 (25 June). Michael Jackson Commemoration. T **276** and similar vert designs. Multicoloured. Litho. P 13½×13.

MS2568 178×127 mm. 2000s.×4 Type **276**; Wearing white T-shirt and dark jacket (facing to left); Wearing white T-shirt and dark jacket (facing forward); Wearing jacket and white T-shirt both with glitter design.. 10·00   11·00

MS2569 178×127 mm. 2000s.×4 Michael Jackson as teenager: Wearing cream jacket and brown shirt (no tie); Wearing blue waistcoat and white shirt; Wearing pale blue jacket; Wearing brown shirt and cream jacket and tie.. 10·00   11·00

277 Q-5

278 Diana, Princess of Wales

2009 (12 Nov). Centenary of Chinese Aviation. T **277** and similar horiz designs showing fighter planes. Multicoloured. Litho. P 14.

MS2570 145×95 mm. 2000s.×4 Type **277**; Q-5C; JH-7A; JH-7 (on ground) .... 11·00   12·00

MS2571 120×80 mm. 4000s. JH-7 taking off (50×38 mm).. 7·50   8·50

(Litho Cardon Printers, Taiwan)

2010 (15 Feb). Diana, Princess of Wales Commemoration. Sheet 160×150 mm containing T **278** and similar vert designs. Multicoloured. P 11½.

MS2572 2000s.×4 Type **278**; Wearing pink floral dress and pink hat; In close-up, wearing white; Carrying bouquet, wearing red jacket... 10·00   11·00

279 Pope John Paul II

(Litho Cardon Printers, Taiwan)

2010 (24 June). Fifth Death Anniv of Pope John Paul II. Sheet 137×138 mm containing T **279** and similar horiz designs. Multicoloured. P 11½.

MS2573 400s. Type **279**; 1600s. With hands raised in blessing; 2000s. Smiling; 4000s. With hand on heart.. 13·00   13·00

280 National Scout Jamboree Emblem and Scout Camp

(Litho Cardon, Taiwan)

2010 (14 Oct). Centenary of the Boy Scouts of America. Sheet 188×114 mm containing T **280** and similar horiz designs. Multicoloured. P 13½.

MS2574 3000s.×3 Type **280**; Philmont Scout Ranch, Cimarron, New Mexico emblem and horseman; Florida High Adventure Sea Base emblem, sailing dinghy and snorkeller.. 12·00   13·00

281 'Treat Livestock against Nagana'

282 Gorilla

(Litho Oriental Security Printing, Bahrain)

2011 (18 Jan). Campaign against Sleeping Sickness (Trypanosomiasis). T **281** and similar multicoloured designs. P 13.

2575	400s. Type **281**	75	30
2576	900s. 'Treat Humans against Sleeping Sickness' (horiz)	1·40	70
2577	1600s. 'War against Tsetse Flies in Uganda' (horiz)	2·50	2·50
2578	3000s. 'Empower Communities against Trypanosomiasis' (horiz)	4·00	4·50
2575/2578 Set of 4		7·75	7·25

(Litho Oriental Security Printing, Bahrain)

2011 (18 Jan). 30th Anniv of PAPU (Pan African Postal Union). Gorillas. T **282** and similar horiz designs. Multicoloured. P 14½.

2579	400s. Type **282**	75	75
	a. Block of 10. Nos. 2579/88	6·75	6·75
2580	400s. Female carrying baby	75	75
2581	400s. Adult and baby	75	75
2582	400s. Head of gorilla, facing left	75	75
2583	400s. Male and female gorillas	75	75
2584	400s. Male gorilla seated	75	75
2585	400s. Close up of face	75	75
2586	400s. Male gorilla among bushes	75	75
2587	400s. Male gorilla feeding, facing right	75	75
2588	400s. Adult on all fours, two young gorillas in foreground	75	75
2589	1000s. Head of male gorilla, mouth open	1·50	1·50
	a. Vert strip of 5. Nos. 2589/93	6·75	6·75
2590	1000s. Gorilla sat in bushes	1·50	1·50
2591	1000s. Gorilla lying on back, mouth open	1·50	1·50
2592	1000s. Gorilla (half length photo)	1·50	1·50
2593	1000s. Head of gorilla (partly obscured by leaves)	1·50	1·50
2594	1600s. Head of gorilla, stalk in mouth	2·00	2·00
	a. Vert strip of 5. Nos. 2594/8	9·00	9·00
2595	1600s. Gorilla in tree	2·00	2·00
2596	1600s. Gorilla seen through vegetation	2·00	2·00
2597	1600s. Head of adult male gorilla, ferns at right	2·00	2·00
2598	1600s. Two young gorillas	2·00	2·00
2579/2598 Set of 20		22·00	22·00

Nos. 2579/88 were printed together, se-tenant, as blocks of ten stamps in sheets of 20.

Nos. 2589/93 and 2594/8 were each printed together, se-tenant, as vertical strips of five stamps in sheets of 20.

283 Rabbit

(Litho)

2011 (1 Feb). Chinese New Year. Year of the Rabbit. Sheet 83×131 mm containing T **283** and similar horiz design. Multicoloured. P 12.

MS2599 2000s. Type **283**; 2000s. Rabbit running .... 3·75   3·75

284 Algeria

(Litho)

2011 (25 Feb). World Cup Football Championship, South Africa (2010). T **284** and similar horiz designs showing teams. Multicoloured. P 12.

MS2600 160×170 mm. 400s. Type **284**; 400s. South Africa; 1600s. Ghana; 1600s. Nigeria; 3000s. Côte d'Ivoire; 3000s. Cameroon...... 8·50 8·50

MS2601 130×190 mm. 900s. Italy; 900s. Brazil; 1100s. Japan; 1100s. New Zealand; 4000s. Australia; 4000s. United States ...... 10·50 10·50

285 Catherine, Duchess of Cambridge arriving at Westminster Abbey

286 Philly Bongoley Lutaaya (1951–89, 'father of positive living')

(Litho C&C Printers)

2011 (29 Apr). Royal Wedding. Two sheets, each 101×119 mm, containing T **285** and similar vert designs. Multicoloured. P 13.

MS2602 600s. Type 285×2; 2500s. Duke and Duchess of Cambridge×2 (all blue borders) ...... 5·00 5·00

MS2603 600s. Duchess of Cambridge waving from carriage×2; 2500s. Duke and Duchess of Cambridge waving×2 ...... 5·00 5·00

(Litho)

2012 (29 Mar). 30th Anniv of the Discovery of HIV/AIDS. T **286** and similar multicoloured designs. P 13.

2604	700s. Type **286**	1·25	1·25
2605	1500s. Couple ('Go together for HIV Testing')...	2·50	2·50
2606	1800s. Scientists in laboratory ('Striving to find an HIV Vaccine')	3·25	3·25
2607	1900s. Four children holding candles ('Prevent HIV, Preserve the Nation')	3·25	3·25
2608	2700s. AIDS ribbon within stamp ('Your Post Office cares. Protect yourself')	4·75	4·75
2609	3400s. Couple with baby ('You too can have an HIV free Child')	6·00	6·00
2604/9 *Set of 6*		18·00	18·00

287 Addax (*Addax nasomaculatus*)

(Litho)

2012 (11 Apr). Endangered Animals of Africa. T **287** and similar horiz designs. Multicoloured. P 14 (**MS**2610) or 12½ (**MS**2611).

MS2610 180×100 mm. 3000s.×5 Type **287**; Cheetah (*Acinonyx jubatus*); Western Lowland Gorilla (*Gorilla gorilla*); Mountain Zebra (*Equus zebra*); Dama Gazelle (*Gazella dama*) ...... 11·50 11·50

MS2611 100×70 mm. 10000s. Ostrich (*Struthio camelus*) (51×38 *mm*) ...... 7·75 7·50

288 Chimpanzee

(Litho)

2012 (11 Apr). 50th Anniv of Jane Goodall?s Work with Chimpanzees, Gombe, Tanzania. Two sheets, each 188×109 mm, containing T **288** and similar horiz designs. Multicoloured. P 12.

MS2612 3500s.×4 Type **288**; Chimpanzee, looking right, twiggy branch in right foreground; Chimpanzee, looking down; Two chimpanzees......... 11·00 11·00

MS2613 3500s.×4 Chimpanzee behind fruiting tree; Close-up of chimpanzee's face; Chimpanzee, looking right; Chimpanzee calling...... 11·00 11·00

289 Panther Cap (*Amanita pantherina*)

290 *Aerangis arachnopus*

(Litho)

2012 (11 Apr). Mushrooms of Africa. T **289** and similar vert designs. Multicoloured. P 13.

MS2614 121×120 mm. 3000s.×6 Type **289**; Death Cap (*Amanita phalloides*); Blusher (*Amanita rubescens*); Penny Bun (*Boletus edulis*); Saffron Milk Cap (*Lactarius deliciosus*); Yellow Morel (*Morchella esculenta*) ...... 14·00 14·00

MS2615 81×79 mm. 5000s. Amethyst Deceiver (*Laccaria amethystina*); 5000s. Mica Cap (*Coprinus micaceus*) ...... 7·75 7·75

(Litho)

2012 (11 Apr). Orchids of Africa. T **290** and similar multicoloured designs. P 12 (**MS**2616) or 12½ (**MS**2617).

MS2616 100×100 mm. 3500s.×4 Type **290**; *Anagraecum leonis*; *Bulbophyllum calyptratum*; *Brachycorythis macrantha* ...... 11·00 11·00

MS2617 71×101 mm. 10000s. *Bulbophyllum sandersonii* (38×51 *mm*) ...... 7·75 7·75

291 Olympic Stadium, London

292 Anniversary Emblem

(Litho)

2012 (3 Aug). Olympic Games, London. T **291** and similar multicoloured designs. P 13.

MS2618 190×151 mm. 1050s. Type 291×4; Wembley Stadium×4; Old Trafford Stadium×4 ...... 9·75 9·75

MS2619 151×180 mm. 1500s. Olympic flame emblem (30×40 *mm*)×8 ...... 9·50 9·50

(Litho)

2012 (9 Oct). 50th Anniv of Independence. T **292** and similar horiz designs. Multicoloured. P 14.

2620	700s. Type **292**	1·25	1·25
2621	1800s. Independence Monument	3·25	3·25
2622	2700s. Uganda flag	4·75	4·75
2620/2 *Set of 3*		8·25	8·25

293 Stephen Kiprotich running Marathon

294 Saddled Horse

(Litho)

2013 (1 Jan). Stephen Kiprotich's Olympic Gold Medal in Men's Marathon, London, 2012, T **293** and similar multicoloured designs. P 13.

2623	700s. Type **293**	1·25	1·25

2624	1900s. Running with Ugandan flag......................	3·25	3·25
2625	2700s. Waving Ugandan flag in triumph (horiz)..	4·75	4·75
2626	3400s. Kneeling at finish, arms raised in triumph (horiz)..	6·00	6·00
2623/6	Set of 4	13·50	13·50

(Litho)

2013 (25 Nov). Chinese New Year. Year of the Horse. T **294** and similar multicoloured designs. P 13½ (2627/8), 14 (**MS**2629) or 12½ (**MS**2630).

| 2627 | 1300s. Type **294** .... | 1·00 | 1·00 |
| 2628 | 1300s. Horse (carrying scrolls with gold streamers) .... | 1·00 | 1·00 |

MS2629 186×95 mm. 2250s.×6 Horse, cantering left (yellow-green background); Horse, standing, facing left (orange-yellow background); Horse, cantering right (brown-rose background); Horse, facing forward (dull orange background); Horse, seen from rear (lavender background); Horse, leaping to left (dull yellowish green background) (all 40×30 mm, showing pen and ink drawings) .... 10·00 10·00

MS2630 101×91 mm. 8800s. Horse, standing, facing right (brown-rose background) (38×51 mm).............. 6·50 6·50

Nos. 2608/9 were issued in sheetlets of 16 containing a block of No. 2627 (4×2) at top, an illustrated horizontal gutter and a block of No. 2628 (4×2) at foot of the sheetlet.

295 Tufted Capuchin (Cebus apella)

(Litho)

2013 (31 Dec). Brasiliana 2013 World Stamp Exhibition, Rio de Janeiro. Animals of Brazil. Sheet 100×150 mm containing T **295** and similar horiz designs. Multicoloured. P 14.

MS2631 3000s.×4 Type **295**; Tayra (Eira Barbara); Brazilian Tapir (Tapirus terrestris); Jaguar (Panthera onca).. 8·75 8·75

296 Catherine, Duchess of Cambridge

(Litho)

2013 (31 Dec). Birth of Prince George of Cambridge. T **296** and similar multicoloured designs. P 14 **MS**2632) or 12½ (**MS**2633).

MS2632 171×121 mm. 3000s.×4 Type **296**; Duke and Duchess of Cambridge with Prince George; Prince George; Prince William, Duke of Cambridge............... 8·75 8·75

MS2633 71×100 mm. 8800s. Duke and Duchess of Cambridge with Prince George (38×51 mm).............. 6·50 6·50

297 Nelson Mandela

(Litho)

2013 (31 Dec). Nelson Mandela Commemoration. T **297** and similar multicoloured designs. P 14 (**MS**2634, **MS**2637) or 13½ (**MS**2635/6).

MS2634 151×151 mm. 3000s.×4 Type **297**; As Type **297** but lake-brown portrait at left; Dull yellow-green portrait at left; Deep grey-blue portrait at left... 8·75 8·75

MS2635 151×151 mm. 4400s.×4 Nelson Mandela waving (black/white photo); With fist raised, in crowd; Smiling, wearing white shirt; Portrait of Nelson Mandela and memorial candles (all 35×35 mm).. 13·00 13·00

MS2636 151×151 mm. 4400s.×4 Nelson Mandela waving (colour photo); In close-up, smiling; On podium addressing crowd; Newspaper headline 'MANDELA GOES FREE TODAY' (all 35×35 mm) .... 13·00 13·00

MS2637 76×106 mm. 8800s. Nelson Mandela holding Nobel Peace Prize (40×30 mm)................................. 6·50 6·50

298 Sikh Emblem–Khanda

(Litho)

2014 (1 Jan). Centenary of Sikh Temple, Kampala. T **298** and similar triangular designs. Multicoloured. P 12½×13.

2638	700s. Type **298**	1·25	1·25
2639	1100s. Standard–Nishan Sahib.................	2·00	2·00
2640	2700s. Golden Temple, Amritsar, India.......	4·75	4·75
2641	3400s. Sikh Temple, Sikh Road, Kampala...........	6·00	6·00
2638/41	Set of 4	12·50	12·50

299 Red-headed Rock Agama (Agama agama)

(Litho)

2014 (1 Apr). Reptiles of Africa. T **299** and similar multicoloured designs. P 12.

MS2642 140×110 mm. 3000s.×4 Type **299**; Nile Crocodile (Crocodylus niloticus); African Spurred Tortoise (Geochelone sulcata); Eastern Green Mamba (Dendroaspis angusticeps) .... 9·00 9·00

MS2643 80×99 mm. 8800s. Cape Cobra (Naja nivea) (vert) .... 6·50 6·50

300 Debrazza's Monkey (Cercopithecus neglectus)

(Litho)

2014 (1 Apr). Animals of Africa. T **300** and similar horiz designs. Multicoloured. P 14 (**MS**2644) or 12 (**MS**2645).

MS2644 150×81 mm. 3000s.×4 Type **300**; Aardvark (Orycteropus afer); African Wild Dog (Lycaon pictus); Okapi (Okapia johnstoni).. 9·00 9·00

MS2645 80×80 mm. 8800s. Antelope (Damaliscus korrigum)... 6·50 6·50

STAMP BOOKLETS

1962 (9 Oct). Black on buff cover. Stitched.

| SB1 | 5s. booklet containing 10c., 15c., 20c., 30c. and 50c. (Nos. 100/4), each in block of 4................. | 6·50 |

1965. Black on blue (No. SB2) or buff (No. SB3) covers. Stitched.

| SB2 | 3s. booklet containing four 15c. and eight 30c. (Nos. 115, 117) in blocks of 4...................... | 10·00 |
| SB3 | 5s. booklet containing four 15c. and 50c., and eight 30c. Nos. 115, 117, 119) in blocks of 4....... | 11·00 |

1970. Black on blue (No. SB4) or buff (No. SB5) covers. Stitched.

| SB4 | 3s. booklet containing four 5c. and 10c., and eight 30c. (Nos. 131/2, 135) in blocks of 4...................... | 15·00 |
| SB5 | 5s. booklet containing four 5c., 10c. and 50c. and eight 30c. (Nos. 131/2, 135, 137) in blocks of 4. | 15·00 |

1971 (15 Dec). Black on salmon (No. SB6) or lilac (No. SB7) covers. Stitched.
SB6	5s. booklet containing four 10c., 15c. and 40c., and eight 30c. (Nos. 132/3, 135/6) in blocks of 4......	9·50	
SB7	10s. booklet containing four 10c., 20c., 30c. and 50c., and eight 70c. (Nos. 132, 134/5, 137, 139) in blocks of 4................	13·00	

B **1**

1975 (9 Oct). Black on blue (No. SB8) or yellow (No. SB9) covers. Stitched.
SB8	5s. booklet containing ten 50c. (No. 153) in two blocks of 4 and one pair as Type B **1**..............	6·00	
SB9	10s. booklet containing four 10c., 20c., 40c. and 80c., and eight 50c. (Nos. 149/50, 152/3, 155) in blocks of 4................	6·50	

POSTAGE DUE STAMPS

The Postage Due stamps of Kenya, Uganda and Tanganyika were used in Uganda until 2 January 1967.

D **1**

LIBERATED
1979
(D **2**)

D **3** Lion

(Litho D.L.R.)

1967 (3 Jan). Chalk-surfaced paper. P 14×13½.
D1	D **1**	5c. scarlet	20	4·50
D2		10c. green	20	5·00
D3		20c. deep blue	35	5·00
D4		30c. red-brown	40	6·50
D5		40c. bright purple	60	15·00
D6		1s. orange	1·50	13·00
D1/6 Set of 6........			3·00	45·00

1970 (31 Mar). As Nos. D1/6, but on glazed ordinary paper. P 14×15.
D7	D **1**	5c. scarlet	15	3·25
D8		10c. green	15	2·50
D9		20c. deep blue	25	3·00
D10		30c. red-brown	35	4·25
D11		40c. bright purple	55	5·50
D7/11 Set of 5........			1·25	17·00

1973 (12 Dec). Glazed, ordinary paper. P 15.
D12	D **1**	5c. scarlet	60	5·00
D13		10c. emerald	60	5·00
D14		20c. deep blue	80	6·00
D15		30c. red-brown	1·00	8·00
D16		40c. bright mauve	1·25	11·00
D17		1s. bright orange	1·75	11·00
D12/17 Set of 6........			5·50	42·00

"UGANDA LIBERATED" OVERPRINTS. Nos. D1/17 were overprinted "UGANDA LIBERATED 1979", in very limited quantities, using a style of overprint similar to Type **32** (*Prices: Nos.* D1/6 *set of 6* £225; D7/11 *set of 5* £75; D12, 14/17 *set of 5* £60; D13 £80, *all mint*).

(Litho Questa)

1979 (Dec). Liberation. As Nos. D1/6 optd with Type D **2**. Chalk surfaced paper. P 13½×14.
D18	D **1**	5c. scarlet	15	40
D19		10c. green	15	40
D20		20c. dull ultramarine ...	20	40
D21		30c. red-brown	20	60
D22		40c. bright purple	20	60
D23		1s. orange	20	60
D18/23 Set of 6........			1·00	2·75

(Litho Questa)

1985 (11 Mar). Animals. Type D **3** and similar vert designs. P 14½×14.
D24	5s. black and bright turquoise-green		15	1·00
D25	10s. black and dull rose-lilac		15	1·00
D26	20s. black and dull orange................		30	1·00
D27	40s. black and bright lilac		80	1·50
D28	50s. black and pale greenish blue..........		80	1·50
D29	100s. black and mauve		1·40	3·00
D24/9 Set of 6........			3·25	8·00

Designs:—10s. African Bufalo; 20s. Koh; 40s. African Elephant; 50s. Common Zebra; 100s. Black Rhinoceros.

TELEGRAPH STAMPS

T **1**   T **2**

1902. Black on coloured paper. Pin perf 12.
T1	T **1**	2a. on *blue-green*................	60·00	45·00
		a. Seriffed "G" in lower "TELEGRAPHS"	£120	
T2		4a. on *yellow*................	70·00	60·00
		a. Seriffed "G" in lower "TELEGRAPHS"	£130	
T3		6a. on *magenta*................	80·00	70·00
		a. "SIK" for "SIX" in upper half...	£140	£130
		b. Seriffed "G" in lower "TELEGRAPHS"	£140	
T4		8a. on *rose*................	90·00	80·00
		a. Seriffed "G" in lower "TELEGRAPHS"	£160	
T5		12a. on *green*................	£140	£120
		a. On *greyish blue*	£170	£150
		b. Seriffed "G" in lower "TELEGRAPHS"	£275	
T6	T **2**	1r. on white laid paper	£170	70·00
		a. Stop for comma after lower "TELEGRAPHS"	£275	
T7		2r. on *yellow*................	£170	80·00
		a. Stop for comma after lower "TELEGRAPHS"	£275	
T8		3r. on *blue-green*................	£300	£180
		a. Stop for comma after lower "TELEGRAPHS"	£400	
T9		4r. on *magenta*................	£400	£225
		a. Stop for comma after lower "TELEGRAPHS"	£600	
T10		5r. on *rose*................	£450	£250
		a. Stop for comma after lower "TELEGRAPHS"	£650	
T11		10r. on *greyish blue*	£750	£500
		a. Stop for comma after lower "TELEGRAPHS"	£1100	
T12		20r. on white laid paper	£1200	£800
		a. Stop for comma after lower "TELEGRAPHS"	£1700	

Nos. T1/5 were printed in sheets of 56 (14×4), from stereotyped plates formed from an original typeset row of seven. Nos. T6/12 were in sheets of 48 (12×4), similarly formed from an original typeset row of six.

No. T3a occurs on the seventh and 14th stamp of each row.

The variety with seriffed "G" occurs on the first and eighth stamp of each row.

Nos. T7/9 are known with the "S" of "RUPEES" omitted but these are of proof status.

Unused prices are for whole stamps. Used prices are for upper halves. The seriffed "G" and "Stop for comma" varieties do not exist in used condition.

Appendix

The following stamps have either been issued in excess of postal needs, or have not been made available to the public in reasonable quantities at face value. Miniature sheets, imperforate stamps, etc., are excluded from this section.

2011
5th Anniv of Pontificate of Pope Benedict XVI. 400s.×2, 1600s.×2, 2000s.×2, 4000s.×2

2012
Fauna of African Great Lakes Region: Wild Cats. 3400s.×2; 4100s.×2
Fauna of African Great Lakes Region: Kingfishers. 3400s.×2; 4100s.×2
Fauna of African Great Lakes Region: Endangered Species. 3400s.×2; 4100s.×2
Fauna of African Great Lakes Region: Owls. 3400s.×2; 4100s.×2
Fauna of African Great Lakes Region: Elephants. 3400s.×2; 4100s.×2
Fauna of African Great Lakes Region: Reptiles. 3400s.×2; 4100s.×2
Fauna of African Great Lakes Region: Primates. 3400s.×2; 4100s.×2
Fauna of African Great Lakes Region: Butterflies. 3400s.×2; 4100s.×2
Fauna of African Great Lakes Region: Fish. 3400s.×2; 4100s.×2
Fauna of African Great Lakes Region: Birds of Prey. 3400s.×2; 4100s.×2
Centenary of Sinking of the *Titanic*. 3000s.×6
Abraham Lincoln Commemoration and 150th Anniversary of the American Civil War. 3500s.×4
Princess Diana Commemoration. 3500s.×3
50th Anniv of the Inauguration of Pres. John F. Kennedy. 3500s.×4
435th Birth Anniv of Peter Paul Rubens (artist). 3400s.×2; 4100s.×2
50th Anniv of First Man in Space (Yuri Gagarin). 3400s.×2; 4100s.×2
35th Birth Anniv of Elvis Presley (1st issue). 3400s.×2; 4100s.×2
15th Anniv of Chess Match between Gary Kasparov and Computer Deep Blue. 3400s.×2; 4100s.×2
Whitney Houston (singer) Commemoration. 3400s.×2; 4100s.×2
35th Death Anniv of Elvis Presley (2nd issue). 3500s.×4
Sailing Boats. 3400s.×2; 4100s.×2
Steam Locomotives. 3400s.×2; 4100s.×2
High Speed Trains. 3400s.×2; 4100s.×2
Non-Motorised Transport. 3400s.×2; 4100s.×2
Motorcycles. 3400s.×2; 4100s.×2
Emergency Vehicles. 3400s.×2; 4100s.×2
Formula 1 Motor Racing. 3400s.×2; 4100s.×2
Projected Automobiles. 3400s.×2; 4100s.×2
Airships. 3400s.×2; 4100s.×2
Passenger Aeroplanes. 3400s.×2; 4100s.×2
WWF. Secretary Bird (*Sagittarius serpentarius*). 3400s.×2; 4100s.×6
Vultures. 3400s.×2; 4100s.×2
African Elephant (*Loxodonta africana*). 3400s.×4; 4100s.×4
Lions (*Panthera leo*). 3400s.×4; 4100s.×4
Cheetah (Acinonyx jubatus). 3400s.×2; 4100s.×2
Gorillas. 3400s.×2; 4100s.×2
Chimpanzee (*Pan troglodytes*). 3400s.×2; 4100s.×2

2013
Dogs. 3000s.×8 Cats. 3000s.×4
World in Stamps: Butterflies. 2500s.×4
World in Stamps: Cats. 2500s.×4
World in Stamps: Dinosaurs. 2500s.×4
World in Stamps: Minerals. 2500s.×4
World in Stamps. Orchids. 2500s.×4
World in Stamps. Owls. 2500s.×4
World in Stamps. Turtles. 2500s.×4
World in Stamps. World Wildlife. 2500s.×4
125th Birth Anniv of Mae Tse Tung. 500s.×6

2014
Pope Francis I. 3000s.×4

Stanley Gibbons
Stamp Catalogues

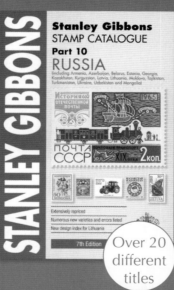
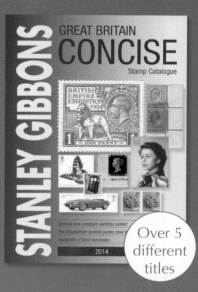

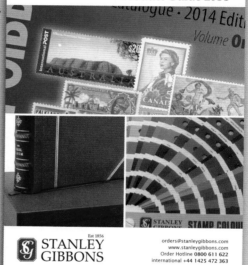

STANLEY GIBBONS
Est 1856

Dear Catalogue User,

As a collector and Stanley Gibbons catalogue user for many years myself, I am only too aware of the need to provide you with the information you seek in an accurate, timely and easily accessible manner. Naturally, I have my own views on where changes could be made, but one thing I learned long ago is that we all have different opinions and requirements.

I would therefore be most grateful if you would complete the form overleaf and return it to me. Please contact Lorraine Holcombe (lholcombe@stanleygibbons.co.uk) if you would like to be emailed the questionnaire.

Very many thanks for your help.

Yours sincerely,

Hugh Jefferies,
Editor.

Hugh Jefferies (Catalogue Editor)
Catalogue Questionnaire Responses
Stanley Gibbons Limited
7 Parkside, Ringwood
Hampshire BH24 3SH
United Kingdom

Questionnaire

2014 East Africa with Egypt and Sudan Catalogue

1. Level of detail

   Do you feel that the level of detail in this catalogue is:

   a. too specialised ○

   b. about right ○

   c. inadequate ○

2. Frequency of issue

   How often would you purchase a new edition of this catalogue?

   a. Annually ○

   b. Every two years ○

   c. Every three to five years ○

   d. Less frequently ○

3. Design and Quality

   How would you describe the layout and appearance of this catalogue?

   a. Excellent ○

   b. Good ○

   c. Adequate ○

   d. Poor ○

4. How important to you are the prices given in the catalogue:

   a. Important ○

   b. Quite important ○

   c. Of little interest ○

   d. Of no interest ○

5. Would you be interested in an online version of this catalogue?

   a. Yes ○

   b. No ○

6. What changes would you suggest to improve the catalogue? E.g. Which other features would you like to see included?

   ....

   ....

   ....

   ....

   ....

7. Would you like us to let you know when the next edition of this catalogue is due to be published?

   a. Yes ○

   b. No ○

   If so please give your contact details below.

   Name: ....

   Address:...

   ....

   ....

   ....

   Email: ....

   Telephone:...

8. Which other Stanley Gibbons Catalogues are you interested in?

   a. ....

   b. ....

   c. ....

   d. ....

   Many thanks for your comments.

Please complete and return it to:
Hugh Jefferies (Catalogue Editor)
Stanley Gibbons Limited, 7 Parkside, Ringwood,
Hampshire BH24 3SH, United Kingdom
or email: lholcombe@stanleygibbons.co.uk to request a soft copy

East Africa with Egypt & Sudan Order Form

STANLEY GIBBONS Est 1856

YOUR ORDER

Stanley Gibbons account number ☐☐☐☐☐☐

Condition (mint/UM/ used)	Country	SG No.	Description	Price	Office use only
			POSTAGE & PACKING	£3.60	
			TOTAL		

The lowest price charged for individual stamps or sets purchased from Stanley Gibbons Ltd, is £1.

Payment & address details

Name

Address (We cannot deliver to PO Boxes)

Postcode

Tel No.

Email

PLEASE NOTE Overseas customers MUST quote a telephone number or the order cannot be dispatched. Please complete ALL sections of this form to allow us to process the order.

☐ Cheque (made payable to Stanley Gibbons)

☐ I authorise you to charge my

☐ Mastercard ☐ Visa ☐ Diners ☐ Amex ☐ Maestro

Card No. ☐☐☐☐☐☐☐☐☐☐☐☐☐☐☐☐ (Maestro only) ☐☐

Valid from ☐☐☐☐ Expiry date ☐☐☐☐ Issue No. (Maestro only) ☐☐ CVC No. (4 if Amex) ☐☐☐☐

CVC No. is the last three digits on the back of your card (4 if Amex)

Signature

Date

4 EASY WAYS TO ORDER

Post to
Lesley Mourne,
Stamp Mail Order
Department, Stanley
Gibbons Ltd, 399
Strand, London,
WC2R 0LX, England

Call
020 7836 8444
+44 (0)20 7836 8444

Fax
020 7557 4499
+44 (0)20 7557 4499

Click
lmourne@
stanleygibbons.com/
co.uk?